Advanced Psychology

Applications, Issues and Perspectives

Christine Brain

Published in 2002 by:
Nelson Thornes Ltd
Delta Place
27 Bath Road
CHELTENHAM
GL53 7TH
United Kingdom

02 03 04 05 06 / 10 9 8 7 6 5 4 3 2 1

A catalogue record for this book is available from the British Library

ISBN 0 17 490058 9

Illustrations by Oxford Designers and Illustrators
Page make-up by Northern Phototypesetting Co. Ltd, Bolton

Printed and bound in Great Britain by Scotprint

Contents

To Paul, Alex and Doug – and not forgetting Kev

Acknowledgements

I am very grateful for all the help and support that I have received in writing this textbook. Special thanks to Nicky Hayes, who spent a great deal of time editing some of the chapters, and offered very helpful advice. Thanks for the patience and support offered by Rick, Carolyn, Louise and Jane at Nelson Thornes, and thanks also to Diana and others at Edexcel. Thanks to colleagues and friends, including Sue Hamza for kindly sending some of her research, and not forgetting friends at Gloscat – amongst them Richard H. for his patience and understanding. I continue to be supported by my wonderful family – Paul, Alex and Doug – who are also my best friends. Thank you.

The author and publishers wish to thank the following for permission to use copyright material:

- Allyn and Bacon for **Fig. 7.15** from R. Gifford (1997) *Environmental Psychology: Principles and Practice,* Second edition, Fig 14.3, p. 351. Copyright ©1997 by Allyn and Bacon
- American Psychiatric Publishing, Inc. for **Table 1.2** from American Psychiatric Association (1994) *Diagnostic and Statistical Manual of Mental Disorders,* Fourth edition, Text Revision. Copyright © 2000 American Psychiatric Association
- Arnold Publishers for **Fig. 2.10** from D. Pennington and P. Hill (1999) *Sound Psychology*, Fig. 4.12, p. 139
- The Continuum International Publishing Group Ltd. for **Fig. 3.6** from D. Child (1997) *Psychology and the Teacher*, Fig. 10.2, p. 283
- Fred E. Fiedler for **Fig. 4.6** from F. E. Fiedler (1967) *A Theory of Leadership Effectiveness*, McGraw-Hill, pp. 40–41
- W H Freeman and Company for **Fig. 6.7** from Michael Cole and Sheila Cole (1996) *The Development of Children*, Fig. 7.1, p. 272. Copyright ©1989, 1993, 1996, 2001 by Michael Cole and Sheila Cole
- Hodder & Stoughton Educational for **Fig. 5.8** from Kevin Wesson *et al* (2000) *Sport and PE: a complete guide to Advanced Level Study*, Second edition, Fig. 26.18, p. 593; **Table 6.2** from C. Flanagan (1996) *Applying Psychology to Early Child Development*, Box 9.1, p. 124; and **Fig. 8.21** from P. Banyard (1996) *Applying Psychology to Health*, Fig. 3.1, p. 33
- Houghton Mifflin Company for **Figs.1.1, 1.10, 1.12, 1.13** from P. C. Kendall and C. Hammer (1995) *Abnormal Psychology*, Fig. 1.2, p. 23, Fig. 6.3, p. 191, Fig. 10.4, p. 307, Fig. 10.6, p. 311
- Human Kinetics for **Fig. 5.12** from R. S. Weinberg and D. Gould (1999) *Foundations of Sport and Exercise Psychology,* Second edition, Fig. 4.2, p. 74
- McGraw-Hill Education for **Figs. 8.11–8.13, 8.15, 8.16, 8.20, 8.27, Table 8.1** from S. Taylor (1999) *Health Psychology*, Fig. 3.4, p.69, Fig. 5.4, p. 150, Fig.2.1, p. 18, Fig. 2.4, p. 25, Fig. 6.3, p. 173, Fig. 7.2, p. 206, Fig. 3.2, p. 65
- Open University Press for **Figs. 8.4–8.6, 8.10, 8.28** from Jane Ogden (2000) *Health Psychology: A Textbook,* Second edition, Fig. 5.4, p. 101, Fig. 5.5, p. 117, Fig. 5.6, p. 118, Fig. 5.7, p. 120, Fig. 2.6, p. 31; and **Figs. 8.1, 8.22, 8.29, Table 8.8** from Wolfgang Stroebe (2000) *Social Psychology and Health, 2E*, Fig. 1.1, p. 3, Fig. 7.3, p. 250, Fig. 2.3, p. 28, Table 7.1, p. 238
- Pearson Education for **Figs. 2.12, 7.16, 7.9, 7.3, Table 7.2** from M. A. Hogg and G. M. Vaughan (1998) *Social Psychology,* Second edition, Fig. 11.5, p. 425, Fig. 5.1, p. 164, Fig. 15.2, p. 561, Fig. 15.5, p. 573, Table 15.2, p. 578
- Pearson Education, Inc. for **Figs. 4.1, 4.3** from Ronald F. Riggio (1999) *Introduction to Industrial Organizational Psychology,* Third edition, Fig. 2.1, p. 22, Fig. 3.1, p. 59
- Taylor and Francis Books Ltd for **Tables 2.1, 2.2, 2.4** from C. R. Hollin (1989) *Psychology and Crime: An Introduction to Criminological Psychology*, Table 2.1, p. 21, Table 6.1, p. 154, Table 6.2, p. 167, Routledge; **Figs. 7.10, 7.5, 7.8, Table 7.5** from D. Halpern (1995) *Mental Health and the Built Environment*, Fig. 21, p. 30, Fig. 3.9, p. 101, Fig. 7.2, p. 196, Table 5.1, pp. 149–50, Taylor and Francis; and **Figs. 3.1–3.3, 3.5, 3.12, 6.6, 7.2** from M. Long (2000) *The Psychology of Education*, Fig.11.1, p. 274, Fig. 2.4, p. 15, Figs. 2.12–2.14, p. 31, Fig. 5.7, p. 127, Fig. 7.3, p. 173, Fig. 4.2, p. 80, Fig. 6.5, p. 138, Falmer Press
- Society for Research in Child Development for **Table 6.1** from J. M. Gottman (1983) 'How children become friends', *Monographs of the Society for Research in Child Development*, 48:3, p. 27
- Wadsworth, an imprint of the Wadsworth Group, a division of Thomson Learning for **Fig. 4.2** from M. G. Aamodt (1999) *Applied Industrial/ Organizational Psychology*, Exhibit 9.02, p. 378; and **Figs. 7.11, 7.12, Table 7.4** from K Deaux and L S Wrightsman (1988) *Social Psychology*, Fig. 17-3, p. 501, Fig. 17-2, p. 500, Table 17-1, p. 521.
- John Wiley & Sons, Inc. for **Figs. 8.2–3, 8.8, 8.17** and **Table 8.9** from E. P. Sarafino (1994) *Health Psychology Biopsychological Interaction*, Second edition, Fig. 1F.1, p. 12, Fig. 1.4, p. 18, Fig. 7.2, p. 212, Table 6.2, p. 188.

Photo credits

- Agence France-Presse, p. 69
- Associated Press, pp. 7,19
- AT&T Archives: Reprinted with permission from AT&T, p. 138
- Atlantic Syndication, p. 64
- British Film Institute, p. 70
- Camera Press, p. 78
- Corbis, p. 18
- Corbis/Bettman, p. 231, p. 281
- Corbis/Anna Clopet, p. 279
- Corbis/Farrell Grehan, p. 202
- Digital Vision (NT), pp. 181, 215
- Format Photographers/Jacky Chapman, p. 212
- Format Photographers /Maggie Murray, p. 229
- Getty Images/FPG International, p. 149
- Harlow Primate Laboratory, University of Wisconsin, p. 198
- Kobal, p. 117 (right)
- Impact Photos/Myong Dong, p. 43
- Magnum Photos/Ferdinando Scianna, p. 218
- Magnum Photos/Ian Berry, p. 227
- Michael O'Brien/Archive Pictures, p. 67
- Photofusion, pp. 273, 282, 288 (bottom), pp. 290, 291
- Popperfoto, pp. 184, 237 (both)
- Rex Features Ltd/Timepix, p. 195
- Science Photolibrary, p.160
- Stephen Wiltshire, p. 117 (left)
- Still Pictures/Mark Edwards, p. 14
- Still Pictures, p. 27
- John Walmsley Photography, p. 159
- Wellcome Trust Medical Photographic Library, pp. 8, 40, 111.

Every effort has been made to trace the copyright holders but if any have been inadvertently overlooked the publishers will be pleased to make the necessary arrangement at the first opportunity.

Introduction – Advice and Planning

This textbook has been written for students studying psychology, and in particular those doing the Edexcel AS and GCE specification. The eight main chapters focus on eight main applications in psychology, which are also studied in other 'A' level specifications, and on other courses too; however, the main focus is on the Edexcel specification. For the Edexcel examination you will only need to study three of the eight main chapters in this book.

Read more than the applications you have chosen

It is hoped that you will take the time to explore beyond what you need to do to pass the exam. If you enjoy the applications you have chosen to study for the exam, consider reading other chapters too. An important point about psychology is that it divides well into sections for study. However, another equally important point is that one theory tends to rest upon another. Psychology focuses on people, and it is hard, for example, to see how we can isolate people at work from those doing sport, and find different theories – both the psychology of work and sport psychology look at theories of motivation, for example. What is learnt for one application can be useful for another, and this applies to many of the applications.

Follow the links between the chapters

Links have been made between chapters, and you should take the time to follow these links. For example, anxiety and arousal are concepts that affect sporting performance, and are also involved in a stress response. In this textbook arousal and stress are examined in Chapter 8, and anxiety and arousal are examined in Chapter 5, so in Chapter 5 the reader is referred to Chapter 8 for more information. It is good practice to read around your chosen subject, to get a better idea of what psychology covers, and to gather important information for your chosen applications.

Recall AS material when asked to

Links have also been made with the AS course. AS is intended to be grounding for the A2 material, so you should try to recall AS material when you tackle the A2.

You will also need to recall AS material for the synoptic parts of the course (Units 5b and 6). When asked to recall AS material, take the time to do so, as it is good practice.

General information about the book

- Each chapter is written to suit the Edexcel A2 specification and uses appropriate headings.
- Boxes are used for various purposes, to help you to learn the material:
  - Study aid boxes give tips
  - Activity boxes suggest things you can do, often in groups, to discuss the issues for yourself
  - Recall AS material boxes are to remind you to use information that you already know, when studying particular areas
  - Synoptic notes boxes are to help you to prepare for Units 5b and 6, the synoptic part of the course, where you are asked to consider various issues and apply knowledge from many areas
  - Self-test question boxes give you essay titles and other questions to work on to test your understanding.
- Exam questions are given as Appendix A, and you should use these to test your understanding of your chosen sections.
- Web sites are included as Appendix C to help in your own research. Although material required for the A2 is covered in this textbook, at this level you will need to do more research, so be prepared to explore areas in more depth.

The Edexcel A2 specification – what material must be covered

For the Edexcel specification:
- You need to study two chapters (two applications) out of the first five chapters.
- You need to study one chapter (that is, one further application) from chapters 6, 7 and 8.
- You need to study chapters 9 and 10.
- You will need to have completed the AS part of the course.
- You will have to recall AS material for some of the A2 exam papers.

Examination requirements

- There are three units for the AS.
- The full A level comprises three AS units and three A2 units.
- Two of the AS units are examined – each exam is 1.5 hours.
- One of the AS units is coursework – marked by the exam board.
- All three of the A2 units are examined – each exam lasts 1.5 hours,
- Exams are available in January and June (in January 2002 Units 5 and 6 are not available).
- Units 5 and 6 must be taken at the end, when the full A level is to be claimed.
- All six units can be taken at the end of the course.
- The full A level cannot be awarded unless the AS units have been taken.
- Each of the six units carries 72 marks.
- At the end, for the full A level, the marks are averaged for a final grade.
- The two AS and three A2 exams are at a different level – in the AS more knowledge and understanding is needed and less evaluation, in the A2 more evaluation is needed and less knowledge and understanding.
- Units 5b and 6 are synoptic units, which means that some of Unit 5 and all of Unit 6 require students to draw on previous knowledge and understanding.

Self-test questions

Self-test questions in the form of essay titles are given in each chapter, and are drawn from the specification. Writing essays in this way will help you organise and learn the material. Essays will also be useful later for revision. These essays can be as long as you like, and you should use as much material as possible, as at this stage you are still exploring the area rather than trying to write a succinct essay.

Revision questions

Appendix A has a list of questions derived from the specification. Use these as revision questions. If you answer all the questions for your chosen applications you will be well prepared for the examinations. Remember that on many occasions you will need to explore the areas in more depth than is given in this textbook.

Preparing for the examination

When you first start a chapter, make sure that you start a new folder for your notes. Keep your notes in order, and date any handouts you receive in class. Don't rely on what you do in class. Read the whole chapter for yourself, and make careful notes as you go. You should read around the area, using web sites and other textbooks. Make separate notes from other sources, but use headings so that you know where this additional material belongs with regard to your own notes. Use the specification so that you are clear about what you need to know, and what headings will be useful. Exam questions are set using the specification, and the wording on the specification is likely to be used.

Once you have read enough of the relevant material, start preparing your essays. Gather up as much information as you can, organise it, then write the essay. Put in as much as you can at this stage. Remember to concentrate on knowledge and understanding, and put in as much evaluation as possible.

Alongside the essays, answer the relevant revision questions in Appendix A. Keep a copy of the specification to hand, and frequently check up on what material is needed. For example, in Chapter 1 schizophrenia, mood disorders, eating disorders and anxiety disorders are all covered, although you need to answer questions on only two of them in the examination. By checking in the specification you can avoid learning unnecessary material, and can make sure you know enough about what is required.

Find at least one copy of a previous examination, so that you can see what format will be used. The A2 contains a question on each application, and within that single question there are three sub-questions in the form of broken essays – you might be asked to describe something for a few marks, and then to evaluate, for example.

1 Clinical psychology

The aims of this chapter

The aims of this chapter are to enable the reader to:

- define abnormality
- describe the DSM classification system
- discuss the diagnosis of mental health issues
- discuss different therapeutic approaches to mental disorders
- distinguish between different therapeutic approaches to mental disorders
- describe the main symptoms of two of the following: schizophrenia, anxiety disorders, mood disorders and eating disorders
- discuss possible causes of physiological, social and psychological factors in two of the following: schizophrenia, anxiety disorders, mood disorders and eating disorders.

STUDY AID

When you have finished working through this chapter you should write an essay about, or at least test yourself on, each of the above points. This will help you to see how good your knowledge and understanding of clinical psychology is.

This chapter covers

INTRODUCTION TO CLINICAL PSYCHOLOGY
What is clinical psychology?
Other related professions
Research methods used in clinical psychology

DEFINING AND CLASSIFYING MENTAL DISORDERS
Abnormality
The DSM classification system
Diagnosis
Cultural factors in diagnosis

Introduction to clinical psychology

What is clinical psychology?

Clinical psychology involves applying psychological knowledge in the clinical context.

Applied psychology involves taking psychological theories and principles that have been derived from careful study, and applying them to problems. In the case of the clinical psychologist, those problems concern abnormal behaviour. Resnick (1991) defines clinical psychology as being concerned with maladjustment, disability and discomfort, assessment and diagnosis. The clinical psychologist is involved in consultation and research and, like other professionals in this area, operates in accordance with a strict set of ethical principles.

In the course of their work, clinical psychologists deal with many issues, including depression, anxiety, psychosis, personality disorder, addictions, learning disabilities, and sexual difficulties. They are involved in diagnosis and assessment much of the time, as well as research, teaching and administration; but one of the more common aspects of their work is psychotherapy, according to various surveys carried out in the USA from 1973 to 1995 (e.g. Norcross and Prochaska, 1982; Norcross et al., 1995).

The kinds of ways a clinical psychologist would be involved in diagnosis and assessment might include something like looking for a learning deficit in a child who is showing disturbed behaviour at home, or testing to see what therapy would be suitable for a certain individual. Their teaching is usually within a hospital or a university, and clinical psychologists also act as supervisors for trainees or nurses taking additional qualifications. Since they are regularly gathering data, clinical psychologists are in a good position to do research, and they also often act as consultants for specific problems. Their work often involves maintaining client records, and they also serve on committees, get research projects cleared and act as heads of department.

Other related professions

Clinical psychologists are neither psychoanalysts nor doctors. They often work closely with **psychiatrists**, who are doctors specialising in the field of mental illness. Since psychiatrists are medically trained, they are able to prescribe medication, whereas a clinical psychologist usually cannot. Some clinical psychologists argue that they should be able to prescribe drugs (DeLeon et al., 1991; Handler, 1988), but others think that they are successful because they are different from psychiatrists and don't use medications as the treatment for problems.

In the psychiatric setting, clinical psychologists are less likely to see themselves in authority over a patient. Instead of telling a patient what is best for them, they are likely to turn away from drugs as a solution, and to look towards alternatives, such as forms of psychotherapy in which the patient is active in his or her own recovery. Clinical psychologists rarely have medical training, but they often have a background in neuroscience, as well as in other areas of psychology, and their training means that they have a very broad knowledge of human behaviour (Kiesler, 1977).

The **psychiatric social worker** is a social worker who often uses psychotherapy and contributes to diagnosis in a similar way to the clinical psychologist. However, there are some major differences between them – in particular, social workers are more likely to deal with day-to-day problems while clinical psychologists aim to address the long-term sources of the problem. Psychiatric social workers also tend to look more at employers, family, work and so on, whereas clinical psychologists will often look more at the individual's own cognitions and behaviour. However, this is not an absolute distinction, because many clinical psychologists are also concerned with family and social factors, and social workers have begun to look at internal psychological factors as well as social and environmental ones.

Another professional who is often involved with problems of mental disturbance is the **counselling psychologist**. This is a psychologist who specialises in 'talking cures' – ways of helping people to come to terms with their problems by talking through them and learning new ways of understanding them. This often overlaps with the role of the clinical psychologist, but counselling psychologists are more likely to work with normal or moderately maladjusted people.

Research methods used in clinical psychology

Research in clinical psychology involves a variety of different types of methods. Because they are concerned with the real problems occurring in people's everyday lives, clinical psychologists rarely conduct 'pure' laboratory research, although they will draw on the findings of that type of research if it is helpful for their work. Mostly, however, they conduct research in a hospital or health service context, which means that their studies tend to be more naturalistic and less strictly controlled than those of an academic researcher.

↻ *Recall AS material*

Recall AS material on method. Think about as many methods and issues involved as you can.

Observations

Systematic observations are those that may eventually lead to a hypothesis that can be tested in some more formal way. Clinical psychologists often gather systematic observational data in their daily work. For example, if in a particular interview an individual struggles to answer a hard question, the clinical psychologist, observing this, might choose to offer an easier question, so that the individual has a better chance of overall success – and to learn more from the interview. In this way the clinical psychologist has observed something, formed a hypothesis, made a systematic change, and then can see the effect of this change.

Evaluation

- No controls, so only limited possibility of generalisation to other situations.
- Limited situation, which again limits generalising.
+ Hypotheses can be generated for testing.

Naturalistic observations are also systematic, but they tend to be carefully planned, in a real-life setting. For example, a clinical psychologist might observe patients just before they undergo ECT (therapies are described later in the chapter). Ten patients might be involved. The problems are that, with only ten patients, only one hospital and only one observer, it might be inaccurate to generalise the findings to all patients about to undergo ECT.

Evaluation

- There is no real control by the observer: the situation controls the observation.
- Often few situations are observed, so little generalisation is possible.
- The observer may affect the situation, so it is not the same as usual.
+ It takes place in a natural setting, which increases validity.
+ Can generate hypotheses for further (perhaps more controlled) studies.

↻ *Recall AS material*

Recall or look up your AS material on method, especially the terms validity, reliability, generalisability, controls, social desirability, demand characteristics.

Controlled observations can take place in the field or a natural setting, but the observer maintains some control over the situation. Controlled observations can be like field experiments in that, in a natural setting, a situation may be arranged so that the required observation can be made. For example, to look at noise, people could be observed in the street, and the observer could arrange for there to be a particular location from which he or she can observe.

Evaluation

- Only a limited situation can be observed, so little generalisation is possible.
- The observational set-up may affect the situation, so it is not the same as usual.
+ It takes place in a natural setting, which increases validity.
+ More control by the observer so it is more apparent what is going on.

Self-test

Do the following statements describe reliability, validity or generalisability?

1 Observations that take place in a natural setting are true to life.

2 Observations often involve few situations, so should not be applied to all situations.

3 Observations which are undertaken with some care not to disturb the situation ought to yield the same results if they are done again.

Answers can be found on p.44.

Case studies

Case studies are intensive explorations of one particular individual or situation. In clinical psychology, this is usually one individual who is undergoing treatment. Interviews, test results and transcripts of treatment sessions can be used as source material for the case study, as well as medical histories, diaries and letters.

Evaluation

- Hard to generalise because only one person being studied.
- Cannot really draw cause and effect conclusions.
- Individuals must be studied singly, which is time-consuming (Allport, 1961).
+ Lots of rich data can be gathered, which it is hard to get any other way.
+ Good to lead to a more controlled investigation.
+ Good for generating testable hypotheses.
+ Davison and Neale (1994) say that case studies are particularly useful for providing descriptions of rare events and can highlight distinctive methods of treating patients.

↻ Recall AS material

Recall one particular case study that you have studied for the AS, or which you have studied in psychology.

Epidemiological research

Epidemiological research refers to the study of the incidence, prevalence and distribution of an illness. The **incidence** refers to how many new cases develop in a given time period, the **prevalence** refers to the overall number of cases there are altogether, and the **distribution** refers to whether the number of cases reported is going up or down. Epidemiological research is done mainly using surveys and interviews, but it may also involve documentary research such as accident statistics or illness records.

An example of an epidemiological study is that carried out by Kessler *et al.* (1994). They used a structured diagnostic interview to find estimates of the 12 month and lifetime prevalence of a variety of mental disorders. Interesting results included some gender differences, in that they found that men are more likely to be diagnosed with a substance use disorder or antisocial personality disorder, whereas women are more frequently diagnosed as having mood disorders or anxiety disorders. One of the implications, if the diagnosis is fair and unbiased, is that men have a greater risk factor for substance use disorder than women (Figure 1.1).

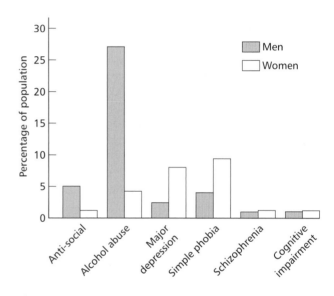

Figure 1.1
Gender differences as a percentage of lifetime occurrence for some mental disorders (Source: Kendall and Hammen, 1995; originally from Robins et al., 1984)

Evaluation

- Difficulties in diagnosing an illness can lead to unreliable data.
- Tends to give correlations, so cause and effect relationships are not found.
- There may be a problem in locating cases, and not all cases may be counted, so the results might not be reliable.
- With surveys demand characteristics or social desirability factors might influence people's answers.
+ Good for identifying groups at risk.
+ Enables identification of general patterns in large amounts of data.

Correlational methods

Surveys and other forms of clinical data collection often give correlational data. For example, the amount of smoking correlates with the likelihood of developing cancer (from the Surgeon General's (1964) study called *Smoking and Health*). Correlational techniques can help us to link one variable with another. To correlate two variables, we need two sets of observations, giving us two sets of scores. For example, if you had both a personality score and a rating for anxiety for each person in a group, then you would be able look at the relationship between those two scores and see whether they correlated.

The main problem with correlation is that, although it can show a relationship, it doesn't show causality. For example, personality may correlate with anxiety, but that would not necessarily mean that a certain sort of personality causes anxiety – or even that anxiety causes a certain sort of personality. There may be some other variable, such as upbringing style, that has caused both the personality and the anxiety.

To give another example, schizophrenia is often associated with (correlated with) high levels of dopamine (schizophrenia is examined in more detail later in this chapter, and the dopamine hypothesis is explored then). Dopamine is a neurotransmitter. So we might say that high levels of dopamine cause schizophrenia, or we might say that schizophrenia causes high levels of dopamine. However, those with schizophrenia often take high levels of anti-schizophrenic drugs, and these drugs often produce high levels of dopamine. So a third variable is implicated. This is sometimes called the third variable problem.

Evaluation

- Even if two variables co-relate, it does not mean that one causes another.
- + Correlations can be more ethical, because variables that already exist can be measured, and variables are not manipulated.
- + Many relationships between variables in real life are correlated but not directly causal, so correlations often have higher validity.
- + Correlation can sometimes be used as a first check for

possible causes. If two variables do not correlate, this can be used as evidence that there is no cause and effect relationship between the two.

Experiments

Experiments are sometimes used in clinical psychology research. Experiments involve manipulation of variables with careful controls. The idea in an experiment is that the controls make sure that only the independent variable (the one that is of interest) is changed or manipulated. So if the dependent variable (the one which is being measured as a result of the manipulation) actually changes, it can be claimed that the reason for that change was the change in the independent variable.

Evaluation

- + Careful controls mean that a cause and effect relationship can be claimed.
- + Careful controls mean that if the study is repeated it is likely that the same results will be found.
- – The careful controls mean that the situation is unlikely to be natural, so the results might not be worth much.
- – Sampling is likely to have been limited, so generalising to a larger population is often difficult.

Overall, then, the range of research methods that clinical psychologists use is very similar to the range of research methods used by other psychologists. The main difference in their research is that it takes place in a naturalistic setting – that is, in the context of psychiatric hospitals, clinics, or other types of institution – rather than in a laboratory.

Defining and classifying mental disorders

Abnormality

Clinical psychology takes theories and research findings that have been arrived at through careful study, using research methods like the ones we have just been looking at. Then these theories are applied to mental health issues, involving abnormal behaviour. But it is important to be clear just what we mean by the term 'abnormality'. We could say that abnormality means anything that is not normal, but that covers too wide a range. Clinical psychologists are not interested in every aspect of abnormality, just in particular abnormalities. So in this section we will look at what abnormal means in clinical psychology.

There are many terms that we could use when we are talking about abnormal behaviour – disability, abnormality, difficulty, problem and difference are just a few. But whatever the term – and there are problems in using certain terminology because of what words come to mean in a society – clinical psychology is interested in the difficulties that arise from some kinds of abnormal behaviour.

It is hard to define exactly what we mean by 'abnormal' for three main reasons:
• There is no shared characteristic of all that we call abnormal – things that are abnormal can have nothing at all in common.
• No single definition is enough to take into account all the different types of behaviour that we might want to call 'abnormal'.
• There is no absolute distinguishing line between normal and abnormal – they often blur into one another.

There are several ways of that people have tried to define abnormality.

Statistical deviation

Statistical deviation from the norm is one approach. It has been suggested that anything that happens infrequently is abnormal – that what is normal is what usually happens. This often implies that any behaviour that does not conform with established standards is called abnormal. For example, if a child's marks and work are of a continually low standard (statistically) when compared with others in the same year group, the child might be referred to a psychologist for evaluation. The child might then be diagnosed as being mentally retarded. But the statistical definition also means that a child with particularly high intelligence would be regarded as abnormal too, and that isn't really what people usually mean when they talk about abnormal behaviour.

Evaluation

+   A single figure can be used as a cut-off point. For example, a score on an intelligence test can be set, below which an individual will be diagnosed as being mentally retarded.
−   It is hard to decide cut off points and to fix an absolute number beyond which the behaviour is called abnormal – having a single cut-off point is often too arbitrary to take account of real situations.
−   If the individual is just under the score, is it justifiable to make the diagnosis?
−   It is hard to decide how many deviations are enough to call someone abnormal, even if the cut-off point is agreed. Would we administer more than one test, for example? It is hard to decide when a strong religious attitude becomes abnormal, for instance.

Social deviation

Deviation from social norms is another way of defining abnormality. For example, if a teenager who has behaved normally starts to exhibit strange behaviour (such as becoming obsessively religious) then she might be referred to a psychiatrist. She might then, following other tests, be diagnosed as being schizophrenic. In this case, her behaviour violated social norms and expectations, although statistically it is not uncommon for teenagers to go through a religious phase.

Evaluation

+   The idea of abnormality being a deviation from social norms is appealing because that is how we think of abnormality. If people are behaving oddly, then we think of them as abnormal.
+   The problem can be diagnosed cumulatively – for instance, a number of different types of behaviour that violate social norms can be recorded and scored, and after a certain number, schizophrenia is diagnosed.
−   Not all incidents of behaviour that don't conform to the social norm show abnormality in the sense it is meant in clinical psychology. For example, those who do exceptionally well at school are not called abnormal, even though their behaviour differs from the social norm.
−   Attitudes and norms vary in different cultures. What is abnormal in one culture may not be abnormal in another, so this does not seem a good definition for diagnosis of abnormality regarding mental health. It is like saying that someone labelled mentally ill in one culture would be normal in another. For example, what Western culture might call obsessively religious might not be thought of as abnormal at all in another culture.

ACTIVITY

Define the term 'abnormal'.

Try this as a group activity. Each member of the group begins by writing down what they think the word 'abnormal' means. Then the whole group discusses each other's definition, and tries to come up with a group definition which everyone can agree with. Note down all the problems you encountered when you were trying to come up with a good definition.

Subjective distress

Another way of defining abnormality in clinical work is to look at it in terms of **subjective distress**. If someone feels they have a problem, and it is so serious that it is disturbing their day-to-day living, this can be used to diagnose abnormality. If a person is suffering from anxiety, even if

Figure 1.2
Making a statement about recycling. Strange behaviour does not necessarily indicate abnormality

someone else would say their anxiety is unnecessary, then from the sufferer's point of view they are in need of help. A person's behaviour might appear to be perfectly 'normal', and yet they could be suffering, psychologically, and in need of help. So the subjective distress of the individual can be a way of measuring abnormality.

Evaluation

+ It allows the individual to affect the diagnosis, which seems an attractive idea. They should know if they need help.
− Not everyone diagnosed as having a disorder agrees with their diagnosis. Not everyone who would be classified as showing abnormality experiences subjective distress, so as a definition of abnormality it is not enough.
− Individuals who show the same behaviours might be diagnosed differently, because they may have different subjective feelings about themselves.
− It is hard to make a clear decision concerning just how much subjective distress would be enough for the diagnosis that the person is disordered.

Disability or dysfunction

A fourth way of defining abnormality in a clinical setting is to see whether the behaviour is causing a problem. For example, everyone has personal fears, and a strong fear of something would not be diagnosed as a phobia that needs treatment unless it was causing problems for the person. If someone was unable to work because of the fear, then it would be causing a **dysfunction**, and so treatment would be needed. But if the fear did not present them with any problems in living, then treatment would be considered unnecessary.

It is usually pretty obvious when a dysfunction of this type is taking place, and readily apparent to both the therapist and the person concerned. But there are objective measures that can also be used. For example, if a person was unable to socialise for some reason, then that would be dysfunctional, even if they had developed ways of coping which didn't require socialising. Often, behaviour that deviates from the social norm also occurs when a problem has become dysfunctional, so this definition links to an extent with that one. However, the key feature is not just that the problem is not 'normal', but that it prevents normal functioning.

Evaluation

+ The problems are often obvious so diagnosis is clearer. It is usually apparent if the person cannot work or their social functioning is being affected.
− There are value judgements involved in deciding what consists of lack of functioning. For example, one person might think everyone ought to socialise frequently, but someone else might not think socialising is important.

Abnormality as the absence of normality

The other way of getting round the problem of deciding just what abnormality is to go about it a completely different way, and look at it in terms of 'normality' instead. It could be said that if 'normality' is defined, then 'abnormal' means not fitting that definition. But even this apparently simple idea gives us problems when we try to examine it more closely. Around one-third of all adults admit to having problems at some time in their lives, according to epidemiological surveys (e.g. Karno *et al.*, 1987). Myers *et al.* (1984) suggest that up to 20% of people in their own survey had a psychological disorder at the time, and considered that this was a fairly typical result for the population as a whole. This suggests that, wherever you are, one in five people around you have a psychological disorder. If that is the case, then suggesting that 'abnormality' is not being 'normal' may not be very sensible. It seems that psychological disorders are common, and so are to an extent 'normal'.

Obviously, then, it is difficult to achieve a clear definition of abnormality. However, the kinds of abnormality that we refer to as mental illnesses do have symptoms – that is, clusters of behaviours which seem to go together. So, although a perfect definition of that disorder might be difficult, diagnosis becomes easier when we look at several abnormal behaviours taken together. For example, someone might be exhibiting unusual behaviours that are against the social norm. They might also be experiencing subjective distress. If that behaviour and experience also leads to one or more dysfunctions, either in their work or their family life, then these different factors would be added together, and would be likely to result in a diagnosis of there being a problem. The challenge then becomes how we combine different groups of 'symptoms' or behaviours, and how many of them we expect to come across to establish a reliable diagnosis. This leads us into the whole question of how mental disorders are diagnosed.

Psychiatric diagnosis means classifying the problem that any particular person is showing. As a result, several classification systems are used by professionals for this purpose. One of the most well-known of these is the DSM system, which stands for the *Diagnostic and Statistical Manual of Mental Disorders*, published by the American Psychiatric Association. It goes through regular revisions, and the current version, produced in 1994, is known as DSM-IV.

DSM-IV defines a mental disorder as a syndrome or pattern that is associated with present distress or disability, or with an important loss of freedom or risk of suffering. As you can see, it uses definitions of abnormality as both subjective distress and evidence of dysfunctioning. The DSM-IV definition goes on to say that whatever the cause of the behaviour, either behavioural, psychological or biological dysfunction(s) must be present in the individual. A simple conflict with social norms is not enough evidence, according to DSM-IV, to diagnose mental disorder.

The DSM system involves the use of explicit criteria for identifying mental disorders, a multiaxial system, an attempt to avoid theoretical bias, and an aim of being useful in treating mental disorders. It was first published in 1952 by the American Psychiatric Association, but

Self-test

Write a timed essay, under exam conditions (or as close as you can manage) using the title 'Discuss ways of defining abnormality'.

The DSM classification system

Clinical psychologists often work with people who have been diagnosed as having some kind of mental illness or psychiatric disorder. If a particular problem or abnormality is to be properly treated, then it has to be diagnosed. So issues of how diagnoses are made are very important – not only for the person who is being diagnosed. The type of help which people receive, for example, can often depend on diagnosis. If you have known someone at school who was diagnosed as dyslexic you will probably know that they could get special help as a result (this is not to suggest that dyslexia is a mental illness, just to illustrate how a diagnosis can be an advantage). But without the label, the official statement and the diagnosis, the person would not have been eligible for help. Also, if the diagnosis is not correct it is unlikely that the person would receive appropriate treatment.

Figure 1.3
Emil Kraepelin, often considered as having founded modern systems of classifying mental disorders

before that there were other systems. One of the first was developed by Kraepelin in 1913 (Figure 1.3), around the same time as others such as Galton and Binet were working on mental tests and intelligence scales. In 1952 the World Health Organization produced its International Statistical Classification of Diseases, Injuries and Causes of Death. We will be looking at other classifications later in this section.

Table 1.1 Classifications of mental disorders used by the Royal Medico-Psychological Association in the 1940s

A. Oligophrenia (amentia, mental deficiency):
   (a) Idiocy
   (b) Imbecility
   (c) Feeblemindedness (moron)
   (d) Moral deficiency

B. Neuroses and psychoneuroses:
   (a) Exhaustion states (including neurasthenia)
   (b) Anxiety states
   (c) Compulsions, obsessions, and phobias
   (d) Hysteria
   (e) Mixed and other forms

C. Schizophrenia psychoses:
   (a) Dementia praecox
      i   Simple
      ii Hebephrenic
      iii Catatonic
      iv Paranoid
   (b) Paraphrenia
   (c) Other forms

D. Psychopathic constitution (including paranoia)

E. Affective psychoses:
   (a) Manic-depressive psychosis (cyclothymia)
      i   Elation
      ii Depression
      iii Stupor
   (b) Involutional melancholia

F. Confusional states

G. Epileptic psychoses

H. General paralysis

I. Other psychoses with organic brain disease

J. Dementia

K. Indeterminate types

A multiaxial system

It was in DSM-III that the **multiaxial system** of diagnosis was first set out. DSM-III was revised in response to a large number of studies and critiques of various diagnostic issues. Eventually, following a trial period of the revised version, DSM-IV was published. A multiaxial

system is where the individual is assessed according to more than one criterion. DSM-IV has a five-axial approach, where five axes or types of information are required.

- *Axis 1* – any clinical disorders or conditions already present, other than personality disorders and mental retardation
- *Axis II* – Personality disorders and mental retardation
- *Axis III* – Other general medical conditions that may affect diagnosis
- *Axis IV* – Psychosocial and/or environmental problems that may affect diagnosis
- *Axis V* – Global assessment of functioning (GAF).

These are described briefly in Table 1.2. The GAF scale involves coding the degree of impairment of general functioning involved. For example, a code of 51–60 implies only moderate symptoms whereas a code of 11–20 means that there is some danger of hurting self or other people.

Diagnosing according to this system means assessing the individual separately on each of the axes. For example, someone might be involved in alcohol and cocaine abuse (Axis I), have some personality disorder (Axis II), have no other condition (Axis III), have educational problems (Axis IV), and be at risk of self-harm (Axis V). Each of these is taken into account in forming the diagnosis, although often only one of them will be labelled as the principal diagnosis, or main problem.

Other classification systems

The DSM system is based on cluster analysis – that is, looking for groups or clusters of symptoms which seem to belong together, and to which a label can be given. There are other systems, also based on cluster analysis of this type. For example, Overall and Gorham (1962) developed the Brief Psychiatric Rating Scale (BPRS), which gives 16 different areas for evaluation. Other systems focus on certain types of disorder rather than attempting to develop general classifications covering all sorts of mental problems. For example, Lorr (1986) helped to develop an interview procedure aimed at identifying psychotic behaviour. The procedure led to patients being given scores on 12 different dimensions, such as hostile belligerence or unsociability.

Another alternative to the DSM makes use of the Five-Factor Model of Personality (FFM) developed by Costa and McCrae in 1992. The five factors are neuroticism, agreeableness, conscientiousness, extraversion and openness to experience, and they are considered to be the basic dimensions of personality. As a result, some people have used them as the basis for diagnosing personality disorders, and researchers

Table 1.2 A condensed version of DSM-IV

Axis I: Clinical disorders or other conditions that may be a focus of clinical attention:
• Disorders usually first diagnosed in infancy, childhood or adolescence (for example, pervasive developmental disorders)
• Delirium, dementia and amnestic and other cognitive disorders
• Mental disorders due to a general medical condition
• Substance-related disorders (for example alcohol abuse, cocaine dependence)
• Schizophrenia and other psychotic disorders
• Mood disorders (for example major depression, bipolar disorder)
• Anxiety disorders (for example, agoraphobia, post-traumatic stress disorder)
• Somatoform disorders (for example hypochondriasis)
• Factitious disorders
• Dissociative disorders (for example dissociative identity disorder)
• Sexual and gender identity disorders (for example vaginismus, fetishism)
• Eating disorders (for example anorexia nervosa)
• Sleep disorders (for example narcolepsy)
• Impulse control disorders (for example kleptomania)
• Adjustment disorders
• Other conditions that may be a focus of clinical attention (for example bereavement)

Axis II: Personality disorders and mental retardation:
• Personality disorders (for example borderline, antisocial, dependent, paranoid)
• Mental retardation

Axis III: General medical conditions that are potentially relevant to the understanding or management of the individual's mental disorder

Axis IV: Psychosocial and environmental problems:
• Problems with primary support group
• Problems related to the social environment
• Educational problems
• Occupational problems
• Housing problems
• Economic problems
• Problems with access to health care services
• Problems related to interaction with the legal system and crime
  Other psychosocial and environmental problems

Axis V: Global assessment of functioning (GAF) scale*

Code	Description
91 to 100	Superior functioning in a wide range of activities
81 to 90	Absent or minimal symptoms (for example, mild anxiety before an exam), good functioning in all areas, interested and involved in a wide range of activities, social effective, generally satisfied with life, no more than everyday problems or concerns (for example, occasional arguments)
71 to 80	If symptoms are present, they are transient, expectable reactions to psychosocial stressors
61 to 70	Some mild symptoms
51 to 60	Moderate symptoms
41 to 50	Serious symptoms (for example suicidal ideation, severe obsessional rituals, frequent shoplifting) or any serious impairment in social, occupational or school functioning (for example no friends, unable to keep a job)
31 to 40	Some impairment in reality testing or communication
21 to 30	Behaviour is considerably influenced by delusions of hallucinations
11 to 20	Some danger of hurting self or others
1 to 10	Persistent danger of severely hurting self or others (for example recurrent violence) or persistent inability to maintain minimal personal hygiene or serious suicidal act with clear expectation of death
0	Inadequate information

*Full descriptions are provided here only for codes 81–90, 41–50 and 1–10.

Source: From American Psychiatric Association (1994) *Diagnostic and Statistical Manual of Mental Disorders*, 4th edition. Reprinted by permission.

have found that diagnoses using this system do correlate with those using the DSM Axis II. For example, Trull (1992) found that the FFM dimensions of neuroticism, extraversion and agreeableness were the ones which linked with the personality disorders diagnosed using DSM-III. If both systems arrive at similar diagnoses for the same patients, this suggests that they are reliable measures.

Costa and Widiger (1994) suggested that the FFM might be a useful substitute for the DSM as a system for personality disorder diagnosis. However, since the FFM was really developed as a way of looking at ordinary personality characteristics, that does present some problems. These include:

- How does the FFM score how maladaptive the disorder is? The DSM uses Axis V for this.
- Where does the FFM give a cut-off point for saying that someone has a disorder or not?
- How is the context of the disorder taken into account? The DSM uses Axis IV for this.
- How would clinicians be trained to use the FFM?

Such issues as these lead to the DSM's continued usage.

The FFM is not the only alternative to the DSM. For example, another classification system is the International Classification of Diseases (ICD) that is published by the World Health Organization and used across the world. ICD-10 was published in 1993. Nonetheless, partly because most of the books and research in clinical psychology and psychiatric diagnoses are American in origin, the DSM is the most widely used system, both in the USA and in the rest of the world.

Issues raised by categorisation systems

1 Categorising means describing, not explaining, but explanations do still tend to be included. For example, it is likely that someone diagnosed with paranoid schizophrenia will be said to have illusions because of it, and this is giving an explanation for the illusions. This can lead to a circular argument – someone has paranoid schizophrenia because they have illusions, and the illusions are explained because the person has paranoid schizophrenia.

2 Categorising suggests that someone either is in the category or is not, whereas mental illnesses tend to fall along a continuum without any clear cut-off point between the two. This means that the difference between normal and abnormal is often a difference of degree: someone can behave a bit oddly without being diagnosed as paranoid, whereas someone else, behaving in a similar but slightly more noticeably 'odd' way, might be diagnosed as mentally ill. The general diagnostic constructs that are often used in equivocal cases, such as

'borderline personality disorder', are not useful because they tend to rely on how many problems a person has, rather than whether they have them or not.

3 There are many different bases for diagnosis. Sometimes people are diagnosed because of their current behaviours or symptoms, and sometimes their past history is used. Sometimes a laboratory test is done and a diagnosis based on biological criteria, and sometimes a self-report measure is used. All this means that two people might be diagnosed in a completely different way, with very little consistency.

4 What counts as an illness is often decided by psychiatrists themselves. Individual psychiatrists have different theoretical stances, social views, and political attitudes, and these can affect what is listed and what is not. For example, homosexuality was considered a disease that needed treatment until society's attitudes changed. Then, however, it was still possible to diagnose it as a disease, under the more vague heading 'sexual disorder not otherwise specified' if the individual wished to change their sexual orientation. The decision to drop homosexuality from the list was eventually made by a vote of the members of the Psychiatric Association, but only after considerable social change in public attitudes had taken place.

5 The DSM gives very explicit descriptions, which can be a useful tool when diagnosing. They are considered to aid *reliability* and *validity*. The idea is that thorough descriptions make it more likely that someone presenting the same symptoms will be diagnosed in the same way by a different user of the manual, which would make the diagnosis more reliable. (Reliability refers to the consistency of judgements across different users of the manual.) Similarly, with detailed descriptions, it is more likely that the diagnosis will be valid, and account for the individual's symptoms. (Validity refers to how true or accurate the diagnosis is. We will be discussing reliability later in this section.)

ACTIVITY

Make a list of behaviours that you would consider odd, but not really evidence of mental illness. Then make a list of behaviours where you would say the person is mentally ill. Do any of them connect? Look at your two lists closely, to see if you can identify a continuum between any of the behaviours.

Diagnosis

Diagnosis is almost always made according to some classification system, such as the ones we have just been looking at. So categorisation is very important. Diagnosis brings with it certain treatments, and perhaps also funding.

If, for example, someone was diagnosed as having a common cold, little treatment and attention might be offered. If, however, they were diagnosed as having meningitis, treatment would be swift, and the treatment would be the medication considered to be most appropriate for the problem, even if that was fairly expensive.

Examples of diagnostic categories

The major diagnostic categories are in axes I and II of DSM-IV. They include:

- *Disorders first diagnosed in infancy, childhood or adolescence.* Examples are separation anxiety disorders, attention deficit/hyperactivity disorders and learning disorders.
- *Substance-related disorders.* Examples are ingestion of alcohol, opiates and cocaine.
- *Schizophrenia and other psychotic disorders.* These include distinguishing between different types of schizophrenia
- *Mood disorders.* These include major depressive disorder, mania and bipolar disorder.
- *Anxiety disorders.* These include phobias, panic disorders, generalised anxiety disorder; obsessive–compulsive disorder and post-traumatic stress disorder.
- *Somatoform disorders.* These are illnesses that seem to have no physical cause but serve a psychological purpose. Examples are pain disorder, hypochondriasis, and body dysmorphic disorder.
- *Dissociative disorder.* Examples are dissociative amnesia or dissociative fugue.
- *Sexual and gender identity disorders.* Examples are paraphilias and sexual dysfunctions.
- *Sleep disorders* such as insomnia or narcolepsy.
- *Eating disorders.* These include bulimia nervosa and anorexia nervosa.
- *Other disorders*, including factitious disorder, adjustment disorder, impulse control disorders, personality disorders.

Advantages of diagnosis

Diagnosis can communicate a great deal of information both to professionals and to the individual. If someone is diagnosed with paranoid schizophrenia, a clinical psychologist will know what symptoms to expect, and this can be useful. Diagnosis also implies that there is some comparability amongst those using the same classification system. According to DSM-IV, diagnoses are free from theoretical biases because they use objective behaviours and sets of symptoms. This means that professionals with different backgrounds and beliefs can use the same classification system, and there should be less bias. However, this is a controversial point, since the behaviour itself has to be interpreted by the person making the diagnosis.

Patients diagnosed as having the same disorder can be compared, observed and research can be carried out. This means that more can be learned about the disorder than if there were no diagnosis linking all the people with the disorder.

Causes for mental illnesses can be looked for much more successfully if everyone with the illness is grouped together under a diagnostic label. Studies can look at common backgrounds, for example, or common experiences.

Diagnoses usually suggest treatments, so if a person is diagnosed with a particular mental disorder, then certain treatments immediately come to mind. But with the wrong diagnosis, the wrong treatment might be administered.

Reliability of diagnosis

A diagnosis is considered to be reliable if more than one psychologist would give the same diagnosis to the same individual. Beck *et al.* (1961) gave two psychiatrists the same 153 patients to diagnose, but the two only agreed in their diagnosis 54% of the time; suggesting that psychiatric diagnosis could be highly unreliable. There are several possible reasons for unreliability in diagnosis:

- Patients gave different psychiatrists different information, for some reason, which highlights the element of *subjectivity* in diagnosis.
- An institution only admits patients with certain diagnoses, and the mental health professional wants them to be admitted. Or perhaps because patients will get more treatment with one diagnosis than with another.
- Insufficient evidence has been gathered, or because the main categories are not used properly. Meehl (1977) argued that, with enough information, by taking diagnosis seriously and by sticking to the thorough descriptions and major categories, diagnosis could be completely reliable.
- Structured interviews are not used in situations where they would be useful. Unstructured interviews are less reliable.
- Some illnesses are hard to diagnose, and some mental health professionals do not have time to gather all the information needed.

ACTIVITY

Imagine that you are carrying out an interview, with a view to diagnosis. Write a few questions that you might consider suitable for a structured interview. Then write a few lines as to how you think an unstructured interview might progress. Make some notes on what the differences in resulting data might be, and how this could affect the reliability of the diagnosis.

Validity of diagnosis

A categorisation system is valid if it predicts what is happening in reality and if it is useful. For example prognosis must be possible – that is, identifying a path for the disease, and what is likely to happen. Treatment must work to an extent, for the diagnosis to be called valid. Robins and Guze (1970) give five criteria for deciding if a diagnosis is valid:

1 There is a clinical description that can go beyond the actual symptoms – for example, if people of the patient's age often suffer from this disease.
2 Laboratory studies support the conclusions – for example, that this particular group of symptoms do usually go together.
3 This particular set of problems is different from other disorders, and the differences are noticeable.
4 Follow-up studies have indicated reliability, for example by using a test–retest method.
5 Family studies suggest that a particular disorder runs in families.

According to Robins and Guze, as long as one or more of these five criteria can be adopted, there should be some validity in the diagnosis.

Other problems with categorisation

There are other problems in the use of a categorisation system. For example, using terms like 'disease', 'symptoms' and 'illnesses' places an emphasis on the need for treatment and a cure, with the individual being a victim. So when some set of behaviours is included in the DSM (for example, dyslexia), this set of behaviours becomes thought of as an illness, which is not always appropriate.

Classifying in itself can be satisfying for professionals, and can seem to give the answers, but it is not really solving anything directly. Also, the fact that a problem has a label can seem to imply that something can easily be done about it, whereas in reality solving mental health problems is not usually at all straightforward.

Self-test

Write a timed essay, under exam conditions (or as close as you can manage) using the title 'Discuss validity and reliability issues in the diagnosis of mental health problems, and the implications which these issues may have'.

Diagnosis means giving someone a label, and labelling in itself can be harmful in society. The label may close more doors than it opens, owing to prejudice, misunderstandings and other such problems. Diagnosis can be helpful in leading to help being available, but it can also lead to loss of employment or other social problems, and this can make the illness worse.

Cultural factors in diagnosis

We have already looked at some sources of bias in diagnosis. Cultural factors are another important source of bias – both in terms of cultural diversity within a society, and in terms of differences between different countries. For example, Davison and Neale (1994) pointed out that if an Asian-American is very withdrawn, it might be necessary to consider that low levels of emotional expressiveness are considered praiseworthy in this particular group. By attending to cultural factors like this, the clinician is able to avoid thinking that a behaviour is abnormal, whereas in reality it is normal for the particular subculture to which that person belongs.

Diagnosis often involves testing, but there are sometimes problems when tests are used on non-English speakers. Differences in language assumptions mean that an interpreter can often unconsciously change the information that they are providing (Sabin, 1975). Also, people often talk more freely to people of their own culture, and might not disclose much to someone from a different background. When these factors are combined with a lack of knowledge about cultural differences, the result can lead to over-diagnosis of mental illness in particular sections of the population. Malgady *et al.* (1987) looked at cultural and language biases in the diagnosis of Hispanics. In Puerto Rican culture believing that evil spirits can possess a person does not mean the one with the belief is schizophrenic, because there is a general belief in that culture that people are surrounded by invisible spirits.

The problem is, though, that it is too easy for a little knowledge to result in stereotyping. The 'evil spirit' example doesn't account for all people from that particular sector of the population, because not all groups in the Hispanic cultures are the same. Cubans, Puerto Ricans, Mexican Americans or other South Americans have more than one belief system, which affects what would be 'normal' for people from their society and what would be considered to be a problem.

There have been several other examples where cultural beliefs lead to certain behaviours that have then been misinterpreted when diagnosing mental health problems. For example, O'Conner (1989) suggested that because of the Native American emphasis on co-operation, there is a different attitude to tests and testing than there is among White Americans. So, for example, when a Native

American child takes an IQ test they may not do so in a competitive way, and their score can reflect this. The result is that their intellectual abilities will be underestimated. Other diagnostic tests, such as the Rorschach, can show similar problems in that the results are affected by cultural beliefs, in that the way that they are interpreted and scored is incompatible with the social assumptions made by the person who is being tested.

Another important source of bias is the general culture within which the diagnosis is taking place. We have seen how homosexuality used to be considered a disorder according to the DSM system, but how changing social attitudes meant that it was removed from the list of disorders, and is no longer regarded as an illness or mental problem. This shows how the attitudes of a culture are likely to affect what is considered to be a disorder, and what needs treatment. Ideally, a classification system ought to be descriptive, and set out in such a way that it would not be biased according to the race, class or gender of the patient. But often the reality is very different. Diagnosis has been shown to have both race bias (Pavkov *et al.*, 1989) and gender bias (Widiger and Spitzer, 1991).

Gender issues

Kaplan (1983) argued that the DSM system emphasises problems in women, making them appear more prone to mental illness and instability than men, although others say that this is not the case (Kass et al., 1983). The main argument centres around that fact that for some mental illnesses more women are diagnosed than men. However, this might not mean that there is a sex bias in the categorisation system so much as that there are biological or genetic reasons for the gender differences in diagnosis. For example, men are more likely to be diagnosed as having anti-social personality disorder but this may be due to biological factors, such as an excess of testosterone. Alternatively, some of the reasons for different diagnosis might be social – for example, a bias due to socially expected behaviours. There may, therefore, be a sex bias in diagnosis which is not necessarily the fault of the diagnostic system itself, but the outcome of bias on the part of the professionals using the system.

Race and ethnicity

Another source of bias in psychiatric diagnosis has to do with issues of culture and ethnicity. For example. different societies have different views about the causes of mental disorders, and, therefore, are likely to have different views about treatments.

China

Chinese views of mental health are different from Western views. Kao (1979) explains how mental illness is seen in China as an imbalance between the forces of yin and yang, which are the dual forces within the universe and include good and bad, men and women, dark and light, positive and negative. Normal healthy living needs a balance between these two forces, and the answer is to follow the ways of nature and society, and to have moderation in thought and deed.

According to this view, disorders come from an imbalance between yin and yang, and treatments are centred around bringing back this balance, using herbal medicines, acupuncture or other traditional treatments. This leads to

Figure 1.4
A Chinese apothecary plays an important role. Cultures vary in their ideas of what causes or treats mental illnes

a completely different approach to mental problems. For example, the idea of *kuang* refers to mental and emotional difficulties arising from an excess of yang, so cooling liquids are prescribed to reduce inner heat and restore internal harmony and balance. The view in traditional Chinese culture was that mental disorders were caused physically, so there was no stigma attached either to the individual or to their families.

In many cultures old belief systems affect current beliefs, so even though modern Chinese medicine doesn't adhere exactly to the traditional approach, there is still a lot of influence. Given the different type of explanation for mental disorders between a Chinese and a Western approach – coming from a different history and different belief systems – it is almost inevitable that different diagnoses, treatments and attitudes exist between two different types of culture.

Middle East

In the Bible, mental disorders are portrayed as impulsive and unreasonable, and controlled by supernatural powers (God, demons). Often mental disorders were said to have been a punishment for sins. So, in places like the Middle East, the cure for mental disorders was to soothe and charm spirits, or have demons cast out. Both the Bible and the Koran teach that obedience to God leads to mental health, and so fundamentalist adherents to both religions tend to regard mental illness as being a religious problem rather than a physical or psychological one.

Later in the history of the Middle East the influence of the Greeks and Romans led to a different approach, and to a greater emphasis on disorders and healing. Europe was also influenced by the Greeks and the Romans, so many similar attitudes to healing exist between the Middle East and Europe. It is interesting to consider how far historical beliefs and ideas affect decisions such as diagnosis of mental disorders.

Africa

In African societies, mental illness was traditionally thought to represent being possessed by demons or angry ancestors, or to have resulted from some kind of spell being put on the individual after a quarrel or dispute with a neighbour. So traditional practitioners often looked for sources of social stress when trying to tackle mental illness. In some African societies, mental disorders were thought to have physical causes. In Africa today mental illness has less social stigma than it does in the Western world, and the members of African societies are more tolerant of it, giving much more family and other social support. Folk healers use herbal remedies and exorcism, and communities sometimes use group therapies such as dance.

Europe

In mediaeval Europe, mental illness was seen as possession by demons and as a punishment for sins or unacceptable behaviour. Gradually, however, a more scientific approach evolved, and various types of treatments were developed. As medical knowledge improved so the emphasis on possession by demons declined. Instead, mental illnesses were seen as having either a physical or a social cause. It was from such thinking that Kraepelin suggested the classification system which we looked at earlier, and Freud developed psychoanalysis.

As we have seen, differences both within and between cultures can produce problems in diagnosis. But taking cultural beliefs into account when making a diagnosis can also lead to problems. One of them is that this can minimise the seriousness of the problems (Lopez, 1989). It could be that less significance is given to hallucinations if the person is African-American, and this could be against the person's best interests, as they may not be then diagnosed as schizophrenic when they ought to be. However, sometimes there can be over-diagnosis. For instance, West Indians in Britain are far more likely to be diagnosed as having mental illnesses than other groups, which is at least partly a result of cultural misunderstandings. Similarly, in America, Blake (1973) found that people were more likely to be diagnosed as schizophrenic if they were African-American than if the person was described as White. How far a professional ought to take cultural and ethnic factors into account, therefore, is a tricky question and one where there are no hard and fast rules.

Approaches and therapies

Many different treatments and therapies are used to tackle mental problems of one sort or another. This is partly because there are so many different approaches to understanding mental problems – different ideas about what is really the cause of the 'problem'. For example, if it is thought that a child's bad behaviour has been learnt through reinforcement, then changing the pattern of reinforcement might be the suggested treatment. It all depends on the particular **paradigm** that the practitioner is adopting.

There are many different paradigms in psychology (Figure 1.5). A paradigm is a set of basic assumptions about how something is thought about, how data is gathered, and what influences there might be. Paradigms in psychology –

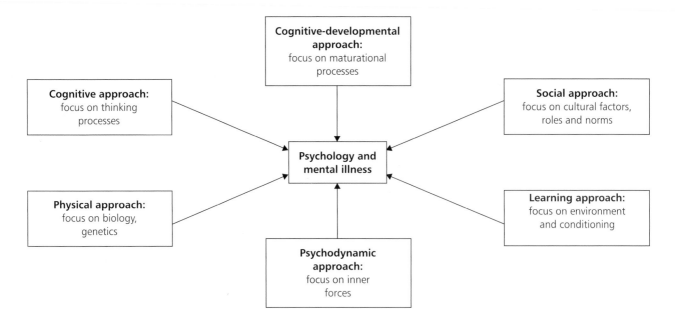

Figure 1.5
The main approaches can help in the understanding and suggested treatment of mental illness, as well as in monitoring mental health

sometimes called approaches – include the biological, learning, cognitive, psychodynamic, humanistic and social approaches or paradigms. We will look at the main assumptions of each of these approaches, and consider the type of treatment or therapy that might be suggested given its assumptions. In what follows, it is assumed that the main approaches (except for the humanistic one) have already been studied for AS level. Within each approach examples of treatments or therapies are given, unless these have been studied already as part of your AS work, or unless they are going to be covered in more detail later in the chapter.

⟳ Recall AS material

Recall your AS material about the different paradigms in psychology – or look them up. These include the main approaches – biological, psychoanalytic, learning, and cognitive. It is from these approaches that the treatments are derived, partly because they determine what is thought to be the cause of the problem.

The medical/biological approach

The biological approach to mental illness assumes that there is a disease that must be treated. This is the medical or disease model, which includes **aetiology** – the study of what causes the disease – as well as the underlying genetic and biochemical factors. Maher (1966) discussed the medical terminology involved when looking at mental health, such as the use of terms such as 'symptoms' for the behaviours that people are showing, and 'treatments' for

the actions people take to help others. The use of these terms tends to assume that there is an illness, comparable to a physical illness, and can also make it difficult for people to look at the problem in any other way.

There have been a number of criticisms of the medical model in the past. Nowadays, the biological approach is less likely to look only at disease, and is more likely to look at disruption of biological functioning. For example, depression is thought to arise sometimes from problems in neural transmission, and anxiety disorders can arise from a problem in the autonomic nervous system.

Evaluation

– A problem with the disease model of mental illness is that such a lot of different symptoms and problems are covered. Even the DSM-IV isn't adequate to cover all the issues.
– Medical diagnosis can easily lead to social labelling, due to general misunderstandings of what mental illness really is.
+ The use of the medical model can make it easier for a person to obtain treatment, and for others to understand what is happening.

⟳ Recall AS material

Recall (or look up) your AS material on the physiological approach on neural transmission, the functioning of the nervous system and on the influence of genetic factors.

Behaviour genetics

Behaviour genetics involves the study of genes, and how differences in behaviour might be attributed to specific genes. The genotype of a person is how they are made up in terms of the genes, and their phenotype is the characteristics exhibited by their genotype and influenced by environmental factors. Some disorders are those of the phenotype, for example, anxiety disorders involve environmental influences. Other disorders can be those of the genotype and are inherited. Many will come from a genetic predisposition that needs a certain environment to trigger the problem.

Ways of studying the question of whether something comes from a person's nature or their nurture include family, twin and adoption studies. These have their own problems and advantages, as you will have studied for the AS part of the course.

↻ Recall AS material

Recall your AS material on ways of studying whether something is caused genetically or from environmental factors, or look them up. This will be important material for Unit 6, the synoptic part of the course.

Biochemistry

Biochemistry of mental illness involves the study of the nervous system, the ways the neurones communicate and act within the nervous system (Figure 1.6), and how neurotransmitters work. Abnormal behaviour can stem from problems in neurotransmitter activity, as has been discussed in the AS part of the course.

↻ Recall AS material

Recall or look up your AS material on how neurotransmitters work.

Biological approaches to treatment

If it is thought that abnormal behaviour is caused either by a genetic predisposition or a biochemical imbalance, then any treatment will have a biological basis. Altering bodily functioning may correct the problem or alleviate the symptoms. For example, drugs can be given to alter the neurotransmitter balance or to mimic a neurotransmitter that is deficient. Phenylketonuria (PKU), for instance, is caused by a lack of an enzyme that lets the body metabolise phenylalanine into tyrosine, and produces mental retardation. This lack of enzyme is genetic in origin, but when it has been identified by genetic testing the imbalance can be corrected through a diet low in

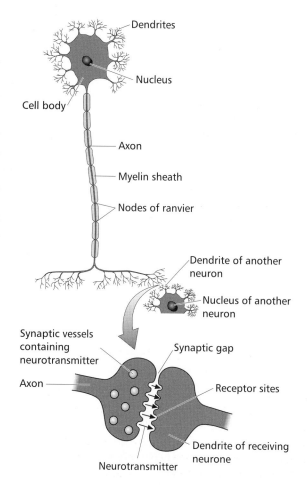

Figure 1.6
A neuron and the synaptic gap

phenylalanine; and so the mental retardation can be avoided.

Other examples of this type of treatment includes giving diazepam (Valium) to reduce tension in anxiety disorders or using other drugs such as lithium to treat bipolar disorder. Some 'biological' treatments include intervening at a physical level and affecting how the neurones actually work, such as by giving electroconvulsive shock treatment (ECT) for severe depression. We will be looking at some other biological approaches to treatment later in this chapter.

Criticisms of the biological model of mental illness

- When dealing with mental problems much of the data are qualitative and not quantitative, but a medical model often assumes that the diagnosis is based on objective measurement, such as measuring a high temperature or carrying out a scan.
- Some symptoms are grouped and labelled a disease as a result; but the disease is only known about by reference to the group of symptoms. This means that the explanation of the disease by reference to its symptoms is circular, and

not all that helpful. However, it might be thought useful to diagnose simply by reference to a set of symptoms, because that would help in later learning, and at some stage a definite cause might be found.

- Szasz (1960) and others argue that the symptoms of a physical disease are objective and can be measured, whereas the symptoms of a mental disease are subjective and cannot. As a result, labelling it as a disease is inaccurate, and it would be more helpful to think of it as 'problems in living' The symptoms can be what a person is thinking, which is subjective, not objective.

- Mental illnesses do not usually have just one specific set of symptoms, and the same physical disease might give different symptoms in different people. Some argue that because of this they should not really be called illnesses. However, it is possible to argue that not all physical diseases have a straightforward, consistent set of symptoms either.

↻ *Recall AS material*

Recall your AS material on method, and distinguish between quantitative and qualitative data; or look this up.

Figure 1.7
Sigmund Freud, well known for developing psychoanalysis, and who emphasised the importance of unconscious forces in driving behaviour

The psychodynamic/psychoanalytic approach

You will already have studied the psychodynamic approach in depth for the AS part of the course. The main point of this paradigm is that problems come from unconscious conflicts and forces. Defence mechanisms are used (unconsciously) to allow the individual to avoid facing up to their unconscious conflicts. Mental illness is thought to occur when the energy used in maintaining defence mechanisms is giving an individual problems.

↻ *Recall AS material*

Recall your AS material on the psychodynamic approach, or look it up. This will also be useful for Unit 6, the synoptic part of the course.

The main method of treatment in this paradigm is to release the unconscious conflicts, getting behind the defence mechanisms, and making thoughts and memories conscious. The idea is that once they have come to conscious awareness there will be no problem, because the individual will be able to learn more open ways of working through their problems and coming to terms with them, and as a result will have freed themselves.

Treatment is by psychoanalysis, although there are variations here. Traditional psychoanalysis involves the therapist not being involved directly. Important issues in treatment include **transference** and **counter-transference**. Transference is where the person undergoing treatment (the analysand) transfers their feelings on to the therapist; counter-transference is where the therapist may transfer feelings on to the analysand. We will be looking at some examples of where psychoanalysis can be used later in this chapter.

↻ *Recall AS material*

Recall your AS material on treatments using the psychodynamic approach, and give an example of the sorts of 'symptoms' an individual might present to the therapist – or look them up.

The behavioural approach

You have already studied the behavioural or learning approach as part of your AS work. The two main types of learning within the behavioural approach are **classical conditioning** and **operant conditioning**, both of which you will have studied in detail for the AS part of the course.

A third type of learning contained within the behavioural approach is **social learning theory**. The main assumptions of this approach are that learning comes from surroundings and environment, and that experiences shape a person's behaviour, attitudes and beliefs. So mental health issues can be understood in terms of a person's learning and experiences, and treatment is likely to be about changing their behaviour – that is, re-learning new ways of acting – to alleviate the problem.

Mental health problems tend to be interpreted as maladaptive behaviour occurring as a result of inappropriate learning experiences. So the idea is that if the behaviour were to be changed, mental health would improve as a result. Ways to change behaviour include behaviour modification and behaviour therapy. We will be looking at some specific examples of these later in this chapter.

Figure 1.8
Behavioural models of psychological treatment follow principles developed by B.F. Skinner

⟳ Recall AS material

Recall your AS material on the learning approach, its assumptions, main concepts and related treatments – or look them up. This will also be useful for Unit 6, the synoptic part of the course.

The cognitive approach

You will already have studied the cognitive approach for AS level. The cognitive approach involves looking at thinking and cognitive processes, and the ways in which people structure information. For your AS work you are likely to have studied mainly memory, but perception, attention, language and thought are also included within the cognitive approach. One problem with the cognitive paradigm when explaining mental health issues is that it does not really do much explaining. Saying that depression comes from sad thoughts is a description of what is happening, but is not much help as an explanation. You can probably see, though, that suggesting that the person attempts to substitute more cheerful thoughts for the gloomy ones, and identifying ways of learning how to do this, might be a successful form of therapy. Quite a lot of modern therapy is based on cognitive restructuring of this type, and stems from the basic assumptions of the cognitive approach.

Cognitive–behavioural therapy

Your AS work for the biological, psychodynamic and learning approaches will have covered some of the treatments and therapies involved. However, work undertaken for the cognitive approach will not have explored the way that it has been used in clinical practice. Cognitive–behavioural therapy is one of the ways in which the cognitive approach leads to a practical application. The idea is that someone uses cognitive restructuring to change the way they think about life, and therefore to change their behaviour and emotions (Davison, 1966).

Rational–emotive behaviour therapy

Ellis (1962) has proposed a different sort of cognitive behavioural therapy. He suggests that irrational beliefs cause maladaptive behaviour. People have mistaken assumptions and, therefore, put pressure on themselves to achieve things they cannot achieve. For example, a woman might think everyone must like her, or a man might think he must always be perfect. Rational–emotive behaviour therapy aims to get people to think more rationally – for example, to admit that they can make a mistake. It combines this with therapeutic efforts to help people to adjust emotionally, and to learn new behaviours.

Cognitive therapy

Beck (1967) also put forward a form of cognitive therapy, emphasising how people distort their experience. Someone who is depressed, for example, is likely to remember or notice only the bad things that happen in a day, and to ignore or discount the positive ones. Beck developed a form of therapy which aimed to encourage people to change the way they see themselves, and the way they interpret what happens to them. Cognitive therapy is very concerned with the attributions and explanations that people use to explain what is happening to them.

↻ Recall AS material

Recall your AS material on the cognitive approach, or look it up. This will also be useful for Unit 6, the synoptic part of the course.

Comparing the cognitive and learning approaches to therapy

There are many similarities between the cognitive and learning approaches to therapy. Both focus on changing behaviour, for example, and both consider that mental disorders stem from maladaptive behaviour. The cognitive approach, however, also focuses on maladaptive thinking. You will have come across Bandura's name in connection with social learning theory, within the learning approach. However, Bandura also advocated changing behaviour through cognitive means, and was the source of some of the close links between these two approaches. In recent years, Bandura has come to emphasise the importance of an individual's sense of **self-efficacy**, which is their belief that they can achieve their desired goals or do what they intend to do.

Bandura's work is usually located within the learning approach partly because of his early work, which emphasised learning through imitation and modelling, and partly also because he sees maladaptive behaviour and sense of self-efficacy as being changed by changing behaviour. However, the work of Beck and others is located within the cognitive approach because they believe change comes essentially from changed thinking patterns, and tend to use behavioural change as a way of achieving or strengthening those different patterns.

The humanistic approach

The humanistic approach was not included in the AS part of the course, so it is outlined briefly here. The focus of this approach is on personal growth, and not so much on mental disorder, which is largely seen as occurring when personal growth is interrupted or stopped for some reason. Those within the humanistic paradigm:
- emphasise free will
- see the most important part of someone's world as being their own view of it
- focus on an individual's strengths, and not their weaknesses

- encourage personal growth rather than relieving distress.

Some important names within the approach include Carl Rogers and Abraham Maslow. For those within the humanistic approach, human nature is basically good, and everyone has a need to self-actualise – that is, to realise their full potential, or strive to do so. Mental health problems arise if this striving for self-actualisation becomes blocked in some way. One problem with the humanistic approach is that for the most part those within that paradigm do not usually think of mental disorders in categories and as needing diagnosis. This sets them apart from many people working in the other approaches. Humanistic therapies have generally been regarded as more appropriate for people with neurotic or anxiety disorders than for those with psychotic problems such as schizophrenia.

Comparing humanistic and psychoanalytic therapies

Humanistic therapies are similar to cognitive therapies, in that they are focused on giving the individual an insight into their own problems. In this way humanistic therapies are also similar to psychoanalytic ones. However, those within the psychoanalytic approach generally see human nature as something that needs to be restrained (the idea of the id), whereas humanists tend to see human nature as basically good and positive. For the humanist, free will is important and, although it can sometimes be destructive, we must use it if we are to achieve mental health and positive mental growth.

Client-centred therapy

Rogers proposed a therapy called **client-centred therapy**, which came from his own experiences as a clinical psychologist. As a humanist, Rogers assumed that healthy people are innately good and effective and can become aware of their behaviour as goal directed and self-directive. So he argued that therapists should create a situation where the individual can become healthy. To do so would mean that they needed to become effective, aware of their behaviour, and able to direct their own goals. However, the person has to do this for themselves, and it is the job of the therapist to create the situation in which this becomes possible. There is an innate drive to self-actualise and this will drive behaviour if the person can avoid social demands from others, including the therapist.

The therapist must have three core qualities:
- *Genuineness* – which means no façade: the therapist must act normally and honestly.
- *Unconditional positive regard* – which means there are no conditions attached by the therapist to the client, in

terms of how the therapist sees them. They will be liked anyway, regardless of what they actually do or say. Even if the therapist does not actually like a particular act or action, he or she must convey unpossessive warmth and respect towards the client, because the client is another human being and therefore a person of worth.
- *Accurate empathic understanding* – having the ability to see through the eyes of the client and to share in their feelings.

Evaluation of psychotherapy

The term 'psychotherapy' covers all treatments involving psychological techniques, such as talking, listening and exploring thinking, from Freud's views to those of Rogers. So the idea of evaluation applies to the therapies of the psychodynamic and humanistic approaches, as well as to cognitive therapies.

One issue is that it could be that someone paying attention to the individual rather than the therapy itself is what helps. This is like a **placebo effect**, where someone is given a sugar pill instead of the drug they think they are taking, but they still improve, presumably because of psychological reasons. However, Lambert *et al.* (1986) studied the effects of psychotherapy in general and found that factors such as warmth, trust and encouragement do have a lasting effect, and this is more than a simple placebo effect.

Similarly, Nicholson and Berman (1983) analysed the results of 67 studies and concluded that the positive effects of psychotherapy lasted for many months after treatment had ceased. However, these conclusions are drawn from meta-analyses, which means combining the results of many different studies. There are problems here in drawing conclusions from studies that used different methods, different patients, and in many cases different therapies.

Another problem which occurs when we are trying to evaluate therapies is what is known as the **deterioration effect**. When a group is studied, although many do improve with psychotherapy, some will always get worse. Combining the results of the group as a whole may obscure any real effects of the therapy, because on average it will appear as though it has not made any difference to the group as a whole. So it is difficult to say for certain that a particular therapy is effective, or better than another.

The social approach – community psychology

The social approach does not directly give rise to treatments in the same way as the other paradigms do.

However, it places an emphasis on a social approach to mental disorders, which is what we will be looking at here. Some researchers have claimed, for example, that schizophrenia is a result of social deprivation, and so social factors are involved in examining schizophrenia, as we will see later in this chapter. But there are several other facets to the social approach.

Community psychology is a relatively new approach, and links in many ways to health psychology. Community psychology emphasises the role of the environment, both in creating problems and in helping to solve them. This is the link to the social approach, as the individual's society and social environment is seen as important. Problems are seen as developing from an interaction between the individual, the social setting and the systems. As a result, considerable emphasis is placed on the community within which everything is occurring. This approach deals with prevention as well as with problem-solving, and as a result it has strong links with **health psychology**, which also stresses the importance of prevention.

A society needs to try to prevent problems, and to solve them with social needs in mind, because problems happen within a community and within a social context. Also, solving mental health problems costs the community both in financial and other terms, so prevention is very helpful to all concerned. Rappaport (1977) suggested that the important factors in this respect are cultural relativity, diversity and ecology. The social approach also emphasises the importance of taking different cultures and a person's ecology – that is, their particular role and activities within their community – into account.

There is, however, recognition of individuality. Community psychology focuses on diversity and the differences between people rather than on social norms, and it also looks closely at the way that the community and the individual interact. There is less emphasis on the inadequacy of a person or on an individual not fitting into rigid social norms, and more on understanding the nature of the interaction between the individual and their community. For community psychology, it is the interaction that is important, and interaction is an important concept in social psychology.

↻ Recall AS material

Recall or look up your AS material on the social approach. This will be useful for linking the concepts of social psychology to community psychology, and also for the synoptic part of the course.

The growth of community psychology

Community psychology has grown considerably during the past couple of decades, particularly in response to the social needs resulting from 'Care in the Community' programmes and other social trends. Some of the factors which led to this growth include:

- *Pressure on treatment facilities.* Mental hospitals were seen as costly and inefficient. Socially oriented mental health professionals wanted alternatives. Drugs became available that would calm patients. This meant that some who would have been admitted to a mental hospital were not admitted, and others were discharged. There was also a shortage of trained therapists in the hospitals, and it was being argued that hospitalisation was not improving the mental health of the patients.
- *Personnel shortage.* Clinical psychologists and psychiatrists were being trained, but not in sufficient numbers to keep up with demand. Therefore new methods of dealing with mental health issues needed to be found.
- *Questions about psychotherapy.* People began to question whether psychotherapy was effective. Also the emphasis on interaction between society and the individual made people think about there being different causes for mental health problems – causes where society may have a role. Social class also seemed to be related to whether people could access psychotherapy.
- *Questions about the medical model.* The medical model was also being questioned. It was seen that mental illness was more complex than simply being a biological problem: social and environmental factors were also important.
- *Emphasis on the environment.* It was realised that social and environmental factors such as poverty, pollution and crowding had effects on people's mental health. An individual's emotional problems were seen as being affected by issues such as employment, family, racism, sexism and educational background.

Community care aims to provide an environment that will enable patients to resume a responsible place in society. For example, it involves setting up halfway houses, where hospitalised patients can learn the skills needed for independent living. Day hospitals are used too, and are less expensive than having hospitals where a patient stays 24 hours.

Crisis intervention

There were other aspects to community care as well as allowing previously hospitalised patients to learn skills and become independent. One of these was the focus on **crisis intervention** – trying to reach people who would previously have been diagnosed as mentally ill and hospitalised before they reached a stage where things became too extreme. Centres in the community that can be easily and quickly reached might be able to help someone in a very stressed condition, and so prevent the need for hospitalisation. However, if these centres are to operate properly they need 24-hour walk-in service and the possibility of immediate attention being given to the person who needs it. In that sort of situation there is little time for a medical opinion or for appointments. As a result, crisis intervention requires a very flexible approach and the traditional mental health profession roles often become blurred.

There have been several ways of attempting to tackle these problems. In the early years, telephone answering services were popular, and they still are used a little. However, this approach is often seen as too slow and too remote, and the favourite alternative is a 24-hour service where professionals answer the calls themselves – although some centres are staffed by volunteers, rather than paid professionals. In the UK, this model has been extended from the mental health field to that of general health as well, as health professionals developed the skills of working in this way. Crisis intervention for mental health, however, is a little different, since it can also involve follow-up calls, face-to-face contact and help with finding temporary shelter, transportation or other kinds of assistance. Sometimes crisis intervention is more short-term but rapid – for example, in a crisis brought about by a major accident such as the Paddington train crash, where community, counselling and clinical psychologists were all active in providing support and help for people traumatised by the disaster.

Is community psychology effective?

In research in the USA, Decker and Stubblebine (1972) found that the number of hospitalisations reduced when crisis intervention was used. However, other researchers found no evidence of improvement when comparing individuals who had received crisis intervention and those who had not. Rappaport (1977) argued there was no evidence that people's mental health improved with community psychology. However, it is now thought that prevention programmes have become much more effective (Felner *et al.*, 1991). This might be because mental health professionals have been learning from early mistakes. In 1994, the American Institute of Medicine published a report describing 39 intervention programmes which had been shown to work. But the report still identified a number of problems with the system, including the number of professionals needed to run such programmes.

Comparing the approaches

There are, as we have seen, some considerable differences between the various approaches. Most clinical psychologists, however, tend to adopt a mixture of paradigms, drawing from different approaches as they appear to be useful. It is possible, though, to draw comparisons between the approaches, although it needs to be borne in mind that a complete knowledge of the paradigm is really needed for understanding, and comparisons may not be useful for a clinician. The main reason for making comparisons is that one approach is often more suitable than others for understanding a particular mental health problem. For example, phobias tend to be seen as learned fears, and so the learning or behavioural approach is often seen as the best way of treating a phobia.

Scientific v. non-scientific

One way of comparing the approaches is to consider whether they are scientific or not. This can affect diagnosis and treatment of a particular mental health issue. There are several different ways of defining what counts as scientific or not, but here we will just consider one of them, which is the idea that 'scientific' can be defined as involving measurement, tests, using controls and drawing conclusions. It would thus be possible to say that the medical or biological approach is scientific – the effect of drugs given to change the balance of neurotransmitters in the brain can be measured, for example (although only indirectly when studying living beings). The learning or behavioural approach is also scientific according to this view, in that it aims at measurable information and intervention where mental health problems are concerned. The cognitive approach, whilst using psychotherapy, and whilst emphasising action such as positive thinking, also rests on measurable data in the sense of using scientific measures where possible. For example, memory problems might be treated using training in thinking and remembering, and measurable tests such as remembering items in a list would be used. So to some extent the cognitive approach can be said to be scientific.

The other approaches, though, would be considered non-scientific according to these criteria. If 'non-scientific' is taken to mean not relying so much on objective testable variables and objective measurable treatments, but looking more at the individual as an individual, then approaches such as the humanistic and psychoanalytic fall into that category. Some cognitive therapies also fall within this category, as they also emphasise the individual and individual functioning. The social approach would also be considered to be more non-scientific than scientific according to these criteria, although research into social issues does use scientific methods.

> **Synoptic Note**
>
> This argument about whether psychology is a science or not is part of what you need for Unit 6, the synoptic part of the course.

Nature v nurture

Another way of comparing approaches is to see how they deal with issues of nature and nurture. The medical or biological approach emphasises the influence of genes and the genotype. A person's nature is important, in that they may have either an inherited problem or an inherited predisposition for a problem. In recent years this approach has increasingly recognised that environmental factors can play a role. Overall, the medical or biological approach emphasises nature. The psychodynamic approach also emphasises the nature side of the debate in many ways, by focusing on unconscious forces and the way that all of us have opposing forces we have to balance. However, nurture is also heavily involved in affecting our development – for example, how our parents relate to us when we are young.

The learning or behavioural approach, on the other hand, deliberately focuses on the influence of nurture and the environment, believing that only external objective acts are important, because only they are measurable. The humanistic approach makes assumptions about human nature, and so to an extent includes nativist ideas, but problems are seen as stemming from our aim to self-actualise and problems in achieving this, which come from our experiences and upbringing – which is nurture. The social approach also emphasises nurture, being interested in the effects of society.

The cognitive approach assumes we all have the same natural means of cognitive functioning, and so might be considered to be on the 'nature' side of the debate, but it also acknowledges that people's problems can often come from inappropriate attributions and beliefs, and these come from experience.

In fact, these nature/nurture issues are much less relevant for the more recent psychological paradigms, since they tend to see nature and nurture as interdependent, rather than being in opposition to one another; and so they tend to build in acknowledgement of both factors.

Types of treatment

It is clear that the different assumptions are likely to produce equally different types of treatment. Another way of comparing the approaches is to look at the different treatments, and this can be a useful way of distinguishing them. For example, drug treatments are likely to be used within the medical or biological approach. Psychotherapy is likely to be used within the psychodynamic, humanistic, social or cognitive approach, but not the behaviourist or medical approach. Systematic desensitisation or a similar method of changing someone's behaviour will be used within the behavioural or learning approach.

Self-test

Write a timed essay, under exam conditions (or as close as you can manage) using the title ' Compare two different therapeutic approaches to mental disorders'.

Specific mental disorders

We mentioned a number of specific mental disorders when we were looking at the DSM-IV categories earlier. In this section, we will examine four of these in more detail: anxiety disorders, schizophrenia, mood disorders, and eating disorders. We will be exploring the nature of the disorders, the various suggestions for possible causes and

ACTIVITY

When looking at therapies, it is important to link them with the major approaches to understanding mental disorder. You need to have at least one example of treatment from each approach – biological, psychodynamic, learning, cognitive and humanistic. Draw up a chart with five columns, for the five approaches. Then make a list of all of the therapies mentioned in this chapter, and classify each one according to the approach within which it originated.

the various therapies that have been used as treatment. In each case, we will examine the relative importance of physiological, social and psychological factors. This will lead us into considering the nature/nurture issue – whether a disorder is genetically given, environmentally caused or comes from a combination of nature and nurture factors.

Anxiety disorders

Anxiety disorders are classified as **neuroses**. These are mental disorders where there is dysfunction, but that dysfunction mainly takes the form of an exaggeration of certain behaviours or symptoms which occur normally in just about everyone. So the person is only different from normal because of the severity or the excessive frequency of their symptoms. Unlike some forms of psychosis, which we will be looking at later, the person is still in touch with reality, and knows that they have a problem.

Anxiety disorders are closely associated with stress. As you may already have learned, anxiety and fear can be useful in evolutionary terms, because the **fight or flight response** prepares the animal (or person) for action when faced with a physical threat, and so helps survival. The physiological changes associated with the fight or flight reaction are involved in both fear and anxiety, but the two emotions are slightly different. Fear is a response to something specific, whereas anxiety is a more general unease. Some anxiety is normal – up to a point – and anxiety only becomes a disorder when it interferes with the person's normal, everyday functioning. Symptoms of anxiety disorder include tension, nervousness, heart palpitations, sweating, dizziness, trembling and concentration problems, which may affect both social and work situations.

Anxiety disorders and symptoms

- *Generalised anxiety disorder* – excessive anxiety that occurs on most days for a period of months. The anxiety usually centres around issues like work and school. Symptoms include fatigue, difficulty in concentrating, muscle tension and sleep disorders.
- *Simple or specific phobia* – persistent, excessive, unreasonable fear about an object.
- *Social phobia* – as with simple phobias, but in response to social situations rather than objects.
- *Panic attack* – a feeling of overwhelming fear that occurs suddenly and unexpectedly. Symptoms include sweating, fear of losing control, trembling, shaking and shortness of breath.
- *Agoraphobia* – fear of being in open places, or places where escape is difficult. It often includes fear of the fear itself.
- *Obsessive–compulsive disorder (OCD)* – obsessions are recurrent, persistent, inappropriate thoughts, and

compulsions are repetitive acts the person feels obliged to perform.

- *Post-traumatic stress disorder (PTSD)* – persistent re-experiencing of a traumatic event. Symptoms include sleep disturbances, difficulty in concentrating and an exaggerated startle response.

Explanations for anxiety disorders

There have been a number of different explanations put forward for anxiety disorders, and these explanations reflect the different approaches to mental disorder we looked at earlier in the chapter.

Biological theories

Anxiety is linked to physiological states, and in particular the state of arousal. The autonomic nervous system prepares the body for a 'fight or flight' reaction (this is sometimes called the emergency reaction). Both hormones and neurotransmitters are involved in this reaction, which is a natural response to perceived threat. Usually the parasympathetic part of the autonomic nervous system allows the body to return to its calmer state. However, if this does not happen, and the alarm or emergency reaction continues, then stress is the result. We will be looking at stress and its physical correlates in more detail in Chapter 8.

Another set of biological explanations emphasises the role of **genetic factors** in anxiety disorders. As we have seen, the readiness of the autonomic nervous system to prepare us for action when a threat is presented is a useful survival trait and is an inherited characteristic of all humans. This predisposes us to excessive fear of certain stimuli, in particular the kind that are common sources of simple phobias. For example, most phobias concern spiders, snakes, heights and so on (Table 1.3). Only rarely do people have phobias about guns and electric sockets, even though we could argue that guns and electricity are just as harmful as spiders and snakes. Seligman (1971) argues that humans are 'prepared' by the process of natural selection to fear certain things that were likely to harm them.

Cook and Mineka (1989) studied monkeys and found they quickly learnt a phobia for snakes by watching other monkeys show fear of snakes. However, the monkeys did not become fearful of artificial flowers when watching other monkeys show fear of artificial flowers. Phobias do seem to be learned (in the above case by observational learning); but there does seem to be a genetic tendency to develop certain phobias rather than others. Preparedness on its own, however, doesn't really explain why some people have such extreme phobias, or why so many people don't have any fear of these specific stimuli.

Table 1.3 Examples of phobias

Label	Fear
Acrophobia	Heights
Aichmophobia	Pointed objects
Ailurophobia	Cats
Algophobia	Pain
Arachnophobia	Spiders
Astraphobia	Storms: thunder and lightning
Autophobia	Oneself
Claustrophobia	Closed spaces; confinement
Euphobia	Good news
Genuphobia	Knees
Gephyrophobia	Bridges
Hematophobia	Blood
Hydrophobia	Water
Linonophobia	String
Nyctophobia	Darkness
Ophidiophobia	Snakes
Pyrophobia	Fire
Thanatophobia	Death
Xenophobia	Strangers

↻ Recall AS material

Recall your AS material from the learning approach where Seligman's ideas about preparedness are discussed – or look it up.

Another genetic feature in the development of anxiety disorders has to do with the fundamental temperament you are born with. Some studies suggest that some children are born with the trait of nervousness, or with a readiness to become nervous. For example, Kagan *et al.* (1988) found that some children were socially inhibited and avoided interacting with others even in their first two years of life. In further studies, Kagan *et al.* found that this trait remained consistent during the first seven years at least, which was as far as their study was able to trace it. It is therefore possible that some people are born with anxiety-related temperaments. Those who are socially inhibited early in life may be more likely to develop anxiety disorders later.

Further evidence for a genetic base for anxiety disorders comes from the way that relatives of children with anxiety disorders are more likely to have them themselves. In one study (Last *et al.* 1991), researchers found that 35% of first-degree relatives of children with an anxiety disorder had a diagnosable anxiety disorder themselves, 23.5% of relatives had such a diagnosis if the children had a different diagnosis (not anxiety disorder), and 16% of relatives had an anxiety disorder of the group where children had no diagnosis at all.

It is generally concluded that there are genetic factors involved in anxiety disorders, since most studies that have looked for genetic contributions, or heritability, have concluded that there is at least some contribution. For example, panic disorder was found in nearly 25% of close relatives of patients with panic disorder, whereas only 2% of the population as a whole experience that particular problem (Crowe *et al.*, 1983). It might be that particular disorders are even more likely to have a genetic basis than others. Generalised anxiety disorder (GAD), for example, seems less likely to be inherited, in that a study of more than 1,000 female twins indicated that GAD does not have a large heritability factor. However, researchers did conclude that 30% of the chance of developing GAD might be due to genetic factors (Kendler *et al.*, 1992a). Simple phobias also seem to run in families, according to a study looking at both close relatives and twin pairs (Kendler *et al.*, 1992b), although further analysis by these researchers suggested that agoraphobia may have the highest genetic component and simple phobia the least.

Evaluation

- We learn from family as well as inherit characteristics from them, so finding that relatives also have anxiety disorders may simply show that observational learning and modelling has taken place, rather than indicating heritability.

Recall AS material

Recall your AS material from the physiological approach on the use of twin studies, or look it up. You can use the criticisms of the method you learned there in evaluating the explanation here.

There is some evidence that **biological reactivity** may be another factor. Some people seem to have a more highly reactive autonomic nervous system than others. When put in a stressful situation where they are challenged (for example, by being forced to hyperventilate), people with panic disorders are more likely to have a panic attack (Barlow, 1988). However, other stressful situations such as doing mental arithmetic or having a pain experience do not appear to trigger off panic attacks, which has been taken as evidence against the idea (Roth *et al.*, 1992). It is therefore an open question whether the idea that some

people are more biologically reactive is a valid explanation for anxiety disorders.

Anther biological explanation for anxiety disorders concerns **endocrinological and neurotransmitter factors** – that is, hormones and brain chemicals. It is thought that some people may lack whatever substances are needed for calm. For example, there are receptors specific to benzodiazepines, which are the chemicals that seem to have a calming effect on people with anxiety, and it is thought that those with anxiety disorders may lack the natural equivalent of benzodiazepines. The neurotransmitter GABA is also said to relate to anxiety disorders.

It is generally agreed that more research is needed in this area before concluding that anxiety is caused by lack of certain chemical substances; but there have been some strikingly effective therapies which have been developed on the basis of this idea. For example, beta-blockers have been very effective treatments for many kinds of anxiety, and it is thought that obsessive-compulsive disorder may be connected to the serotinergic system, because drugs such as Prozac, which block the re-uptake of serotonin, work so effectively with some people. (For more information about neurotransmitters, and how they work, see Chapter 8.)

Psychodynamic theories

Freud distinguished between objective, moral and neurotic anxiety. In **objective anxiety**, the reason for the anxiety is located in the external world. For example, being anxious because someone is pointing a gun at you would count as objective anxiety – the objective reality itself is likely to cause fear. **Moral anxiety** is where the superego causes the worry. For example, an anxiety about being punished if one's behaviour is not moral or up to standard in some way would be an example of the internalised strictness of the superego creating anxiety. **Neurotic anxiety** is when the person is trying not to give in to an uncontrollable urge to do something harmful or socially unacceptable. Repression keeps these urges under control, and stops the person from experiencing anxiety. But repression will only keep the urges unconscious, and will not remove the problem, and the person may experience anxiety or panic attacks as a result.

Later psychodynamic theories emphasise parenting and the early years, and consider situations such as separation from the mother as leading to later anxiety disorders. It has been suggested, for example, that perhaps those with social phobia are re-living early mother–child relationships. The problem is that there is little evidence for this explanation. For example, children separated from their mothers do not seem more likely to develop anxiety disorders than any other children.

Behavioural theories

Behavioural theories suggest that classical conditioning principles, operant conditioning or modelling lead to learned anxieties. One example of the way classical conditioning can lead to phobias occurs in the case of Little Albert, which you may have studied for the AS part of the course. Little Albert showed a natural fear response to a loud noise. When his pet rat was paired with the loud noise, it was not long before Little Albert showed a fear response to the rat as well. He had learned a phobia by means of classical conditioning.

Figure 1.9
The tarantula. It is not uncommon for people to want to avoid spiders. However, phobias are persistent unreasonable fears that interfere with a person's life

Operant conditioning might mean that a fear is learned through reinforcements. Avoiding something unpleasant can be a positive reward. School phobia, for example, can be an escape response learned through the principles of operant conditioning. Modelling can lead to learning too, so someone observing that a girl has escaped bullying by staying away from school (developing a school phobia) might learn to escape bullying in the same way.

⟳ Recall AS material

Recall your AS material from the learning approach. Go through the principles of classical conditioning and in particular the study of Little Albert, who learnt to fear objects through the application of those principles. If you don't remember it, look it up.

Cognitive theories

The cognitive approach explains anxiety by saying that it is a dysfunctional way of seeing the world. People with unhealthy emotional lives have irrational thoughts, or make consistently irrational attributions. These are often self-defeating. For example, if a person thinks they must always be the best, they may become anxious about taking part in a competition for fear of failure. A study of 500 research participants showed that those who believed they should, for example, aim for perfection did tend to have high levels of anxiety (Deffenbacher *et al.*, 1986), which provides some evidence for beliefs and anxiety being closely linked.

Social factors

Beck and Emery (1985) talk about an 'anxious schema'. Social factors can be involved in this schema, and these can also include what a person thinks he or she ought to be like – their self-image and personal standards. It could be argued that this is also true in the psychodynamic explanation, as moral anxiety can be said to stem from worry about conforming to social norms and rules. Similarly, if we say that people learn fears and anxiety, then we could argue that they will be socialised within a certain social structure, and that this social structure affects what is learnt. For example, if a social phobia develops through wanting to avoid unpleasant interactions at school, then it is clear that such learnt behaviour depends on social factors. Cognitive perspectives are also involved here, so these social factors are ones which work with and within the other approaches, rather than instead of them.

Treatment of anxiety disorders

As you might expect, treatments go along with beliefs about the cause of the problem. For example, Little Albert was conditioned to fear furry objects, so to 'treat' his fear extinction would be needed. The furry object would have to be presented without the fearful noise, so that the fear response became unlearned. Little Albert's phobia was caused by conditioning, which is within the learning approach, so it would be to the learning approach that we would look for a treatment.

⟳ Recall AS material

Recall your AS material about the learning approach and check that you understand the process of extinction – or look it up.

The psychodynamic approach – insight therapies

The psychodynamic approach suggests that the defence mechanism of repression prevents the expression of unconscious impulses, and this leads to anxiety. **Insight therapies** are where the therapist wants the client to gain insight, or understanding, of what their problem is so that they can work effectively to reduce their anxiety. Psychoanalysis, an insight therapy, is fairly rigid in structure, and can take a long time, but modern psychodynamic therapies are often more short-term.

Evaluation

- Earlier in this chapter we looked briefly at the effectiveness of psychotherapy. Svartberg and Stiles (1991) reviewed 19 studies of short-term psychodynamic psychotherapy carried out between 1987 and 1988. The participants were all depressed, anxious or personality disordered. Svartberg and Stiles found psychotherapy was good for those described as 'neurotic'. They also found that short-term treatment was better than no treatment, and that interpretations of transference were as effective as other strategies. However, they didn't have enough information to draw conclusions about the effectiveness of the long-term psychodynamic treatments.

- One problem with insight therapies is that the client needs to be in a position to think about themselves fairly rationally in order to gain insight, which might not always be possible. For example, those with psychotic problems, rather than neuroses may have difficulty doing this, so psychotherapy is not always suitable. Similarly, children may not be able to have sufficient insight into the workings of their own unconscious minds, so psychotherapy is not a suitable therapy for children.

🔄 Recall AS material

When you studied the psychodynamic approach for the AS you probably looked at a case study carried out either by Freud or another psycho-analyst. Recall this AS material here, and the details of psychoanalysis which you learned there. Understanding how the psychodynamic approach relates to mental health issues was the key application for that approach, so you should have a clear understanding of what insight therapies are, and how at least one is carried out.

The humanistic approach – existential therapy

Frankl (1960) developed a method of existential therapy known as 'logotherapy', which specifically focused on anxiety disorder and phobias. He believed that anxieties arose from excessive anticipatory anxiety, and that the anticipation of problems gave the client their unwanted symptoms. Frankl suggested using paradoxical intervention, in which the client should wish for exactly what was feared. One example he used was a young medical student who began trembling whenever the anatomy instructor entered the room. Using logotherapy, she decided to tremble on purpose whenever the occasion arose, but found she could

not. Furthermore, the systematic attempt meant that her unwanted trembling also disappeared. Frankl argued that this was because of her changed attitude to the situation. The symptoms persist because the individual is maintaining the problem by continually anticipating it. If they try to create the problem, their anticipation changes and the problem should go away.

Evaluation

- Not much research has been done to evaluate this therapy for treatment of anxiety. However, it does seem to have worked to an extent for stress, depression, agoraphobia, and insomnia. Shoham-Soloman and Rosenthal (1987) have reviewed 12 studies and found that paradoxical interventions, whilst not particularly better than other interventions, did produce beneficial changes.

- Therapy derived from a humanistic approach might not be helpful in cases of severe anxiety, because this type of therapy requires clients to have self-knowledge, and to be in a state where they can evaluate rationally what they are saying and thinking. They also need to be able to change their thought patterns consciously and deliberately. Similar criticisms apply here to those outlined for psychodynamic psychotherapy, because children and some adults may not have sufficient insight to understand how to change their goals. However, for mild anxiety and some phobias existential therapy is of some use.

Behavioural therapies

Some therapies used for anxiety operate from within the learning approach. Treatments such as **systematic desensitisation** and **implosion therapy** (flooding) use learning principles to help the person to re-learn alternatives to maladaptive behaviours. Anxieties and phobias are maladaptive in that they are dysfunctional for the individual, so therapists using this approach take the view that what is needed is to change the sufferer's behaviour.

Systematic desensitisation involves gradually introducing the person to the feared object, perhaps by starting with a picture. For example, if a person has a phobia about spiders, then he or she will be shown pictures of small spiders at first, gradually moving towards producing a real spider for the person to hold. At each step the individual must be relaxed, because the aim is to replace the fear response with a relaxation response. Systematic desensitisation is a slow, gradual process but has been shown to be very effective with this type of anxiety disorder.

ACTIVITY

Write down the conditioning processes involved in developing a fear of spiders, identifying the key concepts of classical conditioning (UCS, UCR, CS and CR). Then write down, in the same way, the processes involved when using systematic desensitisation to treat the phobia.

Implosion therapy takes a different approach. It still uses learning principles, but this time the principle of habituation – the idea that repeated exposure to the same stimulus will weaken the response. In this therapy the anxiety is increased by the therapist 'flooding' the person with what frightens them. For example, someone who has become frightened of cars when crossing the street may be placed in a room surrounded by large video screens showing cars coming at them. The idea is that the individual cannot maintain the alarm response for very long, because it is so physiologically demanding, and so the physical symptoms of their anxiety will decrease. The person interprets this as calming down, and this helps them to control their fear. They learn to replace the fear response with a new calmer behaviour.

The above two examples of therapies use classical conditioning principles but some approaches also use operant conditioning. For example, in **behaviour modification** the person is rewarded with something when they overcome an obstacle. For example, a fear of lifts might be overcome if the individual is rewarded step-by-step as they get near a lift, then when they can do this comfortably, then when they get in one. Behaviour modification techniques often make use of the operant conditioning principle known as behaviour shaping, or successive approximation.

Evaluation

- A problem with behavioural treatments is that, although the behaviour can be changed, they do not tackle any of the underlying causes of the anxiety. These treatments work best with phobias where a specific problem exists, and can work with obsessive–compulsive disorders. But if the individual repeatedly develops obsessions and compulsions, it seems likely that there is some deeper reason for their problem, and changing their surface behaviour may not help. In the long term it leaves the underlying cause unaffected.

Cognitive–behavioural therapies

Behavioural therapies have been particularly effective in developing ways to treat specific problems such as phobias. However, more generalised anxiety disorders are difficult to treat in this way. In practice, a therapist will often use cognitive–behavioural therapies rather than strictly behavioural ones, on the grounds that the client's cognitive functioning is important as well as their behaviour. **Rational–emotive behaviour therapy** was outlined earlier, as was Beck's **cognitive therapy** technique. The main aim is for the therapist to provide structure and guidance so that the client can review their thinking for themselves, and realise that it needs to be altered. The therapist will give the client 'homework' exercises so they can practise changing their thinking patterns, and they will encourage the client to explore the attributions and assumptions they habitually make, so that they can see what needs changing. This general approach has become very popular, and most modern counselling follows the same path.

Evaluation

- Borkovec and Mathews (1988) found that cognitive–behavioural strategies have worked reasonably well for generalised anxiety. Heimberg (1989) found they were successful in treating social phobias, and Clark and Beck (1988) found they seemed to work for panic disorders too. Others have arrived at similar conclusions, which suggests that overall this is an effective form of therapy.

Synoptic Note

This material will be useful for Unit 6 – the synoptic element of the course. For synoptic questions you are required to know about behavioural change and social control. Recall your AS material in the learning approach where the key application was to know about how classical and operant conditioning are used to change human behaviour. There are social and moral issues involved, such as who decides who should change and what those changes should be. You can use this material here too – for example, if people with phobias seek help in changing their behaviour, is it still unethical? Also, in some cases society might want to change a person's behaviour because it is not functional for society, rather than because it is not functional for the person, which might be considered unethical. Try to work through these sorts of arguments as you go through the A2 part of the course.

Biological treatments

There are also some biological treatments for anxiety disorders, based on the use of drugs. Gitlin (1990) points out that drugs such as alcohol help us to relax and to sleep; and many people see it as helpful for anxiety, although research shows that the harm which alcohol does often outweighs its benefits in this area. (We will be looking at alcohol in more detail in Chapter 8.) Manufactured tranquillisers used to treat anxiety disorders include barbiturates and benzodiazepine substances. As we will see in Chapter 8, they can cause problems with addiction, but many psychiatrists prescribe drugs for people with anxiety disorders nonetheless.

Many anti-anxiety drugs contain benzodiazepines, which inhibit the activity of the nervous system. In 1981, Mellenger and Balter estimated that 9–10% of the population use these drugs occasionally over the year, although more recently there has been a move against excessive reliance on benzodiazepines, with the advent of more modern drugs such as beta-blockers and selective serotonin reuptake inhibitors. Benzodiazepines are mainly used for anxiety-provoking situations, insomnia, GAD and panic attacks. Salzman (1991) suggested that long-term users of benzodiazepines can be classified into four main groups:
- Older medically ill patients taking other medicines.
- Psychiatric patients with anxiety disorders.
- Psychiatric patients and others with vague and chronic symptoms.
- People with chronic sleep disorders.

Evaluation

- These drugs do seem to be effective for panic disorders (Ballenger *et al.*, 1988), and it is thought that they reduce panic attacks by restoring the correct balance in neurotransmitters in the brain (see Chapter 8). However, one problem is the side effects. They may cause drowsiness or slowing of cognitive functioning. Another problem is tolerance, which means doses may need to be increased as the person becomes increasingly used to the drug. They can also produce dependence, which leads to withdrawal symptoms when the drugs are discontinued.

- These issues mean that taking medication for anxiety disorders has drawbacks. In one study only 43% could last longer than a week without the drug when it was stopped, and only 38% stayed off the drug for 5 weeks (Rickels *et al.*, 1991). This could be because of the rebound effect, in which discontinuing a medication means the anxiety actually feels worse. Abelson and Curtis (1993) point out that drugs are usually stopped gradually to reduce these problems, but even then around 90% of patients reported withdrawal symptoms and 42% of their sample would not give up the drugs.

Summary

The diagnosis of anxiety disorders may rest on a description of symptoms using the DSM or similar system but the treatments are often quite varied, and depend on the theoretical approach of the therapist. The many paradigms within clinical psychology have produced a variety of different approaches to treatment but most clinical psychologists are able to use combinations of different approaches as they seem appropriate. It is also possible that therapies such as cognitive–behavioural therapy are leading to an integration of different approaches. For example, Freud's psychoanalysis has to some extent given way to a less specific psychotherapy approach, and humanistic ideas about empathy and unconditional positive regard can quite easily be integrated into cognitive therapies. Some therapies such as systematic desensitisation remain specific, but even with these it has been argued that the relationship between the therapist and the client affects the effectiveness of the treatment. Some researchers (e.g. Kendall and Hammen, 1995) have argued that the tendency for therapies to integrate in this way is likely to result in a more complete understanding of anxiety disorders.

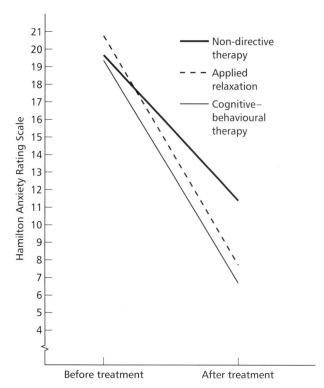

Figure 1.10
Comparison of treatments for generalised anxiety disorder (Source: Kendall and Hammen, 1995; based on Borkovec and Costello, 1993)

▌ *STUDY AID*

You need to know at least one example of a therapy from each of the psychodynamic, behavioural, learning, social, humanistic and cognitive approaches. These were described in this section partly to help in you to understand the disorder, and partly to give you examples for the previous section on treatments and therapies.

Schizophrenia

Anxiety disorders, as we have seen, are classified as neuroses, but schizophrenia is a **psychosis**, which is rather different. Psychoses are mental disorders where the individual is not in touch with reality. Schizophrenia is a specific sort of psychosis, characterised by thought, language and behaviour disturbances. There is more than one type of schizophrenia; and it has been claimed that the term is just a label covering many different conditions, all of which have similar symptoms. We will be looking at this more closely later.

The disorder has been known a long time, though not always by the same name. For example, Kraeplin (1883) used the term *dementia praecox* to describe illnesses where there was mental deterioration that started early in life and involved disassociation from reality. Bleuler (1911) introduced the word 'schizophrenia', meaning split (*schism*) of the mind (*phrenos*). Despite common misunderstandings of the term, the name schizophrenia is not about split personality, but about the splitting of cognition from emotion.

Schizophrenic disorders and symptoms

- *Disturbances of language and thought* – these involve loose associations of ideas (for example, where personal meanings interrupt, and there is lack of coherence) and conceptual difficulties with thinking. Also there can be use of peculiar words, and poor speech in the sense of odd use of words and delusions.
- *Perceptual disturbances* – sensations can be heightened, even small changes in the environment can be noticed very quickly, and there can be hallucinations.
- *Affective disturbances* – the patient may show apathy and lack of pleasure, or inappropriate feelings and emotions.
- *Behavioural disturbances* – there can be peculiar mannerisms and facial expressions, and reduced movements. Inappropriate social behaviour often occurs, and an apparent lack of motivation.

Different people with schizophrenia present different symptoms. Communication is often difficult because the individual cannot recognise that he or she is ill, or that what they are saying and doing is not right. For example, language confusion commonly shown by schizophrenics includes 'clang associations', in which the individual relates words because of their sound, such as 'the duck clucks'; and neologisms, where a word is made up altogether. This disorganised speech is sometimes referred to as 'word salad', and is taken as a major symptom of the disorder. But other types of symptoms are also involved, and they can vary a great deal from one person to another. For one person, the world may be a very confusing place, with lots of ideas and sensory messages combining together. For another, their schizophrenia may involve withdrawal into a private world.

In total, five different kinds of schizophrenia have been identified (Figure 1.12):
- paranoid
- catatonic
- disorganised
- undifferentiated or simple, and
- the most recently identified one, residual schizophrenia.

Incidence of schizophrenia

Although schizophrenia has different sets of symptoms, it is not suggested that the different types have different causes. Schizophrenia is the most common mental illness and is found in every culture and in all parts of the population. About 1% of people, in all populations in all countries, develop schizophrenia, and this percentage appears to be quite stable. It affects all cultural groups, although mental illness (including schizophrenia) in general is usually found more in the poorer sections of a community. Most studies show no gender differences, although Iacono and Beiser (1992) suggest that it is more common or more severe in men. Goldstein (1988) found that women have shorter stays in hospitals and that schizophrenia seems to be less severe in women than in men. There is also an age difference: Lewine (1991) found that schizophrenia tends to show itself between the ages of 14 and 25 in men, whereas women generally experience it between 24 and 35.

Explanations for schizophrenia

There is no single cause of schizophrenia and, as with anxiety disorders, explanations for it tend to fit the main approaches used in clinical psychology. It is possible to draw a general distinction between biological explanations and psychological explanations; but many practitioners will draw on both explanations as they seem to be appropriate. We will begin by looking at the biological explanations, and go on to psychological ones later.

Biological explanations for schizophrenia include genetic factors, biochemical factors and the importance of certain brain structures. It is a dramatic illness, and some have likened it to some of the symptoms of brain injury, but although there are some parallels between certain types of brain injury and schizophrenia, they are often quite different on closer examination.

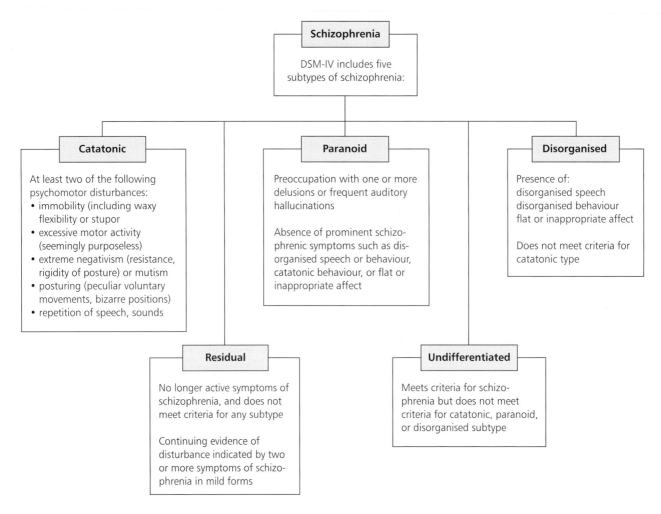

Figure 1.11
Five subtypes of schizophrenia are recognised in DSM-IV. These subgroups are descriptive in nature and do not imply different origins or causal factors (Source: Kendall and Hammen, 1995)

Genetic inheritance

One of the more popular biological explanations for schizophrenia, however, concerns **heritability**. As with anxiety disorders, family and twin studies have shown that there is some element of heritability in schizophrenia, although results vary between studies and it is not possible to draw absolute conclusions. Gottesman (1991) found that close relatives of schizophrenics had a risk factor of 46% – that is, their likelihood of developing schizophrenia themselves was 46%. For identical twins the risk factor was 48% (Figure 1.13). These two figures are quite high compared to the 1% likelihood of developing schizophrenia across the whole population, so it is easy to conclude that there is a high heritability factor in this mental illness. It seems that the closer the relative, the higher the likelihood of getting schizophrenia, that is, the higher the **concordance rate**. The concordance rate for

schizophrenia for identical (monozygous, MZ) twins, as we have seen, is 48% (although other studies give different figures), and the rate for non-identical (dizygous, DZ) twins is 17%, so there seems to be a high heritability factor.

Torrey (1992) reviewed eight twin studies and found that the concordance rate for schizophrenia in MZ twins was on average 28%, with 6% for DZ twins. This is a much lower figure than Gottesman found, but the difference between the rates for DZ and MZ twins is still quite high, so a genetic factor is still likely. McGue (1992) used the same data as Torrey and found a rate of 40% for MZ twins, so it is clear that methodology is important here. The overall conclusion from twin studies is that there is some heritability factor, but exactly how much is still not known.

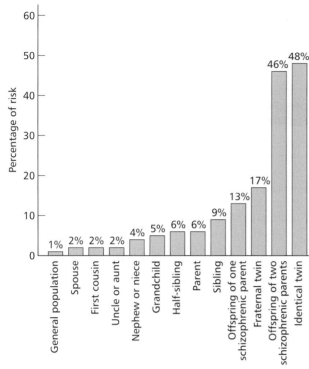

Figure 1.12
Genetic contributions to schizophrenia (Source: Kendall and Hammen, 1995; adapted from Gottesman, 1991)

Adoption studies are useful because a genetic factor can be looked for, and this time the environment of the family members is not shared, as one is adopted and 'reared apart'. It seems that adopted children who develop schizophrenia are more likely to have a biological parent with schizophrenia, and this points to a genetic factor. Even if adopted children are reared in a family where there is a psychotic parent, they are less likely to develop schizophrenia than an adopted child reared in a 'normal' family, but whose biological parent has schizophrenia. This also suggests that there is a genetic influence.

There does seem, therefore, to be a genetic factor in schizophrenia but, as with anxiety disorders, the extent of this factor varies. Sherrington *et al.* (1988) linked schizophrenia to a specific area of chromosome 5, but these are contentious findings which have not been replicated by other researchers.

Evaluation

The problems in searching for a genetic link in schizophrenia are that:

- schizophrenia may be a set of symptoms, but linked to more than one gene

- the methods used to study concordance may be flawed, and

- only some types of schizophrenia may be genetically linked.

There are also problems concluding that something is entirely genetically caused. Unless it is 100% certain that both MZ twins will develop a disorder, then that disorder cannot be completely genetically caused. If there are differences at all (and for schizophrenia there is at least a 52% difference, even according to Gottesman) then other causal factors must also be involved.

Another problem with studying twins is that they are usually brought up in very similar surroundings, so they share not only their genetic make up but also their environment. One reason for comparing MZ and DZ twins is that DZ twins also share their environment, so if there are differences, we can usefully suggest that these differences are in the genes. But it is also possible to claim that MZ twins are treated more similarly than DZ twins.

Recall AS material

Recall your AS material explaining the difference between MZ and DZ twins and their genetic make up. If something is more often linked in MZ twins than in DZ twins, since MZ twins share 100% of their genes and DZ twins share 50% of their genes, then it is usually concluded that this is evidence for their being a heritability factor. If you don't remember it, look it up.

Although one gene might be difficult to identify, as in the case of a gene for schizophrenia, it is sometimes possible to look for **genetic markers**. Researchers sometimes find that another gene is generally found with the one of interest. If this other gene (the marker gene) is more easily identifiable, then finding that gene can help to identify people at risk.

Holzman *et al.* (1988) suggested there is such a marker gene for schizophrenia. They found that eye movement dysfunction (EMD), where the pattern of eye movement when following a moving spot of light differs in some people, occurs in 4 to 5% of the whole population, but is found much more often in schizophrenics and their close relatives. This suggests that perhaps a gene for schizophrenia and the gene for EMD follow the same inheritance pattern. Grove *et al.* (1991) looked at the data on EMD and concluded that the evidence supports the claim that there is a single gene for schizophrenia – or at least, certain types of it – but they argued that other factors are important too.

↻ Recall AS material

Recall or look up your AS material on genes and genetic markers.

Brain abnormalities

The results of different types of brain scan suggest that schizophrenics may have differences in brain structure from 'normal' people. Two differences have been suggested using neuroimaging (scanning).

- It is possible that the ventricles are enlarged.
- Another brain difference is the reduced size of areas of the prefrontal cortex, areas of the temporal lobe, and areas such as the anterior hippocampus-amygdala (Shenton *et al.*, 1992). There is evidence of reduced blood flow, for example, in the frontal areas, and reduced blood flow suggests impaired functioning.

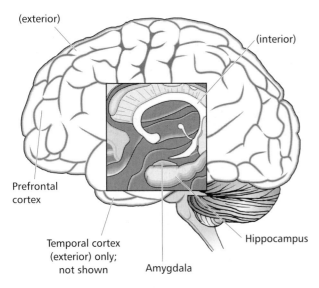

Figure 1.13
Areas of the brain that could be abnormal in schizophrenia. Reduced sizes of areas in the prefrontal cortex, temporal lobe and subcortical regions in the limbic system (such as the anterior hippocampus-amygdala) are the most likely possibilities, reflecting atrophy, neurodevelopmental abnormality or other damage that impairs their normal functioning (Source: Kendall and Hammen, 1995)

Problems in cognitive functioning do seem to be connected to the development of schizophrenia and there could be an element of inheritance in these problems. However, environment may also play a part. For example, some research suggests that viral infection might lead to neurological abnormalities which would show up on brain

scans. Watson (1959) argued that a large number of schizophrenic patients are born in the winter months, which suggests that an environmental stressor connected with winter might also be a causal factor.

Evaluation

- We cannot know whether enlargement of the ventricles might be a causal factor, or whether having schizophrenia, taking medication and so on might have caused the enlargement. Andreasen *et al.* (1990) did find enlargement at an early stage in the development of schizophrenia, so it seems that the brain difference might be a cause. However, another problem is that not all those with schizophrenia have the enlargement – which is largely found in men with cognitive impairment, severe symptoms, and for whom medication has not worked well. It seems possible that the enlargement of ventricles does produce some problems, but not necessarily schizophrenia itself.

↻ Recall AS material

Recall AS material on the physiological approach, where scanning techniques were discussed, or look this up

Biochemical factors

Another set of biological explanations for schizophrenia have focused on **biochemical factors**. In some cases of schizophrenia giving the patient medication helps, which suggests that there might be a biochemical factor – more specifically, a neurotransmitter – involved in schizophrenia. (We will be looking at neurotransmitters more closely in Chapter 8.) Phenothiazine drugs reduce symptoms of schizophrenia, and they are known to work by blocking dopamine receptors. So it is has been suggested that schizophrenia results from excess dopamine in the brain. Blocking dopamine receptors, it was thought, stopped too much dopamine from being taken up by the brain, which implied that the excess dopamine caused the symptoms which occurred without the drug.

The second reason for the **dopamine hypothesis** was the observation that drugs which increase dopamine activity make the symptoms worse. For example, amphetamines produce psychotic-type symptoms, and they indirectly increase dopamine levels in the brain. This evidence also suggests that excess dopamine can cause schizophrenia. However, levels of dopamine in those with schizophrenia can only be measured indirectly, although indirect measures do seem to reinforce the dopamine hypothesis.

Evaluation

- The idea that excess dopamine is a cause of schizophrenia is now thought to be too simplistic. Not all those with schizophrenia respond to drugs that block dopamine receptors. Also the drugs can work with some symptoms, but not all. Davis *et al.* (1991) suggested that in some areas of the brain (e.g. in the areas serving the cortex) there is low dopamine activity where people with schizophrenia are concerned, but that in other areas (e.g. the subcortical system) there is high dopamine activity. It could be that the low level in one area stimulates more activity in others – but more research is needed, because we have relatively little knowledge of the neural pathways used by the working brain. Dopamine does seem to be important, but it isn't a simple explanation for schizophrenia.

- Another problem, of course, is that finding a high level of a chemical in the brain doesn't automatically mean that the chemical causes the problem. It could just as well be a response to it, as the brain attempts to deal with the problem. Exercise, for example, raises noradrenaline levels in the brain; but that doesn't mean it is the noradrenaline which causes the exercise: it is there as a reaction to the exercise, not as the cause of it. It is possible that the same kind of process applies in the case of dopamine and schizophrenia.

↻ *Recall AS material*

Recall your AS material from the physiological approach where neurotransmitters were discussed, or look it up.

Overall, then, there do seem to be biological factors in schizophrenia. There seems to be a genetic element, although one single gene might not be implicated, and there may be different causes for different types of schizophrenia. There do seem to be some brain differences in those with schizophrenia, and these do seem to have occurred before the onset of the illness. However, they may indicate mental problems in general rather than specifically schizophrenia. Also the neurotransmitter dopamine seems to play a part, but exactly what part, and to what extent, is not yet known.

Given the relatively small percentage (less than 50%) of cause given to genetic factors, it is clear that the environment also plays a part, perhaps in triggering the illness in some and not in others. In fact, the general model used most commonly to explain schizophrenia nowadays is an interactive approach, in which biological factors make the person more vulnerable to developing the disease but whether they develop it or not is dependent on environmental stressors and other psychological factors.

Psychological factors in schizophrenia, like the biological factors which have been put forward, are quite varied. It is clear that stressful circumstances have a part to play in triggering or causing schizophrenia; but they don't seem to be the whole story. It may be that the individual must be biologically predisposed to developing schizophrenia, but then needs additional reasons for it to manifest itself in one person and not in another.

Family interaction

One of the first psychological factors in schizophrenia to be identified was the effect of certain types of family interaction. This came particularly to prominence in the 1960s, following the pioneering work of R.D. Laing and his colleagues (Laing, 1967). By highlighting the existence of family conflicts, and particularly challenging family interactions such as double-binds, they showed how schizophrenia, at least in some young people, could be viewed as a reaction to an intolerable set of conflicting social demands. This fitted with some of Freud's ideas, which suggested that schizophrenia might be a regression to a primitive state because of conflict, and with work by Fromm-Reichmann (1948), who looked at the characteristics of mothers who were likely to induce schizophrenia in the child.

Evaluation

- Early theorists argued that mothers of schizophrenics were either overprotective or rejecting, either very hostile or excessively affectionate. In other words the findings appeared to be contradictory, giving both extremes.

- Most of the early studies completely ignored the father's role.

- The findings came from **retrospection** – in other words, asking people to recall their experiences – and this means that the data can be unreliable.

- Studies of schizophrenics often lacked a control group – where non-schizophrenic individuals' childhoods are investigated.

These early perspectives emphasised the role of the mother; but later approaches looked at the family as a whole, leading to **family process theories** as an explanation for schizophrenia. This led researchers to look at the hidden messages or inconsistent communications in family life. One of the examples of disturbed communication in families which was identified by Bateson *et al.*, in 1956 is the double-bind – a situation in which whatever the child or young person does is wrong. A mother might say that she loves the child and accuse it of never showing affection, but then stiffen up and turn away from a kiss whenever the child attempts to be affectionate. This type of inconsistent message can be very disturbing for children, and when carried out over years can produce considerable psychological disturbance, which may lead to schizophrenia.

Research into these types of disturbed communication led to studies of problematic role relationships within the family and other types of disturbed interaction. This highlighted other problems, such as scapegoating, where one individual – usually the one who eventually became mentally ill or showed psychological disturbance – took the blame for what were actually much more extensively disturbed relationships between all of the family members. Ultimately, this led to the development of **family therapy** as a method for dealing with psychological problems.

Researching family processes when it comes to schizophrenics is extremely difficult; but there have been some observations which have supported these ideas. Miklowitz *et al.* (1991) looked at communication within such families, using a Thematic Apperception Test (TAT). This involves asking someone to interpret what is happening in a set of ambiguous pictures. When trying to say that the person in the picture was trying to make a goal of their life, those with schizophrenics in the family said things like 'but the thing is as I said, there's got … you can't drive in the alley'. Another statement was 'it's gonna be up and downwards along the process all the while to go through something like this' (quoted in Kendall and Hammen, 1995). It seems from this example that unclear communication was certainly taking place within those particular families.

In recent years, the emphasis on family difficulties has shifted from disturbed communication to the lack of expressed emotion in such families. Families where the family members are over-protective of the schizophrenic member and demonstratively affectionate are called high in expressed emotion, while those who are colder and more rigid are referred to as low in expressed emotion. Mintz *et al.* (1987) found that there does seem to be a link between both high and low extremes of expressed emotion and schizophrenia.

Evaluation

- Showing that poor communication links with schizophrenia in families does not give a causal link. The communication difficulties might show a genetic link between communication difficulties and schizophrenia, rather than pointing to the communication problems causing the schizophrenia.

- The idea of expressed emotion in families predicting schizophrenia has been criticised, because the type of emotion in the family might arise from there being a schizophrenic member in the family.

The diathesis–stress approach

As we have seen, a genetic predisposition is not enough to account fully for schizophrenia, but there are also criticisms of the theories which suggest that certain types of family interactions cause schizophrenia. It seems that a cause would have to involve both genetic–biological and environmental factors, and most modern practitioners see schizophrenia as resulting from an interaction between the two.

The **diathesis–stress model** includes both 'nature' and 'nurture' as explanations. Diathesis refers to a vulnerability or predisposition to schizophrenia, which may come from genetic and other biological causes (some of the evidence for this has been reviewed above). Stress refers to factors in the environment which mean that normal coping mechanisms are not enough, so that a vulnerable or predisposed person becomes overstretched. Stressors could be family interactions, job difficulties, problematic relationships, poverty and other social class issues, or any other set of negative life events, and tend to be cumulative in their effects. We look more closely at stress and stressors in Chapter 8. It is the combination of a genetic or biological predisposition with environmental stressors which appears to be responsible for the onset of schizophrenia in the individual.

ACTIVITY

Draw up two lists with the headings 'biological causes' and 'psychological causes'. Taking each column separately, note down the main types of causes, and the sorts of studies you might expect to be carried out to investigate them. Draw on what you have already learned for the AS part of the course within the learning and physiological approaches as well as what you have learned here.

Treatment of schizophrenia

There have been several different approaches to the treatment of schizophrenia. Although we will not be going into detail here, this section will discuss some of the main treatments in relation to the different approaches to understanding mental illness.

Biological treatments – the physiological approach

Biological treatments have normally focused on the use of drugs. Phenothiazines are tranquillisers and the first drug used to treat schizophrenia (1952) was chlorpromazine – an 'anti-psychotic', or neuroleptic, drug ('anti-psychotic' means it reduces hallucinations and delusions). Other neuroleptic drugs are now used, and we will be looking more closely at the way these drugs work in Chapter 8, where the working of neurotransmitters is explained.

Evaluation

- Some theorists have argued that the use of drugs simply masks the problem rather than actually treating it, and doesn't help the individual to recover. Kane *et al.*, (1988) found that 10–20% of patients do not improve with drug therapy.

- If discontinued, drug therapies sometimes lead to relapses. Hogarty (1984) found relapse rates of around 40% of patients within six months, and 70% within a year.

- Neuroleptic drugs can have serious side-effects. For example, the muscular tremors and jerking which used to be thought of as symptoms of schizophrenia have actually turned out to be effects of the drugs used to 'treat' the illness.

Psychoanalysis – the psychoanalytic approach
Delusions and thought disorders can be seen as defences against anxiety, or as evidence of repression or regression. This is a psychoanalytic explanation for schizophrenia. Psychoanalysis, including transference, can perhaps make sense of the apparently irrational thoughts of the schizophrenic.

Evaluation

- Psychoanalysis is notably more effective with neurotic disorders than with psychotic problems, because it relies on the person gaining insight into their problem, and this is often not practicable with schizophrenic patients.

↻ Recall AS material

Recall – or look up – your AS material on psychoanalysis and the psychodynamic approach.

Psychotherapy – the humanistic approach
Laing (1967) saw schizophrenia as an attempt by the individual to regain their sense of self faced with intolerable and conflicting social demands. Laing suggested that society and family could engulf the person and take away their control of their 'self'. Given a safe haven, the individual could develop a sense of self and a sense of freedom, and this was the therapy proposed by Laing. Laing proposed that schizophrenics should be treated in safe, supportive therapeutic communities rather than in clinical settings such as hospitals. There, they would be able to receive psychotherapy, and the stress-free environment would also help them to recover.

Evaluation

- The therapeutic community established by Laing had some success, although other similar establishments were more varied in their results. Psychotherapy is not generally used as a therapy today, although many clinicians have found that listening to someone with schizophrenia can give them support and may help recovery.

Cognitive therapy – the cognitive approach
Cognitive impairments shown by schizophrenics are thought to be biologically caused, which is different from saying that schizophrenia is caused by cognitive dysfunction. However, it has been argued that improving cognitive functioning can be a useful therapy. Liberman and Green (1992) reviewed studies that focus on improving language skills and attention with schizophrenics, and found that there is some evidence of success. Perris (1989) taught schizophrenic patients to challenge their delusions, again with a certain amount of success. It has also been thought that the social functioning of schizophrenic patients can be improved by using cognitive methods.

Evaluation

- Bellack (1992) argued that it is hard to see what skills to teach, and questionable whether the patient will transfer such learning to real-life situations.

Token economy programmes – the learning approach
Another type of treatment that focuses on changing the skills of patients is the **token economy programme**, which focuses on altering the person's behaviour so that they can learn more 'normal' ways of acting. The principles of operant conditioning can be applied to specific behaviours which it is thought need to be changed. Desirable behaviours, such as personal grooming, are encouraged by giving tokens that can be exchanged for desirable items such as cigarettes or chocolate. This is a secondary reinforcement system, based on immediacy of reinforcement, as used in operant conditioning. The principles of social learning theory are also involved as staff are also asked to model the desired behaviours (Paul and Lentz, 1977).

Evaluation

- Token economy programmes do seem to work but require a dedicated staff and much effort. Now that community care is often found, patients spend less time in hospital, and this tends to mean that such programmes are no longer suitable.

- Behaviour modification programmes are expensive and, although they would probably still be useful in community care homes, it would be impractical to provide and train staff to do them properly.

Synoptic Note

For Unit 6 you need to learn about the ethics of behaviour change. Using token economy programmes, or attempting to change cognitive functioning or social skills does lead to behaviour change, so you need to look at arguments about who should decide what changes should occur. There is also the question of who decides who should change such behaviour. These are the types of questions you need to address in the synoptic part of the course.

Social skills training programmes – the social approach

Social skills training programmes are similar to cognitive–behavioural ones. They generally focus on helping people with schizophrenia to interpret communications from others correctly, and to identify ways to solve social problems. The main focus is on independent living skills, and ways to identify the emotions of others. The principles of social learning theory are involved, since modelling is used, and homework assignments are also set.

Halford and Hayes (1991) reviewed a number of studies and found that social skills training programmes did work to adapt behaviours, and in this way helped the patients concerned. They also found that a control group of schizophrenics without the training did not show the same level of knowledge about others' behaviour, which suggests that social skills training does work. The researchers concluded that these programmes help to modify behaviour, help general level of functioning, and seem to help to prevent relapse.

Evaluation

- Social skills training may be effective, but it is by no means a cure for schizophrenia. It does not address any fundamental problems or the cause of the condition.

Mood disorders

Mood disorders are disorders of feeling, also known as **affective disorders**. There are two main types of affective disorder:
- unipolar depression
- bipolar depression.

Unipolar depression is where the person has one consistent, recurrent state – generally that of being depressed, although it may also include mania. There are several types of **unipolar disorder**, including major depressive disorder, reactive depression, dysthymic disorder and others.

Bipolar disorder is where the person experiences more than one emotional state as part of their problem – for example, where they are sometimes manic and sometimes depressed. This too has several different types, including bipolar I disorder, bipolar II disorder and cyclothymia. Bipolar means having two extremes, or 'poles' so manic depression is two-sided and known as bipolar, whereas straightforward depression is one-sided, and known as unipolar.

Depression involves persistent negative moods, depleted energy, the altering of sleep habits, and altered motivation and behaviours. As with other disorders, depression is thought of as a problem when it leads to dysfunctional behaviour – it is likely that everyone has depressed feelings at times, but depression becomes a disorder when the symptoms are persistent and the person's normal functioning is affected. Major depressive disorders include:
- *psychotic depression,* where there is departure from reality
- *melancholic depression,* where there are severe physical symptoms
- *seasonal affective disorder,* where depression occurs as a result of persistent environmental conditions such as lack of daylight.

Depression seems to affect women more than men, tends to occur more in young people, and is found in all cultures.

Bipolar disorders include both depression and **mania**. Mania refers to an energetic state in which the person shows increased activity, and often expresses grandiose beliefs along with excessive behaviours. Bipolar disorder used to be called manic depression. Bipolar I disorder involves both mania and depression and affects men and women equally. Bipolar II disorder involves depression and hypomania, which is a milder form of mania. Cyclothymic disorders are mild ups and downs, which are not really out of the normal range but occur frequently enough to be a problem. It is most common for bipolar disorders to recur at intervals with the person being able to function well in the periods between episodes.

Causes of mood disorders

Effectively, two types of causes have been identified for mood disorders: physiological causes, and psychological ones. However, as with schizophrenia, there is often an interaction between the two, so it is unlikely to be the case that one single factor causes the entire problem.

Biological causes for depression

Three main biological causes have been suggested for depression. One is, that it is inherited – the result of **genetic influence**. Family studies, as with other disorders, do suggest a heritability factor in unipolar disorder but this is quite low. Genetic transmission of bipolar disorders seems more likely, in that there appears to be a stronger genetic link for bipolar disorders than for other disorders. Studies of close-knit isolated communities such as the Amish, for example, have shown how bipolar disorder (manic depression) runs in families. However, most researchers agree that it is likely that depressive disorders involve more than one gene – for example, for the different disorders – which makes straightforward conclusions in this area difficult.

Evaluation

- A disorder may be transmitted through family learning rather than through genetic influence. This is particularly likely with moods and emotional reactions, since young children learn behaviours in response to irritations and frustrating situations by imitating the adults around them.

Another possible physiological explanation for depression is the action of **neurotransmitters**. It is thought, for instance, that neurotransmitter functioning or dysfunctioning may be a cause of depression, and research focuses on monoamines such as noradrenaline and serotonin. The hypothalamic–pituitary–thyroid (HPT) axis and the hypothalamic–pituitary–adrenal (HPA) axis seem to be important where depression is concerned.

With regard to bipolar disorders, it is thought that the neurotransmitter dopamine may be important in regulating mood activity. It is possible that the balance of chemicals in the brain becomes altered because of the manic episodes – one theory of the cause of these disorders is that the brain might become more sensitised to the effects of stress. Having become more sensitised, it is possible that the physiological changes then start occurring without the environmental stressor, or with only a minimal stimulus.

Hormonal activity in the body has also been suggested as a possible cause. These are chemicals in the bloodstream which act to maintain emotional states, and they are closely linked with neuronal, or brain activity. There are two major neuroendocrine systems which may be involved here. One of them is the HPA system, which will be described in more detail in Chapter 8, when we look at stress. What it particularly does is produce cortisol – a hormone that prepares the body for stress. If depressed people are given a synthetic cortisol they do react abnormally to challenges, which suggests that depression might come from an abnormal stress response. This abnormal response might be learned, as a result of experience (as we saw above), or could be the result of a genetic tendency.

Hormone activity may be involved in mood disorders in other ways. For example, monoamine neurotransmitters and the HPA system are affected by **circadian rhythms**. Many mood disorders show seasonal patterns and/or sleep disorders, and these might indicate that a problem in circadian rhythm functioning could be the cause of depression. Hormones are also linked with unipolar depression – for example, postpartum blues (after the birth of a baby), which are quite common. However, this type of depression is a little different from other types of depression, and may operate differently in terms of its physiological correlates.

Evaluation

- The symptoms labelled depression do seem to have more than one cause, and depression is probably not one single 'thing'.

↻ *Recall AS material*

Recall your AS material from the physiological approach on circadian rhythms – or look it up.

Psychological causes for depression
Reactive depression – depression that occurs in response to a particular set of events, such as a bereavement or divorce – is something which most people experience at some time in their lives. It can be a short-term thing, lasting only a few weeks, or it might last for a long time, requiring the person eventually to seek treatment. When that happens, it is often because other personal problems have become tangled up with the person's reaction to the events – for example, a lowering of self-esteem resulting from the loss of a relationship; or chronic depressive thought patterns.

Seligman (1975) identified a characteristic **attributional style** that is associated with people who had long-term depression. When they give reasons for why things had happened to them, they tend to make attributions which were global (applying generally to everything rather than just to one particular situation), external (originating outside of the person concerned, stable (that is, likely to persist for a long time), and uncontrollable. As a result of these characteristic attributions, Seligman argued, the depressed person experiences a kind of **learned helplessness**, which leads to their apathy and sense of hopelessness in everyday living, and this is what produces their depression.

Other psychological explanations for depression come from the idea that it stems from a lack of self-worth. Carl Rogers found that many of his depressed clients had become so because they had an unrealistic ideal self which they could never live up to. As a result, they felt they were constant failures and easily became depressed. This overly idealistic set of standards had occurred because they had always experienced conditional positive regard as children, and that had given them the message that they were not really loved; only some ideal child who was never naughty. So they felt they always had to be perfect in order to achieve positive regard from other people.

Brown and Harris (1978) performed an extensive study of depression in young London housewives – housewives as a group tend to be very vulnerable to this problem. They found that the most important factor of all in whether someone developed the disorder was whether they were part of a supportive social network. There were other factors too, such as losing a parent in childhood; but having friends and neighbours who they could talk to when necessary was by far the most important.

Treatment of mood disorders

As with other kinds of mental disorders, mood disorders can be treated either physiologically or psychologically. The general approach used to understand the disorder informs the treatment being used. So, for example, if the disorder is thought to come from an imbalance of neurotransmitter chemicals in the brain, drugs that can adjust that balance would be considered the right kind of treatment. However, if the disorder is thought to arise from habitual depressive thought patterns, then therapy which aims to change those thought patterns would be considered more appropriate.

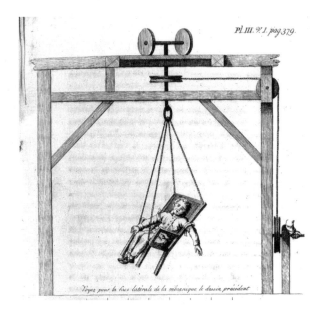

Figure 1.14
In the nineteenth century people were treated for depression by spinning them in a rotating chair

Biological treatments

The most common treatment for unipolar disorders is medication, such as tricyclic antidepressants, monoamine oxidase inhibitors (MAOs) and the newer selective serotonin reuptake inhibitors (SSRIs) such as Prozac. These increase levels of serotonin in the brain by inhibiting its re-uptake (see Chapter 8). These drugs have been found to be effective in some cases, though not all.

Bipolar disorders are generally treated with lithium carbonate, which has been found to suppress the mood swings and produce a more 'flattened' level of emotional response. However, this drug must be used continually, because if a patient stops taking the medication, the episodes recur. Anticonvulsants have also been used to stabilise brain functioning.

Evaluation

- Generally medication is only effective with those with mild or moderately severe depression. This may be because it addresses the physical symptoms, but not the causes of the disorder.

- Lithium carbonate medication can easily produce dependency, because of the need for continual treatment. Also lithium does not work for everyone, and is toxic, which are two more problems with the treatment.

In some cases, and particularly in the case of severe depression, psychiatrists have found that electro-convulsive therapy (ECT) can be more effective than medication, at least in the short term. However, its effects do wear off after time, and the depression often returns. There is no clear reason why it appears to work for short periods, but it has been suggested that the amnesia produced by the ECT allows the person to forget their problems temporarily, and so allows them a short period of relief from their habitual depressive actions and ways of thinking.

Seasonal affective disorder (SAD) is thought to occur mainly as a result of deprivation of sunlight during the winter months. Light therapy, in which the person is exposed to sunlight-simulating lamps for an hour at a time, has been used to treat this problem, and appears to have some success. It has also been found that sleep deprivation can sometimes help in cases of SAD, although it is not clear why this should be the case, apart from producing a general disruption of biological rhythms.

Psychological treatments

There have been several different types of psychological treatments used for depression, and also for manic depression, although they are generally considered to be less successful in the latter case. In the case of reactive depression, of course, time is generally the healer – the depression resulting from a bereavement or divorce generally lessens over time as the individual gradually becomes more used to living without the other person.

Sometimes, though, this doesn't happen because habitual negative thought patterns have developed, like the depressive attributional style which we looked at earlier. Cognitive therapy is often very useful in these cases, because it helps the person to re-learn positive ways of thinking, and they can often get a grip on their depression in this way. Indeed, some kinds of depression seem to vanish altogether as a result of cognitive therapy; although this doesn't apply to all depressions.

Helping the person become more active and in control of their life can also be an important psychological treatment to prevent relapses, in cases of recurrent depression. Rational-emotive behaviour therapy (REBT) has been used to deal with this type of problem. When the person is experiencing a severe bout of depression, they may resort to chemotherapy (drug treatment) to help them in the short term, but may use a stronger kind of psychotherapy like REBT to help them to learn a more positive way of living their life which will help to prevent its recurrence.

Carl Rogers, as we have seen, saw depression as being one outcome of conditional positive regard from parents. He, and other clinical psychologists following his methods, sometimes used **client-centred therapy** to deal with this particular type of problem. By offering the client a relationship based on unconditional positive regard, he helped the person to work through the personal conflicts and feelings of inadequacy which led to their depression, and as a result raise their sense of self-esteem and so remove the root cause of their depression.

Psychotherapy may sometimes be used even in types of bipolar depression which appear to have a biochemical cause. It can work mainly by helping the individual to recognise their symptoms early and to deal with them, and by helping them to learn how to avoid stressors which might trigger their illness. However, this type of psychological intervention is generally thought to be a supplement to conventional medical treatments, rather than a full treatment in itself.

Evaluation

- The problem with many types of depression is that they can result from chronic social problems produced by poverty, inadequate housing and other kinds of factors. It is not possible to remove these by psychotherapy. So there is a limit to how effective psychological interventions can be.

Eating disorders

There are two main types of eating disorder: anorexia nervosa and bulimia nervosa. As a general rule, they start before adulthood, and can then continue into adult life, although there are some cases of adults developing eating disorders in later life with no sign of the problem earlier.

Anorexia nervosa is an illness stemming from an intense fear of becoming fat, and a distorted body image. Symptoms of anorexia include dramatic weight loss, obsessions and neuroses, a need for personal control, depression, low oestrogen levels, and negative attitudes towards sexual activity. Anorexics see themselves as fat, and refuse to maintain their normal body weight, and females with anorexia (anorexia is 11 times more likely in females than males) cease menstruating. Anorexia is a serious mental problem which can even lead to death, although it is estimated that nowadays increased awareness of the disorder means that some two-thirds of anorexics are successfully treated, and less than 5% of cases are actually fatal (Steinhausen, 1994).

The most likely age for the onset of anorexia is between 14 and 18 years. More cases are reported nowadays than there were three or four decades ago, although this might be because of a greater awareness of the disorder rather than because it is actually increasing. It has sometimes been called the 'dieter's disease', but most dieters are not anorexic because they do not have a distorted body image and because they do recognise successful weight loss.

There is considerable variation in the incidence of anorexia in different countries. It is quite rare in China, for example (Lee and Chiu, 1989), but quite common in Japan (Suematsu *et al.*, 1985). Hoek (1991) reported a high incidence of anorexia among teenagers in a Dutch study, while Dolan (1991) pointed out that it is rare amongst black teenagers in the USA. One possible reason for this seems to be the importance placed on slimness or on the value of restricted eating in the cultures concerned. There is some evidence, for example, that it was quite common among monks and nuns in mediaeval times, when fasting was commonplace and some members of religious communities allowed their religious fervour to carry it to extremes.

Bulimia nervosa is characterised by binge eating, where there is little control over how much is taken in. Typically, these binges will be followed by self-induced vomiting, fasting, vigorous exercise, or excessive use of laxatives as the bulimic person tries to prevent weight gain by getting rid of the calories. This is why bulimia is sometimes also known as the 'binge–purge syndrome'. It is not an uncommon behaviour among young people (according to Fairburn and Beglin in 1990 around 1% of the adolescent population had bulimia); so for bulimia to be diagnosed as a disorder in need of treatment, the general criterion operated by clinicians is that there should have been at least two binges a week, over a period of three months.

Anorexia and bulimia seem to be related and about half of those with anorexia show some sign of bulimia, as they often use bingeing and purging techniques rather than simple fasting. Like anorexia, bulimia has been found in a number of countries. For example, it is relatively common in the UK, and binge eating has been identified in Zimbabwe (Hopper and Garner, 1986). Bulimia occurs more often in females than in males, and the average age for onset is 18 years, which is older than the age for anorexia.

Causes of eating disorders

As with the other disorders we have looked at in this chapter, researchers have suggested different causes for the illness. Some of these emphasise biological factors, while others emphasise possible psychological causes of one sort or another.

Biological factors

Malfunctioning of the hypothalamus has been suggested as a possible cause of both anorexia and bulimia, as the hypothalamus is known to influence feelings of satiation, and thought to regulate eating habits. Experiments with animals carried out in the 1960s showed that lesions in a particular part of the hypothalamus could produce over-eating, to the extent that the animal became obese, while lesions in another area of the hypothalamus produced self-starvation, with the animal eating far too little to maintain its body weight. Many researchers have seen this as being very similar to human eating disorders, and proposed that similar mechanisms might apply.

An alternative type of biological explanation is the idea that anorexia and bulimia may result from an imbalance of neurotransmitters in particular parts of the brain. For example, Fava *et al.* (1989) found that when anorexia develops there are also changes in the amount of noradrenaline and serotonin present in the brain, and suggested that this might be a cause of the problem.

It has also been suggested that anorexia and bulimia may result from genetic factors. Scott (1986) reviewed a number of twin studies of anorexia, and found that the concordance rate (where one had it, the other did too) for MZ twins was higher than that for DZ twins, which suggests that there may be a genetic factor. Similarly, Holland *et al.* (1988) found 56% of MZ twins were concordant for anorexia, whereas only 5% of DZ twins were concordant.

Evaluation

- Explanations for eating disorders in terms of brain damage are not particularly useful, as they offer no possibilities for treatment. So clinicians dealing with anorexics or bulimics have tended to adopt different explanations.

- One problem with the neurotransmitter explanation is that the starvation might lead to the neurotransmitter changes, instead of the neurotransmitter changes being the cause of the disorder.

- Calculating heritability from twin studies may ignore psychological factors, such as the emotional closeness between twins which may lead to correlations with emotional problems.

⟳ Recall AS material

Recall your AS material on the use of twin studies, or look it up.

Psychological factors

It is thought that the physical changes, and the challenges, that come with adolescence could be a cause of anorexia. Adolescence is a time when body fat can increase and concerns about weight are important for the individual at the same time. In a society in which advertising models and pop stars are all very slim, concerns about weight are common among young people.

Early **psychoanalytic explanations** see the starvation involved in anorexia as being symbolic of sexual conflicts – for example, that anorexic girls were denying an early childhood fear of impregnation by the father. More modern psychoanalytic explanations argue that girls with anorexia had problems with their early mother–child relationship. As a result, they did not develop a sense of ownership of their own bodies and were attempting to regain control over it through not eating. So the cause of the disorder, in this view, is the disturbed mother–child relationship.

Some psychologists have suggested that there may be **personality traits** which make certain people likely to become anorexics. It has been suggested, for example, that a type of personality where compliance, dependence and perfectionism are found might lead to the development of anorexia nervosa (Steinhausen, 1994). Obsessive–compulsive tendencies are also a part of the disorder; but those with it do not tend to show any problems at school or similar types of disturbance. According to this view, the disorder comes from the type of personality.

One of the more popular modern explanations for anorexia, and for bulimia too, has been that its roots lie in disturbed interactions within the family. Minuchin *et al.* (1978) suggested that the **family system** in which the individual with anorexia lives can be marked by enmeshment, or over-closeness. Individual family members lack separate identities in an enmeshed family, and a child may not be able to develop independence in the way that it should. Refusing to eat is a kind of rebellion by the child, which enables her to assert a kind of independence. So anorexia might be an act of rebellion in order to gain independence from an enmeshed family.

There are also family links with bulimia. When researchers have examined the specific behaviours within the family, they have found that families with anorexic or bulimic daughters tend to show more 'ignoring' and 'walling off' behaviours, rather than the more positive ones of 'helping' and 'trusting'. It has been suggested that the eating disorders may come from having families with such negative behaviours.

Evaluation

- It is possible that negative family behaviours may come from having a child with an eating disorder, rather than the behaviours causing the eating disorder.

Some clinicians have found the **learning approach** to be a useful way of explaining anorexia. The idea is that avoidance of food is associated with anxiety on the part of parents and others, so when an individual avoids food they get attention. The individual learns that not eating brings attention and their fasting behaviour is reinforced. Social learning theory can also provide explanations, in terms of the way that thin models give expectations and help to shape an adolescent's body image. Researchers have shown that the cultural ideal of beauty is changing and becoming thinner (Williamson *et al.*, 1990), which is likely to produce particular pressure on girls to become slimmer, which could be a cause.

Cognitive explanations for anorexia have also been popular. Several studies have shown that anorexics have distorted thinking (e.g. Garner and Bemis, 1984). For example, they make incorrect cognitive evaluations such as thinking they are fat when they are really extremely thin. There are also attributional problems, in that their obsession with thinness becomes a controlling factor in how they see almost everything.

Cognitive factors also seem to be involved in bulimia. For example, those with bulimia seem to ignore hunger signals, and simply eat what they have the opportunity to eat, which sets them up for bingeing. Polivy and Herman (1987)

Figure 1.15
Members of the Boston organisation Boycott Anorexic Marketing believe that using very thin models in advertising encourages the development of eating disorders in young women.

carried out a study where participants drank a filling milk shake thinking the study was about taste preferences. Then they were allowed into another room, where snacks were laid out on tables, and they were told that they could eat whatever they wanted. The 'normal eaters' did not eat much because they were already full from the milk shake. However, the other group, who were habitual dieters, seemed to think that they had broken their diet in any case, so they might as well carry on eating. They appeared to ignore physiological signals that they were full. The researchers suggested that those who develop bulimia may think as these dieters think, but to a greater degree.

Just as for schizophrenia, some suggest that it is not that either biological factors or environmental factors cause anorexia or bulimia, but a combination of both. What researchers and clinicians working in this area general use is the **diathesis–stress model** – the idea that there may be physiological or personality predispositions, but that environmental stressors are needed to 'tip the balance' and lead people to go on to develop the disorder. A person may have a predisposition to anorexia but without the relevant stressors they won't develop the illness.

Treatments of eating disorders

There has been relatively little use of medical treatments for eating disorders, although antidepressants have sometimes been used to treat bulimics, and several clinicians have experimented using appetite stimulants with anorexics. As a general rule, these medications do not seem to be particularly effective, and have sometimes produced their own dependency problems.

Psychoanalytic treatments have been used in both anorexia and bulimia, aiming to uncover problems with early mother–infant relationships. One of the recurrent problems with psychoanalysis as a treatment method is that because psychoanalysis can take years, and because the approach covers such indirect symptoms and sources, it is very difficult to test to see how effective it is.

Behaviour modification programmes appear to have been more successful in treating these disorders, and they have been used extensively. The idea is to change eating habits using rewards as reinforcement, so that the person will start to eat more. In anorexia, the evaluation of the effectiveness of treatment is generally quite simple – has the person gained weight or not? Leon and Phelan (1985) say that behaviour modification does lead to weight gain, but does not address other factors, so it is not a cure and might result in relapses later on.

Cognitive therapies have also been tried, and cognitive–behavioural therapies are often used with bulimic patients, to help to change faulty thinking patterns. Fairburn (1984) explained how cognitive–behavioural therapy looks at moving towards normal eating patterns, and also at challenging any faulty body image; an evaluation study by Wilfley *et al.* (1993) suggested that these methods do work.

Minuchin *et al.* (1978) looked at family systems and claimed that 86% of 53 patients receiving family systems therapy did recover from the anorexia, so it seems that family therapy can be helpful too. Overall, the most successful therapies currently used to treat eating disorders include behaviour modification, family systems approach, and the need for cognitive therapy to challenge distorted thinking patterns.

Self-test

Write a timed essay, under exam conditions (or as close as you can manage) using the title 'Discuss the possible causes of two different mental disorders'.

Suggested reading

Davison, G.C. and Neale, J.M. (1994) *Abnormal Psychology*, Sixth Edition. John Wiley and Sons.

Kendall, P.C. and Hammen, C. (1995) *Abnormal Psychology*. Boston: Houghton Mifflin Company.

Phares, E.J. and Trull, T.J. (1996) *Clinical Psychology*, Fifth Edition. Pacific Grove, California: Brooks/Cole.

Answers to Self-test questions on p. 4:

1 Validity
2 Generalisability
3 Reliability

2 Criminological psychology

The aims of this chapter

The aims of this chapter are to enable the reader to:

- *describe the main principles of criminological psychology*
- *describe studies of eyewitness testimony*
- *discuss how recall is affected by attribution biases*
- *discuss evidence of the use of hypnosis in memory recall*
- *discuss different approaches to offender profiling*
- *describe influences on jury decision-making*
- *discuss social–cognitive processes such as the just world hypothesis and the self-fulfilling prophecy*
- *discuss media influences on aggressive behaviour*
- *describe and discuss methods of controlling aggression*
- *discuss the effectiveness of zero tolerance.*

STUDY AID

When you have finished working through this chapter you should write an essay about, or at least test yourself on, each of the above points. This will help you to see how good your knowledge and understanding of criminological psychology is.

This chapter covers

INTRODUCTION TO CRIMINOLOGICAL PSYCHOLOGY
Defining crime
Finding out about crime
Theories of crime

THE LEGAL ASPECTS OF CRIME
Eyewitness testimony
Offender profiling
Jury decision-making

INFLUENCES ON CRIMINAL BEHAVIOUR
The self-fulfilling prophecy
Other social factors
Media influence

TREATING CRIME
Controlling aggression
The effect of zero tolerance

Introduction to criminological psychology

Psychology has been used to aid investigations of crime for many decades. Psychologists have been involved in prison work, forensic work and the detection of criminals almost since the development of psychology as a profession. But it is only relatively recently that its general importance has come to be recognised by society as a whole.

In modern days, psychological theories and methods play an important role in the field of crime. Their uses include the courtroom, explaining deviance, clinical criminology and the treatment of offenders, and informing prison practices and systems. The British Psychological Society has a Division of Criminological and Legal Psychology, which includes forensic psychology. Criminological psychology is the general term which we use to describe the area of applied psychology dealing with the various aspects of crime. The other two terms – legal psychology and forensic psychology – are more narrow, with the first being concerned with the application of psychology to courts, legislation and sentencing, and the second with identifying, and sometimes tracking down, criminals.

Psychology is not alone in its study of crime and criminal behaviour. Crime is studied in a number of different academic disciplines, including sociology, law, anthropology, medicine and psychology; and there are also general criminology courses which draw on all of these fields. Each discipline is able to contribute its own insights and approaches to the field, and each has proved useful in its own right. In this chapter, though, we are concentrating on the contribution the discipline of psychology makes to understanding of crime and criminal behaviour. Although there is sometimes a little overlap between disciplines – for instance, labelling theory is used in both psychology and sociology – for the most part, psychological knowledge is distinctive in its approach, and the area of criminological psychology is constantly developing.

STUDY AID

If you are studying sociology, you may have studied the area of crime and deviance, and some of what you have covered may be of use here. Recall the three main perspectives in sociology, and throughout the chapter be aware of where concepts and issues within sociology are also relevant to the field of criminological psychology.

Defining crime

Defining crime may seem straightforward, but it is not as easy as all that. There are different ways of looking at crime, using different perspectives.

The consensus view

The **consensus view** of crime uses the functionalist approach – looking at society's functioning within its accepted framework. According to this view, crime is simply a violation of the law, which is disapproved of by members of society because it goes against the general consensus as to what is right, which is reflected in the laws of that society. In other words, the functionalist view operates from the idea that there is consensus about what crime is, and agreement about the laws a society uses to deal with crime.

A crime is, according to this definition, an act which is legally forbidden; and anti-social behaviour is only a crime if a law has been broken and there was criminal intent. This may sound simple, but it does raise questions about the relationship between morals, ethics and crime. Sutherland and Cressey (1960) discussed the way that definitions of crime vary over time. In the past, printing a book and driving with reins were both criminal acts. In the more recent past homosexuality was illegal, but consenting homosexual behaviour between adults is now legal, and there are arguments for the age of consent being lowered to 16. In these examples (and many more), the acts or actions have remained the same, but whether they are counted as criminal or not has changed.

The conflict view of crime

The conflict view of crime has been described as the opposite of the consensus view. Society is seen as being made up of conflicting groups. As people do not have equal power, since they do not have equal wealth, some are poor and dissatisfied. This dissatisfaction leads to conflict, and the conflict promotes crime. But crime is seen as being defined by the interests of certain groups rather than others, because some laws reflect the vested interests of certain groups in society, or give advantages to some groups rather than others. For example, the compulsory purchase legislation used widely in the 1950s and 1960s allowed local authorities to force house-owners to sell their properties, if the land was wanted for other purposes. Although this was generally used to improve urban areas, there were also cases of unfair appropriations, in which it became apparent that the law worked to the advantage of some groups but not others.

The conflict view also raises questions about 'victimless crime'. There is a constant social debate about whether an act that is against the law but does not actually harm anyone should be regarded as criminal behaviour. According to the consensus view, such an act is clearly and simply a crime but according the conflict view it is a very different type of activity from an act which has victims, and defining it as a crime is much more dubious, because it simply reflects the interests of those who made the law, or caused it to be made.

The interactionist view

The interactionist view of crime comes from the symbolic interactionist perspective – the idea that we can understand social behaviour in terms of the roles and role-behaviours which people adopt in day-to-day living. According to this view, people's behaviour is guided by how they interpret events in their lives – the meanings that they place on what happens to them. These interpretations are learned from the reaction of others around them, and people evaluate their own behaviour through other people's reactions.

According to this perspective, therefore, an act itself is not criminal – it is the meaning behind the act that is criminal. For example, from the interactionist perspective, killing someone might not always be a crime, because the act might be done in self-defence. Whether it is deemed to be criminal or not is decided by those in power, who impose their views on others who have less power. This view sounds like the conflict view, but the main difference is that it is not thought that these views come from a desire for power in a political sense.

As a general rule, we will be adopting the consensus view in this chapter, defining crime simply as an act that breaks the law. However, we will also sometimes be referring to the conflict and the interactionist approaches, as they become relevant to specific topics.

Finding out about crime

Like defining crime, finding out about crime is less straightforward than it appears to be on the surface. The rate of crime in the population as a whole is known as the **incidence of crime**, while the statistic describing the percentage of individuals who actually experience crime is known as the **prevalence of crime**. However, many crimes go unreported and never come to the attention of police or the criminal profession. And sometimes changes in the ways that crimes are detected or identified can make it appear that there has been a massive change in the crime rate, when in reality it is simply the official

statistics that have changed. An apparent drop in street crime statistics, for example, may reflect an improvement in social behaviour; but it may simply reflect a police decision not to prosecute minor offences.

Police recording of crime

As we have just seen, not all crimes (acts that break the law) are recorded in **official statistics**, which emphasises some of the problems of identifying crime. Even when people do come forward to report crime, it is not always recorded by the police officers to whom it is reported. Hood and Sparks (1970) suggested that only about two-thirds of the serious crimes that were reported to the police were actually recorded officially. Hough and Mayhew (1985) estimate that only 75% of reported robberies were recorded, and in the case of bicycle theft the figure of reported cases was as low as 27%.

The police have discretion on which crimes to record and which not to record, which means that some crimes, such as domestic violence, often go unreported because the police concerned feel that there is little point. Also, some crimes are reported quite a long time after they have been committed and this can mean they are not recorded, as it does not seem likely that they will be solved. Another factor in whether a crime is reported or not is the victim. If he or she felt that they may have 'deserved' what happened to them, are frightened of offending the perpetrator, or even feel that it will lead to a lot of unnecessary hassle, they may be reluctant to report the crime.

Evaluation

- The problems with crime reports mean that statistics about crime must be carefully analysed. The 'dark figure' in crime statistics refers to crimes that are committed but not recorded, and it can only ever be a guess.

Offender surveys

Another way of finding out about crime is to ask the offenders. Belson (1975) carried out an **offender survey** in which 1445 boys aged 13–16 years were chosen from a London area and interviewed about crime and crime-related acts. The findings suggested that around 70% of the sample had been involved in theft from a shop, with 17% admitting to having stolen from private property. Self-report studies generally suggest that official figures underestimate the extent of crime quite considerably.

Evaluation

- Self-report studies have been criticised because the participants may not tell the truth. Some participants may exaggerate their participation in criminal acts, while others may not admit to having carried out criminal acts.

- There may also be bias in the sampling procedures. For example, if a school population is sampled, those doing the criminal acts may not be in school at the times of the survey.

- Blackmore (1974) compared the results of self-report surveys with police records and found a good level of agreement between the two.

Victim surveys

A third way of finding out about crime is to ask the victims. Household surveys such as the British Crime Survey are becoming increasingly popular, and often allow researchers to discover crimes which have not been reported. **Victim surveys** indicate that, contrary to the impression given by TV and other media, violent crimes are not common. Thefts, especially from a motor vehicle, are the most common form of all. Hough and Mayhew (1983) estimated from their survey that someone over the age of 16 might expect to be burgled once every 40 years, but robbed or assaulted once in every 500 years. It is important to note that about 90% of those surveyed report no experience of crime (Sparks, 1981). Other people, however, report being involved in more than one crime. For example, burglaries are more common in inner city areas, and young males are more likely to be the victims of assault.

Evaluation

- Victim reports tend to ask questions about crimes against the person or against property, and do not focus on **white-collar crime** (which refers to crimes such as fraud).

- As with offender surveys, there is a problem in knowing whether the respondent has told the truth.

- Interviewer characteristics and the way the interview is carried out can affect the reliability of the results of victim surveys.

- However, such reports do yield interesting data, especially when taken together with data gathered from other sources.

Theories of crime

Many of the different approaches within psychology are reflected in criminological psychology, particularly when it comes to the theories that have been developed to help to explain why crime happens. In this section we will look at explanations that draw from the physiological approach, the psychodynamic approach, the learning approach, the cognitive approach, and the social approach.

 Recall AS material

Look up the main approaches in psychology from your AS work. Write a paragraph for each of the approaches that help to explain why people commit crimes, giving what you think the explanation in each case would be.

Physiological theories

The physiological approach, when applied to criminological psychology, covers such issues as inherited characteristics, biochemical factors and biological types. These are all explanations which have been put forward in an attempt to explain why people become criminals, and they have implications for crime prevention and rehabilitation policies.

One recurrent set of ideas about the origins of criminality is the idea that there may be **genetic factors** in criminality. This idea surfaced in the early part of the nineteenth century, when Lombroso suggested that criminals had a different genetic make-up, and that certain types could be identified as criminals on the basis of their physical characteristics, such as body shape and facial characteristics. On the basis of examinations of convicted criminals, he suggested that about one-third of criminality was inherited.

These early ideas about the importance of inherited characteristics had profound social implications. In particular, they implied that the cause of crime was outside an individual's power, being located in his or her genes rather than being something which they could be held consciously accountable for. Schafer (1976) suggested that Lombroso's theory was the beginning of criminology. However, there were considerable problems with drawing these conclusions from the research methods used. For example, the studies were all of convicted criminals, without control groups and without any awareness of the importance of careful sampling. It was considered enough to look at prison populations, and draw out examples on the basis of impressions and limited samples.

More recent studies have considered the investigations for a genetic factor in criminality. **Family studies** indicated that it may run in some families. For example, Osborn and West (1979) found that around 40% of the sons of fathers who were criminals were criminals themselves, whereas only 13% of the sons of non-criminal fathers were criminals. Other family studies have found similar findings; but few of them have looked at the family culture, or its values and social beliefs.

Evaluation

- The problem with family studies is that sons share their environment with their fathers, as well as sharing 50% of their genes. Finding a correlation between fathers and sons does not necessarily show that genetic factors are the cause, because it is just as possible that the way the boys were brought up contributed to their criminality. Using family studies, we cannot claim that genetic factors are any more relevant than the shared environment. There is a problem here in separating nature from nurture.

Another type of study used to investigate a possible genetic component in criminality is the **twin study**. These assess the **concordance rate** between twins on particular characteristics. For example, if a study were comparing twins on driving competence, and found that in half the cases both the twins had good driving skills, but in the other half one twin had good driving skills and the other did not, it would be deemed that there is a 50% concordance rate for driving skills. Since identical (MZ) twins share 100% of their genes while non-identical (DZ) twins share 50% of their genes, then a high concordance for MZ twins and a lower one for DZ twins implies that there may be a genetic component (see Table 2.1).

There have been many studies which have looked at concordance rates for MZ and DZ twins in criminal behaviour. Hollin (1989) reviewed a number of studies and found that on average the concordance rate for criminality is 48% for MZ twins and 20% for DZ twins. This has been taken as implying that there may be a genetic factor involved in criminality.

Evaluation

- One recurrent problem with twin studies is that judgements of whether twins are MZ or DZ were based on their physical appearance. Recent genetic studies suggest that many pairs of twins have been wrongly diagnosed in this respect.

- Both MZ and DZ twins in these studies share the same home environment; but there is some evidence that MZ twins are treated more similarly by other people by virtue of their similar appearance. So, although they share more genes, they also share more of their environmental influences than DZ twins. Again there is a 'nature/nurture' problem here – there is a problem in separating nature from nurture to determine the cause of a behaviour.

> ### Synoptic Note
>
> The 'nature/nurture' debate is examined in Unit 6, the synoptic element. You will need to refer to examples of problems in deciding whether something is caused by 'nature' or 'nurture' (or a combination). A criminal tendency is just such an example.

Another way of looking for a genetic component to criminal behaviour is to look at adopted children. The idea is that the adopted child experiences the environment of the adopted parents, rather than the environment of the natural parents. So if there is a correlation between the behaviour of the child and that of the natural parents, the cause is likely to be genetic rather than environmental.

Mednick *et al.* (1983) studied around 14,500 adopted children and found that an adopted boy with a biological parent who is a criminal was much more likely to have also committed crime. Similarly, Crowe (1974) found that some 50% of adopted children whose natural mothers had a

Table 2.1 Summary of twin study data looking at criminality

	MZ twins		DZ twins	
	No. of pairs	% concordant	No. of pairs	% concordant
Lange (1929)	13	77	17	12
Legras (1932)	4	100	5	0
Rosanoff *et al.* (1934)	37	68	60	10
Kranz (1936)	31	65	43	53
Stumpfl (1936)	18	61	19	37
Borgstrom (1939)	4	75	5	40
Rosanoff *et al.* (1941)	45	78	27	18
Yoshimasu (1961)	28	61	18	11
Yoshimasu (1965)	28	50	26	0
Hayashi (1967)	15	73	5	60
Dalgaard and Kringlen (1976)	31	26	54	15
Christiansen (1977)	85	32	147	12

Source: Hollin (1989)

criminal record had themselves committed a crime by the age of 18, whereas in a control group of adopted children whose natural mothers had no criminal record the figure was only 5%. Evidence from this type of study has been taken to imply that there is a genetic element to criminal behaviour.

Evaluation

- Studies have found environmental as well as genetic factors. For example, an adopted boy is more likely to commit criminal acts when both the biological and the adopting fathers are criminals.

- Many adoption studies show **response bias** in that the research participants are generally the adopting family, who have a vested interest in emphasising the criminality of the biological parent and their own law-abiding nature. Since data is often collected by interview, this can distort the findings.

- Correlation is not causality, and there are often intervening factors in the association between crime and genes. For example, Bohman (1978) found a genetic predisposition to alcoholism, and alcoholism is related to criminal behaviour. Cadoret and Cain (1980) showed that a biological relative who is antisocial or alcoholic is more likely to lead to antisocial behaviour in an adopted child. While this may be interpreted as a genetic factor in criminal behaviour, it is a far cry from being a 'criminal gene' as the term suggests.

ACTIVITY

Write a paragraph each on twin studies, family studies and adoption studies as ways of looking at the causes of criminality, including the strengths and weaknesses of the methods.

Another explanation for criminal behaviour is that criminals may have an extra chromosome. The human genome consists of 23 pairs of chromosomes, and one pair – that which determines sex – is known by its shape rather than by a number. Women have two X chromosomes, and so are described as XX; while men have one X chromosome and one shorter Y chromosome (XY). However, it is not uncommon for people to have an additional chromosome – a fact that was only just being discovered in the early 1960s. In 1961, Sandberg *et al.* reported a study of chromosomal abnormality in a prison population, and argued that some 5% of criminals had **XXY syndrome** – they had an extra X chromosome. They suggested that this may be a factor, particularly in violent crime. The idea was widely publicised, although the fact that XXY people are found in all sorts of walks of life was less well known.

Evaluation

- Owen (1972) challenged Sandberg's findings, arguing that there was a problem in categorising people as XXY, and also there did not seem to be more XXY males in prisons than in the population as a whole.

- Among the few who did have the syndrome, Owen observed that they were more likely to have committed sexual offences than violent crimes. So if there is a link between XXY and criminality (and subsequent research found that this was unlikely) it is not particularly with violent crime as was originally claimed.

Synoptic Note

Methodology is a part of Unit 6, the synoptic element. So knowledge of the methodological issues mentioned here about twin, family and adoption studies is likely to be useful for that part of the course.

Attempts to identify other physiological correlates of criminality have all been distinctly equivocal. It was thought, for example, that **biochemical factors** might be involved: Weiss (1983) suggested that hyperactive children are more likely to become delinquent, and other studies suggested that diet is linked to criminal behaviour. However, more careful research showed that these connections were tenuous at best, and often confused correlation with causality. Dietary factors, for example, were connected more strongly with social class than with criminality as such, though since criminality rates (as measured by these studies) are also connected with social class they inevitably show a correlation.

More specific types of physiological evidence have also been sought, but again with only limited success. It was argued, for example, that it might be possible to use electroencephalograms (EEGs) to detect abnormal brain functioning on the part of criminals; but Loomis *et al.* (1967) found no correlation between EEG patterns and criminal behaviour. Some studies (e.g. Monroe, 1978) have linked brain damage to violent behaviour; but again the evidence for this is not very clear.

Evaluation

- It is difficult to find sufficiently clear data to connect hyperactivity, diet or vitamin deficiency to crime.

- EEG measures are not objective, as they measure live brain activity, and may be affected by the current situation.

Another idea about physiological correlates of criminality came from an extensive study by Sheldon, in 1942, in which he looked at the **body shapes** of 1800 research participants, and argued that they fell into three main types – ectomorphs, who are thin and bony, mesomorphs, who are broad and muscular, and endomorphs, who are large and heavy (Figure 2.1). These shapes, Sheldon argued, linked with personality: ectomorphs tend to be introverted, mesomorphs are adventurous, and endomorphs sociable.

In a follow-up study, Sheldon (1949) looked at 400 males in rehabilitation and found more mesomorphs than any other body type. There were also some endomorphs but few ectomorphs. Although the idea that body type was linked to criminal behaviour became very popular, more recent studies showed that it was not really supported by the evidence.

However, even if body build does not itself produce criminal behaviour, it is still possible for it to be a factor in crime. It is possible, for example, that more muscular and larger individuals may be more likely to be invited to become involved in crime than those deemed as 'weedy'. And on the other side, it has been shown that a certain type of body build can be more likely to lead to arrest (Feldman, 1977), possibly because it fits with police conceptions of a 'typical criminal'. Goldstein *et al.* (1984) argued that stereotyping of this type could often lead to

arrests or convictions. So Sheldon's ideas, although not supported by the evidence, still have an effect in society today.

Psychoanalytic theories

Psychodynamic theories emphasise inner forces as causing criminal behaviour more than social and environmental factors, although social and environmental factors are sometimes also taken into account. According to the psychoanalytic approach, crime can be caused by inner dynamic forces. One of the most important features in this model is the emphasis which it places on childhood experience. For example, Aichorn (1955) argued that environmental factors could not be wholly responsible for crime. Some delinquent tendencies might be innate, but **early emotional experience** was also a powerful factor. The wrong kind of early emotional experience could produce 'latent delinquency'. If the process of socialisation (for example, the development of the ego and the child's acceptance of rules) goes wrong, then latent delinquency could become a dominant state. Aichorn describes this dominant state as 'dissocial'.

Other psychoanalytic theorists used the concept of **sublimation** to help to explain crime. Healy and Bronner (1936) studied children in a child guidance clinic, and found that children who had committed offences were those who also had less stable families and showed more emotional disturbance. They interpreted this finding as

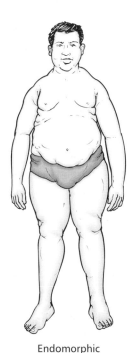
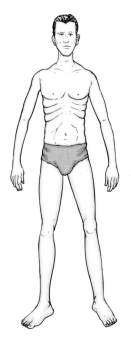

Endomorphic   Mesomorphic   Ectomorphic

Figure 2.1
Human body types: endomorphic, mesomorphic and ectomorphic

evidence for the claim that delinquency can be explained by sublimation. Sublimation refers to the channelling of unacceptable impulses into other thoughts and behaviours. For example, if someone has not experienced strong emotional ties with their parents, their unconscious unsatisfied wishes may become sublimated into criminal acts. Delinquency, according to this view, is sublimating or acting out inner conflicts.

Another explanation from the psychoanalytic approach is the idea that delinquency can result from **over-permissive parenting**. The internalising of parental authority is an important factor in the development of the personality, since it eventually results in the superego – the third part of the personality which balances the impulsive demands of the id with the strict demands of duty and responsibility. If parents are too permissive, the superego of an individual may not be fully developed, and antisocial impulses may be poorly controlled, leading to criminal behaviour.

Evaluation

• 'Standard' evaluations of the psychodynamic approach, such as problems with evidence and research methods, can be used as evaluation points here.

↻ *Recall AS material*

Recall your AS material from the psychodynamic approach, or look it up.

ACTIVITY

Divide a sheet of paper into three columns. Head each column according to the three parts of personality in the psychodynamic approach, and write a brief description of each one in the column below its name.

Learning theories

Where the psychodynamic theorists held that the cause of behaviour is inside the individual, in buried unconscious conflicts or wishes, learning theorists suggest that the cause of behaviour is in the environment. They argue that crime results from an individual's learning and the stimuli offered by the environment.

Operant conditioning principles have been used to explain criminal behaviour. In operant conditioning, the antecedent (what happens before the behaviour) prompts the behaviour, and the behaviour is made more likely to happen by its consequences – the ABC of behavioural theory. The main point of operant conditioning is that behaviour which has desirable consequences is likely to be repeated. The organism – person or animal – operates on the environment through its behaviour. That produces changes that are either desirable, and so strengthen (reinforce) the behaviour, or undesirable, as in punishment.

Behaviour can be reinforced through **positive reinforcement**, when the consequences are pleasant and so the behaviour is repeated, or through **negative reinforcement**, which is when the consequences allow the organism to avoid or escape from unpleasant stimuli, so the behaviour is repeated. Both of these types of reinforcement strengthen the behaviour, and so make it more likely to happen. Punishment weakens the behaviour by producing unpleasant consequences but it is less effective than reinforcement.

↻ *Recall AS material*

Recall – or look up – your AS material from the learning approach, especially the principles of operant conditioning.

One of the ways that learning concepts have been applied in criminological psychology is through **differential association theory**. This was proposed by Sutherland (1939), and suggests that crime is learnt by association, and that people learn whether criminal behaviour is favourable or not as a result of its consequences. According to this approach, criminal behaviour is not learned through associating with criminals, but by learning the methods involved in crime – an individual can learn the methods from their parents even if the parents do not commit crimes. For example, although parents may say it is wrong to steal, if they show examples which contradict this (such as not returning change that is wrongly given to them) they are setting an example of criminal behaviour.

The key points of Sutherland's differential association theory:
• Criminal behaviour is learned.
• The learning comes through association with others. The behaviour is mainly learned from close personal groups.
• The learning involves how to commit crime, as well as drives and motives to do with crime.
• The law is perceived as either favourable or unfavourable through learning, and this learning influences drives and motives.
• An individual turns to crime when their view of crime as favourable outweighs their view of crime as unfavourable.

- Differential associations are learning experiences, and they vary in importance for each individual.
- Criminal behaviour is learned by the same processes other behaviour is learned.
- It is not that need (for example, money) causes crime. Instead, crime is caused by the methods that have been learned.

Differential association theory, then, uses the principles of learning and social learning to explain crime. But it is a social theory as well as a learning one, because it avoids any absolute definition of crime, arguing that crime is defined by those in power rather than reflecting standards of morality or any other principles. Those making the law decide what is deviant, and those committing deviant acts are criminals.

Jeffrey (1965) linked differential association theory with operant conditioning, arguing that these points were very similar to saying that the consequences of a behaviour (such as a criminal act) determine whether it is repeated or not. Jeffrey (1965) suggested that crime is maintained by the consequences for the individual; so if the criminal does not experience negative consequences, criminal behaviour will be repeatedly strengthened.

Evaluation

- Differential association theory does not explain why others, given the same examples, do not learn to commit crime.

- Association as an explanation for criminal behaviour ignores mediating cognitive factors. Cognitive factors such as motivation do seem to play a part in explaining criminal behaviour; as do the internal factors such as vicarious learning and self-reinforcement which are dealt with in social learning theory.

Social learning theory has also been used to explain criminal behaviour. This includes ideas about social motivation as well as behavioural learning. Bandura (1977a) identified three important factors in motivation.
- One factor involves **external reinforcement**, and is the same as the emphasis on consequences proposed in operant conditioning.
- A second factor is **vicarious learning**. This means that an individual can learn from watching another person, and observing whether their behaviour is rewarded or punished. This is one step away from operant conditioning, in that operant conditioning suggests learning is through the consequences of one's own actions, whereas vicarious learning suggests that we can learn through watching what happens to others when they do things such as criminal acts.
- The third aspect of motivation identified by Bandura

involves **self-reinforcement** – personal achievement and meeting one's own standards.

Social learning theory helps to explain behaviour by saying that we model our behaviour on that of others, and that the reinforcement which enables us to continue showing a particular behaviour can be either external or internal. In the context of crime, Bandura suggested that observational learning takes place within the family, the subculture and within the social environment, such as the media; and this represents an important source of cognitive factors that will act alongside the behavioural learning to determine whether criminal acts are carried out or not.

Evaluation

- It has been said that if environmental factors cause crime, this takes emphasis away from the free will of the individual, so people cannot be blamed for their criminal actions. However, the same argument has also been used for genetic theories.

- One criticism of learning as an explanation for criminal behaviour is that the thought of imprisonment should deter individuals from committing criminal acts, whereas this does not seem to be the case. Some theorists have argued that imprisonment may not be such an aversive event for those with a deprived upbringing. As a result the thought of imprisonment, whilst being a deterrent, does not outweigh the possible rewards of the criminal act. However, a more practical explanation is that criminals do not usually believe that they are likely to be caught and so the thought of punishment does not act as a deterrent because it is considered so unlikely.

ACTIVITY

Make a list of the principles of operant conditioning, and write a brief description of each one.

Cognition and crime

Cognition refers to concepts such as memory, reasoning, thought processes and imagery. Yochelson and Samenow (1976) interviewed male offenders and claimed that they had found criminal thinking patterns that characterised all criminals. In a further analysis, Ross and Fabiano (1985) analysed Yochelson and Samenow's findings and suggested that there were 52 characteristic styles of thinking that make up a 'criminal mentality'. These include concrete thinking, failure to empathise with others, irresponsible decision-making, a poor concept of time and seeing themselves as victims.

- Interviewing is sometimes an unreliable method, which means that the validity of the results might be called into question.

- The sample used by Yochelson and Samenow included many criminals who had been judged not guilty by reason of insanity, so it was not a representative sample of the criminal population. So the conclusion that all criminals share these thinking patterns cannot really be justified by the data.

- There is also a possible problem in assuming that thinking styles or patterns can be said to cause behaviour. The link between thinking patterns and behaviour is by no means straightforward.

Other researchers have looked at **cognitive styles** to see if a certain style predicts or explains criminal behaviour. Ahlstrom and Havinghurst (1971) proposed that the root cause of criminal behaviour might be a lack of self-control, which would lead to impulsiveness. Ross and Fabiano argued that impulsivity can be defined as failing to stop to think between having the idea for an action and carrying the action out. This impulsiveness may result from not having learned effective thinking, or not thinking of alternative actions. Rotenberg and Nachshon (1979) found that offenders did seem to be more impulsive than non-offenders, but other researchers did not find these differences (Saunders *et al.*, 1973).

Another aspect of cognition that might be associated with criminal behaviour is the concept of **locus of control**. Offenders seem to think of their behaviour as being externally controlled, for example, by influences outside their control (Kumchy and Sayer, 1980). Again, though, other studies have not replicated these findings.

- Although there does seem to be some evidence that offenders may have characteristic thinking patterns in such areas as locus of control or impulsivity, different studies contradict one another.

- We are a long way from understanding how cognitive processes may lead to criminal behaviour, since there is no straightforward link between the two.

- Arguing that criminals are qualitatively distinctive from 'normal' people – whether by personality trait or by cognitive style – cannot be justified by the data of these studies. It is also of questionable value in really helping us to understand why people become criminals.

Social theories

Another way of looking at the causes of criminal behaviour is to see it as a result of social factors. One of the most well-known social theories of crime is called **labelling theory**. Labelling theory draws on social psychological mechanisms such as the self-fulfilling prophecy to show how the behaviour and assumptions of others often produces behaviour which lives up to negative social expectations.

According to labelling theory, what is criminal is decided by those in power. Authorities, such as teachers, judges and the police, label someone a criminal – and that means that it is the disadvantaged of society who are most likely to receive that label. People who commit white-collar crime, for example, are rarely labelled as 'criminals', even though their actions break the law. According to this model, behaviour is not criminal in itself. It becomes a crime when someone in power in society labels it as such. But once it has been labelled that way, those in authority treat the individual as though they were 'criminal', and this becomes a self-fulfilling prophecy. We will be looking more closely at the self-fulfilling prophecy and labelling theory later in this chapter.

The legal aspects of crime

Legal aspects of crime concern the activities of the police and the courts, including tracking down criminals and sentencing them. In other words, they are not particularly interested in looking at why people commit crimes, or how to prevent people from committing crimes in the first place, but are concerned with dealing with crime once it has taken place. In this section, we will look at three major ways that criminological psychology has contributed to the legal aspects of crime: eyewitness testimony, offender profiling, and jury decision-making.

Eyewitness testimony

Witnesses are often of great importance in finding out who has committed a crime. Even though there may be forensic aspects to crimes which may help to link them with a particular suspect, witness statements are often essential for identifying suspects in the first place. But eyewitness accounts are not straightforward.

Courts often place a great deal of emphasis on an individual's eyewitness account of the circumstances of the crime. However, such accounts have often been questioned, partly because they commonly show inconsistencies, and partly because human memory isn't by any means an accurate recording of what happened. For example, witnesses tend to overestimate the length of time an incident lasts for. In a study done by Buckhout (1974) students thought a staged incident lasted twice as long as it did; which means that it can sometimes be difficult to check on the facts of an incident.

More importantly, witnesses may be very confident about their recall, but their level of confidence does not match the accuracy of what they remember. Clark and Stephenson (1995) asked police officers to recall an event when they were alone, in a pair or in a group of four. They found inaccuracies of memory in each of their experimental situations, and in each case the participants were reasonably confident of their answers. The condition with four people produced more accuracy, as might be expected, but on the other hand, they were even more confident of their accuracy than those in the other groups – even when they were wrong. So witness confidence can't be taken as any indicator of how accurate eyewitness testimony might be.

Understanding memory

Sometimes, eyewitness testimony can be astoundingly inaccurate. For example, Buckhout (1980) studied the effect of a television news programme. Viewers saw a mugging taking place in a New York street and then saw a police line-up using six people, one of whom was the mugger. Viewers then called the police in response to an appeal for identification of the mugger; but only 14% of those who called were correct in their identification. When people taking part in a legal conference were used as participants watching the same piece of film, 20% did correctly identify the mugger, but this was not significantly more. These sorts of studies cast doubt over eyewitness testimony as a way of identifying a criminal (Table 2.2).

Eyewitness testimony is all about memory, so if we are to understand the issues surrounding eyewitnesses we need to have a clear understanding of what memory is and how it works. Eyewitnesses witness the event, wait before giving evidence, and then give the evidence. It has been said that these stages correspond to the three memory stages of encoding, storage, and retrieval.

At the encoding stage, information is selected by paying attention to some things rather than others. This is not a straightforward process, and is easily influenced by bias of one kind or another. It is not possible to pay attention to everything, so some information is lost immediately. There are other problems of bias at the storage stage – in particular, the way we try to make information make sense in terms of our own ideas and existing schemas. Bartlett (1932) suggested that we make sense of information as we store it, and this distorts the information. The final stage, retrieval, can also lead to bias and distortion. Although we may have a clear memory of what we have stored (albeit already reconstructed and distorted), the way we are asked to retrieve information can itself distort the stored information. Leading questions can produce different 'memories' than non-leading questions, for example.

So we only attend to some of the information, we distort or reconstruct what we have attended to, and our

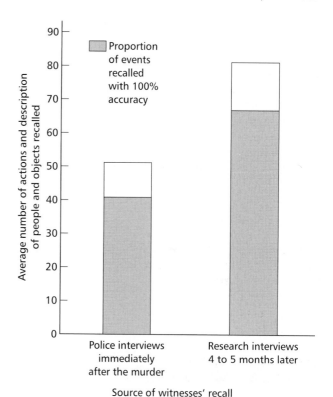

Figure 2.2
Accuracy of witness recall of a murder (Source: Hewstone et al., 1996; based on Yuille and Cutshall, 1986)

Table 2.2   *Variables that affect eyewitness memory*

Social	Situational	Individual	Interrogational
Attitudes	Complexity of event	Age	Artists' sketches
Conformity	Duration of event	Cognitive style	Computer systems
Prejudice	Illumination	Personality	ID parades
Status of interrogator	Time delay	Race	Mugshots
Stereotyping	Type of crime	Sex	Photofits
		Training	

Source: Hollin (1989)

memories can be further distorted by the way that we are asked to recall them. When we really get down to it, our memory for people and events is often extremely inaccurate. Criminological psychologists have spent considerable efforts in trying to understand and explain just how these errors of memory can be understood and addressed.

There are two main models of memory that researchers in this area tend to use. Some researchers (e.g. Anderson, 1990) prefer the **associative network model** of memory. This model suggests that we have nodes or links along which cognitive associations can travel, and a network of cognitive links can spread in this way. Nodes are ideas or propositions such as 'book' or 'reading', and by linking these ideas we form associations. When someone thinks about an association or recalls something, links are activated, and this makes the links or associations stronger. This means that some associations become stronger than others, for example, 'reading' and 'book' would be strongly associated but 'reading' and 'car' might be less so. Associations can be made in all sorts of ways, but the most strongly used ones are the more likely.

According to this model, long-term memory incorporates all the possible nodes and associations which can be triggered off by a particular item of stored information. Short-term memory, on the other hand, is the active memories that are in someone's consciousness at any one time. According to association theory incorrect memories are the result of mixed associations where links are wrongly made between nodes. Wyer and Carlston (1994) looked at how this applies to person memory. They suggested that another implication of the theory is that inconsistent information will be recalled better than predictable or consistent information, because it attracts attention. That produces more cognitive activity, which strengthens links and retrieval routes.

Studies of inconsistency found considerable variation in how effective inconsistencies are. For example, according to Bodenhausen and Lichtenstein (1987), they don't seem to help when the person is making complex judgements. It also doesn't help if the impression of the person has already been well established (Fiske and Neuberg, 1990), or if the person has had a lot of time to think about their impression (Wyer and Martin, 1986). Moreover, some types of inconsistency are more helpful than others – for example, Wyer and Gordon (1982) found that descriptive inconsistencies (e.g. about the person's appearance) were less effective in improving memory than evaluative inconsistencies.

The main alternative way of looking at memory in the context of how we recall people and events is **schema theory**. Schema theory suggests that we use past experiences to help to make sense of what we see. We store our past experience in the form of cognitive structures, which we use as the basis for our own experience in the world and in planning out future actions. Because of this personal relevance, we make an effort to make sense of the information we receive – as in Bartlett's 'effort after meaning'. According to schema theory, incorrect memories come about as a result of our personal reconstruction of events and memories so that what we store makes sense.

Not all of the influence of schemas, though, is about inaccuracy. Christianson *et al.* (1998) asked students, teachers and policemen to watch a video and answer some questions. Policemen were found to have better recall. This might be because they have more experience and could more easily analyse the information. As a result, policemen may have more relevant schemas to link the event on the video to.

Association theory, then, suggests that we use nodes and associations and build up memories through links. Schema theory suggests that we construct meaningful representations of issues, combining information, plans and experience. Both ideas can account for incorrect memories, but in a slightly different way. One difference, for example, is that schema theory takes a 'top-down' approach – suggesting that what we already know about the world is used to make sense of incoming information. Association theory is a bottom-up approach, suggesting that the characteristics of the incoming information affect how we process it. Overall, though, both approaches are useful, so most psychologists working in this area draw on both association theory and schema theory when explaining problems with eyewitness memory and eyewitness testimony.

↻ Recall AS material

Recall your AS material from the cognitive approach, especially material on eyewitness testimony – or look it up.

Studies of eyewitness testimony

One of the main researchers in the area of eyewitness testimony is Elizabeth Loftus. Loftus carried out many experiments using the method of showing participants a short video and then asking questions. In one study, for example, Loftus (1975) showed around 150 students a film of a car accident. Half of the participants were then asked leading questions after the film – questions which included some misleading information designed to encourage the participant to 'remember' something that was not there. For example, one question was 'how fast was the white sports car going when it passed the barn while travelling along the country road?' There was no barn in the video. After a week the group were questioned again, and 17.3% of the group who had been given the misleading question about a barn remembered a barn, compared with 2.7% of those who did not have the misleading or leading question.

In 1978, Loftus carried out a similar study. In this study she used 195 participants, 95 of whom saw a small red Datsun car at a stop sign. The other 100 participants were shown a nearly identical slide, but the car was waiting at a give-way sign. After seeing these and other slides, participants completed a 20-item questionnaire asking about what they had seen. Question 17 was different for the two groups, asking either 'Did another car pass the red Datsun while it was stopped at the stop sign?' or: 'Did another car pass the red Datsun while it was stopped at the give-way sign?' So some participants had a question consistent with the slide they had seen, and some did not. Then the participants did an unrelated task before being asked to identify the slides they had seen. Those with the consistent question selected the correct slide 75% of the time. But those with an inconsistent question only selected the correct slide 41% of the time. It appeared that the misleading question had affected their recall.

Loftus and Palmer (1974) carried out a study using a similar method. Participants saw a film of a car accident and then were asked questions about it. The key question was the same except for the last word. The question was 'how fast were the cars going when they ...?' and the end word was 'bumped', 'hit', 'collided', 'smashed' or 'contacted'. The aim was to see how these different words led to different estimated speeds. The more 'serious' the word, the higher the speed that was estimated. An average of 41 mph was estimated when the word was 'smashed' compared with 32 mph when the word was 'contacted'.

A further test was carried out with the same participants. A week later they were asked 'Did you see any broken glass?' Of those who had been given the word 'smashed' in the original question 32% said they did see broken glass, whereas 14% of those who had the word 'hit' said they saw broken glass. There was no broken glass, but it was consistent with the notion of 'smashed' and the thought that the cars were going quite fast, whereas it was less consistent with the word 'hit', and the lower speed.

These studies raise a number of questions – both about the accuracy of eyewitness testimony and about how easily witness memories can be changed or distorted. However, Loftus (1997) pointed out that it is really only the peripheral detail that can be distorted by other factors and other events. Central details appear to be correctly recalled, but there seems to be a 'misinformation space' where eyewitnesses are willing to accept the introduction of false information and incorporate it into their memory. The tendency to accept misinformation increases over time, so the longer ago the incident, the more likely someone is to incorporate misinformation.

There are also limits to the way that information can be distorted. People do not readily accept unlikely information, for example; and they don't easily change information which was distinctive in the original stimulus. For example, in an experiment where a red purse was stolen, and the colour was very clear, 98% of the participants remembered the colour of the purse. Later all but two of the participants were not misled by a question about a brown purse. They remembered that the purse was red.

Evaluation

- Participants were using information from more than one external source (videos, questionnaires) as well as their previous experience. So they may not be incorrect memories as such, but composite memories based on different sources.

- Baddeley (1995) suggests that the problem with the Loftus and Palmer study is not with the memory trace as such, but with interference in retrieval. The misleading questions interfere with finding the original memory rather than changing it.

- Fiske and Taylor (1991) suggest that problems found in eyewitness testimony might happen because of a confusion between episodic and semantic memories. The video would give episodic memories, because memories would be of the specific events in the video. However, the introduction of a misleading piece of information means that semantic memory is triggered.

Following the Loftus studies, researchers began to investigate the ways that witness memories can be distorted. For example, Garry *et al.* (1994) carried out a study in a shopping mall. A 14-year old was convinced by an older brother that he had been lost in a shopping mall. The older brother talked about other real events that had happened, and at the same time kept mentioning the false shopping mall incident. After about two weeks the 14-year old could 'recall' the incident, including giving false detail, for example, about an elderly man who rescued him. When the 14-year old was debriefed he was upset. False memories had been implanted.

↻ *Recall AS material*

Recall AS material from the cognitive approach, where you may have discussed false memory syndrome. If you can't recall it easily, look it up.

Children have particular problems when it comes to eyewitness testimony. Ceci *et al.* (1994) used children as participants and asked them some times about real events and at other times about made-up events. The study was carried out over a 10-week period. The researchers found that the children's memories had been heavily influenced by what the adults had told them – 58% of the children under school age described false events or stories and 25% invented memories of false events. When psychologists were subsequently shown videotapes of the children recounting their memories, they were not able to tell whether the memories were false or real.

There are also special factors involved in the way that children need to be questioned, because of the imbalance of power between children and adults. For example, children will often change their stories if they are asked the same question twice, because they interpret this as the adult meaning that their first answer was not satisfactory and that they should say something different. With an adult, changing the story often means that the first version was a lie. But with children, it is more likely that the first version was the truth and that later versions are untrue, as the child searches to find something which will satisfy the person asking the questions. Recent investigations have shown that children are surprisingly accurate in their eyewitness accounts; but these and other factors have led to special treatments for child witnesses in the courts.

ACTIVITY

Write a short paragraph describing false memory syndrome, then use the information in this chapter to help to explain how it happens.

In terms of research with adults, Garry *et al.* (1994) identified four different types of memory-distortion studies:
- those using leading questions
- those where a new item is suggested
- those where an object is manipulated that was observed in a different scene
- those that suggest a whole episode which had either happened at some other time or had not happened at all.

Evaluation

- Eyewitness memory research is mainly based on experiments such as those carried out by Loftus and her colleagues. One problem with laboratory studies is that they are not in natural settings and may not resemble real-life situations.

- In laboratory studies the same item is used as the stimulus and for recall. In real life this is unlikely. For example, a photograph of a suspect would involve different clothing, for example, or a different haircut.

- In real-life events are confusing and fast-moving, whereas in laboratory situations they tend to be slower and more explicit.

Factors influencing eyewitness testimony

Researchers have identified a number of different factors that can influence eyewitness testimony. Loftus (1981) distinguished between event and witness factors. **Event factors** are to do with the event itself, while **witness factors** are to do with the person who is the eyewitness. Other researchers have made similar observations. For example, Ellis (1975) identified a number of stimulus factors which could influence eyewitness testimony, such as the length of time the person was at the scene, lighting and distance from the event. Ellis also discussed the influence of subject factors like the age of the witness. As we've seen, interrogational factors (to do with asking questions) can influence eyewitness testimony (Clifford, 1979), and so can social factors such as prejudice and stereotypes. In this section we will look at some of the studies which have investigated these types of influence.

Person memory

The way that we remember other people is often strongly influenced by the **stereotypes** that we hold. Stereotyping can lead to confused associations, where wrong events are associated because of previous associations. Similarly, information can be added to memories because something similar has happened before. For example, Loftus (1979) showed participants a film which began by showing two people talking to one another. Later in the film, the first person was seen committing a burglary with someone else. When recalling the scenes, participants tended to remember the second person (from the first scene) as being the accomplice, even though they did not see the accomplice properly. The first association between the two was enough to prompt the participants to 'remember' those two people as being the ones involved in the crime.

Other factors also influence our memory for people. For example, even when we have only had a glimpse of someone, we often gain an impression of their personality – mainly because we assign personality traits to them.

These traits are often entirely fictitious, and nothing like the real person, but they can influence eyewitness memory: we remember actions which seem to 'fit' those traits. Schneider *et al.* (1979) suggested that we cluster traits according to social desirability (for example 'friendly'), and competence (for example, 'efficient'). This clustering can distort our memories of people by encouraging us to remember them acting in accordance with the traits we think they possess.

Similarly, we make inferences about people on the basis of how they act, and this can distort eyewitness memory. We generally see behaviour as having a purpose; and so when we see someone acting in a particular way we are likely to interpret what they are doing as conscious and planned. Hoffman *et al.* (1981) showed how these inferences about the purpose of the behaviour can distort recall considerably.

We usually remember people's appearance better than their behaviour or traits, which is thought to be because visual information involves a direct sort of memory store – visual, or iconic memory – which doesn't involve the nodes and associations involved in semantic memory. Freides (1974) argued that we can be very good at remembering faces. But this can also be influenced by other social factors. For example, Malpass and Kravitz (1969) found that we are not as good at recalling faces of people of a different ethnic background from ourselves. This has been explained in terms of social identification, and the way that we don't pay as much attention to 'out-group' faces as we do to faces belonging to our 'in-group' (Devine and Malpass, 1985).

⟳ Recall AS material

Recall your AS material from the social approach, and in particular social identity theory, or look it up.

Emotions

Arousal is another factor that can influence eyewitness recall. Being in a high state of excitement, fear or anxiety influences the amount of attention we pay to the world around us, in that high levels of arousal reduce the effectiveness of the attention paid. Even though the person feels that they are remembering the situation vividly, their memories are often inaccurate under that sort of situation – sometimes dramatically so. For example, Hollin (1989) reported that there is systematically less accuracy in reporting violent events than in reporting other kinds, and Loftus *et al.* (1983) found that participants who watched a film of a hospital fire had worse recall when they were reminded of the fire later than people recalling less emotional events. However, that

doesn't seem to apply when the situation has been staged for the purpose of study. Malpass and Devine (1983) found that staged violence actually led to better recall – possibly because it was not real and simply added extra excitement; or possibly because the participants were not emotionally affected.

Being confronted by a weapon is another emotional experience which can influence memory. The **weapon focus effect** is the observation that if there is a weapon in the scene, witnesses are likely to focus on the weapon and not on the offender's face (Figure 2.3). As a result, their recall of appearance and facial features is less clear (Loftus *et al.*, 1987). It was thought that this was because of the emotional implications of violent weaponry, such as knives or guns, but Mitchell *et al.* (1998) found that if an offender carried a piece of celery it was focused on in just the same way as a weapon, so perhaps it is the existence of an unusual or inconsistent stimulus that attracts the witness's attention.

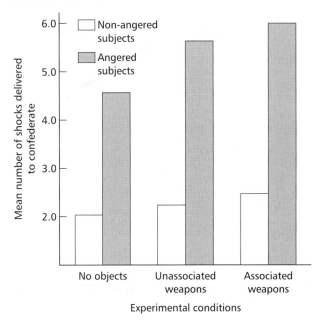

Figure 2.3
Studies show that when a weapon is present in a scene more shocks are delivered. This suggests that the presence of weapons in a scene is noticed (Source: Hewstone et al., 1996; based on Berkowitz and Le Page, 1967)

Attributions

Another factor that influences eyewitness testimony is the way we attribute reasons for our own and others' actions. If actions were clear and there were obvious causes for them, then this would not be a problem. However, often when others are involved the reasons for actions are not clear at all. We have to work out a reason based on many factors, including the situation and the type of person involved, and these **attributions** involve interpreting the situation according to our existing knowledge and how we make sense of the situation. That can produce widely different interpretations – for example, we might say that a robber grabbed hold of a hostage and dragged him off, or we could say that a robber caught hold of a fellow thief and helped him to get away.

Attributions are the reasons we give for behaviour, both our own behaviour and that of others. We can attribute behaviour to external causes, such as the situation or someone else's actions, or we can attribute behaviour to internal causes – factors within the individual such as fear, competence or lack of ability. When we give an internal reason for a behaviour, this is called **dispositional attribution**, because we are considering someone's disposition. When we give an external reason for a behaviour, this is called **situational attribution**, as we are considering the situation as the cause of the behaviour.

Some characteristic errors can be made when giving reasons for actions, and are commonly found in eyewitness testimony. One of them is **hedonic relevance**, or the personal meaning which an event has for us. If an event is personally meaningful, we are more likely to make a dispositional attribution, even if that is inappropriate in the circumstances. For example, if we have an accident in a new car, we are more likely to blame the other person's driving (dispositional attribution) than we are to blame the situation (situational attribution). This is because the car is important to us, and raises the level of hedonic relevance in the situation.

Another characteristic error is known as the **fundamental attribution error**. This refers to the tendency we have to over-emphasise internal factors as causing the behaviour of other people, while we over-emphasise external factors as the cause of our own behaviour. As a result, we often make the mistake of blaming other people personally for their problems and actions, whereas if we were in the same situation we would be looking at the pressures and influences leading us to act that way. Some researchers have argued that giving internal factors as reasons for the actions of others allows us to predict their actions better, making us feel as though we have more control over our environment. If we believed that others do things because of different situations, this would make their behaviour less predictable – although it would make our judgements more accurate.

The **actor–observer effect** can also lead to an attribution error. If we are the actor – the person doing the act – we tend to emphasise external causes for our behaviour. But if we are observing another actor, then we tend to emphasise an internal cause for their behaviour, even if their behaviour is the same as our own. So if we miss the bus we blame the bus for being late, but if someone else misses the bus, we blame them for not getting up in time.

Another type of attribution error is the **self-serving bias**, in which what happens in the situation affects how we attribute cause to what happened. Although we are generally more likely to give external attributions for our own behaviour and internal attributions for the behaviour of others, the self-serving bias means that we give dispositional or internal reasons for our actions when it is in our interest to get credit for doing so. For example, if we got up early and caught the early bus, we are successful and it makes us look good in the eyes of an employer, and so we take credit by giving internal reasons for being early. However, if we are late, and it makes us look bad, then we give external causes, such as missing the bus because it came early.

Hypnosis

Popular 'folk wisdom' tends to assume that hypnosis is a way of gathering accurate, buried memories, and as a result investigative or forensic hypnosis has been used in the USA to try to find out more information from eyewitnesses. Forensic hypnosis is the use of hypnosis to gather information for use as evidence. Those experimenting with the technique believed that the individual can use hypnosis to access 'buried' information, and bring this information into consciousness.

However, hypnosis doesn't actually work like that, and nor does human memory. Even when there has been no attempt to influence the participant, hypnosis is not particularly effective. Sanders and Simmons (1983) asked participants to watch a video of a pick-pocket at work. Then half the participants were hypnotised and interviewed, and an identity parade followed. The other half followed the same procedure but were not hypnotised. The hypnotised participants were actually less accurate in their recall.

In a review of this area, Geiselman and Machlowitz (1987) looked at 38 studies that compared standard police interviews with interviews where hypnosis was used and found that in 21 studies the hypnotised participants did recall more correct information. In 13 studies there was no difference, and four studies showed that less information was given by hypnotised participants. In eight studies there were more errors under hypnosis.

What is of more concern is that a hypnotised person is very relaxed and very suggestible. As a result, it is very easy indeed to implant false memories – and once they have been implanted it is impossible to distinguish them from the 'real' ones (Orne, 1979). The interviewer doesn't even have to be trying to influence the interviewee, either. Because hypnotised participants are so suggestible, they can pick up subtle hints from tone of voice, body posture and other clues, and will fabricate whole memories without realising what they are doing. Gibson (1982) argued that using hypnosis in police interviewing ought to be considered as equivalent to tampering with evidence, because that was the effect it was having on the witness's memory.

Although most research has involved laboratory studies, there has been some real-world research. For example, Yuille and Cutshall (1986) studied witness accounts of a robbery and shooting, and found that even after 5 months there was accuracy of recall. Of the 21 witnesses 13 were traced and asked about the event. Their recall was compared with police reports and was found to be substantially accurate. What errors there were, were due to the witness not being able to see the whole event, and no errors seemed to be caused by recalling false information. The most accurate information was given by those most involved in the incident. While not all real-world studies have produced such optimistic conclusions, studies like this give some grounds for thinking that it may be possible to use our knowledge of influencing factors to improve witness recall.

These are not the only topics studied by researchers. Hollin (1989) summarised several different topics which researchers into eyewitness testimony had investigated:

- Clifford and Richards (1977) found that policemen recalled better after 30 seconds than after 15 seconds.
- Yarmey (1986b) found more accurate recall in daylight and twilight than in the evening or at night.
- Clifford and Hollin (1981) found that recall of appearance of an attacker was less accurate when a scene is violent.
- Clifford and Hollin (1981) found that recall of violent crime was less accurate as the number of attackers increased, but that recall of non-violent crime was not affected by the number of criminals.
- Loftus and Burns (1982) found less accurate recall if a scene involved someone shot and bleeding than if there were shots but no one was hit.
- Leippe *et al.* (1978) found that recall was more accurate if subjects knew that valuable property had been stolen than if they did not know the value of the property. But this is not simply about the seriousness of the crime, because more violent crime leads to less recall. Deffenbacher (1983) suggested that this might be because of arousal: normally, serious offences are better recalled, but recall for violence is made inaccurate because of the emotions of the witnesses.
- Ellis (1984) observed that recall for faces does not seem to deteriorate over time.
- Alper *et al.* (1976) found that group discussion improved identification but also increased inaccuracy, by group members contributing information which wasn't originally there. Similarly, Warnick and Sanders (1980) found that witnesses who had discussed an incident gave better recall, although Loftus and Greene (1980) found that if wrong information is introduced about a target's appearance witnesses do incorporate that incorrect material in their recall. So groups could help, but they could also contaminate evidence.
- Laughery and Fowler (1977) found that making photofits was helped if there had been rehearsal – that is, systematic remembering – soon after the incident.
- Davies *et al.* (1979) found that looking at photographs before a recognition task reduced recognition of faces.
- Gorenstein and Ellsworth (1980) found that once a 'mugshot' has been selected (even if one of an innocent person) then that person is likely to be selected in an identity parade even when the real target is in the parade. Once a choice is made it seems hard to change.
- Loftus and Palmer (1974) and others have shown how the wording of a question can affect recall. For example, asking about a car 'smash' can mean participants in a study, when asked to recall a scene from a video, are more likely to mention broken glass being at the scene. However, other studies (e.g. Zanni and Offerman, 1978) have not replicated these findings.

Evaluation

- Many of the above studies involved artificial conditions, and may not apply to real-life situations.

ACTIVITY

Write short notes on eyewitness testimony, and evaluate how far such testimony should be relied upon in court.

Improving eyewitness testimony

The doubts about eyewitness testimony raised by psychological research have resulted in new techniques for police interviewing, with a view to getting more reliable and accurate information from witnesses to crimes. Studies which highlight sources of inaccuracy also suggest ways that we can improve the accuracy of our recall – by avoiding or controlling the factors which produce problems.

For example, one way to improve memory for faces is to pay more attention (Wells and Turtle, 1988). We do not find it easy to describe the face of someone we do not know who we saw commit a crime (Loftus, 1979). Reasons for this include:

- witnesses do not get a clear look at the offender
- witnesses can be upset, frightened or confused by the crime

• the offender may wear a mask or be disguised in some way.

Shapiro and Penrod (1986) wondered if there were circumstances where a correct identification was more likely. They evaluated more than 100 of the studies in the area of eyewitness testimony. It appeared that the similarity of the situation for recall compared with the situation when the crime took place affected accuracy of recall. The more similar the situation when recalling, the more accurate the recall. Also identification was more difficult if the suspect's appearance had changed since the incident. If the context was the same for recall as it was for the incident, then recall improved.

Table 2.3 Improving the accuracy of eyewitness testimony

Although eyewitness testimony is often unreliable there are ways in which its accuracy can be improved.   • The witness mentally goes back over the scene of the crime to reinstate additional cues.   • The witness has already associated the person's face with other symbolic information.   • The witness was exposed to the person's face for a long time.   • The witness gave testimony a very short time after the crime.   • The witness is habitually attentive to the external environment.   • The witness generally forms vivid mental images.   • The person's face was not altered by disguise.   • The person looked dishonest.

Source: Hogg and Vaughan (1998), based on Shapiro and Penrod (1986)

As a result of this and other studies, police interviewing is now much more sensitive to the ways that recall can be influenced. For example, police interviewers generally encourage the witness to focus on the situation and try to re-create it mentally. They also use interview techniques incorporating mnemonics to help people to remember. Police officers themselves may take training programmes in aspects of witness testimony such as face recognition and interviewing methods.

ACTIVITY

Write short notes on the ethical and practical problems involved in using lie detectors when interviewing witnesses (as opposed to suspects).

Self-test

Write a timed essay, under exam conditions (or as close as you can manage) using the title 'Discuss how recall is affected by attributional biases'.

Offender profiling

Offender profiling involves using forensic evidence to find behavioural information that can help to lead to the identification of suspects. Physical and behavioural evidence is examined, including issues about the scene of a crime and the type of victim, and this intensive analysis is used to inform investigators of specific offender characteristics.

Profilers come from different backgrounds, and there is no specific professional training for the job, although there are different approaches, which we will be looking at later in this chapter. Criminal profiling is a task, rather than a profession, and is done by whoever seems to be the most qualified or suited to do it. For example, in the USA some profilers are FBI employees, while others are forensic psychologists. Training involves developing the ability to carry out clinical interviews and to combine different sources of evidence, but profilers are not usually trained in interpreting physical forensic evidence or in attending actual scenes of crime.

Profilers need to be neutral, so they would not be expected to interview actual suspects or be involved in the realities of a murder hunt. Their contribution needs to be objective and removed from individuals in the case, because if they know about a suspect they might be influenced by this knowledge when suggesting a profile for the criminal. As a result, it is rarely the investigating officers themselves who do profiling, but more commonly an independent expert.

Copson (1996) described offender profiling as any technique where behaviour of an offender is used to draw conclusions about the sort of person that offender is. Similarly, Turco (1993) suggested that offender profiling is 'drawing a sketch' to suggest who the offender might be, with the information for the sketch coming from the crime scene, from knowledge about the victim, and from psychological theory.

Inductive and deductive reasoning

A very early example of profiling is found in the Whitechapel murders case in Britain in 1888. Dr. Phillips, the police surgeon, drew conclusions about the offender's personality from a thorough examination of the wounds of the victims. For example, the wound of one of the victims suggested a professional working in medicine or some similar profession because some of the victim's organs had been removed with great skill.

Traditionally, offender profiling tends to be divided into the inductive type and the deductive type. **Inductive reasoning** is reasoning where information from the environment is considered and weighed up. Information is gathered from many different sources, and then conclusions are drawn.

An example of inductive reasoning might be: 'I see lots of white swans. I have never seen a black swan. Therefore all swans are white'. The problem here is that I only need to see one black swan and my conclusion is incorrect. In inductive reasoning the conclusion will only be true according to our current experiences, and any new experience can change the conclusion. An example of inductive reasoning within criminal profiling might be something like: 'Most known serial murderers are Caucasian. Most known serial murderers are male. Most known serial murderers operate within a comfort zone. Therefore it is likely that any given serial murderer will be Caucasian, male and operating within a comfort zone' (Turvey, 1999).

Deductive reasoning is logical reasoning, and has sometimes been said to be the opposite of inductive reasoning. An example of deductive reasoning might be: 'Every time it rains I get wet. It is raining. Therefore, I get wet.' There is no problem in this reasoning, and if I really do get wet every time it rains (and, of course, this first statement might not be true, because I could use an umbrella), then if it is raining, I will certainly get wet. In deductive reasoning the conclusion is bound to be true if the first statement is true. There is a certainty involved that is not there in inductive reasoning.

Turvey's (1999) example of inductive reasoning was also presented as if it were deductive (i.e. more certain than it really is): 'Most known serial murderers are Caucasian. Most known serial murderers are male. Most known serial murderers operate within a comfort zone. Therefore, the serial murderer will be Caucasian, male and operating within a comfort zone.' The statement has still really been derived inductively, but it is expressed in the form of a deductive statement and sounds much more definite than the openly inductive one.

An **inductive criminal profile** is one that has been reached by looking at statistical data. Correlations are looked for to see where there are shared characteristics between crimes, for example. Educated generalisations

are made based on examination of statistical evidence. There is a discussion below about jury decision-making. It is claimed that jury forepersons are often male, and that men speak more than women in the jury deliberation process. Using inductive reasoning based on statistical information we can say that it is likely that a foreperson will be male and will talk the most. This is an example of inductive reasoning, and not unlike the processes involved in offender profiling.

The statistics come from those who have already been convicted of crimes. Although offender profiling may seem a glamorous job, it entails many hours of analysis of statistics. A criminal profile is usually a generalisation, and is an average profile of the sort of person that the criminal might be.

Evaluation

- A problem with inductive generalisations is that the observations that form the basis of the generalisation are often not checked. Such observations can come from single instances, rather than many observations. Walton (1989) suggests that some profiles are induced from a very small number of observations.

- As offender profiles use inductive and not deductive reasoning, conclusions should always include terms such as 'most likely' or 'probably'.

- Offender profilers use statistical information from public sources such as criminal records and the media. They also use formal and informal studies of known criminals, as well as their own practical experience. These methods are useful in that no practical training is needed, but these sources of data often include bias, which needs to be acknowledged.

A **deductive criminal profile** is one where if the first statement is true then the conclusion must also be true. An example is offered by Turvey (1999). The situation is that the offender disposed of a victim's body in a remote area and tyre tracks were found at the site. The profiler draws the conclusion 'if the tyre tracks belong to the offender, then the offender has access to a vehicle and can drive'.

Evidence for a deductive profile comes from physical evidence (such as tyre tracks), aspects of the scene of the crime, and a study of victim characteristics. The deductive method is scientific in that evidence is gathered and a working hypothesis is put forward. Conclusions are drawn on the basis of whether the evidence fits the hypothesis; and the deductive profile can be changed and amended in the light of new evidence. There is an ongoing process and profiles must reflect this process, rather than claim to be 'truth'.

Aspects of profiling

Profiling is a complex business, and involves definite stages. For example, there are two phases in deductive profiling. The first is the investigative phase, where evidence is gathered. Patterns of known crimes are studied, analysis is made of behavioural evidence, and profilers try to take an objective view. The second phase is the trial phase, in which the profiler aims to gain insights into the case.

The primary goals of the **investigative phase** are to:
• reduce the suspect pool
• help to link crimes to one another
• help to decide if the criminal behaviour is going to escalate into more serious crimes
• give the investigators leads and strategies
• keep the investigation on track.

The primary goals of the **trial phase** are to:
• assist in evaluating the evidence
• assist in planning an interview strategy
• help to gain insight into the criminal's motivations
• help to gain insight into the criminal's state of mind
• help to suggest links between crimes.

Profiling involves looking at many of the different features of the crime, or crimes. One of them is the **corpus delicti** – the 'body of the crime'. This refers to the facts which show that a crime has taken place. For example, fingerprints at a point of entry, broken windows, ransacked rooms, missing valuables. There might also be other evidence – for example, victim's blood, a weapon, wound patterns, torn clothing. All of these provide information that can contribute to the profiling process.

Another source of information comes from the **modus operandi** (MO) – the method of operation used by the criminal. The MO is all the actions and behaviours that were needed to commit the crime. It might remain consistent from one crime to the next, but it can also evolve and change – the offender can become more skilled, for example (Geberth, 1996). To establish a modus operandi, a forensic examiner can look for tools used to gain entry, types of items taken, lack of fingerprints and may also look at the types of restraints used on a victim, or similar types of clue.

Some criminals exhibit **signature behaviours**. These are actions that were not necessary to commit the crime, but which give an indication that two or more criminal acts may be connected or committed by the same person. As these actions are not necessary, they can point to the offender's emotional and psychological needs. A forensic examiner might look for slashing clothing in cupboards, stealing female undergarments, destroying furniture, a specific type of weapon or the level of injury involved.

Ethical problems and profiling

Offender profiling is a powerful tool, and it is important therefore that profilers do not claim that someone is actually the offender or allow their profiles to be used as evidence of guilt. Profiling can suggest the sort of person who is likely to have committed a particular crime, and can lead to an arrest; but it only deals with *types*, not specific individuals. And it can work the other way, in that profiling can point the police in a certain direction, and can be used to suggest that a suspect is not in fact the offender.

However, as with so many criminological techniques, profiling is sometimes interpreted as being more certain than it really is. Turvey (1999) warns against using profiling as anything more than suggesting probabilities. He cites the case of Rachel Nickell, studied by Kocsis *et al.* (1998). In July 1992 Rachel Nickell was stabbed 49 times in front of her two-year old son when they were walking on Wimbledon Common. Paul Britton prepared a psychological profile, and Colin Stagg fitted it. However, there was no evidence. It appears that the police used a female officer to get to know Stagg to try to find evidence, and Britton helped in this enterprise.

Figure 2.4
Paul Britton, an offender profiler working in Britain

Subsequently Stagg was arrested. However, at his trial there were many inconsistencies. For example, Stagg seemed not to know the location of the crime, and said (wrongly) that the victim had been raped. These inconsistencies were ignored by the police, who were certain (from the profiling) that they had got the right man. When it became apparent that they had not, the woman police officer resigned from her job. It has been suggested that the trauma of befriending Stagg, followed by the perceived failure of the operation, led to her resignation. Turvey concludes that this is an example of profiling being taken too far.

Evaluation

- Profiles are generalisations and do not take individual differences into account. It may be that such generalisations come from inappropriate samples, for example.

- Information comes from known criminals, but not from unknown ones, so there is a whole set of missing data – information applying to 'successful' criminals.

- Inaccuracies in the profile can lead to an innocent person being questioned or even convicted.

Approaches to profiling

Offender profiling is particularly popular in the UK and the USA. But the two societies go about it in very different ways. It is often said that the British approach involves 'bottom-up' processing, while the USA approach involves 'top-down' processing. **Bottom-up processing** is where information is gathered and conclusions are drawn strictly from the evidence. Previous knowledge and information is not used. **'Top-down' processing**, by contrast, involves using previous knowledge and information to draw conclusions about a current situation. Previously stored knowledge is used to make judgements.

The British 'bottom-up' approach

Boon and Davies (1992) suggest that the British approach to offender profiling is a 'bottom-up' approach because it involves working with detailed information gathered from the scene of the crime and from information about the crime. From this detailed information a picture of the criminal is suggested. The reasoning involved is inductive reasoning, because the conclusions are only tentative, being formed as they are from what has been observed. Any change in what is observed, or any additional information, can change the conclusion.

The case outlined above, where Paul Britton undertook profiling to try to find the killer of Rachel Nickell is an example of the British 'bottom-up' approach. Another example is given by Gudjonsson and Haward (1998). They outline the Torney case. A police officer was charged with murdering his wife, son and daughter. The officer claimed that his 13-year old son had gone berserk and had murdered his mother and sister, before turning the gun on himself. But profiling evidence suggested that the killings had been executed calmly and efficiently by someone who knew about firearms, and that this did not tie in with the claim that at 13-year old boy had

'gone berserk'. It was more likely that the police officer had committed the murders, and he was in fact convicted of the crimes.

Profilers in Britain are mainly forensic clinicians employed by the Health Service or universities. They take time off from their jobs to carry out profiling when asked to. The arrangements tend to be informal, although Copson (1995) warns that this informal approach, where statements are often verbal and not written, means there can be misunderstandings.

Professor David Canter uses an inductive profiling model based on statistical analysis and use of probabilities, in which information from previous crimes is used to form an empirical base for the development of hypothesis ('Empirical' means using actual evidence). The Informed Offender Profiling System (IOPS) has been developed at the Centre for Investigative Psychology at Liverpool University, where Canter is currently based. In the centre, new crimes are compared with a database of existing crimes and a predictive profile is produced.

There are several aspects of this system. For example, Canter (1998) has described a geographical support tool, which is based on consistencies in the geographical locations an offender is likely to use. This was used in the case of the 'Railway Rapist' (Canter, 1998). Between 1982 and 1986 there were a series of assaults in North London which took place near railway lines. There were also three murders between 1985 and 1986, and from the MO and other features of the crimes, it was thought that the rapes and the murders were linked. Canter drew up a table of all the offences with all the details, and from this information was able to develop a profile. The offender:
- lived in the area defined by the first three cases
- probably lived with a wife or girlfriend, and probably had no children
- was in his mid to late 20s, and right handed
- had a skilled or semi-skilled job, possibly with weekend work
- knew the railway system
- had a criminal record, probably involving violence.

John Duffy was arrested in 1986. He lived in the right area, was separated from his wife, was in his late 20s, was right handed, had raped his wife at knife point and was a travelling carpenter for British Rail. He was originally 1505th out of 2000 suspects, but the profile had meant he was quickly looked upon as a suspect.

The US 'top-down' approach

In 1979 the FBI began to collect data from interviews of convicted serial killers and murderers. They built up a picture of the type of person who would commit such crimes. It was thought, for example, that sex killers were likely to be white, male and unmarried. They would either be unemployed or have unskilled jobs. They tended to have had a history of psychiatric or alcohol problems, and to come from dysfunctional families.

The American approach to offender profiling is referred to as a 'top-down' approach because it involves going from previously known information to a conclusion about the criminal. The American approach is based on data collected from interviews with known criminals. From such interviews, and using the experience of those involved in crimes, a classification system is built up (for example, classifying murders as organised or disorganised), and this forms the basis for drawing up profiles.

Offender profiling in the USA used to rely almost exclusively on the behavioural analysis of crime scenes and information from victims and witnesses. Physical and behavioural evidence within a series of crimes or from similar crimes would be examined, and in this way previous knowledge would be used to set out a set of offender characteristics. The use of previous experience is why the American approach tends to be referred to as 'top-down'. This approach is less rigid now, and profiling is more likely to include intuition and investigative experience, but the overall approach is still maintained.

It is hard to be precise about the differences between 'bottom-up' and 'top-down' approaches to profiling, particularly because there are differences within each of the approaches too. For example, Britton works within the British 'bottom-up' approach, and analyses information from the scene and likely behaviour patterns of the offender. He seems to focus less on statistical analysis than does Canter, who also works within the 'bottom-up' approach. Canter uses information from past crimes, and this is 'top-down' in the sense of using past experience. However, Canter mainly uses information from the crimes being investigated, and collates information from many different ('bottom-up' and empirical) sources.

The American emphasis on 'top-down' processing does involve using past experience, and focuses on what has previously be learned. It has been argued, particularly by David Canter, that relying on interviews with convicted killers, as the US approach does, is not sensible, as serial killers are known to be manipulative and sensation seekers. But nowadays, US profiling also uses information from the scene.

The use of behaviour analysis, that is analysis of previous crimes, is a deductive approach. The use of statistical analysis (preferred by British profilers) is a more inductive approach. Although the use of statistics still involves previous crimes, much more use is made of the evidence and information arising from the particular crime being investigated. Overall, the main points are that offender profiling can use statistical analysis to arrive at possibilities about an offender, and behavioural analysis to see what type of person is involved. It draws on past experience as well as information from the scene.

Studies do suggest that profiling can be effective, at least in certain circumstances. For example, Copson and Holloway (1997) carried out a survey with detectives from 184 cases where offender profiling had been used. They found that it was believed that profiling had led to the identification of the offender in 2.7% of cases, and had helped in solving 16% of cases.

In another study, Pinizzotto and Finkel (1990) asked groups of detectives, students, profilers and clinical psychologists to look at two closed police cases and to draw up profiles. One case was a sex case, and the other a homicide. The profilers did produce more detailed profiles, and were more accurate in the sex case, but the detectives were more accurate in the homicide.

Self-test

Write a timed essay, under exam conditions (or as close as you can manage) using the title 'Compare the British "bottom-up" approach with the US "top-down" approach to offender profiling'.

Jury decision-making

To be on a jury, you need to be over 18, to understand English and to have had no convictions. More than 12 people are asked to attend the court, and from this group 12 people are elected to the jury. There is an examination process (called *voir dire*) where the judge and lawyers question jurors and, if they wish, can make sure any particular individual is not selected. If no reason is given for a juror being rejected, this is called a **peremptory challenge**. If evidence of bias is given as a reason, this is called a **challenge for cause**.

The decisions that juries make have profound implications – in some countries, even to the point of life or death. As a result, there have been a number of studies investigating how juries work, and the various factors that can affect their decision-making processes. In this section we will look at a number of these factors, beginning with those concerning the case itself – publicity, evidence and what the defendant is like. Then we will look at studies relating to witnesses of one sort or another (although we have already looked at the question of eyewitness testimony in some detail, so there is no point repeating it here). Finally, we will look at the ways that juries go about their deliberations, and the factors which can influence their decision-making processes (Figure 2.6).

Table 2.4   Juries can be biased for many reasons

> *Probability that the defendant committed the crime*
> 1 If a suspect runs from the police then he probably committed the crime.
> 2 In most cases where the accused presents a strong defence, it is only because of a good lawyer.
> 3 Out of every 100 people brought to trial, at least 75 are guilty of the crime with which they are charged.
> 4 Defence lawyers don't really care about guilt or innocence; they are just in business to make money.
> 5 Generally the police make an arrest only when they are sure about who committed the crime.
> 6 Circumstantial evidence is too weak to use in court.
> 7 Many accident claims filed against insurance companies are phony.
> 8 The defendant is often a victim of his own bad reputation.
> 9 If the grand jury recommends that a person be brought to trial, then he probably committed the crime.
>
> *Reasonable doubt*
> 1 A defendant should be found guilty if 11 out of 12 jurors vote guilty.
> 2 Too often jurors hesitate to convict someone who is guilty out of pure sympathy.
> 3 The death penalty is cruel and inhumane.
> 4 For serious crimes like murder, a defendant should be found guilty so long as there is a 90% chance that he committed the crime.
> 5 Extenuating circumstances should not be considered – if a person commits a crime then that person should be punished.
> 6 Too many innocent people are wrongfully imprisoned.
> 7 If a majority of the evidence – but not all of it – suggests that the defendant committed the crime, the jury should vote not guilty.
> 8 If the defendant committed a victimless crime like gambling or possession of marijuana he should never be convicted.

Source: Hollin (1989)

Case factors

There are a number of ways that different aspects of the case may influence a jury's decision-making processes (Figure 2.6). These include the amount and nature of pre-trial publicity; the type and nature of the evidence offered, and the characteristics of the defendant.

Figure 2.5
Courtroom scene

Pre-trial publicity

Jurors can be influenced both before and during a trial. Often there is pre-trial publicity, and jurors can be aware of a case before they are elected to be on the jury. They may have factual knowledge and also feelings and personal opinions about the case. The well-known O.J. Simpson case is an example of how pre-trial publicity can affect a trial. Fein *et al.* (1997) used this case and cuttings from newspapers, and set up a mock jury to see if pre-trial publicity would affect a juror's decision. Jurors were more likely to say 'guilty' if they had access to pre-trial publicity, but if the reporting mentioned race jurors were likely not to be affected by the publicity, thinking of it as racist. Around 80% of mock jurors said 'guilty' given pre-trial publicity, but only 45% voted 'guilty' if race were mentioned in the cuttings.

Publicity during a case can be just as damaging. In April 2001, the courts abruptly stopped an expensive prosecution against the footballer Lee Bowyer and some others for what had appeared to be a racist attack on a young Asian man in Leeds. When the case was very nearly completed, the *Sunday Mirror* ran a large article castigating the defendants, which was deemed likely to have influenced the jury. As a result the case had to be dropped, at a cost of millions.

The question, therefore, is just how important this type of influence is; and the evidence suggests that it can be quite powerful. Linz and Penrod (1992) used newspaper cuttings and a mock jury to investigate the effects of reporting of a case before a trial and found that it did affect jury decision-making. As well as pre-trial publicity, it may be that jurors know about previous convictions and this will influence their judgements. In England previous convictions are not allowed as evidence in a trial to avoid this problem, but in high-profile cases it may be difficult to avoid that type of information coming to the surface.

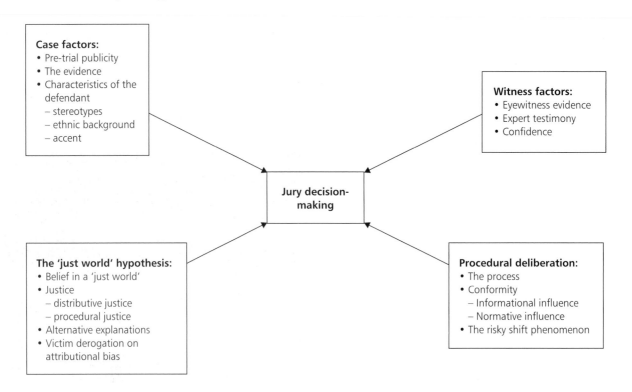

Figure 2.6   Factors affecting jury decision-making

The evidence

It has been shown that the evidence itself has an effect on jury decision-making. Pennington and Hastie (1990) suggest that jurors try to make sense of the evidence, and impose their own story on the information they are given. This 'story model' fits with the claim earlier that we reconstruct evidence to make sense of it (Bartlett, 1932), and that we use schema and earlier associations when assimilating new information (Figure 2.7). In a trial the prosecution and defence teams are each trying to construct different stories. The task of the juror is to reconcile these stories with their own versions – and their own versions come in part from the sense that they have made of the case. So the stories which they tell are significant.

Characteristics of the defendant

Another major set of factors which influences jury decision-making concerns the characteristics of the defendant. For example, Harrower (1998) suggested that when defendants are physically attractive they receive more lenient sentencing. But if they have used their attractiveness as part of the crime – for example, when defrauding someone – then sentencing is not more lenient. One reason for this may be lie in the nature of the **stereotypes** that we use. Dane and Wrightsman (1982) point out that stereotypes of villains are always unattractive, and think that this may explain why more attractive defendants are sentenced less harshly.

Stereotyping also means that we pay attention to what has been emphasised by our culture (Lippmann, 1922). Duncan (1976) showed a film where one man pushed another man. There was no sound to the film, but the researchers varied the ethnic background of the people being shown; and asked their participants to judge whether the push was violent or not. As many as 75% said that the push was violent when a Black man was seen to shove a White man, but only 17% saw the behaviour as violent when a White man pushed a Black man. The participants were White Americans. It was concluded that the stereotype of the culture (at least at the time of the study) was that a Black man is more likely to shove a White man than the other way around.

Another factor is the **ethnic background** of the defendant. As we have seen, when mock jurors 'tried' O.J. Simpson using newspaper publicity, they were less likely to give a guilty verdict if race was mentioned in the publicity. Studies using mock jurors show that the race of a defendant does affect the verdict. For example, Pfeifer and Ogloff (1991) found that White American university students were more likely to say that a Black defendant was guilty than a White defendant, even when the crime was the same. It has also been found that Black defendants are likely to receive more severe sentences for the same crime than White defendants (Stewart, 1980).

Trial evidence

World knowledge about similar events

Knowledge about story structures

Construct stories

Match accepted story to verdict categories

Conclude with particular verdict if fit is good

Instructions on the law

Prior ideas about crime categories

Learn verdict categories

Figure 2.7   Pennington and Hastie's 1990 'story model' for jury decison-making (source: Pennington and Hastie, 1990)

Skolnick and Shaw (1997) set up a mock murder trial using over 200 students as the 'jurors'. They looked at the influence of ethnic background and also of status – whether the person was a celebrity or not. The results were as follows:

- If the juror was Black and the defendant's race was Black, 18.7% returned a guilty verdict and 32.7% said not guilty.
- If the juror was Black, and the defendant White, 33.6% returned a guilty verdict and 15% said not guilty.
- If the juror was White, and the defendant Black 18.7% returned a guilty verdict and 29.2% said not guilty.
- If the juror and defendant were White 22.6% returned a guilty verdict and 29.5% said not guilty.

It appears, therefore, that the ethnic backgrounds of both the juror and the defendant are important. What is interesting, though, is that the black defendant always received fewer guilty verdicts, regardless of whether the juror was Black or White – perhaps because of a change in the general level of racism in society; or possibly because people have become more sensitised to the ways that these issues may affect jury decisions.

Another factor that affects jury decision-making is the defendant's **accent**. For example, a Birmingham accent is seen as having low status. In one study (Mahoney and Dixon, 1997) defendants with 'Brummie' accents were seen as more guilty than defendants with 'non-Brummie' accents. A Black defendant with a 'Brummie' accent was seen as the most guilty of all, regardless of the specific details of the evidence.

Similar results have been found in Australia. Seggie, (1983) found that an Australian with a 'standard' accent

was thought of as more likely to be guilty where white collar crimes were concerned, but an Australian with a 'broad' accent was seen as more likely to be guilty for other types of crime. It is clear, then, that the characteristics of the defendant can exert quite an influence on the ways that juries make decisions.

Figure 2.8   O.J Simpson was famously acquitted of the murder of his wife in 1991

Witness factors

There are a number of ways that witness factors can influence juries. We have already seen how eyewitness testimony itself can be influenced by a range of factors, but nonetheless juries place a great deal of weight on what eyewitnesses have to say. In one study, for example, Loftus (1974) asked participants to act as mock jurors, and to read three summaries of a case with only circumstantial evidence against a defendant. In one summary there was no eyewitness. In a second, the evidence from an eyewitness was there, and not questioned. In a third summary, the evidence came from an eyewitness who was described as having poor eyesight. Loftus found that 18% of the jurors in the condition with no eyewitness said the defendant was guilty, compared with 72% where the testimony was unchallenged; and a surprising 68% in the condition where the eyewitness was said to have poor eyesight. So even if the eyewitness testimony was questionable or discredited, it still counted for a lot with the jury.

Other studies, too, emphasised how important eyewitness testimony seems to be – although, interestingly, they have found that juries pay less attention to eyewitness testimony that does not identify the defendant (McAllister and Bregman, 1986); which may reflect a tendency to pay more attention to positive information than to negative information.

Evaluation

- Many of these studies are laboratory-based experiments, so their validity can be questioned.

- Hollin (1989) argues that in real-life studies jurors do not seem to see eyewitness evidence as influential in their decision-making.

It has been suggested that, given the possible problem with eyewitness reliability, **expert testimony** should be used to increase juror knowledge of these possible problems. Loftus (1980) gave descriptions of two trials to mock jurors. One trial involved a murder, and the other a mild assault. In both cases eyewitness testimony was important. When jurors were told about eyewitness testimony unreliability, 43% said 'guilty' in the murder condition (compared with 68% before the expert testimony about eyewitness reliability) and 35% said 'guilty' in the mild assault condition (47% beforehand).

The **confidence** of a witness can also affect jury decision-making. Some studies (e.g. Wells *et al.*, 1979b) suggest that jurors are more likely to give a 'guilty' verdict if testimony comes from a confident witness whereas they are more likely to say 'not guilty' if a witness is not confident. In fact, Penrod and Cutler (1987) found that witness confidence was the most important factor of all in a jury's evaluation of evidence given by a witness.

The process of deliberation

Reaching a verdict involves a process of deliberation, which is another important aspect of jury decision-making. Strasser *et al.* (1982) found that the decision-making process of 12 people put together in an intense setting (that is, comparable to a jury) often followed a set pattern. The first step was to appoint a foreperson, who is often male, and often elected because they were the first person to be appointed to the jury. A foreperson is usually someone of higher socio-economic status, or who has previously been on a jury. Kerr *et al.* (1982) looked at 179 trials in San Diego and found that 50% of jurors were female, but 90% of the forepersons were male.

The second step involves a show of hands or a secret ballot, which is used to establish the situation at the start of the deliberation process, and only after that does the jury move on to the third step, in which evidence is reviewed, followed by a review of the judge's instruction on the law. Finally, the application of the law to the evidence is reviewed, and then the deliberations begin.

During the deliberation process, it has been observed that men tend to speak more than women, and the foreperson speaks most. Usually the foreperson dominates the discussion, but on some occasions the foreperson is not the leader, and others dominate. There might also be social loafing – a tendency for people to leave the work to others – which we will be looking at in more detail in Chapter 4.

Studies suggest that around one-third of jurors change their mind during the deliberation process, but that the opinions at the start of the deliberation process give the best clue as to the eventual verdict. So if the jury starts with 11 out of the 12 thinking the defendant is guilty, a guilty verdict is more likely than if two or more people think the defendant is not guilty.

Figure 2.9
In the film Twelve Angry Men, *Henry Fonda's character sways the opinion of the rest of the 12-man jury, even though he was a minority of one*

This finding relates to the findings of Asch (1956) in his well-known studies of **conformity**. It is more likely that one person who is not in agreement with a majority will change to the majority view than if more than one person disagrees. With an ally, that is, when there are at least two people not conforming, the non-conformers are more likely to hold out against the majority.

Conformity can occur through **informational influence**, where the juror might be persuaded by what the others say. Conformity can also occur through **normative influence**, where a juror might say they agree with the others, even though privately they disagree. Usually participants go along with the majority view, although occasionally there can be minority influence. We will be looking at all of these processes more closely in Chapter 4.

↺ Recall AS material

Recall AS material from the Social approach, where you may have briefly looked at conformity in relation to obedience, or look it up.

Most jurors appear to have made up their mind during the trial and the deliberation process does not have much effect on their decision, according to Kalven and Zeisel (1966), but other researchers disagree. For example, extreme positions tend to have quite an impact on group decision-making (Kaplan and Schersching, 1981). Groups tend to reach a more extreme view than do individuals, and this is often known as the **risky shift phenomenon**. Again, we will be looking at this more closely in Chapter 4, but it is worth mentioning here as it has relevance for juries as well as for working groups.

In the UK it is not legal to question jurors, so evidence about jury decision-making comes from studies of mock juries. This means that if a mock jury knows that their decision does not really affect an individual in the way that a real jury decision can affect them, they may be likely to make different decisions. However, Kalven and Zeisel (1966) carried out a study on real jurors in the USA, and

found that in 3576 cases jury verdicts agreed with the judge's verdicts 78% of the time (Table 2.5). However, many American states banned the questioning of jurors after that date, so subsequent studies had to use mock juries.

There is some variation in how mock jury studies are carried out. The most effective options seem to involve a realistic situation where a group of people is called for jury service but is not allocated a case. They then listen to a real trial in a courtroom and use a room within the court when deliberating their verdict. However, other techniques are less realistic, sometimes just giving a group of people a written account of a case and asking them for a verdict.

Evaluation

- The main problem for studies of mock trials and mock juries is that they know that their decision will not have real consequences.

- In real studies (such as that done by Kerr, 1982) it seems that those factors that seem to be important in simulations, such as race, have no effect on the verdict. This suggests that there may be demand characteristics in these studies, with participants making the decisions they think that the researchers want.

- Issues such as the prosecuting lawyer's respectfulness seem to have a large effect on a jury's verdict, but these sorts of issues are not studied in simulations.

The 'just world' hypothesis

As we saw earlier in this chapter, we attribute reasons for our own behaviour and for that of others, and sometimes those attributions can be biased. These biases can lead to incorrect judgements about others. We have seen how we sometimes make inaccurate judgements in order to protect ourselves or our self-esteem – the self-serving bias. This sometimes comes in another form, known as **self-handicapping**. This involves giving our behaviour an external cause rather than an internal cause, and doing so before the event itself, in order to protect ourselves from facing up to consequences (Berglas, 1987).

Table 2.5 Comparing the verdicts of judges and juries*

Judge would have	Jury Acquitted	Convicted	Hung	Total
Acquitted	13.4	2.2	1.1	16.7
Convicted	16.9	62.0	4.4	83.3
Total	30.3	64.2	5.5	100.0

*Percentage of verdicts in 3576 trials.
Source: Sabini (1994), using data from Kalven and Zeisel (1966)

For example, someone might feel they were likely to fail an exam, but wouldn't want to admit that the failure would be due to internal reasons such as lack of knowledge. So that person might publicly claim they were going to fail before going into the exam, because they had not been well and so could not revise. Or they might deliberately provoke some situation or crisis, like an argument with a girlfriend, which would prevent them from doing last-minute revision and so give an external excuse for failure.

Another form of attributional bias is a belief in a 'just world'. One way of dealing with the unfairness of the world is to blame victims for their problems. This is to do with how we judge victims of crime, as well as how we judge criminals. If we blame victims, this means that we do not have to focus on problems with society, because we can blame the victim instead. Belief in a 'just world' can mean that victims are thought of as responsible. For example, Davidowicz (1975) suggested that many people blame the six million Jewish victims of the Holocaust for their own fate, although better awareness of history means that this finding is not supported.

Justice
There are two ways of looking at justice. One type of justice is **distributive justice**, which is concerned with whether a trial or similar event has a just outcome. But there can be errors where justice is concerned – errors of eyewitness testimony, for example, or attribution errors – and the criminal justice system has to ensure that these do not unfairly affect the trial. So there is another type of justice, called **procedural justice**, which is concerned with the procedures we use to try to make sure that justice is done. Procedural justice involves trying to avoid errors, so that we can achieve distributive justice through the court system.

It seems that we have an idea of equity and fairness, and people are motivated to produce equitable outcomes. Lerner and Simmons (1966) carried out a major investigation of people's perceptions of justice and fairness. Participants – female students – were tested one at a time, and told that the study was about the perception of emotional cues. Before the study the participants also rated themselves on social attractiveness. Then each participant met an accomplice of the researchers and given to understand that it was another participant, who was taking part in a study on human learning. The real participant was then taken into a room where they could watch through a two-way mirror, while the accomplice went into the next room, where there was a generator, electrodes and other equipment. The accomplice then went through a learning experiment, observed by the genuine participant who was asked to observe the emotional state of the accomplice.

The participant was then shown a 10-minute videotape of the accomplice 'suffering' as they were given shocks for wrong answers (fake shocks, of course, but the participant did not know this). One group of participants was told that this was the half-way point in the study, and that the accomplice would carry on suffering. The other group were told they could choose what would happen next. There were three choices: the accomplice would continue to be punished for incorrect responses; they would be rewarded for correct responses; or a control option in which they could say that the accomplice should neither be rewarded or punished. Then all the participants rated the accomplice using the 'social attractiveness' scale they had previously used on themselves, and rating her as a potential friend.

The findings showed that whenever participants could, they asked for the 'victim' to be rewarded for correct responses (apart from one participant, who chose the control condition). And in that condition, the accomplice was rated higher on social attractiveness and being a friend than for the condition where the participants could not choose and the suffering would continue. It seemed that the participants derogated the accomplice when she would continue to suffer – seeing her as less socially attractive and be less desirable as a friend.

The idea of a 'just world'
Lerner and Simmons interpreted this tendency to derogate as having to do with a belief in a 'just world' – the idea that people get what they deserve. If we did not believe this, much of our behaviour would be a waste of time. For example, if promotion at work is not done fairly, then there is no point in putting in extra hours in the hope of promotion. Therefore, if someone is suffering and does not deserve it, then the world is not fair. When the participants in the above study were able to stop the suffering, they did not have a problem, and could continue to believe in a 'just world'. But when the accomplice had to continue to 'suffer', then their belief in a 'just world' was threatened. To maintain it, they had to conclude that the accomplice must have deserved the punishment in some way.

The **'just world' hypothesis** claims that seeing a victim suffer makes us want to help, and if we can help then we will. But seeing someone suffer and being powerless to help also arouses selfish feelings in us, so that we can preserve our belief that our world is 'just'. Lerner and Simmons introduced another condition where the participant thought the study was over, but had no chance to change the procedure to include reward for correct answers. In this new condition the accomplice was still derogated (to justify her suffering) but not so much as when the participant thought the study would continue. They suggested that this was because continuing suffering also mean that the participant's own discomfort would continue, so additional blame was given to the accomplice for causing suffering for the participant as well as herself. This additional blame made the ratings of social attractiveness and qualities of friendship even lower.

Evaluation

- The Lerner and Simmons study involved deception, and also put the participant under stress, both of which are against ethical guidelines.

- Being a laboratory study, its real-life application can be questioned, although there seems to be no reason to think that the participants knew that the other person was an accomplice.

- Other studies have found that we derogate victims, but have suggested reasons other than the 'just world' hypothesis.

Alternatives to the 'just world' hypothesis

A belief in a 'just world' may be a partial explanation for derogation of a victim, but it is not the only explanation. For example, Cialdini *et al* (1976) suggest that we do not derogate all victims, only the ones we feel we have done harm to. It is as if by blaming the victim we can turn the responsibility – or guilt – away from ourselves.

Responding to this, Lerner and Miller (1978) suggested that we derogate victims only when we feel we might share the same fate. If we think the same thing could happen to us, we do sympathise, but we also need to find a reason for it having happened to the other person. One way of doing that is to blame the victim, because that implies that it happened because of something about them. Since we do not share this characteristic, it won't happen to us.

According to Sabini, what is actually happening with victim blaming is a combination of all of these reasons. People want to see the world as just and fair, and they also blame the victim for their own personal suffering – for example, for the distress they felt when hearing about the event. They feel responsible for the victim's suffering, and they also want to believe they won't be such a victim themselves. All four factors are involved in motivations for victim blaming.

Victim derogation

Overall, the conclusion is that victim derogation is another form of attributional bias, but one which has important consequences. For example, victims of rape are often blamed for being raped. Jones and Aronson (1973) carried out a study where participants were given a description of a rape, with no evidence that the victim was at fault. Participants were asked to allocate a prison sentence to the rapist, and also to say how far they

thought the victim of the rape was to blame. One group of participants was told the victim was a virgin, another was told she was a married woman, and a third group was told she was divorced.

The 'just world' hypothesis predicts that the more respectable a person is thought to be, the more she will be blamed. Belief in a 'just world' means that respectable women cannot be victims, as that would not be 'just'. So there is more need to look for an alternative explanation, other than that she is simply a victim. In accordance with this idea, Jones and Aronson found that the participants blamed the 'married woman' most, and the 'divorced woman' least. But they gave the rapist the longest sentence when the virgin was the victim, implying that they did not blame the virgin.

ACTIVITY

Write a short paragraph on attributions, describing what they are. Then make a list of all of the different ways that attributions can be applied in criminological psychology.

Self-test

Write an timed essay, under exam conditions (or as close as you can manage) using the title 'Discuss influences on decision-making processes as they relate to a jury'.

Influences on criminal behaviour

Social learning theory suggests that much of what we learn is done by imitation and modelling on those around us. As a result, there are both social and media influences on criminal behaviour. The influence of other people is a major factor in our behaviour; and the media are also a major influence on what we learn. A lot of research has been carried out to look at how both social influences and the media affect our behaviour, particularly since it is often claimed that aggressive acts in the media can lead to real-life aggression.

The self-fulfilling prophecy

One of the most important social influences on behaviour, including anti-social behaviour, is the **self-fulfilling**

prophecy. This is used to explain why some people turn to crime. We looked at labelling theory at the start of this chapter, which is the idea that someone only becomes a criminal when labelled a criminal by those in society. It is not what they do, but the way that society labels what they do that matters because when we are labelled in some way we have a tendency to 'become' that label. The process by which this happens is the self-fulfilling prophecy (Figure 2.10). For example, think of someone you know who is popular at parties. Because they are seen by others as the life and soul of the party, they act out that role, so when they are out with other people they become the focus of attention. It is expected from others, and those expectations become self-fulfilling, so the person lives up to them.

Snyder *et al.* (1977) carried out a study to investigate the self-fulfilling prophecy. Male participants were told that they were to talk to a woman on the telephone, and to get acquainted with her. Some were told that the woman was attractive, while others were told she was not. When the participant believed the woman to be attractive (whether it was true or not), the woman he was talking to became more friendly and sociable. But if the woman was thought to be unattractive (even if that was untrue), they responded to the male participants in an aloof manner. The behaviour of the male participants was self-fulfilling, because it led to the required response. They were friendlier and more positive with those they believed to be attractive, and the person responded accordingly,

and they were formal and less positive with those they believed unattractive, which set the tone for those conversations.

Rosenthal and Jacobson (1968) carried out a study that is well known in social psychology. The study was called 'Pygmalion in the classroom'. At the start of an academic year some teachers were allowed to overhear a conversation between two researchers, identifying some 20 children as 'late developers', and about to 'spurt'. All the pupils in the class had had an IQ test before the start of the year, and the teachers believed that the predictions about the pupils came from the results of the test. They were really chosen at random. But when the pupils were tested again at the end of the year, the 20 pupils did indeed have improved IQ scores, and they were higher still after two years. Because the teachers had expected those pupils to do better, they had given them extra attention and additional feedback, so the 'prophecy' came true.

In another study, Eden (1990) looked at the training of 1000 Israeli soldiers, organised into 29 platoons. Some platoon trainers were told their groups had above average potential, but others were not told anything. After ten weeks the performance of all the soldiers was assessed. Both in the written exams and on a weapons test the soldiers who had been said to be above average did better than the others, even though initially all the soldiers had been at an average level.

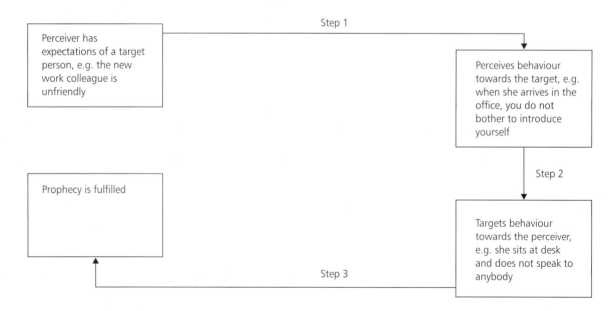

Figure 2.10
Steps in the self-fulfilling prophesy (Source: Pennington et al., 1999)

Evaluation

- The self-fulfilling prophecy works best when those having the expectations and the person being expected to behave in a particular way are not well known to one another.

- It is argued that the self-fulfilling prophecy works only if the expected behaviour does not go too much against how the individual perceives themselves; although studies of social influences on self-esteem and self-image cast some doubt on this.

- Some (e.g. Copeland, 1994) have argued that the expected behaviour may not be carried out if the individual is in a position of low power, as they will focus on doing what they ought to do, and this might clash with the expectation. Some management studies, however, suggest that it works in these cases too.

Self-test

Write a timed essay, under exam conditions (or as close as you can manage) using the title 'Discuss the self-fulfilling prophecy with reference to anti-social behaviour'.

Other social factors

As we've seen, the self-fulfilling prophecy can be a factor in criminal or anti-social behaviour. But it can act in both positive and negative ways. It can be a negative influence by encouraging people to turn to crime, as a result of social expectations from their peer group or local community. This may be particularly true if they have low self-esteem, and are in a criminally minded social group. But it can also be a positive influence. Jussim *et al.* (1996) showed how children from some groups, for example ethnic minorities, can, through the self-fulfilling prophecy of high expectations from teachers, learn to do well. That type of achievement makes them much less at risk, and much less likely to turn to crime.

Other social factors that can be linked to crime include family patterns, child-rearing strategies and the influence of schooling. For example, important aspects of the **family** that might lead to delinquency include the size of the family, the pattern of interactions within the family and disruption within a family. A large family can lead to stress for the parents and a lack of organisation and deprivation for the children (Farrington, 1991). There is also a problem if others in the family are delinquent, as it will be more likely that these will be models for the younger children, who may follow them into delinquency. If there is conflict between the parents or within the family, together with poor communication, this can lead to delinquency. Similarly, broken homes have been linked to delinquency – an issue which we will be looking at in more detail in Chapter 5.

Another social factor that has been linked to criminal behaviour is the way that children are brought up. Certain **child-rearing strategies** are more likely than others to lead to delinquency. Hoffman (1984) lists three patterns of child-rearing:
- **power assertion**, where there are criticisms, threats, maternal deprivation and physical punishment;
- **love withdrawal**, where disapproval is shown by the withholding of affection;
- **induction**, which means explaining to a child what consequences its actions have for other people.

According to McCord (1979), the most usual child-rearing strategy in delinquent families is power assertion. This is partly because of the use of physical punishment, which may lead to delinquency but also because it is often associated with an inconsistent pattern of punishment.

Schooling can be another factor in predicting delinquency, particularly if there are problems at school, and school is a bad experience. Some schools may not engage their pupils well, and pupils' schooling problems may not necessarily come from low intelligence. According to Hargreaves (1980), schools where there are problems seem to have a high staff turnover, social disadvantage in their catchment population and low staff commitment; and they tend to see pupils as having low ability and to use streaming.

Schweinhart and Weikart (1997) suggest that children from deprived backgrounds who receive traditional education are four times more likely to become criminals and have a record at the age of 23 than those with the same background, but who have been at schools which encourage them to plan their own progress. When encouraged to take part in decision-making and reviewing their progress, children from deprived backgrounds did well overall. Initially differences were not particularly noticeable, but they became apparent later in their schooling.

There are more subtle social influences on delinquency too, not least of which is **peer pressure**. Farrington and West (1990) point out the importance of a peer group in governing behaviour, especially for adolescents. Criminal acts in adolescence usually take place in groups, and the members of the group often live near to one another. There can be many reasons for this – one common reason is that the individuals are deprived and rejected at home and not progressing at school, so they opt to follow the norms and rules of their peer group.

↺ Recall AS material

Recall AS material from the learning approach, in particular social learning theory, or look it up.

Media influence

There has always been debate about whether media portrayals of aggression encourage aggression in society as a whole. The problem is that not everyone agrees on a single definition of aggression. Hollin (1989) suggests that aggression is a term referring to the intention to hurt or gain advantage over someone else, but does not necessarily mean that there has been physical injury. Violence, however, does mean the use of physical force against another person. Criminal violence is violence when someone is injured, and the action or actions producing the injury are against the law. Violence can come from aggression, though, so treating crime often involves controlling aggression.

Explanations for media influence

We looked at some theories of aggression and violence earlier in this chapter. As we saw, they can be biological or psychological; but it is not easy to separate the two. Some theorists, for example, suggest that aggression is an instinct. Freud, for instance, described impulses that could lead to violence, and believed that aggression could release such innate impulses. Sometimes the aggression could be harmless, such as aggression as part of sport, but it would absorb the aggressive energies in a socially acceptable way – a process known as **catharsis**. At other times, however, there may be no catharsis, and the impulses may not be released. A situation like that, Freud believed, could lead to criminal violence.

The social learning theory of crime, on the other hand, suggests that we learn through observing others. Bandura (1973a,b) argued that we need to look at how the aggression is acquired, how it is instigated and how it is maintained. According to social learning theory we acquire aggression either directly, by learning processes such as reinforcement, or by observation of others. Bandura also suggested that we sometimes instigate aggression if the outcome is perceived as worth while. If the outcome is desired and the environmental cues are present, then aggressive behaviour is likely. But social learning isn't the only factor. Bandura also suggested that

high temperatures, air pollution and crowding could add to the likelihood of aggression, because then arousal would be higher.

ACTIVITY

Write a short paragraph on social learning theory. Then write a further paragraph on how you think social learning theory can be applied to criminal behaviour.

There are of course many other issues related to violence, including personality, environment and biological inheritance. In this section, however, we will focus on the influence of the media, and the relationship between violence in the media and in real life. Huesmann *et al.* (1984) suggest that being aggressive can become a pattern that can be repeated in generations. It seems that violence in the media might lead to aggressive behaviour, and aggression can run in families. This last claim does not necessarily suggest that such behaviour has a biological basis as children are, according to social learning theory, likely to model themselves on and imitate their parents.

Synoptic Note

Aggression is another example of a situation when we cannot tell whether a behaviour is driven by innate forces or learned through interaction with the environment. These are useful examples when discussing nature/nurture – one of the issues you need to study for Unit 6, the synoptic part of the course.

Cumberbatch (1992) commented on the amount of research in the area of TV violence, and there is a strong feeling that violence on TV, as well as in video games, can be linked to real-life incidents. Cumberbatch suggested that the main concern is to do with violence in the media, and the possible link to violent behaviour. This means looking at the extent of violence in films and on television, and the impact of new technology such as video games. Some examples of violent films that have been linked to real-life crimes include *Child's Play*, *Natural Born Killers*, *Power Rangers* and *A Clockwork Orange*.

There is an argument for banning programmes showing violence. Newson (1994) discussed how so many of the studies that look at a relationship between screen violence and aggressive behaviour suggest that there is a link between the two. But Cumberbatch (1994) criticised

Newson's report as gathering evidence from newspaper articles and giving a simplistic conclusion, rather than being an in-depth analysis. It is a controversial issue among researchers as well as in society as a whole, and there are those who do not accept at all that TV and film violence contributes to real-life aggression.

There are a number of factors which can contribute to the influence of media representations of violence. Although most discussions assume that the problem is simply one of copying the actions on TV or in video games, there are more subtle influences going on. One argument is that watching violence on TV leads to **disinhibition**. – a reduction in the power of the social forces which usually prevent or inhibit certain acts. It means losing one's normal inhibitions. Another argument is that violent TV can produce **desensitisation** – someone might get so used to watching violence that they cease to be offended or moved by it. Perceptions are changed so that the act does not seem all that bad. Huesmann and Eron (1986) traced people's viewing habits over 22 years. The results of this longitudinal study were that they found the more a person watched screen violence, the more likely this person was to have been convicted of a violent crime by the age of 30.

Evaluation

- When experimenters have tried to test factors such as desensitisation, they have had to use mild violence (e.g. Freedman, 1984). This produces validity problems, and may not say much about the type of violence that is really of interest.

Deindividuation may be an influence on aggressive behaviour. It is to do with the way that membership of a large group can mean that people see themselves as losing their individuality, and as not being identifiable. It is possible that this removes the threat of punishment for wrongdoing because, if they cannot be identified, they cannot be punished. Several researchers have shown that aggressive acts are more likely if a person is deindividuated. For example, Lightdale and Prentice (1994) found that men and women behave more aggressively when they are anonymous, and men are no more aggressive than women. In wars many horrific acts are carried out, and one reason could be that soldiers are deindividuated.

Evaluation

- Experimental studies of deindividuation have been rather obvious, and some have suggested that the findings have come from the demand characteristics of the study rather than from deindividuation itself.

ACTIVITY

Use the Internet or other resources such as a CD-ROM containing newspaper articles, and find examples where real-life crimes have been linked either to playing 'violent' video games or to watching violent programmes. Analyse the evidence you have found, and write a short paragraph arguing that there has been an effect from the media, and giving the evidence. Then write another short paragraph suggesting how this evidence might be flawed, or how there might be other explanations.

Studies of TV violence and aggression

There have been many studies of TV violence and aggression – partly because of the increasing amount of violence being shown on TV, and partly because of the increasing importance of TV in day-to-day living. In 1989 children in America watched about 3.5 hours of television each day, and saw on average 33 violent acts in that time (Heymann, 1989). Singer and Singer (1981) gave parents a questionnaire to find out how much television their children watched. The researchers then watched the child's behaviour at school, and found that those who watched the most television were also the children who behaved most aggressively.

In another study, Gerbner *et al.* (1986) found that cartoons had an average of 20 violent acts per hour, with the aggressors often being the heroes. Modelling on heroes is even more likely, according to social learning theory. Bandura (1973a) did find that film and TV violence seem to gloss over the aggressiveness of the acts and the suffering of the victim, which may suggest to the viewer that such actions are not harmful.

Sheehan (1983) found a correlation between a child's TV viewing and aggressive behaviour. Sheehan studied middle-class children aged between 5 and 10 years, with peers rating the child's behaviour according to whether it would physically injure or irritate another person. Data was gathered about the participants' parents, and the researchers also asked about the children's aggressive fantasies. They found correlations between viewing violence and peer-rated aggression for children aged 8–10 years old, with the correlations being stronger for the boys than for the girls. The stronger correlation for boys ties in with social learning theory, as boys are more likely to model on males and often it is the male actor modelling TV violence. However, parental characteristics such as income, rejection of the child, TV viewing habits

Figure 2.11
Vicarious experience – learning to be aggressive. Bandura argued that children can learn violence by observing a model they admire

and use of punishment were also factors; and the researchers found that those children who were more aggressive also tended to have aggressive fantasies.

Evaluation

- Sheehan carried out a field study, which was more valid, because it was more natural.

- A cause and effect relationship between watching violence on TV and behaving aggressively could not be found because of the lack of controlled experimentation.

- This study could look at the correlation only at that particular time. It could not be conclusive about a relationship between viewing habits of a child when younger and its level of aggression when older, although it did suggest that there may be one.

- The many connected variables suggest that concluding that watching TV violence leads to aggressive behaviour may be too simple.

Black and Bevan (1992) gave a questionnaire about aggression to 129 cinema goers. They were asked to complete the questionnaire both before seeing the film and afterwards. Those going to watch a violent film showed higher aggression scores than those who had chosen to watch a non-violent film, and after the film those who had chosen the violent film had even higher aggression scores. This suggests that more aggressive

people are likely to choose to watch violent films, and also that those who watch violent films become even more aggressive. It is not claimed that violence in the media is the only cause of any violence that may follow, but it may be a factor (Figure 2.12).

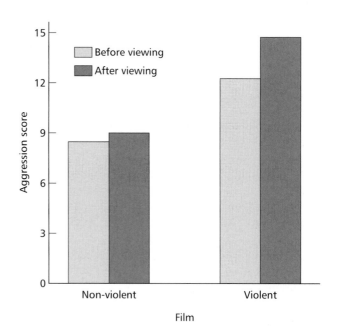

Figure 2.12
Aggression scores before and after watching a non-violent and a violent film (Source: Hogg and Vaughan, 1998)

Evaluation

- Finding a link between the amount of violent TV that was watched and the amount of aggressive acts seen does not show a cause and effect relationship. Other factors may be involved, such as that the aggressive child enjoys watching violence on TV. Another factor could be that those watching most TV tend to be ignored by their parents, which also produces aggressive behaviour.

In a more controlled study, Parke *et al.* (1977) investigated boys in an institution, where they could control the amount of TV watching and what was watched. This was one of a series of three field experiments that were carried out in Belgium and the United States (Leyens *et al.*, 1975; Parke *et al.*, 1977). Juvenile offenders were shown exciting films, some of which included violence and some of which did not. There were trained observers who coded the actual violence the boys exhibited during a normal day. The researchers found that watching violent exciting films increased aggressive behaviour, whereas the boys who watched non-violent exciting films were noticeably less aggressive.

Evaluation

- This was a different type of study because the independent variable (what was watched on TV) could be manipulated by researchers, and there could be controls, such as what the control group watched or did. It did seem to suggest a cause and effect relationship between TV watching and aggression.

- There are still other factors involved, such as the surrounding circumstances and the boys' previous experiences, that might contribute to the observed aggressive behaviour.

Another part of the Parke *et al.* (1977) experiment involved the boys in being able to give 'electric shocks' to someone who had provoked them. Those who had watched the violent films gave more shocks. (The person given the shocks was a confederate of the experimenters, of course, and the shocks were fake, but the boys did not know this.) Similarly, Liebert and Baron (1972) showed that both boys and girls aged between 5 and 9 gave more severe punishments to an opponent if they had watched a film with violent scenes. A control group watched an exciting race instead of the film with violent scenes, and gave fewer 'shocks' to a confederate of the researchers acting as an opponent.

Leyens *et al.* (1975) carried out a field experiment similar to that by Parke *et al.* The researchers manipulated the amount of violent content a group of teenage boys watched on television. The participants were in a boarding school in Belgium living in four dormitories. Their behaviour was recorded before the study began, and the amount of aggression recorded, so that there was a baseline measure; this tended to be higher in two of the dormitories. Then a week was designated 'Movie Week'. Special films were shown, but no other television could be watched. Boys in two of the dormitories – one with the higher aggression levels, and one with lower – watched 'violent' films such as *Bonnie and Clyde* and *The Dirty Dozen*. The boys in the other two dormitories were the control groups and watched non-violent films such as *La Belle Americaine*. Observers then rated the boys' behaviour for aggression during the week and for the week after.

They found that physical aggression had increased for all the boys who watched the violent films. However, verbal aggression increased only in the boys from the 'more aggressive' dormitory; whereas the boys from the non-aggressive dormitory who watched the violent films showed a decrease in verbal aggression. It is possible that the violent films may have had a cathartic effect in that sense.

Evaluation

- Field studies do not have the same controls as laboratory experiments, although most of the studies do show a link between TV watching and subsequent behaviour.

- Leyens *et al.* (1982) argue that most studies tend to single children out, whereas in real life children play in groups and behave interdependently. TV viewing and cinema-going take place in a social context, and individuals talk to one another. Children discuss what films they want to see, and can influence each other to behave aggressively; social factors that are rarely taken into account.

- Laboratory and field experiments look at short-term effects, as the violence is almost always measured very soon after the filmed or TV violence is watched (Huesmann and Miller, 1994). Longitudinal studies look at longer term effects, which also tend to suggest that there is a link between watching violence and carrying out aggressive acts.

As you can see, there have been a lot of studies carried out in this area. Wood *et al.*, (1991) carried out a **meta-analysis** (a statistical analysis of many studies) reviewing 23 experimental studies looking at TV violence and aggression. They found that aggression does seem to increase after watching violent TV or violent films. Similarly, Comstock and Paik (1991) carried out a meta-analysis of over 1000 studies comparing TV violence and aggressive behaviour, including experiments, longitudinal studies and surveys. They concluded that there was a clear short-term effect, and the studies given above illustrate this point. They also concluded that there were long-term effects in that significant positive correlations are consistently found (much like the link between smoking and lung cancer).

Comstock and Paik suggested that the many factors in TV violence which can lead to aggressive behaviour can be grouped into four dimensions:

- **Efficacy** – aggression is portrayed in the media as a way to achieve goals or to be unpunished (in other words, as an effective form of action). So if violence seems to achieve a goal or the perpetrators go unpunished, this is more likely to lead to it being copied.
- **Normativeness** – the violence is shown, but the consequences for the victim are not. Aggression appears to have no consequences, and can even be seen as justified, for example, when carried out by police officers.
- **Pertinence** – viewers see the perpetrator as being in similar circumstances to themselves, or as similar in some other way, which makes this type of action appear pertinent to their own lives. Realistic as opposed to fantasy situations, for example, are more influential for this reason.
- **Susceptibility** – when the viewer is watching they are in a emotional state such as anger or pleasure. This emotional arousal prevents or inhibits reasoned analysis of the situation by the viewer.

Berkowitz (1984), Eron (1994) and Huesmann (1988) have all suggested that it is the way that people process information in response to aggressive scenes that is important. Just thinking about an action may lead to it being carried out (Berkowitz, 1984). So images of violence, for example on TV or in video games, can be enough to lead to violence in real life purely because of **cognitive processes**. **Neo-associationist analysis** – the idea put forward by Berkowitz to explain how this happens – is similar to the idea outlined earlier in this chapter that our memory consists of nodes and associations. A thought moves from node to node through association pathways and this can lead to action. An image can generate a thought. This idea can also explain priming, which is where one image (for example, a gun) can lead to other associative thoughts such as 'shooting'.

Video games

New technology has introduced new fears about the link between watching or imitating violence and real-life aggression. Children and adults now play computer games where the player is actively involved in 'crime and violence'. But there are major differences between video games and watching television. One difference is that playing is active, whereas watching is passive. Video games also require more sustained attention, and they show abstract violence. Television requires less sustained attention, but can show real violence.

Studies have suggested that those children who seem to be addicted to computer games might have a particular personality type, and arousal levels might be important. It is possible that playing violent computer games can lead to desensitisation and isolation. Fisher (1993) has looked at addiction to computer games in children, and Griffiths and Dancaster (1995) have looked at arousal and personality type. Toles (1985) studied arcade games and found 92% had no female roles, although things have changed since the time of that study. Video games are often violent, and a review of studies by Griffiths (1997) concluded that they do have a short-term effect, in that after young children have been playing such games they do behave more aggressively. However, there is need for more systematic research into this area.

Self-test

Write an essay, under exam conditions (or as close as you can manage) using the title 'Discuss studies into the effects of the media on aggressive behaviour'.

Treating crime

Approaches to treating crime have tended to focus on two main areas. The first of these is controlling aggression, and the idea is that the various types of research and analysis carried out on factors leading to aggression may help practitioners to develop better ways of controlling it. The second is to develop community and policing practices which are more effective in controlling crime; and one of the most useful of these appears to have been the idea of **zero tolerance**.

Controlling aggression

As we have seen, there are many different explanations for aggression. In this chapter the focus has been mainly on the effect of watching violent behaviour on television or in films, and the likelihood that this affects the amount of aggression in an individual. The ways of controlling aggression we will be considering in this chapter tend to come from the accepted explanations for the behaviour. As we saw in Chapter 1, the treatment we consider appropriate for a particular disorder is very dependent on where we think that disorder has come from, and the same applies to criminal behaviour.

For example, if we think that aggression is caused by an excess of testosterone, then we might look to drugs to control aggression (following a physiological explanation) but if we think aggression is caused by there being no outlet for inner tensions, then we might look to sport or some way of releasing such inner aggression (following a psychodynamic explanation, perhaps). If we think aggression is caused by imitation and modelling, then we might recommend more coverage of prosocial (helpful) acts on television (following a social learning explanation) but if we think that catharsis or the release of inner tensions is necessary, we might recommend the watching of violence on television (following a psychodynamic explanation).

It is thus important when judging the effect of a way of controlling aggression to consider which approach is being used as an explanation for the aggression. Evaluating the approach can also be an effective way of evaluating the method, as well as looking at whether it works and in what situations. This depends on the theory, for example, watching violence on television could be considered a useful strategy for controlling aggression, or could be thought of as the opposite – that is a cause of aggression. But the studies which we looked at in the previous section tend to suggest that watching more violence is not exactly helpful as a controlling method

Cognitive–behavioural therapy

Cognitive–behavioural therapy (CBT) rests on the assumption that thinking patterns affect behaviour. The implication is therefore that if we change our thinking patterns we are likely to change our behaviour. So if someone can change their attributions about other people, they may be able to change their behaviour towards others. **Self-instructional training** is one way of changing an individual's thought patterns. It often focuses on their self-statements and changes them, for example, by including less criticism of, and more positive statements about, themselves. Self-instructional training

has been shown to improve self-control, and this tends to reduce aggression against others, so it can be a successful technique.

Role-taking also appears to be helpful in reducing aggressive behaviour. Chandler (1973) worked out a programme for young offenders in which they took the role of victim, and a follow-up study after 18 months showed that those on the programme had committed fewer offences than other offenders not on the programme (and acting as a control group).

Evaluation

- Ethically this could be considered dubious, as the offenders not offered the programme might be said to have suffered because of this choice, which is against official guidelines. However, it would never be possible to test out any new procedure if some groups were not selected for initial trials.

- It could be claimed that those chosen for the programme received more attention, so they improved because of the attention and not because of the programme itself. The phenomenon called the 'Hawthorne Effect' predicts that participants selected for study are likely to show changed behaviour just by being selected. We will be looking at this in more detail in Chapter 4.

- The techniques outlined above assume that aggression is caused by cognitive processes. If aggression is attributed to a different cause, such as brain damage after an accident, then cognitive strategies might not be useful.

Anger management

Another way of treating aggressive behaviour, and thus controlling crime, is to use anger management techniques. **Anger control programmes** also focus on cognitive processing, and examining thoughts before an angry attack. It is suggested that thoughts lead to anger, which is then expressed. The expression of the anger is reinforcing in that perhaps it relieves pressure, and so the individual will use anger to release pressure from such thoughts in another situation (Novaco, 1975).

Anger control programmes generally have three stages.
- The first is a stage of **cognitive preparation**, in which the analysis of anger patterns allows the individual to trace their own thought patterns and recognise triggers.
- The second is a stage of **skill acquisition**, in which techniques of self-control and arousal management are taught, as things to do when the identified triggers

arrive. For example, following awareness that a situation that might lead to anger is developing, self-talk might be used to stop an aggressive reaction. Social skills training or assertiveness training can also be useful.

- The third stage consists of **application practice**. In this stage stressful situations are created so that an individual can practice their anger control techniques. Then the therapist and the individual can assess how well the techniques are working, and perhaps reassess the situation (Figure 2.13).

Evaluation

- The method does seem to be effective. For example, McDougall *et al.* (1987) found that when 18 young offenders in prison attended an anger management course offences in prison were reduced.

- This technique is only likely to work for those whose aggression comes from anger, and who are able to learn to identify thought processes involved.

- If the course takes place in a prison situation, and is evaluated as succeeding in that situation, this does not mean that the individual will be able to transfer their learning and the techniques needed to control their aggression to another environment.

Social skills checklist

Here is a list of things that people have to do nearly every day when they meet other people. Which of them are you good at? Which of them are you not so good at? Look at each item in turn and decide how good you are at doing it; then put a tick in the space opposite which is nearest to how good or bad you think you are.

	I am good at this	I am not bad at this	I am not very good at this	I am bad at this
A				
1. Looking people in the face				
2. Being watched by lots of people				
3. Staring people out				
4. Smiling at people I fancy				
5. Keeping a straight face				
6. Not blushing when I am caught out				
7. Looking angry when I feel it				
8. Hiding my disappointment				
9. Knowing what other people are feeling				
10. Standing close to other people				
B				
1. Joining a group of people already talking				
2. Having to tell people who I am				
3. Going into a room full of people				
4. Being interviewed				
5. Starting a conversation with a stranger				
6. Giving people directions in the street				
7. Carrying messages				
8. Saying what I want to say				
9. Understanding what other people say				
10. Answering questions/asking questions				
C				
1. Having an argument				
2. Being told off				
3. Being ordered about				
4. Making a complaint				
5. Refusing to do something				
6. Apologising, making excuses				
7. Giving someone bad news				
8. Praising someone				
9. Responding to praise				
10. Asking for help				

Figure 2.13
A social skills checklist used in training. (Source: McGuire and Priestley, 1983)

Punishment

Punishment can of course be used to control aggression, and may have some effect. For example, when the police in Minneapolis arrested violent partners in domestic disputes only 10% re-offended, compared with 24% who re-offended if the violent partner was just separated from the other person for a cooling-off period (Sherman and Berk, 1984). This suggests that the punishment (being arrested) was more effective than counselling. And there may be a modelling influence too. For example, Bandura *et al.* (1963) showed that when an aggressive model was punished, children watching were less likely to copy that behaviour.

Evaluation

- Punishment can lead to displaced aggression.

- In the Bandura study, the children who watched the punished aggressive model did not reproduce the behaviour at that time. But it could appear later if it was rewarded.

- It is better to reward non-aggressive behaviour than to punish aggressive behaviour. When nursery school teachers were asked to pay attention to desired behaviour and ignore aggressive behaviour, the number of aggressive acts fell from 64 before the experiment to 26 acts two weeks later (Brown and Elliot, 1965).

Evaluating treatments for crimes

Martinson (1974) examined 231 different studies (not all looking at violent crimes, but at crimes in general) and concluded that nothing works. However, Thornton (1987) looked at the same data as Martinson and considered the methods used in the different studies. For example, **recidivism** was defined differently (recidivism means repeated offending, as measured by the rate of going back to crime after a term in prison), and the way groups were allocated to some studies may have affected the conclusions. Thornton found that 34 of the studies were comparable with one another, and in these studies it was possible to compare a group that had treatment to a control group that did not. Of these 34 studies 16 showed that the group with therapy benefited, 17 showed there was no difference and one suggested that the treatment had made the aggression worse.

Hollin (1989) concluded that treatment works with some offenders some of the time, and this is called differential treatment. It can also be influenced by programme drift (in which the aims of a programme gradually shift away from its original ones), programme reversal (in which staff model inappropriate behaviour) and programme non-compliance, where the programme changes half way through. These can all produce problems with treatments.

However, despite these factors some treatments can be effective. In 1992, Hollin showed that Aggression Replacement Training (ART), which involves such treatments as social skills training and anger control, does seem to work. For example, Goldstein *et al.* (1989) found that only 15% of those who had undergone ART were re-arrested, whereas 43% of a control group were re-arrested. Losel (1995) looked at more than 500 studies of this kind, and found that overall treatments had led to a 10% drop in recidivism – although these studies did not all involve violent crime. This suggests that treatments do work to an extent.

Self-test

Write an essay, under exam conditions (or as close as you can manage) using the title 'Discuss two means based on psychological findings of controlling aggression'.

The effect of zero tolerance

Zero tolerance is a concept that has recently arisen as a way of preventing crime. It means not accepting any criminal behaviour, and not 'turning a blind eye' to any misbehaviour. For example, very recently a zero tolerance policy has been announced about going over 70 mph on British motorways. In the past, police would not usually stop someone driving at 80 mph and charge them with speeding, but the zero tolerance policy means that any exceeding of the speed limit would be cause for attention. Other examples of zero tolerance policies in Britain include awareness of domestic violence, for example, Edinburgh City Council used media campaigns which also included an emphasis on rape and child sexual abuse. In Chester there was an advertising campaign to warn people about danger from strangers.

The idea of zero tolerance is that if small crimes are prevented, this will help to stop larger crimes too. It is based on the idea that if smaller crimes are ignored and not punished, then a 'culture of crime' can easily develop, and larger crimes become more likely. Zero tolerance is said to have been started by Wilson and Kelling in an article in 1982. The article was called *Broken Windows* and suggested that the environment could be a factor affecting criminal behaviour. For example, graffiti could suggest that a neighbourhood is not cared for, and this could reduce inhibitions in those living in the area. In

1992 zero tolerance was introduced in a New York district. There was a 25% increase in arrests, but also a reduction in serious crime – in 1991 there were 2166 homicides, and in 1997 there were 767. This is taken as evidence that zero tolerance works.

Evaluation

- In New York there was not only a zero tolerance policy, but also around 7000 more police officers, which may also have contributed to the reduction in crime and the increase in arrests.

- Bowling (1999) suggested that the market for drugs declined around the same time, and that could have affected the reduction in crime.

- Citizen patrols were also introduced at the same time; they, too, could have helped to reduce the crime rate.

As we can see, there are other factors which could have been at work, apart from the zero tolerance policy. But crime is not a simple affair. In this chapter we have looked at some of the many theories of crime, at the legal aspects of crime, at some of the influences on crime, and at some of the ways that have been suggested for treating crime. In all cases there have been arguments and controversy, but the work of criminological psychologists has contributed greatly to the ways that crime can be tackled.

Self-test

Write an essay, under exam conditions (or as close as you can manage) using the title 'Describe what is meant by zero tolerance and consider its effectiveness'.

Suggested reading

Brewer, K. (2000) *Psychology and Crime*. Oxford: Heinemann.

Harrower, J. (1998) *Applying Psychology to Crime*. London: Hodder and Stoughton.

Hogg, M.A. and Vaughan, G.M. (1998) *Social psychology, second edition*. Prentice Hall.

Hollin, C.R. (1989) *Psychology and Crime. An Introduction to Criminological Psychology*. Routledge.

Pennington, D.C., Gillen, K. and Hill, P. (1999) *Social Psychology*. Arnold.

Sabini, J. (1994) *Social Psychology, second edition*. W.W. Norton and Company.

Turvey, B. (1999) *Criminal Profiling: an Introduction to Behavioural Evidence Analysis*. London: Academic Press.

3

The psychology of education

The aims of this chapter

The aims of this chapter are to enable the reader to:

- *describe and evaluate the behavioural approach to learning*
- *discuss the educational implications of Piaget's theory*
- *recall key assumptions of the cognitive approach and evaluate its usefulness when applied to education*
- *describe and discuss teacher influences on student performance, including teaching styles and the effects of teacher attitudes and expectations*
- *understand the relevance of different learning/cognitive styles in the classroom*
- *discuss factors relating to educational assessment, including the measurement of IQ and issues of discrimination through assessment*
- *describe and discuss the process of identifying, categorising and assessing students with special educational needs*
- *describe and discuss issues concerning the identification, assessment and treatment of 'gifted' children.*

STUDY AID

When you have finished working through this chapter you should write an essay about, or at least test yourself on, each of the above points. This will help you to see how good your knowledge and understanding of educational psychology is.

This chapter covers

INTRODUCTION TO THE PSYCHOLOGY OF EDUCATION
    Concepts in the psychology of education
    Methods used in the psychology of education

THEORIES OF LEARNING
    Types of learning
    Behaviourist theories of learning
    The cognitive–developmental approach to education

    The cognitive approach to education

FACTORS AFFECTING STUDENT PERFORMANCE
    Teacher variables
    Student variables

ASSESSMENT
    Assessing intelligence
    Bias in educational assessment
    Special educational needs

Introduction to the psychology of education

Educational psychologists are professional psychologists who have gone on to become qualified teachers and gain teaching experience. Following that, they undertake another 3-year training programme to become a fully qualified educational psychologist. This intensive professional training gives the educational psychologist a wide range of skills and abilities.

Although some are interested in adult learners, most educational psychologists focus on individual children's school experiences and progress. They may, for example, carry out tests on children to see if they have special needs, and they may liaise with families and with the school staff to ensure that a child receives the appropriate kind of teaching. Because of this, they need to be aware of the psychology of education and the different issues which it raises, such as how to assess children, the importance of different learning styles, and the implications of various theories of learning. We will be looking at these issues in this chapter.

↻ Recall AS material

Recall your AS material covering three of the main approaches – cognitive, cognitive-developmental and learning theory. The key assumptions and principles of these three main approaches are the main subject matter of the first part of this chapter. The physiological approach is also referred to briefly, so it would be a good idea to recall that as well. If you don't remember them, look them up.

Concepts in the psychology of education

Some fundamental issues arise when we look at the psychology of education. One of the first of these concerns the focus of interest – whether the focus is on the uniqueness of each individual or on general ideas which apply across the board. Another set of concerns is to do with the paradigms that are being applied – the overall framework of ideas within which the educational process is operating and being understood. We will begin our study of the psychology of education by exploring these concepts.

Nomothetic or idiographic

The psychology of education draws on four of the main approaches to psychology – cognitive, cognitive-developmental, physiological and learning. We will be looking at these more systematically later in this chapter, but it is worth noting here that these approaches generally take a **nomothetic** stance – that is, they are concerned with identifying general laws or principles which can be applied to everyone, or at least in most cases.

However, the psychology of education also includes ideas from the humanistic approach, which emphasises the uniqueness of each individual, and also takes the view that the main goal of each person is to self-actualise – to make real or satisfy all of their personal needs. Maslow outlined a hierarchy of needs, which we will be looking at in detail in Chapter 4, but which you may also find relevant here. The humanistic approach takes an **idiographic** stance, which is to say that it emphasises individuality and uniqueness, and in that respect is different from the nomothetic approach. Another way of explaining the term 'idiographic' is to say that it means there is no wish to develop general laws and to build a theory. The person is looked at as an individual, rather than as an example of a type or category.

By contrast to the idiographic approach, the nomothetic approach looks for general laws of behaviour. The learning approach, for example, uses experiments to generate data about behaviour and general laws about behaviour are proposed on the basis of these data, which makes it nomothetic. The cognitive approach is also nomothetic, as are the cognitive–developmental and social approaches; these three approaches aim to generate general laws from the evidence that is gathered. The physiological approach mainly looks at how we are similar in a biological sense, which is another example of a nomothetic stance. For example, people with brain damage may be examined as individuals by means of case studies, but the findings are generalised to put forward general principles about how the brain works – this makes it a nomothetic approach as well.

The psychodynamic approach is a bit different because individuals are the focus of attention, particularly when it comes to therapy. But the psychodynamic approach also involves generalisations, such as models of personality development. So the psychodynamic approach has an idiographic focus, in that an individual's feelings and problems are the focus of attention, but it also has a nomothetic focus in that it also aims to identify general laws about psychological development and dysfunction.

The psychology of education tends to use general laws about behaviour from which to draw conclusions about individuals, but there is also a recognition that the people who are being educated are all individuals; and the humanistic approach has been influential in this area. So in education in particular, the issue of idiographic or nomothetic orientation can be quite significant, and is useful when evaluating the claims of a particular approach.

In what follows, the nomothetic approach of looking for generalisations that apply to everyone is the main approach. For example, questions are asked such as whether large classes are less effective than smaller ones. This means taking a scientific approach, and building general laws – in other words, adopting a positivist approach and using scientific methods.

However, it is useful to remember the post-modernist idea that reality is socially constructed. We would need to take an idiographic stance to look closely at people's socially constructed worlds if we really wanted to explore the personal and social meanings of education for the individual. This in-depth exploration would add to our understanding significantly, even if it did not generate the type of knowledge from which policy could be formulated. Although what we learn from specific studies about specific individuals may not always transfer to different people in different situations, it still might be useful in helping us to gain a true picture.

> **Synoptic Note**
>
> The question of whether an approach in psychology is idiographic or nomothetic is part of the 'is psychology a science?' debate, so these ideas will also be useful for Unit 6, the synoptic part of the assessment.

Paradigms

Another useful way to look at the psychology of education is to consider the different **paradigms** involved. Paradigms are ways of understanding, and the main approaches in psychology can be thought of as paradigms. Kuhn (1962) defined a paradigm as the shared ideas held by a scientific community – in other words, a general way of understanding a particular body of knowledge. Psychology at the moment encompasses many different paradigms, some of which are very different from one another.

The psychology of education uses many approaches in its explanations for child behaviour, and in its recommendations for what is good practice in education. Educational psychologists historically have worked within different paradigms, and research in the psychology of education reflects these changing ways of understanding education.

For example, if children are thought of as passive receivers of information, as they were in schools at the beginning of the twentieth century, then **didactic teaching**, in which the teacher gives information and the child (hopefully) receives it, would be thought of as the best

approach. If, however, it is believed that children need to be active when learning, then didactic teaching would be frowned upon. The learning approach, if taken as a paradigm, emphasises conditioning, and a didactic approach that took account of this would gain approval. But the cognitive approach generally emphasises active processing, and so would stress the need for the child to take an active part in the teaching and learning process, making a didactic approach unsuitable.

In this chapter we will be considering both the learning and the cognitive paradigms, as well as some others; they have all been useful to some extent. Where one person in psychology may look to the learning approach for an explanation of behaviour, another (perhaps in a different situation) might use the physiological approach. For example, when considering a pupil who is behaving badly in class, we could say that this is due to previously learned behaviour or we could say that there is a biological cause for their behaviour. A paradigm is a current body of knowledge within which researchers in a particular discipline study. The learning approach could be called a paradigm, as could the physiological approach.

Historically, the psychology of education has shifted from an emphasis on conditioning and didactic teaching to an emphasis on cognitive development and an active approach to learning, and now onwards towards a social approach and an emphasis on learning through interaction (Wood, 1998). In the social paradigm the teacher is a facilitator and part of the child's social world. Reality for those working in the social paradigm is socially constructed rather than being 'out there' to be measured, and the role of the teacher is to facilitate that construction. For example, language is used as discourse and there are layers of meaning to words which children need to explore. Also concepts like gender are socially constructed and children learn about such concepts through their socialisation, of which education is part.

> **Synoptic Note**
>
> The debate about what psychology is, and the various paradigms involved, also contributes to discussions about whether psychology is a science. You will therefore also find this material useful for Unit 6, the synoptic part of the course.

Methods used in the psychology of education

Educational researchers use a variety of different methods for evaluating different aspects of the educational process. However, as with most real-world phenomena, it is extremely difficult to come to any absolute conclusions about effectiveness or causality – partly because of the way that real-world events are usually caused by combinations of many factors, and partly also because the most valid research takes place in real classrooms, where there is always a great deal more going on than a researcher could explore.

Experiments have often been used in education. Some of the experiments that have informed classroom practice have been laboratory experiments – for example, research into reading fluency. But more often educational research uses natural experiments, which take place in real schools. Usually, these have taken the form of one group of students experiencing some kind of special or experimental treatment and being compared with other students who did not have the same experience. For example, different class sizes can be set up to try to investigate the effect of class size on performance, or different reading schemes can be introduced to try to assess which is most effective for children who are just learning to read.

Evaluation

- There are ethical problems involved in manipulating school experiences, particularly if children might be deprived of a potentially beneficial experience by being part of a control group.

Observations are less likely to interfere with a child's experiences than experiments. Sometimes educational observations may be similar to natural experiments, because they involve comparing one type of education in one school with a different practice in another school. This could be seen as a natural experiment because the variables are already in place, and have not been manipulated by the researcher. But it is an observation because data are gathered by watching and recording.

Evaluation

- When variables are not manipulated they are unlikely to be controlled, and may differ in other ways (e.g. the amount of class time they take).

- Other factors are also likely to vary – for example, class size, teacher attitude, parental background, school and ethos of the school. So it is not possible to sort out whether the differences have come from the technique being studied or something entirely different.

↺ Recall AS material

Recall, or look up, your AS material on methods, especially experiments, natural experiments and observations.

ACTIVITY

Make notes on the use of experiments, natural experiments, and observations in studying the psychology of education. Write a paragraph summarising the way that each method has been used. Then give at least two advantages and disadvantages of each.

Qualitative or quantitative methods

One of the decisions an educational researcher needs to make is whether to gather qualitative or quantitative data – or both. **Quantitative data** are data which involve numerical measurements of some sort. **Qualitative data** involve meaningful information, usually in the form of words. They may, for example, come from asking about a person's attitudes, emotions, feelings or characteristics in a way that involves description rather than a measurement scale.

Quantitative data can be very useful when trying to make comparisons, because they involve taking measures according to definite procedures (for example, rating someone on a personality trait, or measuring someone's GSR). However, the problem is that procedures may not be fully comparable. For example, GSR may be a reliable measure, but judging someone on a personality trait will probably be done differently by different raters. Therefore, in psychology, the distinction between quantitative and qualitative measures can become a bit blurred (Hayes, 1997).

Qualitative data are likely to have validity, as the person's natural setting is likely to be involved. However, reliability can be weak, as in a different place at a different time different findings may result. Our thoughts, emotions and individual characteristics often vary from day to day, and from time to time.

Researchers in the psychology of education often use a combination of the two approaches. We may look at reading skills, for example, and use quantitative measures such as the number of words correctly identified, or the time taken to read a passage. But we will need qualitative data to get a full idea of a child's reading ability, or the type of mistakes that he or she is making. Combining both quantitative and qualitative data collection enriches the picture the researcher can obtain from the study.

Methodology is part of Unit 6, the synoptic part of the course, and this includes the quantitative or qualitative debate That debate may also be relevant when arguing whether psychology can be called a science or not, another topic which appears in Unit 6, as do ethical issues.

Theories of learning

Learning can involve academic learning, the learning of a new skill or learning how to act in a certain situation. Essentially, learning is an experience that produces a change in behaviour, and we usually expect that change to be reasonably durable (Kimble, 1961). The learning may not always show up immediately – we can also learn something that produces a change in our behaviour later, rather than immediately.

The psychology of education, obviously, places its main emphasis on learning. Although attention is paid to issues such as teaching styles, pattern of assessment, and to practical issues such as class size, underlying all these is the central question of how learning takes place. Bloom (1956) drew up a taxonomy of learning objectives, to identify the many different types of learning which may have relevance in an educational context.

Types of learning

Learning can mean different things to different people. Learning for the behaviourist means associating a new stimulus with a new response. Learning from a cognitive–developmental viewpoint means assimilating and accommodating new information and then amending schemas. Learning from a cognitive viewpoint can mean forming new connections in memory or building a network of new associations, depending on what model of memory is used.

Within the educational system, those developing the curriculum have often found it useful to distinguish between different types of learning. Bloom identified three main types: **cognitive learning** (to do with thinking), **affective learning** (to do with feeling) and **psychomotor learning** (to do with movement skills). These types are all important, and recognised in discussions about the primary curriculum, in particular.

Education at higher levels focuses mainly on cognitive learning. Bloom sub-divided the cognitive domain into six areas: knowledge, comprehension, application, analysis, synthesis and evaluation. However, Gagné *et al.* (1988) proposed a different division, arguing that intellectual skills can be separated into knowledge skills and understanding skills – a division which is commonly used in secondary and higher education.

We will be looking more closely at the behavioural and cognitive domains of learning in the next part of this chapter. As we have seen, the paradigm within which research is taking place governs the sort of conclusions reached. But learning is a broad term covering more than one skill, ability, or psychological domain, and for everyone researching within the psychology of education learning is a central interest.

STUDY AID

In the AS/A2 psychology examinations learning is measured by assessing knowledge and understanding (assessment objective one – AO1), and evaluation and comment (assessment objective two – AO2). The assessment objectives for the Edexcel specification are listed in full on p.7 and you should be aware of how your learning is being measured. There is a third assessment objective (AO3) that measures your ability to carry out studies and understand methods.

Behaviourist theories of learning

Behaviourist theories of learning are concerned with the way that learning produces changes in behaviour. They do not really concern themselves with changes in thinking styles or with knowledge acquisition, but are more concerned with the types of behaviours and skills a child can acquire. As a result, the behaviourist approach to learning tends to focus on conditioning, and the learning of new responses to stimuli.

Principles of conditioning

As you will know from your AS work, there are two main types of conditioning: classical and operant conditioning. Both of these have some relevance in the educational process, although operant conditioning has a broader range of applications in the classroom. In this section we will review some of the main concepts in conditioning, and look at their relevance in education.

Recall AS material

Recall your AS material on the principles of classical and operant conditioning – or look it up.

Classical conditioning

Classical conditioning is concerned with forming straightforward, one-to-one associations between reflexes and stimuli. Some early approaches to teaching, such as those which emphasised rote learning, drew heavily on classical conditioning but its principles are not usually used in modern teaching. However, phobias can be learned through classical conditioning, and school phobia is common. An example of how classical conditioning principles may be used to explain school phobia is given in Table 3.1.

Table 3.1 How classical conditioning principles can be used to explain school phobia

Bullying	Unconditioned stimulus (UCS)	Fear/anxiety	Unconditioned response (UCR)
Bullying + being at school	Unconditioned stimulus (UCS) + conditioned stimulus (CS)	Fear/anxiety	Unconditioned response (UCR) + conditioned stimulus (CR)
Being at school	Conditioned stimulus (CS)	Fear/anxiety	Conditioned response (CR)

Classical conditioning has also been used to explain more subtle forms of phobias – such as reluctance to learn a particular subject, or a feeling of being unable to do so. Many adults, for example, have difficulty with maths, because of having had unpleasant experiences in learning maths when they were at school.

ACTIVITY

Use the learning approach to give two different explanations for how a school phobia could be learned. One of these explanations should use the principles of classical conditioning, and the other should use the principles of operant conditioning and/or modelling and imitation.

Operant conditioning

The principles of **operant conditioning** can also be used to explain learning, and have been more widely used by educationalists and researchers than classical conditioning techniques. Operant conditioning principles suggest that the antecedent (what happens before an incident) leads to the behaviour, which in turn gives the consequences (this has been called 'ABC'). Consequences that are desired or enjoyed by the animal or person producing the behaviour are reinforcing. This means that the behaviour is more likely to be repeated (Figure 3.1).

Reinforcement can be of two kinds: positive or negative. **Positive reinforcement** involves giving a reward of some sort. For example, if a child is praised for some behaviour such as setting the table, the consequences of their action (praise) are desired or at least experienced as pleasant, so the child is likely to repeat the behaviour. This is an example of positive reinforcement.

However, a learned behaviour can also be strengthened if the consequences mean the removal or avoidance of something not desired, or unpleasant. In this case **negative reinforcement** is being used. For example, if a child does something that means they avoid something they don't like – perhaps they don't go to school because they are being bullied – this is an example of negative reinforcement. The child repeats the behaviour (not going to school) and so avoids the unpleasantness (being bullied).

Punishment is not really part of the operant conditioning repertoire, because it is more commonly associated with classical conditioning. It is less useful in learning, for several reasons:

- Punishment does not show a child what the desired behaviour is.
- Punishment can make a child regress to previous behaviour which is equally unacceptable. It suppresses the current behaviour but does not put anything positive in its place.
- The punisher may be seen in a negative light and may not be co-operated with in future. If this is the teacher, this later non-cooperation can be a problem.
- Punishment, particularly if it is harsh or unfair, may lead to aggressive behaviour through modelling. Children may see the behaviour as acceptable, and may imitate it.

Rewards are much more useful in the classroom, as they show children what the desired behaviour is. Moreover, rewarding often involves positive actions, so imitation and modelling are desirable consequences. In addition, the child often develops a positive relationship with the person rewarding them, and if this is the teacher, this can be useful. There are some drawbacks, however:

- Rewards can be seen as bribes, with the child not the teacher being in control.

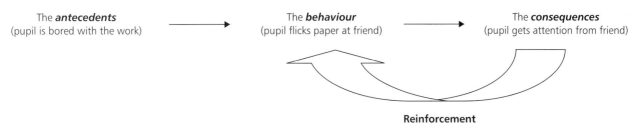

The ***antecedents***
(pupil is bored with the work)

The ***behaviour***
(pupil flicks paper at friend)

The ***consequences***
(pupil gets attention from friend)

Reinforcement

Figure 3.1
'ABC' learning and how behaviour is modified (Source: Long, 2000)

• Care needs to be taken to ensure that rewards accord with efforts. For example, a child who is not working very hard may get more rewards as a teacher tries to get them to work, while another who is working hard and getting fewer rewards may see the system as unjust.

A reward tends to be more successful if given immediately. When starting a new task or dealing with a new class, a teacher may give out many rewards. However, as a new system is established rewards are given only for higher levels of achievement, and there are unlikely to be too many of them. In fact, giving too many rewards may be a problem, because if a teacher always uses rewards, then if for some reason they stop doing so the child may stop the behaviour. Infrequent rewards are less predictable and may be more successful. This links with the material on **schedules of reinforcement** that you have studied in your AS level work, and you may find it useful to apply it here.

ACTIVITY

Give definitions of the following terms:
• *positive reinforcement*
• *negative reinforcement*
• *punishment*
• *schedules of reinforcement*
• *behaviour shaping.*

Teaching methods based on conditioning

Operant conditioning principles are often used in the classroom to encourage learning. Perhaps the most influential discussion of how this can be used was initiated by Skinner, in 1954, who developed the idea of **programmed learning**. This is the idea that learning can proceed by small steps, with the child getting as many opportunities as possible to get the right answer. In that way, the correct behaviour (getting the answer right) is reinforced. The concept of programmed learning underlies a great many educational practices in modern education, in particular structured study programmes.

Programmed learning

At a practical level, the idea of programmed learning is that some material is presented and the child is asked questions about the subject matter. If the answer is correct, a reward is given, such as praise. If the answer is incorrect, more questions may be asked or more information given. The materials and questions could be given in a certain order, which makes it easy for the child to build on its existing knowledge, and means there is only a small step from what has already been achieved to the new task (Figure 3.2).

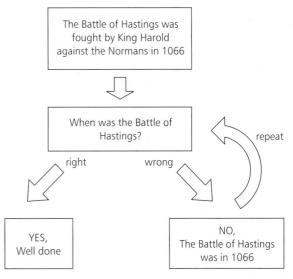

The Battle of Hastings was fought by King Harold against the Normans in 1066

When was the Battle of Hastings?

right

wrong

repeat

YES,
Well done

NO,
The Battle of Hastings was in 1066

Figure 3.2
Sequence of programmed learning (Source: Long, 2000)

There are several advantages to programmed learning techniques:
• Success is emphasised, and easy to achieve.
• Learning is structured and ordered.
• Jamison *et al.* (1974) compared learning by programmed learning with other methods, and found that it was more successful.

Teaching machines

Programmed learning techniques were initially used in class-based tasks and educational textbooks and study guides. However, in an influential article in the *Harvard Educational Review* Skinner argued that they could be used even more efficiently by teaching machines.

In fact, Pressey (1926) had introduced the first teaching machine, which set out multiple choice answers to questions, counted the number of correct answers, and gave a piece of candy to the pupil if the answers were good enough. Following this type of model Skinner (1954) produced the first linear teaching programme, which presented information and assessed the answers to multiple-choice questions. If the answer was wrong, then the pupil was given the chance to try again, and the whole task was presented through small bits of information following a logical sequence. That meant that the pupil was almost guaranteed success by the ease of the questions.

Early approaches used linear teaching programmes, but soon became more sophisticated. In 1955, Crowder used branching teaching programmes for the US Air Force. Again, this used multiple-choice questions; if the student's answer was correct, the student would move on in a linear fashion. However, if the answer was not correct, the student would be taken down another route to practice more of the questions on the same topic (this is a branch). This process of taking the student through remedial loops is known as 'wash back'.

Skinner's teaching machines adopted the same method, and he argued that they could be even more effective than human teachers, because learning could be matched to the pace of the individual. However, although the development of computers has led to more sophisticated programmed learning and some topics, notably statistics, are quite often taught using computer programmes, it is generally recognised that they do not work effectively without a human presence, and that for most subjects human delivery is far more effective.

Evaluation

- The software may be too hard or too easy for its purpose.
- The work can be boring and dehumanising for the learner.
- Students often dislike the isolation of the machines.
- If students work at their own pace, they may not be working to the best of their ability.
- Students can lack motivation once the novelty has worn off.
+ Computers give access to a lot of information.
+ Reward systems can maintain interest.
+ If students work at their own pace, they are not embarrassed by being compared with others.
+ Fewer teachers are needed.

Direct instruction

Other ways of applying operant conditioning to learning have focused on direct instruction from teachers. For example, one of the models used in America in the 1970s was known as the Direct Instructional Systems for Teaching and Remediation (DISTAR). In this method, the teacher was given a script to use, which stated what they were able to say, and included a high frequency of praise as reinforcement. It was mainly used for basic skills training, focusing particularly on numeracy and literacy.

However, although some researchers (e.g. Kennedy, 1978) found that DISTAR could be effective in remedial teaching, enthusiasm for directly scripted approaches fell off during the 1980s. This was partly because of an increased recognition of the social importance of interactions – the scripts were considered to be too artificial and to put children off learning. They are very rarely used in education nowadays.

Evaluation

- One problem with programmed learning is that natural curiosity may be limited by such programmes, and that a child's own motivation is not involved. The child may come to work only for rewards (Lepper and Greene, 1978).

- Children also watch others being praised or punished, and use observational learning. So there is more to programmed instruction than 'pure' operant conditioning.

- Studies have shown that learning can take place without the learned behaviour being acted out immediately (e.g. Tolman, 1932). This implies that cognitive processes are at work, and that learning is more than the principles of operant and classical conditioning imply.

Reducing problem behaviour

Behaviourist principles can also be used to reduce problem behaviour in the classroom. The learning approach has been criticised as focusing too much on behaviour itself, and not enough on cognitive processes or on possible causes of the behaviour, such as biological ones. However, it can be useful because behaviour is often measurable and visible, and as such can be isolated and dealt with.

Behaviour therapy using classical conditioning

Sometimes responses can be changed using the principles of classical conditioning. Classical conditioning is used where reflexive responses are involved, so where education is concerned this usually refers to situations involving some level of fear and anxiety. School phobias, for example, can be dealt with by using **systematic**

desensitisation. This involves gradually getting the child used to going to school, so that eventually he or she can be fully integrated into the school day.

The idea behind systematic desensitisation is to get a child to replace their fear and anxiety with a relaxed response, so he or she is introduced to the idea of going back to school in a step-by-step manner. This might begin by approaching the school, whilst remaining relaxed, and then becoming used to being in the building. The child may then be persuaded to attend one session. As soon as the child becomes too anxious, the gradual introduction to school life is halted until the anxiety has died down and the programme can continue.

The extinction of a phobia can be achieved by using techniques like systematic desensitisation, because the existing response becomes substituted by a new one, and that means it eventually dies out. The conditioned stimulus (for example, attending school) can be paired with a pleasurable stimulus (for example, meeting friends) and the response can be altered. Using classical conditioning principles this means that the phobia can be extinguished (Table 3.2).

Table 3.2

Meeting friends	(UCS)	Pleasurable	(UCR)
Meeting friends + attending school	(UCS) + (CR)	Pleasurable	(UCR)
Attending school	(CS)	Pleasurable	(CR)

Behaviour modification using operant conditioning

Problem behaviour can also be tackled using operant conditioning principles. In these, the undesired responses are replaced by desired responses using rewards, and occasionally punishment to induce avoidance learning.

Rewards, or **positive reinforcement**, can be whatever a child would find desirable. For example, some children like to be allowed to stay with a teacher, but some would prefer to be allowed extra play time. Usually younger children prefer something direct and active, whereas older children prefer to be given more freedom and control, rather than a direct reward. An effective positive reinforcement will be one which is desirable for the child. For example, Harrop and Williams (1992) found that sending information home to parents was a powerful reinforcer for many children; but this would not necessarily be so if the child came from a disturbed or abusive family.

Punishment can also be used, in that undesired behaviour can be ignored or can be punished. In schools punishments are usually such things as keeping a child in at break time. As we have seen, punishment does not always work very well, but it is still used, and one reason is that it is easy to do. Ignoring bad behaviour and praising good behaviour takes longer – it is quicker to punish the bad behaviour. If it is used in conjunction with giving rewards for good actions, then avoiding punishment can sometimes act as negative reinforcement.

The main problem with punishment is that is does not show a child what the right behaviour is, and it can show a child that behaving aggressively is acceptable. However, O'Leary *et al.* (1970) found that private reprimands were successful if the child understands that they could have used an alternative, if feedback is consistent and specific, and if the teacher has a positive relationship with the child.

Negative reinforcement may also be used in the classroom. For example, a child may be able to escape from some negative situation, like taking extra work, by working hard in class. Avoiding punishment, too, as we have seen, may sometimes work as negative reinforcement, as may earning 'extras' like additional playtime (i.e. escape from a boring classroom) for completing a task quickly. However, too much use of negative reinforcement can mean that children feel that they have lost control of their situation, and they may try to regain it through attention-seeking behaviour.

Rather than punishment, many teachers prefer to use **time out** as a technique. Being cut off from opportunities for positive reinforcement can help to stop attention-seeking behaviour or any similar problem behaviour. There are sometimes situations where ignoring problem behaviour may be dangerous, as the child or someone else may come to harm. At those times, taking the child somewhere else for a few minutes and cutting it off from the social activities that are going on can be an effective technique.

However, a problem with using 'time out' is that it can easily become punishment. So it is necessary to be very clear to the child about what the desired behaviour is. Levy and Kahan (1991) described the 'pin down' approach where children in care were kept in their rooms for a long time. It was claimed that this was a recognised behaviour modification method, but since the children were given no clear instructions about how they were to behave in order to be allowed out of their rooms, this was not an effective technique.

Another option is to use the **Premack principle**. This is where a rewarding activity is used to set up a situation where a less rewarding activity will be carried out by the child. For example, a teacher might say to a child 'if you finish your reading, then you can go out to play'. This is a form of positive reinforcement. This is part of the RPI (rules, praise and ignoring) system (outlined below) when considering the effectiveness of behaviour modification).

Extinction is also relevant in the classroom, in that a teacher may be trying to extinguish undesired behaviour as well as encouraging desired behaviour. Ignoring undesired behaviour is a good way of extinguishing it, but the problem is that bad behaviour is hard to completely ignore. If a child is behaving badly in order to gain attention, then any frowns or glances can be reinforcing. A child's behaviour may be reinforced by teacher attention of any sort. Teachers can achieve extinction of undesired behaviour by walking away, turning away, or by paying attention to a child who is behaving correctly even when another child is behaving badly. It is, however, difficult to achieve extinction of undesired behaviour in this way, because of the power of variable reinforcement. Intermittent rewards can be more effective, and if a child finds any attention rewarding, an occasional 'telling off' can be even more reinforcing than if the teacher consistently reprimands the child.

There is also the problem that the bad behaviour will probably increase when the teacher starts ignoring it, as the child tries harder to get attention (if teacher attention is the reward). This increase in the undesired behaviour is called a 'response burst'. It soon disappears, but the teacher needs to be aware that it will happen, so that they do not give up too soon. It is also important that the teacher watches carefully for any desired behaviour and rewards it immediately, so that positive reinforcement is being used alongside ignoring the bad behaviour.

Another problem is that the teacher needs to find out what is reinforcing the bad behaviour. If it is the teacher's attention, then ignoring the bad behaviour might lead to extinction. However, if the reward comes from the child's peers, then ignoring the bad behaviour will not extinguish it. Time out might be more successful, or some other method which interrupts the source of reinforcement. It is important for a child to know exactly what they are doing wrong, and exactly what the right behaviour ought to be.

O'Leary and O'Leary (1977) reviewed various studies using behaviour modification and found that it was generally effective in schools. Following the use of behaviour modification, classroom environments demonstrated more cooperative behaviours and improvements in learning. However, it is apparent that children need clear targets and need to know what they are aiming for, and for this they need regular feedback. Many teachers have found that younger children benefit from being given stickers for good behaviour and the use of a chart to show their progress. Older children, on the other hand, do not need immediate reinforcement quite so often, and can be praised at the end of a session, for example.

Educational research has shown that regular and frequent rewards are best at first, but then it is better to reward less frequently. This may mean that the behaviour tails off for a short while, but it is likely to be more stable in the future. Madsen *et al.* (1968) devised a technique called RPI (rules, praise and ignoring) which was found to be effective by Wheldall and Glynn (1989). RPI involves firstly setting up rules in the classroom. Then the teacher praises children when the rules are followed, and ignores behaviour that breaks the rules.

It is questionable, however, whether behaviour modification of this type is purely behavioural. It does include a cognitive element, in that pupils come to expect certain rewards. This cognitive element can be made use of, and an older child can monitor their own progress. McNamara (1979) looked at the use of self-ratings with children of secondary school age and found that pupils could recognise their own weaknesses and plan improvements for themselves.

Evaluating the behavioural approach

Overall, behavioural techniques have been shown to be effective in the classroom, and the principles of classical conditioning have been used effectively to help children to get over school phobia. The behaviourist approach suggests that we can look at all behaviour by breaking actions down into small pieces and examining them carefully (this can be called a 'reductionist' approach). However, this ignores any intervening thought processes, and these are now thought to be of too much importance to be overlooked.

While behavioural techniques have been useful, researchers have become increasingly aware of the cognitive elements involved in the learning process. For example, it has been shown that children can monitor their own progress, and evaluate themselves. This involves thinking processes, and goes beyond a simple 'stimulus–response' explanation. Cognitive theories of learning involve looking at these, and we will be looking at both cognitive and cognitive–developmental theories of learning next.

Self-test

Write a timed essay, under exam conditions (or as close as you can manage) using the title 'Discuss the usefulness of the behavioural approach to learning'.

The cognitive–developmental approach to learning

The cognitive–developmental processes approach looks at how thinking develops. Theorists within this approach include Piaget, Bruner and Vygotsky. Although Piaget did not directly apply his theory to education, many other researchers did, and Piaget's theory formed important groundwork for what followed. It is Piaget's theory that is examined here.

Piaget's theory

Piaget drew attention to the ways children think. He focused on cognitive processes, and in particular the development of reasoning and logical thinking. However, his emphasis was very clearly on development, and is very different from the cognitive approach itself, which we will be looking at in the next section.

Piaget suggested that a child moves through four **developmental stages** as it develops cognitive abilities:
- At first the baby focuses on motor movements and sensory information.
- Then the child learns more about itself in relation to its environment.
- A young child finds it hard to put itself in the position of another person, and to see things from someone else's point of view. However, when the child has developed a bit more, it can see things from another person's point of view, and can deal with problem solving as long as the topic is not abstract.
- Finally, an older child can manage abstract thought and adult reasoning.

Learning is taking place throughout these stages of cognitive development. Piaget believed that we develop **schemas** (schemata) as we interact with the world. A baby's schemas are very basic, but as the baby manages to interact with the environment it assimilates new information. However, schema development is limited owing to the baby's poor control over muscles and limited physical abilities, which makes it hard for it to interact in a systematic way with the environment. As the child assimilates new information, schemas grow and are adjusted to fit it, and sometimes even sub-divide to form entirely new ones

The child's learning mainly takes the form of establishing new schemas about the world. If the existing schemas do not work, or are not enough to make sense of the child's experience, then there is a lack of (mental) equilibrium, or balance. So the child adjusts its schemas until there is a balance again – a process known as **equilibration**. Through a process of disequilibrium and restoring its mental balance, the child learns about its surroundings, including the people in the environment. The process of adjusting the schema to fit new information is called **accommodation**, and the process of absorbing new information into existing schemas is called **assimilation**. It is through these processes that a child learns, according to Piaget.

Piaget's views about building new schemas can explain some current thinking about education and learning. If young children need to learn though states of disequilibrium, and the opportunity to assimilate and accommodate new information, then they need to be surrounded by new materials and new experiences. The emphasis is on the child, who has to experience the world in order to build schemas. The child must be active in the process – passive learning will not be enough for full schema development.

↻ Recall AS material

Recall your AS material on the cognitive–developmental approach, especially Piaget's theory. If you can't remember, look it up.

Applying Piaget's ideas to teaching

The implications of Piaget's views about how a child learns – by assimilating and accommodating new information – is that education must be appropriate for the stage the child is at. A baby cannot use logical thinking processes, and is not able to take another's point of view, for example. A child in the concrete operational stage needs objects to manipulate, and should not be asked to use complex logical thinking. Young children in the pre-operational stage need materials to aid their experiences, and need to have as many varied experiences as possible, to build schemas.

Piaget's ideas about the development of cognition had a number of other implications for the teaching process. One of these was the idea that curriculum planning needed to take account of the child's stage of development, and children should not be asked to learn something they are not developmentally ready for. It was also argued that the teacher should look out for certain important periods in a child's development, for example, when a child is about to attain a certain conceptual ability. However, this does not mean the teacher should simply sit back and wait for physiological maturation to occur, even though many teachers at the time interpreted it that way.

Another implication of Piaget's theory was that work should be presented in an ordered sequence, and it is implied by Piaget's theory that a child must understand one level of reasoning before moving to the next. This also implied that teaching from around the age of 7 should start from concrete reasoning and build to abstract reasoning. The recommendations of the Nuffield Science programme and the Mathematical Association reflected the idea of using practical work before deductive work. It was also argued that active learning should be promoted by planning practical tasks. Pupils need to experience things for themselves, in concrete situations. Then they can assimilate and accommodate, and build new schemas (Figure 3.3).

Using Piagetian tasks, some researchers (e.g. Lovell, 1961) found that some pupils do not reach the formal operations stage, and argued that this should be taken into account in teaching. Although Piaget did not suggest that verbal instruction would help the learning process, and should go with the experience of the child, other researchers such as Bruner did argue that explanation helped. But Bruner's ideas were based on the work of Vygotsky, which placed far more emphasis on the importance of social interaction and guidance from adults.

Piagetian ideas became very popular in education during the 1970s and 1980s, but they eventually led to under-expectation in many schools. Subsequent re-evaluations of Piagetian theory also suggested that children's abilities had been seriously under-estimated and when the social context and the importance of adult guidance was taken into account both researchers and educationalists found that children were far more capable than had been thought, or than Piagetian theory implied.

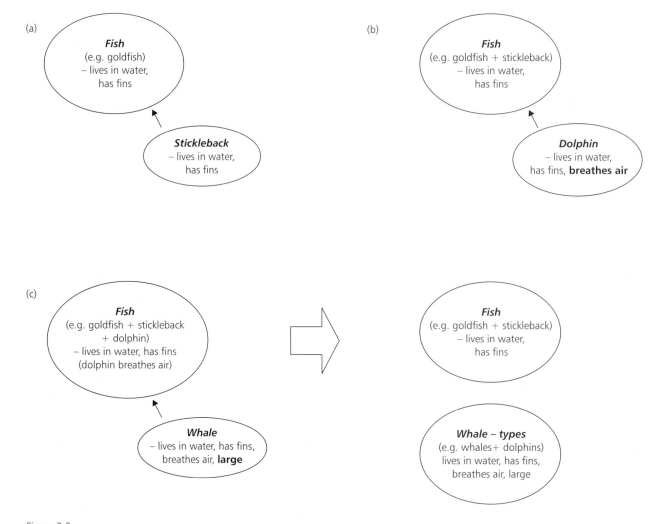

Figure 3.3
Assimilation of information (a) in a state of equilibrium, (b) in a state of disequilibrium. (c) Accommodation of information (Source: Long, 2000)

ACTIVITY

Write a brief summary of the four developmental stages proposed by Piaget. Taking each stage separately, outline its implications for the child's education.

Discovery learning

As we have seen, there are different ways of looking at learning and the psychology of education. One significant view of the learning process concerns the way that learning is not passive. Even when it comes to didactic instruction, in which the teacher instructs the pupils directly, the pupil learns only when they are active in receiving the input – when they are listening, paying attention, and making sense of the information. As attention focused on the child's cognitive development, educationalists began to perceive the active role of the pupil as a key part in the educational process.

Discovery learning is a child-centred approach, which suggests that the student should find key concepts through direct experiences. It was first developed in the 1960s, in response to the challenges presented by Piagetian theory. Bruner (1961b) suggested that students need to build their own system of understanding. Discovery learning is useful because the learning will match the child's developmental level – it will fit with the child's own developing understanding. Bruner argued that learning takes place as a spiral, with the child learning some basic concepts first then building on these basic concepts as it moves into different developmental stages, until it is able to deal with complex issues.

Piaget's theory implied that children are active when learning, and in developing their cognitive processes. The child needs to be active in order to assimilate new information, and accommodate this new information in the form of new or adjusted schemas. This implies that, for young children at least, there should be as many different experiences around as possible, because the child should experience things for itself rather than being told about them. For example, if a child was learning about history, and about the storming of castles, the young child would benefit from a model of a castle, toy soldiers, and 'weapons' to act out a siege. Model-making, visits and project work are needed for the child to actively participate, and then build new schemas. This **active learning** was a major part of the educational implications of the Piagetian approach.

The Plowden Report (1967) on primary education in Britain led to an emphasis on **child-centred education**.

The report suggested that there should be less emphasis on individual subjects in the primary curriculum, because the boundaries between subjects were not very clear in any case. It also recommended that topic approaches with active participation would mean that children were better motivated, and argued that small group work would lead to better learning because children would work together and share ideas.

Discovery learning involves induction (generalising to general laws or principles from specific cases) with the minimum of instruction. For example, a child might learn some properties of water by playing, and then generalise its findings to develop general laws about liquids. Discovery learning also involves trial and error strategies. Lots of mistakes ('errorful' learning) will be made whilst the child discovers for itself.

One well-known example of inductive discovery learning was given by Bruner (1961b). Children aged 10–12 years were given charts of North Central America showing rivers, lakes and natural resources. The children had to show where cities, railways and major roads might be situated, without using other maps or books. The children had some knowledge of geography, and had to generalise from their previous knowledge. At the end of the lesson they were shown the 'right' information on another chart, and found out their mistakes. In this way they learned that cities are founded where there is water and natural resources, and so on.

In practice, 'pure' discovery learning is rare. The teacher always has to give some input, in order to structure the knowledge that the child is acquiring. For example, in Bruner's example, the teacher provided the geographical map, and later provided the answers, so that the children could learn from their mistakes. However, there is not so much input as when direct teaching is taking place.

↻ Recall AS material

Recall or look up your AS material on the assumptions of the cognitive–developmental approach, and also the ideas of Vygotsky and Bruner, if you have studied these theorists.

Rowell *et al.* (1969) compared discovery learning with verbal instruction. They found that verbal instruction worked well, and led to better learning for students in the formal operational stage. It was thought that discovery learning meant that a child had to organise material carefully before learning, whereas in verbal instruction the organisation is already done for the child. However, they did state that discovery learning could be useful for younger children, even if verbal instruction also has merit.

In direct teaching the teacher is the source of the knowledge. Ausubel (1968) argued that teachers need to organise learning, so that the pupils can progress through structured knowledge. A teacher might, for example, give a preview, or **advanced organiser**, so that the student has a framework for their learning and the lesson is placed in context. In one recent observational study, Galton *et al.* (1999) found that teachers use a lot of direct teaching but also use questions to involve their pupils in the learning, and often direct teaching is followed by some supervised practice or experience.

It appears, therefore, that direct teaching and discovery learning can be used together with good results. Mayer (1987) carried out a review of studies which suggested that pure discovery learning can increase motivation but that the learning could be unfocused and could need a lot of time. Direct teaching takes less time, and there is good learning initially, although long-term retention is less effective than discovery learning.

As a result, and also because of an over-emphasis on discovery learning which led to fundamental skills like reading and writing becoming neglected in the primary curriculum, educationalists nowadays have moved towards **guided discovery** teaching. This combines direct teaching with discovery learning and means the teacher sets up learning situations where pupils discover the knowledge. It takes longer than direct teaching, but seems to lead to better retention in the long term. A combination approach can be good for young pupils although, as we saw earlier, Rowell *et al.* (1969) found that verbal instruction can be very effective for older students.

Evaluation

- HMI reports in the 1980s showed that subjects such as English and maths suffered when the 'topic'-based approach was introduced following the Plowden Report. The National Curriculum was introduced to make sure that basic subjects were covered by all schools. However, enquiry methods were still encouraged.
- One problem with discovery learning is identifying just what the aims of the learning are – whether the aim is for the child to learn something, or whether the aim is for the child to learn skills about how to discover.
+ The merits of discovery learning for young children are that it is thought to be more satisfying, can lead to better motivation, encourages problem-solving skills and emphasises the need for the child to take evidence into account, and not to just accept everything.

Cognitive–developmental theories, as we have seen, have led directly to different teaching methods being proposed, and have generated many policy decisions in education.

One important contribution has been the emphasis on discovery learning, and the need for the child to actively explore in order to assimilate and accommodate new information. Another important contribution has been the emphasis on maturation, and the need to take the child's developmental stage into account.

ACTIVITY

The following terms are based on the ideas of Vygotsky and Bruner. If you have studied this material, write a brief definition of each one:

- *discovery learning*
- *scaffolding*
- *reciprocal learning*
- *zone of proximal development.*

The cognitive approach to education

The cognitive approach is based on information processing, and has been used to explain cognitive development (e.g. Klahr and Wallace, 1976). The idea is that input comes into our brains via our senses. That input is then changed in some way – by being stored, or manipulated, or adjusted to fit in with existing knowledge. Following that, there may be an output of some sort. In this way we process information rather than simply receive it. It is the way that we carry out the processing which is the focus of interest in cognitive psychology.

When it comes to applying the cognitive approach to education, the main focus is on the way that memory works. Memory is a key concept in the learning process, and it is also a fundamental part of our knowledge about information processing. There has been a considerable amount of research into ways of structuring and organising information in order to facilitate memory, and also into how we go about storing memory. You are likely to have learned about this as part of your AS level work, and it has relevance here as well.

↻ Recall AS material

Recall your AS material on memory and on the assumptions of the cognitive approach, or look it up if you can't recall it.

Cognitive theories of learning

A number of researchers have explored the ways that cognitive factors influence learning. Perhaps the two most significant of these are Ausubel, who looked particularly at the role of expository or reception learning – that is, learning which has to do with receiving information from others; and Gagné, who focused particularly on the conditions of learning. We will look at both of these approaches in this section.

Ausubel's approach

Ausubel was particularly interested in the way that teachers could optimise the ways that their pupils receive information, in situations where it is the teacher who is telling them. As a result, Ausubel's work is particularly concerned with **meaningful verbal learning**, and the use of advance organisers.

Meaningful verbal learning refers to the fact that the material being imparted to students needs to make sense – that is, it must contain meaning. In order for this to happen, it needs to be related to the student's existing knowledge. This idea links with findings from memory studies, in which it has been consistently found that people are far more able to learn and remember meaningful material than nonsense syllables. Ausubel believed that an explanation from a teacher was the quickest and most effective way of giving information meaning. He did not see discovery learning as particularly useful, arguing that it was time-consuming, and meant that the students learned from their errors, which was not rewarding.

Ensuring that material is meaningful is one part of the approach, but Ausubel also emphasised the need for clear structuring of what was being imparted. One of the main techniques for doing this is through the use of **advance organisers**. These involve introducing the subject matter before the lesson begins and setting the material in a context that the student can relate to. Advance organisers are used to help to explain the important concepts, and to give meaning to the material so that the learning which results is more effective.

There are two types of advance organiser. The first is an **expository organiser** – a kind of simplified outline of the material. Ausubel argued that this is best when a teacher is presenting new material, because it 'primes' relevant schemas and establishes the appropriate kind of mental set, or readiness to receive the information. The second type of advance organiser is the **comparative organiser**, which involves drawing comparisons between the material to be presented and the student's past experiences or learning. This helps the student to perceive the relevance of the material, and to fit it with existing knowledge structures.

There has been a considerable amount of research investigating Ausubel's approach to information. For example, Mayer (1979) found that providing a structure at the start of the lesson was particularly effective when new

topics were being introduced. In fact, many of the ideas which Ausubel put forward have now become standard educational practice. You may have noticed, for example, that at the beginning of each chapter of this book there is an overview of the material to be covered – an example of the use of advance organisers.

Gagné's approach

Gagné (1965) was the other major theorist who applied the cognitive approach to teaching and learning, focusing particularly on **conditions of learning**. Gagné was particularly interested in perception, selective attention and language skills, and the way they were influenced by the conditions of learning. Gagné's emphasis on the conditions of learning, the processes of learning and the capabilities displayed after learning make this approach a clear example of an information-processing model.

Conditions of learning can be either internal or external. Internal conditions of learning, according to Gagné, are the previous learning which the student has undergone, and the processes they use to access previously learned knowledge or skills. External conditions of learning are other factors, such as the way that other people (teachers, particularly) guide the learner, the opportunities they get to rehearse or practise their learning, and motivation.

Conditions of learning are the first step in the educational process, and Gagné argued that a teacher needs to ensure that these have been properly established. The second step concerns the **events of learning** – that is, the way that information is actually taken in and processed. It includes the presentation of information verbally or in other ways, the use of activity or guided methods in the classroom, the exercises or other activities which enable students to clarify or consolidate their learning. In other words, the events of learning are all about information-processing – how the information is taken in and processed.

The third step in Gagné's approach is concerned with the **outcomes of learning** – that is, the capabilities which the student has achieved through the learning that has taken place. Gagné identified five types of learning outcome: intellectual skills; cognitive strategies; verbal information; motor skills; and attitudes. Since the main focus of education, according to Gagné, was on the acquisition of intellectual skills, the model went on to explore these in some detail.

Intellectual skills, according to Gagné, can be structured hierarchically. At the bottom of the hierarchy are the basic forms of learning – signal learning, stimulus–response learning, motor chaining, and verbal associations. As well as these basic forms, there are higher levels of intellectual skill, such as discrimination or concepts, while at the top of the hierarchy is the application of higher-order rules

Table 3.3 Gagné's hierarchy of intellectual skills

Higher-order rule learning, or problem solving	The ability to combine two or more rules to achieve a novel solution
Rule learning	Linking together two or more concepts
Concept learning	Correctly responding to groups and categories of information
Discrimination learning	The student is able to select appropriate responses to different but connected stimuli
Verbal chaining or association	When two established verbal stimulus–response associations are linked, such as when learning a foreign language
Motor chaining	The development of sensory motor skills, such as using a pen
Stimulus–response learning	Based on operant conditioning, with a stimulus becoming associated with a voluntary response
Signal learning	Based on classical conditioning, in which a signal elicits a reflexive response

and problem-solving. It was necessary, Gagné believed, for children to master the 'lower level' intellectual skills in order to progress to the higher ones. For example, a child would need a grasp of number concepts before it would be able to understand mathematical rules. Gagné's hierarchy drew on concepts from the psychology of learning, as well as on concepts from cognitive psychology. The full hierarchy is given in Table 3.3.

Gagné developed the idea of **learning task analysis**, which is a way of identifying the steps needed to obtain a specific learning outcome through a particular type of learning task (Figure 3.4). A learning task analysis involved developing a flow chart of the steps needed to achieve the outcome. The first step is to identify the learning outcomes. The next is to generate a verb to match the outcome. For example, if the teacher wants children to learn to distinguish between different types of farm animal, the verb would probably be 'discriminates'. Finally, the teacher needs to identify a task which will show that the outcome has been achieved.

Planning the flow chart is time-consuming, but it is a useful strategy when a teacher is first tackling a topic; and some aspects of learning task analysis have become well established in educational practice. You may have noticed, for example, that each chapter of this book begins with a list of the educational outcomes which you should be able to achieve on completing the chapter. This is an example of the way that some of Gagné's ideas have been put into practice (Table 3.4).

Educational research has suggested that Gagné's analysis of skill development also seems to have direct relevance for the educational process. For example, Airasian and Bart (1975) showed that students' learning does seem to follow the progression predicted by Gagné. Learning skills such as mathematics showed a progression from simple understanding to being able to use rules. The model is useful for the teaching of reading, too, in that children have to have basic understanding and familiarity with the stimuli (such as letters of the alphabet) before being able to use more complex rules.

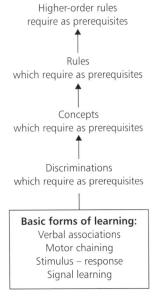

Figure 3.4
Gagné's hierarchy (source: Gagné, 1965)

ACTIVITY

Write three paragraphs on how the idea of information processing might guide teachers to improve their students' learning. Deal with a different technique or implication in each paragraph.

Table 3.4   *Illustrations from some of Gagné's learning outcomes*

Capability	Verb	Example
Intellectual skill Discrimination	Discriminates	Discriminates, by comparing outlines, the difference between oak and chestnut leaves
Concrete concept	Identifies	Identifies, by pointing, named countries on a map
Defined concept	Classifies	Classifies, by writing lists. the phyla of a given number of animal species
Rule	Demonstrates	Demonstrates, by writing down the arrangement of 'i' and 'e' after 'c'
Higher-order rule (problem solving)	Generates	Generates, by building up the steps in the arrangement, the solution to a quadratic problem
Motor skill	Executes	Executes a hand stand
Attitude	Chooses	Chooses, on leaving school, a job which does not involve manual labour

Source: Gagné (1965)

Applying the cognitive approach

Mandler (1983) suggested that the information-processing approach is stage-like, in that we discriminate by picking out information from the flow from our senses (the first stage), we see regularities in the information coming in (the second stage), and then we use problem-solving processes (the third stage). These stages, according to Mandler, are useful because they can help to explain why some people are quicker than others, for example when learning mathematics. These people may be able to discriminate, see regularities and problem-solve more efficiently than others, at least when it comes to numbers.

Other researchers, however, have challenged the stage idea. For example, Klahr (1982) argued that development is more continuous than stage-like, and that information is constantly being received and sorted by the individual. The reason for the popularity of stages was the way that Piaget's cognitive–developmental theory, as we saw above, involved stages, and many educationalists found this to be a useful way of conceptualising a child's education. But other researchers saw it as being a contentious issue, because it meant that the actual capabilities of a child were often ignored if they didn't fit perfectly into the 'stage' he or she was considered to be in.

Ausubel emphasised the need for meaning when learning, and the value of giving outlines before a lesson to help a student to link new material to old. This was a valuable contribution to educational practice. In the classroom, it seems to be most effective when new topics are introduced. But it has also been implemented in the development of educational resource material.

Gagné's contribution to educational practice was partly in the identification and structuring of intellectual skills, which enabled teachers to see more clearly what a particular task involved and which basic concepts needed to be understood before rules could be applied. The most influential contribution, however, was the idea of learning task analysis, allowing learning outcomes to be set and evaluated, so a teacher can see what learning has occurred. This also formed the basis for the modern educational use of learning and assessment objectives.

Cognitive theories may be criticised as neglecting other approaches to learning – for example, there is no mention of the use of praise or punishment. But, on the other hand, the learning approach makes no mention of cognitive factors. If we are to achieve a full understanding of the educational process we need to be able to draw on all three approaches – the learning approach, the cognitive–developmental approach and the cognitive approach.

Self-test

Write a timed essay, under exam conditions (or as close as you can manage) using the title 'Discuss the usefulness of the cognitive approach to education'.

Factors affecting student performance

There are many factors that can influence how students perform in the classroom. As we have seen above, the approach to teaching and learning can make a difference, but there are individual variables as well, which all have their effect. Some of these are to do with the teacher – the teaching style they use, and their attitudes and expectations. Others are to do with the student, and in particular the cognitive and learning styles they adopt in the classroom. In this section we will look at how these psychological factors can have an impact on the educational process.

Teacher variables

Student learning can be affected by issues such as whether programmed learning or discovery learning is the chosen method of instruction, but it can also be affected by individual teachers and the way that they go about their task. For example, teachers vary in the style of teaching they adopt with their class, and this can influence student performance. They also have different expectations and attitudes towards their students, and this can lead to labelling and stereotyping. The action of the self-fulfilling prophecy can mean that these have a dramatic effect on the student's performance and subsequent achievement.

Teaching style

There are two different ways of looking at teaching style. One way is to consider the classroom setting and the style the teacher prefers to use in class; the other way is to look at the teacher's own learning or cognitive style. We will be looking at learning/cognitive styles when we look at student variables, but they also apply to teachers and the way that they approach information.

Effectively, there are two main **classroom teaching styles**. One style – the **didactic style** – tends to be teacher-centred, and often involves a fairly formal approach in which the focus is on the subject matter that must be delivered. The other – the **student-centred style** – tends to be more informal, and is generally focused on learning skills rather than on the subject matter. These two styles are outlined below but it is important to remember that they are very general categories. The classification 'didactic', for example, covers 'formal', 'direct' and 'whole class' teaching; while the 'student-centred' classification covers 'progressive', 'discovery' and 'group work'. In practice, of course, most teachers use a combination of styles depending on the requirements of their situation.

Comparing didactic and student-centred styles

A number of dimensions can be used to identify or compare didactic and student-centred styles. One of these is whether the approach is **formal** or **progressive**. Formal teaching tends to be teacher-directed and didactic. Progressive teaching, on the other hand, emphasises discovery in learning and some freedom to explore.

Another dimension is whether the teacher's style favours **discovery learning** or **direct teaching**. A progressive style tends to favour discovery learning, which is also child-centred. The pupil is an active independent learner, and the use of discovery learning is matched with the child's developmental stage. Direct teaching is where the teacher provides the knowledge and facts are focused upon. But there is still an emphasis on matching the teaching to the developmental stage of the child, through the use of structuring techniques such as Ausubel's advance organisers, and setting the material in context.

Bruner (1961) criticised didactic teaching, on the grounds that it would not enable a pupil to apply knowledge to a new situation. He argued that student-centred learning encourages children to build their own understanding structures, so that they can apply understanding to novel situations. Others, however, have argued in favour of direct teaching. Mayer (1987) suggested that using the discovery approach does motivate pupils, but takes quite a lot of time and can be unfocused. Direct teaching does not need so much time and learning is good at the start, although in the long term retention of the knowledge can be poor and transfer of learning is not good. On the other hand, if direct teaching is unstructured, and the teacher is giving facts without links to previous knowledge, then direct teaching is not very effective.

Overall, it seems that a combination of direct and progressive teaching styles can be beneficial. Guided discovery is the term for combining direct and student-centred styles. The teacher sets up the situation where discovery takes place.

As we saw earlier in the chapter Rowell *et al.* (1969) found that with older students direct verbal instruction lead to quick learning and good retention. But direct teaching isn't necessarily as arbitrary as its critics have suggested. Galton *et al.* (1999) found that teachers who use direct teaching also check their students' knowledge by means of questions. This questioning ensures that students are engaged in the learning process. Also, after the direct instruction, students would be given tasks to use to practice their knowledge, and to help the teacher check their learning.

Whole-class or small group styles

A third dimension for comparing didactic and student-centred styles is whether they involve whole-class or small-group work. As a general rule, didactic styles tend to involve whole-class work, while student-centred styles tend to involve small groups – although this isn't inevitably the case. Small groups can be chosen by ability or selected to cooperate and investigate, depending on the subject the students are learning. In maths, for example, selecting groups by ability can be a useful strategy, as children of similar ability are more able to work together. Whether group work is successful can depend on how the groups are formed, as well as on the subject being taught.

Brophy and Evertson (1976) found that whole-class lessons gave better results. Whole-class style meant that the teacher presented the material to the whole class, and then individuals practised the work. However, Good and Grouws (1977) found that to be successful whole-class teaching needed to be well managed, with clear instruction, moving at a good pace, and involving students actively by means of question and answer sessions. A problem with whole-class teaching is that some students opt out, and it can be difficult for a teacher to notice this (Galton *et al.*, 1999).

Certainly for secondary education, whole-class teaching is often effective. Reynolds and Farrell (1996) have found that countries that use whole-class teaching methods often have better results; but the problem with this sort of study is that the whole culture is different. For example, countries around the Pacific Rim have a more 'cooperative' culture, whereas in the UK there is more emphasis on the individual, so small-group work will have different educational and personal significance in the two countries.

Bennett and Dunne (1989) found that 88% of the discussions children had when working in small groups were about the task they were undertaking – the children in the groups were closely involved in what they were doing. Mixed-ability groups also seem to work well, for both the children of lower ability and those of higher ability. So group work does seem to be effective. However, cooperative work means a lot of preparation for the teacher and has to be well organised, so busy teachers tend to choose individual learning methods.

The emphasis on Piagetian approaches to education and the influence of the Plowden report meant that most primary education in the 1980s tended to be small group work. However, an influential paper by Alexander *et al.* (1992) suggested that there were disadvantages to using this method of teaching exclusively. They argued that whole-class teaching in primary education could also be effective, and should become part of the school day.

Galton *et al.* (1999) reported that primary teachers in the UK had responded to the paper by increasing whole-class teaching from 15.1% of the time to 31.3% over a four-year period. The rest of the time, however, was still spent on group work, and teachers reported many benefits from combining the two teaching styles and so varying the children's experience of learning.

Aronson *et al.* (1978) developed the idea of the **jigsaw classroom**, where the class is divided into groups and each group is given part of the whole topic. The idea is that each group has to find out about its part of the assignment, and then the groups feed back to build the whole 'answer'. It was found that those with different abilities were able to help each other, and the children also mixed well socially.

Effectiveness of teaching style

Evaluating different teaching styles is not easy, because there are so many variables involved. For example, younger teachers are said to use a more progressive style. If an evaluation attempts to compare progressive style with formal style using a sample of teachers who habitually adopt each one, then any differences they find might not be due to the style, but to the length of teaching experience.

Nonetheless, some educational researchers have undertaken evaluation studies. For example, Bennett (1976) carried out a questionnaire study of 468 primary school teachers, and identified 12 different teaching styles, with most teachers using a combination of formal and informal approaches. A comparison of the 12 most formal classes with 13 of the most informal ones showed that children generally do better in maths, reading and English if the teacher style is formal, teacher-centred and subject-oriented than if they are in a child-centred, discovery-oriented setting.

This also depends on the individual teacher. The researchers found that one of the most informal classes, for example, showed the highest gains in mathematics, reading and English. This teacher monitored the children's progress closely and structured their learning experiences carefully, and the researchers suggested that it might have been the high structure and close monitoring which gave the gains, rather than the formal or informal teaching style. It is possible, too, that a formal style usually means more structure and closer monitoring, which might account for the more general result.

Some subjects seemed to be unaffected by teacher style. Bennett found that creative activities such as story writing were not affected by the formality of the classroom setting. But some styles seemed to suit particular children more – for example, insecure children seemed to work harder in a formal classroom setting.

Bennett's findings suggested that structure was what really counted, regardless of whether the classroom teaching style was formal or informal. Tasks need to be planned, and the teacher needs to be sure that students are attending to the task at hand. Structuring of the learning is also needed, in the sense of linking what is to be learned with previous understanding.

Although most educationalists would agree with these conclusions, there have been some criticisms of Bennet's findings, and in particular of the conclusions drawn from the data. There was also some criticism of the method, in that some researchers suggested that more capable children had been in the formal class groupings. Aitkin *et al.* (1981) reviewed Bennett's data and found that with re-grouping of the classes, informal styles did not produce results that were particularly different from formal styles.

Mixing styles

The ORACLE project (Observational Research and Classroom Learning Evaluation) which was carried out at Leicester University during the late 1970s also looked at classroom teaching styles (Galton and Simon, 1980). The findings suggested that teachers used four main styles:

- **Individual monitors** – The teacher monitors the pupil's work, tells the pupil what to do, and does not ask many questions.
- **Class enquirers** – Questioning is seen as important. Teachers walk amongst the pupils asking and answering questions.
- **Group instructors** – There is a lot of transfer of information from teacher to pupil. Teachers structure group work and then discuss the material.
- **Style changers** – Half of all teachers were found to be style changers. Style changers spend more time hearing pupils read, and they make more statements controlling the tasks and asking questions. The ORACLE project identified three types of style changer. One type, an **infrequent changer**, is ready to change style if circumstances demand, but does not do so automatically. **Rotating changers** set up different tasks and groups of pupils moved from one task to another. **Habitual changers** swapped between instructing the whole class and instructing individuals without having any particular plan or system to the changes.

Overall, the research project found that teachers using the class enquirer style seemed to get better results with mathematics and languages, whereas infrequent changers seemed to get better reading results, while rotating changers seemed to get the worst results overall.

What all this seems to add up to is that different styles are appropriate for different situations. They are also of different value, depending on the subject being taught. Some subjects seem to be learned well if a direct style is used, while other subjects benefit from a progressive style. Most teachers, as we have seen, use a mixture of styles rather than one, which appears to be by far the best kind of strategy

Self-test

Write a timed essay, under exam conditions (or as close as you can manage) using the title 'Discuss the possible effects of two teaching styles on student performance'.

Teacher attitudes and expectations

Another important teacher variable comes from the attitude of the teacher towards his or her students. Teacher expectations have been shown to have an effect on the learning and development of an individual, as the result of several different psychological processes, including the self-fulfilling prophecy, labelling, and stereotyping. We looked at all of these processes in Chapter 2, but they have relevance for the psychology of education as well as in criminological psychology.

The self-fulfilling prophecy

The idea of the self-fulfilling prophecy became widely recognised as a result of a study by Rosenthal and Jacobson, in 1968. All the children in a particular school were tested by researchers at the start of a school year. The test used was the Harvard Test of Inflected Acquisition, and teachers were told that it was a special test that could detect unrecognised academic potential. The researchers then selected 20% of the children. They didn't talk directly to the teachers, but deliberately allowed them to overhear a conversation in the staff room between the researchers doing the project. During the conversation, the children they had selected were named as being 'late bloomers', and, according to the test, likely to show a sudden spurt in achievement during the forthcoming year. In fact, the children had been chosen randomly, and the test results had not been used at all.

At the end of the school year, the children were tested again, and those who had been predicted as 'late bloomers' had improved considerably. As they had been chosen randomly, the researchers concluded that the teacher had communicated to the chosen children in some way that they were expected to improve. The teacher's expectations seem to have led each child to try harder; and this increased effort was sustained by the increased attention they received from their teacher. This idea, that a statement comes true simply because it has been made, is known as the **self-fulfilling prophecy**.

There were some criticisms of the study. For example, Claiborn (1969) replicated the study and did not find the same results, arguing that this showed that the results were simply a product of the experimental situation. Snow (1969) suggested that the design of the study was weak. The teachers themselves tested the children at the end of the year, and Snow argued that their expectations might have somehow biased the results. It was also claimed that the tests were unreliable, although they had undergone the same rigorous development process as other psychometric tests, so this does not seem to be a particularly valid argument. Other researchers concluded that many of the challenges to the Rosenthal findings came from educationalists who did not want to recognise just how influential a teacher's attitudes and expectations could be in the classroom.

Expectations don't just apply to individuals. Sometimes, they apply to whole social groups, and many educationalists see the under-achievement of children from ethnic minorities as influenced by negative attitudes towards their group. In an investigation of this, a teacher suggested to a class that children with brown eyes were the least able in the class. The teacher and the other children then treated those with brown eyes as if they were of lower ability. The brown-eyed children stopped trying and became very resentful. They were very negative about class work. Then the teacher changed the criteria, and this time it was those with blue eyes who were described as being less capable. They also stopped trying to work, and became very negative, while the brown-eyed children, who were now receiving all of the attention and help from the teacher, blossomed.

This is an example of the self-fulfilling prophecy. The self-fulfilling prophecy means that when something is expected of an individual by others it becomes true, because of how the individual is treated. The blue-eyed children really did under-achieve in their school work, and become less confident in their learning, as a result of how they were treated by the teacher and the rest of the class. When they were treated as lacking ability, the children paid less attention, learned less, and would have become less able if the experiment had continued. The study was shown in a film called *The Eye of the Storm*, which illustrated just how important teacher expectations about social groups can be to educational achievement.

↻ *Recall AS material*

Recall your AS material from the social approach, particularly material on prejudice – or look it up.

Labelling

In Chapter 2 we saw how labelling can influence deviance and criminal behaviour. The same process can happen in education – as we have seen, through the actions of the self-fulfilling prophecy, someone who has been labelled as unintelligent by others may become less intelligent, as measured by school achievement or IQ tests. Becker (1963) argued that a label is not neutral, but always contains an evaluative element; and it has a 'master status', which means that it overrides other social characteristics. For example, someone might have many social roles such as parent or worker, but if they are labelled 'deviant' then this label will override the others. In the same way, getting the label of deviant in the classroom can override all other characteristics.

A label has special importance. Negative teacher expectations often come from labelling; and labelling almost always leads to stereotyping. If someone has been labelled, the tendency is to assume that they also have all the other characteristics that go with the label. If it is powerful enough, it can also affect the person's self-concept, in that they may come to see themselves in terms of the label. For example, children labelled as troublemakers in class may come to see themselves as troublemakers, and cause trouble as part of living up to that label.

One way in which teachers can label children is through their language use. Bernstein (1961) proposed that working-class children use a restricted language code, in which the immediate context is referred to, and language is simplified. He suggested that middle-class children, on the other hand, use elaborated codes, which have more complex grammar structures, and involve more use of abstract ideas. A child using elaborated code, when describing a picture, for example, goes beyond the immediate context, and elaborates, which is the sort of activity that is desired and reinforced by the educational process. Language codes are learned at home, but Bernstein argued that these different language codes meant that some children – that is, middle-class ones – were better equipped to take advantage of educational opportunities.

Labelling a child according to their language use is a form of stereotyping. There is no evidence to suggest that those using restricted code are less intelligent (Stones, 1984); but teachers can often construe it that way, because less verbal children may not respond to the teacher in the way that is desired. Labov (1972) argued that restricted code is just as powerful in its own way, and not inferior to elaborated code – it is like using a dialect, and should not be seen as inferior. However, labelling by language code can mean that a teacher expects less of a child using restricted language – and, as we have seen, lower expectations can lead to lower achievement.

Stereotyping

Stereotyping involves applying generalised information to form judgements about people, regardless of their individual qualities. When teaching a pupil for the first time, a teacher is likely to draw on whatever information they have available in order to process new information and link it with their previous knowledge. They may use their ideas about gender, race and parental occupation when building expectations of a new pupil. And the actions of the self-fulfilling prophecy mean that these ideas are not likely to change, as they will be reinforced by the child's response to its treatment.

Teacher expectations arise from previous contact with other students, as well as previous knowledge about individuals. So a teacher is likely to draw on information about a sibling or relative in an earlier class when making judgements about a new child. Records and comments from other teachers also affect how a teacher views a pupil. Baker and Crist (1971) show that the higher the academic achievement of an older sibling, the higher the academic achievement of a younger sibling, if they both had the same teacher (Figure 3.5). This connection, however, does not happen if the two siblings had different teachers. This suggests that teachers transfer the expectations they have of an older sibling onto the younger sibling, with a clear effect on academic achievement.

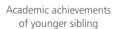

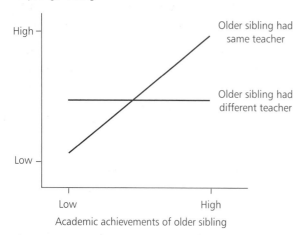

Figure 3.5
How teacher expectations based on the achievements of an older sibling can affect the achievements of the younger child (Source: Long, 2000; based on Baker and Crist, 1971)

Rogers (1982) suggested that there are four stages for teacher expectations influencing the child's performance.
• Firstly, the teacher forms an impression of the child, from which expectations are derived. This can often involve labelling and stereotyping, although it may be based on personal dislikes as well.
• Secondly, the teacher's behaviour is affected by the expectations.
• Thirdly, the child consciously or unconsciously recognises the expectations of the teacher.
• Fourthly, the child's behaviour starts to match the expectations, and the negative prophecy made by the teacher about the child's low capability is fulfilled.

Evaluation

• Rosenthal (1985) suggested that teacher effects are only 3% of the overall factors that affect student achievement. However, expectations can last a long time, and have a long-term effect, and many researchers would set the figure much higher. Brophy and Good (1974) reviewed the findings of studies looking at teacher expectations and found that overall teacher expectations did affect student achievement, while Brattesanti *et al.* (1984) argued that the main effect comes from the way that teacher expectations influence students' own self-concepts. They found that 12% of the factors that account for a student's expectations about their own performance could be attributed to teacher expectations.

• Expectations can be positive too, and when they are they can make just as much difference in the other direction. Rutter *et al.* (1979) showed how higher expectations with regard to a student's achievements lead to higher academic achievement. However, there is always an interaction between expectations and other factors. Just expecting more of a student will not inevitably lead to higher academic achievement: it is the way that high expectations are linked to other educational factors, such as better explanations and more patience with student difficulties, which enable children to acquire the educational skills and knowledge required for high achievement.

ACTIVITY

Use the explanations of stereotyping you learned for AS level to show how teachers might use stereotypes when making judgements about students.

Student variables

Learnng is affected by student variables as well as by the style or attitudes of the teacher. One of the ways that students vary is in their choice of learning style. It is claimed, for example, that learning is better if the student's learning style matches the teacher style. In this section we will look at some of the different learning styles that have been identified, and how they may manifest in the educational context. We will begin this by looking at those aspects of learning styles which are specifically to do with cognition, and are therefore often described as **cognitive styles**.

Cognitive styles

Effectively, cognitive style refers to the way a person processes information. There are a number of different ways that people go about processing information, and researchers have identified a number of dimensions, which we will look at briefly in this section. As a general rule, cognitive styles tend to be described as 'either–or' pairs – someone may be said to have either a focusing or a scanning style, for example. This is partly because of the way that research into cognitive styles tends to be carried out, because it involves contrasting the ways that different people tackle cognitive tasks. But as with most of these simple distinctions, many people use a mixture of the two styles in practice.

Field–dependence

One way of considering cognitive style is to separate those who demonstrate **field-dependence** from those who demonstrate **field-independence**. Those who see their surroundings as a whole are called 'field-dependent', while those who habitually separate figures from backgrounds and focus on the figures themselves are called 'field-independent' (Witkin, 1965). For example, if you are more likely to notice the person as standing out from their background as in a photograph, then you are demonstrating field-independence. Witkin believed that those who can easily separate figure from background when perceiving, are also likely to use a 'field-independent' strategy when processing information intellectually.

Field-dependence versus field-independence has also been referred to as global versus articulated. Those who use a **global style** are field-dependent, and those who use an **articulated style** are field-independent. Vernon (1969) suggested from research that field-independent people are better at maths, science and spatial tasks, and also tend to be more self-sufficient, assertive and independent thinkers.

> ## ACTIVITY
>
> *It is possible to test field-dependence by asking people to study photographs and find out if they notice background or if they focus more on the 'figure'. A good way of doing this is to pick a set of photographs in which there are clear figures in the foreground, and distinctive features in the background. Many holiday snaps are like this. Develop a set of questions, some of which ask about the foreground, and some of which ask about the background. Two questions for each photograph should be enough. Show someone the photographs, then ask them to answer the questions, without looking at the photos again. Their answers will tell you whether they remember the foreground or the whole picture more clearly.*
>
> *You could follow this up with a questionnaire looking at maths or science abilities, or assertiveness.*

Impulsivity may also be a cognitive style. If a person habitually makes decisions in an impulsive fashion – that is, quickly and without weighing things up – then they may be using an **impulsive style**. If, however, someone tends to weigh things up and think carefully about the accuracy of their answers, they may be showing a **reflective style** (Kagan, 1971). Kagan argued that the reflective style is characteristic of someone who takes an analytical approach to problem solving.

Another cognitive style is to do with seeing the complete picture from the outset, or preferring to build it up from smaller pieces. Those who like to see things as a whole are called **holists** and those who prefer putting things into sequence and building up a complete picture gradually are called **serialists** (Pask; cited by Child, 1999). This is very obvious in the classroom – some students prefer to have an overview of the whole thing when they are beginning a new topic – taking a holistic approach – whereas others prefer to learn things step-by-step – that is, using a serialist approach.

Convergent and divergent thinking

Guilford (1959) identified a significant distinction between convergent and divergent thinking. Effectively, **convergent thinkers** like to focus in on problems, so they are good at dealing with problems that have a single solution, which can be found from the information available. Other people have more wide-ranging ways of thinking, and they are more able to deal with problems

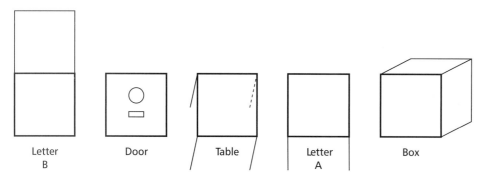

Figure 3.6
Some answers to the 'squares test' of divergent thinking. Those being tested needed to come up with ideas of what a square could represent (Source: Child, 1997)

requiring novel or creative approaches. They are known as **divergent thinkers**. A divergent thinker is good at problems where there is more than one possible solution, or where more than one answer is required.

Hudson (1966) argued that the education system tends to favour convergent thinkers rather than divergent ones. For example, intelligence tests typically only have one right answer to each item, and require straight-line logical thinking, of the sort that convergent thinkers are good at. But even though divergent thinkers are good at open-ended problems, and can generate a lot of good ideas, they may appear to be less capable than they really are, because there are no items on intelligence tests which would enable those skills to be used.

Focusing and scanning

One of the first cognitive styles to be identified is to do with the way that people formulate hypotheses when they are trying to solve problems. Bruner *et al.* (1956) showed how some people like to gather as much evidence as possible before formulating a hypothesis about a problem. This approach was named **focusing**. Other people adopt a **scanning** approach, which involves forming a hypothesis very quickly, and then looking for evidence to test it.

Bruner *et al.* found that using a scanning approach can sometimes mean that the person reaches a solution quickly, but that it can also be time-consuming if some evidence is missed out, or the hypothesis has to be abandoned because it is wrong. Focusing is likely to be more accurate in the long run, but can take longer. The same applies in the classroom, where pupils using a focusing approach may take too long to decide on a solution, while the scanners rush in too quickly and are often inaccurate.

Learning styles

Educationalists often use the terms learning style and cognitive style as if they were completely interchangeable.

While this is largely true in practice, there are slight differences between them. For example, a learning style is particularly concerned with a person's approach to problem-solving or to tackling learning tasks, whereas a cognitive style has to do with a person's characteristic ways of perceiving information, and their thinking strategies. Cognitive style may be part of a person's learning style, but learning style also has an affective element, concerned with the person's feelings and emotions. But often cognitive styles are referred to as learning styles, and the distinction is not really a crucial one.

Kirton (1976) distinguished between **adaptors** and **innovators** in the classroom. The differences between the two styles are summed up in Table 3.5. Effectively, what Kirton discovered is that adaptors tend to go about tasks in an orthodox way, using tried and tested methods; while innovators are more likely to think laterally and focus on the overall goal they have to reach, which means that they may adopt entirely unorthodox methods for reaching it. Kirton claimed that whether a person is an adaptor or an innovator is not linked to intelligence, but is a way of going about learning – a learning style. Adapting or innovating are ways of tackling problems, rather than showing any special ability.

Another way of looking at learning style is to consider cultural effects. Some cultures emphasise cooperation, and students have the whole group in mind with regards to achievement, for example. Other cultures emphasise competitive learning, where the individual is supposed to succeed, and is in competition with others in the group. This difference in emphasis between **competitive learning** and **cooperative learning** has been said to affect whether the teaching style adopted by the class teacher is likely to lead to successful learning or not.

For example, around the Pacific Rim, most cultures have a cooperative emphasis, whereas Western countries place emphasis on individual achievement. Reynolds and Farrell

Table 3.5 Comparing adaptors and innovators

Adaptors	Innovators
Precise, reliable, efficient	Think laterally, undisciplined
Focus on the means of achieving as well as the goal	Focus on the goal, not the means
Use tried and tested ways of solving problems	Manipulate problems
Have high self-doubt and are conformist	Have low self-doubt and generate ideas
Sound and dependable	Impractical and unsound

(1996) showed that whole-class teaching in countries where cooperation is emphasised leads to very high educational attainment and standards. Caplan *et al.* (1992) showed that individuals who emigrated from South-East Asia to the USA did very well in educational terms, even though they had poor language skills and had to adjust to a different culture. It appeared that it was family support and the family's emphasis on the need to succeed that led to these children doing well at school. In the USA the children did well because emphasis was on them to succeed as individuals.

The researchers' conclusion was that teaching style tends to suit the needs of the culture. If the culture emphasises cooperation, then a whole-class teaching style might be the best. If, however, the culture emphasises competition between individuals, then active learning by the individual might be the best. This conclusion is a bit simplistic, but shows that cultural factors need to be taken into account.

Another way of looking at individual and cooperative learning is to look at differences between individuals rather than between cultures. Whole-class teaching has been compared with group work, and it could be said that whole-class teaching leaves the individual to learn alone, whereas group work needs cooperative learning. This may have different effects, and we explored some of the issues earlier in this chapter. Johnson and Johnson (1987), for example, suggested that cooperative learning, that is learning with other students, can be successful. Galton *et al.* (1999), however, found that most of the time children worked independently, and worked cooperatively for only 13.5% of the time. Much of classroom work is competitive too, so cooperation is even less likely.

Effects of learning style

It is clear that learning or cognitive styles can have a considerable effect on a learner's achievement, depending on the tasks the learners are being asked to do. For example, divergent thinkers are best if a problem has lots of solutions and the aim is to generate a lot of useful suggestions. If accuracy is desired, then a reflective thinker may be best. Similarly, if someone is a holistic thinker, then they need an overview and a framework in order to learn. However, if someone thinks in a serialist way, then lists and a step-by-step approach may be more useful.

However, the style of the learner is only part of the picture. Teacher style is also important, and the two can interact. For example, Joyce and Hudson (1968) have looked at whether medical students were convergent or divergent thinkers. Their findings suggested that examination results were better for those students whose learning style matched the teacher's style. Also, as we have seen, the classroom teaching style is important as well. So it is clear that any single style on its own isn't what matters – it is how the whole set of styles, and the task's requirements, fit together that matters.

Self-test

Write a timed essay, under exam conditions (or as close as you can manage), using the title 'Discuss the effectiveness of two learning/cognitive styles'.

Assessment

There are many factors to do with assessment, and many different types of educational assessment have been studied and evaluated. We have touched on some of them already, such as the use of assessment objectives in teaching. However, in this section we will look at only a few aspects of educational assessment – at the question of assessing intelligence; at issues of bias in assessment, and at the assessment of special needs in education.

Assessing intelligence

One of the major issues in educational assessment has been the question of intelligence. On the surface, it seems like a very straightforward issue: surely those who are more intelligent are likely to do better in education? But when we try to pin down what that idea actually means in practice, things get a bit more difficult. Some problems come up when we try to define exactly what we mean by intelligence; others come up when we try to develop ways of testing intelligence; and a third set of questions is raised by social bias and other issues. We will look at that last set of questions in the next section but here we will look at some of the issues raised by attempts to define and test intelligence.

Defining intelligence

Intelligence was described by Heim (1970) as 'grasping the essentials of a situation and responding to them appropriately', which sums up most of what it seems to be about, although this definition is perhaps a little too vague to be of much practical use when it comes to assessment.

In 1960 Vernon argued that intelligence is probably best thought of as intelligent behaviour rather than as some kind of mental quality. He suggested that it has a biological, a psychological and an operational side. The biological side to intelligence seems to be a capacity to adapt to environmental stimuli. This fits with the ideas of other researchers. For example, Hebb thought that intelligence was linked to neurological connections in the brain, and believed that high intelligence resulted from having a good (well-exercised) brain and central nervous system.

The psychological side to intelligence refers to mental efficiency, and ability to undertake abstract reasoning. The operational side to intelligence is where intelligent behaviour must be operationalised in order to test it and measure it. Operationalising in this context refers to means identifying examples of intelligent behaviour which can be measured.

> ### Synoptic Note
>
> Issues about methodology are needed for Unit 6, the synoptic part of the course. Operationalisation of variables is such a methodological issue.

Types of intelligence

Several theorists have argued that there is more than one type of intelligence. For example, Hebb suggested that

intelligence A is the intelligence of the genotype, the genetic part, representing our innate potential. *Intelligence B*, on the other hand, is the phenotype, the intelligence we actually develop – a combination of the potential (intelligence A) and the effects of learning and environment.

It is impossible to measure intelligence A, as this is only genetic potential. It is also difficult to measure intelligence B with any certainty, because intelligence B changes as we proceed through life, and as our experiences change us. Vernon suggested that, really, all we can measure is *intelligence C*, which is the part of intelligence B that intelligence tests sample. Intelligence C, in other words, is what we measure using intelligence tests; but we would be seriously misled to think that this accounts for the whole of someone's intelligence.

So tests do not measure the whole of intelligence. They measure intelligence C, which is a sample of our genetic capabilities after interaction with the environment. Depending on the theoretical model on which the test is based, the version of intelligence C which is assessed can include a number of different abilities. As a general rule, most intelligence tests include verbal reasoning, spatial reasoning, and non-verbal reasoning, but some have a wider range of other kinds of tasks; and some limit themselves to just one or two types of task which seem to be indicative of intelligence in some way.

But there is also uncertainty as to what intelligence consists of. Some researchers suggest, for example, that creative writing should be a measure of intelligence, while others consider musical and artistic abilities to be part of what is called intelligence. Gardner (1990) proposed that there are actually six different kinds of human intelligence: linguistic, logical–mathematical, spatial, musical, bodily–kinaesthetic, and personal. If we were really to develop effective intelligence testing, Gardner argued, we would need to assess each of these separately, using appropriate tests, some of which would be very different from the existing ones.

Measuring intelligence, then, is a challenge, and one which many people prefer to side-step. The problem is that we can never be quite sure exactly what is being measured by any particular test; and we can always think of kinds of intelligence that are not sampled by tests. But nonetheless, many researchers use IQ – the score obtained from intelligence tests – as a measure of intelligence in their research, and most researchers in this area tend to fall back on the operational definition that intelligence is what intelligence tests measure.

ACTIVITY

Operational definitions are an important part of the research process. In your coursework, for example, you will have carried out a study that required you to operationalise your variables. This means you had to choose to study something, such as prejudice, and then find a way of measuring it. Write a paragraph explaining what operationalisation means, and then two more paragraphs, one outlining the advantages of operationalisation and the other outlining its disadvantages.

IQ testing

Intelligence tests began with the work of Binet, in France, in order to identify children who needed additional educational support. However, they quickly became used as 'gatekeepers' – for educational access, immigration, and a number of other purposes. In recent times, intelligence tests are sometimes used to select personnel for jobs, and they are still sometimes used to select children for certain types of education.

Binet (1905) (Figure 3.7) devised tests to select those children who would not benefit from normal school education, so that they could be provided with specialist schooling. He did this by developing test items that 75% of children in a certain age group could answer. The middle 50% in terms of ability would be able to solve the problems, and so would the top 25%, so 75% can succeed. So the test could be used to identify children who were below the **norm** – the 25% of children who were not able to complete the various test items for their particular age group.

Binet's test was **standardised**, which means that the questions were tested on many children of different age groups. If 75% of children of a certain age succeeded at one set of tasks, those tasks were said to be the right level for that age group. Binet used a variety of different types of test items, such as naming parts of the body or identifying rhyming words, which children of different ages could usually manage. Then he tested children on the tasks, and refined them, until they gave consistent typical results for each age group.

This led to the idea of **mental age**. If a child could succeed at tasks standardised for seven, eight and nine-

year-olds, but not those for ten-year-olds, then it was said that that child's mental age was 9. But mental age, Binet argued, didn't depend on physical age. A child could have a chronological age (their actual age) of 13 and a mental age of 9. Or a chronological age which was lower than their mental age, if they were particularly bright.

The idea of mental age led to the idea that it would be possible to describe the relationship between a child's mental age and its chronological age using a single figure. Stern developed the idea of the IQ score, which would be a child's mental age divided by its chronological age. If the two were the same, then the child's score would be 1. But Terman proposed multiplying the answer by 100, to make the numbers easier to handle. So if a 9-year old (chronological age) had a mental age of 9, instead of an IQ of 1, the IQ would be 100. This is the formula used today.

$$IQ = \frac{\text{Mental age}}{\text{Chronological age}} \times 100$$

Figure 3.7
Alfred Binet

Evaluation

- The concept of IQ based on mental age can apply only to developing children. Standardised tests are only reliable up to the age of around 15 years. Mental development after that age is less regular, so different criteria have to be used when developing tests for older people. Weschler developed a test of adult intelligence which included performance measures as well as verbal tests, and which was commonly used for this purpose to establish standards for testing people of all age groups.

Some IQ tests

Binet's IQ test for children rapidly became accepted, with a version known as the Standford–Binet becoming widely used in the English-speaking world. Since that time, IQ tests have been updated, but the basic idea behind IQ testing has remained the same.

Binet's test was an individual one, involving several tasks to be administered to the child taking the test; and this pattern is also followed in some modern IQ tests, such as the British Ability Scales or the Wechsler intelligence tests for children or for adults. These individual ability tests give detailed results, which can also be used for diagnosis, and as a result many of them are closed tests – that is, they can be used only by suitably trained and qualified professionals. For example, the Weschler Intelligence Scale for Children (WISC) is a closed test that has both verbal and performance subtests. The profile of results it gives can often be an indicator of more subtle disorders such as dyslexia, but these have to be interpreted by trained professionals, who will understand fully what the test profile means.

Many IQ tests, however, are group tests, which can be given to several people at the same time. The AH test series is popular for this purpose, and there are different versions depending on the characteristics of the population being tested. College graduates, for example, would need a slightly different kind of IQ test than adults who had been out of the educational system for many years. Table 3.6 gives some typical test items.

There are other types of group test too. For example, SATs (Scholastic Aptitude Tests) are now used in all UK schools to measure whether the school is coming up to scratch, and they are also taken to indicate a child's progress. The 11+ examination, which used to be used in the UK to determine the type of secondary schooling a child should receive, was a combination of maths and English tests, combined with a general IQ test. Its results were thought to indicate whether a child would benefit most from the practically oriented education provided by secondary modern schools, the more academically oriented education provided by grammar school, or (in some areas) the technically oriented education provided by the technical grammars.

Some tests are more specialised. For example, the British Picture Vocabulary Scale is a specific test for language, which investigates it by asking for responses to different pictures (Dunn *et al.*, 1997); and the Effective Reading Tests (1985) provide diagnostic information about a child's reading competences. Other IQ tests concentrate entirely on non-verbal abilities. One of the most commonly used examples of the latter is the Raven's Progressive Matrices test (Raven, 1993) (Figure 3.8). This test can be administered to groups or individuals, it covers all ages from 5 to adult, and gives a single score. The matrices involve geometric shapes, and the task is to pick one from others offered, to follow the pattern.

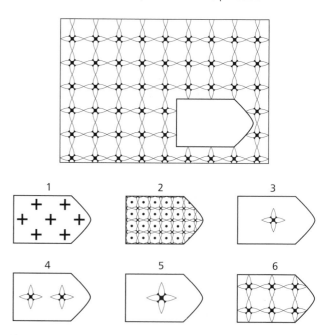

Figure 3.8
An example item from the Raven Matrices test. The task is to find the pattern that fits into the empty space. (Source: Gleitman, 1994)

Norm-referencing

IQ tests are **norm-referenced**. That is, their results don't indicate an absolute measure, but rather a comparison between the individual person's score and the norm, or standard, for their particular group. IQ test results are designed to produce a **normal distribution**, which means that if lots of them were plotted on a graph they would give a typical bell-shaped curve. That curve allows us to say how typical any one single IQ result is.

As we have seen, the mean, or average IQ is 100. The standard deviation, which indicates the typical range of scores, is 15. This means that about two-thirds of the population will fall within one standard deviation of the

Table 3.6 Some examples of test items

Some examples of test items
a. Choose the right alternative:

Synonyms	e.g. slake	(grow, drink, quench, pour, loose)
Autonyms	e.g. easy, soft	(putty, hard, simple, brittle)

b. Ordering and classification:

Arrange the following in descending order according to complexity	carnivore, vertebrate, animal, domestic cat, feline animals

Source: Child (1999)

mean, and about 96% within two standard deviations. Only 2% of the population will have more extreme scores than that.

What this means in practical terms is that about two-thirds of the population will have an IQ between 85 and 115; because 85 is one standard deviation below the mean and 115 is one standard deviation above it. We also know that 96% of the population will score between 70 and 130; and that anyone with a score of over 130 will have an unusually high IQ score. Similarly, anyone with a score of under 70 will have a very low one (Figure 3.9).

Figure 3.9
A normal distribution score for IQ. SD = standard deviation

IQ tests therefore have to be carefully **standardised** to make sure that they give the appropriate kinds of results. That process of standardisation takes a long time, and involves a great deal of checking and testing. For example, each test item needs to be tested and re-tested to make sure that it will give the same kinds of results when used with different groups of people.

Also, the test as a whole needs to be evaluated on different samples, to make sure that the typical results for those kinds of people have been taken into account. IQs are not simply the scores obtained from the tests. Each test result has to be looked up in a table of **population norms**, to find out the IQ that would be indicated by that score. There are different population norms for different groups of people – adult males, for example, or school-age girls. These population norms are part of the way that the test has been standardised.

Evaluation

- When standardising tests, it is important that the sample is representative of the population it is trying to illustrate. For example, if all the children being used for standardisation had high ability, the results would not represent a norm in terms of what that age group could normally do.

- A problem with some tests is that they were standardised quite some time ago, and their population norms may have changed.

- Many tests were standardised in just one area or part of the country, so again they may not be representative of the whole population.

- Some of the more well established IQ tests that were devised some time ago use words such as 'shepherd' or 'parlour', which may not be well understood today. However, most professional tests are revised and brought up to date at fairly regular intervals.

- Some group IQ tests provide only a single score, which may not be particularly helpful, although individual IQ tests provide profiles of their sub-tests which are much more useful as diagnostic information.

Reliability in testing

Psychology can be seen as an attempt to build a body of knowledge about people – about their minds, their motivations, and their behaviours. There are many accepted ways of adding to the body of knowledge, including observations, surveys and experiments. Whatever the method, issues of validity and reliability are always important. A reliable test is one that can be repeated and the same results will be found. A valid test is one that measures what it claims to measure. If a method is not reliable or valid, then it would be hard to add to an overall body of knowledge with any certainty.

Reliability is all about dependability – that is, whether a test will give the same result if it is done again under the same conditions and with the same people. The idea is that tests which give different results when they are repeated cannot be very good measures of what is being tested. For example, if a child obtained an IQ score of 115 on one occasion, and an IQ score of 100 on a second occasion, using the same test, then we could conclude that something had happened to the child, or that the test was unreliable, because it was giving inconsistent results. We could only find out whether it was the test or the child by using a test which we knew was normally reliable. So evaluating the general reliability of the test is an important part of test development.

In Chapter 5 we will be looking at studies of severely deprived children. One of these concerns twin boys in Czechoslovakia who were very badly neglected, and had no opportunity for the normal everyday learning that children do during their first 7 years or so. The boys were discovered, went to school and were fostered in a very caring way. Their IQs were tested and found to be very low. After a couple of years of their 'new' lives, their IQs were tested again and found to be much more normal – almost exactly 100, in fact. The test was reliable, so the researchers were able to conclude that the boys' intelligence had increased because of good quality care. If they had not known whether the test was reliable, no real conclusions could have been drawn.

↺ Recall AS material

Recall your AS material on reliability and validity from your study of methodology. If you have trouble remembering, look it up

Assessing reliability
Reliability, then, is all about the consistency of the results a test or measure gives. There are three different techniques we can use to assess how reliable a test is: the test–retest method, the split-half method, and the parallel forms method. Table 3.7 summarises the three methods, but we will look into them in more detail here.

The way that the reliability of a test is expressed is by using a correlation coefficient. You will have looked at correlations in your AS course, so it may be helpful to look it up for more detail. In summary, a correlation is a number between –1 and +1 which expresses the pattern of similarity between two sets of scores. With a positive correlation, as one score rises, so the other rises. A negative correlation means that high scores on one measure are associated with low scores on the other. A perfect correlation (which means that every pair of scores follows the predicted path) is scored as either –1 or +1, and the closer the correlation coefficient is to either of those extremes, the stronger it is. Most professional IQ tests have reliability coefficients of around +0.8.

↺ Recall AS material

Recall your AS material on correlations, or look it up.

Assessing the reliability of a test, then, involves measuring the correlation between two sets of scores. The simplest way of doing this is known as the **test–retest method**. It involves doing the test twice and testing for a correlation using an appropriate statistical test. A test would be deemed reliable if a child who obtained a high score the first time obtained a high score the second time and a child who obtained a low score the first time obtained a low score the second time. There has to be a delay between the tests, usually of several days or weeks, because otherwise the person might remember their answers on the first occasion, or the scores might be affected by fatigue or boredom.

One problem of using test–retest as a way of assessing reliability is the way that people learn from their experience, and often they will remember test items even after some time. So test developers tend to prefer ways of assessing reliability which mean that the person has not encountered the test items themselves before. One way of doing this is known as the **split-half method**. Using this method, the person takes half of the test on one occasion, and the other half on another occasion. If the two halves show a close correlation, then the test is deemed to be reliable.

However, it isn't quite as simple as this account makes it appear. For example, both halves of the test must be exactly matched – it wouldn't work, for instance, if one half was easier then the other in an IQ test, or if most of the questions for one subscale were clustered in one of the half-tests and not the other, because we might easily draw the wrong conclusions. So each test item needs to be paired up with another one of equal value and meaning; and the new half-tests constructed so that one from each pair goes into each test. It is almost like developing an entirely new test; but it does mean that unless the individual has changed dramatically during the interval their results on one half-test should correlate closely with their results on the other.

The third way of testing reliability is to have two exactly equivalent versions of the same test. This is known as the **parallel-forms method**, or sometimes the **alternate-forms method**. The person can complete both tests on separate occasions, and then their scores can be correlated. This is a common form of testing reliability, and most often-used psychological tests have more than one form. Developing them is expensive, of course, because each version of the test has to go through the same standardisation test and have its population norms assessed; but once it has been done the two versions of the test are available to researchers, and they are often useful for other kinds of research which might involve measuring the same psychological characteristic twice.

ACTIVITY

Write a set of short notes about reliability, making sure that they include information which would answer the following questions:

a How is reliability defined?
b How can reliability be tested?
c Why is reliability important?'

Table 3.7 Testing reliability

Test–retest	Doing the same test twice on two separate occasions, and correlating the two sets of scores
Split-half reliability	Splitting the test into two halves, then administering the halves on separate occasions and correlating the scores
Parallel forms	Doing two different forms of the test on two separate occasions, and correlating the scores

Validity in testing

The results of a test are valid if the test measures what it claims to measure. But that isn't quite as simple as it seems. For example, if we wanted to obtain a valid measure of intelligence, we would have to be sure that

our test really was measuring intelligence, and not, say, learning. But to do that we would need to be extremely clear about what we thought intelligence actually was, or we would need to use some other indicator of intelligence, which we were happy with, as a kind of 'yardstick' to check validity. But all tests have their own problems. In this section we will look at the four main types of validity – face validity, content validity, criterion validity and construct validity.

Face validity

Face validity is sometimes called surface validity, and it is to do with how a particular measure appears on the surface – whether it looks as though it measures what it should be measuring. For example, a test might ask: 'Which is the odd one out: cklab; gernoa; ehtiw; eengr; bleta'. If you think that being able to pick out the odd one out is something to do with intelligence, then for you this question would have face validity as an item for an intelligence test.

However, it might be that when the item was rigorously scrutinised, it gave results which were not about intelligence but about learning. Regular *Countdown* viewers, for example, are used to solving anagrams and might score more highly with a question like this than other people of the same intelligence would. That would mean that it wasn't exactly a good measure of intelligence, and more a measure of learned skills in anagram-solving.

Face validity, then, isn't really a very good indicator of whether a measure really is valid. Something may seem plausible on the surface, but actually fail to measure the thing in question. During the last century some researchers believed that measuring the size of the skull – the brain-case – would be a good measure of intelligence, because they believed that the larger the brain, the higher the intelligence. Nowadays we know that the brain doesn't work like that, and that some of the most intelligent people don't have particularly large brains. The idea had surface validity, but it wasn't really a good measure.

Content validity

As a result, researchers have focused more on other ways of defining validity. One of these is content validity, which is all to do with whether the content of the test items is appropriate for the purpose. A test for 9-year olds, for example, must have items that a 9-year old can understand; or an A level exam for a particular subject must contain only items that are on the specification. So content validity refers to the nature of the questions which are being asked, and whether they reflect the purpose or aim of the test or measure.

Criterion validity

Criterion validity is arrived at by comparing scores from a test with scores from some other measure – by checking them against some other criterion, or standard. That measure might be something which is tested at the same time or is already available, which would be a test of **concurrent validity**. For example, if a child's IQ has already been measured by one test, then a score obtained from another test can be compared with the first score. If the scores are similar, then the second test would be thought to have criterion-related validity.

Alternatively, a score might be compared with some other score obtained at a later date. This is known as **predictive validity**. For example, a child's IQ might be tested when he or she is 7 years old, and then re-tested at 15. If the two IQ scores match, then the first test would be said to have predictive validity. There are a number of cases where particular scores are used to make decisions, because they are thought to have predictive validity. For example, many university admissions tutors use A level results to decide who will be accepted on their degree course, believing that the grade of A level indicates how well they will do on their degree. But Peers and Johnston (1994) showed that there is only a low correlation between A level results and final degree classifications. Some people who achieve quite modest A level results do very well in their degree, which is not the predicted outcome.

Construct validity

Construct validity is all about whether the test items match the theoretical constructs underlying the test items. For example, if you had a theory of intelligence which asserted that the ability to identify patterns and odd-one-outs is the key to all intelligent behaviour, then you would be likely to develop an intelligence test based on odd-one-outs and patterns. That test would have construct validity, because it would reflect the theory underlying the test. If, on the other hand, you believed (as Guilford did) that intelligence consists of over 100 different skills, then your IQ test would have to contain all sorts of different kinds of test items, to reflect these different skills. So construct validity depends on having a very clear theoretical model, and whether the measure is really appropriate for the situation depends on how appropriate the theory itself is.

Those are the main types of validity, and as you can see, none is particularly concerned with 'the truth'. That's because the truth is hard to get at, and researchers often have to make operational definitions – doing the best they can under the circumstances. In recent years, people have begun to become more concerned with **ecological validity**, which is to do with how much a test or measure reflects reality, or at least real-life situations. But ecological validity is hard to measure, and often has to be treated simply as a more rigorous version of face validity.

Table 3.8 Types of validity

Face validity	The item appears, 'on the face of it', to test what it claims to test
Content validity	Whether the content of the items in a test is appropriate for that test
Criterion validity	How the test compares with other, well established, measures
Concurrent validity	How the score compares with another already existing score
Predictive validity	How the score matches a score obtained on a later occasion
Construct validity	How closely the test items fit their underlying theoretical constructs

Synoptic Note

Issues of validity and reliability are important for Units 5b and 6, the synoptic parts of the course.

ACTIVITY

Write a paragraph on each of the following types of validity, giving an example of each:

- *face validity*
- *concurrent validity*
- *predictive validity*
- *construct validity*
- *content validity*
- *ecological validity.*

Bias in educational assessment

Controversy about using intelligence tests in education has mainly focused around the purpose to which the test results will be put. It may be useful to measure intelligence, for example, if the information is used by a teacher to choose tasks which suit the educational level of the child. Children's ability cannot always be judged from their school work, and tests may be useful in that respect.

Sometimes, though, IQ tests can be used for more negative purposes, such as restricting access to courses or schools. And as we have seen, when tests were used in the Rosenthal and Jacobson study their results led to changes in teacher expectations, which affected the children's education considerably. In this section we will be looking at the question of bias in educational assessment, and the implications it may have for education in general. Then we will go on to look at the specific implications of gender bias in IQ testing, and its consequences.

Bias in IQ tests

It has been claimed that educational assessment involves bias, and particularly if it involves judgements based on IQ. For example, the 11+ was very widely used to select children for special schooling in grammar schools. It was heavily based on an IQ test, which some children were deliberately coached to pass. This **training effect**, which enabled some children to learn how to do well at intelligence tests, meant that the tests ended up discriminating in favour of better-off families who could afford the extra time and tuition.

Is intelligence a useful concept?

Howe (1988) argues that there are low correlations between intelligence and some learning and memory tasks, and questions whether intelligence is a useful construct at all. Sternberg (1988) suggested that there is a correlation between learning and intelligence in a broader sense than Howe's specific memory tasks; but Sternberg was also using a broader definition of intelligence, and not one which is reflected in the IQ tests currently used.

It isn't just about general intelligence, either. For example, some people score very badly on IQ tests but have very high achievement in a specific area. Some autistic people have an amazing ability in a certain area. For example, one autistic person can draw anything he sees and the perspective and detail are perfect; another can reproduce any music she hears; others are able to perform complex mathematical calculations This evidence suggests that there is not just one 'general ability factor' that means someone is intelligent, and some researchers believe that intelligence as a specific ability may not exist.

This raises another source of bias, which is what happens when intelligence is accepted as something measurable and genetic, and decisions are based on the results of tests. Since experience shows that these results can be affected by experience and training, that means that the decisions that have been made – such as the type of schooling offered – have been biased, and will have disadvantaged certain individuals.

Figure 3.11
A scene from the film Rainman, *which featured an autistic person who had extraordinary numerical gifts. For example he could keep track of all the cards in a casino game. From* Rainman, *with Dustin Hoffman and Tom Cruise*

Figure 3.10
Canary Wharf, London, as drawn by Stephen Wiltshire, an autistic person

Culture-fair tests

It is not just individuals who are disadvantaged: there has also been controversy over the way that biased IQ tests can disadvantage whole cultures (Sarason, 1973). For example, intelligence tests such as the ones we have been describing were designed to test the IQs of White people, and were also closely oriented towards middle-class values and knowledge. As a result, people from other cultures are likely to do badly on these tests. An ideal test would be **culture-fair** – that is, it would be equal for everyone, regardless of cultural background. But in reality IQ tests don't often reach that standard.

A great many of the studies looking at whether tests are culture-fair concern IQ tests. However, there is also concern about other assessments in education, which might also be considered not to be culture-fair. Tests or exams might also give different results for different cultures because of cultural bias built into the them. There are different ways in which a test can lack cultural fairness:

- The items in the test may not understood by people from some cultures.
- The language used in the test may favour certain cultural groups and disadvantage others (Labov, 1970).
- The tester may affect the results. For example, children respond better in a situation where they feel at ease with the tester, and they may feel more at ease if the tester is from the same cultural group.

It is generally accepted that there can be cultural bias in test results because either items can be culturally specific, or the way the test is administered can be biased against certain cultures. However, some researchers argue that this does not account for all the difference between cultures where IQ tests are concerned. For example, when the Stanford-Binet test was translated into Black English and given orally to Black children by a Black examiner the children received the same sort of scores as did children given the usual Stanford-Binet test in the usual way (Quay, 1971). Other researchers challenged these findings, arguing that the content of the test items was the same, and still reflected White middle-class values and ideas even though they had been dressed up in 'Black' language.

Bias through environmental factors

It does seem that Black children do not do as well as White children on IQ tests, even when the tests are altered to allow for cultural differences. But this group difference seems to be due to environmental factors, not to anything genetic. Black people traditionally experience a more deprived environment and a greater share of unemployment in developed countries, and this can be reflected when comparing group scores. When Black and White people with the same environmental conditions are compared, the differences disappear.

Loehlin et al. (1975) identified two groups of children with the same environment and matched for a number of factors: education, parents' education, parents' income, occupational level and so on. One group of children was Black and the other group was White. The differences between the Black and White children were much smaller in this study than they had been in studies that had simply compared groups of Black and White children without bothering to match up the samples.

The conclusion from these sorts of studies is that it is environment that leads to differences in test scores rather than some genetic component. However, there are often still some slight differences between the scores of Black and White children. Some have suggested that this is because some inherited factor is involved, but there are many other explanations for group difference of this kind – not least of which is the question of cultural bias in the tests themselves. And there are more subtle environmental factors that can come into play, too. Just being Black or White is a difference that affects how a person is treated by society, so no match could be exact.

Gender inequalities

There have also been systematic group differences between boys and girls on intelligence tests. Ever since IQ tests were first developed, girls have scored more than boys on the same tests. But instead of it being argued that this shows that girls were more intelligent, the population norms on IQ tests were adjusted so that they give similar results. In a typical IQ test, a girl has to get more answers right than a boy of the same age to achieve the same IQ.

Other forms of educational assessment may also have been biased in favour of boys. Until relatively recently, boys tended to do better in assessment, especially in the more technical areas. Maccoby and Jacklin (1974) found that the curriculum favours technical areas, mathematics and science, which are subjects at which boys used to be expected to do better. That also seemed to be reflected in teacher expectations: Bilton et al. (1996) found that illustrations in science books, for example, showed four boys for every girl. Single-sex schools for girls generally achieve good academic results, but Arnot et al. (1998) have suggested that this is because their intake is selective rather than for any other reason.

In more recent years, girls have begun to do better than boys in examinations (Figure 3.12). Throughout the 1990s the GCSE results for girls were around 10% better than for boys; and educational concern is now focused on improving the results obtained by boys at school. This included looking closely at what happens in the classroom. For example, it was claimed at one stage that girls receive about one-third of the teacher's time (Spender, 1982). However, Croll and Moses (1990) found that it is more balanced than that: in their study, girls received about 46% of the teacher time. However, boys were also more likely to be involved in negative interaction with the teacher, so even though the girls had roughly the same amount of attention, theirs may have been more positive, and more helpful to their education.

Researchers have put forward a number of reasons for gender differences. Inevitably, some have emphasised **biological differences** in the brains of males and females (Brannon, 1996). For example, adult male brains

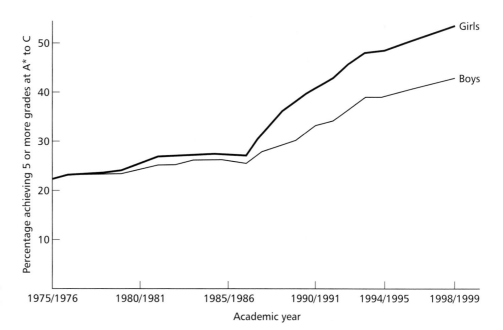

Figure 3.12
Comparison of GCSE achievements of boys and girls over time (Source: Long, 2000)

are larger than female brains, and females have a larger corpus callosum. Part of the hypothalamus is larger in males and male brains seem to be more affected by lateralisation (the tendency of the two halves of the brain to have different functions), and some researchers have claimed that this tendency is more marked for males, although the evidence is not very strong.

There are some systematic differences. For example, girls tend not to do so well on spatial items when they are tested, and some researchers see this as an expression of biological differences in brain functioning. However, Brannon (1996) suggested that it could equally well be because they practise spatial skills less than boys, and not because they are biologically not suited to these sorts of tasks.

The problem is that there is no real evidence to show what difference in attainment and behaviour these differences might produce. Bee (1992), suggested that baby boys are more active, which may lead parents into playing more active games with them and lead on to other kinds of parental encouragement. But there are only very few temperament differences between babies according to gender, and little evidence to show that biological differences cause specific behavioural differences.

Another possibility is **socialisation**. It does seem that parents do encourage the behaviour that 'suits' the gender of the child (Frisch, 1977). When young, children seem to be given 'gender-appropriate' toys – for example, boys are given construction toys and technical ones, whereas girls are given dolls and drawing materials (Unger and Crawford, 1992). There is also evidence that mothers talk more to girl babies than they do to boys, and that

they play in very different ways with them; which may account for the way that girls tend to be more fluent in language than boys, while boys are (generally speaking) more likely to engage in active rough-and-tumble play.

Another reason why there might be gender differences in attainment is the way that the expectations of others are likely to be fulfilled (we looked at the **self-fulfilling prophecy** earlier in this chapter). If girls are expected to be good at certain items in a test or at certain skills, then they are likely to become good at them. Also if boys are expected to do well in certain skills, then it is likely that they will do well at those skills, because that is how they earn praise and encouragement in the school system.

> **Synoptic Note**
>
> Explanations for differences in educational achievement between boys and girls is another example of the 'nature/nurture' debate, which is in the synoptic part of the course, assessed in Unit 6.

It has been argued that different assessment types can favour girls. For example, GCSEs involve quite a lot of coursework, and since teenage girls appear to be more conscientious and hard-working than boys, they may be more likely to do better at coursework. However, after 1994, coursework marks for GCSEs were reduced so that for most exams they were not more than 50%, yet the gender differences in results remained. Arnot *et al.* (1998) suggested that girls began to do well when strategies were introduced in schools in the early 1980s to counter inequalities. Sexism was discouraged, equal access to the curriculum was encouraged, and perceptions of gender roles changed. As a result, girls received more encouragement to achieve than they would have done before.

Another possible explanation for why boys are not doing as well as girls in education could be because they are less conforming. Croll and Moses (1990) found that teachers thought of girls as more helpful, and tended to like girls more. Boys might therefore not do well at school because they conform less to educational norms. But these, of course are generalisations. Some boys do better than girls because their motivation is intrinsic (within them), rather than being due to expected norms. They enjoy learning, so they work hard. Overall, the spread of boys' achievement is wider than the spread of achievement for girls – some boys do extremely well, while others do extremely badly. This also provides some evidence for the claim that boys may be simply less conforming to educational norms.

Special educational needs

Special educational needs is a term that refers to the additional educational support which some children require in order to help them to benefit from their schooling. Children who have difficulties that prevent normal progress in school are said to have special educational needs, and these difficulties include emotional, behavioural, physical and learning problems. The UK's 1996 Education Act holds that a child has special needs if he or she has significantly more difficulty in learning than another child of the same age would have. As a result, 'normal' teaching is not thought to be sufficient, and additional resources are needed. It was this sort of thinking that Binet was following back at the beginning of the twentieth century, when he devised the first IQ test.

One of the most important parts of an educational psychologist's job is to identify children who have special educational needs. Such children require an official Statement of Special Educational Needs from an educational psychologist before their local authority can obtain the additional funding required to give them the type of education they need. According to the Audit Commission, 15% of the money spent in schools in Britain during 1998 was for the support required by children with special educational needs.

There are five stages involved in obtaining a Statement of Special Educational Needs:
- **Stage 1** – The teacher identifies a special educational need and registers it with the school Special Educational Needs (SEN) coordinator.
- **Stage 2** – The school SEN coordinator gathers information and works with the teachers to learn more about that child.
- **Stage 3** – Specialists from outside the school are brought in to support the SEN coordinator and the teachers. These

may be educational psychologists, education welfare officers, or other professionals.
- **Stage 4** – The local educational authority (LEA) considers the need for a Statement, and if it believes the need is there will call on its team of educational psychologists to make an assessment.
- **Stage 5** – The educational psychologist undertakes testing and diagnosis, makes a Statement if appropriate, and the LEA then puts provision in place.

The Warnock Report on Special Educational Needs in 1978 argued that 20% of children in schools would need special provision at some time during their education. In 1996, some 16.4% of children in schools had been identified as having special educational needs; and by 1999 this figure had risen to 19.9%. This is quite a high figure, but it includes those who need special provision for only a short period of time.

Overall, though, the demand for educational resources to satisfy special educational needs continues to grow. In 1994 the DfEE's Code of Practice on the Identification and Assessment of Special Educational Needs proposed that no more than 2% of the school population should require Statements carried out – that they should only be done in a small number of cases. The figure is now closer to 3%, and shows no sign of decreasing. Given the financial incentive for schools to have Statements, this is not really surprising. Other ways of calculating SEN provision have been suggested, but the diagnosis of individual children is always going to be the determining factor, so it is difficult to see how the present trends could be changed.

Defining special needs

Defining special educational needs is a challenging task – mainly because it is a matter of drawing fairly arbitrary lines. It is not simply that some children have difficulty and some are 'normal'. For example, children are not simply divided into those who can read and those who can't: there are lots of children at in-between stages. It is hard to draw a line between 'normal' ability and 'special needs', and hard to distinguish between special needs of different forms. In its current usage, the term 'special needs' covers a range of abilities from very low to poor.

One way of attempting to define special needs has been to look at it statistically. As we saw when we looked at normal distributions earlier in this chapter, roughly 2% of the school population would be expected to fall two standard deviations below the mean. It is also the case that 2% of the school population are in special schools; and these children are often well below average in IQ (Gipps and Stobart, 1990). However, choosing the two-standard deviation point is quite arbitrary: it would be equally possible to choose one standard deviation below

STAGE ONE (removed in 2001)
The class teacher becomes concerned that a child may have some problems, monitors his or her progress, seeks support from the special educational needs co-ordinator and alters teaching approaches to help the child

STAGE TWO (renamed in 2001)
If a child continues to have problems then the responsibilty passes to the special educational needs co-ordinator. An ***Individual Educational Plan*** (IEP) is now generated which can utilise resources and expertise available in the school as a whole. This might, for example, involve teaching or non-teaching time out of the school's own budget

STAGE THREE (renamed in 2001)
If problems continue, then the child is referred for asessment and help outside of the school and this would result in a further IEP. This advice or support would at first be from a peripatetic support teacher, who would assess the child's level of problems and give advice on teaching approaches and/or some teaching time. Educational psychologists tend to become involved in cases which are either more severe or where a number of factors are involved; they carry out assessments of level of functioning and give advice on teaching and management

STAGE FOUR
With the more severe and intractable problems, the child is referred to the education authority to consider whether statutory assessment is appropriate. If this is agreed (and the majority are at this stage), then reports are gathered from the professionals involved

STAGE FIVE
The various reports and assessments are now considered by the education authority who usually issue a ***Statement of Special Educational Needs***, with the appropriate support or school placement. Statements are regularly reviewed (at least yearly), and these can be modified if the child's needs change

Figure 3.13
The formal process of special education (Source: Long (2000), based on the code of practice (DfEE, 1998))

the mean instead, which would include about 16% of children, and could just as well be deemed to be the point where special provision should begin, if a statistical definition is followed.

However, most educationalists don't use a statistical definition of special needs. Instead, they look at what children need to be able to do to function 'normally'. A child who does not have some necessary basic skills can be defined as having special needs. Children with moderate or severe learning difficulties, for example, might be unable to use public facilities, or unable to recognise danger signals. Learning to read properly is important. Bynner and Parsons (1997) conducted a study including over 1,500 adults of 37 years of age, and found that over 6% of them were below the level of a 9 year old in a basic literacy task. Nowadays, we would consider that older children who cannot fill out forms or read a newspaper have special needs, because of the difficulties that these inabilities will cause them in adult life.

Categorising special needs
Terms such as 'moderate learning difficulties' arose from the 1978 Warnock Report on Special Educational Needs.

Before that, children had been categorised using terms such as educationally sub-normal (ESN) or severely sub-normal (SSN) – that is, in terms of comparison with a 'norm' of the rest of their age group. However, this type of categorisation rapidly led to labelling and stereotyping; and was also found to be too general to describe most children's problems. Quite a lot of children only need help in specific areas, and are as competent as other children of their age in other respects.

Because of this, the Warnock report focused on a child's educational needs, rather than on categorising it by comparison with 'normal' children. In that context the report identified five different types of problem which might mean that the child would require special educational provision: learning difficulties, emotional and behavioural difficulties, language difficulties, physical problems and sensory problems

Learning difficulties
Learning difficulties have been divided into three groups – mild, moderate, and severe. A child with **mild learning difficulties** can cope with normal schooling but is likely to have some difficulty with the work. Such

children usually stay at an ordinary school, but have some additional support and some special work. Many of the schoolchildren in Britain with a Statement of Special Needs have mild learning difficulties which can be catered for in normal schools.

Children with **moderate learning difficulties** are not likely to reach a normal level of attainment in basic skills such as literacy, even with extra help. They can be educated in normal schools but need considerable extra support and some are considered to be better off in special schools. At the time of writing, public policy is to avoid labelling and segregation by keeping these children in ordinary schools as much as possible.

Children with **severe learning difficulties** not only have difficulties with school work, but with other basic skills such as being independent and communicating with others. These children are usually educated in special schools, although when they are younger they are sometimes placed in mainstream schools for a few years, to aid their social development as far as possible. But the curriculum they follow is often linked with early developmental stages, and they are not expected to achieve a great deal.

Another set of learning difficulties includes specific learning difficulties such as dyslexia. Statements of special needs are often obtained for children with dyslexia, and in 1994 the DfEE code of practice (1994) encouraged this. But since then, the controversy about children being over-diagnosed with dyslexia, and the disorder being used to hide or justify inadequate teaching meant that official attitudes changed, so that in 1997 a DfEE Green Paper required that Statements for those with dyslexia should be carried out only under special or extreme circumstances.

Emotional and behavioural difficulties
Learning difficulties is the largest category of special needs, but **emotional and behavioural difficulties (EBD)** is the next largest category. Usually disruptive behaviour is the problem, but anxiety and depression are also difficulties for some children. Emotional and behavioural difficulties are often linked to home and social problems, which means that these difficulties sometimes disappear when these other problems are solved. It is therefore thought that there should be little intervention at school level. Emotional and behavioural problems tend to be dealt with by involving parents, giving extra support and getting specialist advice. Some children attend special residential schools, but most remain in mainstream schooling.

Language difficulties
Language difficulties represent another source of special educational need. Problems with speech and language can cause difficulties in educational attainment, because education is almost entirely based on language competence. Speech therapists can help, but they tend to work in the health service rather than the education service, which requires joint planning between authorities. Currently, the emphasis is on working with the child on their communication, and making sure that the context has meaning for the child. This reflects the current psychological understanding of the ways that children obtain and use language.

Physical problems
Physical problems are another source of special educational need, which are often practical ones that need to be overcome. For example, mobility problems can mean that a child has restricted access to the curriculum, in that he or she may not be able to access the special rooms required for technological subjects. However, recent legislation has meant that this problem will need to be addressed by all educational providers.

Some more extreme physical problems also need to be tackled, if all children are to receive the education to which they are legally entitled. Children with cerebral palsy – in which physical coordination and control problems come from early brain damage – often have learning problems, depending on which area of the brain is damaged. Some, however, have 'normal' abilities to learn, but physical problems that make it hard for them to achieve their potential. Spasticity is the most common problem here. It comes from damage to the motor cortex, giving difficulty with movement. Ataxia comes from damage to the cerebellum, giving problems with walking, and making the individual appear clumsy; athetosis is caused by damage to the basal ganglia and can lead to involuntary movements, dribbling and difficulty in speaking.

Physical problems of this type can be so severe that the individual needs to attend a special school where the teachers will be able to attend to them properly. But there are other physical problems, such as epilepsy, that can affect attainment but can be dealt with in the ordinary school system. Medication is needed for some conditions, and this can lead to drowsiness or difficulty with concentration; but if teachers are alerted to this they can allow for these problems in dealing with the child. In these cases structured programmes are useful so that a child who has had to be away from school for medical reasons can take up where they left off.

Sensory problems
Sensory problems may also give children special educational needs. For example, hearing difficulties can cause considerable problems, since much of modern

education depends on listening to the teacher or other classroom stimuli. Murphy (1976) estimated that some 20% of primary school children may have some temporary hearing loss, and this can affect language development. In another study, Gottlieb *et al.* (1980) found that 46% of the children who needed help with reading were found to have middle ear problems.

Some children have permanent sensory problems and attend special schools, for the deaf or for the blind, where such children can follow a normal curriculum in a way that is suited to their needs. According to Best (1992) there are 3 blind children and 4.3 partially sighted children for every 10 000 school-age children, which adds up to quite a lot of children overall.

Explaining special needs

Several explanations have been put forward for why children have special educational needs. These discussions are mainly concerned with learning difficulties, and rarely include physical or sensory problems. But some theorists see severe learning difficulties as having **biological origins**. Simonoff *et al.* (1996) suggested that around 33% of those classified as having severe learning difficulties have genetic abnormalities such as Down's syndrome. About 20% of those with severe learning difficulties have more than one congenital problem, and the other children with that level of difficulty often have some sort of brain damage.

Evaluation

- Those classified as having mild or moderate learning difficulties do not have physical problems – although these might be present but not identifiable.

Another possible biological factor which has been put forward is **gender**. There tend to be more boys amongst children needing special provision – for example, Male (1996) found twice as many boys as girls in a school for moderate learning difficulties. But this is consistent with the gender effects we observed in the last section – there are more boys at both extremes of the scale, while girls tend to cluster in the middle. If gender is a factor in special educational needs, it could be due to either biological or environmental factors.

Other types of explanation for special educational needs have emphasised environmental factors. Most children with special needs (except where there are physical problems) come from deprived areas, where they may not get the parental attention, resources and toys which will help them to learn. It has been suggested that a high proportion of moderate learning difficulties are caused by social deprivation (Dunn, 1968).

One argument against special needs being caused by environmental effects used to be that programmes put on to give more help (such as the Head Start educational enrichment programme in the USA) did not seem to succeed. Jensen (1973) used this evidence to argue that extra help to overcome social disadvantages did not work, and was evidence that those problems were genetic and not caused by a poor environment. However, later studies showed that there were good effects from Head Start in the long term (Barnett, 1995), and that the role of parents is really important in tackling these problems. So it does seem that environmental factors have an influence on learning, and may lead to some children experiencing learning difficulties.

Synoptic Note

The 'nature/nurture' debate is part of the synoptic part of the course, assessed in Unit 6.

Problems with special needs assessment

There are a number of problems with Special Needs assessment. As we have seen, Statements of Special Needs mean that additional resources are provided to schools. Without a Statement there is usually no additional funding. So there is a powerful incentive for schools to obtain Statements for their more challenging pupils, in order to obtain the resources they need.

Another problem is the difficulty of using testing to identify special needs. Educational psychologists have the responsibility of identifying such children, and of drawing up an Individual Education Plan for them. There are, however, relatively few educational psychologists in Britain, and they are each responsible for a large number of children. The types of tests which are used for this process are the individual diagnostic tests such as the Weschler Intelligence Scale for Children or the British Ability Scales and other, more specialised tests. The criticisms of such tests (which we looked at earlier in this chapter) highlight some of the problems in identifying special needs in this way – although it should be pointed out that the clinical skills of the educational psychologist are used in addition to the test results themselves.

Knowing where to draw a line between 'normal' functioning and 'special needs' is another recurrent problem. One child's difficulties may be so extreme as to need a Statement, while another, very similar child may be just good enough to manage without a Statement being necessary.

The first stage of identifying special educational needs comes through the direct observation of a child's behaviour or abilities. This relies on a teacher or parent suggesting that there is a difficulty. It may not be a problem in many cases, but in other cases – for example, where there is a mild learning difficulty or a mild hearing disorder – the problem can go unnoticed. Detailed professional exploration of potential problems doesn't happen until after a need has been identified, so it is easy for non-severe problems to be overlooked.

As we have seen, the old title of 'educationally sub-normal' (ESN) was dropped because it produced problems with labelling. Labels are at first given to describe a group, but they soon acquire other, more negative meanings, and so labels are frequently changed. Labelling can be a problem if the label comes to mean something different; and children often pick up on labels and use them as insults. Stereotyping is involved here (stereotyping was discussed earlier in this chapter).

There is also a problem in that it is easy for a child's abilities to be underestimated. For example, a child might be a slow reader because of sensory difficulties such as problems with sight and hearing rather than learning difficulties as such. It is not always easy for a busy teacher to work out the cause of a problem, so bringing in the school SEN co-ordinator is often useful, in that more investigation can be carried out to avoid underestimating a child's potential or ability.

Similarly, a child with physical difficulties may not be able to carry out certain tasks, but this might not mean that understanding is not there. It is partly because of the possibility that a child's abilities might be underestimated that many parents believe that their child will be better off in mainstream schooling, where it is felt they will be treated more 'normally'. On the other hand, this can sometimes have the opposite effect, since mainstream schools usually have far greater numbers in each class, and a child is more easily 'lost'. Class sizes in special schools are much smaller, and the pupil–teacher ratio is smaller, so children get more individual attention.

Self-test

Write a timed essay, under exam conditions (or as close as you can manage) using the title 'Discuss the process of identifying, categorising, and assessing students with special educational needs'.

Gifted children

Our discussion of special educational needs has focused on the 2% of the school population who are likely to have an IQ score of less than 70. However, another 2% of the population score at the other end of the distribution – children with an IQ score of more than 130. Although it might be assumed that having a very high IQ score is an advantage, gifted children can be classed as having special needs too. Like all children, they need an education that will enable them to make the most of their abilities, and develop their skills effectively.

Defining giftedness

As with special needs, any line drawn between being gifted and not being gifted is an arbitrary one, in that it is a matter of choice depending on what is being examined and where the boundary is set. Terman (1925) defined it as being those with an IQ of 140 or higher; whereas Freeman (1991) defined 'giftedness' as having an IQ of 130 or above. In Terman's USA longitudinal study of giftedness, IQ was measured using the Terman–Merrill Intelligence Test. But giftedness is not confined to having a high IQ. Some autistic children are very talented in one particular area, as we saw earlier in this chapter, although they need special educational support in others. Gardner (1983) talked about multiple intelligences, and argued that high levels of achievement are often in one area only, so it might be that giftedness and having a high level of general ability do not go together.

The National Association for Gifted Children suggests that a gifted child learns more quickly, has a retentive memory, concentrates well, has a wide general knowledge and interest, enjoys problem solving, has an odd sense of humour, sets high standards and has an good imagination. One difficulty is that a child's giftedness can go undetected if the child is bored at school, or if abilities are deliberately hidden in order to be accepted. Freeman (1991) suggested that teachers failed to identify about 24% of children with high IQ scores.

There are other checklists of what to look out for in a gifted child. For example, a gifted child is said to have keen powers of observation, a good memory, a special interest in music or art, and plenty of ideas. Shore and Kanevsky (1993) define gifted learners as having:
- Memory and knowledge base – they know more and can use what they know.
- Metacognition – they can monitor their strategies.
- Speed – they spend longer planning but work at great speed.
- Problem categorisation – they exclude irrelevant information and know when they need more.
- Procedural knowledge – they know how to use their knowledge.

- Flexibility – they can do lateral thinking and problem solving.
- Preference for complexity – they prefer complex problems.

Do gifted children have special educational needs?

Although on the face of it gifted children have advantages in our educational system, in other ways they also have special needs. If giftedness is having a high IQ, this should mean academic success; but too often it can lead to social isolation and boredom at school instead. Terman's longitudinal study, started in 1925, did not find that gifted children were isolated, but Freeman (1991) suggested that Terman had selected advantaged children, and that other gifted children without such an advantaged background might be more isolated.

Freeman studied less privileged children, taking a sample of 70 children from the register of the National Association of Gifted Children, and studying them again 10 years later. The measure of IQ was Raven's Progressive Matrices, which is a reasonably culture-fair test. The children came from several different schools, and Freeman gave the test to all the children in each selected child's class. The complete study involved three groups, each of 70 children: the original sample of 70 from the register of gifted children, another 70 with similar IQ but who had not been identified as gifted, and a third sample of 70 were chosen at random. Interviews as well as other tests were carried out with the children.

Freeman found that the children who had been given the label 'gifted' often had social difficulties. Many were sensitive, lonely and bored. The other group of children, who had equivalent IQs but had not been identified as gifted, seemed to have fewer problems regarding mixing with their friends, and Freeman concluded that being identified by parents as gifted may be what causes a child's problems, rather than having a high IQ. Another finding was that a child with a good educational environment but normal ability could get as good an IQ score as a child with good ability but a poor environment.

Another study was carried out by Marshall (1995) using the Mensa membership list (Mensa is an association for those with high IQ). Marshall found that its members often had social and emotional problems, but they did not seem to be caused by having a high IQ. Having different experiences in education, such children were mainly concerned about being part of the group, and about not being different.

Helping gifted children

In the USA, gifted children are identified and given extra support. They are either put into groups to work together ('pulled out') or go to special schools. In Britain being 'gifted' is not considered a special need in the sense of attracting funding and support. However, children can be put into groups above their age level, and a more advanced curriculum can be offered. Kulik and Kulik (1992) found that usually this involved setting additional work. It was unusual to find such children put into special groups to help one another.

Subotnik *et al.* (1993) followed the progress of some gifted children in the USA with an average IQ of 157. They did not do especially well in their careers, however, although they did well enough. In 1968 Oden retested some of those who had been in Terman's original study. She compared the top and bottom 100 men when looking at the type of job, income and amount of authority (this was the top 100 in status, and the bottom 100 in status). In an in-depth interview it was found that the top group had experienced more stable homes when they were children, and less illness. They also had more support from home, and it was thought that this background had helped them to develop a higher need to achieve.

A problem in assessing giftedness is that it is probably not one thing in any case. An autistic child can have special needs and be gifted in the sense of having an outstanding talent. However, that child is likely to have a low IQ as measured by tests. Giftedness can be high IQ, high ability, an exceptional talent, creative thinking, or a proficient use of divergent thinking. These are not all measured in the same way, and there is no clear definition, so there are sure to be problems in assessing giftedness.

Some researchers have identified creativity as the essence of giftedness; but this presents its own problems. Eysenck (1993a, b) assumed that creativity is a trait, so that a person can score as 'creative' using tests such as divergent thinking tests. But not many of the people thought of by society as creative – musicians, artists and the like – do very well on these tests. Another way of defining creativity is to look for some exceptional talent in mathematics, art, science, music or writing. It is hard to think of a test that will find out if someone has exceptional talent, and this is a problem in assessing gifted children in order to provide for their special educational needs.

There are some other problems involved in attempting to assess creativity using tests. For example, tests are usually timed and taken under exam-like conditions, whereas creativity may need time and a relaxed atmosphere. Wallach and Kogan (1965) established a relaxed atmosphere and a situation like playing, and found that divergent thinking scores matched IQ more closely than previous studies had found. And there is also the problem that not all novel responses show creativity. Someone might be mentally ill, for example, and their responses could be distinctly unorthodox without indicating that they were particularly creative. Most creativity tests have an element of subjectivity in the marking, although they are standardised with population norms and other criteria. But the element of judgement is still there.

We can see, then, that defining giftedness can be a problem, and ensuring that gifted children obtain an education which will enable them to develop their talents to the full is tricky. The UK is only just coming round to the idea of establishing special provision for those with exceptional sporting talent; many hope that once this has become accepted it can generalise to other areas of exceptional achievement. But in the meantime, as we have seen, it is an open question whether gifted children actually benefit from being identified as such.

Self-test

Write a timed essay, under exam conditions (or as close as you can manage) using the title 'Discuss issues surrounding the identification and assessment of gifted children'.

Suggested reading

Childs, D. (1999) *Psychology and the Teacher*, sixth edition. Cassell Education.

Fontana, D. (1988) *Psychology for Teachers*, second edition. BPS Books.

Haralambos, M. & Holborn, M. (2000) *Sociology Themes and Perspectives*, fifth edition. Hammersmith: HarperCollins.

Long, M. (2000) *The Psychology of Education*. London: Routledge Falmer.

4 The psychology of work

The aims of this chapter

The aims of this chapter are to enable the reader to:

- *understand the concept of work and its importance in adult life*
- *outline and discuss a theory of work motivation*
- *discuss two methods used to select personnel*
- *discuss the use of psychometric tests for recruitment*
- *identify types of leadership and their effects*
- *discuss one theory of leadership effectiveness*
- *describe the processes involved in group dynamics and decision making at work*
- *discuss the psychological implications for the individual of unemployment, redundancy, retirement and increased leisure time*
- *outline and discuss two factors causing stress at work, and identify specific stressful occupations.*

STUDY AID

When you have finished working through this chapter you should write an essay about, or at least test yourself on, each of the above points. This will help you to see how good your knowledge and understanding of work psychology is.

This chapter covers

THE PSYCHOLOGY OF WORK
  Defining work psychology
  Work motivation
  Job selection and assessment

LEADERSHIP AND GROUPS
  Leadership
  Working groups

THE INDIVIDUAL AT WORK
  Stress at work
  Changes in working life

The psychology of work

This chapter covers a wide range of issues from organisational psychology and occupational psychology. The title 'The Psychology of Work' includes both of these areas, which have become quite distinct in recent years, although in older texts you may come across the terms 'occupational psychology', 'organisational psychology' and 'work psychology' being used interchangeably. Occupational psychology tends to focus on the individual at work whereas organisational psychology is more concerned with the organisation as a whole; however, both are relevant to the study of the psychology of work and working life.

For the most part, psychologists tend to adopt a fairly pragmatic approach to work, but it is worth exploring some of the relevant sociological perspectives that can influence the way we understand what it is all about. Karl Marx, for example, believed that work is the way that people find fulfilment and happiness ('work' in this context is the production of goods and services). But if what the individual produces is not complete, or if they are selling their labour to others without having a satisfying end product, then they become alienated, and estranged from that source of personal satisfaction and fulfilment. Organisations, Marx believed, led almost automatically to alienation, because the person was working in a way that divorced them from a sense of involvement with their own productivity, resulting in dissatisfaction and unhappiness.

Organisational psychology, as a general rule, works within a more functionalist viewpoint, although many of the recent initiatives in both occupational and organisational psychology, such as job enrichment strategies and empowerment, do draw on ideas based on Marx's. The functionalist view of work is that there is solidarity in industrial society, and this solidarity is based on differences between people – different specialised roles which allow the organisation or society to function. Roles and economic goals are connected to work output by the people who work and participate in that organisation or society, which means that work is an important part of any social system.

Within each organisation there are roles, hierarchies and economic goals. The membership of the organisation is the people that work there, and its structure is the relationship of those people to one another. Within an organisation there are usually top managers, middle managers and an operating body of people. There can be a tall structure, where there are many roles within the hierarchy, or there can be a flat structure, where individuals tend to be experts and there are few layers in the hierarchy. The organisation

has economic goals, such as making a profit. However, it often has societal goals too, such as contributing to the wider community. The interlinking of roles, relationships and goals mirrors the way that society is organised, and contributes to the solidarity and overall functioning of the organisation. We will be looking at roles and working groups later in this chapter.

Defining work psychology

Defining work psychology is probably easier than defining work itself, which is more difficult than it might appear. Grint (1991) showed how all definitions of work have their own problems.

- We could say, for example, that work is paid employment, but then housework and other such activities would not be classified as work, whereas many would feel that they should be.
- We could say that work is what we do to survive but, although this might have been true in the distant past, nowadays things are different. For example, we regularly work for rewards that are over and above what we need for pure survival.
- We could define work as something we have to do, but there are things we have to do (such as eating) that we do not call work.
- We could say that work is activities that are not leisure, but some people combine leisure activities with work – for example, discussing a business deal over a round of golf.

For the most part, we tend to consider work as paid employment, and to ignore some of the arguments above. Grint (1991) concluded that work is socially defined, in that any definition of work has to be located in a particular society and at a particular time. Although much of what follows in this chapter looks at work within organisational structures, it is important to remember that this is a particular cultural view. In other societies, work can be a very different thing – for example, farming land and looking after livestock.

Types of work psychology

Landy (1997) suggested that industrial and organisational psychology began in the USA with the study of individual differences – differences between people. Psychological testing was used by the American army in 1919, and areas of interest at that time included tests of mental ability, performance rating, job standards and preparing training materials (Katzell and Austin, 1992). However, despite a handful of books on the subject, it was not until 1945 that the American Psychological Association formed a division for industrial and business psychology. This had 756 members in 1960, but 2005 members by 1980 – and by the 1980s organisational psychology had become widely recognised.

In the 1930s, a set of pioneering studies at the Hawthorne Electric Plant in Illinois raised interest in topics such as morale, leadership and group dynamics. Between the Second World War and the 1960s interest focused on performance appraisal, training, selection of personnel and also on the job satisfaction of workers. From the 1960s to the 1980s, criticisms of the actual tests being used began to come to the fore, mainly concerning their validity and fairness; and work motivation became a popular research topic.

Shimmin and Wallis (1994) looked at how occupational psychology developed in Britain. The issues it covered included hours of work, industrial accidents, selection procedures, time and motion studies, methods of work and psychological testing. Specific studies were carried out, such as the effects of fatigue on pilot skill. Shimmin and Wallis identified some of the main areas of interest of occupational psychologists in the UK between the 1970s and the 1990s, which are listed in Table 4.1. Many of these mirrored areas of interest in the USA.

Table 4.1 Areas of interest to occupational psychologists

> • Personnel selection
> • Job satisfaction
> • Design of work
> • Quality of working life
> • Occupational stress
> • Stress management
> • Unemployment
> • Absence and accidents
> • Unfair discrimination
> • Training
> • Occupational guidance and counselling.

Organisational psychologists, on the other hand, tend to focus on the social side of work and the impact which different management practices may have on the functioning of the organisation as a whole. Table 4.2 lists some of the areas of interest of organisational psychologists.

Table 4.2 Areas of interest to organisational psychologists

> • Work motivation
> • Organisational communication
> • Teamworking
> • Leadership styles
> • Empowerment and delegation
> • Organisational culture
> • Group dynamics and group influences
> • Organisational commitment
> • Organisational change
> • Innovation
> • The psychological contract at work

The emphasis in each of these areas is quite different but until recently both came under the same heading – occupational psychology. For example, the British Psychological Society's *Journal of Occupational Psychology* was founded in 1971, and for its first 20 years included organisational psychology as part of occupational psychology. In the early 1990s, however, it changed its title to the *British Journal of Occupational and Organisational Psychology* – reflecting the way that the two parts of work psychology had come to be seen as entirely separate.

The European Network of Organisational and Work Psychologists produced a curriculum for use as a frame of reference for work and occupational psychologists. Around 20 European countries form this network, and the idea is to organise research in such a way as to encourage international collaboration. It divides work psychology into three separate areas:

• **Personnel psychology** is about relationships between people and the organisation, particularly with regard to establishing a relationship between the individual and the company, and also concerning the termination of this relationship. Recruitment, training and performance appraisal come within this area.

• **Work psychology** is about the processes and tasks people do at work, and includes issues such as workload, environment and equipment design, and ergonomics.

• **Organisational psychology** is concerned with how people behave in groups, and topics include leadership and work motivation.

The British Psychological Society has had a division of occupational psychology since 1971, which had three main aims:

• To promote high standards of competence and behaviour among occupational psychologists.

• To increase public awareness of what occupational psychologists do, and of the area of work.

• To develop the practice of occupational psychology.

These aims were written at a time when the term 'occupational psychology' included organisational psychology, so the list of skills the Division considers that occupational psychologists will have includes aspects of work psychology such as personnel selection and assessment; organisational change and development, interviewing techniques, and group processes. At the time of writing the Division is changing both its name and its lists of specified skills, to clarify the distinction between organisational and occupational psychology, and to reflect the increasing specialisation and complexity involved in applying the psychology of work.

Methods used in work psychology

Whether they are occupational or organisational in their focus, psychologists studying people at work have used a range of research methods including experiments, observational studies, interviews, surveys, and case studies. Some methods are more common than others. Organisational psychologists, for example, often use questionnaires, because they are a very efficient method of obtaining information from people working throughout an organisation. Occupational psychologists use psychometric tests, and interviews, quite often.

Both types of psychologist will sometimes carry out experiments or observational studies, although these tend to be rather different from the types of experiment carried out by, say, cognitive psychologists working in the laboratory. Because they use real-world research, it is often not possible to control variables to the extent that a laboratory allows, so there is always room for other influences to creep in. Nonetheless, many kinds of experiments have been carried out in the working environment – experiments on different levels of lighting, for example, or on introducing different methods of working, such as teamworking.

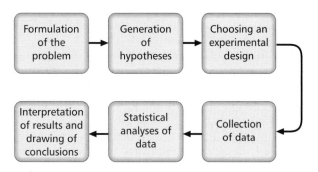

Figure 4.1
Steps in the research process (Source: Adapted from Riggio, 2000)

Most of the experiments in the early days of work psychology involved looking at the ways that people worked, to see if there were more efficient ways of going about it. But the problems with trying to carry out controlled experiments in a working environment is that all sorts of other factors – particularly social ones – come into play. In the studies carried out in the Hawthorne Electric Plant in Illinois in the 1930s, the experimenters tried varying all sorts of working conditions but they often found that what caused increases in productivity was something quite different from what they thought they were studying. In one section of the plant, for example, they measured the typical productivity rate, and then increased the lighting levels. Productivity went up, suggesting that better lighting helped people work. But then, as a control, they tried lowering the lighting levels, and productivity went up again – not down, as they had

expected. Finally, they put the lighting levels back to how they had been originally, and productivity became higher than ever! When they looked more deeply into what was going on, they found that what had really made the difference was the fact that someone was actually paying attention to the workforce, and was concerned about their conditions of work. The actual conditions didn't matter – it was the interest from the researchers that made the difference.

Modern work psychologists have learned to deal with such problems, and use a range of research methods designed to allow them to study both the social and the physical aspects of the working situation. Interviews are used quite often, as are questionnaires and field experiments. Because of the richness of the data, work psychologists are increasingly using qualitative as well as quantitative methods to analyse their findings. A typical organisational case study will involve bringing together several different methods rather than just using one single approach.

⟲ Recall AS material

Recall your AS material on type of research method, and on the distinction between quantitative and qualitative methods. Look it up if you can't recall.

ACTIVITY

Make a list of the main research methods used by work psychologists, and give two advantages and two disadvantages of each. This may also be useful when you come to deal with Unit 6, the synoptic element of the course.

Work motivation

Most adults work. Some are in paid employment, while others do voluntary work, which is also part of the social system even though it is not paid. It is usually assumed that most people prefer to work, and that they also prefer to enjoy their work. Later in this chapter we will be looking at some of the effects of changes in the work situation, particularly unemployment and retirement, and we will see that these can often be psychologically damaging. Work is clearly important to us.

In any organisation motivation of the workforce can be a problem, depending on what is being asked of them, and the ways they are treated. The theories of motivation that are outlined below are used by organisational psychologists as tools to help managers to motivate their workforce. When you are reading about the theories, it is also useful to think of practical ways in which they can be used or applied.

Steers and Porter (1991) suggest that motivation serves three functions:
- To cause people to act – to energise their behaviour.
- To direct people's actions towards attaining specific goals – to ensure that their behaviour is in some way relevant to their overall motives.
- To make sure that a person maintains the effort they need to reach their specific goals. These goals will be different for different people – some might be motivated by money, some by interacting with people, others by power and influence, for example.

Like many other areas of applied psychology, the question of motivation at work can be approached from a number of perspectives.
- **Need theories** see people as driven to satisfy physiological and psychological needs.
- **Behaviour-based theories** suggest that we act in the way we do because of various patterns of reinforcements or the circumstances in which we find ourselves.
- **Job-design theories** of motivation see motivation as being closely linked with the ways that work is organised and with the expectations and ideas held by the management and workforce.

The different theories can be tentatively linked with some of the basic approaches in psychology. Need theories tend to relate biological needs (hunger, thirst, warmth, human contact) to drives that motivate us to behave in ways that will satisfy the need. Need theories thus have assumptions similar to those within the physiological approach, even though they include social needs. In addition, Maslow's need theory is part of the humanistic approach, which assumes that an individual is motivated to self-actualise. Behavioural theories of motivation, on the other hand, suggest that we are motivated to behave by positive reinforcements or similar factors, and these ideas link with the learning approach. Often the theories work together rather than contradict one another; saying something similar but with a different emphasis.

↻ Recall AS material

Recall AS material on the assumptions of the main approaches – or look it up.

Need theories of motivation

Need theories work on the principle that ordinary living involves physiological and/or psychological deficiencies that emerge as resources become used up or situations

develop. These deficiencies create an imbalance, which creates drives – pressures to satisfy them. People then have to reduce those pressures or drives by acting in a way that will satisfy them. Physiological needs are thought of as biological drives in the case of needs such as hunger and thirst. Other needs, such as the need for contact with others, are thought of as psychological needs. In essence, then, need theories of motivation propose that we are motivated to do something because of interactions between our various needs and the drives to satisfy them.

Synoptic Note

There is room here for a discussion on the 'nature/nurture' issue. It is hard to prove which drives are innate – although it is clear that hunger and thirst are – and which drives have been learned through socialisation. The problem of deciding what is innate or inborn and what we learn through interaction with our environment is one you will have come across before. Make a note whenever such issues arise, because a discussion about the nature/nurture problems is part of Unit 6, the synoptic part of the course.

Maslow's need hierarchy theory

Maslow's need hierarchy theory is one of the most popular theories of motivation in management; mainly because it seems to be able to explain how some people are never satisfied with what they have, but always want something more or different. There are various versions of Maslow's theory. The original version proposed seven sets of needs, but the more common version argues that human needs can be organised hierarchically into five sets, ranging from lower-order needs at the bottom to higher-order needs at the top.

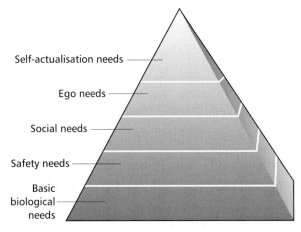

Figure 4.2
Maslow's hierarchy of needs (Source: Aamodt, 1999)

Lower-order needs include physiological needs, safety needs and social needs. These are often grouped together as **deficiency needs**, because they arise in response to a clear lack or deficiency in the person's life. Deficiency needs, according to Maslow, must be satisfied first, before higher-order needs can be met. Higher-order needs include esteem and self-actualisation, and are often referred to as **growth needs**, referring to the psychological growth that occurs as we satisfy these needs. The highest level of Maslow's hierarchy is all about **self-actualisation** (achieving one's highest potential and feeling fulfilled). According to the humanistic approach, it is the ultimate goal of every individual, and in the organisational context the idea is often linked with job satisfaction.

Maslow believed that many people don't get as far as satisfying their higher-order needs because their attention has to be focused on satisfying deficiency needs. But once deficiency needs have been satisfied, people begin to want to satisfy the higher-order needs too. People are motivated at work, according to this theory, because as each level of need becomes satisfied the next level becomes important. This is what motivates people to strive for better jobs, better working conditions and so on.

Maslow's approach was very popular, and several researchers attempted improvements on his basic ideas. For example, Alderfer (1972) proposed a theory with three categories instead of Maslow's five (or seven): existence needs (Maslow's physiological and safety needs), relatedness needs (Maslow's social needs) and growth needs (to do with fulfilling one's potential and self-actualisation). Alderfer also discussed why unsatisfied lower needs interfere with higher ones, arguing that this is because of the frustration that is felt when lower-order needs cannot be met, so the individual cannot reach the higher levels.

Evaluation

- The main problem with need motivation theories such as those of Maslow and Alderfer is that they are not supported by the evidence. Murrell (1976) points out that very little research has been carried out to test Maslow's theory.

- What evidence does exist suggests that higher-order needs may not always wait until deficiency needs are satisfied. Some people aim for self-actualisation even when their physiological needs are not fully met.

- There is no real way of measuring self-actualisation. In fact, Muchinsky (1993) states that Maslow's theory is more philosophical than empirical, which means that it is extremely hard to test.

- Furnham (1997) argues that the theory has useful ideas such as emphasis on an individual's different needs.

Rollinson *et al.* (1998) suggested that the theory prompts managers to consider their workers' needs, which in itself is a good thing.

STUDY AID

If you have studied clinical psychology as part of the course, or have read Chapter 1 (which covers clinical psychology), then recall the basic assumptions of the humanistic approach.

McClelland's achievement motivation theory

McClelland (1961, 1975) developed a theory of motivation at work which also emphasised needs. But, unlike Maslow's and Alderfer's theories, McClelland's theory is more closely linked to organisational psychology, in that its main concerns are what motivates people at work rather than motivation in general.

McClelland suggested that three needs are central when considering work motivation – need for achievement, need for power and need for affiliation. His theory was called achievement motivation theory because at first he emphasised the need for achievement above other needs. Later, though, he gave similar emphasis to the needs for power and affiliation.

- **Need for achievement (nAch)** is the drive to succeed and get the job done. People with a high need for achievement enjoy the challenge of work, and are motivated to get ahead and to solve problems. They are task-oriented rather than relationship-oriented – terms we will be meeting again later in this chapter, when we look at leadership. Task-oriented means focusing on the task itself, whereas relationship-oriented means focusing on relationships between people, to help to get the job done.

- **Need for power (nPow)** is the need to control the activities of others and to be in control. Those with a high need for power are more interested in having power than in achieving the task they are doing. Their main motivation for working is to have high status or influence within their organisation. McClelland distinguished between **personal power** (the power to achieve one's own ends) and **institutional power** (the power to achieve the targets or goals of the organisation).

- **Need for affiliation (nAff)** is the need to be liked by, and to interact in positive ways with, other people. Those with a high need for affiliation work to maintain friendships and prefer working with others. Their main motivation for working has to do with the social context within which their work takes place, and as a general rule they are more readily motivated by co-operation in the workplace, rather than by competition.

McClelland argued that we all have these three needs to different extents. One person might have a high need for power and a high need for affiliation but not such a high need for achievement. He or she might become a popular team leader or departmental head but might not aim for promotion; someone else with an equally high need for power but high achievement motivation would try to rise through the various status levels in the organisation.

If a worker is to succeed, the type of work they do must match their own type of motivation. Someone with a high need for achievement might do better if they were allowed to solve problems for themselves, in jobs within engineering or science for example. They might do well in sales, where they are rewarded by commission for sales achieved. McClelland and Franz (1993) found a correlation between high achievers and high income. A person with a high need for achievement may not do well in a team because they prefer not to delegate or work as part of a unit.

Those with a high need for affiliation work better as part of a team or in jobs where they must relate well to others – for example, in public relations or in counselling. Those with a high need for power work better in positions of power, such as in management. Leaders and managers, McClelland argued, need to be aware of the different needs of the individuals within the group if they are to keep up their employees' motivation.

It is possible to have too high a need for achievement, which affects leisure time and family life. Machlowitz (1976) argued that some people seem to be achievement addicted, and referred to these people as **workaholics**. Some companies encourage 'workaholics' and promote them, as they are useful to the company; but this can be rather short-sighted because they are also vulnerable to stress disorders and burnout. Machlowitz identified 15 characteristics as applying to workaholics (Table 4.3).

Table 4.3 Machlowitz's characteristics of workaholics

- An ongoing work style
- A broad view of what a job requires
- A sense of lack of time
- The use of lists
- Long work days
- Little sleep
- Quick meals
- An awareness of what their own work can achieve
- Cannot enjoy idleness
- A desire to excel
- Dreading retirement
- Lots of energy
- Can work anywhere
- Initiative
- Work and leisure overlap

Evaluation

- Locke and Henne (1986) suggested that motivational needs need to be translated into particular goals for the individual, and one weakness of McClelland's theory is that it does not give any clues as to how this can be done.

- Rollinson *et al.* (1998) argued that McClelland's suggestion that people can be trained to focus more on having a higher need for achievement, is inconsistent with the original claim that an individual's specific needs were developed in early childhood.

- There is a cultural bias in the theory, in that it seems to apply more in the USA where it originated than in European or other cultures.

Measuring achievement motivation

The fact that different people respond to different types of motivational goals means that it might be sensible to measure someone's type of motivation and use that measure to match the person to a job. Another application of McClelland's theory may be to teach people who are in jobs that require a high need for achievement to be more achievement oriented – by role-play for instance. There are several other possible applications. However, we need a way of measuring achievement motivation.

McClelland used the **Thematic Apperception Test (TAT)** to find out the particular pattern of needs held by specific individuals. The test involves showing people ambiguous pictures and asking them to interpret what the picture represents, usually by writing their own version of the 'stories' that the pictures are telling. The TAT is a **projective test**, in that individuals project their inner thoughts and motivational needs onto the pictures to relate the story. By examining the kinds of themes and ideas that the person brings to the story, the psychologist is able to identify their main motives and anxieties.

Evaluation

- The researcher has to interpret the story and this can sometimes mean that scoring is unreliable, although most responses are standardised.

- Some researchers suggest that those who write longer stories are also more likely to be given a higher score on achievement motivation.

- Spangler (1992) analysed results of the TAT and found it is quite a good measurement tool, despite these criticisms.

Behaviour-based theories of motivation

Behaviour-based theories of motivation are concerned with the outcomes of actions. The idea is that each action produces an outcome, which can become the motivation for the person to repeat the action. The focus in these theories is what happens as a result of particular actions, or behaviour.

Self-test

Write a timed essay, under exam conditions (or as close as you can manage) using the title 'How adequate are need theories for explaining motivation at work?'.

Reinforcement theory

The reinforcement theory of motivation draws on operant conditioning theory, which suggests that behaviour is motivated by its consequences. If the action produces desired consequences, it will probably be repeated; if the consequences are not desired, the behaviour is not likely to happen again. It is not usual in the work situation for a worker to be continuously reinforced for their actions (workers who are paid weekly are paid by a fixed-interval schedule, for example) but operant conditioning also shows how partial reinforcement (reinforcing behaviour now and again rather than every time it happens) is often stronger than continuous reinforcement.

Reinforcers may be positive or negative. In the case of positive reinforcers, the individual is motivated to act because their actions may bring them rewards. In the case of negative reinforcers, the individual acts to avoid or escape something unpleasant. For example, someone may act to avoid a noisy environment (negative reinforcement) or achieve a peaceful environment (positive reinforcement).

Another principle of operant conditioning is that punishment weakens an action. If someone receives punishment when acting in a certain way, they are less likely to act in that way again. Punishment may therefore also be a motivator, although positive and negative reinforcers are better motivators because they lead to repetition of the desired behaviour. Punishment is not a good motivator because, although it weakens undesired behaviour, it does not lead to the desired actions.

Punishment is not a good strategy for a manager who wishes to motivate their workforce. Organisational psychologists have identified several reasons for this:
- It does not lead to the required actions.
- It creates feelings of hostility and lowers morale.
- Workers may try to punish their supervisors in retaliation.
- Without the threat of punishment the undesired behaviour may continue, because the worker has not learnt to replace the undesired behaviour with the desired behaviour.

- Supervisors often become inefficient because they spend all their time watching out for undesired behaviour that must be punished.

Evaluation

- Criticisms of the reinforcement theory of motivation are the same criticisms as those of operant conditioning in general. For example, the problem with extinction is important. If the reinforcements are not maintained the behaviour will be extinguished, but this doesn't always happen.
- Reinforcement theory is also criticised because it emphasises **extrinsic motivation** – factors other than the work itself are motivators. But researchers have found that workers often find intrinsic factors motivating, such as satisfaction in creating the product.
- Evaluations of programmes of organisational behaviour modification in which target behaviours are set and rewarded show that such programmes have been successful in motivating workers to be more productive (Mawhinney, 1992).

↺ Recall AS material

Recall AS material from the learning approach, in particular principles of operant conditioning. Look it up if you can't recall easily.

Goal-setting theory

Developed by Locke (1968) and Locke and Latham (1990a), goal-setting theory emphasises setting per-formance goals for the worker. Because it is about actions – performance – it is also classified as a behaviour-based theory of motivation. Effectively, this theory is all to do with setting targets (goals), which make the working task seem more manageable and something the individual can achieve without too much trouble.

Goal-setting theory is based on three basic principles.
- The first is that difficult goals lead to higher performance than easy ones. If we find something too easy, we are not particularly motivated to do it again. But if we find it challenging but manage to achieve it, we develop a sense of personal satisfaction which motivates us to try the same thing again.
- The second principle of goal-setting theory is that specific goals lead to higher performance than broad, general goals, for reasons which we will look into.
- The third principle concerns the importance of feedback. In particular, feedback on performance is essential when aiming to achieve difficult goals, so that the person is able to appreciate how much they have done and how effective it is.

The challenge of the goal-setting approach is to make sure that goals are always clear and attainable. This requires measures of what has been achieved, and what is still to be achieved, so that the person can measure their own attainment against the target. General goals, such as 'doing better' are not usually successful because they are not measurable. If a goal is too large, too challenging or too difficult, it needs to be broken down into a series of smaller, manageable goals. Some researchers have also found that extrinsic rewards such as bonuses can increase people's commitment

Researchers exploring goal-setting have identified a number of factors that can affect its success as a motivator. Locke *et al.* (1981) found that it is important that an individual should accept the goals if they are challenging or difficult, although Yearta *et al.* (1995) found that where there are multiple goals that are a long way off, then goal difficulty does not mean improved performance. Erez and Arad (1986) found that it was most highly motivating if workers participated in the goal-setting, and further work by the same research group found that commitment to the goals on the part of the workforce was essential. Erez and Zidon (1984) found, similarly, that goals have to be achievable – there is no point setting goals which are so ambitious that they are impossible to achieve.

Recent research has not looked so much at whether goal-setting is an effective technique, but more at why it works. Setting goals may lead to better planning by workers, for example (Vance and Colella, 1990). Smith *et al.* (1990) found that good planning led to better achievement of goals. Feedback also seems to improve performance, as if people are learning through trial and error, with feedback leading to adaptations and improvements. Goal-setting techniques have become widely known, and are used in many areas, such as in sport training, or weight-control programmes.

Evaluation

- Meta-analyses suggests that goal-setting is an effective motivating technique (Wofford *et al.*, 1992).

- However, although goal-setting theory has generated much research, a lot of this has been carried out on college students, so it is unclear how far the findings can be generalised.

- Goal-setting is also often studied using simulated work situations in laboratory settings, which raises questions about validity.

- There has been recent field research, however, and Arnold *et al.* (1995) suggest that goal-setting theory seems to be the most consistently supported theory in the area of work psychology.

- Managerial techniques such as 'management by objectives' (MBO) are consistent with goal-setting theory and a measure of its usefulness as a theory.

STUDY AID

The idea of goal-setting as a motivator can be used when studying. If you think of all the material you need to study for a particular subject as one goal, you are likely to feel overwhelmed by the task. But breaking this large and challenging goal into sub-goals, such as mastering one chapter of a book at a time, is likely to be more motivating.

Job design theories of motivation

Job design theories of motivation emphasise the design of the job itself, and the structure of the job as a motivator. If a job is well designed and the worker finds satisfaction for both physiological and psychological needs from the job, then the worker will be motivated. According to this approach, it is not the need or drive itself that is the motivation (as in need theories), or the outcome of the behaviour (as in behaviour-based theories), but the design and structure of the job itself.

Job-design approaches have recently become very popular and have often broadened into other aspects of working life. Where they initially tended to focus purely on the characteristics of the job itself, there is now great interest in how these characteristics and other aspects of life in the organisation – such as the organisation's culture or managerial practices – contribute to the **quality of work life (QWL)**.

Someone's QWL does depend on their working conditions and the payment benefits they receive, but that is not the whole story. It also depends on other factors, such as their opportunities to participate and advance in the organisation, how much job security they have, the type of work they do, and the type of organisation to which they belong. Adams *et al.* (1996) discussed how QWL links with the quality of people's relationships outside work, including their general health and wellbeing.

Herzberg's two-factor theory

Bringing all of these factors together can be a tricky task, and understanding how they work together can be even more challenging. Herzberg's **two-factor theory** is one of the few theories that has tried to tackle this area (Herzberg, 1966). Herzberg argued that job satisfaction is very far from being a simple continuum. Instead, Herzberg suggested that job satisfaction might be produced by entirely different factors from the ones which produce job dissatisfaction – that they are not connected along a simple line ranging from high to low satisfaction. This is why the theory is called the 'two-factor' theory, because Herzberg saw job satisfaction as one factor and job dissatisfaction as a different one.

Herzberg's initial conclusions were drawn from surveys with white-collar professional workers (accountants and engineers) in Pittsburgh (Herzberg *et al.*, 1959) and was backed up by later research in the UK and USA. Employees were asked what they thought of as good or bad about their jobs, and the different aspects of their replies were classified according to whether they contributed to job satisfaction or to dissatisfaction.

The factors that led to job satisfaction were called **motivators**, and those which led to job dissatisfaction if they were not present **hygiene factors**. Motivators, Herzberg found, are part of the content of the job itself – for example, level of responsibility, type of work and opportunity for advancement. Hygiene factors tend to be concerned with the context of the job, such as working conditions, benefits, salary and company policy. If the hygiene factors were not right, employees would feel dissatisfied, which would give management problems such as high levels of sickness, absenteeism and high staff turnover. Under correct hygiene factors employees would do their work more competently, but still might or might not feel a sense of satisfaction from doing it – this depended on the motivators.

Herzberg's approach had implications for managers, in that a manager who concentrated only on hygiene factors might reduce job dissatisfaction but still not have a high level of job satisfaction among the workforce. High levels of job satisfaction will be achieved only if the manager is also careful to provide motivators.

Evaluation

- It is not always easy to separate hygiene factors and motivators. Salary is a hygiene factor, but can be a motivator if it is indicative of status within the company, for example.

- It can be claimed that the two-factor theory applies more to white-collar and professional workers (and, indeed, these formed the initial sample).

- The theory is important because it goes away from simplistic ideas about job satisfaction. Research resulting from the theory has led to interest in job enrichment, and formed the basis for many new managerial initiatives.

ACTIVITY

If you have a full-time or part-time job, sort the various features of your working life into factors that give you job dissatisfaction (or would do if they were worse) and factors that help you to find your work satisfying. Make a list of what could be improved to give you more job satisfaction. How well does your list of hygiene factors and motivators relate to the ones that would be predicted by Herzberg?

Self-test

Write a timed essay, under exam conditions (or as close as you can manage) using the title 'Compare and contrast two theories of work motivation'.

Job selection and assessment

One of the most important things for any organisation is to have the right people in the right jobs. The process of identifying the right kind of person for the demands of a particular job or jobs is known as **personnel selection**. This is important for the organisation, but just as important for the person concerned. As we have seen, job satisfaction comes from within the job itself, so being suited to the job in some way is important.

Different organisations have different needs regarding the people they need in their key roles. For example, in an organisation with a flat structure, with experts in different roles, people with a high need for achievement in their areas of expertise might be best suited to the jobs that come up. But people with a high need for achievement in terms of status and position wouldn't be, because a 'flat' organisation with very few management layers wouldn't provide opportunities for promotion. Recruitment programmes, testing and screening are all expensive for the organisation, but so is taking on the wrong sort of people, so the cost usually outweighs the cost of hiring the wrong person for the job.

Cook (1993) identified two approaches to personnel selection.
- In the **predictivist** perspective the job is a given entity and the person who is best suited to fit it must be chosen: the person–job fit is important. The predictivist perspective tends to fit the North American model, and looks at job analysis, person specification, selection criteria, recruitment and selection, some of which are

outlined below. In this perspective, the person must fit the role, and is subjected to the selection methods that the organisation chooses.

- The other perspective is the **constructivist** perspective, in which the emphasis is on the individual candidates for the job. This is a more European perspective, which emphasises how both the organisation and the candidate construct a view of each other during the selection process. This view will help not only in their decisions but also in their future dealings with one another (Dachler, 1994). The constructivist perspective sees job selection as looking at prospective candidates for jobs in terms of what they can bring to the organisation. It involves looking at the person–job fit, the person–organisation fit, and then person–team fit (Anderson and Ostroff, 1997).

Choosing people for jobs is a challenging task, and there are several different techniques that prospective employers can use. Personnel selection has three major areas.

1 Job analysis, which involves identifying the important features of the tasks the person is going to be asked to do, and identifying particular qualities they would need in order to do it.
2 Selecting the candidate through applications and job selection interviews.
3 Psychometric testing.

Job analysis

Job analysis is the first stage of personnel selection (Figure 4.3). It involves identifying the duties, tasks and responsibilities of the job and developing an understanding of the knowledge, skills and abilities needed to do the job.

Wheaton and Whetzel (1997) discussed how vital job analysis is for personnel selection, because only up-to-date job analyses make sure that the rest of the personnel selection process is appropriate. As jobs can change over time, they argued that it is important that job analyses should be carried out regularly, and kept up to date.

Methods used in job analysis include drawing up a job description, which lists the tasks and responsibilities of the worker, the equipment needed to do the job and the output required. The job description may include an objective measurement of the work being done, interviews with workers, and other ways of collecting information. Once the job description has been completed, a job specification will be worked out, which provides information about the type of person needed to carry out that particular job – such as the type of experience and education they should have, and in some cases personality qualities which seem appropriate. A job evaluation might also be produced to assess how worthwhile the job is for the organisation, and to determine salary level. The final stage in job analysis is to establish performance criteria, which are used to see how well someone is performing in the job.

Job analyses, bringing with them job descriptions, evaluations, person specifications and performance criteria, are useful for the organisation. They are also useful for the employee, as the job description makes it clear what he or she is expected to do and what rights they have. For example, discrimination on the grounds of disability is not allowed, and people with physical or mental disabilities have to be accommodated so they can do their job. Some job analyses must therefore take such disabilities into consideration.

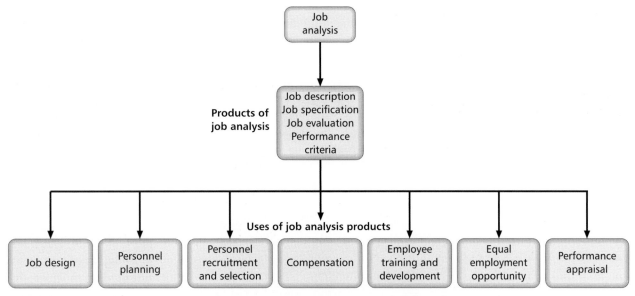

Figure 4.3
How job analysis and personnel functions are linked (Source: Riggio, 2000; based on Ghorpade, 1988)

ACTIVITY

If you have a full-time or part-time job, try carrying out a job analysis. First, write out a job description, detailing the tasks you do, the equipment you need and the minimum qualifications needed. Then write out a person specification, describing the type of person you think is needed for the job. Once you have done that, have a go at a job evaluation, making notes about the usefulness of your work to the company. Finally make a list of what you think the ideal personal qualities for your job would be. How far do you match up with your job?

Methods used in job analysis

There are a number of different methods used in job analysis. One of the most important is **observation.** Trained job analysts use observation a great deal, watching the person doing the job over a period of time – at different times and on different days. Sometimes, video cameras are used for more detailed analysis. Observation is not suitable for all types of jobs, of course – many managerial and professional jobs, for example, involve decision-making and strategies which are not easily observed. It is most useful for jobs where there are distinct and measurable tasks.

One disadvantage of observation is that the observer might affect the situation. One of the early findings of organisational psychologists was the way that workers often perform better simply because they are being observed – an effect known as the **Hawthorne Effect** (from the experiments carried out by Mayo (1933) at the Hawthorne Electric Plant in Illinois, which we looked at earlier in this chapter). However, other studies have shown

that being part of an observation can cause reduction in productivity – for example, if the workers believe that the tests will lead to more demands on them (Roethlisberger and Dickson, 1939). Either way, the observer has influenced the findings, which experienced job analysts need to take into account.

An alternative to observation is **participation**. The job analyser carries out the actual job for a period of time, noting what it involves and its actual tasks; and this technique can be very useful for certain types of jobs. However, it is generally considered to have only a limited value, partly because of the need in some jobs for specific training and experience, and partly because not everyone carrying out a job analysis would be able to do the actual job – particularly the more demanding types of manual work.

Another way of carrying out a job analysis is to look at **existing data**. Sometimes a job analysis can be carried out using the company's statistics, previous job analyses, or analyses of similar jobs together with supervisors' reports and other such information. It has also been known for job analysts to use profiles obtained from similar jobs in other organisations, but this is always a little uncertain, because of the differences between organisations. Information taken from other organisations needs to be carefully checked for accuracy, as the job may have changed since the original data was gathered.

Interviews are useful ways of finding out about a job. Ammerman (1965) suggested a job analysis interview technique for use with small organisations which involved five basic steps:

1 Convene a panel of experts with representatives from all levels.
2 The panel identifies the objectives and standards an ideal person would achieve.

Figure 4.4
Workers in the original Hawthorne studies

3 The panel lists specific behaviours needed to achieve these objectives and standards.
4 The panel identifies which of these behaviours are critical for the objectives to be achieved.
5 The panel ranks the objectives according to importance.

Most of the time interviews are much less formal, and involve open-ended questions in which the interviewers simply ask people about the work they are doing. However, interviews are expensive to carry out, and ideally a job analyst will interview several employees, unless the job is only ever done by one person (which is not very likely). But even then, they would need to interview both the person doing the work and their supervisor to get a full perspective of what is involved and what it is actually for.

Job analysts often use **survey techniques** when they are dealing with jobs that are quite common in an organisation. Questionnaires are relatively cheap to produce, and can be circulated to any number of employees. The advantage is that a survey allows for more than one set of data to be collected at once, and this saves both time and money. Also the survey can be anonymous, which means that workers might be more willing to give information. However, the information that can be obtained is limited by the questions asked, and open-ended questions are notoriously unsuccessful in surveys. In an interview, the interviewer can explore different themes and ask open-ended questions as much as they think is appropriate.

One of the more specific techniques used for job analysis is the use of **job diaries**, the person doing the job keeping a diary recording day-to-day activities. Their main advantage is that they can give detailed information over a period of time, but keeping a diary is time-consuming both for the person writing down the information and for the person analysing it.

↻ *Recall AS material*

Recall – or look up – AS material on methods used in psychology, including criticisms of the different research techniques.

As well as the general methods used above, there are also some specific techniques used for job analysis. One of these is known as the **job elements method**, in which the knowledge, skills, abilities and other characteristics required for the job are identified, and rated according to their importance for the job. This helps recruiters know what qualities will be required in the person needed for the job (Primoff, 1975).

Functional job analysis (FJA) is another fairly widely used technique, particularly in America, although its rather mechanistic approach has attracted some criticisms. FJA was designed in 1991 to help develop the *Dictionary of Occupational Titles* in the USA, in which over 40,000 jobs were described. Jobs were classified using a nine-digit code, with the middle three digits being the ones that give the job description, focusing on data, people and things (Table 4.4). In this system, 'Data' refers to what the job entails (what they have to do); 'people' refers to the amount of interaction with others that is needed; 'things' are the equipment and things that a person has to interact with. For example, if the digits are 107, this means that the job requires not much co-ordination of data (1), not much mentoring people (0) but quite a lot of handling things (7) – '0' tends to mean little contact, and '9' means a lot of contact (Fine and Getkate, 1995).

Table 4.4 Hierarchy of work functions used in functional job analysis

Data (4th digit)		People (5th digit)		Things (6th digit)	
0	Synthesising	0	Mentoring	0	Setting up
1	Co-ordinating	1	Negotiating	1	Precision working
2	Analysing	2	Instructing	2	Operating-controlling
3	Compiling	3	Supervising	3	Driving-operating
4	Computing	4	Diverting	4	Manipulating
5	Copying	5	Persuading	5	Tending
6	Comparing	6	Speaking, signalling	6	Feeding, off bearing
		7	Serving	7	Handling
		8	Taking instruction, helping		

Source: Riggio (2000)

A third specific technique used for job analysis (particularly in America) is the **position analysis questionnaire.** This organises 187 job elements into six categories (Table 4.5). Each element is analysed according to how important it is for the job, the amount of time the employee spends doing it, and how likely it is to occur. The idea is that it provides a more straightforward method for comparing jobs within different organisations than interviews (McCormick, 1979). However, research suggests that it is only a reliable measure when used by expert job analysts, not if it is used by people doing the jobs themselves (Harvey and Lozada-Larsen, 1988). Some researchers have suggested that this might be because the job analysts have better verbal skills, but others maintain that a system that cannot be used by those who know the work best is of doubtful validity.

Table 4.5 Categories of the position analysis questionnaire

Information input – where the employee gets information required to perform the job.

Mental processes – what kind of thinking and reasoning is needed to perform the job.

Work output – the tasks to be done and the equipment needed.

Relationships with other persons – what interactions and contacts are needed to perform the job.

Job context – the physical and social contexts the job is performed in.

Other job characteristics – other relevant activities or conditions.

We can see, then, that there are many different ways of approaching job analysis. Many of these reflect the methods used by organisational researchers and other applied psychologists, and so may be familiar to you. However, no technique is absolutely perfect – in fact, Morgeson and Campion (1997) listed 16 different ways in which job analyses might be inaccurate. Some are inaccuracies from the analysts themselves – who might make mistakes when analysing data, or might overestimate the importance of certain areas, for example. But other problems are inherent in the methods chosen.

Synoptic Note

The examples of research methods used here may also be useful for Unit 6, the synoptic part of the course.

Applications and interviews

Applications and interviews are all about obtaining information from the candidates who are applying for the job. Prospective employers can ask for information in several different ways – some ask only for a letter of application, while others ask for a curriculum vitae (CV) or expect the candidate to fill in a standard application form.

There are advantages and disadvantages to each method. Letters of application enable an employer to judge the candidate's ability to express themselves in written English and to look at presentation style, neatness and sometimes even handwriting. Application forms ask for pre-set categories of information, and have the advantage of presenting information about the candidates in ways that can easily be compared. The CV is a personal way of organising information which allows the candidate to emphasise their strengths and expertise in ways that might not be possible on a standard application form. They can be more informative than application forms, but make comparing candidates more difficult.

Both application forms and CVs are popular in the UK, in Denmark CVs are more popular than standard forms, whereas in Germany standard application forms are more popular (Shackleton and Newell, 1997). In France, hand-written letters of application are frequently requested, and graphologists are often consulted to interpret the handwriting and give their analysis of the person's character. Job advertisements for manual and blue-collar jobs often ask candidates not to submit a CV because they are often more concerned with routine jobs which don't require distinctive personal qualities. But a CV is generally expected for professional and managerial positions.

In the UK, equal opportunities legislation means that application forms must not include questions about race, religion or disability, in case the information is used for job selection (which would be illegal discrimination). However, these questions can be asked on a separate sheet for the purposes of monitoring – for example, large organisations are supposed to employ a certain minimal percentage of registered disabled staff.

First impressions count, and the way the information is presented on the application form, letter or CV often forms an impression that lasts throughout the selection process (Macan and Dipboye, 1994). The most important role of this information, of course, is to provide **biodata** – biographical information about what a person has been doing with their life – which can be used to screen applicants and develop a short-list for a particular job. Many personnel researchers see biographical data as the best predictor of future performance (e.g. Knouse, 1994).

ACTIVITY

Collect a set of advertisements for jobs of various types (try your local newspaper, a national tabloid, and a national broadsheet such as the Telegraph or Guardian). Look at the different types of information requested. How many ask for each type? Then see whether different types of job ask for different types of information. What explanations can you suggest for your findings?

As a general rule, **interviews** take place after an initial sorting of candidates on the basis of written information. Their main purpose is to fill in gaps in information, to measure factors such as appearance and communication skills, to provide applicants with information so that they can see if they want the job or not, and to act as public relations for the company. In a large survey of employers, Shackleton and Newell (1997) found that the interview seems to be by far the most popular way of assessing a candidate.

Job interviews are usually used alongside other techniques. This is probably just as well: organisational research suggests that interviews are not a very reliable or valid means of selecting people for jobs because they are so dependent on individual impressions and other factors such as nervousness (Hunter and Hunter, 1984). But that doesn't stop them from being very widely used, and some researchers have argued that if they are conducted

properly, they might be more valid that was previously thought (e.g. Anderson, 1997).

 **Recall AS material**

Recall your AS material on reliability and validity, or look it up.

Improving interviews

Researchers have identified a number of different techniques for improving the effectiveness of job interviews. One of these is the **situational interview**. In this, the interviewers provide hypothetical situations, and the interviewee has to suggest how he or she would deal with that situation (the situations, of course, are aimed to reflect the kind of challenges which the person is likely to encounter when doing the job). Motowidlo *et al.* (1990) argued that using these can make job interviews much more effective.

Another technique, **structured behavioural interviews** (Motowidlo *et al.*, 1992) is also a way of making job interviewing more effective. These are sometimes referred to as **behaviour description interviews**, and involve interviewees drawing on what they have done in the past to show how they would deal with a situation they might be presented with in the future.

Structured interviews are preferred in job selection because all candidates are asked the same questions, making it easier to make fair comparisons (Dipboye,

Table 4.6 Types of validity and reliability

Predictive validity	The extent to which selection scores predict future job performance. Successful applicants are tracked through the selection process and after a period of employment with the organisation a subsequent measure of performance is obtained. The selection and criterion ratings are correlated
Concurrent validity	The extent to which selection scores predict current performance. Selection techniques are administered to existing job incumbents and correlated with ratings of job performance taken over the same time period
Construct validity	The extent to which selection accurately measures the constructs or dimensions it was designed to assess. The selection method is correlated with another method which is known to accurately reflect the construct
Content validity	The extent to which the selection process adequately samples all the important dimensions of the job. This requires a thorough examination of the job description and job specification
Face validity	The extent to which the applicant perceives the selection method to be relevant to the job
Parallel reliability	Measurement consistency. Each candidate completes two equivalent selection methods and the two scores are correlated
Test–retest reliability	Measurement consistency. Candidates complete the same selection method at two times. The two scores are then correlated
Split-half reliability	Measurement consistency. Items from a measure are divided into two halves (e.g. odd-numbered versus even-numbered items) and the scores from each half correlated

Source: Chmiel (2000)

1994). Using a panel of interviewers also seems to improve reliability, but validity can still be a problem, as stereotypes can easily be shared – and there is always the risk of 'groupthink' (a problem of shared group assumptions which we will be looking at later in this chapter). A panel of interviewers can be expensive, though not as expensive as multiple interviews, in which an interviewee is interviewed separately by several people.

It is generally taken for granted that interview questions must be job-related, and this is borne out by research findings which suggest that interviews using hypothetical situations or similar job-related exercises seem to be more successful in choosing the right candidates (Latham and Saari, 1984). Some researchers argue that good interviews also use a scoring system for candidates' answers, and recommend the adoption of rating scales, although this is a little more contentious. Some training for interviewers does seem to be effective (Stevens, 1998), although the evidence for this is not conclusive (Howard and Ferris, 1996).

Evaluation

- Reliability of the interview may be a problem, not only because the judgements of the interviewer are likely to bias their opinions, and because the interviewee might not perform well due to nerves.

- Interviewers are often biased because of gender, race, physical disability, and/or physical attractiveness (e.g. Wright and Multon, 1995).

Figure 4.5
One problem with hiring interviews is that interviewers tend to make snap decisions based on first impressions or limited information

- Interviews are very vulnerable to other types of bias, such as snap judgements (when the rest of the interview is interpreted as confirming the initial opinion) or the contrast effect in which an applicant following a very good (or a very bad) candidate might be evaluated more negatively (or favourably) in contrast.

- An interview is not always useful, because interviews test a person according to their communication and social skills, and how well they present themselves – skills that might not be important for certain jobs.

- People with good cognitive abilities tend to do better in interviews – although sometimes good cognitive abilities mean that a person will be good at the job, so this may not be too much of a problem (Huffcutt *et al.*, 1996).

ACTIVITY

Write a sentence or two on what might make an interview more reliable, and how you would test this. Then write a short account of what might make an interview more valid, and how you would test this. These issues are useful in evaluation, and may also be useful for Unit 6, the synoptic part of the course.

Psychometric testing

Another means of selecting personnel is to use **psychometric testing**. Psychometric tests are standardised measures divided into cognitive ability tests and personality tests. Britain, Belgium and Portugal make a lot of use of both cognitive ability tests and personality tests, whereas Germany and Italy use them less (Shackleton and Newell, 1997). There are many tests on the market and the British Psychological Society (BPS) has published several reviews to help people to decide which test to use (e.g. Bartram *et al.*, 1997).

Psychometric tests are usually used in recruitment, to try to find the right person for the job. They are also sometimes used when considering someone for promotion, and some tests have been produced which have specialised uses, like the tests that look for managerial potential. However, psychological tests are rarely used entirely on their own – they are always used alongside interviews, managers' reports or other kinds of information – and they are never supposed to be used for demotion (when someone is considered not suitable for the post they occupy, and allocated a lower-status position). Demotion is not supposed to happen anyway, because there are employment laws to protect employees.

Psychometric tests measure psychological abilities and characteristics, and several different types are used.

Cognitive tests test either general intelligence or specific cognitive skills. **Ability and aptitude tests** look either at mechanical ability – the ability to recognise and apply mechanical principles – or at other motor and sensory skills or potential. These tests often include timed performances to do with the manipulation of small parts, or similar tasks, to explore someone's suitability for certain types of work. **Personality tests** measure the psychological characteristics of employees. They are very popular, but often misunderstood, because they depend very strongly on the model of personality held by those who developed the test.

Cognitive tests

Cognitive tests look at a person's mental abilities or potential. Sometimes they involve specific skills such as decision-making or problem-solving, so that they can detect people who appear to have the right kinds of abilities for responsible managerial positions. Sometimes they are simply tests of general intelligence. These are often taken as pencil–and-paper tests, administered in groups or by computer. They tend to assess factors such as basic verbal and numerical abilities to see if a person can learn simple jobs and follow instructions. One such test is the Otis self-administering test of mental ability (Otis, 1929).

Evaluation

- When measuring general intelligence, the results can show general abilities, but these may not be specific enough for the required task. However, some researchers argue that these tests do tend to be reasonable predictors of job success, even though they don't work in every case (Hunter and Hunter, 1984).

- Another disadvantage is that general intelligence tests are performed better by people with more education or of a higher social class. This has caused problems in the employment context, because the tests may discriminate against some ethnic minority groups, because members of these groups are found more in lower economic groups.

- Not only might some groups perform less well because of the education and social class but Chan *et al.* (1997) argued that some ethnic groups may be less motivated to perform well in such tests, which again may be a source of discrimination.

Aptitude and ability tests

Such tests are designed to identify a person's specific skills or their potential to learn particular types of skills.

Mechanical ability tests measure abilities such as identifying and applying mechanical principles. These tests may be particularly useful when selecting trainee engineers, or when looking for employees to work in areas such as construction and repairing of machinery. One such test is the Bennett mechanical comprehension test (BMCT). Muchinsky (1993) argued that the BMCT is the best predictor of job performance in groups such as those involved in the manufacture of electromechanical components.

Motor and sensory tests detect how good someone is (or could become) at physical or sensory skills. For example, they may focus on the sophisticated muscular control needed for high-tech assembly tasks – involving tests such as the Crawford small parts dexterity test (Crawford, 1981), which measures motor abilities and consists of timed tests in which the person is required to handle and manipulate very small parts. Alternatively, they may focus on sensory abilities. Every telephone engineer, for example, has to have a colour vision test, because of the complex colour-coding used in telephone systems. Prospective air pilots also need perfect colour vision, so a test to detect this is included as part of the entry criteria for the RAF. Other tests may explore other types of sensory ability, for example the Snellen Eye Chart for visual acuity, and other tests have been developed for hearing and the other senses.

Personality tests

Personality tests are attempts to look at the type of person who is applying for a particular job in order to match personality characteristics to the job requirements. A personality test is always based on a theory of personality, and the test itself will reflect the assumptions of that theory. For example, the Myers–Briggs test is based on the theory of Carl Jung, and has four scales reflecting aspects of that theory, such as intuitiveness. By contrast, the Edwards personal preference schedule, which has 15 dimensions, is based on a theory by Murray identifying different personality traits; and projective tests such as the TAT, are based on psychodynamic principles.

Projective tests – unstructured tasks such as pictures or inkblots that have to be interpreted – are relatively uncommon in the work situation, because they are normally concerned with detecting abnormality, and most occupations require tests which evaluate normal personality. They are also time-consuming and expensive, so are used only in rather special situations. Most of the tests used in occupational selection are more conventional ones, often based on trait theories of personality, such as the five-factor theory which tests for the five personality factors outlined (Table 4.7).

Robertson and Kinder (1993) argued that some work-related personality characteristics are quite good predictors of job performance, especially when the

Table 4.7 The five-factor model of personality

> **Neuroticism** (insecure, anxious, depressed versus emotionally stable)
>
> **Extroversion** (assertive and sociable versus timid and reserved)
>
> **Openness to experience** (curious and creative versus narrow in interests and practical)
>
> **Agreeableness** (co-operative and likeable versus antagonistic)
>
> **Conscientiousness** (dependable and hard-working versus disorganised and lazy)

personality characteristics required have been ascertained by a thorough analysis of the job. The most common tests which are used in this context are tests of general personality such as the Minnesota Multiphasic Personality Inventory (MMPI) or the Occupational Personality Questionnaire (OPQ). These tests provide a personality profile, which shows the person's stronger and weaker traits. They can be used to look for positive or negative qualities and help to identify people who would not be suitable for certain jobs, such as police work (Hathaway and McKinley, 1970).

A number of tests have been devised for specific jobs, and tend to focus on more specific characteristics – for example, in the USA (though not in the UK), dominance and extraversion have been found to be good predictors of success as a manager (Barrick and Mount, 1993). Some tests, such as the California Psychological Inventory (CPI) developed by Gough (1987), use such findings to look for people with management potential. This test also has a work orientation scale to predict employee performance in general; and such scales use other information about personality characteristics such as the way that dependability and conscientiousness appear to be good predictors of job ability, and of attendance at work (Barrick *et al.*, 1994).

Administering tests

Administration of tests is a complex task, for which people need to be specially trained. Each test, for example, comes with a set of standardised instructions, and should be taken under appropriate conditions. The BPS administers a Certificate of Competence in Occupational Testing, which qualifies non-psychologists such as personnel officers or recruitment specialists to administer psychometric tests for employment purposes. The BPS certificate also introduces prospective trainers to the ethical aspects of testing, which are important if they are to be used to make serious decisions.

Computer-based testing (CBT) is sometimes used rather than paper and pencil tests. Tests administered in this way can be immediately scored using the computer and the results fed back to the decision-makers. Many researchers feel that CBT is both practical and cost-effective, particularly for organisations that do a great deal of recruitment or job selection (Schmitt *et al.*, 1993).

A variant on CBT is known as computer-adaptive testing (CAT). This is becoming popular in the USA. These are known as 'smart' tests, because the computer adjusts the level of difficulty for the person taking the test. If a few questions are found to be giving difficulty, for example, the computer asks easier questions. CAT is used in tests which have knowledge-based questions, with right or wrong answers. They are often more informative than other computer-administered tests, because the computer can take the wrong answers into account when making an assessment.

Many modern tests involve work simulations of some kind, some using video technology to create a work situation in which the candidate has to suggest a solution to a problem. The candidate can also be asked to perform work-related tasks in this virtual environment. This is a realistic test, but it is an expensive way of testing. Other tests look at specific aspects of a working situation in a rather less expensive way, such as the popular 'in-basket exercise' test, in which prospective managers are asked to prioritise different tasks for the day. The decisions they make help the job selectors to identify their working styles, and also perhaps their potential for specific types of work.

Some of the tests used in occupational selection may have low validity, as they are often very general and are not carried out in a real-life setting. However, some researchers have found that employment tests are often better predictors than other selection methods such as interviews and using biographical information (Hunter and Hunter, 1984). As jobs are complex, and usually involve more than one skill, employment screening tests are often grouped into sets, known as **test batteries**, and scores from several different tests are combined (Ackerman and Kanfer, 1993).

Self-test

Write a timed essay, under exam conditions (or as close as you can manage) using the title 'Discuss two methods employed in selecting personnel'.

Leadership and groups

Organisational psychology, as we have seen, is concerned with the ways that people work within the organisation. Although we tend to think of work as mainly to do with performing specific tasks, the social aspects of working life can make all the difference between whether we enjoy work, whether we are motivated to work hard or diligently, or whether we simply see work as something we have to put up with in order to reach the weekend. Most people work alongside others, and have to co-operate with them in order to do their work (we will look at some aspects of working in groups later in this section). Another crucial aspect of working life has to do with organisational leadership – the directors and managers of an organisation, and how they interact with employees.

Leadership

Yukl and Van Fleet (1992) defined **leadership** as where a leader uses his or her influence to help the group to reach its goals. Some leaders emerge from within the group, and some leaders are leaders because of their role, such as the supervisor of the work group, or a manager. The style of the leader is of great importance to the decisions or success of the group. Sometimes appointed leaders are not the true leader of the group, because their leadership is not effective.

There have been a number of different types of theories of leadership. Early theories of leadership were called **universalist theories** because studies looked for the universal characteristics of a good leader – the personality traits or styles that seem to make leaders effective. Later research led to **behavioural theories**, looking at the behaviour of effective leaders rather than their personal characteristics, on the grounds that the secret of good leadership is in actions. More modern research tends to lead to **contingency theories**, which emphasise the relationship between the characteristics of the leader and the work situation. Using this approach, factors such as the personality of the leader or their behaviour are seen as being contingent on other factors, such as the demands of the particular working situation.

Researchers have used a number of different approaches to studying leadership. Some have adopted an experimental approach, in which variables are manipulated in order to produce different effects (later in this section we will be looking at a study by Lewin *et al.* which followed this approach). Others have used observational methods – looking at leaders in action and attempting to identify distinctive characteristics. Organisational researchers have also used case studies of successful leaders to attempt to single out factors that might be important.

One of the most common ways in which leadership has been studied falls back on the old universalist approach, which attempts to identify the personality characteristics of successful leaders. A common method is to give personality tests to a group of participants, to ask peers, supervisors or other observers to rate the effectiveness of these participants as leaders and to look for correlations between the personality found and the leadership effectiveness rating. Research of this type has typically found that, since many different personality traits seemed to correlate with leadership effectiveness, many different types of people can be leaders – there is no single 'leadership trait'.

Leadership has been studied using survey techniques. Questionnaires yield a lot of data, which is usually analysed using **factor analysis**, a statistical procedure that helps a researcher to identify groups or clusters of items which seem to be connected in some way. The idea is that if participants answer one item in a negative way, they are likely to answer related items in a similar manner. Complex computer analysis identifies the clusters of scores in the data, and can alert a researcher to the way that different behaviours seem to go together, and may be indicating a significant factor underlying the behaviour. For example, enjoying helping out newcomers, going to organisational social events, and preferring to discuss work problems rather than solving them alone might all cluster together and be indications of an underlying factor of extraversion. Factor analysis is used to find those factors which might correlate with effective leadership – if someone has those factors, he or she is a good leader. Unfortunately, as with psychometric research, there seem to be many different factors affecting leadership, and no single one holds the key to success.

Leadership styles

When it was found that there was no single leadership personality characteristic, the focus of research shifted to the behaviour of leaders, and in particular the styles of behaviour they adopted with their employees (this way of looking at leader style is part of the behavioural approach to the study of leadership). Research into leadership style has given a number of insights into leadership effectiveness, and researchers have identified a number of different dimensions that contribute to effective leadership.

One of these dimensions is whether the leader is **employee-centred** or **job-centred.** Research at Michigan University in the 1960s looked at a large number of effective and ineffective leaders in production industries and, rather surprisingly, found that the managers who concentrated most on production had the least productive departments. Those that were employee-centred – interested in and concerned about their subordinates – were much more effective than those who simply focused on the task (were job-centred).

At the same time researchers at Ohio University (e.g. Stodgill, 1974) asked employees of various organisations, including military ones, to describe their boss's style. The research was carried out using questionnaires, and included questions about how the boss helped with personal problems, or whether the employees/subordinates were criticised as poor workers. Factor analysis was used.

The Ohio study identified four main factors in effective leadership:

1 **Consideration**: how much subordinates and leaders show consideration towards one another.
2 **Initiating structure**: how far the leader gives clear-cut roles and responsibility when a goal is to be achieved.
3 **Production emphasis**: how far the leader is influenced by production targets.
4 **Sensitivity**: how far the leader is sensitive to the needs of the subordinates.

In the really effective leaders all four of these factors appear to be combined.

More recent studies have also identified consideration and initiating structure as important factors in effective leadership. These factors are now more commonly referred to as **relationship-oriented/employee-centred** (consideration) and **task-oriented/production centred** (initiating structure). Leaders are either relationship-oriented (in which case they are good leaders from the employee's viewpoint) or they are task-oriented (in which case they often appear to be good leaders from the employer's viewpoint, although more complex analyses which take into account staff retention and morale suggests that they are not very effective in the long run, because taking on new people or covering for absences is also costly to the organisation).

Blake and Mouton (1964) developed a scale in which a manager could plot their own style. Their findings implied that leaders could be high both on relationship-orientation and task-orientation and still be good leaders. Blake and McCanse (1991) developed a leadership grid which also focused on the leader's own interpretation of their style, and which looked particularly at concern for people and concern for the task. They defined five main leadership styles and described them numerically, using a system in which the first figure is concern for people and the second, concern for task.

1 Team management (9.9 style). Leaders and followers all want the same goal (the task) and work towards the goal with mutual trust and respect.

2 Middle of the road management (5.5 style). The leader balances the need to get the job done with the need to keep up good morale.
3 Impoverished or laissez-faire management (1.1 style). The leader puts in the least amount of effort to get the job done and keep the group together.
4 Country club management (1.9 style). A friendly atmosphere is the main goal.
5 Task management (9.1 style). The job is done with any human elements affecting it as little as possible.

They assumed that the 'team management' (9.9) style is best, but other researchers have argued that this might not always be the case. People are different in different situations, and different tasks need different approaches.

Authoritarianism

Another set of research into leadership style focused on **authoritarianism**. Some researchers compared **autocratic** leaders with ones who were more **democratic**. This refers to how much the leader lets subordinates have a say in decision-making. The autocratic leader takes all decisions, while a democratic leader lets others give their opinions and help make decisions. Another factor connected with this type of research concerned **permissive** versus **directive**, which refers to how far leaders direct what is going on. Directive leaders give the orders while permissive leaders let their subordinates direct activities. The subordinate is important here, as the success of a style can depend on how good the subordinates are. If they can make good decisions, a democratic and permissive style might be the best one.

One of the most well-known studies of leadership style was carried out by Lewin *et al.* in 1939. They investigated leadership style in after-school clubs among 10-year-old boys who undertook model making in the clubs. The adults leading the boys acted in one of three ways. There were three separate groups, each with one leader. Every 7 weeks the leader changed style, so all the boys experienced all the styles but only one leader. This was so that the boys' responses could be said to be caused by the style and not the characteristics of the leader.

- The **democratic** group met 2 days earlier than the other groups and the leader discussed various possibilities regarding projects. The boys chose their workmates and made their own decisions. The leader explained what he was saying and joined in with the group. The boys got on well with one another and seemed to like each other better than the group with an autocratic leader. They got less work done, but the group did focus on the task, and the boys continued to work when the leader left the room. They also co-operated with each other if something went wrong.

- The **autocratic** leader told the boys what model they would make and who they would work with. They praised or blamed the boys, but did not explain their comments. The leaders were friendly, but impersonal. The boys became aggressive when mistakes were made, and their approaches to the leader were often attention-seeking. They did make good models, though, and got on with the task.
- The **laissez-faire** leader left the boys to get on with making the models and only offered help when asked for it. They were not often asked. They did not praise or blame the boys. These boys were aggressive, though not as much as the autocratic group. Very little work was done and the boys became discouraged when things went wrong.

The democratic style of leader was by far the most effective; the boys got most done and were happier. The autocratic leaders got things done too, but the boys were less co-operative. The laissez-faire style meant that little was achieved.

The study was widely quoted to show the effectiveness of the democratic approach, although some researchers (e.g. Brown, 1985) argued that the democratic style was best at that time because that was the style that the boys were used to, from their parents and teachers.

Evaluation

- There is a problem in saying that the leader's style causes the success of the task, because it is difficult to sort out causality. The style may correlate with the effectiveness of the leader, but this does not mean that one causes the other. For example, Greene (1975) suggested that work output can affect managerial style, rather than style affecting the output.
- The leader's general behaviour can be described, but it is hard to record the different behaviours that a leader might have when interacting with different members of the group.
- Informal leadership from other members of the group might affect the task outcome.
- Situational variables may also affect the outcome. The style approach does not look at situational variables and how situations can influence the ways that people interact.
- No one style has been shown to be the best in all circumstances, which shows how important situations and social factors can be. As a result, the behavioural approach of looking at styles has moved on to a contingency approach, which looks at styles, situations and social interactions.

Self-test

Write a timed essay, under exam conditions (or as close as you can manage) using the title 'Discuss different styles of leadership'.

The contingency approach

As we have seen, universalist approaches looked for the personality traits that would make a good leader, while behavioural approaches looked for the actions which would make a good leader. But neither of these was sufficient in themselves. Nowadays, the widely accepted theories of leadership tend to follow the **contingency approach**, which looks at how environment, leadership styles and situations interact.

In this section we will look at two theories that fall within the contingency approach – Fiedler's Contingency Model, which is a well known theory of leadership effectiveness, and House's path-goal theory of leadership. Contingency theories do not look for one best style of leadership, but suggest that leader effectiveness is contingent upon (depends on) the interaction between the leader's behaviour and the situation.

Fiedler's contingency model of leadership effectiveness

According to Fiedler (1967) effective leadership depends on how far the situation gives the leader control, and on the leader's behavioural style. What the leader does must fit with the demands of the situation. Fiedler took the idea of there being two main styles – task oriented and relationship oriented. He also believed that these were relatively stable traits – a leader would either always be task oriented (focusing on getting the job done) or always relationship oriented (focusing on maintaining good relations within the working group).

In order to measure the leader's orientation, and in particular to find out whether a particular leader was task oriented or relationship oriented, Fiedler developed his LPC measure ('least preferred co-worker') measure. Someone completing the LPC scale is asked to choose their least preferred co-worker ('the person with whom you had the most difficulty in getting a job done') and to evaluate them according to a number of bipolar dimensions such as 'pleasant/unpleasant' or 'friendly/unfriendly'. These particular bipolar scales are simple either-or measures, with no options in between. The total LPC score is calculated by adding all the scores from the bipolar scales. A low score means bad ratings for the person chosen, while a high score means the least preferred co-worker is rated highly on at least some of the various dimensions.

People differ in the ways they think about those with whom they work. This may be important in working with others. Please give your immediate, first reaction to the items on the following two pages.

Below are pairs of words which are opposite in meaning, such as 'Very neat' and 'Not so neat.' You are asked to describe someone with whom you have worked by placing an X in one of the eight spaces on the line between the two words.

Each space represents how well the adjective fits the person you are describing, as if it were written.

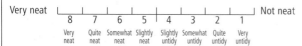

For example: If you were to describe the person with whom you are able to work least well, and you ordinarily think of him or her as being *quite neat* you would put an X in the second space from the words Very neat, like this:

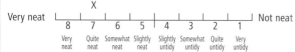

If you ordinarily think of the person with whom you can work least well as being only *slightly neat*, you would put your X as follows:

If you think of the person as being *very untidy*, you would use the space nearest the word 'Not neat':

Look at the words at both ends of the line before you put in your X. Please remember that there are *no right or wrong answers*. Work rapidly, your first answer is likely to be the best. Please do not omit any items, and mark each item only once.

LPC

Think of the person *with whom you can work least well*. He or she may be someone you work with now or someone you knew in the past.

He or she does not have to be the person you like least well, but should be the person with whom you had the most difficulty in getting a job done. Describe this person as he or she appears to you.

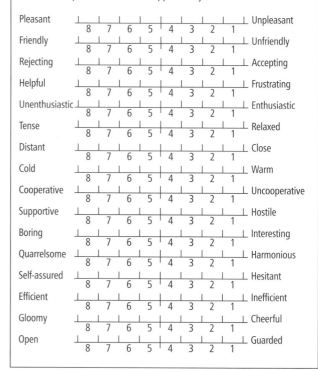

Figure 4.6
Fiedler's Least Preferred Co-worker (LPC) measure (Source: Fiedler, 1967)

Fiedler argued that a task-oriented person would rate the LPC harshly, because they would focus on getting the job done, whereas a relationship-oriented person would be more likely to rate the LPC quite highly because he or she would be inclined to separate the least preferred co-worker's personality from their work performance. The LPC measure would thus give a way of finding out a leader's basic orientation.

Different types of work situation, Fiedler argued, suited different leadership orientations. The work situation could be favourable for the leader, unfavourable for the leader, or neither favourable nor unfavourable. Fiedler identified three variables to define the work situation:

• **Leader-member relations** refers to the relationship between the leader and the followers – is the leader well-liked, and trusted by subordinates? This measure is assessed by asking group members rate their loyalty to their leader.

• **Task structure** looks at how clearly the job itself is organised and structured. It is assessed by looking at how well-defined the group's goals are, and whether there are clear procedures for the task.

• **Position power** refers to the leader's power over subordinates – for example, their ability to discipline, reward, hire or dismiss employees.

These variables combine to create a situation, which affects whether a particular leader's style will be suitable or not. A situation that is favourable for the leader would involve good position power, good leader–member relations, and a clear task structure. An unfavourable situation would involve bad position power, poor leader–member relations and an unclear task structure. Fiedler argued that task-oriented leaders are effective if the situation is either highly favourable or highly unfavourable whereas relationship-oriented leaders are most effective when the situation is neither highly

Figure 4.7
Leader–member relations show the respect workers have for their leader

favourable nor highly unfavourable (where the leader's power, the leader–member relations, and the task structures are neither very good nor very bad).

In favourable situations relationships are already good so a task-oriented leader can succeed. In unfavourable situations a task-oriented leader has nothing to lose, and will get the job done in a difficult situation. However, in the middle situation, a relationship-oriented leader can persuade the followers to perform better, and will be a better choice of leader. It is in these middle situations that problems between individuals may arise, so the relationship-oriented leader is best equipped to deal with these situations.

Fiedler's model was one of the first detailed theories of leadership to deal with the interaction between the leader and the situation. Ayman *et al.* (1995) argued that it is useful because it highlights the relationship between the leader's style and the work situation. Fiedler and Chemers (1984) used the model to develop an application called Leader Match, which teaches managers to recognise their own style and trains them to recognise the situations where they may succeed. Leister *et al.* (1977) argued that the programme is successful in increasing effectiveness but others feel that Leader Match does not follow the predictions made by the model (Kabanoff, 1981)

Evaluation

+   The model generated a lot of research, so is useful from that point of view. A number of studies have supported the model (Strube and Garcia, 1981).
−   Some studies have not supported Fiedler's predictions (Vecchio, 1977); and Peters *et al.* (1985) found that its

predictions are supported better in laboratory situations than in real-life situations.
−   Ashour (1973) argued that the LPC is not a clear measure as it derives the leaders' style only from looking at feelings towards the least preferred co-worker, and not from any behavioural observations or other data.
+   The model does not consider those with a middle LPC score, although Kennedy (1982) found that leaders with a middle score were effective in a range of situations.

Path–goal theory

Path–goal theory (House, 1971) also explores the differences between task-oriented leaders and relationship-oriented ones. However, House sees the leader as a guide who helps the group through problems and blocks to achieve their goals. The goals involve job satisfaction, which the leader helps the group to attain; so worker motivation is an important part of the theory.

To help the workers to attain their goals, including satisfaction and motivation, the leader can adopt one of four categories of behaviour:
*   **Directive behaviour** – the leader provides instructions for getting the job done.
*   **Achievement-oriented behaviour** – the leader sets challenging goals and measures outcomes.
*   **Supportive behaviour** – the leader is caring towards the workers and makes the work environment friendly.
*   **Participative behaviour** – the leader takes an active role, and takes suggestions from workers, for example.

Directive and achievement-oriented behaviours are both task-oriented, and are also known as initiating behaviours. Supportive and participative behaviours are both relationship-oriented or consideration behaviours. In some situations directive behaviour may be best – for example, where the task is complex and the worker lacks experience. In other situations supportive behaviours are better – for example, where the task is routine and the workers do not need direction.

Evaluation

- Research into the path–goal theory has produced mixed results (House, 1996). Researchers (e.g. Wofford and Liska, 1993) have argued that the model does link leader behaviour to differences in situation, which is useful; also that it helps researchers to look more closely at task-oriented and relationship-oriented behaviour. On the other hand, Yukl (1989) argued that the model seems unable to make specific predictions in work settings – and Miner (1984) criticised it on the grounds that the theory has not led to an application. However, many organisational psychologists have found that the path–goal theory of leadership gives a useful way of expressing some of the basic concerns of management and the way that leaders and subordinates interact.

Self-test

Write a timed essay, under exam conditions (or as close as you can manage) using the title 'Discuss two theories of leadership effectiveness'.

Working groups

Organisations are made up of individual people, but much of working life actually takes place in work groups, as opposed to as a solitary venture. A work group might be a department, a team or a set of people doing the same job. Work groups often provide professional identities, and at a psychological level they also provide for a person's social needs. As a result, the study of work groups has become important in organisational psychology (Sanna and Parks, 1997).

Technically, a 'group' refers to two or more people achieving some goal by means of social interaction. Usually, though, in an organisational context we mean something a bit larger when we talk of a group. Two people constitute a dyad, three people a triad; small groups tend to be between 4 and 20 people (Forsyth, 1990). Groups at work usually (though not always) have a work-related goal to achieve, and they be formal or informal.

Gordon (1983) suggested four criteria that must be met for there to be a group:
- the members must see themselves as a unit
- rewards must be provided for the members
- anything that happens to one member affects the others
- members must share a common goal.

Some working groups are much more loosely organised than this, but it is in the closely knit, common-purpose

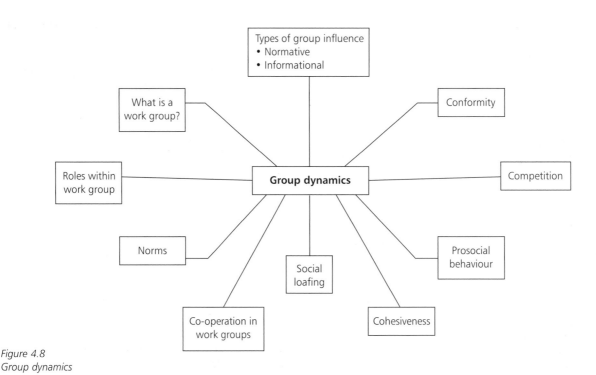

Figure 4.8
Group dynamics

groups that we see the full effect of what has become known as **group dynamics** – the special ways that groups act and interact.

Group dynamics are the processes by which groups function. Factors involved in group dynamics affect leadership decisions, and are important influences on what happens in the work place. Since most work organisations are made up of small groups, an understanding of group dynamics is very important when trying to understand how an organisation functions.

Group dynamics

Group dynamics is the name given to the various social processes that take place when people are acting or working in groups. They include the ways that social roles and group norms affect how people behave, issues concerning co-operation, competition and prosocial behaviour, the negative process known as social loafing, and a number of different aspects of conformity and cohesiveness (Figure 4.8).

Social facilitation

It has been found that people react differently just because others are present. **Social facilitation** refers to the way in which a practised response (one that someone can do well) is done better with an audience (Zajonc, 1965). In contrast, when we are not good at something, we do it even less well with an audience. From this we can assume that being part of a group will itself affect an individual's performance.

Zajonc suggested that simply being in the presence of others leads to an arousal response. This response is automatic and unavoidable: it is in our nature. This means that when in a group we are likely to be under some sort of stress, as stress occurs when our arousal response is activated. If we are confident in what we are doing, we should do better when in a group – but if we are not confident, we may do worse in a group than when alone. Social facilitation is also discussed in Chapter 5.

Evaluation

+   Some say that Zajonc's is a simple explanation, and simple explanations are appealing.
+   It seems likely that members of a species do react to the mere presence of others of that species. This reaction could be a useful survival trait.
−   However, others think that Zajonc's explanation does not pay enough attention to cognitive aspects, such as the state of mind of the person at the time.

↻ Recall AS material

Recall AS material from the biological approach, in particular arousal. Or look it up.

Roles and norms

Social roles are the parts people act out as members of society – such as parent, policeman, teenager, football enthusiast. Each social role carries its own set of expectations about how the person should behave, and the people playing those roles learn to act in accordance with those expectations. Social roles can develop in more specific contexts, and one of these contexts is within working groups. Benne and Sheats (1948) identified three categories of group roles which have relevance for modern working life:

*   **Group task roles** are related to getting the job done. There are roles such as information giver, evaluator-critic and procedural technician.
*   **Group building and maintenance roles** deal with maintaining interpersonal relations. There are roles such as harmoniser, encourager and compromiser.
*   **Self-centred roles** involve satisfying personal goals rather than group goals. There are recognition seekers, help seekers and aggressors.

Not every role is clear-cut, of course. It is not at all uncommon for people to experience **role ambiguity** – being unclear about the roles they are required to play in the work place. Role ambiguity can be a significant source of stress. Sometimes a person is expected to behave in different ways because they have more than one role, and if the expected behaviours are contradictory this can produce **role conflict**. Role conflict is not uncommon when someone is a member of more than one work group (not uncommon in modern working life).

Group roles are important, partly because they can be a significant factor in maintaining **group cohesiveness** – the tendency of the group members to stick together and co-operate with one another. People tend to learn the requirements of each role within the group – the role expectations – very quickly. As a working group develops with time, people take up different roles and learn about them – a process known as role differentiation. For example, a new group member might begin by acting out the role of novice, but then, showing themselves to have a good sense of humour, may take up the role of joker within the group.

Behaviour that is considered appropriate for group roles is often associated with maintaining **group norms** – 'rules' that show what is appropriate and what is not. Some norms are formal and written down, but many are informal. Norms can govern the speed in which a job is completed, the clothes that are worn and what are considered appropriate topics of conversation. Norms also help to make group behaviour more predictable, for example, in governing turns in speaking or time of speaking for each member.

Feldman (1984) argued that group norms at work develop from supervisor comments and from leader's examples, but many organisational psychologists would question this, because informal norms often emerge within the working group without a leader's influence. Some norms emerge as a result of the group's history – for example, things that have gone wrong in the past may have led to existing norms. Also norms may be transmitted from one working group to another, particularly if people move between the two groups.

Conformity

Group norms appear as a result of **conformity** – going along with the behaviour of others, and acting in the same way. Conformity can also sometimes mean acting against your beliefs, although conformity in the sense of what holds a group together usually means that the members of the group all agree with the group's norms. They are not just showing compliance (which means they go along with what is decided) – they are internalising the rules and norms of the group, and they are adopting group ideas and ideals as their own.

Asch (1956) carried out a well-known study of conformity, in which he asked participants to compare the length of lines, in a very simple task which he said was part of a study on perception. Participants worked with a group of about six others, who (unknown to the participants) were Asch's helpers. The helpers sat in a row, and the participant was placed at the end of the row, or second from the end. Then Asch showed four lines on a screen. The members of the group had to say which of the first three lines was the same length as the fourth line, and the answers were obvious. When Asch's helpers gave what was clearly the wrong answer, in about one-third of trials the participant agreed with the helpers and also gave the wrong answer. This was clearly a case of conformity to a group (although we do have to remember that about two-thirds of the participants did *not* conform).

In a variation on the study Asch tried a condition where one of the helpers gave the correct answer; in that situation participants always also gave the right answer – with just one person's support, the participant would hold out against the group.

Other studies showed that personality affects conformity – for instance, those who are authoritarian conform more (Crutchfield, 1955). Females tend to conform a bit more than males do (Eagly and Carli, 1981). So how the group is made up may also influence whether group members conform.

In the Asch study, participants knew the right answer but conformed to the group, rather than believing or internalising group norms. Sometimes, however, people go along with the group because they really believe that the group is more likely to be right than they are. Two types of group influence have been suggested:

- **Normative influence** occurs when participants in situations like Asch's accept the answers of the group because they think others will laugh at them, or because they think they will be threatened by the group if they do not conform. Effectively, they are responding to normative pressure – pressure to conform to the group's social norms.
- **Informational influence** occurs when participants in situations like the one Asch devised accept the group's answers as being right because they believe that the group is more knowledgeable than they are. Effectively, they are responding to informational pressure – that the information the group gives is the right information.

In another condition Asch told the participant that they were late for the study but could still take part. He or she was asked to note down the answers of the others in the group, and then write down their own answer. They were under no normative pressure, so if they still conformed they were responding to informational influence. Participants in this condition gave fewer wrong answers than those who had to give their answers aloud; but gave more wrong answers then those who did the tasks without knowing the group's answers. It seems that both informational and normative pressure were present in that situation. Both of these pressures can be important factors at work.

Minority influences

Conformity is not always inevitable. Minority pressure groups have managed to have an effect on policy making – for example, when women campaigned to be allowed to vote. Einstein was also only one person, yet he successfully challenged the scientific beliefs of his day. Moscovici *et al.* (1969) conducted a series of studies into the ways that a minority could affect social behaviour, using coloured light in a laboratory situation. He used a colour that most participants, when alone, called 'blue'. Then he included confederates (helpers) who called the colour of the light 'green' – but unlike Asch's study, the confederates were a minority of the group. Moscovici wanted to see what the effect of this minority would be on the majority. The colour was a bit like 'green', even though most people called it 'blue', so, unlike Asch's participants, Moscovici's participants would find the answer 'green' an acceptable one (participants who were colour blind were excluded). When confederates consistently said the colour was 'green' 8.4% of the participants answered 'green'. So there was a minority influence, as only 0.25% answered 'green' when alone. Participants changed their views directly (the **direct effect**) when, having previously said the light was blue, they called the light 'green'. They were also found to have changed their view of what was green and what was blue:

this is called a **latent effect**. This was found in a later experiment where participants had to decide where a line could be drawn between blue and green (they were shown many shades in between).

A dissenting minority can keep up a task-related conflict (by disagreeing) for a long time, which can change the attitude of the whole group (e.g. Nemeth and Owens, 1996). If the minority is more than one, this consistent disagreement with the majority view can affect decision making. The pressure from the minority within the group can be cognitive or social; but the disagreement makes other team members continually reassess their opinions. If the minority's arguments are consistent and clear they can eventually bring about a change in the group's approach to a problem.

 ### Recall AS material

Recall (or look up) AS material from the social approach, in particular conformity.

Co-operation and prosocial behaviour

Conformity is one of the social processes which helps us to **co-operate** with one another; and co-operation is probably the single most important factor in any organisation. People have to work together, doing their part of the work so that others can do theirs, and this permeates the whole organisation. As a result, the study of co-operation has been an area of interest in organisational psychology.

Sometimes organisations find it beneficial to promote competition. Competition involves members working against each other to achieve their own individual goals – if it is mishandled it can be very damaging, but at times competition can be healthy (salespersons, for example, often compete to be the top salesperson for the month, week or year). However, competition has to be handled carefully if it is not to become demotivating – Campbell and Furrer (1995), for example, found that introducing competition in a group where goals were already set decreased performance, so it is not always a good motivating strategy.

In working groups, co-operation is the norm, and competition is usually counterproductive. Workers are generally expected to co-ordinate their efforts as a team. For example, when one group member goes on a lunch break, the others will cover for them. Gouldner (1960) described a **reciprocity rule**, which means that individuals tend to help the other members of the group because they expect help when they themselves need it. This can be quite a significant factor in work co-operation. Co-operation in work groups is also higher when there is

a high degree of **task interdependence** (the performance of one individual is affected by others in the group) (Wageman and Baker, 1997). Some researchers also argue that rewarding workers increases their satisfaction within the group, so co-operation becomes more likely. Rewards also often depend on the performance of the group.

Group co-operation often goes hand in hand with **prosocial behaviour**, behaviour that benefits the group but not always the individual themselves. Prosocial behaviours go beyond the requirements of the work role (such as suggesting actions to improve safety), even when the individuals will not themselves benefit (Bateman and Organ, 1983). A number of researchers have found that prosocial behaviour seems to improve job satisfaction (e.g. Organ, 1988).

 ### Recall AS material

Recall AS material on social identity theory, or look it up. Social identification is strongly connected with group cohesiveness.

Social loafing

Some group members do not co-operate or behave in a prosocial way – some actually do *less* when they are working in a group than when working alone – this is known as **social loafing** (Latané et al., 1979). The observation has a long history: in a study by Ringleman, participants pulled as hard as they could on a rope whilst Ringleman measured their exerted force (Moede, 1927). His participants then did the task in pairs. Ringleman thought that the force exerted by the pair would be twice that of the force exerted by a single participant but he found that less force was exerted by a pair. Similarly, Latane (1981) found that in a restaurant customers' tips were around 19% of the bill if they dined alone, 16% of the bill if they were with one other person, and 13% of the bill if they were with five other people.

Social loafing seems to occur more when individuals do not think their own contribution is being measured, and when the tasks are simple. With more complex tasks or when the individual believes his or her contribution is known, then social loafing is less likely to occur (Comer, 1995). Punishing social loafers does not always work (George, 1995), but social loafing can be decreased if people can see that their personal input is being measured or taken note of in some way.

A number of different reasons have been put forward to explain social loafing. Kerr and Bruun (1983) suggested that when things are going well the individual thinks their contribution is not necessary. This is called the 'free rider theory'. Robbins (1995) found that group members who perceived other group members as engaging in social loafing were more likely to do it too. This may link with another explanation, suggested by Kerr (1983) and known as the 'sucker-effect theory'. The idea is that if an individual thinks the others are not pulling their weight he feels taken in by them, and his work performance falls to match their performance. However, organisational psychologists have discovered that social loafing can be reduced by increasing the cohesiveness of the working group (Karau and Hart, 1998), perhaps because the sense of 'belonging' to a group helps motivation.

Self-test

Write a timed essay, under exam conditions (or as close as you can manage) using the title 'Discuss group dynamics in the context of leadership'.

Group decision making

Group decision making involves establishing group goals, choosing a course of action, selecting new members, and evolving norms.

In **autocratic decision making** the group leader makes the decisions alone, using the information that he or she has. This is a fast way of making decisions but has the disadvantage that, since the decisions are made only on the basis of what the leader knows, the knowledge of those in the group is not used and the quality of the decision may be poor. The decision is good only if the leader has all the necessary knowledge. Autocratic decision making should be thought of as similar to autocratic leadership.

Consultative decision making, on the other hand, is when a leader is making the decisions but asks for information from the group before making the decision alone. This might lead to a better quality decision than if the leader does not have the necessary knowledge, but still uses an autocratic decision-making technique.

Another alternative is **democratic decision making**, which involves all the members taking part in discussion and then voting on what action to take. Democratic decision making is usually based on the rule of the majority, and uses the knowledge and experience of all the group members. Alternative decisions are likely to be considered, and the members are more likely to agree with the decision (and abide by it) because they have had their say. However, democratic decision making is time-consuming, and can encourage conflict. It is generally an inefficient way of making decisions, and members who do not agree with the majority decision might not go along with the plan of action.

In **consensus decision making** everyone has to agree on the course of action, not just a majority. This is particularly time-consuming, but sometimes is necessary – juries, for example, use this approach because of the importance of their decision. Such decisions are usually of high quality and backed by everyone; however, the time taken to reach a consensus is a problem and sometimes it is not possible to reach a consensus.

Each of these types of decision-making is found in organisational life. Group decisions (or team decisions) are often best because knowledge and experience of all members is pooled, and is available to the whole group. However, sometimes the individual with the most information can make a better decision (Miner, 1984), and sometimes the leader has more influence than at other times, so the group decision can be strongly affected by either an individual or the leader. In a crisis it is often better for a strong individual or a leader to make the decision, as group decisions tend to be slow.

Organisational researchers have developed some techniques to enhance decision making. One, which is particularly effective when a group is seeking an entirely novel solution to a problem, is known as **brainstorming**. Osborn (1957) developed this technique, in which a number of group members (ideally between six and ten) generate ideas or solutions to the problem. The climate in which the ideas are generated is all-important: the atmosphere, in the first stage at least, must be non-critical and all ideas, no matter how obscure, collected. The rules for the first stage of brainstorming are:
- No idea is too far out.
- Criticisms are not allowed.
- The more ideas the better.
- Members should build on each other's ideas.

Following the initial idea-generating stage, the group evaluates the different ideas and explores their practicality.

Brainstorming is very popular in organisational life, particularly in advertising and promotional work. However, some researchers (e.g. Yetton and Bottger, 1982) argue that brainstorming is not very effective as a way of problem solving. A problem is that the group dynamics may be powerful, as seen above, and individuals do not really feel free to contribute their ideas. Paulus and Dzindolet (1993) suggest that brainstorming does not produce better ideas than the individuals can produce on their own, but that it continues to be popular because the members of the group do believe it to be useful.

In a new technique – electronic brainstorming – group members exchange ideas over a computer network (Gallupe *et al.*, 1991). The developers argued that this technique seems to work well, perhaps because group dynamics are not present when the group is communicating via computer (Cooper *et al.*, 1998). However, it has attracted only limited take-up, and it remains to be seen how effective it turns out to be with time.

Groups, then, can sometimes enhance decision making, or at least make people feel that their decision making has been enhanced. But sometimes, the presence of a strong cohesive group can create problems.

Groupthink

Where groups come to high-quality decisions it is often because alternatives have been considered and a consensus reached. However, sometimes the evaluation process is not gone through; sometimes decisions are hasty and premature. These decisions are often low-quality ones, and the situation is called **groupthink** (Janis, 1972; 1982). Groupthink tends to occur in highly cohesive groups where it is generally the norm to arrive at an early decision. Bernthal and Insko (1993) suggest that groupthink occurs more in groups where the cohesiveness is relationship-based rather then task-based.

In coming up with the concept of groupthink, Janis looked at high-level decisions which were very bad decisions. For instance, the 'Bay of Pigs' debacle was a decision to invade Cuba in 1961, made by John Kennedy (then US President) and a team of expert advisors. The invasion involved a small group of badly trained exiles and the US Air Force. Kennedy's expert group were a very cohesive group isolated from the opinions of others, and the leader of the group favoured the attack. The invasion failed within days and Kennedy acknowledged that it had been a bad decision. A fiasco in business was the decision to market the drug Thalidomide, which caused birth deformations. A more recent fiasco was the decision to launch the Challenger space shuttle. Janis came up with symptoms of groupthink from studying examples like these (Table 4.8).

To break up a group so that groupthink does not occur – and to obtain better decisions – outsiders can be brought in to put an alternative viewpoint. Another strategy is to have one or more members playing the role of 'devil's advocate', which means that they voice an alternative view even if they don't believe it.

Not all researchers believe in groupthink, of course – researchers rarely agree completely with one another. Aldag and Fuller (1993) question the groupthink phenomenon, and have said that if there were such a thing, it might not be as bad as Janis suggests. However, most organisational psychologists regard groupthink as a very real problem in organisational life, and one that needs specific measures to prevent.

Table 4.8 Symptoms of groupthink

1 Illusion of invulnerability – the group sees themselves as invincible. They have faith in the group and so ignore possible disastrous outcomes of their decisions
2 Illusion of morality – the group is seen as morally correct, and members see themselves as the 'good guys' against 'the rest'
3 Shared negative stereotypes – there is less likelihood of contradictory views in the group because the members have developed similar beliefs
4 Collective rationalisations – members explain away anything that goes against what is being decided
5 Self-censorship – members suppress their own doubts
6 Illusion of unanimity – members think that the decision is a consensus, even when this is not true. Opposing views are not voiced (but may be held) so members think no one disagrees
7 Direct conformity pressure – direct pressure is put on a person with an opposing view to agree with the majority
8 Mindguards – particular members insulate the group from any negative input

ACTIVITY

In your study of social identity theory you should have come across the idea of the in-group and the out-group. Relate these concepts to the concept of groupthink, and make notes comparing the two theories.

Group polarisation and risky shift

Group polarisation is the name given to an effect that was first observed in organisational life under the name of the **risky shift phenomenon** – the observation that groups sometimes made much riskier decisions than the members of the group would have made if they were acting alone. The phenomenon was first discovered by a graduate student named Stoner, and followed up by Wallach *et al.* (1962). It surprised organisational psychologists when it was first discovered, because they had always assumed that group decisions would be more conservative.

In the risky shift research, individuals had to make either an attractive but risky decision to solve a problem or a less risky but less attractive decision. They then formed groups, which also had to make those decisions and the group decision was compared with the individual decisions.

The application of the idea of there being a risky shift is that businesses and others making decisions became concerned that a group is likely to make a riskier decision. However, there is also evidence that some groups become more cautious when making a decision, rather than riskier. Lamm (1988) suggested that group discussion tends to make individuals more extreme, but that they can become riskier or more cautious. Accordingly, the risky shift phenomenon was re-named **group polarisation** – the tendency for groups to make decisions that are more extreme than the decision each individual would have made (Myers and Lamm, 1976).

Group polarisation occurs more in groups where there is a lot of agreement in the first place than in groups where individuals tend to disagree (Williams and Taormina, 1992). A number of explanations have been put forward for group polarisation. One is the idea that the individual hears arguments from other group members that boost their own ideas (either to be more risky or more cautious), so the group becomes more extreme as the individual's opinions are supported and boosted. Another is the idea that individuals adopt the values of the group, and so decisions are stronger (more extreme) in whatever direction the group goes in.

Evaluation

- Studies of group polarisation have often used artificial groups with artificial tasks (e.g. Stoner, 1961). These studies were reliable, as they were controlled experiments, but may lack validity, being artificial problems in an artificial setting.
+ Some group decisions studied were real decisions made by real groups. These studies were more valid, although they lacked the controls of the experiments.

ACTIVITY

In the situations used in studies of group polarisation, dilemmas or problems with no specific answer are presented and given a score (for example, 0 could be the cautious decision and 10 the most risky decision). The participant has to indicate what score represents the decision they could make. The group decision is usually nearer one end of the scoring scale (10–0) and is compared with the average of the scores of the individuals that make up the group. The individual decisions range more around the middle.

Try developing your own set of risky situations, and see whether you can also find group polarisation.

The individual at work

Occupational psychology, as we saw earlier in this chapter, is mainly concerned with the individual at work, while organisational psychologists are concerned with the social processes that make working life possible. In the previous section we explored some of the issues concerning organisational psychologists; but we will now go on to look at two of the areas of interest to occupational psychologists – the question of stress at work and the question of how people cope with changes in working life and experience.

Stress at work

Research into stress at work has been carried out for the sake of both the employee (to try to improve their conditions) and the employer (many working days are lost because of stress). Stress at work is an important area within occupational psychology.

Defining worker stress

Stress can be seen as a physiological response to a threatening environment or events (Selye, 1976). The term usually refers to continuation of a normal physiological response called the 'alarm reaction' (experienced when an organism needs energy to tackle a threatening situation). Usually the alarm reaction ceases when the situation changes, but if a threatening situation continues, and the physiological response continues, 'stress' is the result.

A threatening situation at work is not likely to be life-threatening (as, for example, a plane crash would be) – 'threatening' used in the context of work is more likely to mean 'the ability of the person does not match the demands of the job'. The situation is threatening to that individual, and if it continues stress is likely to result.

Lazarus (1991) has a transactional view of worker stress, and sees stress as coming from a worker's perception that the situation is threatening. This helps to explain why one person may find a job situation threatening and the other may not – with different skills and abilities, one may be able to cope with the demands of the job (and not be stressed), whereas the other (without the skills) becomes stressed.

Riggio (2000) defines worker stress as 'physiological and/or psychological reactions to an event that is perceived to be threatening or taxing.' The effects of stress can be both positive and negative. For example, the skills and abilities to cope, though missing in a new job where someone has just received promotion, may be quickly gained, and the promotion may be very welcome. There are positive feelings – for example, pleasure from the challenge – and negative feelings such as anxiety from having to do unfamiliar things. Some (e.g. Shanahan and Mortimer, 1996) have called negative stress '**distress**' and positive stress '**eustress**'. Table 4.9 lists ways in which we are affected by stress.

Table 4.9 Stress responses

Physiological responses	Increased heart rate and breathing rate, increased blood pressure and sweating
Psychological responses	Anxiety, fear, despair, and mental preparation – thinking about the problem and trying to deal with it
Stressors	It is hard to list stressors as a lot depends on the perception of the individual. What one person perceives as stressful another person looks forward to (for example, shopping) Some events, however, are stressful for most people – such as planning a wedding or having an operation
Stress-related illnesses	*Physiologically based* stress-related illnesses include ulcers, colitis, migraine, asthma attacks, heart disease and hypertension
	Psychologically based stress-related illnesses include fatigue, anxiety, depression and mental strain

STUDY AID

The issue of stress and the alarm reaction is explored in chapters 5 and 8. You could read the relevant sections in those chapters to extend your understanding.

Sources of worker stress

Stress can come from the individual (**dispositional stress**) or from the situation (**situational stress**). Situational stressors are found both at work and at home so all areas of a person's life need to be considered when looking for causes of stress. Dispositional stress comes from the character of the individual.

Specific stressful occupations

Stressful occupations include air traffic controllers, those in health care, firefighters, policemen and postal workers.

- Mohler (1983) found that air-traffic controllers experienced high levels of worker-related stress.
- Krakowski (1982) found high levels of stress amongst medical doctors.
- Shouksmith and Burrough (1988) found that air traffic controllers' jobs are stressful because of heavy workload, fear of causing accidents, poor work environments and poor equipment.
- DiMatteo *et al.* (1993) found high levels of stress amongst dentists. They suggest that dentists' stress comes from difficult patients, heavy workloads and from the dentists' idea that others held negative views about them.
- It might be thought that high levels of stress went with responsibility at work, but Wolfgang (1988) compared physicians, pharmacists and nurses and found more stress amongst nurses, who would appear to have less responsibility.
- Although it may be seen that police officers and firefighters are stressed from the physical dangers of their jobs:
  Jermier *et al.* (1989) and Riggio and Cole (1995) found that the physical danger seems to be motivating and exciting;
  Brown *et al.* (1996) found police officers suffered stress from workloads and increased responsibility, as did others in other occupations

Factors producing stress at work

Studies of particularly stressful occupations demonstrate that, although there are some stressors specific to the job (for example, dentists' view of how others perceive them), many jobs have similar stressors (for example, heavy workload).

Sources of stress at work are often divided into organisational and individual sources (similar to situational and dispositional factors within the individual). **Organisational stressors** can be thought of as coming from either work tasks or work roles. Individual sources of stress can come from characteristics of the individual, their behavioural patterns or from poor experiences of stress.

Organisational sources of stress – situational stressors
Work task stressors

Work **overload** occurs when excessive concentration, output or speed is needed. It is often thought of as the greatest cause of work stress. Research (e.g. Cobb and Rose, 1973) suggests that work overload causes high heart rate and elevated serum cholesterol; it also relates to

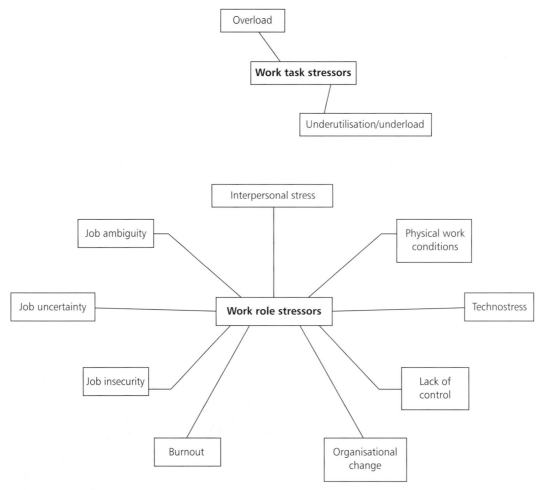

Figure 4.9
Work task and work role stressors

psychological measures of stress (e.g. Spector, 1987) and to job dissatisfaction (Kirmeyer and Dougherty, 1988). Work overload has been linked with stress in many occupations including clerical workers, air traffic controllers, health workers and soldiers (e.g. Bliese and Halverson, 1996; Shouksmith and Burrough, 1988).

Having too little to do can also be stressful; this is called **underutilisation** (Ganster *et al.*, 1986). Underutilisation is not just having too little to do; it includes boring jobs and jobs where the worker feels their skills are not being fully used (Melamed *et al.*, 1995). For example, college graduates in low-level clerical jobs may experience stress from underutilisation (e.g. French *et al.*, 1982).

Work role stressors

When the tasks and requirements of a job are not clearly outlined **job ambiguity** occurs, and this can be a source of stress (Beehr, 1985). Sometimes this is called **job**

uncertainty, although this also means having poor feedback (a worker does not know if they are doing well or not). Supervisors can reduce job uncertainty by clarifying job duties (Schaubroeck *et al.*, 1993; O'Driscoll and Beehr, 1994). Conflict of roles can also be a source of stress (Greenhaus and Beutell, 1985). A worker may have conflicting roles at work, or their job role may entail overtime, which can lead to conflict between the job role and family roles.

If a worker experiences **lack of control** at work, this too can result in stress. Low-level jobs and jobs in highly structured organisations often mean a worker has little control, and individuals – particularly those who want to have some input – can become stressed (Dwyer and Ganster, 1991). Jackson (1983) found that giving workers a say in decision-making and letting them plan their own work tasks reduces stress. However, lack of control does not cause stress for everyone Carayon (1994). Some workers want control more than others, and personality may be a factor.

Sethi *et al.* (1987) discuss **technostress**, by which they mean stress that comes from uncertainty caused by changes in technology. For instance, computers are useful in that they can often take care of work that used to be boring and repetitive but the coming of computers has changed some jobs a great deal. Job uncertainty may be a factor as some workers fear they will lose their job. Korunka *et al.* (1993) looked at the introduction of new technology into seven Austrian companies. It caused higher levels of stress, especially for those not involved in its planning and implementation. Carayon (1994) suggests that stress related to the technology may come from high workload, underutilisation, lack of control and lack of supervisor support. If a worker is inputting data for long hours without any clear idea of why, this may well lead to stress. Both Carayon (1994) and Korunka *et al.* (1993) found higher levels of stress in the 'lower' level jobs and less stress in professional or supervisor jobs. Depression, illness and some types of substance abuse can come from lack of control – for example, if the worker is not involved in timetabling tasks (Karasek, 1979).

Frese and Zapf (1988) talk about **physical conditions** in the environment as sources of stress. These include loud noise, poor ventilation, poor lighting and extremes of temperature. Dangerous work conditions are also sources of stress.

STUDY AID

The issue of physical work conditions is studied in other areas of psychology. Physical factors that might cause stress at work (including noise, temperature, lighting and ventilation) are considered in Chapter 7. You could read the relevant sections there to extend your understanding.

Interpersonal relations (relations between people) at work can be a source of stress. For example, a worker might not get on with their boss or there may be conflict between two people competing for promotion.

In general people prefer predictable and stable lives, and studies have shown that stress comes from major changes in the work environment (e.g. Leiter and Harvie, 1998). Marks and Mirvis (1998), for example, found that a company merger or reorganisation is likely to be seen as stressful by many of the workers in the company.

Burnout refers to the stage of becoming less committed to the job and gradually withdrawing from the work. Withdrawal can include lateness and absenteeism as well as decreased work quality. The Maslach Burnout Inventory

Human Service Survey (Maslach and Jackson, 1986) assesses 'burnout'. Burnout seems high in 'caring and helping' jobs such as health workers, teachers and policemen (e.g. Cherniss, 1980; Byrne, 1993; Leiter and Maslach, 1988; Leiter and Schaufeli, 1996). However, some disagree over the definition of burnout (e.g. Evans and Fischer, 1993).

Burnout is likely to occur when:
- there are unresolved interpersonal conflicts
- clearly defined work tasks and responsibilities are lacking
- overwork is extreme
- appropriate rewards are not given
- inappropriate punishment is meted out.

Figure 4.10
Research indicates that job burnout particularly occurs in the human service professions such as teaching

There are three stages to burnout:
1 Emotional exhaustion
2 Depersonalisation (insensitive attitude to others in the workplace)
3 Feeling of low personal accomplishment (feelings of frustration and helplessness)

Individual sources of stress – dispositional stressors

Type A personality
Someone with a **Type A personality** according to Friedman and Rosenman (1974) is competitive, has drive, and has a sense of urgency and impatience. Those with this behaviour pattern also seem more likely to suffer stress-related coronary heart disease (Schaubroeck *et al.*, 1994). Some studies suggested that the competitive drive and hard work were the causes of stress, but later studies indicate that repressed hostility is an important factor (e.g.

Smith and Pope, 1990). Rosenman (1990) and other recent researchers point to a combination of competitiveness, impatience and hostility (negative emotions) as the likely cause of stress. Alternatively, it could be that those with Type A personality feel more stress given the same workload, or have stronger physiological responses to stressful situations, and those stronger reactions may give the health risk.

STUDY AID

Issues such as the Type A personality are studied in other areas of psychology – for instance health psychology (Chapter 8). You could read the relevant section there to extend your understanding.

Susceptibility/resistance to stress

Some people are more susceptible or more resistant to stress than others. **Hardiness** is the ability to deal with stressful events successfully; one way of doing this is to see a stressful event as a challenge, not a threat. People who are resistant to stress seem to have more control over their lives and are more likely to be committed to their jobs.

Self-efficacy (a belief the individual has that they can engage in actions that will lead to desired outcomes; Bandura, 1997) is also likely to lead to resistance to stress. Studies done by Saks (1994) and VanYperen (1998) suggest that self-efficacy can help to reduce stress in the work place.

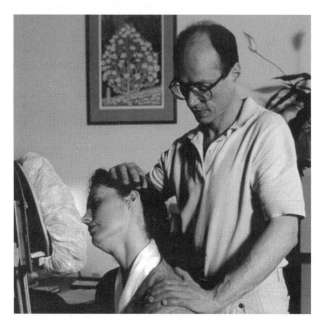

Figure 4.11
Relaxation techniques may serve as useful coping strategies, although their effectiveness in the workplace has been questioned

STUDY AID

The concept of self-efficacy is studied in other areas of psychology, and Chapter 5 examines self-efficacy in more detail. Read the relevant sections there to extend your understanding.

Evaluation

- Many of the above studies have been done in the USA, although conclusions seem to apply to workers in Britain.

- Findings from many studies support one another, and the idea of there being both situational and dispositional factors that cause stress seems to be well supported by the evidence.

- Issues such as work overload, job control and adverse physical environments do seem to be important when looking at job-related stress.

Self-test

Write an essay under exam conditions (or as close as you can manage) using the title 'Discuss three factors which produce stress at work'.

Changes in working life

Critical life events do occur that are not related to work – for instance marriage, divorce, having children, bereavement – although many critical life events *are* related to the work situation. These include unemployment, redundancy, retirement and the increased leisure time a person may have when they no longer work.

Adult development tends to be seen as involving stages, with starting work as the first stage. It is expected that an adult will continue to work until retirement, although there are exceptions, for example, when a woman gives up work to bring up children (some see bringing up children as work, and as one of the stages). Retirement can be seen as a normal stage in adult development, as can the increased leisure time that comes with it. However, other critical life events such as unemployment and redundancy are not seen as normal stages. It might be thought, therefore, that retirement would be less stressful for an individual than unemployment or redundancy. Occupational psychologists consider such issues as which life events are stressful, and whether there are certain stages that an adult goes through when retiring.

Evaluation

- The idea that adults move through stages of development has been criticised because it does not allow for differences between people. One way of evaluating general statements about how people are affected by unemployment or retirement – such as that these events are stages – is to suggest that considering the problems such life events bring in general ignores differences between people.

Unemployment and redundancy

The difference between unemployment and retirement is that, whereas we can prepare for retirement, unemployment is unexpected, (Raphael, 1984). Loss of work can be like any other form of bereavement. Firstly, there is shock and a feeling of disbelief. Then the individual is likely to start thinking it was all for the best, and might start blaming their employer. This is a form of rationalisation, and these thoughts can be comforting. The rationalisation stage will be reached more quickly if other work is available. However, a sense of loss is still probable. If a job was valued, and hard to replace, grieving is likely to be more intense.

Argyle's (1989) review of unemployment and mental ill health brought up several points:
- Depression is usually higher amongst the unemployed (Warr, 1984). There is a feeling of learned helplessness and people blame themselves.
- Suicide is more common amongst the unemployed, perhaps because of depression, poverty, reduced social support and alcoholism.
- Physical health can suffer because of unemployment. However, Warr (1984) found that although 27% of the 954 unemployed British men in his study said their health had got worse, 11% said it had improved. Mortality rate is higher for unemployed people.
- Unemployment brings financial difficulties and loss of self-esteem. In families with dependent children, emotional distress from unemployment is higher, possibly because there are more financial difficulties (Warr, 1984).

Argyle identified the following factors that affect how far unemployment causes distress:
- level of financial hardship
- length of unemployment
- level of social support from family
- perception of the cause of the unemployment
- how far the person was committed to their work.

Kelvin and Jarrett (1985) suggest that people who become unemployed go through specific stages:
1 Shock, anger and incomprehension.
2 Optimism, a holiday feeling, and active job searching.
3 Pessimism, anxiety about the future (as job searches fail).
4 Fatalism, hopelessness and apathy (as job searching is abandoned).

Unemployment tends to be more stressful for middle-aged people, as they are more likely to have been attached to their job. Work is often a source of social relationships, so social support from family can help to alleviate stress caused by unemployment. People who are unemployed but keep active tend to suffer less from stress. Being out of work can be seen as a failure, although in a recession this feeling is not as bad, as others are in the same situation. When many are unemployed individuals can feel less to blame for their situation, which alleviates the stress felt.

Retirement

Retirement is planned loss of work, and produces different feelings from unemployment However, retirement does bring losses – for example, loss of friendships, loss of income, loss of personal identity. Some people feel they are too young to retire, and can experience a greater sense of loss. When a person retires they lose the pattern to their day, which can lead to a feeling of emptiness (Raphael, 1984).

It can be difficult to adjust at home, especially if a partner is also at home. Couples must adjust to increased time together. Often people move house when they retire, which makes things more difficult because they have to make new friendships. Another problem with retirement is that a person's social role is often removed when they leave work, and he or she has no clearly defined role in life.

Retirement can result in loss of self-esteem. People cope better if they have planned their retirement, and can continue with the interests they had (Turner and Helms, 1989) such as science, writing, academic and leisure pursuits.

According to Atchley and Robinson (1982) there are six phases to retirement:
1 **Pre-retirement phase**
   - Remote subphase – retirement is seen as being in the future.
   - Near subphase – friends and colleagues start to retire, and anxiety develops.
2 **Honeymoon phase** – Just after retirement new-found freedom brings relief and happiness.
3 **Disenchantment phase** – In this stage there are feelings of being let down. If health and finances decline, depression in this stage is worse. This phase can be a problem if the individual had unrealistic expectations about retirement.

4 Reorientation phase – A more realistic approach develops. Individuals look for ways to work in the community, and ways to be useful.

5 Stability phase – Life settles down to a comfortable and ordered existence. There is mastery of the retirement role.

6 Termination phase – Illness and disability can make looking after oneself impossible, so the retirement role becomes a disabled role.

There is less of a problem in adjusting to voluntary retirement, but involuntary retirement is likely to bring depression. Argyle suggests that being satisfied with retirement depends on:

- health
- finance
- purpose in life
- having interests
- education and social class
- whether the retirement is voluntary and planned
- gender (married women have least difficulty).

Disengagement theory

As an individual ages he or she starts to **disengage** from society (Cummings and Henry, 1961), and retirement could be part of that process, as the individual no longer has a work role. This is a biological process in which a person gradually withdraws from some parts of society. This includes withdrawal from the workplace. It has been suggested that this withdrawal is preparing the ageing person for death.

Evaluation

- One important point is that people are retiring from work younger and early retirement is being used as a way of reducing or changing the work force. However, some people who take early retirement find work in another area, and do not withdraw from society.

- In some cultures older people are sought out for their wisdom and advice, which does not support the idea that there is a biological disengagement. The elders are called upon to make decisions and solve disputes, so they are as much involved in society as anyone.

- In Western society disengagement is not something that is chosen; our social structure often does not allow the retired person to engage in society. Disengagement, if it occurs, is not then a choice, driven by biological forces, but is forced upon the individual by the social structure.

- Where there is opportunity to engage with society, retired people do so. If we accept the ideas of disengagement theory, we would not expect this to happen.

Activity theory

Activity theory suggests that people who remain involved in society will be happier and healthier (Havinghurst, 1964). When at work, a person is fulfilling several social roles, and retirement means losing one or more of these roles. It is seen as important for the individual to take on new social roles, and to remain active in society to maintain their self-esteem. Activity theory sees ageing as a positive process, as opposed to the negative view of disengagement theory.

Social exchange theory

Some people enjoy the increased activity that retirement can bring; others prefer to slow down and take a rest. Evidence can be found for both activity theory and disengagement theory. It has been suggested that there is an exchange between society and the individual, and there are two sides of a contract. Social exchange theory suggests that this contract involves the older person in agreeing to take less part in society, so leaving their place free for a young person to fill it. The other part of the contract is for society to agree to let that person have more leisure time, and to allow them to enjoy it without feeling guilty. Social exchange theory explains why some people can enjoy more activity, whereas others are able to disengage. Social class could be a factor here. Teachers tend to re-engage, whereas working-class men often disengage (Atchley, 1976).

Table 4.10 Comparing unemployment and retirement

Both involve being out of work, a lower income and increased leisure time. However:
• Retired people don't look for work • Retired people go out less • Retired people are happier (they may get bored and lonely, but they are less depressed and usually in better health)

Increased leisure time

As suggested by the activity theory (outlined above), increased leisure time can lead to a more active life, and many who retire involve themselves in new pursuits, taking on different social roles. Social exchange theory proposes that society allows the retired person to enjoy their new leisure time and not to feel guilty about it because, in return, he or she agrees to opt out of society to an extent, especially with regard to work role, leaving the way clear for young people to take on the jobs they need. This contract means that those who have retired can enjoy increased leisure time. However, others prefer not to re-engage in new activities when they retire – they take a rest.

People who are unemployed or who have just been made redundant, however, do not have this permission to enjoy their new leisure time. Although their loss of social roles is similar to the loss experienced by the newly retired, they are supposed to have a work role, and so are under pressure to rejoin the workforce. Their leisure time is not allowed. Stress and depression often result. As outlined above, unemployment increases the likelihood of developing a mental health problem.

Self-test

Write an essay under exam conditions (or as close as you can manage), using the title 'Discuss the psychological implications for the individual of two out of: unemployment, redundancy, increased leisure time and retirement'.

Suggested reading

Aamodt, M.G. (1999) *Applied Industrial/Organisational Psychology*, third edition. Belmont, CA: Wadsworth Publishing Company.

Chmiel, N. (ed.) (2000) *Introduction to Work and Organizational Psychology*. Oxford: Blackwell.

Hayward, S. (1996) *Applying Psychology to Organisations*. London: Hodder and Stoughton.

Riggio, R.E. (2000) *Introduction to Industrial/Organisational Psychology*, third edition. New Jersey: Prentice Hall.

5

Sport psychology

The aims of this chapter

The aims of this chapter are to enable the reader to:

- discuss the trait approach to personality, including the work of Eysenck and Cattell
- discuss research linking personality traits to choice of sport/sporting success
- describe social learning theory, and individual differences in behaviour
- define socialising influences with regard to sporting behaviour, including gender, family and culture, and sport as an influence on social development
- describe theories of motivation, including intrinsic and extrinsic motivation
- discuss achievement motivation and its application to sports psychology
- discuss self-efficacy and motivation in sport
- discuss attribution theory and motivation in sport
- offer explanations of social facilitation, including those of Zajonc and Cottrell
- understand the relationship between team cohesion and performance
- describe possible negative effects of team membership on individual performance, including social loafing
- discuss the effects of anxiety and arousal on sporting performance.

STUDY AID

When you have finished working through this chapter you should write an essay about, or at least test yourself on, each of the above points. This would help you to see how good your knowledge and understanding of sport psychology is.

This chapter covers

WHAT IS SPORT PSYCHOLOGY?

INDIVIDUAL DIFFERENCES AND SPORT
    Introduction
    The psychometric approach

Trait approaches
Linking personality traits to choice of sport and sporting success
Sport and socialisation
Socialising influences, and sport as an influence on social development

What is sport psychology?

Sport psychology is a relatively new field within psychology. Although, as far back as 1898, Triplett looked at social facilitation and the effect of others on performance, he was working within the field of social psychology, and sport psychology had yet to develop. In the 1920s in America books were written about the psychology of coaching and the psychology of athletics but it was not until 1967 that the North American Society for the Psychology of Sport and Physical Activity (NASPSPA) was formed, and it was from around this time that the speciality of sports psychology started. In Europe the International Society of Sport Psychology (ISSP) was formed in 1965, and the *International Journal of Sport Psychology* was first published in 1970.

One difficulty in this relatively new field is in relating theory to practice. The theories are those used in other fields of psychology (for example theories of motivation are used within organisational psychology) – it is the *application* of these theories to sport that is new. There is a problem here in that the application of the theory has not always been tested – and, when it is tested, the theory does not always match the practice. Learning is often on a trial-and-error basis, and Martens (1987) points out that theory must be tested in real-world sport.

One problem in linking theory to practice is in the research methods that must be used. Psychologists would need to study sporting performance in action, and not only on the training ground. However, sporting performance could be affected by such studies, which would not be ethical (or allowed by coaches) because athletes would not want their performance to suffer just because they are being studied in a real event. Experimental design is also difficult, as the control group may be denied access to some help that the study group was getting. This could make the control group's performance worse, which would not be ethical.

Given these difficulties sport psychologists have begun to move away from research methods such as experiments and correlations, using in-depth interviews as well as case studies. This has led to a greater emphasis on the applied side of sport psychology.

Individual differences and sport

Introduction

It is sometimes thought that only a certain type of personality takes up sport. Early in sport psychology research focused on personality, looking mainly at trait approaches and social learning theory. It is interesting that other approaches to personality, for example, the psychodynamic approach, or the humanistic approach, have largely been ignored in sport psychology.

There is disagreement as to whether studying personality in sport is useful; for example, Cox (1994) feels that it is, whereas Vealey (1992) points to inconsistencies in findings. Questions asked include whether personalities of top-class performers differ from the personalities of those who do not succeed, and whether we can predict sporting success from a study of an individual's personality. It is also interesting to see whether players of different sports have different characteristics.

Morgan (1980b) suggests that personality is a factor in sporting success. This is sometimes called a **credulous view**, which means that it has real meaning for people. Others, however, hold a **sceptical view**, and suggest that personality has no relevance to sporting performance. We cannot see or measure someone's personality, we can only assume it from their behaviour or what they say: in some ways it does not really exist. Personality is a **hypothetical construct** – it cannot be observed, but only inferred from behaviour.

↻ Recall AS material

Recall your AS material about the psychodynamic approach, especially its focus on personality, or look it up. Write a short paragraph linking it to sporting achievement. For example, consider the function of the id, and the function of the superego: would a strong superego be a limiting factor in sporting achievement, for instance?

Defining personality

Lazarus and Monat (1979) define personality as 'the underlying relatively stable psychological structures and processes that shape someone's actions and reactions'. Gross (1992) suggests that personality involves the relatively stable aspects that make individuals unique, but which can also be used to liken people to others. Both definitions focus on some characteristics that are stable, and that shape a person's actions. Questions arise as to whether such characteristics are innate or learned, and whether they can be changed.

Nomothetic or idiographic – a useful distinction regarding personality theories

A **nomothetic approach** to the study of people is to look for general laws that apply to everyone. An example of a nomothetic approach is the multistore model of memory, which suggests that everyone possesses general structures such as short-term and long-term memory, and does not consider individual differences. The theories of personality put forward by Eysenck and Cattell both take a nomothetic approach.

An **idiographic approach** looks at the differences between people, and is interested in an individual's unique characteristics. A humanistic approach would be idiographic, as people are studied as individuals, whereas the trait approach is nomothetic, seeking general laws about people. As sport psychology is interested in general laws – for example, which type of person makes a successful sportsperson – it is likely that the nomothetic approach to study is used.

Synoptic Note

The division of theories and research into nomothetic or idiographic is helpful when discussing whether psychology is a science, and this information is useful for Unit 6.

STUDY AID

The issue of whether an approach is nomothetic or idiographic in emphasis is also studied in other areas of psychology. It is explored in Chapter 3, and you could read the relevant sections there to extend your understanding.

The psychometric approach

A psychometric approach sees personality as something measurable. Trait approaches are psychometric approaches, because they measure personality. A psychometric test should be reliable, valid, standardised and have a wide distribution of scores. A psychometric approach is also nomothetic, because people are treated as being subject to general laws (and not as individuals).

↻ Recall AS material

Recall your AS material on methodology, or look it up if you can't remember. Write definitions of 'reliable' and 'valid' as used in psychology. You may have already come across psychometric testing – for example, within the psychology of work.

Reliability, validity, standardisation

If a test has **reliability**, repeating it will give similar results. A **valid** test measures what it claims to measure, and can be successfully used in real-life situations. If a test is **standardised**, sufficient people have been tested to ensure that the whole population's range of scores is catered for by the test. Once a test has been standardised against a large population, any individual's score can be judged against this standard, and this standard will be normal. To standardise a test needs a wide variety of individuals to ensure that results are representative of the target population.

Factor analysis

Personality tests yield a lot of information about individuals, and it would be difficult to discuss personality if we had to make lists of all the characteristics. By using **factor analysis**, a few factors can be used to summarise these many different characteristics, so factor analysis allows us to draw conclusions about personality and compare people.

Factor analysis means that lots of data about people is analysed to see if there are any common factors. For example, if all those people who say that they are aggressive also say they are excitable these two characteristics could be said to go together. Factor analysis is a method of finding out which traits or characteristics go together. Certain characteristics that go together can be called a factor – someone who is aggressive and excitable might be called 'unstable', for example, and this could be considered a factor in their personality.

Orthogonal v oblique methods

In factor analysis, an **orthogonal** method aims to find a small number of powerful factors that are not connected to one another, but go to make up the individual. Eysenck's approach uses an orthogonal method. An **oblique** method tries to find a small number of factors that are not separate, but go together to make up the individual. Cattell's approach uses the oblique method.

Oblique factors can be either first-order factors or second-order factors. First-order factors are those discovered before factor analysis. Second-order factors are discovered through factor analysis. Eysenck's second-order factors are called types, and Cattell's second-order factors are called source traits. Eysenck believed that a set of uncorrelated factors was the simplest idea, and so thought this was the right approach, whereas most factor analysts prefer the oblique approach, where factors are connected.

STUDY AID

The issue of psychometric testing is studied in other areas of psychology, for example in Chapter 4 where the psychology of work is discussed. You could read the relevant sections there to extend your understanding.

Trait approaches

Research into personality using the trait approach dominated sport psychology in the 1960s and 1970s. Traits are **dispositional characteristics** – those within a person – whereas **situational characteristics** are those to do with the situation, and are outside a person. Traits are relatively stable and enduring characteristics that can be used to predict a person's behaviour in given situations. For example, if someone is seen as aggressive, they are likely to be aggressive in most situations because this trait is stable and enduring.

Eysenck's type theory of personality

The ancient Greeks thought that individuals fell into one of four categories or types (Table 5.1). When using the term 'type' to apply to someone it means a person belongs to one category or another, but not to both. These types can be linked to Eysenck's personality dimensions.

Table 5.1 The four humours according to the ancient Greeks

Choleric – excess of yellow bile
Sanguine – excess of blood
Melancholic – excess of black bile
Phlegmatic – excess of phlegm

Eysenck's personality dimensions are not entirely separate as the Greeks' types were. A type is a combination of traits, and is formed when traits correlate. Eysenck's types are not 'all or nothing' factors, but form dimensions, and personalities come somewhere along these dimensions. The overall type is at the top of a hierarchy, with the traits below it, and the specific behaviours from which we derive the traits are at the bottom of the hierarchy (Figure 5.1).

Eysenck (1947) used factor analysis, having gathered information from 700 neurotic soldiers. He first checked that they did not have mental or physical illnesses. He used 39 items and found two orthogonal factors (factors that did not correlate or go together) – introversion–extroversion (E) and neuroticism–stability (N). Saying these two factors do not correlate means that someone could be stable and an extrovert or stable and an introvert, for example.

Typical introverts are quiet, introspective and reserved towards others. They plan ahead and distrust impulses.

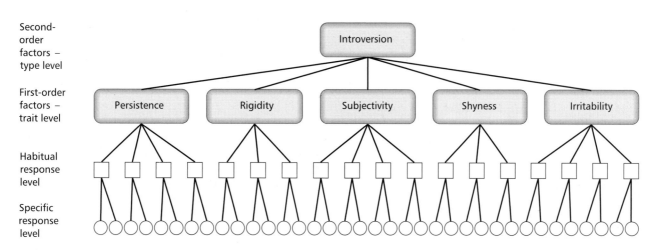

Figure 5.1
Eysenck's hierarchical model of personality in relation to the introversion dimension (Source: Gross, 1996; from Eysenck, 1953)

They keep their feelings under control and set store by ethical standards. Typical extroverts are sociable and have many friends. They don't like studying by themselves and crave excitement. They are easy-going and prefer doing things. They are not always reliable. A high scorer on the neurotic scale is anxious, moody and worries, and is likely to sleep badly and be over-emotional. A low scorer on the neurotic scale is slow to arouse in an emotional sense and is usually calm and unworried.

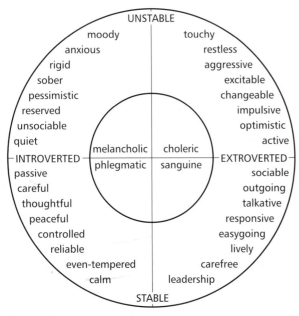

Figure 5.2
Eysenck's dimensions of personality (Source: Gross, 1996; from Eysenck, 1965)

Further research led to the addition of another dimension, which was called psychoticism (P) (Eysenck and Eysenck, 1985). High scorers on the psychoticism scale would be solitary and not care about others. They might be cruel, lack feelings, like odd and unusual things and have a disregard for danger.

Eysenck's methodology

Eysenck's original questionnaire was the Maudsley Medical Questionnaire (MMQ), which measured only N. Then the Maudsley Personality Inventory (MPI) was developed, which measured E and N. The Eysenck Personality Inventory (EPI) added a Lie scale, as it was thought that answers might be socially desirable (**social desirability** means that the respondent gives the answers they think they ought to give, and those that are socially acceptable). The Eysenck Personality Questionnaire (EPQ) added a P scale. The questions all required 'yes' or 'no' answers and the questionnaires are thought to be both valid and reliable. One way of testing the validity of the questionnaires is to give them to those who seem to fit the types measured, and to see if the conclusions fit. For example, someone who is considered to fit the introvert type should have a score that means they are called introvert.

Biological basis

Eysenck's theory does not just classify personalities into different types, but also offers a biological explanation for people belonging to their particular type. It is suggested that these characteristics are inherited.

Eysenck suggests that E concerns the balance between excitation and inhibition, which involve nervous system processes. The ascending reticular activating system (ARAS, found in the brainstem) maintains the level of arousal that an organism needs. To maintain the right level the ARAS can either dampen down (inhibit) the incoming sensory data or enhance (excite) it.

> ### STUDY AID
>
> The issue of arousal and the role of the nervous system is also studied in other areas of psychology. It is explored in Chapter 8, which discusses health psychology, and you could read the relevant sections there to extend your understanding.

Extroverts have a strong nervous system, and their ARAS tends to inhibit impulses. Extroverts tend to be under-aroused, because inhibition builds up quickly but dissipates slowly, so the inhibition tends to be the main state for an extrovert. An introvert, however, is the opposite: their ARAS tends to excite more, because it is weaker. Excitation builds up quickly, and inhibition develops slowly, so the introvert tends to be over-aroused, and in a state of excitation of impulses. So an extrovert will seek excitement while an introvert does not.

N concerns the autonomic nervous system (ANS) and differences in the limbic system. The sympathetic branch of the ANS activates the 'fight or flight' syndrome and prepares the organism for action. The activation of the sympathetic branch of the ANS leads to raised heart rate, increased breathing rate, sweating, increased blood pressure and production of adrenaline. A person who scores highly on the N scale has an ANS that reacts quickly to stressful situations, and where the alarm reaction is quickly activated. A more stable individual reacts more slowly.

P might be related to male hormones such as testosterone, but this is not certain.

Evaluation

- Eysenck claims that our biological make up, and in particular the way our ARAS and ANS work, give us our personality characteristics. Evidence for these claims comes from biological tests. For example, those who tend to have an inhibited system might be thought to tire more easily, as they 'work harder' to excite the nervous system. Extroverts, therefore, might be thought to tire more easily, which has been found (Eysenck, 1967). Harkins and Green (1975) found that introverts do better at tasks where they need to concentrate for long periods. Extroverts also change jobs and partners more often than introverts, which is in line with the theory, as they are more likely to seek change because existing stimuli lose their arousal value. Extroverts in general search for new stimuli more often, whereas introverts do not need to.

• It might also be thought that extroverts are less easily conditioned, as they are less likely to respond to new stimuli, needing a stronger stimulus to arouse them. However, evidence for this is mixed. Kline (1983) thinks that there is no real evidence for extroverts being harder to condition, when considering laboratory experiments involving responses such as eye-blinking. Care should be taken when generalising findings from laboratory studies to real-life situations.

• Wilson (1976) asked if introverts are less easily sedated using drugs, as they are more aroused. Claridge and Herrington (1963) suggest that introverted neurotics were more difficult to sedate than extroverted neurotics. Eysenck (1995) claims that studies have shown that drugs affect introverts and extroverts differently, and in line with his ideas.

> ### Synoptic Note
>
> The area of personality can be used as an example of a nature/nurture debate. If personality is inherited, and has a biological basis, our personality is in our nature and cannot be changed by upbringing (by nurture). Eysenck's personality theory suggests that personality is inherited but other theories (such as social learning theory) suggest that personality comes from nurture. In Unit 6, which is the synoptic part of the course, you will be asked to discuss the nature/nurture debate, and you could use personality as an example.

Criminality

Eysenck suggests that criminals are neurotic extroverts, because the extrovert is more difficult to condition and so would have a weaker conscience (this is assuming that our conscience comes from socialisation and conditioning). Cochrane (1974), however, found that prisoners, when tested on the EPI, are not more extrovert. They do score higher on N, but some studies find them to be more introvert. So evidence for this claim is mixed.

Evaluation

– The lack of evidence that introverts are easier to condition is a weakness of Eysenck's type theory as a

whole. The important thing about conditionability is that it looks at innate characteristics as well as considering external factors such as socialisation.

– Heim (1970) criticises the questionnaires themselves, and in particular the EPQ where only 'yes' and 'no' answers are possible. This forced choice leaves no room for individual differences, and is bound to lead to simplistic answers.

– Testing seems to focus on people at either end of the scales, for example, those that score high or low on N. There is little evidence about those whose scores fall in the middle of the scales.

+ The theory has generated a lot of research (Shackleton and Fletcher, 1984) and the types do seem to have stood the test of time.

Cattell's trait theory

Cattell (1965) considers that there are surface traits, and that underneath these there are traits like second-order source traits, which are the fundamental dimensions of personality. Cattell uses the oblique approach, and holds that these source traits are correlated, and do connect with one another (unlike Eysenck's separate types). Surface traits are the way we normally describe people, but the source traits underlie these normal descriptions. To understand someone's personality, we need to look at their source traits.

Cattell suggested three sources of data, when thinking of the methods used to collect data. He called these sources of data L-data (life), Q-data (questionnaire) and T-data (tests).

• L-data comes from observations. Cattell started by listing all the words that describe personality that he could find. Then he took out the words that were synonyms (those meaning the same thing). He trained observers to study a small sample of students for 6 months, and to rate the students on all the traits that he had listed. Factor analysis suggested that all these traits led to 15 first-order traits. These 15 were called source traits or primary traits.

• Q-data comes from the results of personality questionnaires, which used questions based on the 15 source traits. Following factor analysis, 16 source traits were found, 12 of which were the same as those found from the L-data, and four were new (Figure 5.3). The Cattell 16PF (personality factor) questionnaire then tested for these 16 traits. Cattell included 'yes' and 'no' questions, but also allowed other answers such as 'occasionally'.

• T-data are gathered from objective tests such as galvanic skin response (which measures such responses as sweating) and reaction time. These tests are called 'objective' because the participant does not know what result is required. Factor analysis of this sort of data has given 21 factors.

Factor	Low Score Description	High Score Description
A	RESERVED, DETACHED, CRITICAL, ALOOF (sizothymia)	OUTGOING, WARMHEARTED, EASY-GOING, PARTICIPATING (affectothymia, formerly cyclothymia)
B	LESS INTELLIGENT, CONCRETE-THINKING (lower scholastic mental capacity)	MORE INTELLIGENT, ABSTRACT-THINKING, BRIGHT (high scholastic mental capacity)
C	AFFECTED BY FEELINGS, EMOTIONALLY LESS STABLE, EASILY UPSET (lower ego strength)	EMOTIONALLY STABLE, FACES REALITY, CALM, MATURE (higher ego strength)
E	HUMBLE, MILD, ACCOMMODATING CONFORMING (submissiveness)	ASSERTIVE, AGGRESSIVE, STUBBORN, COMPETITIVE (dominance)
F	SOBER, PRUDENT, SERIOUS, TACITURN (desurgency)	HAPPY-GO-LUCKY, IMPULSIVELY LIVELY, GAY, ENTHUSIASTIC (surgency)
G	EXPEDIENT, DISREGARDS RULES, FEELS FEW OBLIGATIONS (weaker superego strength)	CONSCIENTIOUS, PERSEVERING, STAID, MORALISTIC (stronger superego strength)
H	SHY, RESTRAINED, TIMID, THREAT-SENSITIVE (threctia)	VENTURESOME, SOCIALLY BOLD, UNINHIBITED, SPONTANEOUS (parmia)
I	TOUGH-MINDED, SELF-RELIANT, REALISTIC, NO-NONSENSE (harria)	TENDER-MINDED, CLINGING, OVER-PROTECTED, SENSITIVE (premsia)
L	TRUSTING, ADAPTABLE, FREE OF JEALOUSY, EASY TO GET ALONG WITH (alaxia)	SUSPICIOUS, SELF-OPINIONATED, HARD TO FOOL (protension)
M	PRACTICAL, CAREFUL, CONVENTIONAL, REGULATED BY EXTERNAL REALITIES, PROPER (praxemia)	IMAGINATIVE, WRAPPED UP IN INNER URGENCIES, CARELESS OF PRACTICAL MATTERS, BOHEMIAN (autia)
N	FORTHRIGHT, NATURAL, ARTLESS, UNPRETENTIOUS (artlessness)	SHREWD, CALCULATING, WORLDLY, PENETRATING (shrewdness)
O	SELF-ASSURED, CONFIDENT, SERENE (untroubled adequacy)	APPREHENSIVE, SELF-REPROACHING, WORRYING, TROUBLED (guilt proneness)
Q₁	CONSERVATIVE, RESPECTING ESTABLISHED IDEAS, TOLERANT OF TRADITIONAL DIFFICULTIES (conservatism)	EXPERIMENTING, LIBERAL, ANALYTICAL, FREE-THINKING (radicalism)
Q₂	GROUP-DEPENDENT, A 'JOINER' AND SOUND FOLLOWER (group adherence)	SELF-SUFFICIENT, PREFERS OWN DECISIONS, RESOURCEFUL (self-sufficiency)
Q₃	UNDISCIPLINED SELF-CONFLICT, FOLLOWS OWN URGES, CARELESS OF PROTOCOL (low integration)	CONTROLLED, SOCIALLY PRECISE, FOLLOWING SELF-IMAGE (high self-concept control)
Q₄	RELAXED, TRANQUIL, UNFRUSTRATED (low ergic tension)	TENSE, FRUSTRATED, DRIVEN, OVERWROUGHT (high ergic tension)

STANDARD TEN SCORE (STEN) — AVERAGE 5

a score of	1	2	3	4	5	6	7	8	9	10
by about	2.3%	4.4%	9.2%	15.0%	19.1%	19.1%	15.0%	9.2%	4.4%	2.3%

is obtained of adults

Figure 5.3
Cattell's 16-point personality traits (Source: Wesson et al; 2000, from Cattell, 1965)

- There is low test–retest reliability for the questionnaire data. Cattell assumes that variations in traits occur over time, so he would not expect good test–retest reliability. According to Cattell, traits are not biologically determined.

- Cattell found two surface traits – exvia/invia and anxiety – that seem to correspond with Eysenck's E and N, and this tends to give validity to the 16PF.

Personality and behaviour

Cattell looks at mood factors, state factors and motivational factors. Within motivational factors Cattell suggests there are ergs, which are innate drives, and sentiments, which are culturally acquired drives. Ergs include exploration, assertiveness and gregariousness. Motive according to Cattell has different parts, including alpha (id, or 'I want'), beta (ego, or concerned with information) and gamma (superego, or 'I ought').

Linking personality traits to choice of sport and sporting success

Extroverts/introverts and sporting success

From Eysenck's theory (extroverts are said to be less aroused than introverts), it can be suggested that extroverts can cope with pain more easily, since they seek new stimuli and are more likely to be already inhibiting sense data. They are more likely to cope with stressful situations, for similar reasons, and can cope better when there are distracting stimuli around, such as an audience. So extroverts should be better at sport in general. Extroverts are less likely to enjoy sport where there is an element of continuousness, for example, marathon or cross-country running.

Introverts, on the other hand, need less arousal, and should be better at sport needing precision and concentration, such as shooting and archery.

Personality and sport injuries

Research into sport injuries has looked at personality. For example, Ogilvie and Tutko (1966) suggested that sport injuries might come from personal characteristics, and research has suggested traits such as determination to punish others, fear of success, need for sympathy or wish to avoid training can lead to sport injuries.

Valliant (1981) reported that runners who said they had been injured seemed to be less tough-minded and less forthright as measured on the 16PF.

- Valliant's study used quite a small sample.

- There was a poor response rate. This is a common criticism of the use of questionnaires.

- Participants had to remember about their injuries, and retrospective studies can be criticised because they rely on memory.

- Kolt and Kirkby (1991) suggested that Valliant's study is not useful because it cannot show whether the personality type caused the injury, or whether the participants showed such characteristics as lack of tough-mindedness because of their injury.

- Jackson *et al.* (1978) assessed 110 high school players at the start of the football season and then collected injury data. This was a prospective study, and was better in that it did not rely on retrospective data, as Valliant's study did. This research found that those who scored as tender-minded were more likely to be injured. However, there is some doubt about the statistical testing of this study. It can, however, be used in evaluation of Valliant's work and it could be suggested that being tender-minded is likely to lead to sport injuries.

- Brown (1971) did a study similar to that of Jackson *et al.* (1978) and found no link between the personalities and whether there was a sport injury or not.

- The general conclusion is that personality is not a predictor of sport injury.

Personality and choice of sport

Cooper (1969) found that international athletes did share some personality traits – they were more competitive, more socially outgoing and more self-confident than non-athletes. However, it might be a mistake to look for these traits when choosing athletes for a team. In Hemery's (1986) interviews of 63 international athletes 89% said they were shy and introverted when they started out as athletes.

Kroll and Crenshaw (1970) used the 16PF to compare American footballers, wrestlers, gymnasts and those good at karate. The footballers and wrestlers had similar personalities, whereas the gymnasts and those doing karate were different from one another, and from the wrestlers and footballers. So it seems that different personality types are successful in different sports, rather than there being one good personality profile for sport in general.

Williams and Parkin (1980) wondered if players at international level for a particular sport differed in personality from those who remained at club level, and looked at male hockey players using the 16PF. The international players differed greatly from the club-level players, but national-level players and club players were not so different.

Evaluation

- When considering trait approaches to personality, and evaluating them within the area of sport psychology, it is important to remember that there are other ways of talking about personality, such as the psychodynamic and humanistic approaches. As these suggest different ways of looking at personality, they can be used to evaluate other approaches.

- Martens (1975) criticised the research methods used, saying that research was not based on theory, but on giving questionnaires to athletes and then looking at the results. The research was often not based on a clear hypothesis. This meant that the results were gathered, and then theories were examined to see what could explain them. This methodology led to findings that did not support one another, and there was no consistent pattern.

- Psychometric approaches to personality use factor analysis but as there are so many solutions that can be found using factor analysis Heim (1975) thought it should not be used. However, others argue that if the most simple number of factors is always chosen, this is a reasonable approach (Kline, 1981). **Parsimony** is an accepted way of deciding what is acceptable when building theories. Parsimony refers to choosing the most elegant and simple solution or theory. This is often found to be the most likely to be 'true'.

- Trait theory is often seen as too simplistic and giving a limited view to personality. There is no recognition that individuals are involved in constructing their own personalities. There is also no recognition of the different external situations that can affect an individual.

- The methods used tend to be self-reports, which can be criticised because a person might not answer the questions honestly. There are issues of social desirability and demand characteristics (demand characteristics mean that a person may answer as he or she thinks the researcher wants them to answer to achieve the researcher's aims). The personality of the researcher, or even the time of day, might affect the results.

- 'Credulous' thinkers believe that personality is a good predictor of sport performance. However, they tend to be early theorists, and criticisms of the methods they used have tended to mean that most theorists are now sceptical about the link between personality and success in sport.

Can personality predict sport success or sport choice?

Sport coaches might like to use a personality test to determine who is likely to become successful, and who is likely to drop out. The advantage of using tests to choose people is that there are often limited funds, and the funds that are available are best spent on the 'right' person, if that person can be identified. If the funds are not 'wasted' on drop outs, and instead are concentrated on the few who might succeed, this would be a more efficient course of action.

However, research seems to suggest that there is no such personality. Vealey (1992) says that no systematic correspondence has been found between personality and sport choice, and that there is no consistent evidence that a particular personality profile goes with superior performance.

There are still those who do think that a specific personality links with sporting success. They criticise previous methods, and feel that research into personality in sport might yield useful results. For example, Vealey suggests that personality develops over a person's lifespan. Most of the research looking at personality and sporting success has focused on college students, whereas research looking at younger children or at adults might be fruitful.

Although a particular personality might not be important, personality could be one of the variables that affects sporting success, so is still worth investigating.

Self-test

Write a timed essay under exam conditions (or as close as you can manage), using the title 'Discuss research linking personality traits to choice of sport and sporting success'.

Sport and socialisation

Personality research tends to suggest that we have a certain sort of personality, and that this is a stable and enduring condition. As outlined above, Eysenck suggests that our personality is part of our nature, and there is a biological basis for it. However, others have suggested that nurture also affects personality – for example, we learn through reinforcement; we tend to repeat behaviour for which we have been rewarded and tend not to repeat behaviour for which we have been punished; we use others around us as a reference point, and learn from them. Social learning theory suggests that we develop as individuals through learning and socialisation. This idea is different from the idea that we have an innate personality, which might or might not lead us to be good at sport. This section looks at social learning theory, how we might learn as individuals, and how individual differences might make us good or bad in sport.

What is socialisation?

Socialisation refers to passing on cultural norms and values of a society. **Primary socialisation** takes place in the family, and **secondary socialisation** occurs within other areas of society such as education, work and the media. Role models are found in all these places, and socialisation comes from many different sources. Sport can act as an agent of socialisation, as the norms and values of a society are reflected in sporting situations. Performers are socialised into the norms and values of a particular sport, so sporting situations are socialisers. It is argued that by taking part in sport children are learning cultural values, as well as motor and cognitive skills. Leadership roles are learnt in sporting situations, as are co-operation, moral behaviour and social roles.

Mischel's (1968) situational approach

The social learning view of personality sees individuals as being shaped by their experiences in a social world. Unlike the trait approach, where personality is seen as stable, the social learning view suggests that our personalities are continually changing and developing in response to our daily experiences. Social roles play a large part in governing an individual's behaviour – someone can be aggressive, for example, in one situation but not aggressive in a different situation. Mischel (1968) gives the example of a boy who is interested in tennis. He watches a good tennis player on television, retains the player's behaviour, practices it when himself playing tennis and feels more confident if his newly learnt behaviour works. The boy has not developed a confident personality but, when he is playing tennis, he is now more confident. This is a situational approach, because the personality depends on a particular situation.

There are four stages of learning by observation, which are outlined later in the chapter.

Evaluation

+ Many agree that the situational approach is useful in moving away from the trait approach to personality. It does seem that people act differently in different situations.
− However, some feel that the situational approach goes too far the other way, and that there must be some stability in an individual's personality.

Social learning theory

Social learning theory suggests that we learn through imitation and modelling as well as through reinforcement.

Bandura carried out a lot of research in this area and concluded that as well as learning through direct reinforcement (for example, praise) we learn through vicarious reinforcement – from observing others and imitating them. We learn in a social setting, with others around, and these others affect what we learn.

Observational learning involves watching a model (the person being observed), and much teaching in sport involves a coach demonstrating what is to be done and the players observing. In various studies Bandura (e.g. 1977a) found that whether a model was copied or not depended on factors such as whether the model's behaviour was rewarded, and whether the model was similar to the observer (for example, regarding age and/or gender). When an observer imitates an observed behaviour – even if this is later – they are said to have socially learned that behaviour.

STUDY AID

Social learning theory is studied in other areas of psychology as well as here. It is explored in the AS part of the course, and also in Chapter 2. You could read the relevant sections there to extend your understanding.

Characteristics of models

- *Appropriate* – If the observer sees the model's behaviour as appropriate in relation to acceptable norms, then the behaviour is more likely to be imitated. For example, aggressive behaviour is more acceptable in males than in females, so males are more likely to copy the behaviour of aggressive male models.
- *Relevant* – Males might be more likely to imitate male aggressive behaviour because this is an acceptable part of the male role, at least in Western society. The behaviour is seen as relevant by the observer, and even more so if the behaviour is 'live' rather than on video. People are more likely to imitate 'live' behaviour than televised behaviour.
- *Similar* – Gender roles are also important. Children start to identify with their gender, and from that time are more likely to imitate models of the same gender.
- *Nurturing* – Models that are kind and friendly are more likely to be imitated.
- *Reinforced* – If a behaviour is reinforced, the observer is more likely to imitate that behaviour.
- *Powerful* – More powerful or skilled models are more likely to be copied.
- *Consistent* – If the behaviour is consistent it is more likely to be imitated.

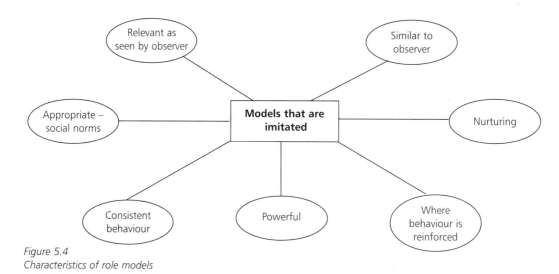

Figure 5.4
Characteristics of role models

Bandura's model of observational learning – in sport

Bandura's research into observational learning can be used in coaching and training. The above characteristics are important – for example, young males will imitate a male sports personality more, given appropriateness, relevance and similarity. If the sports personality is seen to get rewards for their behaviour – and they often are – then the behaviour is more likely to be modelled. Similarly the model is likely to be skilled and therefore powerful, and is also likely to be consistently good. All these factors mean that young people model on successful sport personalities, a fact that is used in advertising.

There are four stages, according to Bandura's model.

Stage 1 – Attention

The model must be perceived as high status, successful and attractive. When someone is starting out in a sport, the model's behaviour must be clear and focus on specific details, as too much information can detract from the initial message. The coach (who should be successful in the field, attractive and of high status if possible) must give a demonstration that can be clearly seen, is accurate, focuses on specific details and maintains motivation. The required actions must be attended to by the observer.

Stage 2 – Retention

Memory of what has been observed is important, and memory for meaningful events is better than if there is no meaning. Therefore a demonstration should be meaningful and relevant. The required actions must be retained by the observer.

Stage 3 – Motor production

At this stage a person must reproduce the behaviour of the model, and the modelled behaviour must be within the observer's capabilities.

Stage 4 – Motivation

If the observer successfully carries out the imitated behaviour the behaviour will be reinforced, and the observer will be motivated to reproduce the actions when needed. Bandura says that the level of motivation depends on the level of external reinforcement (such as praise), the level of vicarious reinforcement, the level of self-reinforcement (such as pride in achievement), the perceived status of the model, and the perceived importance of the task.

Table 5.2 *Making demonstrations effective in a sporting situation*

- Ensure that the learner sees the relevance of the demonstrated skill
- Refer to a high-status model
- Make sure the observer can see and hear well
- Allow time for rehearsal, to aid memory
- Highlight the main points of the technique
- Have a short time between the demonstration and the practice
- Reinforce successful performance

Learning and performance

It appears that if something has been learned it can be performed, although the relationship between learning and performance is not straightforward. Performance is a motor skill; however, learning is an internal process. Learning is supposed to lead to change in behaviour but learning is hard to measure. An athlete may perform badly even though he or she has learned a skill. Variables that might affect performance of a well learned behaviour include boredom, tiredness and lack of arousal as well as motivational factors (looked at later in this chapter).

The performance curve

A performance curve is what results from measuring a skill over a period of time. The quality of performance should improve over time, but there are different stages in this improvement. There are different types of performance curve.

- The linear curve – improvement is steady, and there are no stumbling blocks. As time goes on, the performance gets steadily better.
- The negatively accelerated curve – there is a lot of improvement early on and then the speed of improvement levels off.
- The positively accelerated curve – there is a small level of improvement early on, but then the speed of improvement picks up.
- The Ogive or S-shaped curve – there are small gains in performance, then a steady improvement, which then levels off .

The learning plateau

There is also often a learning plateau (levelling off with no improvement). This can be caused by loss of motivation, and making practice more interesting can help to get a person over the problem. Tiredness and lack of confidence can also lead to a learning plateau, and a rest from practice, or more support, can help in this situation. A lack of understanding can also lead to a learning plateau, so clearer directions and more feedback can help.

Socialising influences, and sport as an influence on social development

Family and culture

Family is a primary socialising agent in our society. A great deal of research in sport psychology focuses on children, because they will be the athletes of tomorrow. It is thought that childhood experiences can turn children away from sport, and these demotivating experiences need to be addressed if more children are to be encouraged to participate.

The family is the main socialising agent for the child. Moral issues and values such as fair play and shared achievement are first demonstrated within a family structure. Within one culture, values are shared and passed on by means of socialisation. By the time a child has reached school, many norms and values have already been demonstrated to the child.

The family has an influence on the child even after the child has started to interact with secondary socialising agents. For example if a father shows his child that aggressive behaviour is not acceptable, it is unlikely that a coach who is encouraging aggression on the sports field is going to be able to encourage that child to become more aggressive, at least when the father is present.

Physical development is important for the very young child, and between the ages of around 6 and 12 there is a period of fairly steady growth (Kirchner, 1992). In schools physical education programmes help with the refinement of motor skills, and have great importance. At this stage the family, although important, is not the only influence when it comes to socialisation. Peers are also important role models, as are television personalities and adults in school. Harter (1978) points out that a child's peers are important to the child's sense of identity and ability to socialise. Games can help to give a child a moral sense, for example, by showing fair play. Team games can help a child share collective achievement.

Through sport a child can learn what is acceptable, what is important and what is valued in society – in Western society this includes success, co-operation, pleasing others and acquiring skills. The child also learns how people behave to one another, what is expected of others, how to interact with others, and what particular behaviour is acceptable in certain settings.

Gender

Although a child might learn through socialisation what is expected of others according to their age, social class, culture, etc., one of the main ways of dividing people in Western society is by gender.

One way that gender affects our socialisation has already been outlined – we are more likely to model on those of the same gender as ourselves. A coach is more likely to be imitated if he or she is of the same gender as the observers. However, this cannot be completely true as, although there are many female sports and PE teachers in schools, adolescent girls appear less interested in sport than boys. There must be other factors at work.

Surveys show gender differences in motivation towards sport, and these differences might come from socialisation. For example, Gill and Deeter (1988) carried out a survey to measure competitiveness, and found that females tended to have a little more goal orientation (goal orientation is the desire to reach personal goals in sport). Males scored higher on competitiveness and win orientation (competitiveness is the desire to seek and strive for success, and win orientation is the desire to win interpersonal competitive sporting events).

Another area where gender differences are found is in **attributions** – the way people attribute causes to events. Females have lower expectations of success than males (Lenney, 1977) and are more likely to attribute their success to luck than males are. Females also attribute their failure to their lack of ability. On the other hand, males tend to attribute their success to internal factors such as ability and their failure to external factors such as bad luck. Even in very young participants these gender differences are noticeable. Bird and Williams (1980) found that 13-year-old boys usually explained success as being due to their own effort, whereas girls of the same age attributed success to luck. These studies suggest that females are lower in self-confidence. Males did have higher levels of self-confidence, but these differences seem to appear only at around the age of 12. Attribution and self-confidence are discussed again later in this chapter.

There are also gender differences in coaching style. Females prefer a democratic coaching style – they prefer to have a say in the decision making. This tendency could come from socialisation. There are also gender differences in leadership styles in general, and females are often said to be more relationship oriented. Perhaps this comes from observational learning of the family situation, or of role models at school or on television. Horn and Glenn (1988) found that female athletes who were anxious preferred coaches who gave strong support and positive feedback.

Factors that tend to lead to a negative attitude to sport include disapproval of family and peers, as well as socialisation against the activity.

- For example, if socialisation patterns suggest that rugby is not for females, it is likely that females will not want to play rugby.
- Similarly, age and gender constraints are understood through socialisation, and can have a strong effect on attitude.
- Negative role models can also lead to a negative attitude. As role models are those who are successful in a particular sport, and are likely to be the socially approved gender, change is difficult, as role models need to be changed.

Gender and competitiveness

One area where there are said to be gender differences is the area of competitiveness. Competitiveness links with achievement motivation, which is discussed later in this chapter. Martens (1976) suggests that the motive to succeed combined with the motive to avoid failure leads to a measure of **competitiveness**.

Competitive trait anxiety is the motive to avoid failure. Competitiveness is the motive to gain success, and is made up of three parts: competitiveness (working towards success), **win orientation** (wanting to win competitions between individuals) and **goal orientation** (the desire to reach personal goals). Male athletes score higher on competitiveness and win orientation; females score higher on goal orientation.

Sport as an influence on social development

Children are exposed to organised competitive sport from a young age (Walsh and Snyder, 1982). In a study in Australia (Clough *et al.*, 1993) boys chose sport as the most preferred leisure activity, girls ranked sport as equal with 'being with friends'; so it can be seen that (in Australia at least) both boys and girls see sport as very important. Children who are involved in sport are seen to have improved physical, social, emotional and psychomotor development. Advantages of being involved in sport include the chance to mix with and make friends with others, to enjoy increased status and to have improved standards of fitness (Passer, 1981).

Others (e.g. Martens, 1976; Scanlan, 1984) have suggested that some damage can be done when children are involved too young in competitive sport. Problems they highlight include physical injury and the stress involved.

Often parents are involved as coaches, and this can mean good family involvement; however, sometimes a coach does not understand the needs of a child (with regards, for example, to physical development), and needs to pay attention to appropriate practice of skills. The child's self-image and attention span must also be considered. With the wrong coaching a child may become demotivated (Evans, 1986).

Alexander (1991) suggests that children receive mixed messages from taking part in competitive sport, where the emphasis is often on winning. Models may be seen to be cheating, but still held up as good examples. If there is an emphasis on competition and winning, these values can be the ones learned and put into practice. So, although sport can be a useful socialising influence, some of the lessons that children learn are not so useful from society's viewpoint.

Self-test

Write a timed essay under exam conditions (or as close as you can manage), using the title 'Discuss sport as an influence on social development'.

Participation and motivation in sport

Introduction

Not only can children learn from taking part in sport; some sports can benefit from children taking part in an organised way at an early age, especially sports such as gymnastics or swimming. Other sports, however, such as cricket and football, may not be played better by those who take part in organised school games, because the skills needed can be learned by informal play in a local park. Participation is important. A problem is that children do not always keep the sport up, as they develop other interests or become demotivated. Motivation is an important factor when considering sporting success, and participation in sport.

Roberts (1992) stresses that the important thing about behaviour is *why* it is carried out. Both the uniqueness of the individual and the wider social values need to be studied in order to find out why something happens. The study of motivation involves identifying personal and social factors that are linked to some reward or incentive – what makes something a motivator? Motivation can be both intrinsic (from within the person) and extrinsic (from external factors). Different approaches to psychology have different views about why actions are carried out. Sport psychology takes ideas from these different approaches.

For example, the psychodynamic approach suggests that we are motivated by innate biological drives, which are really aggressive impulses struggling for recognition. It could be said, for example, that aggressive impulses are found more in males. The motivation to participate in sport could be seen as a natural expression of male aggression. For many years females have been restricted to certain sports, and this can be seen as supporting the view that aggressive impulses give motivation for actions. The humanistic view, however, might suggest that we are motivated to take part in sport because we need acceptance, recognition and love from others. Participating in sport gives an individual the opportunity to receive such acceptance and admiration. The individual's self-concept can be improved through sporting success. The behaviourist view is more likely to look at extrinsic motivation, in the form of rewards. Thomas (1978), however, suggests that rewards alone do not account for sport participation, and there must be other motivational forces present.

⟳ Recall AS material

Recall (or look up) your AS material on the approaches to theories of motivation – looking at the 'why' of the behaviour. Freud, for example, thought we are motivated by instinctual drives. The behaviourists think we are motivated by a system of rewards and punishments. You may also have looked at other approaches, such as the humanistic approach. Rogers, from the humanistic viewpoint, thought that individuals were motivated by a drive to self-actualise. It is clear that different approaches have different views on motivation.

Defining motivation

Motivation can be said to direct our efforts, and we can become more motivated given more effort. However, the view that motivation drives our efforts, and is under our control, can be too simplistic (Weinberg and Gould, 1995). We are motivated when ready to act in a particular way, and motivation relates to the direction the behaviour will go in. This means that as well as involving intrinsic and extrinsic mechanisms, motivation also involves our state of arousal and whether our goals are clear.

Primary and secondary motivation

Motives can be divided into **primary motives**, where the organism is motivated to get what it needs for survival, and **secondary motives**, which are learned. It is not always easy to see what are primary drives or motives, and what are secondary ones. For example, the need to self-actualise could be learned but could also be claimed to be an innate drive.

Intrinsic motivation

Biological drives

Intrinsic motivation comes from within us, and so to an extent is innate. Examples of intrinsic motivation are hunger and the drive to eat, thirst and the drive to drink, and possibly aggression and the drive to release such feelings. Intrinsic motivation is primary in that it is likely to stem from internal mechanisms, and these are likely to have arisen through evolutionary processes and biological drives.

Thinking patterns

Intrinsic motivation links to cognitive psychology because it refers not only to internal biological drives but also to the thoughts of the individual and how far that person is determined to succeed.

Introducing an element of competition also acts as intrinsic motivation. Deci *et al.* (1981) carried out a study where half the participants taking part in a task were told to try to beat the others, whereas the other half of the participants were not given this instruction. Both groups were allowed to win. Later the participants were given a choice of activities, and those who had been given an element of competition were the most motivated to continue with the activities. It seems as if competition acts as an intrinsic motivator. Competitiveness was discussed earlier in this chapter.

Intrinsic motivation and improving motivation in sport

A sportsperson with intrinsic motivation is said to have a **mastery orientation**. This means that they take part in the sport for its own sake, and are inwardly motivated. They don't do it for money or external reward. They are

Table 5.3 The flow experience (intrinsic motivation)

The flow experience involves:	The flow experience can come from:
Complete absorption	Positive mental attitude
Apparent loss of consciousness	Relaxed attitude, controlled anxiety
Effortless movement	Enjoying optimum arousal
Merging of action and awareness	Focusing on appropriate aspects
Feeling of self-control	Physical readiness
No extrinsic motivation	

likely to pursue excellence, and push themselves to improve. Intrinsic motivation is found in competent, self-confident athletes. Maslow's theory of motivation, which refers to a hierarchy of needs, suggests that the 'highest' need is the achievement of self-actualisation, and Csikszentmihalyi (1975) talks about the flow experience (a peak of internal motivation) – see Table 5.3. The flow experience has been said to be self-actualisation.

Extrinsic motivation

Extrinsic motivation comes from outside us, and such drives and motivation would be learned through interaction with the environment. Examples are the need to achieve at work, or the need to be friends with a lot of people. It is not easy to decide what motivation is intrinsic and what is extrinsic. External motives are likely to be secondary motives, as they have been learned.

The behaviourist view of motivation suggests that reinforcers are important, and that motivation is learned. These reinforcers could be called external motivators. Effective Contingency Management refers to using such reinforcers well and successfully.

External rewards can be tangible and intangible. Tangible rewards are trophies, medals, money, badges and certificates – rewards that are real. Intangible rewards (those that one cannot 'touch') include praise, smiles, social status, approval from others, social reinforcements, and national recognition.

Smith *et al.* (1979) compared the behaviour of performers who were encouraged by their coaches when they made mistakes with that of performers whose coaches did not give such reinforcement. The participants were children. Children given encouragement showed more enjoyment than those who were not encouraged, particularly those who started with low self-esteem. It seems that extrinsic factors such as encouragement and reinforcement can be strong motivators.

🔄 Recall AS material

Recall – or look up – material from the learning approach, particularly with relation to schedules of reinforcement within operant conditioning. Questions can be asked here as to what schedules work best when looking at extrinsic motivators for those who participate in sport. What do you think?

Improving motivation in sport

- Avoid the use of punishment
- Use positive rewards wherever possible
- Use rewards and reinforcement that have meaning for the participant
- At first use continuous reinforcement and immediate reinforcement
- Intermittent reinforcement can be successful later
- Reward performance, not just winning
- Use shaping techniques (successive approximations)
- Provide feedback

Interactionist view – intrinsic plus extrinsic motivation

If you look at individual achievement, you will probably find both intrinsic and extrinsic motivators. Performers often respond to praise and perform for a reward, although most also need intrinsic motivation, such as the desire to succeed. Most sports have tangible rewards – cups, medals, financial rewards, etc. – but the individual needs to put in extra effort that simple rewards could not elicit.

Evaluation

- Some research (e.g. Orlick and Mosher, 1978) suggests that if intrinsic motivation is high, adding extrinsic motivation can actually decrease the level of performance. It is possible that the performer might see the reward as meaning that someone or something else was taking control away from them, and might be demotivated because they feel they have less control. Coaches and advisors should involve the athlete in any decision making, so that they do not feel this loss of control. An extrinsic reward might be a motivator if the performer succeeds and receives the reward. However, if the reward is not achieved, the extrinsic motivator may have had the opposite effect, and might actually lower motivation.

Cognitive evaluation theory

Deci and Ryan (1985) propose the cognitive evaluation theory, which emphasises mainly intrinsic motivation. The theory suggests that we need to evaluate our performance against that of others, and sports settings allow this to happen. By having a standard, feedback can be meaningful, and someone is more likely to be motivated to do better if they have a measure against which to evaluate their performance. By practising and getting better against this measure the individual gains control, and so intrinsic motivation can rise. If feedback is negative, however, and the individual is not succeeding when evaluating their performance against that of others, intrinsic motivation can be lost. Coaches and others should emphasise what was done well, rather than focus on a poor performance.

The cognitive evaluation theory holds that events that affect the individual's perception of competence, and how much they think their own efforts can help them to succeed, affect their intrinsic motivation (Weiss and Chaumeton, 1992). These events can be rewards or feedback about their performance, often relative to others. The most important factor about rewards and feedback is that the control is not taken from the athlete. For example, if a coach praises a player for achieving something difficult but does not praise effort in other areas where perhaps success was not so obvious, the athlete may feel that the control is with the coach. It might seem that the coach is only measuring what he or she wants, rather than measuring the performance. If an athlete achieves financial support (perhaps a scholarship), they need to feel that this has been earned. If, however, the scholarship is seen as a way of controlling the athlete, then intrinsic motivation can be lowered.

Summary – the use of rewards to develop intrinsic motivation

As has been seen, rewards can lower intrinsic motivation, particularly if the individual sees the rewards as leading to a loss of control over the situation.

Successful strategies for using rewards to improve intrinsic motivation are:
- ensuring that rewards come from the performance itself
- emphasising praise
- setting realistic goals, where the individual can succeed and be rewarded
- manipulation of the environment so that there will be success
- allowing the individual to take part in the decision making
- setting up lots of opportunities for learning and practice.

Self-test

Write a timed essay in exam conditions (or as close as you can manage), using the title 'Distinguish between intrinsic and extrinsic motivation and discuss how each might be related to sport psychology'.

Achievement motivation

A further way of defining motivation is to look at what has been called 'achievement motivation', or the need for achievement. Some sportspeople succeed and others of equal ability do not, which is often put down to achievement motivation – some people seem to want to achieve more than others do. Murray (1938) linked a person's need for achievement to their personality. Some people seem more willing to put themselves in situations where their performance can be measured against that of others, and they are often said to have more achievement motivation.

McClelland (1961) developed a motivation theory that included a need for achievement, and Atkinson (1964) also talked about this need. Atkinson thought that both personality and the situation had a role to play in whether a person has a strong need for achievement (nAch).

Synoptic Note

Recall any areas that you have studied where the nature/nurture debate has arisen. You will be able to apply this debate to the discussion about motivation.

STUDY AID

The issue of motivation, including McClelland's theory, is studied in other areas of psychology, as well as here. It is explored in Chapter 4, and you could read the relevant sections there to extend your understanding.

Atkinson's theory of motivation

Atkinson's theory is an interactionist one, in that he looks at situational and personality factors. The idea is that an individual has two underlying motives.
- The need for success (nAch), which means that a person wants to succeed for reasons such a pride and satisfaction (intrinsic motivation).
- The need to avoid failure (nAf) where, in order to avoid feeling shame and humiliation, the person is motivated not to fail.

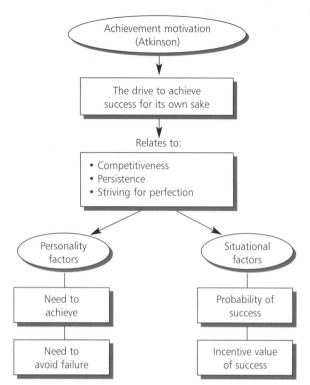

Figure 5.5 Atkinson's theory of achievement motivation (Source: Wesson et al., 2000)

People who do well in sport have a high nAch and a low nAf, and those who do not do well seem to have a high nAf and a low nAch (Table 5.4).

Alongside these intrinsic factors are extrinsic factors such as the likelihood of success and the importance of success or failure to the individual. The more a person is likely to succeed (perhaps because the opponent is weak), the less the importance of success; the less the person is likely to succeed, the greater the incentive.

Achievement motivation = (motive to succeed – motive to avoid failure) × (probability of success × incentive value of success)

A person who is **task goal oriented** focuses on their own performance and examines their own achievement without

reference to others. Someone who is **outcome goal oriented** focuses on winning, and what the outcome is, rather than on their own performance. These ideas link to the idea of competitiveness, which was outlined earlier.

Evaluation

- It is difficult to measure achievement motivation, and often participants are asked either to say what their attitudes are or to use attitude scales. These measures can be unreliable.

- Achievement motivation is calculated by taking the need not to fail from the need to achieve, and most research is done on people with a high nAch, or a high nAf. Those with a middle score tend not to be studied as much.

- Test results do not always support the claim that high achievement motivation leads to better performance.

- There may be different aspects to achievement motivation that are important to different people or in different sports. Achievement motivation is a large concept, which could be more useful if divided in some way.

Development of achievement motivation

Veroff (1969) lists three stages to the development of achievement motivation.

Autonomous competence stage

At between 3 and 4 years of age children focus on mastering skills in the environment and testing themselves. As personal competence grows, autonomous evaluation builds. 'Autonomous' means under one's own power.

Social comparison stage

By 5 years old children start to compare themselves with others of the same age, and start to want to be better than others. Normative comparisons mean focusing on winning (being above the norm), whereas the informative value of comparisons means evaluating their own skills, and how good they are.

Table 5.4 Motivation to succeed or to fail: comparing nAch and nAf

A person motivated to succeed:	A person motivated to avoid failure:
Looks for challenge	Avoids challenges
Feels that standards are important	Gives up easily
Likes feedback	Does not like feedback
Is not afraid of failure	Attributes failure to external factors (e.g. luck)
Is optimistic	Is pessimistic
Is confident	Lacks confidence
Is task goal oriented	Is outcome goal oriented

Integrated stage

In the integrated stage a person has autonomous competence and uses social comparison. Some people may not reach this stage, and those who do can be of any age.

Self-efficacy

Atkinson's theory of achievement motivation is a very broad concept, and can usefully be broken down into specific motivating factors. For example, someone could have a high achievement motivation, which included a low need not to fail, but this motivation involved academic success rather than sporting success. Someone else could be highly motivated to achieve success as a runner, but not be interested in achieving success in another field. Factors other than such a broad concept as achievement motivation might have an effect on sporting success.

Figure 5.6
Self-efficacy refers to confidence in a given situation. A skier may have high self-efficacy regarding downhill skiing but low self-efficacy with regard to tight turns

One factor that has been looked at with reference to sporting success is **self-efficacy**. Bandura (1977b) suggested that as we learn to do something well we develop a feeling of self-efficacy – we expect to do well in that task. Self-confidence is an overall term for feeling comfortable about your performance, but self-efficacy is the belief a person has in their capability of performing a particular task (Bandura, 1986). If someone has high self-efficacy they will carry on trying for longer, and will try harder. Someone with low self-efficacy gives up quite easily, is likely to blame themselves for failure, and tend to be prone to depression or anxiety. Bandura (1982) thinks that we prefer the feeling of self-efficacy to the feeling of failure, and that if we want to encourage others to take part in sporting activities we need to encourage self-efficacy.

Feltz *et al.* (1979) applied self-efficacy to sport, and in 1992 Feltz reviewed research linking self-efficacy to motivation in sport. McAuley (1992) looked at exercise psychology and self-efficacy. Exercise psychology is a field examining the use of exercise to help those with an illness, or those in sedentary occupations.

A performer's sense of self-efficacy will affect their choice of activity, the degree of effort and the level of persistence. At first, research suggested that a high level of self-efficacy was enough for someone to succeed, but later studies showed that the performer must also want to succeed (this links to the material on achievement motivation given above) and must have the necessary level of skill. Cognitive processes such as attribution are also important.

Social cognitive theory

Bandura (1977a, b) suggested that learning a behaviour is not enough for it to be carried out. There has to be some motivation for the person to act out the behaviour. Social learning theory explains how learning takes place, and social cognitive theory examines the cognitive processes that are necessary for that learning to be put into practice. A person needs an incentive to do something, and the incentive depends on what he or she perceives the outcome of the action to be. For example, a man might not enjoy running, but realises that the outcome of going for a run will be an improvement in his health, so continues with the exercise.

Four antecedents of self-efficacy

Bandura (1986) discussed four main antecedents of self-efficacy, factors that influence the level and strength of self-efficacy:

- Past accomplishments (which affect what the individual is feeling).
- Other experiences (including the person's experience of models and their observational learning).
- Verbal persuasion received from the coach or trainer.
- The level of emotional arousal.

Past accomplishments

The main factor in determining the level of self-efficacy is past accomplishments (Feltz, 1992). Previous failure can lead to low self-efficacy, and high self-efficacy has been shown to improve achievement. If someone has done well already, they are likely to have a high feeling of self-efficacy. This link would be even stronger if the past successes were seen by the individual as being under their own control. Your coach telling you that you are doing well would not have as strong an effect as realising for yourself that you are doing well. A trainer could make sure that a beginner succeeds – for example, by setting a tennis net lower or by shortening a match.

- Techniques involving performance accomplishments have improved self-efficacy (e.g. McAuley, 1985b).

Vicarious experience

A vicarious experience is an experience achieved through watching someone else achieve. If a performer sees someone with similar ability achieving the necessary skill this will raise their feeling of self-efficacy. Their anxiety might also be lowered – if someone else can do it, there is more hope that they can do it too.

Evaluation

- When performance is attempted after the modelling has taken place, self-efficacy improves (Feltz *et al.*, 1979). Modelling alone also improves self-efficacy (e.g. McAuley, 1985a), but it is better if the performer acts out the task after the modelling. One study by George *et al.* (1992) asked female college students to watch a video of a model performing a leg extension endurance task then to perform the same task. Before the study, the participants carried out a self-efficacy questionnaire, and only those who said it was at least moderately important for them to do well were included in the study. There were different conditions within the study, and different models were used (an athletic male, an athletic female, a non-athletic male, a non-athletic female and a control condition with no model). A model similar to the observer improved results. However, Gould and Weiss (1981) replicated the study and found that similarity of ability was more important than similarity of gender.

Verbal persuasion

Many trainers keep reassuring performers that they can do a particular feat. This can work, but it depends on who is doing the persuading. This idea links back to social learning theory where, for example, models of the same gender are most likely to be copied, as are models with high status.

It is important not to use verbal persuasion to make the performer think they are better than they are, because this can decrease self-efficacy, especially if the performer fails at the task. Feltz (1992) thought that performers should use self-talk and imagery as well as other cognitive strategies.

Evaluation

- Wilkes and Summers (1984) looked at whether persuasion could improve confidence and change an individual's interpretations about their levels of arousal. They found performance did improve, but self-efficacy did not seem to be involved in this improvement. Feltz (1992) found that self-talk and imagery, rather than verbal persuasion by others, did work to an extent.

- Yan Lan and Gill (1984) tried to persuade performers that a heightened arousal level meant their performance would be good, but this did not seem to increase self-efficacy. A criticism of their study is that the participants may not have believed the false feedback – they may not have believed they were in a state of heightened arousal.

- Fitzsimmons *et al.* (1991) studied experienced weightlifters (they wondered whether previous research, which was done on novices, might not have revealed information that research carried out on experienced performers would show). The lifters had to perform a bench press. Participants were randomly assigned to one of three conditions: (1) false positive feedback (participants were told they had lifted more than they had), (2) false negative feedback (participants were told they had lifted less than they had) and (3) accurate information was given. Performance was improved by false positive feedback, although previous weightlifting experience was the most important factor in whether later performances improved or not – participants were able to judge their own performance, and this affected subsequent lifts.

Emotional arousal

Arousal can have a good effect on performance, and this area will be investigated further later in this chapter. However, arousal can also make performance worse. If individuals feel anxious, and can tell that their heartbeat is faster and that they are sweating, they may interpret these signs in a negative way. Their self-efficacy can be lowered. Relaxation and stress-management techniques can help to overcome these fears. Alternatively, the individual can learn about arousal, and realise that it is not necessarily a bad thing.

Evaluation

- Feltz (1992) looked at a high avoidance task, and chose the performing of a back dive. She measured physiological arousal and perceived autonomic arousal. The actual level of arousal did not seem to affect performance, although the *perceived* level of arousal did. Perceived level of arousal involves cognitive processing, and this is linked to self-efficacy. However, in this study, the actual performance had more effect on self-efficacy. Although it seems obvious to say so, the main factor affecting whether we think we are going to be good at something (self-efficacy) is whether we have done it well before. Kavanagh and Hausfeld (1986) tried to put participants in either a happy or a sad mood to see if self-efficacy was affected by mood, but they did not find self-efficacy changed with mood state.

Table 5.5 Improving self-efficacy, and therefore improving performance

- Provide situations where the individual experiences success
- Use goal setting, so that players experience success – set achievable goals
- Encourage confidence by what is said
- Ensure performers are well-prepared for the event
- Make sure performers use internal attributions for their success (they take credit)
- Emphasise performance, not the outcome

Self-test

Write a timed essay under exam conditions (or as close as you can manage), using the title 'Discuss self-efficacy and how it can be used to boost motivation in sport'.

Attribution

Attribution refers to the way we give a cause to something. **Internal attribution** means we see the cause as coming from within us (perhaps thinking that we are a failure). **External attribution** means giving an external cause for something – for example, we might see failure as being due to bad luck, or poor track surface rather than poor performance.

Attribution theory looks at the way in which individuals evaluate their success and failure, including in performance situations. The causes that a person attributes to their failure or success can affect their performance, their hopes for the future, their actual achievement, their motivation and their future participation. We attribute causes not only to our own behaviour but also to that of others. This in turn can affect our behaviour.

Weiner's two-dimensional model of attribution

Weiner (1972) developed a model involving four categories of causal attributions – ability, effort, task difficulty and luck. These categories are then fitted into two dimensions – the stability dimension and the locus of causality dimension (Figure 5.7).

The stability dimension refers to whether causes are permanent or changing. Ability and task difficulty are seen as relatively stable, whereas effort and luck are changeable. Ability will be a relatively stable cause for success and can be used over time. Similarly, lack of ability is a relatively stable cause for failure.

The locus of causality dimension refers to whether attributions are internal or external. Ability and effort are internal, whereas task difficulty and luck are external.

In 1986 Weiner added a further dimension called 'locus of control', which considers how far an individual feels that the cause was within their control. If a performer thinks their success was due to the task being simple and to them having luck then their satisfaction won't be very high. If, however, they think they did well by trying hard at a difficult task, then their satisfaction will be higher. So if success is attributed to external control, their satisfaction is reduced. If failure is attributed to internal control, the performer would blame him- or herself (Figure 5.8).

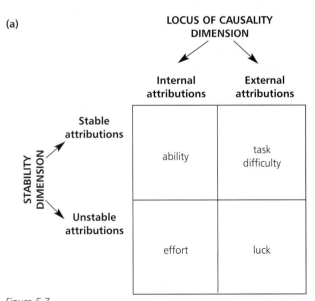

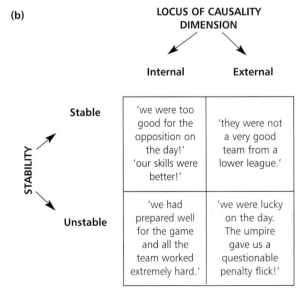

Figure 5.7
(a) Weiner's model. (b) An example of Weiner's model with attributions included – why we won (Source: Wesson et al., 2000; from Weiner, 1986)

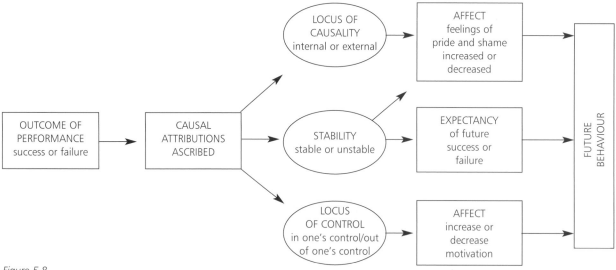

Figure 5.8
A revised model of attribution (Source: Wesson et al., 2000)

Applying attribution theory to sport

Within attribution theory there are biases. In general, for example, we tend to take credit for our successes, giving both internal cause and internal control as causal factors. We also tend to blame our failures on external causes and external control. This bias is called **self-serving bias**.

High achievers think that they are successful due to personal disposition and high ability (internal factors), and are motivated to continue. They attribute failure to external factors such as difficulty and are motivated to continue, but to try harder. Low achievers, however, attribute success to external factors such as luck and attribute failure to internal factors such as lack of ability. They are less motivated to continue.

Figure 5.9
Self-serving bias: John McEnroe protests

Another factor that affects attributions is whether a person is motivated by mastery goals or outcome goals. If a person is motivated by outcome goals ('I lost') as opposed to mastery goals ('I need to work on my backhand, but my ground strokes were good') this affects their attributions and their motivation.

Learned helplessness

Learned helplessness is a reaction learnt by a performer who feels that they have no control over the situation. Someone becomes conditioned to a certain behaviour and sticks to this pattern of behaviour rather than trying to change it, even though changing it would improve things – they learn to be helpless. Performers might learn to fail in this way. If they attribute failure to lack of ability and see the task as very difficult, then they could well stop trying. This type of performer is usually outcome oriented and has had bad experiences. They feel incompetent and are reluctant to try out new skills.

Dweck (1975) studied learned helplessness in children who saw failure as inevitable. Half of the group were given easy tasks, so experienced success, and the other half had some tasks where they were successful and some in which they failed. At this stage the children were encouraged to see their failure as lack of effort, which is an unstable attribution that they can do something about. The children who had been encouraged to change their attributions and improve their effort performed better overall on later tasks. It was as if they had changed their attributions, from seeing themselves as helpless to seeing that there was something they could do to change.

⟲ *Recall AS material*

Recall AS material about learned helplessness, or look it up. Conditioning could be so strong that, even when a situation changed and behaviour could change, the learnt pattern continued. This learned helplessness can mean that someone is not motivated to change their behaviour, even when it is possible.

Fundamental attribution errors

The coach and the performer might attribute different reasons for a situation – the performer is likely to blame external factors for their failure, but the coach will probably blame internal factors. This tendency to blame others' disposition (their character) for their failure and yet blame the situation when it comes to ourselves is called the 'fundamental attribution error'. A coach needs to be aware that they are likely to blame the individual, and must counter this by looking carefully at the situation.

Attribution retraining – improving sporting performance

Attribution retraining is needed if attributions are holding someone back (Dweck, 1975). Strategies include:
- Avoiding attributing lack of success to lack of ability.
- Attributing failure to something the performer can do something about, such as trying harder, understanding more, making better tactical decisions.
- Emphasising task goals.
- Ensuring that coaches and trainers do not make negative comments about performance.
- Noting that the observer tends to blame the individual, whereas the individual will blame the situation. Coaches need to be aware of this tendency, and to counteract it by looking at the situation.
- Helping the performer to see failure as due to external unstable factors – things that the person can change.
- Making sure that verbal comments are used to give positive feedback.

STUDY AID

Attributional biases are studied in other areas of psychology, as well as in sport psychology. They are explored in Chapter 2, and you could read the relevant sections there to extend your understanding.

Self-test

Write a timed essay under exam conditions (or as close as you can manage) with the title 'Discuss how attribution has been applied to improving motivation in sport'.

Influences on sporting performance

Much of what has been discussed so far in this chapter has involved looking at the performer – their personality, the influence of socialisation, motivation, self-efficacy, attributional style, the ways a person perceives success or failure, and how this perception affects whether they continue with the sport or not.

In this section social influences are examined. The mere presence of others can affect performance, as can team membership. Another area that can affect sporting achievement is anxiety and arousal.

Social influences

Sport usually takes place in the presence of others, rather than in isolation, and the effect of the presence of others on our performance is known as **social facilitation**. An audience could improve the performance, or make it worse. Other social influences include being part of a team.

Social facilitation

Social facilitation refers to how the presence of others (the audience) affects performance. Others can be **primary spectators**, who are actually present, or **secondary spectators**, who are watching the event on television or reading about it. Passive spectators are on nobody's side, supportive spectators are supporting the individual. Others present besides the audience are **coactors** – people who are also taking part in the event.

Triplett (1898) studied the effect of others on the performance of cyclists. He found that performance was affected by whether cyclists were alone, in pairs, or in groups. He also did a laboratory study using children winding fishing reels. Children seemed to compete with one another – their performance improved when they were not alone. Other research, however, has suggested that it is not the competition that produces the improved performance, but just the presence of others (e.g. Dalshiell 1935). Coaction (acting with other performers present, rather than acting in the presence of an audience) appears to improve performance.

Zajonc's drive theory

Zajonc (1965), who studied social facilitation, thought the performance in the presence of others depended on the nature of the task and that the mere presence of others is enough to raise an individual's level of arousal. With the level of arousal increased, the level of drive would increase. As a skill becomes well learned (it becomes the dominant response) it requires less drive or arousal to perform it – this is the **drive-reduction theory**. When we get good at something we could become bored, as our arousal level has reduced. Having an audience will lift the level of arousal and so lift the drive, and the well-learned skill will be performed better.

However, something that the individual finds difficult will probably be done less well when others are present. This is because the level of arousal is quite high already, as the task is difficult (it is a non-dominant response), and the extra arousal given by the presence of others will decrease performance. An increase in drive from the audience's presence will increase the number of errors. The drive-reduction theory can be explained using the inverted-U hypothesis (this is explained later in this chapter).

When someone is learning something, the behaviour is not yet a dominant response but once the skill is well learned it becomes a dominant response. The theory says that a non-dominant response is performed less well with others present, and a dominant response is performed better with others present.

Evaluation

- Zajonc's view focuses on the task difficulty, but seems to assume that differences in audiences will not have an effect on performance. Others have said that there is no such thing as a passive audience (Gahagan, 1975). For example, there is the difference in performance between a 'home' and an 'away' match.

Cottrell's evaluation apprehension theory

Cottrell's theory looks at the effect of the audience on performance. Cottrell (1968) focused on the type of audience, rather than the type of task. Cottrell argued that whether a performance improved in front of others depended on whether the individual saw the others as supportive or not. Evaluation apprehension refers to whether they think they are being evaluated by others around or not. The performer's feelings of evaluation apprehension affect the effects of social facilitation. If they think they are being evaluated, this increases their apprehension and their arousal.

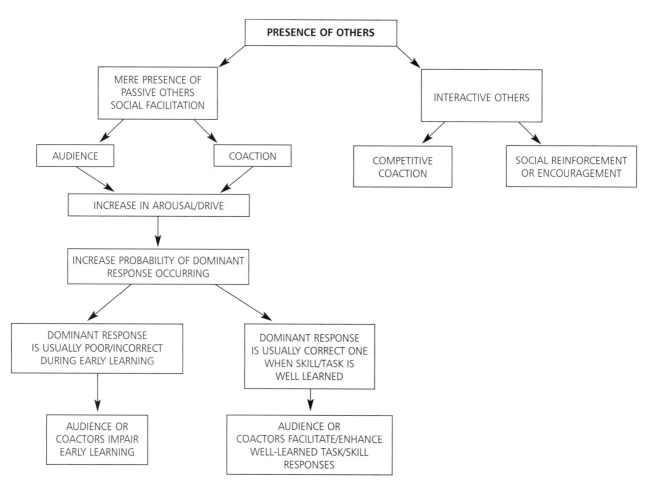

Figure 5.10
The relationship between drive theory and social facilitation according to Zajonc (Source: Wesson et al., 2000)

It might be thought that a team would perform better at a 'home' match, but they can actually do less well as they perceive the audience as evaluating their performance more, so their evaluation apprehension is higher. Cottrell suggested that the more expert an audience is the more performance decreases, and takes this as evidence that anxiety at being judged decreases performance.

Table 5.6 Applying social facilitation theory to sporting performance

- Training alongside others can help to put effort into training
- When learning new skills it is better to try alone
- Techniques for shutting out distractions from the crowd would be useful

Team cohesion and performance

In many sports performers are part of a team of people who interact – team members should have some positive feelings towards each other, there should be a collective identity and usually a sense of shared purpose. There are different types of sporting teams – in some the members do not change but there are also groups where membership changes frequently, such as in a climbing club.

It is usually thought that people perform differently when part of a group. One way of defining a group is to think of the 'Six I's' – interaction, interdependence, interpersonal relationships, identical goals, identity and independence.

Tuckman (1965) suggests that a group must go through four stages to become a team:
1 Forming – people get to know one another and understand roles and relationships within the group.
2 Storming – members start to challenge the status of the leader and there is competition for power.
3 Norming – the group begins to work together and see the need for common goals.
4 Performing – members identify with the team. They are aware of the roles of the others in the group and the feel that they can all contribute.

Roles within groups and teams include formal roles (such as captain), formal task or performance roles (such as goalkeeper) and informal roles (such as team comedian). There are also group norms that the individual has to adhere to.

It is not always the case that a group of the best athletes for a particular sport will be the best team. Steiner (1972) said that the team result is often more than the 'sum of its parts' (the total of the talent in the team). A team's success is due to the talent of the individuals, but can also be affected by the cohesion of the team (or lack of it) and the motivation of individuals within the team.

The resources of a team include the player's abilities, skill levels, the group's skill level, general resources such as fitness and individual and group mental resources. There are also social resources such as age, education, religion, occupation, gender, race and socialisation experiences.

The team with the better individuals has the greater potential for succeeding, but success also depends on the type of activity, specific skills needed and expectations about the game. Reasons why the 'best' (i.e. most talented) team might not always win include co-ordination losses, where the team strategies break down, and motivational losses, where individuals or the team lose confidence.

Cohesion

One important aspect of a team is its **cohesion**. Cohesion is the tendency of a group to stay together to achieve goals, and is a dynamic or continuously changing process. Festinger *et al.* (1950) say that cohesion is the total field of forces that encourage members to stay part of a particular team or group. Success might give the team cohesion, or cohesion might lead to success. Research suggests that both these statements are correct. When team members feel that the team has good cohesion, then there is greater satisfaction with the group, and success is more likely. Success also leads to satisfaction with the group – and, again, further successes are then more likely.

Cohesion can come from the attractiveness of the group or from the benefits individuals can gain from the group. **Interactive teams**, like basketball teams and hockey teams, have a high division of labour and individuals have specialist roles within the team. In interactive teams cohesion is important for success. In **coactive teams** (teams like rowing teams and swimming teams) members rely less on each other, and only have to do their task successfully. Cohesion is seen as less important for coactive teams.

Cohesion has been divided into **task cohesion** – how well the team works together to achieve the required goal – and **social cohesion** (how much the team members like one another). Carron (1982) proposed a model of the antecedents (the pre-existing variables, or whatever is already in place) that could influence the development of group cohesion. There are thought to be four main categories of antecedents ('antecedent' refers to what leads to group cohesion):

- situational/environmental elements
- personal elements
- team elements
- leadership elements.

Widmeyer *et al.* (1990) enlarged on Carron's idea. They saw that there was a circular relationship between success and cohesion in that success leads to cohesion and cohesion leads to success. Leadership and team elements were seen as social, whereas environmental and personal elements were seen as to do with the task. The group's integration and the individuals' attitudes to the task work within these four elements and affect the performance of the group.

Cohesion could work in a way similar to Tajfel's (1978) social identity theory, where the in-group individuals boost the in-group at the expense of the out-group to raise their self-esteem.

STUDY AID

Groups (and leadership) are also studied in other areas of psychology – for example, in Chapter 4. You could read the relevant sections there to extend your understanding.

↻ Recall AS material

Recall AS material from the social approach, in particular Tajfel's work and social identity theory. Look it up if you can't remember easily. The individuals of an in-group maintain self-esteem by boosting the achievements of the in-group and denigrating the out-group. Teams can act in this way too. The team is the in-group, and maintains self-esteem by banding together against the out-group.

Factors associated with group cohesion

- Type of sport – interactive teams perform better if they are cohesive, but this is not the case for coactive teams.
- Stability – greater group stability means it is more likely that members stay and get to know one another.
- Size of group – smaller groups have more cohesion, perhaps because members get to know one another better.
- External threats – members band together to fight against external threats, and so do not notice internal divisions so much.
- Similarity – similarity of age, gender, status and skill level tends to increase cohesion.
- Satisfaction – being satisfied with other team members means individuals are more likely to do better.
- Success – success goes with good team cohesion.

Applying research on cohesion to sporting performance

Improving team cohesion is likely to improve sporting performance. Here are some suggestions on how to improve cohesion.

- Get players to get to know one another.
- Make all players feel important, and encourage them to take part in team decisions.
- Encourage group identity, using club T-shirts, etc.
- Develop training practices that involve team interaction.
- Set clearly defined goals that are performance based.
- Encourage open communication between team members.
- Make sure players all know their own role and the roles of others.

Social loafing and negative effects

Although being part of a team or group enhances performance, there are negative effects from being part of a team. For instance, being part of a group can also lead to **social loafing**. Social loafing is a term meaning that some individuals within a group can sit back and let others get on with it rather than pulling their weight. This is the **Ringelmann effect**, so called because Ringelmann in the late nineteenth century measured how much effort was being put into a tug-of-war contest. Ringelmann found that the more men there were in the tug-of-war team the less each individual exerted himself: if there was only one person on each side he gave 100% effort, when there were two people per team they gave 93% effort each, three people gave 85% effort each, four people gave 77%, five 70%, six 65%, seven 58% and eight 49% of their potential. So as the size of the team grew, each individual's input grew less. This is an example of social loafing.

Some explanations for social loafing:

- The individual thinks others are not fully committed so feels taken for granted if they put in too much effort.
- The individual thinks others will cover up for his or her lack of effort. If the outcome is important to the individual, they will put the effort in.
- The individual thinks their own lack of effort won't be noticed in the crowd. Latané *et al.* (1980) created a simulated swim in which there were competitors, spectators and prizes. When lap times were not going to be announced (and they were not always announced) participants swam slower in the relay than they did as individuals. However, when lap times were going to be announced, the swimmers swam faster in the relay than individually. Latané *et al.* said that performers demonstrated allocation strategies and minimising strategies. Allocation strategies mean that the individual allocates effort, and keeps best efforts until it benefits them as individuals more (that is when

they are alone). The other strategy is that individuals are motivated to give as little effort as possible (that is the minimum effort) to achieve the task.

STUDY AID

Social loafing is studied in other areas of psychology, as well as in sport psychology. It is explored in Chapter 4, and you could read the relevant sections there to extend your understanding.

Applying research on social loafing to sporting performance

Coaches and trainers need to make sure they are attending to individuals when trying to improve team success. They must make sure social loafing cannot take place, that individuals cannot hide in the crowd, monitor individual performance and give feedback.

Group size

Group size can also be a problem, and if a group is too large its success can be affected. If there are many talented individuals in a large group, the coach has to bring together all the skills of the individuals, which can be difficult. At some stage a team may have all the necessary skills, and adding more does not mean increased success. Roles can be duplicated and there is a risk of social loafing.

Self-test

Write a timed essay under exam conditions (or as close as you can manage), using the title 'Discuss the possible negative effects of team membership on individual performance'.

Arousal and anxiety, and their links to performance

Arousal

Arousal is an important factor in sporting performance and success. Zajonc (1965) thought that levels of arousal affected performance, and that the presence of others changed levels of arousal. Cottrell (1968) thought that the type of audience affected arousal, and, therefore, affected performance. Both these ideas were discussed earlier when looking at social facilitation.

Arousal refers to a physiological response controlled by the autonomic nervous system (ANS), particularly the sympathetic and parasympathetic parts. We have evolved an alarm reaction (sometimes called the emergency reaction) in which the sympathetic part of the ANS is activated when we need to take quick action, possibly against a predator in the past. Physiological changes that occur include raised heart rate and pulse rate, dilation of pupils and sweating, preparing us for some immediate action. These physiological changes are what is called arousal. In the past action was likely to be fighting or fleeing from danger, and the alarm reaction is often called the 'fight or flight' response.

Arousal theories suggest that we need to be in a balanced state (a state of homeostasis). The sympathetic division of the ANS creates the aroused state by drawing on the hormonal and endocrine systems to get the body ready for action. The parasympathetic part of the ANS works to restore the system back to a less energised state, ready for the next time.

Arousal in itself is not good or bad; it is just the energised state. When aroused we are in an energised state, and our drives can be increased by this excess energy. So arousal can be useful. However, being in an increased energised state and suffering from anxiety can worsen performance. A person's psychological state can trigger the reaction.

The reticular activating system (RAS) maintains a general level of arousal in the body, and helps to maintain this balance by inhibiting or exciting incoming sensory information. These processes were discussed earlier when looking at Eysenck's personality theory (page 168). A person becomes aroused when physical demands are made on them, for example, but also when he or she is anxious or worried, so there is clearly a connection between the physical state and the psychological state. The level of arousal must be right for a sportsperson – he or she needs to be aroused enough to have the drive to succeed but not too aroused by anxiety that their performance suffers.

Anxiety is the negative emotional state associated with feelings of worry and caused by arousal. If the state of arousal is maintained for too long, strain will result, and a person will become stressed if the parasympathetic part of their ANS does not cancel out the reactions the sympathetic part triggered.

STUDY AID

The issue of arousal, the role of the nervous system, and issues of stress and strain are also studied in other areas of psychology. It is explored in Chapter 8, for example. You could read the relevant sections there to extend your understanding.

Drive theory

At the time that Hull (1943) and then Spence (1956) developed their drive theory it was thought that performance improved as arousal increased. The drive theory proposed that arousal brought more drive and more energy, so performance would get better. This is a learning theory in that performance is linked to habit strength as well as to drive (habit strength is the strength of the learning). So performance improved with improved drive and improved learning of the skill. The better someone was at doing something, and the more aroused they were, the better the performance.

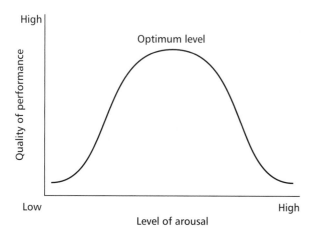

Figure 5.11
The inverted U relationship between arousal and performance

This is a very similar idea to that of Zajonc, who said that performance increased when there were others around, because arousal increases when others are around. Zajonc also thought that performance increased, not only with the arousal that the presence of others gave but also with increased skill. The dominant response is the one that will occur in times of arousal. This works if a skilled performer is aroused and the dominant response is the required one (which it will be if the skill is well practised and is the habitual response) – but in times of arousal a beginner's dominant response might be an earlier (and wrong) way of doing things. In this case, the performance will be hindered by arousal.

Evaluation

- Observations of real-life situations show that arousal does not always improve performance. There have been many examples where a person who is excellent at their sport puts in a surprisingly bad performance, even in conditions where they are likely to have had high levels of arousal.

The inverted U hypothesis

Yerkes and Dodson (separately in 1908) found that complex tasks are performed better when arousal is low,

but simple tasks are performed better when arousal is high. Both over-arousal and under-arousal can be bad for performance. There is an optimum level of arousal for the best performance, and this level varies according to task and to the individual. After an optimum level of arousal is reached there is a gradual falling off of performance. When the preparation is right, the right decisions have been made, and the arousal level that these circumstances are likely to lead to is right, then performance can be excellent. However, if any of these factors goes wrong it can lead to excess arousal and a poor performance.

Usually motor skills need quite a high level of arousal, and if the task requires little decision making (like weightlifting) then high arousal gives a good performance. However, complex tasks that involve decision making or accurate skills are done better with a slightly lower level of arousal. Beginners usually do better with low levels of arousal, and this should be taken into account by coaches and trainers. The beginner needs to process a lot of information, whereas an experienced performer will not need to give so much attention to the processes involved. The beginner experiences what is called **perceptual narrowing** and **cue utilisation**. By trying to use relevant cues (cue utilisation) and focusing carefully on the task (perceptual narrowing) the individual needs to have a low level of arousal, as attention is hard to focus if arousal is high. If the attention needed is very high because the performer has a lot to attend to, or there are unusual cues, the perceptual narrowing can be so great that hypervigilance (or 'blind panic') can occur.

Catastrophe theory

Fazey and Hardy (1988) have suggested the catastrophe theory as a way of explaining arousal, and as a modification of the inverted U hypothesis. The catastrophe theory shows that after the optimum level of arousal there is a sudden loss of performance, not a gradual one. When physiological arousal is combined with cognitive anxiety this combination can result in a sudden deterioration in performance that is very hard to recover from.

Anxiety

Anxiety is the negative emotional feeling that comes with arousal and stress. Anxiety has cognitive and somatic (physical) components. Some different types of anxiety are outlined below.

- *Cognitive anxiety* – Cognitive anxiety refers to negative thoughts a person can develop about achieving, and also negative expectations.
- *Somatic anxiety* – Some worry experienced is due not to thoughts but to physical reactions such as increased sweating, and having a queasy stomach. These physical symptoms make the person anxious, and this type of

anxiety is called somatic anxiety. Some people accept a little anxiety as normal when being asked to take part in a competition but others become very anxious.

- *State anxiety* – State anxiety is a perceived anxiety that occurs only in certain situations. Cognitive or somatic anxiety can also be state anxiety. For instance, during a match a player may be only slightly anxious, but may develop state anxiety at crucial points in the match. State anxiety is not related to arousal itself, but to the person's perception of their anxiety.
- *Trait anxiety* – Trait anxiety refers to the stable trait of anxiety that some people have as part of their personality. If someone has a high level of trait anxiety, they are likely to become anxious quite quickly, and are also likely to become aroused easily.
- *Competitive anxiety* – Anxiety at the point of competition can negatively affect a performer's concentration and level of processing information. It is not true that experienced performers do not experience competitive anxiety – they just seem more able to control this anxiety than beginners.

Self-report tests (e.g. Speilberger's STAI) can be used to measure state and trait anxiety, State anxiety is measured in particular circumstances, whereas trait anxiety refers to an individual's predisposition to worry. People who have high trait anxiety seem to perceive some competitive situations as very worrying, so they have high trait anxiety and high state anxiety, and their performance is likely to be adversely affected. However, the level of state anxiety is also affected by the particular situation, so a performer may experience more overall anxiety in one situation than in another. There is an interactionist relationship between the level of trait anxiety and the situation, and these two factors give the level of state anxiety (state anxiety is often referred to as A-state).

Before a competition, state anxiety can be affected by the fear of failing, the fear of being evaluated, the fear of the event itself and its importance, the fear of injury or the lack of control (perhaps due to the opposition's skill, or the poor environment). During the competition, state anxiety can be affected by the evaluation of others, interaction with others, injury during the competition, environmental influences, type of task, or how things are going.

Martens refers to global competitive trait anxiety, a general anxiety that competitions in themselves bring to some people. His sport competition anxiety test (SCAT) uses 15 items where participants use self-reports to give a measure of their personality, which could help coaches predict a performer's likely anxiety strength for a competition. An updated version of the SCAT uses separate measures for cognitive and somatic anxiety, and is called the competitive state anxiety inventory (CSAI2).

Evaluation

- SCAT is easy to administer, and can be used with large groups.
- It can be open to bias as participants might answer as they think they should answer (it shows demand characteristics).
- Responses can be misinterpreted.
- Administration of the questionnaire can itself make someone anxious.

TRAIT

Trait anxiety
A motive or acquired behavioural disposition that predisposes a person to perceive a wide range of objectively non-dangerous circumstances as threatening and to respond to these with state anxiety levels disproportionate in intensity and magnitude to the objective threat.

STATES

Arousal
A general physiological and psychological activation of the organism that varies on a continuum from deep sleep to intense excitement.

↓

State anxiety
Moment-to-moment changes in feelings of nervousness, worry, and apprehension associated with arousal of the body.

Cognitive state anxiety	**Somatic state anxiety**
Moment-to-moment changes in worries and negative thoughts.	Moment-to-moment changes in perceived physiological arousal.

Figure 5.12
Trait anxiety and state anxiety (Source: Wesson et al.*, 2000; from Weinberg and Gould, 1995)*

- It is assumed that high 'anxiety' scores are bad, but this is not necessarily true.

- One problem is that a questionnaire administered before the competition may not be a reliable measure of anxiety state during the competition, as arousal can rise at the start of the competition.

Self-test

Write a timed essay under exam conditions (or as close as you can manage), using the title 'Discuss the effects of anxiety and arousal on sporting performance'.

Suggested reading

Gross, R.D. (1996) *Psychology, The Science of Mind and Behaviour*. London: Hodder & Stoughton.

Morris, T. and Summers, J. (eds) *Sport Psychology, Theory, Application and Issues*. Australia: John Wiley & Sons.

Wesson, K., Wiggins, N., Thompson, G. and Harrison, S. (2000) *Sport and PE, A Complete Guide to Advanced Level Study*, 2nd edition. London: Hodder & Stoughton.

Woods, B. (1998) *Applying Psychology to Sport*. London: Hodder & Stoughton.

6

Child psychology

The aims of this chapter

The aims of this chapter are to enable the reader to:

- *discuss Bowlby's theory of attachment and the evolutionary basis of attachment*
- *discuss different attachment types, including cross-cultural studies and research involving the strange situation task*
- *discuss criticisms of attachment research, including the relationship between attachment types and caring style*
- *outline possible effects of short-term deprivation*
- *discuss research into the effects of day care, including studies of intellectual and social/emotional development*
- *discuss possible effects of long-term deprivation and privation*
- *distinguish between different categories of play*
- *discuss theoretical perspectives on play and the therapeutic value of play*
- *describe developmental trends and cultural differences in peer relationships*
- *discuss research into the popularity of individual children.*

STUDY AID

When you have finished working through this chapter you should write an essay about, or at least test yourself on, each of the above points. This will help you to see how good your knowledge and understanding of child psychology is.

This chapter covers

WHAT IS CHILD PSYCHOLOGY?

ATTACHMENT
    Attachment and definition of terms
    Explanations of attachment
    Attachment types
    Criticisms of research into attachment
    Attachments with people other than the mother (including caring style)

DEPRIVATION AND PRIVATION
    Short-term deprivation
    Research findings into the effects of daycare
    Long-term deprivation and privation

SOCIAL DEVELOPMENT
    Play
    Friendships

What is child psychology?

Child psychology involves studying all aspects of child development and what affects it. Many psychologists, including clinical psychologists, health psychologists, and educational psychologists are involved in applying the theories of psychology to help children and young people, although they may not be called 'child psychologists'.

Child psychology focuses mainly on what might affect 'normal' development, although there is interest in how children develop in general. The application of child psychology involves studying areas where development might go wrong, and looking at possible ways in which a child might recover. Children can be deprived of care or appropriate socialisation, for example. **Privation** is when a child does not have the opportunity to form an attachment, and **deprivation** is when a child may have had some care and attention but it is removed or lost, and so the child is affected. **Socialisation** refers to the processes that affect us and make us into social beings – processes such as learning the rules, learning about social roles, learning how to interact with others, and understanding spoken language, as well as appropriate body language.

Child psychology starts with the newborn baby, and studies 'normal' progression through childhood. It also involves studying the effects of an upbringing that is not 'normal'. In this chapter the effects on a child's development of play behaviour and relationships are also studied.

↻ Recall AS material

For this chapter it will be useful to recall the following areas of your AS material:

- The cognitive–developmental approach, including Piaget's ideas, which link to ideas about play.

- The psychodynamic approach, including Freud's ideas, as Bowlby worked within a psychodynamic framework.

- Methods, especially when considering evaluation of studies.

- The physiological approach, especially regarding the theory of natural selection and survival of the fittest.

Attachment

Attachment and definition of terms

Grossman and Grossman (1990) observe that children from about 7 months old get upset when separated from their main caregivers, and this is taken as evidence that these children have become attached to those caregivers. The processes of bonding and **attachment** begin early in the growth of the infant – during pregnancy. It is not easy to study these processes, but much can be learned from examining the development of attachments and the effects of a breakdown in attachment and **bonding** (which is forming relationships with those around).

Bonding and imprinting – and the study of animals

Ethological studies – studies of animals in their natural setting – are done with the assumption that every behaviour is there for a reason, which is linked to that animal's chances of survival. The process of attachment between human babies and their caregivers might be a survival instinct. Lorenz (1935) investigated imprinting in **precocial** animals (precocial means that the young can move about and have well developed sense organs). **Imprinting** can be seen as a type of bonding, which links with the way human babies form attachments.

Lorenz, within an ethological framework, observed an imprinting response in geese. Newborn birds follow the first moving object they perceive, which is usually their mother. It seems that the tendency to imprint is genetically determined. In one experiment Lorenz placed half of a set of goose eggs that were about to hatch under the goose mother and the other half of the eggs beside him. When the eggs hatched, the goslings that were with the goose mother followed her, but the ones that hatched by Lorenz followed him, as he was the first moving object they saw. In another stage of the study, Lorenz mixed the goslings up again. When they were released, the goslings followed their attachment figure – the goose mother or Lorenz.

Critical and sensitive periods

Imprinting seems to occur as animals are born or hatch. Researchers originally thought that imprinting had to happen at this time or would never occur – that there is a **critical period** after which the behaviour will not occur. Lorenz (1935) thought that imprinting had to happen within the first 5–24 hours of 'birth', or not at all. Other researchers (e.g. Sluckin, 1965) suggest that there is a best time for something to occur, but that it can still happen later – there is a **sensitive period** rather than a critical period. The evidence that, if a gosling is kept isolated immediately after hatching and not allowed to imprint, it will imprint when it does eventually come across its first moving object even if this is beyond the critical period makes a sensitive period more likely.

*Figure 6.1
Because they had been
allowed to imprint on him, young
goslings followed Lorenz as if he
was their mother*

Imprinting or attachment in human babies

There is evidence to suggest that human babies form attachments as if they are imprinting. MacFarlane (1975) found that a human infant can differentiate its mother's breast pad from others by 3 days after birth, and Mehler *et al.* (1978) suggest that the infant can pick out its mother's voice by 30 days.

Bonding – the parental investment theory

Attachment and bonding is a two-way process, and involves the caregiver as well as the infant – the caregiver must take on their caring role. The **parental investment theory** (Kenrick, 1994) proposes that where the female of a species invests a lot of time and effort into an offspring, that investment is likely to include taking care of the offspring. In humans, a 9-month pregnancy and the fact that there are few offspring (relative to other species) is a large effort, which must be protected – and it makes sense biologically that the mother will bond with her infant. Klaus and Kennell (1976) discovered that newborn infants who were given extra skin-to-skin contact with their mothers during the early days seemed to form stronger attachments. However, this extra contact had to be within hours of birth to have an effect, which suggests that there is a biological basis to bonding and attachment.

Evaluation

• Rutter (1979) suggests that the bonding between a caregiver and a baby is a process that gradually builds, and his ideas go against the idea of a critical period in which bonding has to take place.

Evolutionary basis of attachment

Those who suggest that there is a biological basis for the bonding between an infant and its caregiver explain this process by saying that it is a survival trait. Those working within an ethological framework think that every behaviour has a function with regard to survival (of the genes). Imprinting seems to have a safety function because it keeps the young and parents together. An element of anxiety may be involved in the biological motivation for imprinting – anxiety might add extra motivation for the young to stay near to the parents and to survive long enough to reproduce. According to the idea of natural selection, any genetically driven behaviour that improves an organism's chances of survival is likely to persist because more of the organisms with genes producing that behaviour will survive and have a better chance passing the gene on.

It has been claimed that the bonding seen in human infants is **innate**, and a survival trait. Through this process infants will get the care they need, and the caregiver will be encouraged to remain close by. Evidence for bonding is that when a human infant reaches crawling age and is able to move away from its caregiver (around 6 or 7 months) it experiences **separation anxiety** and **stranger fear**. These anxieties help to keep the infant close to its caregiver, and persuade the caregiver to remain close by the infant. Both these behaviours are likely to aid survival of the infant, and both are part of attachment.

Evaluation

• Imprinting, bonding, attachment, the experience of stranger fear, and separation anxiety are all likely to improve the survival of the infant by closely connecting it with its caregiver. However, there is no definite proof that these processes are innate or genetically driven – they could have developed through the rules and norms of human society, which state that parents should look after their offspring in certain ways. These assumptions have been reinforced through socialisation, so the behaviours may not be as much natural as given by the environment.

• It is implied that the caregiver is the natural mother, but others close to the infant can be the main attachment figure (just as Lorenz was to his geese). It has also been claimed that human infants can have more than one attachment figure and that the forming of attachments is not just a survival trait to connect the infant to the natural mother.

↻ *Recall AS material*

Recall your AS material from the physiological approach, especially where evolution was discussed, and the idea of survival of the fittest. Look this up if you can't recall.

(Synoptic Note)

There is an example here of the problem in deciding what behaviours are 'natural' and which are given through nurture. This issue of nature/nurture is part of the material needed for the synoptic element of the course, and it is worth gathering examples of 'nature/nurture' problems, ready for that section.

Explanations of attachment

One explanation of attachment is that is has an evolutionary basis but there are other explanations, such as those of Freud and Erikson – both working within the psychodynamic approach. Many of the current ideas on attachment come from conclusions reached by Bowlby, one of the main 'names' in this area, who drew his ideas from the work of ethologists such as Lorenz, and from psychodynamic ideas.

Freud's drive-reduction explanation

Freud thought that attachment and the interactions between parents and the child early in the child's life were very important in the child's later development. He proposed that the motivation for our actions comes mainly from biological drives. We seek to satisfy these drives, and derive pleasure from doing so. For instance the infant's hunger needs to be satisfied, and the infant will seek to satisfy such urges (though not consciously). Freud thought that other drives need satisfying in the same way,

and that seeking pleasure by satisfying our drives is the purpose of our existence. According to Freud the first stage of development is the oral stage, in which pleasure comes from the mouth, and the infant will become attached to whoever satisfies that drive – usually the mother. With the arrival of the second stage of development – the anal stage – the child should be seeking independence.

Evaluation

• Evidence does not support Freud's claim that the infant attaches to the person who feeds it, and children at the anal stage are not always comfortable with independence.

• There are general criticisms of Freud's ideas, and these can be used in evaluation here.

↻ *Recall AS material*

Recall – or look up – your AS material on the psychodynamic approach, including the main assumptions of Freud. If you have studied Erikson's approach as part of the psychodynamic approach, recall that here too, ready for what follows. Include criticisms of psychodynamic ideas, as they can be used in evaluation.

Erikson's psychosocial explanation

Erikson (1963) worked within the psychodynamic approach. He proposed eight stages of development which occur throughout an individual's lifetime. As a person works through each of these stages, they develop a new skill after resolving a particular conflict that characterises that stage. The first stage is that of the conflict between trust and mistrust – a child must learn to trust that their caregiver will be around when needed, and attachment is important in the process of learning trust. In the second stage, the child must learn autonomy and independence.

Evaluation

• Erikson's ideas can be linked to the idea of the development of attachment. The child is mistrustful, and this mistrust is seen in separation anxiety and stranger fear. However, if an attachment is present trust can be built as the child learns that even if it strays from its caregiver he or she will still support it. This explains how separation anxiety and stranger fear (both of which are described later in this chapter) gradually disappear.

Bowlby's theory

John Bowlby is an influential figure in early child psychology. He was interested in the relationship between the child and its mother, and he was asked by the World Health Organization in 1950 to look at the consequences of an early childhood where the pattern of the mother providing the care was broken. This was just after the end of World War II and there was general concern about the effects of deprivation. Bowlby looked at evidence gathered from observations of children in hospitals, in care and in nurseries. He was interested in children who had lost their parents or had been separated from them for some time. He also looked at evidence gathered from clinical interviews with young people and adolescents.

Bowlby (1969) found that when children were first separated from their mothers (and it is likely at that time that the natural mother was the main attachment figure) they became very distressed, crying loudly and appearing angry. If the separation continued, the child became despairing and depressed. Finally, if the mother did not return, the child seemed to become resigned to the separation, but seemed to lack interest in others, which Bowlby called **disattachment.** Bowlby also studied mother/child interactions in species such as ground-living apes. In such species, infancy lasts a long time and groups bond together as defence against predators. The infants often cling to their mothers although they also play and explore, frequently returning to 'base'. The infant leaves the mother for longer and longer periods as it grows, but when a certain level of anxiety is reached rushes back to the safety of its mother. Bowlby's ideas come from an evolutionary perspective, where it is thought that behaviours such as attachment come through the process of natural selection.

↻ Recall AS material

Recall your AS material on the psychodynamic approach and the cognitive-developmental approach, especially material on method, where clinical interview was discussed. Bowlby used clinical interviews to gather his data.

Monotropy

Bowlby's emphasis on the instinctive nature of attachment led him to suggest that the mother or mother-figure would be the single caregiver. He thought that both infants and their mothers instinctively bond to one another as a survival trait. An infant tends to attach to one main figure (this tendency is called **monotropy**), but this main figure does not have to be the natural mother. This particular attachment is different in quality to other attachments the infant may form.

Stranger fear

Young babies from around 6 months old are frightened when a stranger approaches, and they cling to their mother or main attachment figure. Bowlby suggests that this is a survival trait – infants that are afraid of strangers and cling to a safe base would have had a better chance of surviving to reproduce and pass on such behaviour. Clinging to the attachment figure also helps to strengthen bonding.

Critical period

Bowlby took an evolutionary perspective, believing that any behaviour that improves the chance of survival is likely to be passed on. He thought that there was a critical period for attachment to take place in the first year of the baby's life. Bowlby stated that mothering that first occurs after 1 year old is not much use, and after the age of about 2½ is useless. Later in this chapter you will see that where attachment is non-existent or delayed the individual does seem to develop problems, which could be taken as evidence for Bowlby's main claims.

Bowlby's maternal deprivation hypothesis

From observing children who had been separated from their mothers Bowlby developed his idea of monotropy, the child having one special caregiver, which was likely to be the natural mother. Bowlby claimed that if the mother–child (or main caregiver and child) attachment was broken during the critical period there would be severe consequences for the child. Bowlby looked at other studies such as those of Goldfarb (1943) and Spitz (1945) and concluded that long-term maternal deprivation was detrimental to the wellbeing of the child.

Goldfarb's (1943) study

Goldfarb (1943) studied 30 children, 15 of whom were brought up in an institution from 6 months to 3½ years and fostered after that age, and 15 had been fostered immediately after leaving their mothers. The two groups were matched for their mothers' level of education and occupations, and for genetic factors. The 'institution' group were isolated and looked after in groups rather than as individuals. When the groups were tested for intelligence, social maturity and language use at the age of 3½ the institution group was behind in all measures. They were re-tested at 10 and when they were 14, and again the institution group was behind (average IQ, for example, was 72 for the institution group, 95 for the fostered group). It was concluded that the time in the institution caused the slow development.

Evaluation

- There may have other been factors that made the two groups differ – for example, the 15 that were fostered immediately might have been in some way more attractive, which is why they did not spend time in the institution.

Spitz's (1945) study

Spitz (1945) visited orphanages in South America. Children in the orphanages had little attention from staff. They were apathetic, and had poor appetites, and it was concluded that lack of an attachment figure led to these problems in development. Spitz also looked at children in hospital, and found physical and mental deterioration caused by being in hospital and deprived from their mother for a long time. Deprivation appears to lead to problems in development.

Evaluation

- It is important to note that not only were the children studied suffering from maternal deprivation (they were deprived of their mother's care and attention) but they were also in an unstimulating environment. Rutter (1981) pointed out that general deprivation may have caused the problems as much as maternal deprivation.

- Another problem with the idea of maternal deprivation is that it does not recognise the difference between being deprived of an attachment figure and never having had an attachment figure. Being deprived of the main caregiver is often a short-term situation, whereas long-term effects are usually caused by privation, which means no attachment was formed at all.

Harlow and Harlow's (1969) animal studies

Bowlby also used evidence from animal studies in developing his theory. Harlow and Harlow (1969) tested Freud's drive-reduction theory of attachments (page 196) by studying rhesus monkeys.

In one study eight rhesus monkey babies were separated from their mothers within 12 hours of birth. The researchers set up cages in which there were two surrogate 'mothers', one made of wire, and the other made of a type of cloth like towelling. Four of the monkeys could get milk from the wire 'mother' and four from the cloth 'mother', and all eight monkeys were able to get sufficient food. The monkeys were with these surrogate mothers for 165 days, and all preferred the cloth 'mother', even those who received food from the wire 'mother'. If the drive-reduction theory were right, then the monkeys would prefer the 'mother' that fed them, but this was not the case. The monkeys seemed to need comfort as well as food. This conclusion has been extended to apply to human babies, and it is thought that the comfort they receive from bonding and attaching to a caregiver is important.

In another study, Harlow and Harlow used the monkeys that had been fed from the wire 'mother'. A mechanical teddy bear that marched up and down beating a drum was placed in the cage. The monkeys were very frightened of the teddy bear and rushed to the cloth 'mother',

clinging to it. However, after clinging to the cloth 'mother' for a little while, the monkeys looked back at the teddy bear as if curious, and some left the secure base to investigate further. It was as if they had received reassurance from the cloth 'mother'. This showed that the monkeys had formed an attachment with the cloth 'mother' (the one giving comfort) rather than with the 'wire' mother (the one giving food). Bowlby used these findings in his conclusion that attachments were important in 'normal' development.

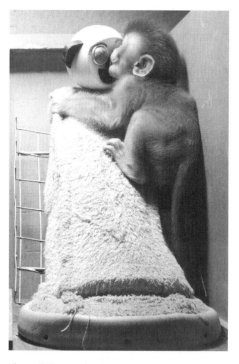

Figure 6.2
In the Harlow (1969) studies, young rhesus monkeys formed attachments to their cloth 'mothers'

Evaluation

- It seemed that a secure base was very important to the monkeys. However, this cannot be enough, because when the monkeys were older they were abusive to other monkeys and did not form normal relationships. This supports Bowlby's claim that the attachment process is two-way and that the infant needs feedback from the caregiver so that the attachment process can become an internal model for relationships. Monkeys brought up without a proper caregiver did not develop normal relationships.

- Applying the results from a study using non-human animals to humans can only be tentative, as species differences might be important.

- It would not be ethical to deprive human babies in this way. Some would also say it is not ethical to use non-human animals in this way.

↻ Recall AS material

Recall (or look up) your AS material about ethical issues – especially concerning ethical principles when using non-human animals in research, and arguments for and against the use of non-human animals in research. Apply these arguments to evaluate the work of Harlow and Harlow.

Bowlby's stages of attachment

Klaus and Kennel (1976) carried out a study in which they concluded that more skin-to-skin contact with its mother led to the child being more secure in their attachment. Studies such as this suggest that the human infant starts the attachment process within hours of birth, and that the bonding is with the natural mother. However, others propose that there is a sensitive, not a critical, period (see page 194), and that the process of forming attachments is more complex.

Bowlby (1969) suggested four stages in the development of attachments (Cole and Cole, 1996).
- *The preattachment phase (birth to 6 weeks)* – In the first few weeks the infant is in very close contact with the caregiver and receives food and comfort. When the caregiver is not present, the infant does not seem to be aware of it.
- *The 'attachment-in-the making' phase (6 weeks to 6–8 months)* – The child starts to show concern if others are around, and responds differently to those they know and to strangers.
- *The 'clear-cut attachment' phase (6–8 months to 18–24 months)* – Separation anxiety begins to occur. The child becomes upset when the caregiver leaves the room. There seems to be a distance between the child and caregiver with which they are both content and outside which the child gets upset. The mother is a secure base from which the child can explore, returning for renewed contact.
- *The phase of reciprocal relationships (18–24 months and onwards)* – The attached child is more confident to explore and the caregiver and child work to maintain a balance between separation and independence and the idea of a secure base.

Bowlby suggests that a child adopts this attachment pattern as an internal working model for making new relationships.

Self-test

Write a timed essay under exam conditions (or as close as you can manage), using the title 'Discuss Bowlby's theory of attachment, including the evolutionary basis of attachment'.

Attachment types

It seems from what has been said so far that there is only one pattern in the formation of attachments, but Mary Ainsworth has looked closely at patterns in mother/child interactions in Africa and the USA, and found differences. There seem to be distinct attachment types and patterns that are established by the third year of the relationship.

The strange situation test

Ainsworth developed this test on children of around 12 months to observe a child with its mother, and when a stranger appears. What follows gives a typical test.
- Observer brings mother, who is carrying the child, into a room equipped with toys.
- Mother puts child down to play, and sits in a chair.
- Observer leaves the room.
- After 3 minutes, a stranger enters the room, greets the mother, then sits down in a chair.
- Stranger and mother talk, and stranger approaches child, offering toy.
- Mother leaves the room whilst stranger distracts the child.
- Mother returns.
- Stranger leaves the room.
- Mother leaves again, leaving the child alone.
- Stranger returns and interacts with child.
- Mother returns.

The observer watches the reactions of the child during these different phases. Ainsworth proposed that there were certain types of attachments, shown by different patterns of reactions. Studies on attachment types have been carried out by Ainsworth *et al.* (1978), Ainsworth (1993) and Isabella (1993).

Types of attachment

Anxious/avoidant

One type of attachment is called **anxious/avoidant**. When the mother and child play together, without anyone else in the room, anxious/avoidant children do not keep checking where their mother is sitting. They do not always cry when the mother leaves the room, and strangers are able to comfort them. When the mother returns, the child may turn away from her. This type of attachment, according to Ainsworth *et al.* (1978) appears in about 23% of the American middle-class children tested.

Securely attached

The **securely attached** child plays happily with the mother present, even when a stranger is also there. However, these children cry a lot and become very upset when the mother leaves the room. The stranger cannot comfort them, and when the mother reappears they go to her straight away, needing comfort. With her there they quite soon resume playing. This type of attachment appears in about 65% of the American middle-class children tested.

Anxious/resistant

Anxious/resistant children seem anxious throughout the test, stay close to their mothers and seem worried even when the mother is present. They become very upset when the mother leaves, but do not seem comforted when she returns. They seek contact with her on her return, and at the same time try to pull away. Around 12% of the children observed in the American sample showed this type of attachment.

Evaluation

- There are ethical considerations when using this test, because the children do get very upset when the mother leaves the room, and many are upset when a stranger is present. Ethical guidelines – for example, not causing distress – need to be considered when such studies are carried out.

- It is important also to look at cultural differences. When carried out with middle-class American participants this test suggested the above three types of attachment, but cultural differences in behaviour could mean that findings from studies done elsewhere will be very different – and indeed this has been found.

Reasons for differences in attachment types (including caring style)

Cross-cultural studies and cultural differences

Different child-rearing practices may cause different patterns of attachment.

Ainsworth's Uganda and Baltimore studies

Mary Ainsworth (who was at the Tavistock Clinic where Bowlby worked, and at the same time) carried out two studies, one in Uganda and one in Baltimore. It was from these studies that the strange situation test developed. Ainsworth visited the Ugandan participants one afternoon every 3 weeks, and the Baltimore families for one 4-hour visit every 3 weeks to (Ainsworth, 1967). She found three different patterns of attachment among the Ugandan people (whom she studied first): securely attached, insecurely attached or not-yet-attached. In the Baltimore study she called these three patterns secure, resistant and avoidant, as outlined above. In the Ugandan study, the mothers who were good sources of information about their babies, and who gave lots of information about them, also showed patterns of secure attachment with them. Those children who were not-yet-attached had mothers who used less physical contact and were not around so much as those whose children had secure attachments. Ainsworth concluded from these studies that mothers who were more responsive early on had babies who cried less and used more vocalisations and gestures.

Kibbutzim in Israel (Sagi et al., 1985)

In Israeli kibbutzim people live in a communal fashion, on a type of collective farm. Children are brought up by a non-family member (a *metapelet*), although they see their family daily. When such children are put into a strange situation (as outlined above) they tend to become very upset and half are classified as anxious/resistant; 37% seem to be securely attached.

Evaluation

- Sagi's (1985) figure is lower than that Ainsworth *et al.* (1978) found in their USA study, and it could be claimed that not having the continuous mother figure present all day had affected the development of a secure attachment.

- Alternatively, it could be concluded that cultural differences led to different attachment patterns, but not that children from other cultures were worse off than those in the USA (which saying they are not so securely attached seems to imply).

- Another interpretation is that the strange situation is suitable for studying within the culture in which it was developed, but not in other cultures.

Germany

Germany also has a low percentage of securely attached children when the strange situation is used (Grossman *et al.*, 1985). Of the German children 49% were anxious/avoidant, and 33% were securely attached, compared with 65% in the American sample.

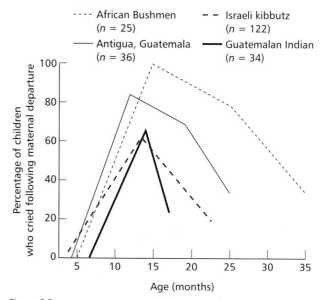

Figure 6.3
Difference in the percentage of children who cried after their mothers left the room in the strange situation test (Source: Cole and Cole, 1996; from Kagan, Kearsley and Zelazo, 1978)

Evaluation

- It was suggested that German parents are more insensitive to their children; however, others suggested that cultural differences were the reasons for the different results. In Germany there is a larger interpersonal distance, and babies are weaned from body contact early in life. German mothers aim to develop an independent non-clinging infant who obeys the commands of its parents.

Japan

Miyake *et al.* (1985) found no anxious/avoidant children when using the strange situation test, but found many who were anxious/resistant. They noted that Japanese mothers rarely leave their child with anyone else and encourage dependency in the child. This means that being alone with a stranger is very upsetting for a child. These conclusions are reinforced by the findings of another study, using a sample of working Japanese mothers and their children (Durrett *et al.*, 1984). This study found patterns similar to those in the USA so it does seem that cultural traditions (which are different amongst traditional and modern Japanese families) affect attachment types and patterns.

Evaluation

- The problem is that we cannot separate the effect of cultural differences on attachments from the effect of the actual test. It could be that it is the meaning of the test that differs, and criticism of the methodology is important.

Differences in the behaviour of the mother

Ainsworth and Bell (1969) looked at differences in the behaviour of the mother to try to explain the different attachment types. They suggested that some mothers are more responsive than others. The baby of a mother who reacted quickly to its cries when it was 3 months old and was sensitive to the baby's feeding needs was more likely to be securely attached at 12 months. Other studies have agreed that securely attached children are likely to have had mothers who are more involved with the child, more responsive to signals, more positive in emotional expressions and give more appropriate responses.

Different characteristics in different children

The relationship between the mother and young child achieves what is called **interactional synchrony**. This can be observed by watching a young baby and its mother mirroring each other's responses (for example, if the mother sticks out her tongue, the young baby will do the same). This suggests that for a secure attachment to be formed both a responsive mother and positive responses from the baby are necessary. The child's temperament may be important, and a child who is easy to establish a relationship with may be more likely to have sensitive mothering. However, there have been mixed findings in this area, and temperament needs to be adequately measured.

Criticisms of research into attachment

It seems that attachment type is affected by the temperament of the child, the cultural context, the family circumstances and the caregiver's behaviour and caring style.

- Ethical concerns have been raised. It was claimed, for example, that the children from traditional Japanese families were very upset by the strange situation test, and this goes against ethical principles.
- Other criticisms include the claim that cultural differences affect how the strange situation is perceived, so it might not be suitable to use a test developed in one culture (in this case the USA) to test children from a different culture.
- A further criticism is that some research (for example, that done by Harlow and Harlow) used non-human animals, and care should be taken when generalising to humans because of species differences.
- In favour of the conclusions from the strange situation test is the claim from some studies (for example, Lyons-Ruth *et al.*, 1991) that the type of attachment found is likely to remain stable. In other words, when tested again, the children would probably show the same attachment type.
- However, this stability in attachment type seems to rely on unchanged family circumstances. If the family is going through a difficult period, the child's attachment type could change (Vaughn *et al.*, 1989).
- An important point to note, in spite of criticisms of attachment research, is that attachments do seem to happen in all cultures and at the same stages. For example, 5-month old babies are not likely to show distress when their mother leaves in the strange situation test, whereas those at 7 or 8 months do. The babies are more likely to get distressed in that situation up to about 15 months, when the child grows more independent. This pattern is found in many studies, in many cultures, and is evidence that bonding and attachment is part of a baby's development.

Attachments with people other than the mother (including caring style)

Usually the mother is involved most with the infant so it is clear why a lot of research has focused on the interaction between mother and child; however, other attachment figures are important. Babies do not only form attachments with their mothers – there can be multiple attachments, and fathers also have a role to play.

The role of the father

Lamb *et al.* (1987) examined the role of the father and the process of attachment between a child and its father. In two-parent families where the father works and the mother does not work outside the home, fathers spend around 25% of the time the mother spends in one-to-one interaction with the child. However, when fathers do feed their infants, they appear to do so as sensitively as the mother and infants who receive sensitive caring from their fathers seem to be as securely attached to their fathers as to their mothers (Cox *et al.*, 1992). According to Lamb fathers spend a lot of their time playing with rather than caring for their child, so their role is different. It does appear that infants are attached to both parents (Isabella, 1993) and researchers should remember that the father–child relationship is also important. However, Lamb's (1976) findings suggest that when needing comfort a child is more likely to turn to its mother.

Multiple attachments

Fox *et al.* (1991) found that infants who were securely attached to their mother were also likely to be securely attached to their father. They form a working model to use when forming other relationships (this links back to Bowlby's idea of an internal working model, page 199).

Babies also form attachments with significant others (people that are important to us). In some cultures babies are cared for by older siblings and form attachments to them as well as to their parents. Dunn (1984) found that babies are less upset in strange surroundings when an older sibling is present. Rutter (1981) points out that some attachment behaviours are shown when a child is with a person other than the main attachment figure, which strongly suggests that the child has attachment figures other than the main one. Some children even show similar attachment behaviours regarding inanimate objects, such as a favourite toy.

The quality of the attachment might be stronger with the main attachment figure, as Bowlby says, although others (such as Schaffer and Emerson, 1964) show that the main caregiver is not always the main attachment figure. By 7 months 29% of the babies Schaffer and Emerson studied had more than one attachment figure. They measured attachment by the amount of protest shown when the child was separated from that person, and whether the baby fussed and cried when left in a room by itself. At 10 months 59% had formed more than one attachment, and by 18 months 87% had done so. The father was the main attachment figure for about a third of the children studied.

↻ Recall AS material

Recall your AS material on the cognitive-developmental approach, especially Piaget's idea that the baby develops schemata through assimilation and accommodation – or look this up. Perhaps the baby forms a schema of the attachment relationship it has with the mother, and this schema could be said to be the working model that Bowlby was talking about. The baby could use this schema when forming other relationships. In this way Bowlby's ideas can be related to Piaget's.

Self-test

Write a timed essay under exam conditions (or as close as you can manage), using the title 'Discuss the relationship between attachment types and caring style'.

Deprivation and privation

Short-term deprivation

The term **deprivation** means that there is (or has been) a main attachment figure, and that the individual has somehow been deprived of that person's attention. **Privation** means that a child has not attached to anyone at all – this person has not been deprived of care; he or she did not receive care in the first place. 'Short-term' deprivation means that the attachment figure goes away for some reason and then returns (the deprivation lasts for a short while only) – it refers to separation. Goldfarb's

Figure 6.4
Jean Piaget

institution study and Spitz's orphanage and hospital studies are all about long-term deprivation or privation. Short-term deprivation is seen as lasting for days or weeks; if deprivation goes into months it is more likely to be thought of as long-term.

STUDY AID

In many books studies called 'deprivation studies' are really about 'privation'. It is difficult to be precise about whether deprivation or privation is being considered because usually there are many different factors involved when looking at problems a child has had in early upbringing, and it is not usual that a child is totally privated. Try to distinguish whether the child is deprived, in the sense of having had an attachment, or privated, as in never having had an attachment at all.

Effects of short-term deprivation – protest, despair, detachment

Bowlby looked at the distress experienced by children who were deprived (short-term) of their main attachment figure, often because either the child or the caregiver had to go into hospital. He characterised this distress as having three stages – protest, despair and detachment.
- At first the child protests, cries and is clearly unhappy.
- If the separation continues the child becomes calmer, but is still angry (this shows despair).
- If the separation continues further the child seems to be responding to others and improving, but this is the stage of detachment, and on being reunited with the main caregiver the attachment may need to be made all over again.

Factors affecting the effects of short-term deprivation

Age of the child
A child around 7 months old is likely to be more distressed, but by the age of 3 years the child is likely to be less distressed (possibly having become more independent). It is likely that by the age of 3 the child can understand explanations of what it happening (Maccoby, 1980).

Gender
Boys do seem to become more distressed than girls.

Usual behaviour of the child
Children who are uncommunicative or aggressive may show more distress on being separated from the main caregiver. Those with a more stable relationship with the main caregiver are more likely to cope better with the separation. Over-protected children may find separation worse because they are not used to it.

Previous experience of separation
Previous experience of separation can help. Stacey *et al.* (1970) found that 4-year-old children having a short stay in hospital coped better if they had previously been separated from their caregiver, for example by staying with grandparents or friends.

Having multiple attachments
Children with multiple attachments seem to cope better. Kotelchuck (1976) found that those who had an attachment with their fathers fared better when separated from them, and protest was less if the child had been cared for by both parents.

Effects of short-term deprivation – the Robertsons' studies

Robertson and Robertson (1968) focused on factors that may alleviate the distress or anxiety felt because of the separation. They looked at four children who were separated from their attachment figures: a boy who stayed in hospital, another boy who stayed in a residential nursery, and two girls who stayed with the Robertsons, whom they had met previously.

The two girls had visited the Robertsons with their mothers before they went to stay, and this helped to reduce the anxiety they may have felt during the separation. The two girls were much less distressed by the separation than the two boys. As the boys had experienced bond disruption, but the girls did not (their mothers and the Robertsons had helped to provide substituted care), it was concluded that distress from separation only comes from bond disruption.

Evaluation
- Only four children were studied.
- Some of the conclusions could have been subjective, for example, the amount of distress experienced.
- Being in hospital or in a residential nursery may have been more upsetting than being in a strange house.

Research findings into the effects of daycare

General findings from research into daycare

Daycare can be thought of in one sense as short-term deprivation. Children differ in the ways they react to daycare. Some children are more distressed than others. It is thought that the quality of the substitute provision and the stability of the arrangement are both important factors. Clarke-Stewart (1989) points out the positive side, in that children gain confidence from experience of daycare, as well as knowledge. Kagan *et al.* (1980) carried out a longitudinal 5-year study of children aged between 3½ and 29 months who were in daycare for 7 hours a day, 5 days a week, testing them for relationships with other children and attachment to their mothers. There were no significant differences between the study group and a control group who did not experience daycare – as long as the daycare was well equipped and well staffed. However, poor daycare centres can do harm. Hoffman (1974) looked at 122 studies of working mothers, finding that dissatisfied mothers appear less adequate, and that the role of work is important in the mother's satisfaction with life. There is an argument that a dissatisfied mother taking care of her children compares poorly to good quality daycare.

Overall there is disagreement as to whether daycare has a bad or good effect on a child's development. Kontos *et al.* (1994) claim that good-quality daycare can be a good experience, whereas others (e.g. Fraiberg, 1977) claim it leads to separation and is bad for the child.

Evaluation

- One problem is that studies tend to be carried out in university daycare facilities, which may not be representative of all daycare centres.

- The daycare centres studied are different, as are the backgrounds of the families studied, which makes it difficult to sort out the different factors involved when comparing studies.

- Tests tend to study one moment in time, not long-term effects, and follow-up studies are rare. It is thus hard to compare studies and therefore to arrive at sound conclusions.

Intellectual effects of daycare

Many studies compare the intellectual abilities of children experiencing daycare with those who do not (e.g. Clarke-Stewart, 1993). The intelligence of 2 year olds from low-income families seems to fall from birth but daycare appears to add to intellectual ability (Caughy *et al.*, 1994). The conclusion here is that daycare can be good, but only if it is good-quality daycare, with a well-equipped centre, and good-quality staff.

Evaluation

- IQ tests usually measure only intellectual ability over the age of 2 years, as before that the measure is usually 'DQ' (developmental quotient), so the above might not *actually* be measuring the intellectual effects of daycare.

The effects of daycare on social development

Some studies in the USA show that children attending daycare centres are more independent, more helpful and co-operative with peers, use better language and are happier in new situations. However, they can also be less polite, less compliant with adults and more aggressive (Howes and Olenick, 1986). Honig and Park (1993) have suggested that the longer a child spends in daycare the more their behaviour is likely to be aggressive, so daycare centres may be considered bad.

Involvement of parents in daycare

It is difficult to measure effects of daycare without taking into account the involvement of parents with their children, and in the daycare provision. Children who attend poor-quality daycare seem likely to have parents with more stressful lives and who involve themselves less with their children. However, parents using high-quality daycare are more likely to be involved in their children's activities. So when it is concluded that high-quality daycare is best, there may be a confounding factor, in that probably the children in such daycare are getting more support at home. Government initiatives to improve daycare provision in deprived areas might go some way to changing differences suggested by the above studies.

Daycare provision

The child at home is more likely to get individual attention, and to have its needs both understood and fulfilled. When in daycare the child is not with adults who know its precise needs, and has to interact with many other children. The plus side to the involvement with peers is that children can learn about their own strengths and weaknesses compared with others, can form a sense of identity and belonging, develop their language skills and improve social interactions. Rubin (1980) points out that a child of 2½ can pay attention, take turns and be responsive to others, so is learning social skills, all processes that can be experienced in daycare provision. Daycare also provides friends, which gives experience in co-operation.

Self-test

Write a timed essay under exam conditions (or as close as you can manage), using the title 'Discuss research findings into the effects of day-care'.

Long-term deprivation and privation

Long-term deprivation is usually taken to mean that the child does not return to their main caregiver, so the attachment is broken. Privation refers to there having been no forming of an attachment in the first place. Studies of privation involve children who have been in institutions from birth, whereas deprivation studies involve children who have had a broken attachment, for example, on the death of a parent, and the effects are apparently similar.

Possible effects of parental separation/divorce/death

Separation anxiety

Bowlby examined what he called **separation anxiety**. He thought that a child who has experienced separation (this would be deprivation, because an attachment had been formed) would become anxious, fearing another separation. The child could exhibit increased aggressive behaviour and become more demanding. He or she is likely to be clinging and might show detachment (see page 203). Bowlby thought that school phobia could be due to separation anxiety, which could arise following a real separation, or from the mother threatening, for example, to leave home.

Parental death

The death of a parent does not affect a child in the same way that divorce does, because there was probably no conflict before the event. Bifulco *et al.* (1992) looked at 249 women who before the age of 17 had lost their mother either through separation or death. Overall the participants were twice as likely as normal to be suffering from depression or anxiety; however, it was noticeable that those whose mothers had died before they were aged 6 had more depression than those who had experienced separation before the age of 6. This suggests that 6 is an important age and that separation is less stressful than death of a parent. In the Robertsons' study mentioned earlier (page 203) the two boys who were separated from their mothers without good substitute care suffered more, which reinforces the conclusion that those who are separated do go through a form of grieving. However, the quality of the substitute care is important.

Comparison of the effects of divorce and death of a parent

By 1986 20% of children under 19 in England and Wales were affected by divorce (Gross, 1996). Children of parents who are divorcing show separation anxiety – for example, by refusing to stay at school. The experience of divorce seems to affect children more than a parent's death (Richards, 1987), which could be partly because the child is angry when a parent leaves because of divorce (the child could feel the parent is going against what the child wants). When a parent dies the child is likely to realise that this was not something their parents chose and so is less angry than one going through divorce. A child may be more affected by divorce because the remaining parent is likely to be negative about the one who left the family,

whereas a parent who dies is likely to be praised and remembered positively. When a parent dies, the remaining family is likely to unite to take care of the child, whereas when one parent leaves due to divorce, their family is likely to lose touch with the child, who will have less support. When divorce is involved one or both parents may remarry, which can be stressful for the child.

Hetherington *et al.* (1979) studied the effects of divorce on 4 year olds, which appear to be in two phases:

1. The crisis phase – The participants all lived with their mothers and saw their fathers regularly. The mothers became more demanding and less affectionate, and the children became more aggressive. Fathers indulged their children more. This can last about 2 years.
2. The adjustment phase – After about 2 years the mother starts to become more patient, and communicates better with the child. There is a better plan between the mother and the father, and a structure is set in place.

It seems that a good relationship between the mother and father helps the child during and after divorce, and could avert the crisis phase. It is the amount of conflict that seems to be the problem, rather than the divorce itself. Rutter (1970) studied 9–12 year olds on the Isle of Wight and found that children could be well adjusted even if they had been separated from their mothers when young. He found that problems were more likely to be caused by family problems than the separation itself. For example, the most badly affected children were likely to have been separated by the psychiatric illness of a parent, whereas those who were less affected were separated by physical illness or housing problems. Rutter concluded that it was the reason for the separation that was important, not the separation itself.

Evaluation

- Rutter's findings can be used to criticise Bowlby's idea that maternal deprivation causes later problems. It seems that it is not the deprivation that is the problem, but the situation causing the deprivation.

Effects of family order and re-ordering on children

The position of a child in the family, and also when step-children are brought together, can affect the development of all the children. A child's brothers and sisters have a great effect on a child, acting as friends and teachers.

The effect on older children when a second child is born

An important study in this area is that of Dunn and Kendrick (1982), who looked at the effect on the oldest child of a family of the arrival of siblings. They studied 44 children whose mother was expecting her second child. With the birth of a second child the mother paid less attention to the firstborn child, who sometimes became more childlike – perhaps to gain attention. If the father spent more time with the child, or the mother included the child in caring for the baby, this seemed to help to avoid jealous feelings. However, Dunn and Kendrick found that an older child who received too much attention when a second child was born developed feelings of hostility towards the younger child.

Teti *et al.* (1996) looked at 194 families where a second child was expected when the first child was between 1 and 5 years old. The security of the older child's attachment was reduced by the arrival of the second child, and the decrease in security was larger if the older child was older than 2 when the second child was born. If the mother involved the older child, and if the home was harmonious (in the sense of the two parents not arguing), then the security of the older child was less affected by the new arrival.

The effect on the child who has an older brother or sister

There is an advantage to a child in having an older brother or sister, who can become an attachment figure. Stewart (1983) used the strange situation test to look at attachments between 54 pairs of siblings. It was found that around 50% did comfort their younger brother or sister when the mother left, and anxiety was reduced.

The older children act as friends as well as role models to their younger siblings, teaching them social relationships and cognitive skills. Shaffer (1993) found that younger children (those with at least one older brother or sister) are

often preferred as friends by their peers, and this may be because they have the opportunity to learn social behaviour from their older siblings. However, Miller and Maruyama (1976) found firstborns are more popular, perhaps because they are less demanding and more friendly.

STUDY AID

Popularity and friendships are discussed in the next section, and this material will be also useful for that section.

Effects of divorce and family re-ordering

Flanagan (1996) outlines a study by Cockett and Tripp (1994) on whether a child is happier after its parents divorce because the family rows before the divorce caused more stress than the divorce itself. They studied 152 children and their parents. Some children were from re-ordered families (they had step-brothers and sisters), others lived with their natural parents. The groups were matched for socioeconomic status, age and gender. Children living with their natural parents were the control group – some had a home life with no conflict, some had parents who argued regularly.

Children from re-ordered families had more difficulties, including health problems and difficulties at school. They also showed low self-esteem. Those in natural families that argued also had problems, but not as many as those in re-ordered families. Children living with their natural families with little conflict did best. So arguments between parents do seem to cause anxiety and difficulty, although divorce brings more problems.

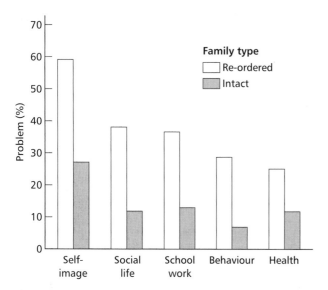

Figure 6.5
Children from intact families seemed to have fewer problems than children from re-ordered families (Source: Flanagan, 1996; from Cockett and Tripp, 1994)

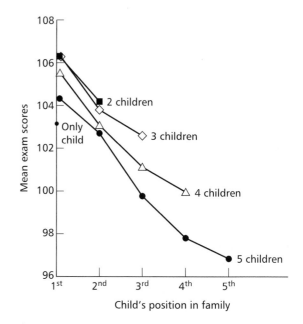

Figure 6.6
Abilities of children according to family size (Source: Long, 2000; from Storfer, 1990)

Evaluation

- The divorce itself may be less of a problem than fitting into a re-ordered family.

- Although correlations are found, this does not mean that some factor (e.g. divorce) causes another (e.g. poor health and school difficulties).

- Re-ordered families are likely to have a low income and financial worries, which could be the cause of the child's problems

Amato (1993) suggests that divorce may lead to maladjustment for more than one reason – such as absence of one parent, poor adjustment of the remaining parent, stressful economic and personal conditions, conflict between the two parents. Also children react differently: some children have more resources for coping, and their reactions also depend on the relationship with their parents. There are communication problems and sometimes children do not get an explanation for the separation. These factors all need to be taken into account when drawing conclusions about the effects of divorce and family re-ordering on a child's development.

There is a positive side to family re-ordering. Surveys have found that there is better communication in step-families, and a more pragmatic approach to problems, although step-families can be less cohesive and more stressful (Carr, 1999). Hetherington *et al.* (1993) found that a child's adjustment to their parents' remarriage is affected by the child's age, their gender and the parents' emotional state. There is good adjustment if the child is in adolescence or early adulthood; however, all children resist the new 'parent' (children between 10 and 15 years old appear to resist the most). Remarriage seems to be more disruptive for girls than for boys. Boys whose mothers remarry benefit from the mother's improved happiness and the presence of the step-father but girls find that the step-father disrupts the supportive relationship they have formed with their mother.

Possible effects of institutional care and adoption
Goldfarb and the Spitz *et al.* study – effects not reversible
Both Goldfarb and Spitz *et al.* concluded that maternal deprivation led to later problems, so there are problems with long-term deprivation.

Evaluation

- It should be noted that both studies focused on the lack of mothering, and did not look at the circumstances surrounding the privation. A study by Skeels and Dye (1939) suggested that the stimulation and care the child received affected their later development, including their intellectual development. Rutter (1970) also pointed to

the importance of the situation, rather than the separation itself. Therefore, a criticism of the studies of Goldfarb, Spitz *et al.*, and Bowlby (whose study is outlined below) is that they focused too much on the maternal deprivation, and too little on the circumstances of the separation. The Harlow studies were taken to mean that monkeys needed affection from a mother figure; however, they missed the stimulation and interaction they would have had from 'normal' upbringing, so the same criticisms apply.

Bowlby's juvenile thieves study – effects not reversible
Bowlby used the findings of the Harlows, Goldfarb and Spitz *et al.* when proposing his theory of maternal deprivation. His own studies (Bowlby, 1946) reinforced his idea that it was separation from the mother figure that caused the problems. Bowlby studied 44 juvenile delinquents who were thieves and compared them with a control group of disturbed juveniles but who had not committed a crime. Of the 44 'thieves' 14 had a character that was called 'affectionless' (an example of being 'affectionless' is that they did not show guilt because they were thieves), seven of the 14 had been separated from their mothers for 6 months or more during the first 5 years of their lives, two more had been in hospital for 9 months when they were 2 years old. Only two of the control group (those who had not committed a crime) had experienced similar separations. Bowlby called the 'affectionless' character 'affectionless psychopathy', and concluded that because 9 of the 14 who showed this character had been separated from their mother or mother figure, then this affectionless psychopathy came from maternal deprivation.

Evaluation

- Rutter (1981) suggested that the juvenile thieves in Bowlby's study were not maternally deprived, but had suffered privation. They had had little opportunity to form attachments, and received little stimulation and consistent care.

- Also only 14 of the thieves had been deprived or privated – the other 30 had not suffered such separations, so it was difficult to justify Bowlby's conclusion that the maternal deprivation had caused the problem (although only this 14 had the affectionless psychopathy Bowlby was looking at, so his claims may have some foundation).

- Another problem is that the data gathered from the participants meant that they had to remember past separations, and retrospective studies that rely on memory can be unreliable.

Research into the effects of privation – Skeels and Dye (1939) – effects reversible
Someone is said to be privated when no attachment has been formed, and often this means the baby is in an

institution from birth. Skeels and Dye (1939) studied 25 children in the USA who were privated until the age of around 2 years. This meant that they had little stimulation and little social interaction, so no attachments were formed. Skeels arranged for 13 of the children at 2 years old to go to another institution (the Glenwood State School), which was for retarded adult women from 18 to 50 years old. These children were cared for by older girls at the school, were given stimulation and equipment to play with, and had staff to interact with. When they left the orphanage to go to the school their average IQ was 64.3. The average IQ of the control group (the 12 children who remained in the orphanage) before the children were split was 86.7. The 13 who went to the school were either adopted at around 3½ or returned to the orphanage, and at this stage the IQ of both groups was measured. The control group's average IQ had fallen to 60.5 whereas the more stimulated group's average had risen to 92.8. The children were assessed again when aged 7: the control group's IQ had dropped by 21 more points, whereas that of the 13 more stimulated children had risen 36 more points.

It was concluded from this study that stimulation and care increased intellectual functioning, and that lack of stimulation and care (privation) caused a loss in intellectual functioning. The findings are supported by another study in 1966 when Skeels revisited some of the participants. All of the experimental group (the more stimulated children) had had more education than the group that remained behind, and about one-third of the more stimulated children were married and were self-supporting. Those in the control group were not self-supporting and were still mentally retarded.

The effects of privation – reversibility?

In the Skeels and Dye study, the experimental group received more stimulation and care between the ages of 2 and 3½ years. Even though their care had been extremely poor before that age, good-quality later care was able to compensate for the early poor attention, suggesting that the effects of deprivation and privation can be reversed. It is important to note that the reversing process (the extra stimulation and care) started from the age of between 2 and 3½ years old. Another study that emphasises the importance of the age of the child is the Goldfarb study mentioned earlier, in which children who were fostered or adopted after the age of 3½ years remained developmentally behind the control group who were fostered at 6 months. This also suggests that age is important. The effects of deprivation might thus be reversible only if the additional stimulation comes by the age of 3½. Another study that reinforces this conclusion (Dennis, 1960) looked at children in orphanages in Iran and found that children adopted after the age of 2 years were not able to improve in intellectual development and reach a

'normal' level, although those adopted before that age could 'catch up'. These studies suggest that there is a critical period for forming attachments and receiving appropriate stimulation and care, from birth to around 2 years.

Tizard and Hodges (1978) carried out a longitudinal study of children brought up in an institution without good-quality care or a single caregiver. Before the age of 2 these children were considered privated, not having had the opportunity to form attachments. Between the ages of 2 and 7 the children were either adopted or returned to their own families. By the age of 8 most of the adopted children and some of those who went back to their own families had formed attachments. The adopted children were more likely to have formed attachments, possibly because the adoptive parents put a lot into the relationship. By the age of 16 the adopted group still seemed to have formed good attachments and relationships with others, but those who had returned to their own families still had difficulties with family relationships. Both groups had some problems with peer relationships. It seems that the attachments made are with the adults in the family, because the adults put in extra nurturing. It is possible that with extra quality care, the effects of early deprivation can be overcome, although there might still be long-term problems, for example regarding relationships with others. Hodges and Tizard's study involved children who started to receive the care they needed at the age of around 2 years, so it is still not clear whether the effects of privation or deprivation can be reversed after that stage.

Can a privated child develop 'normal' intellectual functioning and 'normal' patterns of development if stimulated and socialised after the age of around 2 years old? Some studies suggest that this can happen. If extreme privation can be overcome, then it seems as if the timing of forming attachments is not as important as the quality and strength of the relationship, and it looks as though there is no critical period.

An adoption study – Romanian children

Ames *et al.* (1990) studied Romanian children who had been adopted by families in British Columbia. There were three groups in the study:

1 46 children who had spent at least 8 months in a Romanian orphanage.
2 29 children adopted directly from their families or a hospital before they were 4 months old.
3 46 Canadian children matched to the Romanian group in age and gender.

The children were assessed when they had been in their adoptive homes for 11 months, and then again when they were about 4½ years old.

The findings were that 78% of group 1 were developmentally delayed in all areas (motor movements, social interactions and language) when they were first adopted. They were small and many had medical problems (Chisholm *et al.*, 1995). On both assessment occasions only 37% of the orphanage children had developed secure attachments, compared with 58% of the Canadian-born children and 67% of those who were adopted early. A third of the group 1 children showed insecure attachments, compared with 4% of the early adopted group and 7% of the Canadian-born group. Insecure attachments were associated with developmental delay and behavioural problems, and the parents reported more stress. So it appears that early adoption can be very successful, but late adoption (or the experience of the orphanage) seems to lead to insecure attachments and developmental delays.

Studies of extreme privation

Koluchova (1972)
One study that looks at a case of extreme privation is that carried out by Jarmila Koluchova (1972, 1976) in Czechoslovakia. In 1960 identical twin boys were born, but their mother died soon afterwards and they spent the next 11 months in an institution. Their father remarried when the boys were 1½ years old. Their step-mother did not like them and they had to live in a small closet without light or adequate food. They were rarely visited and were not allowed to mix with the rest of the family. They were mistreated, apparently mainly by their stepmother, although it is reported that their father also beat them. When they were 6 years old the authorities became aware of their existence. They were small for their age, and suffering vitamin deficiency. They could not talk much and were terrified of things around them. They were then placed in a children's home, with children younger than them. This was a non-threatening environment, and they were well cared for. The boys started to learn to speak, gained weight, and became interested in things around them. After some time in the institution, they were fostered in the care of two sisters. The twins were given love and stimulation, and extra care. At the age of 8 their IQ was below normal but by 14 they showed normal IQ scores (Figure 6.7). By the age of 20 (Gross, 1996) they were of above average intelligence, had completed apprenticeships and had good relationships with adults and peers.

It seems that the effects of severe early privation can be overcome by careful nurturing. The twins were over the age of 2 years when they started to receive the extra quality care, so it looks as if there is no critical period when a child must receive extra stimulation to reverse the effects of privation or deprivation.

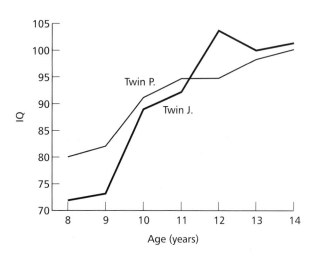

Figure 6.7
When the twins studied by Koluchuva received high-quality care their intellectual abilities showed gradual recovery until they were normal. (Source: Cole and Cole, 1996; adapted from Koluchova, 1976)

Evaluation

- These boys were twins, so were not completely alone during their removal from normal socialisation processes. This might have meant that they could attach to each other, although clearly they would still have suffered privation as they did not experience 'normal' interactions between people.

- It is also important to note that the care the boys did receive from the sisters was above average. This extra quality care could have led to the rise in IQ and catching up in development. Koluchova thought that this was the reason for the improvement, and evidence for his conclusion is that the sisters also fostered another child, who made great progress with them (Hayes, 2000).

- However, the other child did not completely recover from her privation, and may have suffered brain damage from her early ill treatment, whereas the twins did seem to completely catch up in their development. Perhaps having each other did help them.

Curtiss (1977)
'Genie' was locked in her room before she was 2 years old, was chained to a potty during the day and tied up in a sleeping bag at night. No one spoke to her. Her father brought her food, but did not speak and only growled at her. She was found, aged 13 years old, severely undernourished, weighing 59 pounds. She was only 4 feet 6 inches tall, made few sounds, and was not toilet trained. She did not walk normally but shuffled and swayed.

If good care could help Genie to recover from her experiences, it might be concluded that the effects of early privation can be overcome, and that there is no critical period for this recovery. If, however, Genie did not recover, then it seems as if there might be a critical period for forming attachments and for being stimulated and socialised.

Genie seemed to have normal ability to perceive and normal spatial awareness, so it looks as if those abilities are genetically given – or at least her surroundings enabled this sort of development. However, in other ways she was developmentally retarded. Having been given some care, she did learn to control her bowels and to walk more or less normally. However, she did not learn normal language, and, although some of her social behaviour became appropriate, it was not 'normal'. She has needed special care, and has not developed sufficiently to manage on her own. She did have quite a lot of attention from the psychologists studying her, and she lived in their homes. She was given a lot of stimulation (because they wanted to try to teach her normal language use, to see if there was a critical or sensitive period for language development, or if it could develop at any time). However, even with good care Genie did not develop normally. Therefore it is hard to conclude that such early privation can be overcome by good care.

Evaluation

- The twins that Koluchova studied were in an institution for the first 11 months of their lives, so their abilities had been studied, and they were thought to be normal. However, Genie had not been tested early on, so it was not clear whether she started off with problems in the first place.

↺ Recall AS material

Recall your AS material, where you may have studied the case of Genie. There is a video of a programme made by the *Horizon* team which features the case study of Genie. It is worth watching.

Self-test

Imagine that you are in charge of an orphanage. Write a report on what you think would be good practice for the orphanage (ignoring possible cost and staffing factors). Consider what would be good practice for children of different ages, and why, and also whether fostering or adoption would be appropriate. Consider the privated child, who has never experienced attachments, as well as the deprived child who has had but lost one or more attachment figures. Write about what would be ideal care, and how this might be provided for children who are experiencing privation or deprivation.

Social development

An important factor in a child's development is their social development. Cases such as that of Genie or the twins, and the studies of the Harlows, show that normal development takes place in a social setting, and that without normal socialisation there is developmental delay. Social interactions are important for the developing child.

Play

Babies and play

Young babies in their first year of life often do not have much opportunity to interact with babies of their own age, although they often have older siblings to play and interact with. Hartup (1983) found that about 25% of 6-month old babies have never interacted with another infant, and 20% only have contact about once a week. This varies in different cultures, and where there are extended families infant–infant contact is more likely. When there is such contact, there seems to be a pattern to its development, just as there is a pattern in other kinds of development. Infants seem to be aware of one another, and react to each other's cries at around 3 months of age (Field, 1979). They smile at other infants by about 6 months old (Vandell and Meuller, 1980) and become more social with one another when there are toys around (Hay *et al.*, 1983).

Defining play

It is difficult to define play. Rubin *et al.* (1983) and Smith and Vollstedt (1985) have listed five ways in which play is described:

1 Intrinsic motivation – to be called play the behaviour has to be done for its own sake.
2 Positive affect – to be called play the behaviour has to be fun.
3 Non-laterality – the behaviour does not follow a sequence or pattern, and there is an element of pretend about it.
4 Means/ends – the means are important, not the ends. The behaviour is more interesting than the outcome(s).
5 Flexibility – the behaviour is not rigid and is changed in changing situations.

An example of play would be using toy animals flexibly, with no goal in mind, pretending some situation and enjoying the experience.

↺ Recall AS material

Recall or look up your AS material on cognitive development, especially with regard to Piaget's stages of development.

Why do children play?

It is often thought that play has a function and is done for a reason – to help children manipulate objects or in their social interactions. Some ethologists talk about an **exploration–play–application** sequence. The exploration is checking something out to make sure it is safe, and could have an advantage with regards to survival (indeed it might have originally evolved for this purpose). Birch (1945) suggested that chimpanzees have to play with sticks, for example, in order to be able to use them appropriately when necessary.

Categories of play

Parten (1932) observed six kinds of play behaviour.
- Unoccupied behaviour.
- **Solitary play** – playing alone. This can be educational and can focus on muscle activity.
- **Onlooker play** – watching others but not participating.
- **Parallel play** – playing alongside other children, but not interacting. This can mean that other children are imitated so social rules are learnt ready for associative play.
- **Associative play** – playing and sharing with other children.
- **Co-operative play** – playing structured games with other children according to rules.

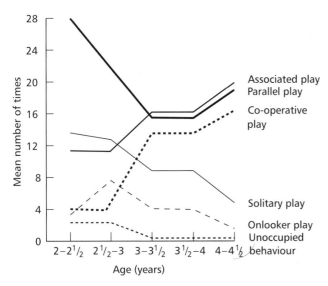

Figure 6.8
Play patterns change with age. Social types of play increase and solitary forms decrease as children age. (Source:Parten, 1932)

Parten undertook 60 one-minute observations of children's play, and found that older children engaged in social play, which includes associative and co-operative play. Younger children were more likely to be involved in parallel or solitary play.

Evaluation

- Cohen (1987) points out that a child can engage in more than one type of play in a typical day, or at any one time.

- Cohen also points out that the types come from observations of children in playgroups and nursery schools, and that the type of play in these situations might be artificial. Most play occurs within a family setting, and play takes place amongst adults and children of different ages.

Reality, fantasy and social fantasy play

There are other ways of categorising play. **Reality play** is the most common form of play amongst 2 year olds, and fantasy play becomes more likely by the age of 3. **Fantasy play** needs the child to have developed certain cognitive abilities and object permanence. **Social fantasy play** develops when fantasy play merges with social play, and then children play together and agree fantasy themes. Connolly and Doyle (1984) found that children who engage a lot in social play are more popular both with peers and with teachers.

↻ Recall AS material

Recall your AS material on Piaget's cognitive-developmental theory, especially the development of object permanence, or look it up. Children need to have the idea of object permanence before they can engage in the above types of play.

Factors affecting children's play

Gender

Children prefer to play with those of their own sex and race. Similarity and proximity are two important factors when making friends, and the same goes for choosing playmates. Children prefer those of the same gender, at least for quite some time, probably because they share so many things. Researchers in this area are Schofield and Francis (1982) and Sagar *et al.* (1983).

Environmental structure

The environmental structure affects the type of play. In a study by Vandenberg (1981) children were placed in an environment containing toys that were aimed at large-muscle use or at fine-muscle co-ordination. Their play was examined to see if the different environment affected the type of play. When playing with the toys needing large muscle action there was much more activity, and the social play carried out involved large groups, playing more roughly. Where the toys needed finer motor co-ordination, the groups were smaller, stayed in one place and played quietly. Vandenberg concluded that environment affects the type of play.

Figure 6.9
There is often very marked sex-role stereotyping in the play of pre-school children

Parental encouragement

Sutton-Smith (1981) studied children's play in New Zealand during the period 1840–1950. At first parents, being pioneers, were busy and needing to settle into a new country, so children developed their own play and games. However, later on adults tended to organise the children's games, and the games themselves became more organised. This was when rugby became a national game, and leadership skills were emphasised. Currently, much of a child's play is organised – through television and commercial toys, so there is less variety.

Curry and Arnaud (1984) suggest that adults ask questions of a child when it is playing, and take part by encouraging them with ideas. Slade (1987) looked at pretend play in 2- and 3-year-old children and found that they played longer when the mother joined in. Also Cohen (1993) says that children gain from parental support. By accepting what the child is doing, parents can encourage pretend play, and the child can try out different roles with confidence. Therefore parental encouragement is an important part of a child's development through play.

Theoretical perspectives on play

Play as surplus energy

Spencer (1873) thought that an organism uses up energy as it copes with its environment. Any surplus energy left over is used in play. Spencer thought that some animals had more energy to use than others, and these would be the ones to play most. The type of play is an extension of the animal's instincts, for example, rough and tumble play might be an extension of survival fighting.

Evaluation

- We do not seem to have a 'tank' of energy that needs filling up as we use energy – when active, someone does not generally become less and less energetic. It is almost as if the more active we are the more active we become, which does not seem to tie in with Spencer's idea.

Cognitive–developmental approach

Piaget linked types of play to stage of development. The four stages of development according to Piaget are the sensorimotor stage, preoperational stage, the concrete operational stage, and the formal operational stage. Piaget thought that the type of play was determined by a child's stage of cognitive development – a child who has attained formal reasoning will be able to use the rules of a game in a way that a child who is still at a preoperational level cannot. The level of cognitive development would limit the child's understanding, for example of rules.

A child in the sensorimotor stage is said by Piaget to engage in **mastery play**, which helps him or her to learn to master their environment. This type of play helps the child to co-ordinate muscle movement, which is an important task within the sensorimotor stage. When moving into the preoperational stage, the child starts to engage in **symbolic play**, in pretend games. In the concrete operational stage the child's play involves rules, although there is no flexibility in the rules. Only the older child is able to use formal reasoning. Play, according to the cognitive perspective, is an important way of practising skills cognitive and motor skills. When faced with a new situation, a child can learn a lot through play.

↻ *Recall AS material*

Recall your AS material on the cognitive–developmental theory and Piaget's stages of development, or look this up.

Psychodynamic approach

In the psychodynamic approach, play is thought to be an expression of some underlying problem or conflict. Melanie Klein and Anna Freud extended Freud's own views to the role of play in uncovering problems that a child may be having. The child needs to resolve issues to maintain a balance between the demands of the id and of the ego and can use play to resolve problems by acting them out. This idea has been extended to a type of therapy that uses play to help the child resolve issues of concern. The main aim is to uncover anxieties hidden in the unconscious, so that the child's problems can be better understood.

Play can be cathartic, in releasing emotions, and can also give the opportunity for defence mechanisms to work. For example, playing with dolls can be an example of projection, where feelings are projected onto another. Similarly, a child can work through previous emotions (regression), and can transfer feelings onto another through displacement during play.

⤳ *Recall AS material*

Recall AS material on the psychodynamic approach, especially the idea of the power of unconscious urges, and the problem in finding out what is being repressed.

Self-test

Write a timed essay under exam conditions (or as close as you can manage), using the title 'Describe and evaluate theoretical perspectives on play'.

Therapeutic value of play

Play therapy has been developed from psychodynamic ideas. Through play the child can act out conflicts and find ways to resolve them. The child is given a secure environment and provided with toys. The therapist then observes the play behaviour and uses the information to try to find any underlying anxieties, and understand a child's problems better. Axline (1971) carried out a case study on a child she called 'Dibs', who was very disturbed. Axline watched his play behaviour to try to understand any family conflicts and resolve problems. Dibs seemed to show hostility to his father – by burying a doll that seemed to represent his father face down in a sandpit, for example. The therapist gained understanding, and some of Dibs' hostility was released through some of the play actions.

Friendships

Defining friendship

Much interest has focused on the development of **friendships** in children. Although children younger than 2 do play together, actual friendships do not seem to start until after this age. By the age of 3 many children are starting to join in with other children when they are playing, and this is when friendships start.

Friendship is described as a relationship where there is affection, reciprocity and commitment between people who see themselves as equals (Hartup, 1992). Hartup gives four functions of friendships:
• To provide a context for developing social skills such as communication, co-operation and the ability to enter a group.
• To provide children with information about themselves, others and the world.
• To provide fun and relieve stress.
• To provide models for later relationships.

Howes (1983) says that friendship is a mutual preference for interaction, a shared positive feeling and an ability to be able to share in play. Selman *et al.* (1983) have shown that by the age of 6 most children know that they are different from others, and can therefore appreciate that others might not feel the same as they do. Younger children, however, tend to have 'best' friends, and expect them to like the same things they do.

When friends first meet they exchange information and establish common ground, explore similarities and differences, and find ways of resolving conflict. Girls share more intimate details of their lives than boys (Furman, 1987). Gottman (1983) carried out a study of pairs of children of the same age who met to play together in one of the children's homes. The children were aged between 3 and 9 years. The mothers completed a questionnaire to say if the children became friends. Gottman analysed tapes of the sessions and found five aspects of interaction that seemed to distinguish whether a child became friends with another or not (Table 6.1).
• Common ground activity.
• Clear communication.
• Exchange of information.
• Resolution of conflicts.
• Reciprocity – when one of the pair contributed positively the other did too.

Factors leading to the formation of friendships include proximity (Epstein, 1989) and similarity (Rubin *et al.*, 1994). So friendships tend to be between those of the same sex, age, race and interests.

Developmental trends in peer relationships

The development of friendships and peer relationships can be traced through examining the different types of play. As play becomes more social, so peer relationships are developed. Roopnarine and Johnson (1984) point out that between the ages of 7 and 9 friendships tend to be with peers of the same sex and age. The older a child is, the

Table 6.1 Examples of children establishing initial relationships

Category	Example
Information	**exchange**
Success	A: What's this?
	B: This is my room right here. This is my farm here. Look how very, very large.
Failure	A: How come we can't get this off?
	B: You know, I'm gonna get the rolling pin so we can roll this.
Common-ground	**activity**
Success: a joint activity is successfully initiated	A: And you make those for after we get in together, okay?
	B: 'Kay.
	A: Have to make those.
	B: Pretend like those little roll cookies, I mean.
	A: And make, um, make a, um, pancake too.
	B: Oh rats, this is a little pancake.
	A: Yeah, let's play house.
	B: Okay, play house.
Failure: initiation is ignored or disagreed with; activity does not develop	A: Let's play house.
	B: Nope, nope, nope, nope, nope nope.
	A: Because you're colouring that brick wall?
	B: Yep.
Conflict	A: This is stretchy.
	B: No, it's not.
	A: Uh huh.
	B: Yes.
	A: Uh huh.
	B: It's dirty.
	A: Uh huh.
	B: Uh huh.
	A: Uh uh.
	B: Uh huh.
	A: Uh uh.
	B: Uh huh.
	A: Uh uh. It's not dirty.

Source: Dworetsky and Davis (1989)

more likely they are to share friends, rather than having a 'best' friend (Table 6.2). Boggiano *et al.* (1986) suggest that a 5-year old is likely to want to make friends with another child because of a toy that that child can share but a 9-year old is likely to want to make friends because someone is nice. Peers also tend to become models.

Corsaro (1985) observed friendships between children in a university child-study centre. Children of 3 and 4 years did play together, but the relationships were fragile, with interactions lasting less than 10 minutes, and often ending suddenly. Children at that age tried to enter other groups, but were often rebuffed. In order to enter a group, the child has to know what is going on, the structure of the group and how to fit in with the group's activities. They also need good communication skills, and should not ask inappropriate questions.

Popularity of individual children

Factors leading to popularity

Children are often classified in psychology as being popular, rejected, neglected or average. This section considers popularity, and the factors that lead to unpopularity. Black and Hazen (1990) suggest that it is the first meeting that is important. Children who can fit in straight away, and can immediately engage in communication, are those that are most popular. Children who have the social skills to make their peers laugh are also valued. Such children are also often academically competent, and perhaps have good ideas as to what to do (Masten, 1986). Youngblade and Belsky (1992) found that children who have the most positive relationships with their parents also form the most positive friendships.

Figure 6.10
Children who form friendships do many things together, including forming emotional ties with one another

rejected so much as neglected. They display neither aggressive nor inappropriate behaviour, but are not accepted. They tend to be shy and rarely play socially, although they are often liked by teachers and do well academically (Wentzel and Asher, 1995). Shy children are often rejected, but there seems to be a cultural element to who is popular. Chinese children are often shy, but shyness there does not lead to rejection (Chen *et al.*, 1992).

Physically attractive children are likely to be popular (Dion, 1973). Langlois *et al.* (1990) show that infants at 12 months old already show a preference for attractive strangers. There might be evidence of a self-fulfilling prophecy here, where children who are liked are confident enough to behave well, and so become popular. A child's name can lead to acceptance or rejection, and those with popular names are likely to be more popular. Name, race, sex and physical attractiveness are thus all factors that affect the popularity of individual children, although the character of a child becomes important later.

Dodge *et al.* (1983) watched how 5-year olds playing in a school playground tried to join in a group of others who were already playing. Popular children stood and waited, watching what was happening, then would gradually move into the group using appropriate behaviour. Neglected children also watched, but did not attempt to join the group. Rejected children were aggressive when trying to join the group. They were unco-operative and disrupted the play of the group. They seemed to lack social skills.

Once a child has been accepted, even inappropriate things they do will still be accepted. However, if a child has been rejected, they remain rejected, even if any inappropriate behaviour is mild (Hymel, 1986). Some children are not

Table 6.2 *The stages of friendship*

Age (approx.)	Description of peer interactions
0–2	Infants show an interest in peers from an early age; at the age of one they will look more at another unfamiliar baby than an unfamiliar adult.
2–4	By the age of two children are ready for nursery school and activities involving their peers, although much of it is parallel, not co-operative play. They have very little understanding of another's feelings. 'Friends' are not necessarily the same sex, though they are aware of gender-appropriate behaviour.
4–7	Children have their first mutual friendships. Play with friends is different from play with acquaintances. Friends show each other affection and approval, but the relationship still lacks empathy. Friendship largely involves common activity, proximity, sharing things. A friend is someone who does things for you.
8–11	Friends have psychological similarity, shared interests, traits and motives. There is now an element of trust and responding to others' needs. Friendships are more genuine, though they tend to be 'fair weather', lasting only as long as is pleasing to both friends. Emergence of the peer group and loosely formed gangs. These gradually become more elaborate, involving membership requirements.
10–12	Friendship involves reciprocal emotional commitment. Deeper, more enduring friendships, where thoughts, feelings and secrets are shared. This is related to the development of empathy. Friends give comfort and support, act as confidants and therapists.
12+	Relationships incorporate the conventions of the society.

Source: Flanagan (1996)

Inappropriate behaviour is rejected

Some peer groups value aggression and others value co-operation. What makes a child popular thus varies between groups. However, some generalisations can be made. Dodge *et al.* (1990) have found that children who are rejected tend to have been more aggressive and to have used inappropriate behaviour. Only those who are both aggressive and use inappropriate behaviour are rejected, and aggressive children are often accepted, so it is not just aggression that leads to the rejection. In fact, 9 year olds who act aggressively in reaction to provocation are likely to have high peer status. Pope *et al.* (1991) show that hyperactive children are often rejected because their behaviour is inappropriate, not because it is aggressive.

Cultural differences in peer relationships

There are cultural differences in peer relationships (for example Chinese children are often shy, but are not rejected because of it). Children prefer to be with others of their own sex and race (Schofield and Francis, 1982) because they are likely to be at the same level of achievement and the same social level, which are important factors in peer relationships.

Collectivism v individualism

Studies have been done to see if the underlying social behaviour of a particular culture or group affects the type of friendships and play that develops. Shapira and Madsen (1969) looked at two groups of Israeli children – one from kibbutzim and the other from a middle-class area. Middle-class Israelis encourage individual achievements in their children, whereas in the kibbutz co-operation is encouraged. The children from the kibbutzim would have the example of **collectivism** as a cultural goal, and the middle-class children would aim for individualism.

Children between 6 and 10 years old from these two communities were brought together to play, and their play behaviour was seen to differ greatly. Shapira and Madsen set the children to play a game in groups of four. The game involved co-operation and unless the group work together the aim would not be achieved. The groups of four played the game six times. For the first three runs the children were told that each would get a prize if the group succeeded in the overall aim but if the task was not completed no-one would get a prize. In the last three trials, the children were told they would be rewarded for part of the task that involved them behaving as an individual. The group still needed to co-operate to achieve to overall aim but the individuals received more reward if they worked for themselves. The cultural differences between the two groups showed in the way the children organised their play. The children from kibbutzim set up co-operative rules in both conditions, so that the overall aim could be achieved. They also set up rules to make sure that all the prizes were shared. However, children from the individualist culture set about gaining the most prizes for themselves.

These studies have been repeated in other cultures, and it is found that the pattern of socialisation affects the rules of the game, and affects peer relationships.

Self-test

1 Write a timed essay under exam conditions (or as close as you can manage), using the title 'Discuss research into the popularity of individual children'.

2 Write a timed essay under exam conditions (or as close as you can manage), using the title 'Discuss cultural differences in peer relationships'.

Suggested reading

Cole, M. and Cole, S.R. (1996) *The Development of Children, Third Edition*. New York: W.H. Freeman and Company.

Gross, R.D. (1996) *Psychology, The Science of Mind and Behaviour, Third Edition*. London: Hodder & Stoughton.

Flanagan, C. (1996) *Applying Psychology to Early Child Development*. London: Hodder & Stoughton.

Carr, A. (1999) *The Handbook of Child and Adolescent Clinical Psychology*. London: Routledge.

Goldberg, S. (2000) *Attachment and Development*. London: Arnold.

Hayes, N. (2000) *Foundations of Psychology, Third Edition*. London: Thomson Learning.

Dworetsky, J.P. and Davis, N.J. (1989) *Human Development: A Lifespan Approach*. New York: West Publishing Company.

Dworetsky, J.P. (1996) *Introduction to Child Development, Sixth Edition*, St. Paul: West Publishing Company.

7 Environmental psychology

The aims of this chapter

The aims of this chapter are, with regard to environmental psychology, to enable the reader to discuss:

- individual and cultural differences in personal space
- consequences of the invasion of personal space
- importance of territory, including two functions of territory
- effect of architecture on communication and on residential satisfaction
- defensible space and the work of Oscar Newman
- good and bad practice in architectural design with regard to defensible space
- sources of environmental stressors, and the effects of environmental stress
- strategies for coping with environmental stressors
- the effects of crowding in animals
- the effects of high-density living on humans
- theories of crowding
- why behaviour is not always environmentally friendly, especially with regard to recycling
- ways of changing attitudes, especially with regard to recycling.

This chapter covers

Introduction to environmental psychology

What environmental psychology is

Environmental psychology is the 'study of transactions between individuals and their physical settings' (Gifford, 1997, p1). It looks at the interaction between the physical world and the behaviour of humans: we change our environment and it changes and affects us. Environmental psychology is a very new field within psychology, although some of the areas covered have been studied for some time. For example, Le Bon looked at crowding as early as 1895, and personal space is a well-researched area. Research in many of the areas now studied by environmental psychologists is to be found in the field of social psychology and crowding and personal space are no exceptions. It has been partly due to a focus on environmental problems that environmental psychology has developed as a field separate from social psychology.

Figure 7.1
Sociofugal space. In waiting areas, such as this airport concourse, chairs are arranged in rigid rows facing in opposite directions, which deters conversation

Some issues of interest within environmental psychology include territoriality, the effect of architecture on behaviour, coping with high-density living, crowd behaviour and encouraging environmentally responsible behaviour. The central issue for environmental psychologists is the transaction between the person and their environment. Environment includes natural surroundings, and artificial environments such as offices and houses. Interest is not really on developing theory for its own sake, but in using findings from studies to solve environmental problems.

History of environmental psychology

Brunswik (1943) is said to have first used the term 'environmental psychology' (Gifford, 1997), and he was interested specifically in how the physical environment affects an individual's behaviour.

In 1943, Lewin's idea of action research – focusing on using research to make social changes – became a starting point for environmental psychologists. Lewin called the physical environment – that is, whatever is not within a person's awareness – the 'foreign hull', and suggested that the study of this area should be called psychological ecology. Studies within environmental psychology became more numerous in the 1960s, and in the last three decades many studies have been carried out. According to Bonnes and Secchiaroli (1995) the term 'environmental psychology' was also used in 1964 in a New York conference about hospital planning.

Barker and Wright (1955) studied behaviour settings – which included the physical settings that surround an individual. An example of a behaviour setting would be a classroom. Social rules are part of a person's behaviour settings. Instead of doing experiments looking at a child's progress, Barker and Wright thought it was important to look at the settings and physical conditions surrounding the child, to have a fuller understanding. They suggested that behaviour could not be studied without taking into account the behaviour setting.

Before Brunswik and Lewin separately advocated looking at physical settings some studies did look at physical conditions, although these were not yet within a field called 'environmental psychology'. For example, Mayo (1933) studied the effect of lighting levels at work on work output. However, it is interesting that he is better known for the conclusion that being part of a group chosen in a study is more likely to give improvements than any light changes, although issues such as light have been shown to affect behaviour. Another area studied before environmental psychology was developed as a separate field was personal space and territoriality (Sommer studied personal space in 1959).

Main theories within environmental psychology (Gifford, 1997)

Unlike some applications of psychology, where the main approaches appear to underpin explanations, environmental psychology draws on approaches or theories that are for the most part not the usual main ones. These are briefly outlined below to help with understanding the material that follows.

The operant approach

The operant approach follows the principles of operant conditioning and focuses on modifying behaviour that is giving environmental problems. Positive reinforcements are used to try to improve the 'environmentally unfriendly' behaviour.

The environment-centred approach

The environment-centred approach looks at the quality of the environment rather the individual. Questions are asked such as whether we should use the environment to satisfy our needs, or whether we should use the environment to improve our values. Within this approach there is also 'green psychology', which focuses on conserving and preserving the environment.

Control theories

Control theories question how much control we have over environmental issues (theories such as 'learned helplessness' are control theories). Control is being examined when areas such as territoriality and personal space are studied, and are looked at in more depth later in this chapter.

Recall AS material

Recall your AS material from the learning approach (or look it up); in particular define 'learned helplessness'.

Behaviour setting theories

A behaviour setting is the environmental setting within which a behaviour takes place. The idea is that there are set patterns of behaviour in particular settings, such as a classroom. Special customs, rules and expected activities are all of interest. Staffing is a major concern when studying behaviour settings.

Stimulation theories

Stimulation theories see the environment as stimulating and adding to sense data. We can be stimulated by factors from our environment such as heat, light and noise, but our senses can also be stimulated by buildings and other people. Arousal theories look at our physiological arousal – arousal leads to stress and the environment can be a source of stress.

Integral theories

Integral theories look at the interaction between the individual and the environment. Chein (1954) proposed a framework for what he called the **geo-behavioural environment**, which means the whole environment including the individual and physical surroundings. The environment contains:

- Instigators – stimuli that trigger behaviours.
- Goal objects – situations where needs are satisfied. If pain is produced, goal objects are called noxients.
- Supports and constraints – physical aspects that aid behaviour (roads or lights) or restrict behaviour (fences or wilderness).
- Directors – environmental features telling us what to do or where to go.
- Global environment – general environmental characteristics (e.g. rainforests are wet).

Interactionism and **transactionalism** are two more integral theories. Interactionism holds that the person and the environment are separate but constantly interact. Transactionalism suggests that the person and their environment are one entity. A person cannot be defined without considering their environment.

Evaluation

- It is hard to test integral theories, as different methods mean that separate variables need to be identified for testing. If the variables were isolated, the integrated whole could not be studied.

Research methods used in environmental psychology

The aim of those working in the field of environmental psychology is to solve problems and find ways to improve our transactions with the environment. Therefore it is perhaps obvious that the preferred methods look at the environment (i.e. use natural settings). Laboratory experiments have been performed – for example, Calhoun (1962) studied the effect of crowding on animals in a laboratory setting (Calhoun's study is outlined in more detail later in this chapter) – but usually were earlier studies carried out within another area such as social psychology.

Environmental psychology is not itself one **paradigm** (a set of assumptions within which research is carried out), and so is likely to use many different methods. Psychology is said to have many paradigms, such as the assumptions, methods and beliefs of those working within a psychodynamic framework, or the claims of social representation theory. It would, however, not be true to claim that environmental psychology is a paradigm – as has already been outlined there are many different theories about the relationship between humans and the environment. Paradigms are overall views of what a body of knowledge is, and this includes assumptions and methods. Within environmental psychology there are many paradigms, and many methods are used (e.g. naturalistic observation, laboratory experiments and interviews). Field studies are popular as they are likely to have good external validity – so the study's findings can be extended to other settings, which is important given the aims of environmental psychologists – and are well controlled, so can be reliable. Quasi-experiments (experiments that may use a natural setting but for some reason are not 'real' experiments) are also often used – for example, important variables might not be controllable.

> ### Synoptic Note
>
> Psychology is said to have many paradigms. Chapter 3 gives a fuller explanation of what paradigms are, and what it means to say that psychology has many paradigms. These sorts of issues are needed for Unit 6, the synoptic part of the course.

Personal space and territoriality

Personal space

What personal space is

'**Personal space**' refers to the area around a person into which others 'may not enter' – or at least if they do we feel uncomfortable. The size of your personal space depends on factors such as how well you know the person entering your 'space'. Personal space is really *inter*personal space, as it involves interactions with others. Personal space includes the way people approach one another – for example, a comfortable distance for two people side by

side will be different from that for face-to-face contact. Katz (1937) is said to have first used the term 'personal space'. Gifford and Price (1979) suggest that there is **alpha personal space**, which is the actual measured distance, and **beta personal space**, which is a subjective estimate of the distance.

Our personal space defines our **territory**, and depends on many factors – it is not just a case of a boundary like a fence around a person. It links to animals' tendency to mark out their territory or to space themselves according to food and mate availability. It is also a way of communicating to others about types of relationships. Hall (1966) listed eight categories of distance according to type of relationship (Table 7.1).

Table 7.1 Hall's categories of distance (based on observations of White, middle-class Americans)

> **1a** *Intimate distance – near phase* (0–15 cm)
> For loving and intimate contact (or obeying rules such as in wrestling); where there are strong negative emotions too (e.g. fights)
>
> **1b** *Intimate distance – far phase* (15–45 cm)
> Where individuals are on very close terms
>
> **2a** *Personal distance – near phase* (45–75 cm)
> Where individuals know one another and are on good terms
>
> **2b** *Personal distance – far phase* (75–120 cm)
> Involving social interactions between friends and acquaintances
>
> **3a** *Social distance – near phase* (1.2–2 m)
> Individuals negotiating with shop assistants or meeting a friend's friend
>
> **3b** *Social distance – far phase* (2–3.5 m)
> For those in business transactions with no desire to become friends
>
> **4a** *Public distance – near phase* (3.5–7 m)
> The distance used by a lecturer with an audience of 30-40
>
> **4b** *Public distance – far phase* (over 7 m)
> The distance used when someone meets someone of much higher authority. Normal conversation is not possible

Evaluation

- It is difficult to generalise from data gathered in one culture or one group, and to say that the same information (in this case distances with regard to personal space) applies to all cultures and groups.

- Hall said that different individuals and cultures vary with regard to the distance they find comfortable, so these distances are only a guide.

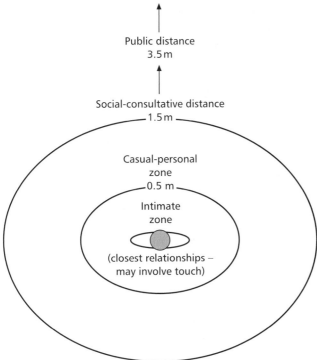

Figure 7.2
Hall's zones of personal space (Source: Long, 2000; based on Hall, 1966)

We learn about these distances in our own culture, probably just as we learn other social skills, and in different cultures people learn different rules. Hall suggested that the order of the zones is the same in all cultures – in other words intimate distance is shortest – even though the actual distances vary. Watson and Graves (1966) looked at cultural differences in personal space. Their study is outlined later, where culture as a factor in personal space is looked at in more detail.

Not only do we not really know how we develop our own personal space but we do not normally notice what distance we feel comfortable with. However, an important

point is that we do feel discomfort if our space is invaded, even though we don't think of it in these terms. We may have negative feelings towards someone because they 'get too close for comfort' but might not realise why we have these negative feelings. It is useful, to take our own concept of personal space into account when making judgements about others.

Measuring personal space

Alpha personal space can be measured in a number of ways.

Simulations

In simulations individuals are asked to place silhouette figures an appropriate distance away (Kuethe, 1962). Duke and Nowicki (1972) suggest a different technique called the Comfortable Interpersonal Distance Scale (CID), where people mark the place on a line where they would want someone to stop approaching them.

Evaluation

- Simulations may not be valid measures because they *are* simulations, and a real person is not present.

Laboratory method

In the laboratory a real person approaches the individual, who asks them to stop when they get closer than comfortable.

ACTIVITY

It will make people uncomfortable if you deliberately invade their personal space, and this is not ethical. However, you could observe people interacting, and guess their relationship from the distance they maintain between them. Note that you must observe in a public place to comply with ethical guidelines. You could also observe your own actions, and judge the distance you maintain between yourself and others, depending on your relationships. Was Hall right?

- This is a reliable method but is not valid because the participants can guess the purposes of the study, which could affect results.

Naturalistic observation

Naturalistic observations study people in public places and analyse distances. Actual distances can be measured from video recordings. It is useful to be able to prepare the area using tape so that distance can be measured more easily, although floor tiles can make a good measure.

Evaluation

+ This method is likely to obtain valid data as it collects real information and participants do not know they are being watched.
− Precise measures are difficult if photographs or video film is used.
− There are uncontrolled variables: crowding in a public place may push two people closer together than comfortable, or they may have to get nearer together to hear each other in a noisy place.
− There are ethical problems involved in naturalistic observations, as the participants have not given consent and do not have the right to withdraw.

Factors affecting personal space

Personal, situational and cultural factors all affect personal space. Situational factors include social and physical factors. Some of these factors are outlined below.

Gender

Children learn personal space distances just as they learn other social skills. Girls seem to develop stable boundaries sooner than boys, but by 16 years there are no differences (Guardo and Meisels, 1971). It has been suggested that men become more upset than women when their personal space is invaded (Garfinkel, 1964), and it seems that men have larger **body buffer zones** than women (Mehrabian and Diamond, 1971). A body buffer zone is the area of personal space surrounding an individual.

ACTIVITY

Test out the idea that men have larger body buffer zones than women by observing behaviour in a public place. Note down the distance when men chat to men, women chat to women, and men chat to women. Generally male/male pairs keep the furthest apart, then female/female pairs and then male/female pairs.

- Gender is not the only factor. Severy *et al.* (1979) did a study that looked at gender, race and age and found that gender influenced personal space only in conjunction with race and age.

Age

As a child ages, their personal space increases (Hayduk, 1983). Tennis and Dabbs (1975) did a study of children from 5 to 18 years old, and found that the older the child the larger the personal space. However, gender was also a factor. Older boys had a larger personal space than older girls, but gender was not a factor for the younger children, and younger boys and girls had similar personal space.

Mental illness/stigmata

People who are mentally ill or schizophrenic seem to have more variability in their personal space distances than usual. Horowitz *et al.* (1964) found that schizophrenic patients tended to choose either larger or smaller seating distances than hospital staff or non-schizophrenic patients – their personal space is not always larger according to this study. Srivastava and Mandal (1990), however, found that schizophrenics *do* choose larger distances and Horowitz (1968) discovered that the size of personal space varies with the degree of schizophrenia – people who had just been admitted for treatment had a larger body buffer zone. If it is accepted that schizophrenic patients who are newly admitted to hospital are the most disturbed, then personal space is larger for those who are more disturbed. The personal space of the same patients became gradually smaller as their treatment progressed.

Evaluation

- As the weeks went on the patients would perhaps have become more comfortable with the surroundings and people at the hospital, which could have led to the reduction in their personal space, rather than the difference being due to reduction in symptoms.

Prisoners with high levels of aggression seem to have larger body buffer zones (Kinzel, 1970). Perhaps these people are aggressive because aggression goes with 'large' personal space. Perhaps others invade their space unknowingly, expecting the individual to have a smaller body buffer zone, and this causes the aggression. Eastwood (1985) found that only violent prisoners who are not good at understanding non-verbal communication and who are more or less psychotic have this large body buffer zone.

Wolfgang and Wolfgang (1968) studied personal space and those with **stigmata** (visible or non-visible difficulties) – such as amputees, mentally ill people or those with epilepsy. People with non-visible stigmata were kept at a greater distance than those with visible stigmata. For example, a person with a broken arm was allowed nearest to others whilst obese people were kept furthest away.

Evaluation

- This study was carried out quite some time ago, and it would be necessary to test whether the same 'prejudices' apply. It seems fair to call the above behaviour prejudice, although this label was not applied at the time.

Jones (1985) found that children with hearing impairments use larger distances than children with no hearing impairment.

Culture

Watson and Graves (1966) found that there are personal space differences between cultures in a study of four male students in a laboratory, two Arabs and two Americans. The average distance maintained by the Arabs was about half an extended arm, but the Americans kept further away when interacting and the Arabs touched each other more.

Mazur (1977) and Forston and Larson (1968) studied the amount and style of touching in people of different cultures. They found that people in Spain, Morocco and Latin America make no more physical contact than American culture (a non-contact culture), although other studies (e.g. Watson (1970) decided that Spain, Morocco and Latin America are contact cultures, whereas America is not. Shuter (1976) found differences between people from different Latin American countries – for example, Costa Ricans choose smaller distances than do those from Panama or Columbia.

Sommer (1968) found no differences between American, Swedish and English groups. Aiello and Pagan (1982) studied Puerto Ricans and found that children in Puerto Rico increase their personal space at a later age than do Puerto Rican children living in New York. Sanders *et al.* (1985) found that male Arabs and Americans have similar personal space, which goes against Watson and Graves's (1966) study; however, female Arabs and Americans do have different distances, and this again suggests gender differences in personal space.

Evaluation

- One problem is that 'culture' is a term covering different factors. For example, Balogun (1991) suggests that religion affects personal space, and carried out a study in Nigeria. Personal space was larger when people of two different religions interacted than two people of the same

religion. Therefore, it may not be culture that is affecting the personal space so much as religion – or some perceived differences.

- Baxter (1970) found that Mexican Americans are closest to each other when outdoors, whereas African Americans are closest to each other indoors. So the situation can also affect the interaction, and studies need to take this into account.

> ### Synoptic Note
>
> The above are example of cross-cultural studies being used to test if an attribute is learned or innate. If the distances that individuals feel comfortable with depending on their relationship with another are the same within one culture, but differ from other cultures, then these distances are probably learned. In general humans have genetically similar attributes and abilities, so if something is genetically acquired all cultures would demonstrate that ability or attribute. Using cross-cultural studies is a way of testing 'nature/nurture' issues. You need to know about such issues and studies for Unit 6, the synoptic part of the course.

Other influences

Attraction can affect personal space. As perceived similarity and pleasantness increase, personal space, as might be expected, decreases (Mandal and Maitra, 1985). People also choose larger distances if they feel insecure (Skorjanc, 1991). Sommer (1969) suggested that whether we are in competition or co-operating affects our personal space – people sit closer together when they are co-operating. Rosenfeld *et al.* (1987) found that people kept further away from someone with high status, so clearly status and power affect personal space. Physical environment also affects personal distance, and when lighting is less bright, people sit further apart (Adams and Zuckerman, 1991).

Physical proximity affects friendship choices

Festinger *et al.* (1950) carried out a study that showed that physical proximity affects choice of friends (**sociometric choice**). Their study was done in a housing project of 17 apartment buildings for married students on a university campus. Sociometric choices are measured by asking people, for example, who they like most, and who they interact with. People on the same floor were more likely to become friends, and those in the apartments near the stairs were more likely to have friends on the upper floors (which adds weight to the idea that physical proximity affects choice of friends, as those near the stairs were more likely to interact with people using the stairs).

Festinger *et al.* (1950) realised that another factor, which they called **functional distance**, is also important. Functional distance is the way the design of a building means that some people are more likely to interact (such as those living near the stairs are more likely to meet people using the stairs). Personal space and privacy are affected by the relationship the individual has with the person possibly invading their space. Festinger's ideas about functional distance suggest that relationships are affected by building design – in other words by their environment.

Evaluation

- This study was done in 1950. Since then there has been a lot of interest in building design. The work of Oscar Newman is particularly relevant.

The consequences of invading personal space

If a person's space is invaded, he or she may perceive the invader as aggressive, and may see someone who keeps too far away as aloof and 'distant'. As a result there can be communication difficulties.

Negative emotions when space is 'wrong'

Shaw (1976) found that we become emotional in some way when our personal space is invaded – even when in a crowded lift, for example, where personal space is almost sure to be threatened. It has been suggested that when someone's space is invaded they respond with the 'fight or flight' response. Sommer (1969) carried out a well known study into this effect: he would sit about 20 cm from the side of an unknown man and observe his reaction. About 30% of the men studied moved away after a minute, as if using a flight response. After 10 minutes half of the participants had moved away. Sommer's control group were men sitting on their own but not having their space invaded. After one minute none had moved away, and only 25% had moved away after ten minutes, so it seemed that invading someone's space does lead them to move away more quickly. Barash (1973) found that if the person invading the space was dressed as a university faculty member, in other words had high status, people moved away even more quickly.

Evaluation

- Somer's observation simply measured the behaviour, and not the negative feelings. When Baker and Shaw (1980) asked people how they felt when they were asked to stand too close to each other, too far or about right, they found that people said they felt more negative when standing too far apart. However, in this study there was no suggestion as to why the participants did not feel uncomfortable when too close together. Findings from many studies such as Sommer's show that people move

apart when they are 'too' close, and so it seems likely that negative emotions are experienced. Perhaps there was a problem in Baker and Shaw's study because they used self-reports.

Knowles and Brickner (1981) studied the effect of invasion of personal space on arousal (the physiological state associated with the fight or flight reaction). They set up a hidden camera in a urinal and measured how long it took men to start urinating, and how long to finish when men were alone, using adjacent urinals or one urinal apart. When men were closest it took longer to begin to urinate and took less time for them to finish. They concluded that arousal from being close had made participants more tense.

Evaluation

- It is not clear how permission was asked for this study, which is clearly a covert study. Presumably it was thought that participants were in a public place and so likely to be observed. However, some might consider this type of observation unethical.

↻ *Recall AS material*

Recall (or look up) your AS material about ethics and about methodology, to remind yourself about ethical guidelines, and about different types of observation (e.g. overt and covert).

STUDY AID

The issue of the fight or flight response and arousal is studied in many other areas of psychology. You will find it discussed in chapters 4, 5 and 8. Read the relevant sections there to extend your understanding.

Attraction when space is 'right'

There seems to be a connection between attraction and getting the personal distance right. The angle of the approach (whether someone is face-to-face, across from someone, or side-by-side) is also important. Fisher and Byrne (1975) looked at the importance of the angle of approach. In a number of trials, a researcher would choose a person who was alone, and sit down alongside them, one seat away or in a seat across from them. When the researcher had left, after 'reading' for a while, another researcher went to ask the participant questions. Male and female participants liked the female researcher who had sat next to them better than they liked the male researcher who had sat close to them. Female participants said they were more attracted to a person who sat across from them, but male participants preferred a person who sat next to them. It seems that gender differences are involved when considering positive feelings and their relationship to personal space.

Interpersonal distance and social influence
Rivano-Fischer (1984) showed participants films of discussions and then asked questions about the discussions. It was found that the actors in the films who used smaller interpersonal distances and who used less direct orientations (which meant they tended to interact side-by-side rather than face-to-face) were judged to be more persuasive. It was concluded that moving closer to someone, but not being directly in front of them, might lead to greater social influence.

Evaluation

- Only the perceptions of the participants were tested, and then only perceptions of what they thought was going on in a film, so there was little validity here. Albert and Dabbs (1970) set up a situation where a speaker voiced an opinion and used three conditions: near, the right distance or further away. The speaker had more influence when further away, which goes against the idea that people are persuasive when nearer. This suggests that perception does not match behaviour – in other words what we say is not the same as what we do.

Helping behaviour and 'space invasion'
Kopnecni *et al.* (1975) found that when a confederate was walking alongside a moving pedestrian and dropped something, the pedestrian was more likely to pick it up when their space was not invaded than when it was. It seems that helping behaviour is less when space is invaded.

Evaluation

- Baron and Bell (1976) found that people were more helpful if their space *was* invaded, so findings are

contradictory. It has been suggested that a lot depends on the attribution of the participant – what they think of the person needing help. If the invader is seen as unpleasant, then help may not be given, and there could have been different attributions in the two studies. This shows the problem of isolating variables to study.

Baron (1978) then did a different but similar study. Again a researcher invaded a participant's space and observed who helped. 'Invaders' pretended to be students who had dropped their coursework. If the invader stood near and pleaded for help because the coursework was essential most help was given. If the invader stood near but did not ask for help, least help was given. With the invader far away and pleading for help they received less help than when they did not ask.

Evaluation

- This study shows the need to study more than one variable. It is not enough just to see if help is given, as there are other variables such as whether it is asked for, and how important it seems, as well as how close the invader gets.

Territory

When an owner of space controls what happens in or near that space, this is their **territory**. Territory is a way of maintaining the privacy needed to reflect and build a concept of self in relation to others. Altman suggests that territorial behaviour can help to regulate social interaction and avoid conflict. According to Altman (1975) there are three sorts of territory:

- **Primary territory** – the area of territory associated with a primary group like the family (a group that is central to us with regard to protecting our privacy). Primary territory is the most hotly defended.
- **Secondary territory** – the area that is not personally owned, but is not public either. It can be a bar in a pub,

Table 7.2 Types of human territories

Type	Occupants	Control and privacy	Use	Examples
Primary	Individual, family, other primary group	Regular and frequent use, long-term occupancy, personal or important activities	High by members	Private room, residence, flat, private office
Secondary	Secondary group	Regular use for varying periods	Moderate, by non-members	A local hotel, church, park, apartment building, hostel
Public	Individual or group	Temporary use for a limited period	Limited	Table at a restaurant, bench at bus stop, theatre seat

Source: Hogg and Vaughan (1998); based on Altman (1975)

where locals usually gather. Strangers can be glared at or mocked, in an effort to maintain some ownership over secondary territory (Cavan, 1963).
- **Public territory** – an area that anyone can access. Territorial markers are used such as hedges and fences to deter intruders. For example, people can leave a bag on a chair in a restaurant as a marker.

Territory does not have to be place, although usually it is. Altman also described how we can defend objects (such as a car or books) as we defend our territory. Ideas can also be territories, and we defend them by copyright rules against plagiarism. In human research, the term 'territory' does not have to be physical space, although **territoriality** (used in animal research) does refer to physical space.

Lyman and Scott (1967) suggest that there are two types of territory:
- **Interactional territory**, where a group of interacting people temporarily have control, for example, classrooms or football pitches.
- **Body territory**, the physical self – the boundary is one's self. This is not the same as personal space, where the boundary is some distance away. People personalise their body territories with jewellery, tattoos and clothing.

Influences on territory

Gender
Protection of territory varies according to age, gender and personality. Males seem to claim larger territories (Hayduk, 1983). Gifford and Sacilotto (1993) carried out a study on dormitory residents who shared a room. Residents drew maps of their rooms, and marked out what they thought was their own territory and what was space shared with their roommate. Males drew larger personal territories than females did. In another study, Barnard and Bell (1982) studied Israeli parents and found that both mothers and fathers agreed that a kitchen is the woman's territory, although over 30% of the fathers interviewed claimed that the whole home was their territory. Then again 48% of the fathers (but only 27% of the mothers) said that they had no place of their own at home. These are apparently contradictory findings. In general mothers did claim that the home was shared territory but that the kitchen was their territory.

ACTIVITY

Barnard and Bell's (1982) study could be partially replicated by using a questionnaire and asking about space within the family home, and whose territory which room is. You could compare their findings in Israel with your culture.

Personality and gender
Gifford (1982) looked at whether certain personality types were more territorial than others. It did seem that in dormitory rooms the more intelligent residents, of both sexes, marked off more territory for themselves. Gender and personality thus seem to play a joint role in determining territoriality.

Physical context
Physical context also affects territoriality, and is investigated further later in this chapter, where architecture is looked at. Newman discusses the idea of **defensible space**. He argues that if people accept that areas surrounding their building are secondary territory (and therefore should be defended) crime in those areas will be less. If someone accepts responsibility for an area – for example, the lobby in a block of flats – then they will 'defend' it.

Competition for resources
It would be expected that where there was competition for fewer resources there would be more territorial behaviour. However, Altman (1975) suggests that the opposite could be true, and that when resources are greater there will be more territorial behaviour because there is more worth protecting. So it could be that we are more territorial when resources are low, or more territorial when resources are high.

Studies of animal behaviour show that if resources are few animals are less likely to engage in territorial behaviour. This seems to be because they would have to spend a great deal of energy to defend what would have to be a large territory (to encompass sufficient resources) – in which case they might as well abandon the idea of territoriality and just get what they can. This is the **cost–benefit model**. Where there are sufficient resources to make defending territory worthwhile, then it *is* defended – the cost of defending in terms of energy spent is worth the benefits from the resources. When there are insufficient resources, any territory would have to be large, and it is not defended because the cost of defending is more than the benefit gained. The cost–benefit model seems to apply to humans only in some cases. Balogun (1991) reports a study carried out on African Bushmen, where Cashdan says territorial behaviour occurs because of competition for resources. When there are plenty of resources, territories are small, and the Bushmen defend the territory by perimeter displays. When resources are scarce, perimeter defending is not practicable, because there is not a small area of good resources to defend. This agrees with the cost-benefit model. However, there are other less direct ways of defending territory. For example, the Bushmen invite visitors, but then develop rituals for gaining access, which limits access. In practice Bushmen tended to allow access only when resources were plentiful, and defended more when they were scarce. This goes against the cost–benefit model, but does appeal to common sense, as well as agreeing with Altman's claim made above, that we defend more when there is more to defend.

Consequences of invasion of territory

Reaction to territorial invasion depends on the type of territory. Primary territory is usually legally owned, so its invasion can involve taking legal action by calling the police. It is hard to deal with invasion of secondary territory, because it is not privately owned. Informal methods of dealing with invasion include giving hostile looks and behaving in an unwelcoming manner. Sometimes the only way to react to an invasion of public territory is to move on and look for somewhere else.

Lyman and Scott (1967) consider that there are three ways in which territory can be accessed:

- Invasion is only one form, and refers to physical invasion, usually where there is an intention to take control from the owner.
- Violation is more temporary and the aim is not to take over ownership but to inflict harm. Violation can be deliberate or unplanned. Kagehiro (1990) points out that if an owner enters a rented flat to seize property because they have been given legal right to do so, the owner may not see this as invasion of the resident's territory, but the resident may see it as invasion. Whether an action is violation or not depends on the individual's perspective.
- Contamination means that another person's territory is fouled, for example, an insecticide spray may drift into a person's garden.

Functions of territory

Using territory to obtain privacy

Altman (1975) discusses personal space and the idea of territory, and suggests that **privacy** is an important concept. Privacy is about the way a person makes himself or herself available to others, and personal space and territory are important in determining levels of privacy. **Desired privacy** is what someone wants in the way of interaction with others, and **achieved privacy** is what they actually get. People are dissatisfied if achieved privacy falls short of desired privacy. Altman suggests that when we develop an idea of self, when we are children, we also develop control over boundaries between ourselves and others. Social comparison takes place; a child compares itself with others whilst building its concept of self. In order to evaluate ourselves and to compare ourselves to others (which is how we evaluate ourselves) we need to step back and reflect. This is done by finding privacy. Our culture defines how we set the boundaries to gain this privacy.

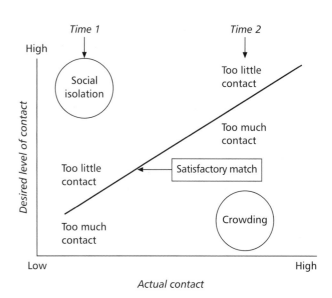

Figure 7.3
Privacy is an optimisation process. The desired level of contact with others can vary, so feelings of social isolation or crowding are relative. You aim for a match between desired and actual levels of privacy (Source: Hogg and Vaughan, 1998)

Figure 7.4
Privacy in public places mainly means avoiding unwanted interactions. To do this we use non-verbal behaviour, such as facing away from strangers

Altman looked at other cultures for information and comparisons of privacy and setting boundaries. In Java, for example, people move through each others' homes with freedom, just as through a public street. There are no doors and the walls are thin. However, people speak quietly and do not like showing emotion, so there seem to be psychological barriers where there are no physical barriers.

Regulation of privacy is the way people make themselves more or less available to others. Altman (1993) argues that there is a transaction between social interaction and the physical environment. Social relationships have meaning and symbolism, and the physical environment can be part of these meanings. Our verbal and non-verbal behaviour help to regulate social interaction. In libraries, for instance, the closer someone comes to another person the more they erect barriers such as piles of books. People also use body language to erect barriers, such as placing their elbows between them and the other person (e.g. Patterson *et al.*, 1971).

Westin (1970) proposed four types of privacy:
- **Solitude** – being alone.
- **Intimacy** – being in a small group separated from others.
- **Anonymity** – being with others, but detached from them.
- **Reserve** – keeping mental distance from others.

Using territory as a social organiser

Knowing about territory allows us to know how to behave in different environments. It can be difficult to manage in a different culture without knowing the rules, including the rules of personal space, territory and privacy. As Altman suggests, we may obtain our idea of self, and our self-esteem, from territorial behaviour and from establishing ways to be private. This helps to shape social interactions, and to shape society itself (Edney, 1975). The example given above of how Bushmen regulated visitors by inventing rituals is an example of how territory can shape social interactions.

It could be that conflict, rather than territory, is the central issue. By using the concept of territory we can avoid conflict. Schrodt (1981) suggests the **street-gang theory** of territory development, where it is suggested that territory is owned by units such as gangs or families. When two different units are next to one another conflict can occur and the territory can change hands. Eventually, if this process continued, one gang would control most of one territory, and another gang would control most of another; fewer gangs would be next to one another so fewer conflicts would occur. In this way territory can be a social organiser. Another way in which territory acts as a social organiser is that we can work out where people are, which makes communication easier. Territories provide access to people.

Using territory to protect resources

Defence of territory can depend on the amount of resources available. If there are many resources, animals defend more (although humans are expected to share more); if there are fewer resources, animals do better if they just take what they can get, but humans are more likely to defend territory. In either case, one of the functions of territoriality can be to protect or obtain sufficient resources to survive.

Self-test

1 Write a timed essay under exam conditions (or as close as you can manage), using the title 'Discuss individual and cultural differences in personal space, and the consequences of invasion of personal space'.

2 Briefly write about two functions of territory.

The effect of architecture on behaviour

Architectural design and resident satisfaction

Buildings are designed to fulfil certain functions, and need to be fit for their purpose: for instance, a church requires a spiritual response, whereas a prison is there to keep people in rather than to be attractive. Buildings also have social and cultural significance, and if blocks of flats are designed to be functional without taking into account the needs of those who live there, resident satisfaction is likely to be low. Patri (1971) examined the effect of new housing on people in Guam who had been used to living in one-room houses – they continued to use only one room in their new houses. The design of the building did not lead to resident satisfaction because it did not take into account the habits and customs of the people.

Building design may affect behaviour in a number of ways:
- **Architectural determinism** suggests that building design can itself affect behaviour. Newman's ideas about this, and the way some buildings can encourage crime, are outlined below.
- **Environmental possibilism** suggests that the environment sets limits to our behaviour and sets the possibilities. The individual helps to shape his or her own behaviour, within a physical environment.
- **Environmental probabilism** suggests that we can look at both the design of the physical environment and psychological factors and predict behaviour that is likely to come from mixing the two.

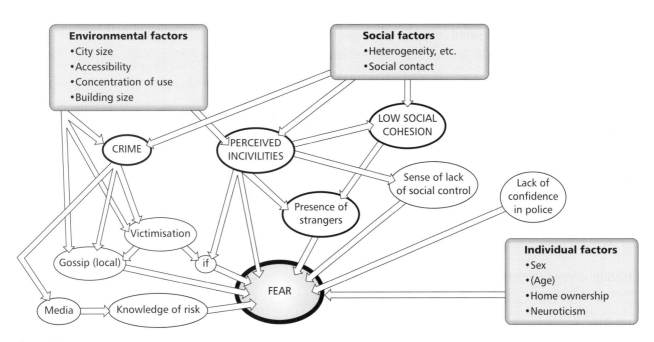

Figure 7.5
What leads to fear of crime in residential settings (Source: Halpern, 1995)

In Britain and the USA people mainly prefer a detached family suburban home (Cooper, 1972). This seems to be to avoid conflict with neighbours, and links back to the ideas of territory and privacy (Michelson, 1977). However, when measuring satisfaction, it is important to take into account economic and practical factors. Gifford (1997) shows how people look at the objective features of a house, then use some subjective impressions, which are affected by factors such as age, occupation, personality and social class. Finally, with these objective and subjective impressions in mind, a person will decide what level of satisfaction they get from this place as a home. More on building design and resident satisfaction is found later in this chapter.

Figure 7.6
Higher crime ratios are found in high-rise housing than in low-rise developments

Social homogeneity can lead to slum areas

Both from a social viewpoint and from a political stance balanced communities are considered desirable. For example, planners do not want a city to be divided into rich and poor areas, or black and white areas: boundaries lead to territory disputes. However, people do like to live in homogenous areas, and in this case homogenous means like-minded groups. Social homogeneity means where there are like-minded people together, and it can lead to a good neighbourhood, where there is sharing and positive relationships. A well planned neighbourhood may not work if there is no social homogeneity.

Breaking areas up into neighbourhoods of similar people can lead to a lack of balance. For example, an area where people are poorer may have fewer amenities, which can lead to conflict. However, even if the planning does not allow for social homogeneity, given the bad effects this can produce, it will tend to happen in any case as people naturally move to areas where they feel comfortable, and which they can afford. 'Good' and 'bad' areas are likely to develop in any case. Fischer (1982) suggests that the higher the level of ethnic segregation, the more group conflicts are likely to occur. There can also be a problem if an area attracts people in the same stage of the life cycle, for example, all young families, as tended to happen in the British 'new towns'; this can lead to particular demands on primary schools at one time, followed by uneven demand for secondary schools and so on. Currently in the new towns there is pressure on housing as the second generation looks for homes of their own.

Mixed areas or grid designs could solve the problem

The problem of social homogeneity is that, although people want to live in homogenous groups, this causes problems such as 'good' and 'bad' areas, and unbalanced demands on resources. To solve this problem some planners have designed areas where there is a mix of types of people (Altman and Chemers, 1984). In a different idea a city does not have a clear centre, but is based on a grid design. One such city is Barcelona. The idea of a grid design is that different areas have their own centres. This should mean there is less social inequality, in that all areas would be the same size, determined by the grid size, and there would be no single centre and no main street, so no area should become a slum.

Building design and the concept of territory – Oscar Newman

Invasion of territory or personal space can be caused by building design – for example, tables too close together in a crowded restaurant can mean that space is invaded. Design of public territory, whether a building or an open space, needs to take account of factors such as territoriality and personal space. Oscar Newman (1973) suggests that secondary space also needs to be carefully designed with these factors in mind. Newman suggests that crime in blocks of flats can be directly related to the way the buildings are designed. Buildings should be designed to encourage occupants to take responsibility for any public territory, which would then become secondary territory. If residents had a sense of ownership over secondary territory such as stairwells, lobbies and lifts, there would be less crime in those areas, as they would be 'defended'. Newman called this sort of area '**defensible space**' – an area that residents place value on.

Newman suggests that to create this defensible space designers should:
* Make sure common space is overlooked.
* Create symbolic markers such as low walls to establish territory.
* Improve appearance of housing so that the residents have a sense of pride and ownership.

Cose (1994) discussed a neighbourhood in Dayton, Ohio, with a high crime rate. In 1991 Newman advised that they closed many of the entrances to the area, installed speed bumps, and divided the area into five smaller neighbourhoods with physical barriers. Traffic was down 67% by 1993 and violent crime had halved, so it seemed that Newman's ideas worked.

Evaluation

* Some studies have shown that with the above changes crime rates increased. Kohn *et al.* (1975) could not replicate Newman's findings. The studies are field studies, and all variables cannot be controlled. They are hard to replicate, and it is difficult to pinpoint causes with so many variables involved.

* A problem with the idea that having defensible space reduces crime is that not all defensible space is defended. If a neighbourhood is not acting as one, then space may not be defended as Newman envisaged it would be.

* Another problem with the idea of changing the environment to give defensible space that is then defended is that some criminals do not pay attention to the environment. Therefore, changes such as physical barriers may not have an effect.

* Defensible space principles tend to work better if the area is already defined, such as with a shop. For example, when a chain of stores cleared windows of advertising and put tills nearer to the window, to give better visibility, there were 30% fewer robberies than in other stores where these changes were not made (Krupat and Kubzansky, 1987).

The Pruitt-Igoe Housing Project – bad planning

Studies of planning disasters highlight the importance of environmental psychology. Yancey (1971) reported on a housing project in St. Louis, Missouri, called the Pruitt-Igoe housing project. This was an estate of 43 buildings, each 11 storeys high, housing 12,000 people. The buildings were put up in the 1950s, and there were around 3,000 apartments intended for families with low income. The planners used plenty of room, and planned pleasant grounds for the flats; indeed the project received planning awards. The design was thought to be good partly because of some cost-cutting measures, for example, the lifts only stopped at every third floor. However, within three years there were many broken windows, stairwells smelt of urine, juvenile delinquents squatted in the apartments and only about 30% were occupied. Clearly the project had failed. The buildings were demolished in 1972.

After interviewing the residents Yancey (1971) suggested that the problem had been the design itself: 78% of the residents were satisfied with the apartments themselves, compared with 55% who had been satisfied with the slums they had moved from, so it was not the actual apartment that was a problem. The design had not taken into account the way the people behaved. The galleries provided for informal meetings had, for example, been placed a long way from the apartments and hallways, so these informal meetings did not really take place. When the families lived in their 'slums' they had chatted in their 'back yards' and this chat could not longer take place. Residents became lonely, and children could not be supervised. There were hiding places in the corridors and stairwells, and children could play there. There was '**atomisation**', a term that means that friendships did not build, and everyone had to look out for themselves.

Figure 7.7
The Pruitt-Igoe public housing project

Evaluation

- It has been suggested that a problem with the Pruitt-Igoe housing project was that many residents were on welfare and did not want to mix too much with neighbours in case too much became known about their business. However, other housing projects have worked better, even though many residents claim benefits. Wilner *et al.* (1962) studied a project in Baltimore of six blocks, each having eleven storeys, with ten flats on each floor. Unlike Pruitt-Igoe some semi-private space was planned, including a common play area on each floor. There was more visiting between neighbours and help between people than amongst those living on the Pruitt-Igoe project. It did seem, therefore, that the planning of the Pruitt-Igoe project was wrong in not allowing for the needs of the residents.

Eastlake housing estate – good planning

Halpern (1995) describes the Eastlake housing estate in England, an area of 712 houses and flats developed in the 1960s. The Department of the Environment in 1989 used this estate to see if improvements in the environment could improve mental health. A questionnaire was undertaken to see what the people living there wanted in the way of improvements and the questionnaires were followed by interviews. The work started with repairs, then tackled minor alterations, finally dealing with major alterations. The residents helped to establish priorities. In terms of mental health the idea seemed to be a success. Mental health was measured by asking residents such questions as how helpful they thought their neighbours would be if he or she was burgled, wanted someone to talk to, or if they were bored.

Renovation of a hospital wing – good planning

Becker and Poe (1980) studied an example of social design where renovation of a hospital wing involved patients,

staff and visitors in the design. Decisions about the renovation involved an attempt to gain consensus between all the interested groups. It was possible to evaluate the effects of the change as the hospital had two similar wings that had not been altered. The morale and the mood of the staff on the renovated wing improved a lot compared with the unimproved wings, although the morale and mood of patients and visitors showed less improvement. A questionnaire was used to assess attitude

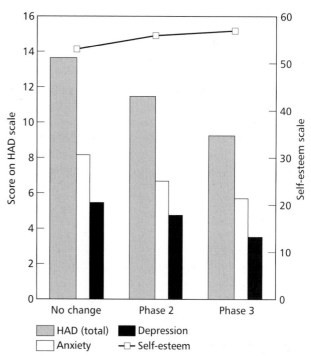

Figure 7.8
Mental health of residents by phases of redevelopment. HAD = Hospital anxiety and depression scale (Source: Halpern, 1995)

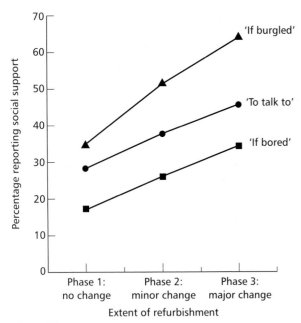

Figure 7.9
How social support from neighbours is perceived following change to the environment (Source: Hogg and Vaughan, 1998)

to the renovated and unchanged wings. All users preferred the renovated wing, with staff giving the best rating. The solarium was considered the most improved area of the wing, and it was used more than it was before the renovation. The visitors were the least pleased with the changes, even though their views had also been taken into account, which was surprising.

Ambient conditions and architectural features

Two main categories of variables must be considered when studying the effect of architectural environment on behaviour – the ambient conditions and the architectural features. The ambient conditions are physical aspects such as light, noise, and temperature. Architectural features are more permanent physical conditions such as size and layout. One example of a study of the effect of ambient conditions was an experiment carried out by Baron (1990) in which it was found that a pleasant air freshener led participants to be more friendly and set higher goals when

Self-test

1 Write a timed essay under exam conditions (or as close as you can manage) using the title 'Discuss the effect of architecture on communication and on residential satisfaction'.

2 Briefly describe examples of good and bad practice in architectural design with respect to defensible space.

carrying out a clerical task. The architectural features of a setting can rarely all be taken in so we select certain features. By arranging furniture in a certain way, for example, we can make a room seem friendlier, just because the arrangement enables people to interact better.

Stress, crowding and urban living

Sources of environmental stressors and effects on behaviour

As outlined above, the properties of our environment can affect how we feel, our health, and our behaviour. Stress is a state of physiological arousal in which we feel unable to cope with the demands of the situation. **Environmental stressors** are factors in our environment, often in the background, that can lead to stress, and can affect performance. Physical disasters such as a volcano erupting or a flood are environmental stressors, but less obvious stressors can also be found. Noise, heat, sunlight, and wind have all been identified as environmental stressors (Halpern, 1995).

	Minor	*Major*
Acute	Daily hassles (e.g. problem at work, with car)	Significant life events (e.g. death of close friend or relative)
Chronic	Many environmental stressors (e.g. ongoing noise, pollutants, crowding)	Major on-going difficulty (e.g. long-term problem with health, poverty)

Figure 7.10
Classes of stressors (Source: Halpern, 1995)

STUDY AID

The issue of stress is studied in many other areas of psychology, as well as here, such as the psychology of health (Chapter 8), the psychology of work (Chapter 4), and sport psychology (Chapter 5). You could read the relevant sections there to extend your understanding.

Noise

Noise is a feature of our society that has been shown to cause stress. Sundstrom *et al.* (1994) suggest that in an office the noise of keyboards can be put up with, but the noise of a telephone ringing or of colleagues chattering can be unbearable. Noise can be defined as sounds that the listener does not want to hear, and even quiet sounds can bring irritation, for example, if someone is trying to sleep. We do adapt to noise. It seems that we can adapt to an office noise that is greater than the noise we can adapt to at home, so the setting is important. Where a person has warning that a loud noise will happen, and can prepare for it, it will not affect them (Broadbent, 1979). Tasks that are well practised are not affected by noise (Harris, 1973). Even when noise stops it can give stress. Complex tasks are affected by continuous noise. It is as if more attention must be paid to the required task in a noisy environment, so with well learned tasks, which need little attention, there is less problem. However, a complicated task needs careful attention, and background noise can affect performance.

Environmental after-effects – Glass and Singer (1972)

Glass and Singer (1972) looked at the effect of noise on performance. The participants did simple tasks involving mathematical addition and verbal reasoning. Whilst doing the tasks they were subjected to either loud or soft noise that was either random or regular. Some participants had a button they could press to stop the noise, and this introduced a control factor. So some participants had random, unpredictable noise, some had regular predictable noise, some had loud sounds, some had soft sounds, and some had control over the noise.

In the second phase participants in a quiet room attempted to solve puzzles, two of which did not have a solution (this was to measure a participant's tolerance of frustration) and had to proofread some text. The participants subjected to the loud, unpredictable and uncontrollable noise found fewest errors in the manuscript and showed the least tolerance of frustration. This is called an **environmental after-effect**.

Long-term exposure to noise affects scholastic achievement

Glass and Singer's study was a laboratory experiment, and the noise was manipulated rather than real. Often field studies are carried out, studying real conditions. For example, Maser *et al.* (1978) studied schoolchildren near the Seattle-Tacoma airport and found that those with low aptitude test scores achieved less than a control group achieved in a different, quieter, area. Similarly Bronzaft and McCarthy (1975) found that in a classroom near a railway line the children nearest to the line did less well on reading tests. Short-term exposure to noise does not seem to affect performance, so laboratory experiments might not demonstrate that noise affects achievement. However, long-term exposure to noise does seem to affect achievement, and this suggests that cognitive processing is affected by the noise. Cohen *et al.* (1973) found that children from apartment buildings by busy roads tested in quiet surroundings did not do as well as children who lived in the quiet areas. It was not the immediate surroundings that affected the results, but the long-term exposure to noise.

Noise affects social behaviour

Mathews and Canon (1975) carried out studies looking at helping behaviour. In one condition the experimenter's arm was in a plaster cast and there was a noisy lawn mower nearby. In another condition the arm was in plaster, but there was no lawn mower. People gave more help when the mower was absent, but when the study was tried with and without the cast, there was no difference in helping behaviour – that is the noise still affected results, but the cast did not. The suggestion is that there is stimulus overload, which is where stimulation is so fast that everything cannot be processed. Noise is part of this stimulus overload, which can be linked to the physiological affects of arousal.

Appleyard and Lintell (1972) carried out a field study using three San Fransisco streets, one with light traffic, one with moderate traffic and one with heavy traffic. Their question was whether noise of traffic affected social interaction. On the street with heavy traffic there was no social activity, and the residents said that living in the area was lonely. However, when the traffic was light there was casual social interaction, and residents said it was a friendly place.

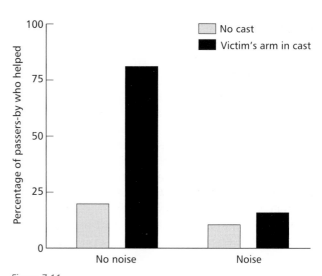

Figure 7.11
Percentage of passers by who stopped to help a pedestrian who had dropped books. The pedestrian either wore a cast on his arm or did not and the conditions were noisy or quiet. Noise apparently deterred altruism and led passers by to overlook the arm cast (Source: Deaux and Wrightsman, 1988)

Moser (1988) used a confederate to carry out acts like dropping keys. The study took place in Paris. There was less helping behaviour when the streets were congested or there were loud roadworks.

Heat

Heat is another stressor. Harries and Stadler (1983) analysed around 4,000 cases of aggravated assault in Dallas and discovered a relationship between violence and 'thermal discomfort' – heat plus humidity. Even where the climate is normally very hot, such as in India, people are in a more negative mood on the hottest days (Ruback and Pandey, 1992).

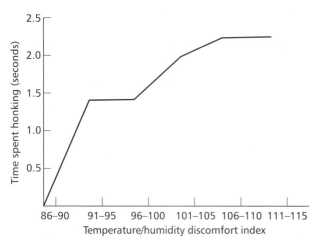

Figure 7.12
Average amount of time drivers spent honking their horns behind a car stopped at a green light in Phoenix, Arizona varied with temperature/humidity (Source: Deaux and Wrightsman, 1988)

Heat and aggression – an inverted-U relationship

Laboratory studies have tested people in various ways in hot and cool conditions. Page (1978) found that when conditions were hot people were less helpful to others, and Griffit (1970) found that attraction to a stranger is less if conditions are hot and humid. There is a inverted-U relationship between heat and aggression. At first aggression and hostility increase steadily as temperature rises but as it gets hotter still, aggression starts to fall. Real-world studies have replicated these laboratory results. For example, Bell and Greene (1982) show that aggression (measured by behaviours ranging from major riots to hooting horns in traffic) goes up as heat rises, but then falls as it gets even hotter. Bell and Fusco (1989) show that the number of assaults per day rose to a peak when the heat was around 97°F, and then fell. Halpern (1995) reviewed studies that looked at a rise in aggression as heat and humidity rose. It was suggested that aggression rises as heat rises, but only up to a point. When it gets really hot, aggression tends to fall.

Evaluation

- Although there is a relationship between violent crime and heat in that there is more violent crime as it gets hotter, this is not true of all crimes. Rotton (1993) found that there was no relationship between rape and the surrounding temperature.

Heat, helpfulness and mental illness

Cunningham (1979) discovered that people in the streets were more willing to be interviewed if conditions were pleasant than if conditions were hot. However, Fisher *et al.* (1984) found that people were more willing to help in the very cold winter months, so it seems that helpfulness is less only in extremes of heat, rather than at extremes of temperature.

Rotton and Frey (1984), taking into account the time of year and day of the week, found that there were more psychiatric emergencies on warm days than on cool days.

Air pollution

Although heat and noise can have positive effects as well as being environmental stressors, air pollution is always seen as having negative effects. Pollutants can have bad smells, and can irritate. Pollution usually involves nitrogen and sulphur oxides, smog (photochemical oxidants), carbon monoxide and particulates. These chemicals can lead to respiratory or cardiovascular diseases (Evans and Jacobs, 1982). Mendelsohn and Orcutt (1979) note that many deaths in the USA are caused by pollution, and Bown's report in 1994 suggests that around 10,000 people in Britain each year die prematurely because of particulates. Lave and Seskin (1970) postulate that at least $200 million could be saved from US health costs if pollution was cut by 50%. The Royal Commission on Environmental Pollution in 1995 concluded that traffic pollution was costing the UK from 0.4% to 1% of GDP (£40 billion per year) (Halpern, 1995). Long-term exposure to pollution seems to lead to desensitisation and denial. People do seem to be able to habituate to pollution, but only to an extent. DeGroot (1967) found that people are satisfied with the air quality in their own area, but this may only be because they have nothing to compare it with.

Air quality and mental health – a survey

Klitzman and Stellman (1989) carried out a survey of 2,000 office workers on four sites, and found that perceived air quality was an important factor when people were rating their mental health. The researchers controlled for age, gender, marital status and occupation (by matching respondents), and found that air quality, noise and ergonomic factors were the three most important aspects of the environment when considering mental health.

Evaluation

- It could be that those with poorer mental health complained more. Surveys do give correlations, but a cause and effect relationship should not then be assumed.

Air quality and mental health – objective measures

Bullinger (1989) measured actual air quality, not just a person's perception of the air quality, and actual measures can lead to conclusions about cause and effect relationships. He found that people living in a polluted area in Bulgaria consistently reported more negative moods than a control group living in an unpolluted area.

Evaluation

- Air pollution is not the only factor involved, so there could be another cause for the negative moods. For example, the quality of housing could vary. It is likely that poorer people are to be found in polluted areas, given that the cost of housing and the cost of living could be lower.

Evans *et al.* (1987) looked at the effects of ozone on people in Los Angeles. Those who lived in the more polluted areas seemed to react more to negative life events. It seems that pollution itself did not worsen mental health, but was an additional stressor. When added to other stressors, it had an adverse effect on an individual's mental health.

Daily pollutant levels and psychiatric emergencies

Rotton and Frey (1984), Brière *et al.* (1983), and Strahilevitz *et al.* (1979) did a series of studies to look at the relationship between pollutants and mental illness. They all found evidence to show that daily pollutant levels linked to psychiatric hospital admissions. The photochemical oxidants and nitrogen dioxide gave the strongest links, and sulphur dioxide gave a less strong link. The weakest link was with particulates and hydrocarbons, so it seems that the type of pollutant is important.

Evaluation

- Strahilevitz *et al.* (1979) found the strongest link between pollutants and psychiatric admissions, but their study did not control well for temperature and weather conditions. However, overall there does seem to be a link between pollution and mental illness, depending on the pollutant.

Smells

Pollutants may lead to increased anxiety, and this could be what leads to the increase in psychiatric emergencies. Laboratory studies suggest that unpleasant smells can lead to higher levels of aggression and lower levels of interpersonal attraction (Rotton and Frey, 1984). However, odourless pollutants such as ozone and carbon monoxide can still cause irritation, so smell is not the only problem. The main factor, however, seems to be mood (which is self-reported), and a negative mood seems to be most linked to the presence of pollution.

Bad smells do seem to impair performance on some complex tasks such as proofreading. However, with less complex tasks such as simple arithmetic, there seems to be little effect (Rotton, 1983). Similarly, bad smells in the air reduce how much we like paintings and photographs, but increase attraction to others if we expect to interact with them (Rotton *et al.*, 1978). Aggression is also increased by unpleasant smells (Rotton *et al.*, 1979). So it seems that the relationship between air pollution and behaviour is a complex one.

Strategies for coping with environmental stressors

It is interesting to look at strategies for coping with such problems. Not much can be done about the outdoor temperature, but heat can be controlled in schools, prisons and other areas. In response to the above findings it seems sensible to suggest that the environment should be carefully controlled, where possible.

Changing environmental stressors

One way of reducing mental health problems related to environmental stressors is to remove the source of stress, however, this is often not within the individual's power. The source of stress is often difficult to remove, as it may not be within any one person's or body's power, although efforts to reduce pollution are being made. Planning and design of buildings can be one way of reducing problems. As has been suggested above, fear of crime can be reduced if buildings are designed taking into account Newman's suggestions with regard to defensible space. Building less high-density living accommodation can reduce stress from overcrowding. Providing common meeting or play areas can reduce loneliness or lack of privacy. Noise can be reduced, and there are laws to tackle this, as there are laws to tackle pollution.

Using coping mechanisms

Another way of reducing anxiety is to discover ways of coping with environmental stressors. It has been shown that noise can lead to stress and to mental illness. However, some people, although finding noise an irritant, do not become mentally ill. This could be because people have different coping mechanisms. Strategies for coping with stress in general can be applied to coping with environmental stressors, and there has been quite a lot of research looking at coping with stress. Coping mechanisms have been divided into two main categories: practical or emotional. Usually practical coping mechanisms are thought of as best; however, in some situations emotional coping mechanisms can be useful (more information on coping mechanisms is given in Chapter 8, which looks at stress in much more detail).

STUDY AID

The issue of using coping mechanisms to cope with stress is examined in other areas of psychology, as well as here. It is explored in the psychology of health, for instance (Chapter 8). You could read the relevant sections there to extend your understanding.

Coping mechanisms can be inappropriate

Coping mechanisms can be inappropriate if the individual thinks that the arousal is caused by something other than the stressor. Schacter and Singer (1962) found that how a state of arousal is felt depends on the perceived cause of the arousal. In Schacter and Singer's study, participants received an injection of adrenaline and were told it was a vitamin compound. Some participants were told the truth – that the injection would activate the sympathetic nervous system – and some were either not told the effect of the injection or were told it would activate the parasympathetic nervous system. After the injection the participants went to a waiting room where there was a confederate of the experimenter. The confederate behaved in a cheerful or angry manner, whichever condition had been agreed with the experimenter. The participants who had been told the cause of their arousal, which was that their sympathetic nervous system had been activated by the injection, did not pick up on the mood of the confederate: these participants had a reason for their feelings. However, the participants who either had no explanation or the wrong explanation were aroused by the injection, but did not know the reason for their arousal. These participants did report feelings similar to the mood the confederate was conveying. They picked up on the confederate's mood to explain to themselves their feelings.

It seems from Schacter and Singer's study that it is not that the arousal is purely a physiological phenomenon, but there is also a cognitive element – to do with what the person thinks is causing the problem. Perhaps if an individual knows that there is overcrowding because their large family is living together in a limited space, this is an adequate explanation, and their feelings of anxiety are accounted for. If, however, a person cannot easily explain the feeling of crowding, because they live alone, but in a small flat in a high-rise block, they may pick up on mood around them to explain their feelings. Then they might attribute anxiety to negative mood, rather than to crowding, and depression might be the result. If noise or pollution is unnoticed, then the individuals cannot explain their anxiety or arousal, and so look for other reasons. This means that one person can experience stress in the physiological sense but accept it, because they have a reason for it. Someone else might experience strain (stress in the physiological sense) from the same stressor but have a different response to it depending on what reason they give themselves for being stressed. Their subjective experience of stress can be an important way of coping with it. If someone is giving their arousal the wrong cause (as they have not realised the air pollution levels perhaps) then their coping is likely to be inappropriate.

STUDY AID

The issue of stress and strain, and the roles of the sympathetic and parasympathetic parts of the autonomic nervous system, is explored in Chapter 8. Read the relevant sections there to extend your understanding.

Coping with crowding

Crowding is discussed in detail later in this chapter. Crowding in animals has been shown to lead to stress, and findings have been generalised to humans. Many studies have shown that crowding gives stress in humans. There are ways of alleviating this stress.

People cope better with stress from crowding if:
- They have control over the situation.
- They have social support from family or friends.
- They withdraw from a situation – even if they cannot physically withdraw, they can avoid eye contact.
- They sit in a corner position, to withdraw from a crowd.
- They know that a crowding situation is likely, because this knowledge gives them some control (Baum *et al.*, 1981).

Other ways of coping include changes to the environment, although this is not always possible. Rohner (1974) showed that people in dormitories prefer bunk beds because this gives more space and room mates are out of sight at night.

City living

City living can lead to stimulus overload from the busy environment. Smith (1991) suggests that city dwellers need to learn to attend only to important stimuli. Milgram (1977) proposes some strategies for coping with city living, and the overload experienced by living with so many people (outlined in Hogg and Vaughan, 1998):
- Allocate less time to each person met (for example, give superficial greetings).
- Disregard low priority people (for example, ignore drunks).
- Shift responsibility (for example, a bus driver wants passengers to have the exact fare).
- Block contact with others (for example, use an unlisted telephone number).
- Reduce involvement (for example, avoid telling others about yourself, and listening to others).
- Heighten availability of other institutions (for example, use institutions such as social welfare and telephone information services).

High-density living

Classical environmental stressors such as noise, temperature and air pollution have already been outlined. Social environmental stressors are sources of stress that are social, and to do with people. Crowding is not just the number of people in a given space; it also concerns the emotions of individuals – we have to feel crowded. We can be in a large space with very many people and feel less crowded than in a smaller place with fewer people.

Some definitions – crowding and density

Crowding is not the same as density. **Density** is the measure of physical space per person within a dwelling (household density) or within an area (neighbourhood density or population density). **Crowding** includes density, but is more than that. Crowding depends on an individual's perception of the density – does it feel crowded, for example? **Social density** refers to the number of people, so an increase in social density means more people for the space. **Spatial density** refers to the size of the area, so an increase in spatial density means less space for the same number of people (Halpern, 1995). Someone living alone in a small room is in high-density conditions, but this would be called cramped, rather than crowded.

Crowding – three components

Sundstrom (1978) and Aiello and Thompson (1980) discuss three components to crowding:

- Crowding comes from some situation such as too many people getting too close, or space being taken up by a visitor (situational component).
- Crowding implies some negative emotion (affective component).
- Crowding produces some behaviour such as aggression, avoiding eye contact, leaving the scene or withdrawing from social interaction (behavioural component).

Table 7.3 Density and crowding

- Density is the number of people per unit of area
- Crowding is a person's experience of the number of people around
- Perceived density is what we think the density of a place is
- Affective density is our emotional response to feeling that there are a lot of people around
- Functional density is when we are pleased that a lot of people are in the place (e.g. at a wedding)
- Crowding is negative affective density, when we are not pleased that there are a lot of people in a place
- Social density is when there is a fixed space available for more and more people
- Spatial density is when there is a smaller space available for a fixed number of people
- Indoor density refers to the number of people in inside rooms
- Outdoor density refers to the number of people that need to use outside space around buildings

The effect of crowding in animals

Calhoun (1962) carried out a well known study, which concluded that crowding in animals can lead to disastrous consequences. Calhoun set up a 'rat universe' using Norway rats. This universe was 10 ft × 14 ft, and divided into four equal cells. Female rats distributed themselves evenly between the four pens, but a few dominant male rats controlled each of two pens. The other males had to live in the other two pens, and density was greater in these two pens, which were called behavioural sinks. As the population of rats rose, disease and behavioural disturbances followed. There was also a high infant mortality rate. In the behavioural sinks packs of males become cannibalistic, hyperactive, hypersensitive and homosexual (Halpern, 1995).

Calhoun carried out another study in 1973 using mice. He left a colony of mice in a large enclosure that contained enough water, food and nesting materials for 4,000 mice. However, the population peaked at 2,200, which was arrived at by the 500th day. The last infant mouse was born

Figure 7.13
Spatial density (crowding) may be perceived as unpleasant (left) or pleasant (right)

Table 7.4 Models of crowding

Model of crowding	Experience in high population density	Immediate reactions	Long-term consequences
Overload	Overstimulation or excess cognitive load from too many people, close interpersonal proximity	Withdrawal: avoidance of social contact; inattention to social cues	With continued social overload, habitual withdrawal from social contact
Arousal	Physiological, psychological arousal (from close interpersonal proximity, fear, uncertainty)	Improved performance of simple tasks; degraded performance of complex or difficult tasks	None predicted
Interference	Frustration from people constraining behaviour, interfering with activities, or blocking access to resources	Negative feelings, hostility	Increased likelihood of violent, aggressive response to provocation
Control	Inability to control sources of overload, interference	Psychological stress	With persistent failure to achieve personal control, learned helplessness
Privacy regulation	Inability to optimise individual level of interpersonal interaction	Use of privacy regulation mechanisms to reduce social contact (personal space, territory, non-verbal communication)	With persistent failure of privacy regulation, severe stress, loss of personal identity

Source: Deaux and Wrightsman (1988)

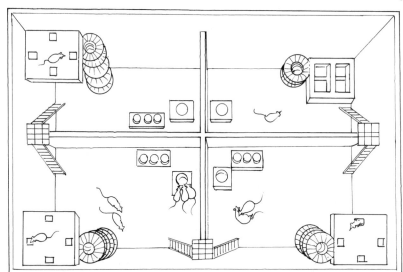

*Figure 7.14
The rat's universe used
by Calhoun*

on the 600th day. The population fell and by day 1,600 all the mice were dead. Environmental issues such as climate and predators were controlled for, and it was concluded that the death of the colony was caused by overcrowding alone.

Studies carried out in natural surroundings also find that there is a maximum animal population according to space available. Some studies found that density caused self-destructive behaviour (e.g. Dubos, 1965), and others found that there was decreased fertility (e.g. Snyder, 1966). Myers *et al.* (1971) found other physiological changes arising from crowding. Christian *et al.* (1960) studied sika deer in their natural environment. The population at one time was 300 deer, which was about one deer per acre. There was plenty of food. However, about half the deer died in the winter two years later and more died the next year, until there were about 80 deer in the herd, which stabilised at this number. The deer who died had enlarged adrenal glands, said to be a sign of prolonged stress. It was concluded that crowding was stressful, and led to the death of some of the deer until a reasonable size of herd was established.

Evaluation

- When applying findings from studies of animals to humans, we need to note that animals may be predetermined by their genes to respond to crowding in a certain way (Calhoun, 1971). There are important differences between animals and humans that need to be taken into account when considering the effect of crowding. Humans are influenced by social and cognitive factors, and can usually escape from a crowded environment, whereas the animals in the studies mentioned above could not escape. Another criticism of laboratory studies looking at crowding in animals is that they are unethical.

↻ Recall AS material

Recall AS material on ethics, and make a list of ethical principles regarding research using animals.

Self-test

Using the information above about Calhoun's studies, compare what Calhoun did with the ethical principles for using animals in research. Discuss whether his research was unethical, and why.

The effects of high-density living in humans

Laboratory studies

Some laboratory studies have been carried out to see what effect crowding has on humans. Evans (1978) found that participants in high-density situations have higher anxiety. Those who have control over the situation, even in high-density situations, are less anxious (Rodin *et al.*, 1978). Men seem more stressed by increases in spatial density, whereas women seem more anxious when social density increases (Fisher *et al.*, 1984). Marshall and Heslin (1975) found that high-density situations were less stressful if the group was oriented to the same goal, so the task is also an important variable.

Evaluation

- Laboratory studies are artificial, and are not valid. Crowding is a social phenomenon and needs to be studied in a real-life social setting. For example, the goals of the group are important and factors such as motivation are important. Laboratory studies isolate variables, and are unlikely to get valid findings. Some variables, such as gender and motivation, for example, go together, and a method where the whole situation is studied might be better.

Studying crowding in homes

There was a discussion earlier in this chapter about high-density living in humans, when the effects of architecture on resident satisfaction were examined. Newman explains the idea of defensible space, and how flats should not be in blocks too large for the residents to take ownership – not only of the flats, but also of the more public areas. Therefore, blocks of six flats, with only two storeys could be satisfactory. Large high-rise buildings, however, would not allow residents to take ownership of public areas. Halpern (1995) suggests that high-rise blocks lead to more mental illness amongst residents, especially in females. Usually it is in high-rise flats that the most high-density living is found.

Stokols *et al.* (1979) points out that crowding at home can have more serious consequences than crowding in a public place. For example, Riemer (1948) found that dissatisfaction of residents in Seattle was linked more to high-density living than to income or family size. In Riemer's survey, when density was 0.4 people per room or less (there were more rooms than people) 7% of the possible complaints on the survey were made. However, when density was more than 1 person per room (there were more people than rooms), 33% of the possible complaints were made. Kellett (1989) shows that high-density living gives more mental illness and psychological distress, and Tryon (1985) found more substance abuse. Galle and Gove (1979) reported more juvenile delinquency and higher fertility and mortality rates amongst those in high-density living. However, with social support these outcomes could be staved off (Evans *et al.*, 1989). Living alone, which also occurs in high-density living, can mean an individual has fewer social contacts and so less support when needed (Koller and Gosden, 1984).

Gottfried and Gottfried (1984) found that cognitive development of children was slower when in densely populated housing, although this was more true for boys than for girls. A case study also found that toddlers seem to be less approachable and less adaptable if they live in high-density housing (Wachs, 1988). Although some people are able to move from high-density housing, those who do not, and who have less choice about moving, report more symptoms of illness that those who can move (Stokols *et al.*, 1983).

In a crowded household children may receive less constructive attention, but could be hit more (Booth and Edwards, 1976). This might mean they spend more time out of doors and get into trouble on the streets. Such children also seem less able to take control when given the option than do children from low-density living (Rodin, 1976).

Table 7.5 Summary of studies on the effects of flat dwelling

Research	Effect of flat dwelling	Summary of results
Wilner *et al.* (1962)	Positive	Slum dwellers moved into new flats showed reduced accidents, slight improvement in health and very slight improvement in self-concept (USA)
Fanning (1967)	Negative	Army wives and children showed worse mental health in flats than houses. Strong methodology
DoE (1972)	Mixed	'No clear pattern' for differing designs in levels of psychosomatic symptoms
Bagley (1974)	Negative	Demographically similar house dwellers less neurotic and consulted their GPs less often for a 'nervous complaint' than flat dwellers
Moore (1974)	Mixed	Non-significant tendency for army wives to have higher symptoms and see GP more often, but compounded with other population differences
Goodman (1974)	Negative	Elevated episode rate in 0–4 year olds in deck-access flats, higher rates of mental illness in 45–60 year olds and higher rates of illness by height
Ineichen and Hooper (1974)	Mixed	Elevated behaviour problems with children in high rise, but physical and mental health of wives often even worse among house renters in urban centre
Richman (1974)	Negative	Matched families: higher levels of depression for women in flats but, if anything, worse rates in low rise. However, high-rise dwellers most dissatisfied
Moore (1976)	Negative	Same population as in Moore 1974. Found flat dwellers significantly more neurotic (personality scale) than house dwellers
Gittus (1976)	Negative	Mothers in flats reported significantly more psychosomatic symptoms than those in houses and more problems for children under 5, especially with more than one
Gillis (1977)	Mixed	Floor level positively associated with psychological strain in women, but negatively associated with strain in men
Saegert (1980)	Negative	Children in 14-storey buildings were more disturbed than equivalent children in a three-storey building
Edwards *et al.* (1982)	Negative	Men living in flats had elevated levels of symptoms (Langner-22) but no significant difference for women. Arguments with partners and children more frequent in flats
Hannay (1984)	Negative	Having controlled for age and sex, those living on the fifth floor or above were found to have significantly more psychiatric symptoms than those living on lower floors or in houses
Byrne *et al.* (1986)	Mixed	No main effect of housing type but strong interaction: levels of psychological distress significantly higher in bad areas when high rises

Source: Halpern (1995)

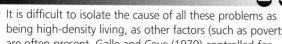

Evaluation

• It is difficult to isolate the cause of all these problems as being high-density living, as other factors (such as poverty) are often present. Galle and Cove (1979) controlled for poverty and found that rates of admission to mental hospital were related to density alone, as was, to a lesser extent, juvenile delinquency. Therefore, the link between mental illness and high-density living is quite strong. However, it was concluded that poverty is an important variable and hard to separate from high-density living.

- Other environmental stressors are also often present – for example, in high-rise flats there may only be one common entrance to many dwellings, and environmental features such as those criticised by Newman may be a large part of the problem. Terraced housing is a form of high-density living, but does not have the same levels of vandalism as high-rise flats; this is evidence that Newman is right when discussing the need for defensible space.

- Another factor associated with high-rise flats, which include high-density living, is the lack of social support. This lack of support was highlighted when looking at problems with the Pruitt-Igoe project. Studies suggest that blocks of flats can lead to more loneliness especially for women (e.g. Moore, 1975), although other studies have shown that in flats people can be less lonely (Churchman and Ginsburg, 1984; Moore, 1975). Problems with high-density living might not be due to the number of people involved but to the perceptions of the residents: they feel lonely, but at the same time lack privacy. So surveys tend to show that there is both loneliness and more social contact, and these problems could be causing any stress experienced, rather than the high-density living itself. If people living in flats either have to stay in the flat or be in the public areas, without any middle choice, then they are likely to be both lonely and lacking privacy. In flats where areas like play areas were planned in, there was more resident satisfaction.

- In Mitchell's (1971) study in Hong Kong (where there is a high density in households) no emotional distress was found. It was thought that cultural attitudes are also important. When dwellings were shared by people other than family, emotional problems due to overcrowding were found, so it seems that the family structure in Hong Kong means that a high-density household containing only family members is accepted.

Self-test

Write a timed essay under exam conditions (or as close as you can manage), using the title 'Discuss the effects of several sources of environmental stressors, and include a description of at least one study looking into the effects of environmental stress'.

Crowds and crowding

Theories of crowding

There are different theories of crowding. Some theories look at what makes an individual label a situation as 'crowded', and others focus on psychological processes that occur when someone feels crowded. Edney (1977) discusses theories of crowding and points out that theories differ in complexity, as well as underlying assumptions.

Freedman (1975) – density-intensity theory (a social theory)

Density is the focus of Freedman's (1975) theory; crowding is incidental. Freedman says that density is not itself harmful, but serves to focus on what is harmful. For example, density in prisons is a problem, but this is because prisons are bad places, not because of density itself – inmates have not chosen to be there, some of the population are unpleasant (to say the least) and architecturally prisons are not pleasing. If the atmosphere of any situation is pleasant, it will be a pleasant place even with high-density living.

Knowles (1983) – Social-physics model (a social theory)

Knowles argues that people are not distributed evenly, whereas measures of density assume that they are. Knowles suggests that there are other factors involved besides actual density – the distances between people are important, but whether there is crowding depends on whether the others form an audience, or whether the distance is short but there is a wall between. Social influence depends on the number of others and their distance from the individual. This approach uses physics to work out distances, and there is an area called psychophysics that uses similar laws.

Manning (1985) – another social theory

Manning suggests that who you meet and what they are doing is important – you will feel crowded if the people are different from you – for instance, if you are a hiker, and others are mountain bikers you may feel more crowded than if the others are hikers too. Other factors – such as if others are noisy and you are quiet, others are in a large group and you are on your own or in a small group – will increase the likelihood that you will feel crowded.

Barker (1968) and Wicker (1979) – a physical theory

Barker (1968) and Wicker (1979) discuss overstaffing, which is an ecological term referring to resource shortages. Physical resources can be desks in a school or computers in an office. Access to the available resources must be restricted to avoid crowding. Space must be similarly restricted, and if it is not overstaffing is like high-density living. Fischer (1976) shows how a shortage of space is only one type of crowding, and other shortages of resources can give the same feelings. Too many people or a shortage of resources are both 'overstaffing' or crowding. Whether we look at shortage of resources or too many people depends on which is the most easily changed.

Schmidt and Keating (1979) – crowding and personal control (a psychological theory)

Schmidt and Keating put forward the idea that there are three types of control, and if someone had any one of these types of control, then they would feel the effects of crowding less.

- **Cognitive control** – Information about crowding, such as letting someone know that it is going to happen, can give cognitive control. In these sorts of situations emotions about crowding are less negative.
- **Behavioural control** is when someone can act to avoid the crowding. For example, in a football match someone might not feel crowded when they are enjoying the game, but in the crush to get out of the match, they lose behavioural control as they are jostled, and then feel more negative emotion.
- When you have **decisional control**, for example, in a crowded cinema you can decide where to sit, then you feel less crowded. However, if there is only one seat left, and you cannot see the screen well, you may have more negative emotions.

Overload – a psychological theory

Another theory that looks at crowding as a psychological process is the idea that information overload gives the negative emotions. Milgram (1970) and Cohen (1978) talk about cities as places where there is stimulus overload, and too much information to take in. A person has a certain ability to process information and a preferred level of stimulation. If their ability to process information is not sufficient, or if the level of stimulation exceeds their preferred level, then they feel crowded. If neither of these conditions is the case then, even in a densely populated city, they will not feel crowded.

Theories of crowd behaviour

Crowd behaviour v. crowding

Theories of crowd behaviour are not the same as theories of crowding. 'Crowding' involves negative feelings, whereas 'crowd behaviour' refers to the actions of a crowd. People can feel crowded with only a few people around, or can be part of a crowd and not feel crowded – for example, if they are with like-minded people at a football match. 'Crowd behaviour' necessarily involves a lot of people. The feeling of crowding has to do with control, and with management of incoming information, whereas crowd behaviour is to do with what happens when someone is part of a group.

Theories of collective behaviour

Another term for crowd behaviour is **collective behaviour**, and this perhaps helps to distinguish theories of crowd behaviour from theories of crowding. Collective behaviour refers to large numbers of people acting in the same place at the same time in the same way, and where

there are strong emotions. Studies of crowd behaviour are not really linked to studies of crowding, although it could be argued that environmental conditions affect crowd behaviour. For example, if amount of control affects whether there is a negative feeling of being crowded, then a large group of individuals who feel they have no control over a situation may experience a great deal of negative emotion, which can lead to aggression and violence.

 Recall AS material

Recall your AS material especially from the social approach, where you may have studied crowd behaviour. If you can, define the term 'deindividuation'. Also note down theories of crowd behaviour if you already know about them. You have probably come across social identity theory, and should recall this theory now.

Contagion theory

LeBon (1903) was very concerned when he read about the crowds in the French Revolution, and realised that apparently civilised people seemed to become savages in such crowds. He suggested that just by being part of a crowd, humans become creatures acting on barbarian instinct. Crowds lead to primitive homogenous (similar) behaviour because:

- members are anonymous and so not responsible for their actions,
- ideas spread quickly through contagion, and
- unconscious antisocial motives are released.

LeBon's theory can be related to Freud's ideas, where the crowd unlocks unconscious desires. Civilised behaviour is in the superego, but in crowds the superego is replaced by the crowd leader, so superego control over each individual is lost, and the leader can release the impulses of the id.

Deindividuation

Another theory of crowd behaviour is **deindividuation**, which means that in a crowd people no longer act as individuals. Although the theory of deindividuation moves away from the idea that people in a crowd revert to primitive impulses, it agrees with LeBon in thinking that the anonymity of individuals in a crowd is important. Jung (1946) defined '**individuation**' as differentiating between individuals in order for their individual personality to develop, and Festinger et al. (1952) coined the word 'deindividuation' to mean individuals not being differentiated as having individual personalities. Zimbardo (1970) discussed the concept of deindividuation and developed the idea. In a large group individuals are anonymous and experience a loss of identity. Responsibility for actions and the consequences of actions can be shelved because the individual cannot be identified and held responsible. Deindividuation is this loss of identity, and means that behaviour becomes impulsive, irrational and disinhibited.

Festinger *et al.* (1952) found that participants who were dressed in a grey labcoat and were in a poorly lit room made more negative comments about their parents than when they were in ordinary lighting and ordinary clothing. Singer *et al.* (1965) found that participants in labcoats made more obscene comments when discussing erotic literature than did more easily identifiable participants. Zimbardo (1970) deindividuated participants by getting them to wear Ku Klux Klan type hoods and cloaks. In one of his studies female participants dressed in the cloaks and hoods gave electric shocks to a female confederate that were twice as long as the shocks given by female participants who were not deindividuated, and who wore normal clothing. In another study Zimbardo found that participants who were deindividuated as 'guards' were prepared to be quite brutal towards other participants who were 'prisoners'.

Diener *et al.* (1976) used children who were trick-or-treating on Halloween night. Children were invited into 27 homes, either alone or in groups, and told to take one of the sweets from the table. Half of the children were asked their names and where they lived, so that they were not deindividuated. The other half was deindividuated, because their names were not known. When in groups the children were to an extent also deindividuated. The researchers watched to see who took more than one of the sweets – which children disobeyed. When children were in groups or deindividuated they were more likely to take more than one sweet – around 8% of the individuated children took more than one sweet, whereas up to 80% of deindividuated children did so.

Evaluation

- These studies conclude that being anonymous increases the likelihood of antisocial behaviour – however, there are studies that have disputed the above claims.

- Zimbardo (1970) used his deindividuation procedure, where participants with hoods and cloaks gave shocks to confederates, on Belgian soldiers. Wearing the cloaks and hoods (when deindividuated), the soldiers gave fewer shocks. It was thought that soldiers were already in a group and deindividuated because of the uniform and the role, so when a disguise was used they were in some ways less deindividuated.

- Johnson and Downing (1979) used a similar procedure to Zimbardo's but had a nurse's uniform as well as the hood and cloak disguise. Half of the participants also wore a name badge to reduce deindividuation. In this study deindividuation did not increase aggression (measured by

the participant giving increased electric shocks). Those in the hood and cloak gave no difference in level of shock whether they were deindividuated or not (meaning whether they had a name badge or not). People wearing the nurse's uniform gave fewer shocks if deindividuated by not having a name badge. This last finding contradicts Zimbardo's original study.

- It is concluded that aggression and antisocial behaviour do not automatically occur when someone is anonymous.

- Expectations about the situation also affect behaviour. Those in Zimbardo's original experiment may have thought that as they had been dressed as Ku Klux Klan members they ought to act in an antisocial manner; the people wearing nurse's uniforms may have thought that they ought to act in a prosocial manner. It is not quite clear, however, why those who had no name badge and wore the nurse's uniform were even less antisocial.

- Jahoda (1982) points out that wearing the hood and cloak is similar to wearing the chadoor – a full-length veil worn by women in some Islamic countries. The chadoor brings with it very clear social responsibilities and a social role about how to behave. Clothing can give information about roles and expected behaviour, and this backs up the point above that the participants may have behaved in an expected manner.

The environment and deindividuation
The main claim about deindividuation is that it can lead to more aggressive and antisocial behaviour, so people in crowds may behave in a way they would not behave in when alone. Prentice-Dunn and Rogers (1982) found that participants working on a group task who could not become self-aware because they had to listen to loud rock music, and were in a dark room, gave stronger electric shocks to a learner than participants who worked in a quiet well-lit room. If the environment leads to feelings of deindividuation, more antisocial or aggressive behaviour may result. The design of an area needs to take this into account, and to attend to issues such as lighting and areas where people can be anonymous. Newman's ideas of defensible space included the suggestion that public areas should be overlooked by residents so that they become secondary territory, where people are not anonymous and deindividuated.

Emergent norm theory
A crowd may initially have no norms but norms may emerge. Crowd behaviour, according to emergent norm theory, is not instinctive, but is collective behaviour that will be governed by norms just like any other behaviour (Turner, 1974). It is assumed that people in a crowd have at first no clear norms, but that they attend to certain distinctive individuals within the crowd. Once there are distinctive behaviours, this gives a norm, and acting in a different manner to this norm would then not be conforming. Also if the majority do not do anything, this

will confirm that the distinctive behaviour is the norm, and there will be even more pressure for the rest to conform. These distinctive behaviours must be noticeable and unusual, and are, therefore, often antisocial and aggressive. These aggressive acts can then emerge as the norm, and this explains why people in crowds do things they would not do as individuals.

Evaluation

- Diener (1980) points out that to follow norms in this way the people in the crowd must be self-aware, and it seems that they are not – usually they are deindividuated.

- Reicher (1982) points out that crowds do not often get together without a reason, and if there is a reason, then there are norms.

Convergent theory

Usually group norms converge towards a common norm. This can happen in a crowd, and can explain crowd behaviour. Hoekstra and Wilke (1972) studied how managers made recommendations about the wages of workers. First the managers made the recommendations individually, and then worked in groups of about five. A total of 432 managers participated; they took into account the output of each worker when making recommendations. Overall the group decision was an average of the individual recommendations so it seemed that there was a convergence, and all the individual recommendations were taken into account. This was a cross-cultural study and there were interesting cultural differences in the group decisions. People from Belgium, the USA and Holland were less generous in their recommendations than those from the UK, Greece, Spain and Italy. So it seems that groups converge to a common norm, but also that individual views, as well as variables like cultural factors, affect group norms.

The environment and crowd behaviour

When designing buildings and areas, issues such as crowd behaviour – indeed issues about social interactions as a whole – are important because crowds can show antisocial, aggressive behaviour. Whether norms converge or emerge, it is likely that aggressive behaviour results, and planners want to design areas that are pleasant for people to live in. Cities such as Barcelona were planned on a grid system so that there was no central place and all areas had an equal amount of land and equal access to resources. It was hoped that ghettos would be avoided. However, elsewhere it has been shown that the way territory is defended tends to mean that people group together in like-minded groups, so it is likely in some ways that ghettos will develop. Attempts are made to see that large groups of disadvantaged people are not put together – to prevent norms from being established –

where such norms could be aggressive or antisocial behaviour. These sorts of issues were also tackled by Newman's ideas of defensible space. If people are not deindividuated, but areas are overlooked and ownership is taken of them, then aggressive collective behaviour is less likely.

Self-test

1　Write a timed essay under exam conditions (or as close as you can manage), using the title 'Discuss the effects of high-density living on humans'.

2　Write a timed essay under exam conditions (or as close as you can manage), using the title 'Discuss two theories of crowding' – remember to note the difference between theories of crowding and theories of crowd behaviour. For this question, only give theories of crowding.

Changing behaviour to save the environment

Why behaviour is not environmentally friendly

Most people agree that there is a need for us to manage environmental resources – to manage the rate and quality of each person's use of natural resources (including manufactured items made using natural resources). Management is done at a macrolevel by governments and organisations, and also at a microlevel by individuals and small groups. Environmental psychology focuses on a microlevel first. As individuals we tend to watch our own use of resources, observe how this affects the environment, and have an understanding of what resources other people are using.

Short-term self-interest v long-term public interest

When resources are limited and held in common – not owned by any one person – there is a problem. If there is free access to resources, people will make consistently higher demands upon the resources, if they pursue their own interests. The term '**commons**' is used to describe any resource held by a group of individuals, rather than owned by one individual. Where the resource does not renew itself quickly, there is even more of a problem. 'Commons' was a term applied to an area of land in a village that anyone could use. Although in theory all villagers would benefit equally from this free use of land, in practice some would benefit more. For example, if they grazed cattle on the land they could perhaps afford more cattle, and would put greater demand upon the commons. In this way resources can easily be depleted. Gifford (1997) explains how we are actually depleting resources more quickly since becoming environmentally aware in the 1970s. Hardin (1968a, b) has examined the 'tragedy of the commons' and says we need to stop free access to resources. This idea is looked at in more detail below.

Others say that individuals will not selfishly take resources but will act in the public interest, for example, using litterbins or turning down thermostats. However, in the short-term it is more rewarding to act in one's own self-interest. This can be done by '**taking**' or '**harvesting**', for example, cutting down a protected tree – or by '**giving**', for example, dumping rubbish on the side of a road. Acting in the public interest, for example, taking rubbish to a rubbish tip, is more time-consuming and difficult, so is less rewarding. It could, therefore, be concluded that self-serving behaviour is natural, and from there it can be concluded that it is a permanent part of human nature.

Commons dilemmas, social traps and social dilemmas

There are two ways that environmental psychologists have looked at the problem of resource management. One group of psychologists looks at decision-making in general, and another looks at resource management directly from the viewpoint of environmental concerns. Some of this second group, which is the group focused on here, looks at the 'commons dilemma', others look at the idea of a 'social trap', and others look at a 'social dilemma'.

These three terms are defined as:
- **Commons dilemma** – the way natural resources are overused because there is a conflict between individual interests and group interests, as outlined earlier.
- **Social trap** – the time trap where, when people act in order to get immediate rewards, there is some gradually building cost, rather than an immediate large cost due to their behaviour. Examples are smoking and overeating. The use of the insecticide DDT is an example of a social trap, as it kills mosquitoes but gradually reduces the fertility of the birds that eat the insects (Gifford, 1997).
- **Social dilemma** – a term covering the commons dilemma and social traps. Something is a social dilemma when (a) a person receives more for choosing self-interest over public interest, (b) a group of people benefit more if they act in the public interest than in

self-interest. This is a dilemma in that an individual benefits by being selfish, but when part of a group he or she benefits more by acting in the public interest.

The question is, when will people act in the public interest? In order to persuade people not to act in their own interest, but to manage resources to help everyone, it is necessary to understand such questions. There are four main influences on people when deciding whether to act in an environmentally friendly manner:
- Is the resource important, plentiful or scarce? (Focus on the resource.)
- Are the individuals young, experienced, old, holding competitive values? (Focus on the people.)
- Are the individuals acting as a group, do they know about one another, and do they trust each other? (Focus on the group.)
- Are the individuals told about the social trap, are they communicating, is there a leader? (Focus on the situation.)

Evaluation

- Methods used tend to be simulations and games. People are given resources, and asked to make decisions. Sometimes they 'play' alone, and sometimes in groups. There are problems in drawing conclusions from simulations about real-life decision making. For example, consider the idea of people escaping from a burning plane. We can see if they are self-interested or if they help one another, and we are likely to find out more if we look at a real situation than if we ask participants to role play the situation. Similarly if they role play in a real plane, with simulated smoke and so on, we might obtain more valid information than if a board game is used. These sorts of criticisms are useful when evaluating the studies that follow, and which draw conclusions about whether people are likely to be environmentally friendly or not.

Behaviour and the environment

Many different factors affect whether people act in an environmentally friendly way or not. Some of these are examined briefly below.

Environmentally friendly behaviour is less likely if the resource is in demand

There is no problem if the resource is not desired. Mintz (1951) carried out a study where groups of 15–21 participants were asked to pull small cones through the narrow neck of a bottle. There were strings attached to the cones, and all participants had to get their cones through the same bottle neck. When there was no reward for pulling the cones out, there was no 'bottleneck' – that is cones were not queued up waiting to be pulled through – as nobody was in a hurry to pull the cones out, and waited their turn. However, when rewards of 10–25 cents were

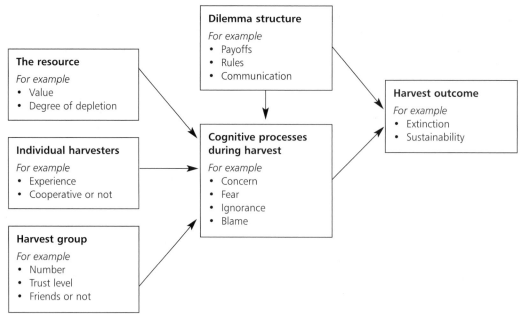

Figure 7.15
An overview of the natural resource management process (Source: Gifford, 1997)

given per cone, and fines of 1–10 cents imposed for failing to get cones out, then there were frequent 'traffic jams' as individuals competed to pull the cones out of the neck of the bottle. The resource is the neck of the bottle, and when rewards are low, the resource is not in demand and group co-operation is high. However, when the rewards are higher, the resource is in demand and co-operation in the group is low. So environmentally friendly behaviour is likely to be lower when the resource is in demand.

A real-life example of the above situation is when there is a fire and fresh air and space are valuable resources as everyone tries to escape. Given the above explanation, it is expected (and found) that in this situation co-operation is low, and there are often tragic consequences. If people realise that co-operation will lead to greater gain – for example, the group realise they will get more cones or have a better chance of escaping from the fire by co-operating – then they will co-operate. However, the value of co-operation might not be realised.

Behaviour becomes more environmentally friendly when the resource is half damaged

Studies have examined a situation where the resource is half damaged to see if there is co-operation to stop destroying the resource altogether, or self-interest where the individual gets what he or she can while there is the opportunity. For example, if pollution already exists, will the users continue to degrade it (pollute) even more, or will they co-operate to stop the situation getting worse? Watzke *et al.* (1972) found that there is co-operation in a half-degraded situation, which suggests that behaviour becomes environmentally friendly once the situation has

deteriorated enough. However, it seems that we act selfishly until there is a problem. In a real-life situation then, when a problem gets bad enough we are likely to get together to stop it getting worse but until then we act in our own interest.

Behaviour becomes less environmentally friendly when the resource starts to diminish

If the resource is half used up (as in lack of oil for fuel) rather than damaged (as in polluted air), then behaviour is different. It seems that we co-operate until the resource begins to be used up and then as the resource becomes scarce we stop co-operating (Brechner, 1976). Resources decline at different rates, and this affects whether people start to take more for themselves. Brann and Foddy (1987) found that if individuals are trusting they will start to take more as time goes on and the resource starts to diminish. However, if they are less trusting, people take the resource at the same rate, and do not adjust their taking according to how quickly the resource is diminishing. So an individual's character is important, and possibly their past experiences.

Behaviour is more environmentally friendly if we think the resource is depleting through natural causes, but less environmentally friendly if we think other people are causing the depletion

Rutte *et al.* (1987) found that people were willing to take less if they thought a resource was diminishing due to natural causes. However, if they thought that other people were causing the resource to diminish, they wanted more of it too. So it seems that the cause of the loss of the resource affects people's behaviour.

Behaviour is less environmentally friendly if we do not know how much of the resource is left, but we think it is diminishing

Hine and Gifford (1993) found that if people were not sure if the resource was diminishing, they were more likely to take it. This could be because people don't believe that the resource is diminishing or because they are acting in self-interest. Uncertainty leads them to continue in their own way, rather than to co-operate to prevent loss of the resource.

Older children (up to the age of 14) are more environmentally friendly, in that they will co-operate over resources

Nursery school children tend to be self-interested. Gifford (1982) carried out a study using children aged from 3 to 16 years and found that the older the child the more he or she would co-operate. At the age of 14 the best use of resources was made but at 16 there was a drop in co-operation. Edney (1979) found in a study of 18–20 year olds that co-operation dropped in the older participants. Bixenstein and Douglas (1967) found, however, that co-operation increased slightly between the ages of 18 and 40. It does seem that young children will act in self-interest whereas older children will co-operate. However, findings of studies are a bit contradictory.

Knowledge of environmental issues leads to more environmentally friendly behaviour

Knowledge of the commons dilemma, or a better understanding of the issues, means more co-operation (Tindall and O'Connor, 1987). Also, if knowledge has involved managing a commons dilemma single-handedly, then this leads to better management next time (Allison and Messick, 1985). It is possible that if an individual deals with the problem, they learn more about the overall situation. Knowledge of environmental issues is also more likely to lead to responsible behaviour (Hines *et al.*, 1986). This links back to the idea of uncertainty (it was said earlier that if someone is uncertain about whether a resource is depleting, they are likely to continue to act in their own self-interest).

Environmental behaviour is often conforming to what others are doing

Conformity is likely in the commons dilemma situations, because when people are not sure of all the issues they are likely to conform (e.g. Fleishman, 1988). If others are acting in self-interest (and it seems that when people are uncertain they do), then those conforming will also act in self-interest. However, if people are acting in an environmentally friendly way – because they have knowledge of the issues, for example – then others will conform to this environmentally friendly behaviour.

Environmentally friendly behaviour decreases as the group size increases

Co-operation decreases as the group size increases (Dawes, 1980). This seems to be because as the group gets bigger any problems caused by one person acting in self-interest are less noticeable. Also it does less harm, and it is harder for the group to sustain negative feedback to prevent defection. Edney (1981) suggests that after a group reaches 150 members' defection becomes more likely. It seems that in larger commons, such as cities, co-operation is unlikely and self-interest is more likely.

Changing attitudes and behaviour

It has been claimed that people conform to the behaviour of others, and that knowledge of environmental issues can promote environmentally friendly behaviour. Changing attitudes is one way of improving environmentally friendly behaviour, and planning a system of rewards and punishments is another.

Using rewards and punishments to encourage environmentally friendly behaviour

If the reward is high enough there is no dilemma

Whether people act in an environmentally responsible way depends on issues such as previous knowledge, understanding of the issues, the particular resource and the patterns of reward and punishment for taking the resource. It might be worth rewarding environmentally friendly behaviour and setting a penalty for non-co-operation. Dawes (1980), however, points out that if the reward for co-operation is high enough then there is no dilemma. The dilemma is whether to act in one's own interests for short-term gain, or to co-operate (against one's own short-term interests) for everyone's greater good in the long term. If the reward for acting against one's own interests is high enough, then the dilemma no longer exists. However, it is unlikely that there is sufficient reward available to reach that state. For example, governments could not afford to pay poachers as much as they would get for selling rhino horns (Gifford, 1997). Allison and Messick (1990) suggest that smaller rewards (for example, a lower price for rhino horns) leads to less plundering of the resource, and higher rewards (for example, higher prices) leads to more harvesting of the resource. If rewards for environmentally friendly behaviour are high enough, there is no problem. Alternatively, if rewards are higher for not behaving in an environmentally friendly manner there is no dilemma – the person simply acts in their own well rewarded self-interest.

Positive incentives are better than punishment – but findings of studies are contradictory

Positive incentives to stop individuals from using up resources can work, and are more useful than negative incentives (Komorita and Barth, 1985). However, Wit and Wilke (1990) found that punishments and rewards were equally effective.

Evaluation

• Note that all these studies are using *simulations* of the commons dilemma and not the real thing, so findings must be interpreted with the lack of validity in mind.

Rewards are relative

It may not be the actual size of the reward that is important but the relative size. Kelley and Grzelak (1972) varied the size of individual rewards and the size of the reward for the group. Increasing the reward for the whole group had less effect on individual selfish behaviour than if the reward for the individual only was increased. It seems that if an individual receives a reward that is large in relation to the reward for others, co-operation is more likely. However, in other studies (e.g. Edney and Bell, 1983) individuals were told that the winnings of the whole group would be equally divided at the end, and this gave more co-operation than if the reward structure was that each individual won as much as they could.

Evaluation

• There might be a problem with the simulation here, in that the rules are too complex (Edney and Harper, 1978). It might be that the participants simply acted in self-interest because they only understood some of the rules, rather than choosing that course of action.

Table 7.6 Use of rewards and punishments to encourage environmentally friendly behaviour

• If rewards for not acting in a self-interested manner are great enough there is no problem, but governments cannot afford this course of action
• If rewards are high for acting in a self-interested manner then people are likely to continue to do so
• Positive rewards are better then punishment, although both can work
• Rewards must be compared with what others get. It is not the reward itself but whether it is more than can be obtained in other ways
• An example of increasing environmentally friendly behaviour is to encourage people to use public transport by ensuring that it is cheaper than private transport, and to punish the use of private transport, for example, by making it expensive. Rewards could be offered when people use car pools, car tax has been reduced for cars with small engines, and special lanes to help traffic to flow more easily are being considered for cars with more than one passenger.

Evaluation

• A problem is that, although behaviour may change, it may change only as long as the rewards and punishments remain. Attitudes may not have changed, and individuals might revert to the original behaviour. In the short-term the change to environmentally friendly behaviour may help, but in the long-term it is better to change attitudes.

• Studies have been done to see how far a reward system works to encourage environmentally friendly behaviour. Later in this chapter studies looking at recycling are used to evaluate how useful rewards are.

Changing attitudes

Dawes (1980) suggests that if individuals are told about the situation – for example, about the benefits of co-operation, about public interest, about resource exploitation – they would co-operate more.

Communication

Communication between individuals increases co-operation (e.g. Brechner, 1976) – people can clarify the payoffs, reach agreements on who takes what, reduce distrust, enhance group identity, encourage commitment to co-operation, agree to penalties for not co-operating, and make others promise to co-operate (Gifford, 1997). Communication can also hold a group together. In simulations when a confederate is introduced into the game and is selfish, the others do not stop co-operating if communication is good (Jerdee and Rosen, 1974). However, in the real world communication is often not easy. Someone has to take the time to plan the communication and to make it happen.

Persuasive communication – The Yale model

According to Schwerin and Newell (1981), behavioural change cannot occur without a change in attitude. Although a system of rewards and punishments can change behaviour, this change is more likely to be a stable one if attitudes have changed. Persuasive communication refers to a message intended to change an attitude, as well as the behaviours of an audience. Hovland worked at Yale University and investigated wartime propaganda on

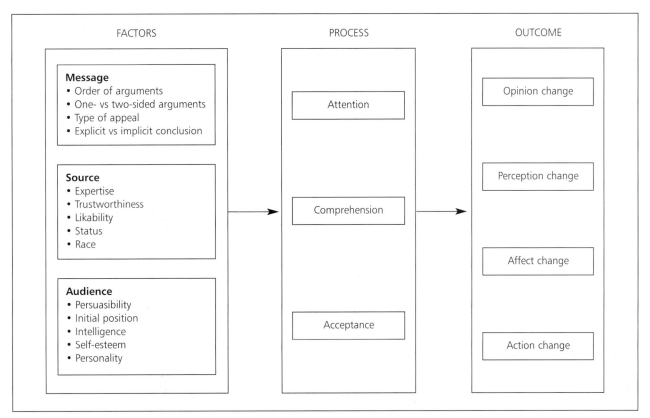

Figure 7.16
The Yale approach to communication and persuasion (Source: Hogg and Vaughan, 1998; based on Fishbein and Ajzen, 1975)

behalf of the US War Department. He was the first to look at the social psychology of persuasion. It was thought that to understand how to change attitudes it was necessary to look at the person giving the message, the content of the message, and characteristics of the receiver of the message (Hovland *et al.*, 1953).

The Yale approach looks at the source, the message and the audience. The Yale model suggests that there are four steps in the process of persuasion:
- attention (the message must be attended to)
- comprehension (the message must be understood)
- acceptance (the message must be accepted)
- retention (the message must be retained and remembered).

Many people think that advertising and other sorts of persuasive communication work only with other people, and not with themselves. This is called the **third-person effect** (e.g. Duck *et al.*, 1995).

Various factors affect how well attitudes are changed by persuasive communication (Hogg and Vaughan, 1998):
- Experts are believed more than non-experts (Hovland and Weiss, 1952).
- Rapid speakers are believed more than slow speakers (Miller *et al.*, 1976).

- Messages that are not thought to be intended to persuade us are better believed (Walster and Festinger, 1962).
- Popular and attractive speakers are better believed (Kiesler and Kiesler, 1969).
- People with low self-esteem are more easily persuaded (Janis, 1954).
- Messages involving fear persuade people more easily (Leventhal *et al.*, 1965).
- Simple messages persuade more easily if someone is not paying full attention (Allyn and Festinger, 1961).
- Presenting both sides of a message is more effective if the audience is hostile (Hovland *et al.*, 1949).
- People are more easily persuaded if the speaker is similar to the receiver in some way (Petty and Cacioppo, 1981), but only when the message is about likes and dislikes. When the message is about facts, speakers that are dissimilar are believed more (Goethals and Nelson, 1973).

Evaluation

- Many of the above studies took place in laboratory or unnatural conditions. This means that generalising from the findings to real-life examples such as trying to encourage environmentally friendly behaviour should be done with care.

- Mainly single variables are isolated for study, whereas interactions between people, such as communicating to persuade, involve many different variables. Some studies have been done where more than one variable has been studied, but these are still done by isolating variables rather than by studying the whole situation, and could lose sight of what is actually of interest.

- Messages studied are usually to do with persuading someone to buy a certain product, which concern people in different ways from messages about the environment.

- Lewin (1943) suggested that persuasion was best done by action research, where those whose attitude 'needs' to change are actively involved in researching the message. This suggests that to persuade people to change to more environmentally friendly behaviour they must discuss the issues, rather than being told about them. Action research considers the interactional part of persuasion more than Hovland and his colleagues did.

Changing attitudes – encouraging environmentally friendly behaviour

The above studies give some idea of the sorts of variables that need to be attended to when considering how to use persuasive communication to change attitudes. There are many other variables, such as the gender of the speaker and the receiver, and whether facts are more persuasive than appealing to someone's feelings. Promotional literature must take into account such factors if attitudes are to change.

For example, a factual message about resource depletion might be more persuasive if given by an expert. However, if the message aims to change someone's feelings, then the message might be believed more if given by someone similar to the receiver. Similarly, the message is better received if given by someone attractive and popular, and if the speaker talks quickly it will seem that they know what they are talking about, so they will be better believed.

Evaluation

- Studies have been done that look at different sorts of behaviour to do with the environment. Recycling is considered below, and studies looking at how to improve recycling behaviour also evaluate the usefulness of promotional literature and other forms of persuasion.

Recycling

It is in our own interests to get rid of the rubbish that we build up, and the easiest way is to throw everything away for others to collect. However, it is in the public interest that we recycle whatever is possible. Reusing resources is in the interest of the majority, and there is a need to change attitudes, and make people recycle more.

Resource recovery, recycling and reclamation

- **Resource recovery** involves recycling and reclamation.
- **Recycling** processes rubbish back into the original product using the same resources.
- **Reclamation** is when the waste material is used again but to make a different product (Geller *et al.*, 1982).

For example, recycled paper can be used to make toilet paper and bags. Reclaimed tyres can be used to make paving mix. Often the word 'recycling' is used to mean any sort of resource recovery.

Recycling by technical means or behavioural means

Resources can be recovered either by technical means or by behavioural means. Technical means of resource recovery involve sorting and recovery of materials at a central plant. This can be expensive, but the consumer does not have to change his or her behaviour. This is therefore, in the short-term, an attractive solution. Most individuals will not consider the long-term cost to them, although it is quite high.

If resource recovery is seen as a behaviour problem, then focus is on persuading consumers to change their behaviour. Individuals must reduce their use of materials, separate their rubbish according to the materials involved, and deliver their prepared rubbish to some central place perhaps. In the short-term this is a less attractive option for the consumer than to simply put all their waste materials in the bin. However, the public choice would be the behavioural means of resource recovery, as it is less expensive overall.

Recycling – a commons dilemma

Recycling/reclamation (in what follows, the term 'recycling' is used to mean both recycling and reclamation unless otherwise stated) is a commons dilemma. A commons dilemma is the term used in environmental psychology to refer to the way natural resources are overused because there is a conflict between individual interests and group interests. The waste materials are commons, in that they are resources not owned by an individual. If the individual acts in their own self-interest, they will discard waste materials without sorting them. If the individual acts for the public good, and in an environmentally friendly manner, then they will sort their waste materials ready for recycling and reclamation. The dilemma is whether to act for self-interest or the public good.

Gifford (1997) suggests that one community of around 200,000 people would save 70,000 trees in one year if the recycling rate was about 68%. This community's actions would divert about 4% of the waste material to being recycled. In the USA the average percentage of rubbish that is recycled and reclaimed is 2.5%.

Who recycles?

About 81% of college students said they recycled (Williams, 1991) and about 58% of community householders said they recycled (Oskamp *et al.*, 1991). However, self-reports may not be accurate. The claims about recycling made by householders with high incomes are higher than those made by low-income householders, but these claims are not always true (McGuire, 1984). Many studies (e.g. Lansana, 1992) found that those who knew more about environmental issues recycled more. This ties in with what was claimed earlier – that those who are more aware of environmental issues act in a more environmentally friendly manner. People who recycle also have higher incomes and more education (Katsev *et al.*, 1993). In the USA it seems that White people recycle most, then Black, and then Hispanic, but Howenstine (1993) points out that this may be more due to access to recycling facilities than to race differences.

Encouraging recycling – evaluating persuasion and reward systems

Hopper and Nielson (1991), Burn and Oskamp (1986) and DeYoung *et al.* (1993) all found that persuasion, in the form of speeches, personal communication and pamphlets, works. Katzev and Mishima (1992) found that reminding people to recycle by using labels also worked. Shrum *et al.* (1994) suggest that techniques used in advertising to sell products should be used to sell recycling.

Diamond and Loewy (1991) found that positive reinforcement changed attitudes (the use of reinforcement in general was discussed earlier in this chapter). Lord (1994) found that positive reinforcement changed attitudes, and a negative message changed behaviour.

A study to persuade people to recycle was carried out in a Virginia university (Witmer and Geller, 1976). This study used persuasion with promotional literature and reward systems. Although the university already had an educational campaign about recycling, leaflets were delivered to all students in two dormitories once a week. Less than 3% of the residents responded, but by recycling, these people produced about 20 kg of paper each week. Two reward systems were also used. In one a $15 prize was offered to the dormitory that recycled the most paper. This reward system yielded around 250 kg of paper, which is a lot more than was produced by flyers alone. In the second reward system raffle tickets were given out for each half kilo of paper recycled. There was $80 worth of prizes. This system yielded 370 kg a week.

- Rewards increased recycling, but without the prizes recycling behaviour fell back to the original level.

- Prompting recycling behaviour, for example by using signs, seemed to work for longer. Austin *et al.* (1993) found that signs close to bins can increase recycling behaviour, although the signs must be placed in the right place.

- The reward system is not very suitable: the prizes for being the best dormitory cost $45 but the paper brought in was sold for only $20; the raffle prizes cost $240 but the paper was sold for only around $40. Winkler and Winett (1982) suggest that we need to make the rewards less than the value of the recycled materials for a reward system to be effective, especially considering the rewards have to be kept up.

- Studies are done out of interest, and labour costs, for example, are not taken into account. However, if a reward system were to be used as a way of encouraging environmentally friendly behaviour in general, then labour costs would need to be covered – and this would be too expensive.

- It seems that signs and reminders are the cheapest and most effective way of changing recycling behaviour.

Using block leaders to encourage recycling

Another way of encouraging environmentally friendly behaviour is to nominate one person to encourage neighbours to recycle (Hopper and Neilson, 1991). Burn (1991) found that if block leaders approached neighbours to encourage recycling, this worked well. Using block leaders was more successful than sending written requests. Kahle and Beatty (1987) found that environmentally friendly behaviour increased even more when the person encouraging such behaviour was a 'significant other', which means the person was important to the person being encouraged.

Making a commitment to recycling, and being given feedback

Making a commitment to recycle materials also works (Burn and Oskamp, 1986). Wang and Katsev (1990) found that recycling behaviour increased by 47% if residents were asked as a group to make a commitment. When students were asked to make a personal commitment the recycling behaviour increased more than when they made a commitment when in a group, so personal commitments count for more. Making a personal commitment means the recycling behaviour lasts longer than if rewards are given, which is good news given that making a commitment is cheaper. Goldenhar (1991) found that people given feedback about the amount recycled showed more recycling behaviour than those educated about the need for recycling, so feedback about actual behaviour is more effective than education.

ACTIVITY

Choose an example of environmentally unfriendly behaviour, such as tankers leaking oil and causing oil pollution. Decide how a reward and punishment system could encourage environmentally friendly behaviour, and how promotional literature might work. You might be able to find an example of where these two strategies have been used (for example, in encouraging car sharing or the use of public transport). Compare the advantages and disadvantages of each strategy, given the evaluations outlined above.

Self-test

1 Link the ideas of operant conditioning to what was said earlier in this chapter about the use of a system of rewards and punishments to encourage environmentally friendly behaviour. Think about how often rewards need to be given, and whether punishment is less effective than positive reward. Draw some advice from the theory as to how a reward and punishment system could operate.

2 Link ideas from the social learning approach to claims that a personal approach from someone in the community can encourage recycling behaviour. Should this be someone similar to the person who needs encouraging? Earlier in this section it was said that those who are similar to the 'audience' do better in encouraging different ideas and attitudes, but that if facts are needed, then someone different (an expert) is better. Link these claims to the underlying assumptions and claims of social learning theory (e.g. what type of model is best?)

Synoptic Note

In Unit 6, the synoptic part of the course, you will need to think about issues such as the contribution a particular approach has made either to research or to society. It could be claimed that suggesting a system

of rewards and punishments to encourage recycling behaviour is an example of a contribution of the learning approach. Similarly, the social learning approach is drawn upon when considering who is a good model for giving a message in an advertising campaign, for example. You could use this material when answering a question for Unit 6.

Air pollution

Adding to air pollution is a 'giving' dilemma, whereas using up resources and not recycling is a 'taking' dilemma. Using up resources like trees (when using paper) and not trying to cut down on this use (by recycling or reclamation) is 'taking' from the environment. Adding to air pollution is 'giving' to the environment (in a negative sense).

Myths about air pollution (Gifford, 1997)

* *Air pollution is a big city problem* – Stewart et al. (1974) found air pollution residues in the blood samples of people living in the country.
* *Air pollution is a new problem* – Air quality is better now than it was in many industrial cities 100 years ago.
* *Air pollution is an outdoor problem* – There is air pollution indoors as well as outside.
* *Factories cause most air pollution* – Rose and Rose (1971) showed that 80 million tons of carbon monoxide are released into the atmosphere in North America each year from transport sources.
* *Incineration works to destroy toxins* – Burning does not destroy poisons, and particulates go into the air.

Effects of air pollution

Sommers et al. (1976) showed that air pollution causes health problems – and it also causes behaviour problems. For example, behaviour can be constrained by air pollution, if children cannot go outside to play. There are cognitive effects, for example, excessive levels of carbon monoxide can mean slower reaction time or arithmetic ability (Schulte, 1963). Slower reaction time can mean worse driving ability, so these cognitive impairments may have important consequences. Studies looked at car accidents to see if there were more at times of the day when carbon monoxide levels might be higher, for example, at rush hour. Findings are inconclusive, although some studies show small but significant correlations between accident rates and carbon monoxide levels (Sommers *et al.*, 1976). Jones and Bogat (1978) compared participants who had been exposed to cigarette smoke and those who had not and found that those who had were more aggressive. Briere *et al.* (1983) found that a psychiatric emergency room was more full when air pollution was higher. Even though their study was only a correlational study, and does not mean that air pollution causes mental health problems, it might show that air pollution is a factor that adds to mental health problems.

Demanding cleaner air

In general people do not demand cleaner air. It seems that we adapt without realising it because air pollution arises gradually. Sommer (1972) suggests that some air pollution in clean air will be noticed, but when air quality is poor in any case, a small rise in pollution is not noticed. This could apply to all areas of resource management – a small amount of litter in a clean area would be frowned upon, but a bit more litter in a messy area might not be noticed. Another problem is the cost of doing something about pollution. Wall (1973) points out that people do not want to complain about a factory if their jobs depend on that factory. Also someone may want to cycle to work but the 'cost' in terms of time, lack of comfort, and inconvenience is too great. This is the commons dilemma – where self-interest means environmentally friendly behaviour is less likely.

Self-test

1 Write a timed essay under exam conditions (or as close as you can manage) using the title 'Discuss why behaviour is often not environmentally friendly in terms of recycling'.

2 Write a timed essay under exam conditions (or as close as you can manage) using the title 'Discuss ways of changing attitudes by use of promotional literature, and link these to environmental issues such as recycling'.

Suggested reading

Cave, S. (1998) *Applying Psychology to the Environment*. London: Hodder & Stoughton.

Gifford, R. (1997) *Environmental Psychology*, Second Edition. Boston: Allyn and Bacon.

Halpern, D. (1995) *Mental Health and the Built Environment. More than Bricks and Mortar?* London: Taylor and Francis.

Hewstone, M., Stroebe, W. and Stephenson, G.M. (1996) *Introduction to Social Psychology*. Oxford: Blackwell Publishers.

Hogg, M.A. and Vaughan, G.M. (1998) *Social Psychology*, Second Edition. Englewood Cliffs, N.J.: Prentice Hall.

8 Health psychology

The aims of this chapter

The aims of this chapter are to enable the reader to:

- *give an account of what health psychology is*
- *define terms involved when looking at substance abuse*
- *describe how drugs work in terms of neurotransmitters and synaptic functioning*
- *discuss effects and consequences, including addiction, of taking drugs*
- *understand the concept of stress*
- *discuss some causes of stress*
- *discuss coping strategies and resources in coping with stress*
- *discuss primary prevention and health education programmes*
- *discuss the health belief model and the theory of reasoned action.*

STUDY AID

When you have finished working through this chapter you should write an essay about, or at least test yourself on, each of the above points. This will help you to see how good your knowledge and understanding of health psychology is.

This chapter covers

In preparation for this chapter, recall or look up your AS material covering:
- the physiological approach, especially neurones and synaptic transmission, and DNA
- methodology
- the principles of classical conditioning
- ethical principles involved in changing behaviour and ethics involved in doing research.

Introduction to health psychology

Health psychology is a relatively new field in psychology but at degree level many courses have modules on health psychology, and it is growing in popularity. Changes in society and in our medical knowledge have shaped the development of health psychology, which looks at why people become ill, how we can stay healthy and how we cope with illness. Health psychology is a wide field focusing on issues such as health promotion and maintaining good health, prevention and treatment of illnesses, the origins and causes of illness (**aetiology**), health care in society and policy issues.

Reasons for the development of health psychology

Changing patterns of illness, arising from improved medical knowledge, as well as changing social patterns, have led to an increased emphasis on psychological factors in illness, and these changing patterns have contributed to the development of health psychology. As well as these other changes, psychology itself has changed, and different models and paradigms have developed, themselves leading to changes in the interests and focuses of psychologists.

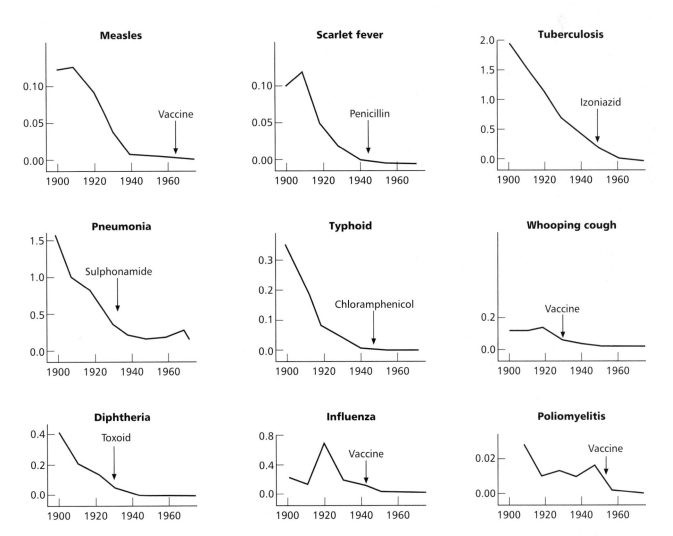

Figure 8.1
The fall in the standardised death rate (per 1000 population) for nine common infectious diseases when considering specific medical measures in the USA, 1900–1973 (Source: Stroebe, 2000)

Changing patterns of illness – from acute to chronic

Until the beginning of the twentieth century the main causes of death were **acute** (short-term) diseases and illnesses such as pneumonia and tuberculosis. During the twentieth century cures were found for many of these illnesses. Vaccinations were used, and people now are more likely to die from **chronic** diseases than from acute ones. Chronic illnesses develop slowly and sufferers can live for quite some time. Heart disease, cancers and diabetes are chronic diseases. These are 'modern' causes of death, and chronic diseases are those health psychologists are usually interested in.

Table 8.1 shows the changes in causes of death during the twentieth century in the USA. Britain follows a similar pattern. The 'modern' list includes many psychological and social factors. For example, diet and smoking are linked to heart disease, and sexual activity is linked to the development of AIDS. These psychological and social factors are very much the focus of health psychology.

Statistics are used to look at changing patterns of illness. **Epidemiology** is the study of how often and where certain diseases occur. For example, epidemiologists look at who has what kind of cancer, and study factors such as gender and social class. They also look for geographical clusters for particular types of illness. Epidemiologists look at morbidity and mortality. **Mortality** refers to how many people have died from a particular cause, **morbidity** how many people have that disease at a certain point in time (its **prevalence**) or how many new cases there are. Health psychologists need to know what diseases lead to early death, as they use health promotion to try to reduce these diseases.

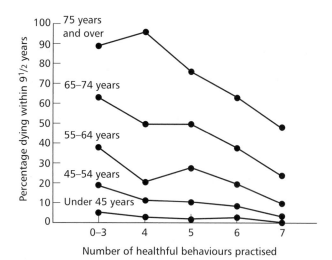

Figure 8.2
Percentage of men who died within 9½ years as a function of the number of healthful behaviours they reported practising and of their ages (at the start of the study in 1965). The decreases in deaths associated with increasing healthful behaviours were not as sharp for women. (Source: Sarafino, 1994)

They also need to know what diseases are prevalent, particularly chronic ones, so that they can see what is needed in the way of health support (Kaplan, 1990). For example, a health promotion campaign might focus on factors leading to heart disease, which seems to lead to early death. Smoking is one such factor; others are exercise, weight loss and diet (McGinnis *et al.*, 1992).

Changing social patterns

A changing society also means changing areas of interest for psychologists. Our population consists more and more of older people as people live longer. From an economic viewpoint we need to ensure that our population is as fit

Table 8.1 *Ten leading causes of death in the USA in 1900 and 1994*

1900		1994	
Death rate per 100,000 of population	**Cause of death**	**Death rate per 100,000 of population**	**Cause of death**
202.2	Flu and pneumonia	285.9	Heart disease
194.4	Tuberculosis	204.1	Cancers
142.7	Gastro-enteritis	56.9	Stroke
137.4	Heart disease	35.9	Chronic obstructive pulmonary disease
106.9	Vascular lesions of the central nervous system	35.4	Accident
81.0	Chronic nephritis	30.9	Pneumonia, flu
72.3	Accident	19.4	Diabetes
64	Cancers	12.2	Suicide
62.6	Infancy diseases	11.7	HIV infection
40.3	Diphtheria	10.5	Homicide

Source: Adapted from Taylor (1999)

as possible. It is in a government's interest to save money by encouraging good health, and health promotion, an important part of health psychology, is a way of doing this. People want to know how to reduce the likelihood of developing such illnesses as AIDS or cancer. Campaigns often focus on smoking and drinking alcohol, for example, as these behaviours have been linked to many diseases.

ACTIVITY

Research a health promotion campaign. Imagine that you have to inform a group of people about an issue of your choosing. Prepare a poster or presentation. State the group being targeted, and explain how your poster/presentation will achieve the aims of the campaign. This would make a good group activity.

Changing knowledge

As knowledge changes, health psychologists face new directions and new challenges. For example, when a link was established between smoking and health many new issues arose such as how tobacco companies have had to pay out compensation, and will probably have to pay out more. Health psychologists are now involved in helping individuals to come to terms with having damaged their health by smoking early in their lives. Health psychologists can also help those who wish to stop smoking.

A current example of how changes in knowledge affect our attitudes to health is the human genome project. As people discover more about genes and their role in health, they can make more choices. It is said now that cause of death can to a large extent be predicted. For example, if there is a trend in your family for men to die quite young (between 40 and 50) from a heart attack, and you are male, then your death from a heart attack is more likely than for someone where there is no such trend. This is only a prediction of course, and there are many other factors to take into account (including whether you smoke or not).

Many people now undergo genetic testing. For example, if one member of a family develops Huntington's disease, then close family members are offered genetic testing to see if they will develop the disease or not. Health psychologists can help in the choice of taking the test or not. If the person will develop the disease, health psychologists can help them to come to terms with the implications. Pregnant women are offered tests to look for

problems with the developing baby and may have to decide whether abort the pregnancy if the fetus is not developing normally. Health psychologists investigate these sorts of decisions to see where help can be given. Helping people to make difficult and informed decisions comes within the field of psychology.

ACTIVITY

Search through some newspapers or magazines. Find an example where someone had to make a life-threatening decision. Describe the example, and then make a list of ways in which you think a health psychologist might help.

Changing research models

As patterns of illness change, so do the research interests of psychologists. During the first half of the twentieth century, the biomedical model was used, whereas current interest focuses on the biopsychosocial model. You can trace the changes of interest – and the growth of health psychology – by tracking changes in the models used in research.

The biomedical model

The **biomedical model** of illness makes the assumption that all illnesses have physiological causes, and that cures are physiological. Those who are ill have symptoms for which cures are sought. Social and psychological factors might be accepted as being of interest, but not with regard to the actual disease.

↻ **Recall AS material**

Recall the assumptions of the physiological approach – look it up if you can't recall it.

In the biomedical model illnesses come from such things as disorders in cells, in blood structure, in the nervous system or in any physical structure of the body. This is a **reductionist** approach, which means that the overall illness would be studied by looking at the parts that make up the whole illness. For example, if you kept getting very strong headaches, the biomedical model would lead a medical practitioner to start testing perhaps your eyesight, or your blood pressure. The problem (for example, the headaches) would be reduced or broken down into parts or symptoms, and these individual symptoms would be examined.

- Continuing with the above example, the biomedical model can be criticised because headaches could be caused by other factors such as stress, and social and psychological factors could be important.
- Another criticism of the biomedical model is that illness and disease are emphasised instead of health.
- The biomedical model cannot explain why the same set of physical circumstances does not always lead to the same outcome. For example, not everyone who is exposed to an infection develops it; some people in families where heart attacks are 'common' do not develop heart disease while others do. Health psychologists are interested in social and psychological factors, as well as in physiological ones.

The psychodyamic model

Freud discussed **hysteria**, where a physical problem (such as blindness) seems to have no physical cause, and yet is a real problem. Freud thought that the person had a psychological problem that was causing the physical problem, which needed to be dealt with to effect a cure. Repressed experiences were causing physical problems, and the repression needed to be revealed to the individual. This was a quite different approach to that of the biomedical model, and led to the conclusion that psychological factors were not only important in illness, but could actually be the cause of the illness.

⟳ Recall AS material

Recall your AS material on the psychodynamic approach, or look it up.

The biopsychosocial model

Health psychology is best understood within the **biopsychosocial model**, which sees causes of illnesses as complex, and involving biological, psychological and social factors (Table 8.2). For example, an illness could be caused by a virus, but affected by a person's behaviour, their beliefs and their occupation. The biopsychosocial model was developed by Engel (1977, 1980).

ACTIVITY

This would make a good group activity. Using Table 8.2, expand each point, explaining what is meant and giving an example. You could work in three groups, each taking one of the three main groupings, and then share your work in a group discussion.

Systems theory

Within the biopsychosocial model researchers use **systems theory,** which suggests that all factors are linked and (for example) changes in cell structure can be linked to social factors such as social class as well as to psychological factors like high stress (Figure 8.3). According to this model both diagnosis and treatment should reflect all three levels. This means that in health psychology a team approach is appropriate.

Research methods used in health psychology

Experiments

Experiments are used in health psychology. For example, researchers might want to find out if a self-help group is useful in combating some illness. If doing an experiment, the researchers would find people with the illness and then interfere in some way, perhaps by offering one group some sort of treatment and using the other group (without the treatment) as a control group. Then observations, questionnaires or interviews can be used to see how the disease is being coped with, and to see if those in the group are doing better.

- It would not be ethical not to offer to everyone something that is known to help, so experiments can be quite difficult to carry out. For example, it would be unethical to offer half of a group counselling, if the other half received no help at all. It would, perhaps, be possible to offer two different sorts of counselling.

Table 8.2 Some factors affecting health and illness according to the biopsychosocial model

Biological	Psychological	Social
Genetics Viruses Physical structural defects Drugs	Expectations Fear Beliefs Attitudes Behaviour (e.g. coping strategies) Stress	Class Job Race/ethnicity Social norms Social pressures (e.g. peer pressure) Social values on health

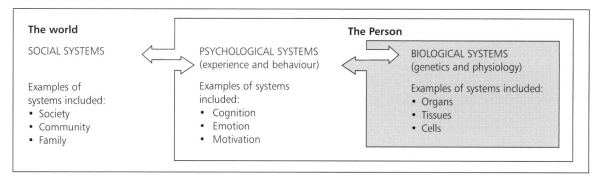

Figure 8.3
The interplay of systems in the biopsychosocial model. The person consists of biological and psychological systems, which interrelate. Each system includes component systems. The person interrelates with the social systems of his or her world. Each system can affect and be affected by any of the other systems (Source: Sarafino, 1994)

Correlational research

Correlational research is also used in health psychology. Without changing anything a health psychologist looks at one variable to see how it varies in relation to another. For example, they could look at people in self-help groups and see if the more they attend and talk, the less medical attention they need. These two variables are measurable (the number of times a person attends a group or talks to one or more of the members can be measured, as can the number of times the person attends a medical appointment).

Alternatively, the medical specialist helping that person could make a judgement about their progress at certain points in the treatment, and use that judgement to produce a score for each variable, then compare the scores for each person. If it turns out that the more a person attends the self-help group the less treatment they have it could be claimed that there was a correlation between attending self-help groups and good health.

Evaluation

+ Figures that are already available can be used, and any measure does not mean changing the person's way of life, as can happen with experiments.
− We cannot discover a cause and effect relationship. We might see that self-help groups mean better health, but we cannot claim that they cause the better health. Some other factor may be involved – for example, that people who access the help of others have a more positive attitude, which is what leads to better health.

Prospective research

Prospective research involves studying how a relationship between two variables changes over time, and adds to the information gained from correlational analysis. For example, if we say that personality is related to heart disease, but it is hard to know whether the disease causes the personality trait or the trait causes the disease, we can look forward from early years to see what developed first. If the trait was present in childhood, and

Self-test

Recall (or look up) your AS material giving the difference between a positive and a negative correlation. Is the example given above about self-help groups an example of a positive or a negative correlation?

If it is found that self-help groups mean fewer medical visits, then this is a **negative correlation**, because the more they attend the group, the fewer visits they make. An example of a **positive correlation** might be that the more hostile a person is the higher the likelihood that they develop heart disease – the more they act aggressively, the more likely they are to be diagnosed with heart disease.

the heart disease developed later, it is likely that the trait caused the disease, not the other way around.

An example of prospective research is where a health psychologist might suggest a special diet for one group, and not for another, and then see the effect the diet has – this would be an experimental study. Looking at people's diets and their health over time to see if health and diet show a co-relationship would be correlational prospective research. The difference between experimental prospective research and correlational prospective research is that in an experiment the researcher does the manipulation, whereas in a correlation the researcher measures variables that already occur.

To do prospective research a **longitudinal study** is needed, in which the same people are followed over a quite a long period. An example might be gathering information over a long period about a group of young women whose mothers have developed breast cancer and analysing the data. Women in the sample who developed breast cancer could be compared with those who did not, to see if there were differences between the two groups – for example, in diet or exercise habits.

Retrospective research

Retrospective research means looking back in the lives of sufferers of a certain illness to see what common factors there were. For example, many people suffering from AIDS have certain sexual habits in common. Researchers were able to say that these habits linked with AIDS even before they really knew what AIDS was.

↻ Recall AS material

Recall or look up methods you studied for the AS. Make a list of the main methods used in psychology, and briefly note down two advantages of each method and two disadvantages. This will help in the synoptic questions in Unit 6.

What health psychologists do

Health psychology looks at health risk behaviours, health protection, cognitive factors, health care and the effects of illness.

ACTIVITY

Find what you can about health psychology by logging on to the Internet. You could look at the Health Psychology Division of the BPS, or try using a search engine such as www.google.com, for example.

Becoming a health psychologist

Some students take degrees in health psychology, others take modules in health psychology as part of another degree course, such as medicine. Some graduates take a higher degree in health psychology. To be a health psychologist you need a degree with BPS Graduate Basis for Registration. After achieving this degree you need a Masters in Health Psychology and 2 years of experience or a PhD in an appropriate area.

The clinical health psychologist

A clinical psychologist could train in health psychology and then specialise in fields such as stress and pain management, or helping those with chronic diseases such as cancer or HIV (Belar and Deardorff, 1995).

The professional health psychologist

Chartered Health Psychologists are chartered by the British Psychological Society. A professional health psychologist is usually involved in research, teaching and treatment/consulting. Their work can be academic, giving advice in education, or working within the health service.

Where health psychologists work

Health psychologists work in NHS trusts, health authorities, universities, private consultancies, rehabilitation units, surgeries in hospitals, and physiotherapy units.

ACTIVITY

This would make a good group activity.

Choose one aspect of what a health psychologist might be interested in. Write out a short description of an individual involved in an issue (it might be someone with an illness, or someone who would benefit from a healthier lifestyle). If you are able to work in a small group, one person should take the role of the person needing help, another that of the health psychologist; a third can be a historian and should take notes as the other two act out the situation. The historian comments on the performance, and all three can discuss issues. If you are able to work in a classroom situation, different groups can then feed back on their 'situation' and the role of the health psychologist in their case.

Health psychology and you

Whilst studying health psychology, you will read about issues that relate to your own experiences, which should make this area interesting for you. However, you may have questions, and you will need to pursue these issues if they cause you concern. For example, if you are a smoker you might want to explore the effect it already has had; if there is a trend in your family towards a particular illness or disease, you might want to know more about it. We all have genetic and environmental factors that will affect our lives, so the material that follows is bound to affect everyone in some way. If questions concern you, it is a good idea to seek clarification from a professional.

Factors affecting health – the nature/nurture issue

ACTIVITY

Ask an older family member to answer the questions in the following questionnaire (which is really aimed at older people), or try it yourself. Make sure no one is too upset by this task.

1 Start by working out the respondent's basic life expectancy. For men this is 67 and for women 75, so you start with the figure according to your gender. If you are in your 50s or 60s, add 10 years, because you have already lived so long. If you are an active person over 60 add another 2 years. So starting figures would be:

- normally   m = 67; f = 75
- If over 50,   m = 77; f = 85
- If active over 60, m = 79; f = 87.

2 Now read the questionnaire and decide how each item applies.

3 Add or subtract the appropriate figures to work out total life expectancy (the number of years to add or subtract is shown in brackets after each point).

LIFE EXPECTANCY QUESTIONNAIRE

1 Family history
- Two or more grandparents lived to 80+ (+5)
- Parent, grandparent, brother, sister died of heart attack or stroke before 50 (–4)
- Parent, grandparent, brother, sister died of heart attack or stroke before 60 (–2)
- Parents or grandparents having diabetes, asthma, thyroid problems, bronchitis, breast cancer, cancer of digestive system – for each case (–3)

2 Marital status
- Married male (+10)
- Married female (+4)
- Over 25 and not married for each unwedded decade (–1)

3 Economic status
- Poor most of your life (–3)

4 Physique
- For every 10 pounds overweight (–1)
- For each inch waist exceeds chest measurement (–2)

5 Exercise
- Regular moderate exercise (3 times jogging per week) (+3)
- Regular vigorous (long distance running 3 times per week) (+5)
- Sedentary job (–3)
- Active job (+3)

6 Alcohol
- 1–3 drinks a day (+2)
- More than 4 drinks a day (heavy) (–5 to –10)
- Teetotal (–1)

7 Smoking
- Two or more packets of cigarettes per day (–8)
- One to two packets per day (–4)
- Less than one packet per day (–2)
- Regular cigar or pipe smoker (–2)

8 Disposition
- Reasoned, practical person (–2)
- Aggressive, intense (–2)
- Basically happy and content (+1 to +5)

9 Environment
- Most of life in rural environment (+4)
- Most of life in urban environment (–2)

10 Sleep
- More than 9 hours a day (–5)

11 Temperature
- Thermostat at home set at no more than 68°F (+2)

12 Health care
- Regular medical and dental check-ups (+3)
- Frequently ill (-2)

Source: Adapted from Taylor (1999).

Make two lists from the items in the above questionnaire. One list should give good health practice, and one should give bad health practice. Compare your list with the one in Table 8.3.

Table 8.3 *Some good and bad health practices/circumstances*

Good health practice/situation	Bad health practice/situation
Longevity (long life) in the family	A history of heart attack or stroke in the family
Being a married man	Diabetes, thyroid problems, digestive problems or asthma in the family
Being a married woman	
Active job	Breast cancer in the family
Taking plenty of exercise	Being unmarried and over 25
Being a light drinker	Sedentary (sitting) job
Not smoking	Being poor most of your life
Being a reasoned, practical person	Heavy drinking
Being basically happy and content with life	Being teetotal
Living in a rural environment	Smoking cigarettes, cigar or pipe
Having regular medical check-ups	Being aggressive or intense
Having regular dental check-ups	Living in an urban environment
Having your heating at home less than 68°F	Sleeping more than 9 hours a day
	Being frequently ill (!)

From the lists you produced, and Table 8.3, make two more lists. One should give genetic or inherited/biological factors affecting how long you might live (nature), and the other should give environmental or behavioural factors affecting how long you might live (nurture). Compare your lists with Table 8.4.

Table 8.4 *Examples of 'nature' and 'nurture' effects on health*

Genetic/inherited factors	Environmental/behavioural factors
Longevity (long life) in the family	Marital status
The type of person you are – your temperament	Type of job
A history of heart attack or stroke in the family	Whether you take exercise
Diabetes, thyroid problems, digestive problems or asthma in the family	Drinking alcohol
Breast cancer in the family	Being poor most of your life
	Smoking or not smoking
	Living in a rural or urban environment
	Taking regular medical check-ups
	The temperature of your home
	Sleeping too much
	Being frequently ill

It is clear that many factors within our environment or our behaviour affect our health. This is evidence that the biopsychosocial model is more useful for health psychologists than is the biomedical model. Table 8.4 also helps to highlight what health psychologists do, and what they are interested in.

Recall AS material

Recall discussion about the ' nature/nurture' issue, for example, within the physiological approach. This will also be useful for the synoptic questions in Unit 6.

Self-test

Write a timed essay under exam conditions (or as close as you can manage) with the title 'Discuss how far factors other than biological ones might contribute to health and illness'.

Health and substance abuse

What is substance abuse?

This section looks at health and abuse of substances such as nicotine, alcohol and cocaine. 'Abuse' means that the substances are being taken for purposes for which they were not originally intended.

Many the substances that will be discussed can be used for appropriate medical purposes – for example, cocaine is good as an anaesthetic, and heroin (the medical term is diamorphine) is widely used in medicine for the control of severe pain. Most people who drink a lot of coffee would not call themselves substance abusers, even though caffeine is a drug. The life expectancy questionnaire on page 261 suggested that moderate drinking is good for us; however, alcohol is also a drug. Nicotine can also be used for medical purposes, even though it is now generally thought of as bad for us. Cannabis is thought by many to be bad, although others say that is should not be banned, and it too can be used for medical purposes such as for the management of multiple sclerosis. What follows looks at substance *abuse*, rather than the substance itself. Substances like glue can be abused when sniffed, so it is not the substance itself, but the use that is made of it that is of interest.

Rosenhan and Seligman (1984) define substance abuse using three criteria:

1 Heavy daily use and not being able to stop using the substance.
2 Problems with social life and general functioning resulting from its use, for example, loss of job or friends.
3 Having problems such as those listed in 1 and 2 for a month or more.

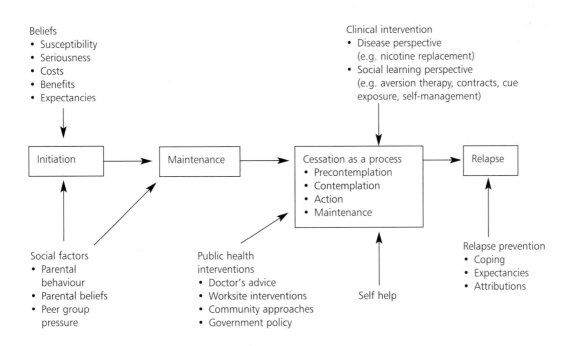

Figure 8.4
The stages of substance abuse (Source: Ogden, 2000)

Health psychologists would use the above definition, but would focus more on resulting health problems.

When is substance abuse likely to begin?

Health-compromising behaviour usually begins in adolescence (Donovan and Jessor, 1985 talk about a 'problem behaviour syndrome'). Drinking to excess, smoking, eating disorders, drug use, unsafe sex, tanning and other risk-taking behaviours often start in adolescence. This could be because of peer pressure – adolescence is a time of life when the peer group has a strong influence. Most teenagers want to be like others, and self-presentation becomes important. If it is cool to be slim, to smoke, to drink and to use drugs, teenagers are likely to do it. This is an important point when considering health promotion. The behaviours also tend to be pleasurable, at least at first, and so teenagers are likely to take part.

↻ *Recall AS material*

Use social learning theory to explain the above suggestion that teenagers seem to want to be like others. This is a good way of linking approaches to practical applications, such as reasons for substance abuse. It is also useful to recall the main approaches, ready for the synoptic questions in Unit 6.

Drug dependency

When a body has got used to a substance and its use has become part of the normal functioning of the body **physical dependency** has developed. Some substances are more likely to lead to physical dependence than others – for heroin it is highly likely, but for LSD it is less likely (Winger *et al.*, 1992).

When people feel compelled to take a substance even when they are not physically dependent upon it they have developed **psychological dependence**. When psychologically dependent on a substance, someone will rely on it to help them to feel good, to help them in their life, and many of their activities will centre around the substance. There is a tendency to become psychologically dependent on a substance before becoming physically dependent upon it. For example, people might centre their lives around drinking alcohol, and then become physically dependent on it as they develop a tolerance for it. Heroin and cocaine seem to produce high psychological dependence, and LSD low dependency.

When someone is either physiologically or psychologically dependent (or both) on a substance they have been using over a period of time they have become **addicted**.

Tolerance is part of physical dependence and refers to the way the body continues to adapt to a substance. To have the same effect, more and more of the substance is needed, although a plateau is eventually reached. For example, at first one pint of beer might have an effect, but soon the individual will need to drink more to get the same effect.

Withdrawal is also part of physical dependence and is the term for the miserable symptoms that are experienced when someone stops using a substance on which they have become physically or psychologically dependent. Symptoms include headaches, irritability, feeling sick, anxiety, cravings, shaking and sometimes hallucinations.

Craving is the very strong desire to consume a substance. Craving comes from physical dependence and also from conditioning. The substance is paired with environmental cues, which act as stimuli to trigger the response of consuming the substance.

↻ *Recall AS material*

Recall the principles of classical conditioning from the AS material you have learnt (or look them up). You could set out the above situation in terms of UCS, UCR, CS, and CR, to link the current material to the behaviourist approach

---

A **relapse** is when someone has managed to stop using the substance and then returns to it.

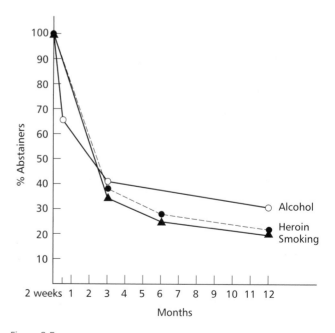

Figure 8.5
Relapse rates for individuals treated for heroin, smoking and alcohol addiction (Source: Ogden, 2000)

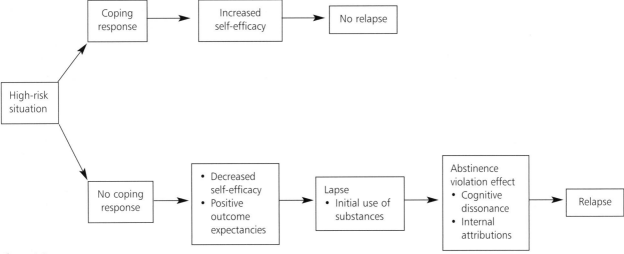

Figure 8.6
The relapse process (Source: Ogden, 2000)

Neurotransmitters and synaptic functioning

The nervous system consists of the brain and the spinal column (the central nervous system) and the peripheral nervous system, which you will study later when looking at stress. It is the central nervous system that is of interest here.

Information travels to different parts of our body largely via the nervous system through billions of cells called neurones, although other ways, such as hormones, are also used.

↻ *Recall AS material*

Recall (or look up) your AS material on the physiological approach, including how the nervous system and neurotransmitters work.

Neuronal and synaptic transmission

Neurones exist in many different shapes and sizes, but they work in the same way. A typical neuron is shown in Figure 8.7. Dendrites receive messages from connecting neurons and lead to the cell body, which contains the nucleus. From the cell body, an axon takes the message to terminal buttons at the synapse at the end of the axon. The synapse is a gap between neurons and the electrochemical message, which stops at the terminal buttons, is either continued across the gap in the form of neurotransmitters or is not continued. The myelin sheath protects the axon, and Nodes of Ranvier (areas where the myelin sheath is missing), speed up the message. The axon is made up of protoplasm.

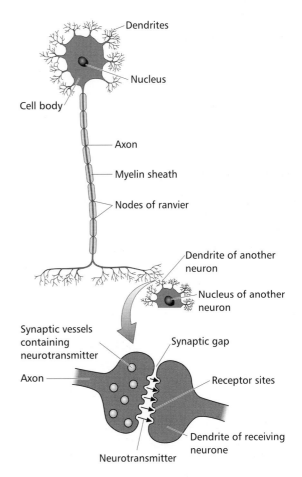

Figure 8.7
An idealised diagram of a neuron and some of its major parts

Initiation of nerve impulses

The electrochemical signal that passes along the axon is called an **action potential**. The neuron contains positively charged potassium ions and negatively charged protein molecules. The fluid surrounding the neuron contains positively charged sodium ions and negatively charged chloride ions. The negatively charged protein molecules are trapped inside the neuron, whereas potassium–sodium pumps allow the smaller potassium and sodium ions in and out. At rest, the sodium ions are kept out of the cell, so the inside of the neuron is negatively charged compared with the outside (by 70 millivolts). This is called the **resting** potential.

When a nerve is stimulated, sodium channels open and sodium ions flood into the cell; the inside of the neuron very briefly becomes positively charged (+40 millivolts). The sodium channels immediately close again and potassium channels open, allowing potassium ions to flow out and restoring the neuron to its resting potential. The action potential jumps down the axon via the nodes of Ranvier (where there is no protective myelin sheath) to speed up the signal. This jumping is called **saltatory conduction**. The action potential will terminate at a synapse unless it can continue across (see below).

It may seem as though all messages at the synapse tell the neuron to fire but some synapses stop the neuron from firing – some are excitatory, and some are inhibitory. Neurons receive messages from both types of synapse, so there is a sort of adding up of instructions (this is known as **summation**). We need inhibitory synapses to control the flow of messages (it is possible, for example, that epilepsy is caused by too many excitatory synapses and not enough inhibitory ones). The stimulus to the neuron must be sufficient to cross a **threshold** level – if enough excitatory synapses are fired the message starts, so there either is a message or there is not one. There is no such thing as a weak message; there either is an action potential or there is not. However, how often the neuron 'fires' (changes from negative to positive and back again) affects the strength of the stimulus, as does the number of neurons stimulated. Therefore there can be strong and weak signals in this sense.

Local anaesthetic drugs such as lignocaine prevent sodium ions from entering the cell by attaching to the sodium gates through which the sodium passes. Such drugs block any action potential (impulse) and prevent the message from being passed. General anaesthetics such as chloroform open potassium gates, increasing the flow of potassium out of the neuron. The likelihood of an action potential is decreased because the balance of potassium and sodium is not right. This is a different way of preventing the impulse from occurring (and preventing the pain message from being sent).

Transmission across the synapse
The action potential cannot travel across a synapse because this junction between neurons is a gap – the two cells do not physically contact.

At the synapse **neurotransmitters** are stored in synaptic vesicles. The electrochemical message stimulates the synaptic vesicles to release their neurotransmitter into the synaptic gap. The dendrites of the opposite neuron have special receptors to receive the neurotransmitter, and when the right neurotransmitter is received (where the chemical 'shape' of the neurotransmitter 'fits' the receptor) it fires these receptors, continuing the message up the dendrites of the receiving neuron to the next synapse – and so the process continues. Once it has crossed the synapse a neurotransmitter is destroyed by special enzymes (**deactivation**), or is taken back up by the axon (**re-uptake**). There are different neurotransmitters: some make a synapse inhibitory, some make it excitatory.

There are dozens of chemicals that work as neurotransmitters, and the list is constantly being added to (Snyder, 1984). The three main types of neurotransmitter are biogenic amines, amino acids and peptides. Usually the brain maintains regular levels of each neurotransmitter, but diet affects the process, and slightly more or less of a neurotransmitter may be produced under special circumstances. Examples of neurotransmitters are serotonin, dopamine, adrenaline, acetylcholine and noradrenaline, and all these are biogenic amines. Neurotransmitters are made from materials in our diet – for example, acetylcholine is synthesised from choline, found in cauliflower and milk; eating carbohydrates can increase levels of tryptophan, which is used to produce serotonin.

Neurotransmitters have a direct influence, but also **neuromodulators** prepare the neurons so that later neurotransmitters will act in specific ways. For example, endorphins (sometimes called the brain's natural painkillers) act like opiate drugs such as heroin and morphine, by preventing the release of neurotransmitters from neurons that send information about pain.

Neurotransmitters and behaviour

There are many different neurotransmitters, and one neurotransmitter can have different effects at different places in the brain, for different purposes. There are also many different types of receptor for a transmitter, for example serotonin has at least ten types of receptor (Humphrey *et al.*, 1993), which means that serotonin is linked to different types of behaviour. For example, stimulation of serotonin receptors type 2C gives different types of behaviour than when 1F receptors are stimulated. This also means that if people have different numbers of different receptors they would be affected in different ways by a particular drug – they would experience different side effects, for example. Table 8.5 gives a few examples of neurotransmitters and their effects.

Table 8.5 Examples of neurotransmitters and their effects on behaviour

Neurotransmitter	Inhibitory or excitatory	Behaviour affected
Dopamine	Both	Parkinson's disease is caused by decay of neurons that release dopamine Schizophrenia might be due to too much dopamine in particular areas of the brain.
Serotonin	Both	Sleep patterns
Noradrenaline	Both, depending on area of brain Connects with eating and emotions Low levels may cause depression High levels may cause mania	Arousal

When studying psychology you will study explanations for behaviour that involve drugs. For example, excess dopamine could be a cause of schizophrenia, and excess noradrenaline might cause mania. If you think of drugs as chemicals, then imagine drugs in the brain as being like neurotransmitters. Drugs will often act in the same way as neurotransmitters, and will 'excite' the receptors to pass a message on, or 'inhibit' the receptors to prevent messages from travelling.

How drugs work

ACTIVITY

Take a short while to review theory that you can apply so far in this chapter. Not only do you want to learn about the theoretical way drugs work, but also about what this means for the individual. This chapter is about applying theory, especially with regard to health psychology. Make a list of any disorder or problem that you have read about in this chapter so far. By the side of each example, note down what you have learnt about it. Applying theory means noting real life situations, and then linking theoretical findings to the situation, possibly to help an individual or improve our knowledge of that situation. Table 8.6 gives some ideas.

If you are working in a group, this would make a good brainstorming exercise.

Table 8.6

Situation/behaviour	Consequences
Smoking	Contributes to many causes of death
Drinking alcohol	Healthy in moderation but can be a health problem
Acute disease	Used to be common cause of death, but vaccines now help in most cases
Chronic disease	Long-term disease, often no cure, needs to be come to terms with
Heroin addiction	Involves the whole family, drug use is continued to avoid withdrawal symptoms
Breast cancer	Involves many emotions, need not lead to death, involves complex decision making
New-variant CJD	No cure, can happen in clusters, relates to BSE/beef, needs to be coped with
Depression	Linked to low levels of noradrenaline
Mania	Linked with high levels of noradrenaline
Schizophrenia	Linked with excess dopamine
Parkinson's disease	Links to low levels of dopamine
Sleep patterns	Links to serotonin
Eating patterns	Linked to noradrenaline
Epilepsy	Too many excitatory synapses, insufficient inhibitory synapses

The list in Table 8.6 should make you realise that knowing how drugs work is an important part of health psychology. Table 8.7 looks at how drugs work with regard to neurotransmitters, and their effects on behaviour. Study the table, keeping in mind the way neurotransmitters work at the synapse.

Table 8.7 Drugs, neurotransmitters, and effects on behaviour

Drug(s)	Neurotransmitter	Effect on behaviour
Amphetamines ('speed' – e.g. Benzedrine)	Block re-uptake of dopamine and noradrenaline, so the drugs are effective for longer (re-uptake cancels their effect at the synapse, and means they are absorbed). Also increase the release of noradrenaline	Increase alertness, give confidence, reduce lethargy, suppress appetite. High doses give behaviour like that of a paranoid schizophrenic
Hallucinogenic drugs (LSD)	Similar to serotonin	Gives calm, inner peace, contentment. Hallucinations and problems with perception. Overdose of LSD gives psychotic reactions. Can cause schizophrenia-like behaviour
Cannabis	Similar to dopamine and noradrenaline. Blocks effects of serotonin (which inhibits thinking and emotions).	Gives illusions of calm etc., as with LSD
Angel Dust (PCP)	Prevents serotonin receptors from receiving serotonin because the drugs block those receptors. Feelings become distanced and less focused	Gives hallucinations, inner peace, as LSD
Stimulants (e.g. Caffeine, nicotine, cocaine)	Either stimulating or relaxing	Nicotine can be either stimulating or relaxing. Cocaine acts like amphetamines, but is addictive. Nicotine is addictive
Barbiturates, alcohol	Hypnotics. Bring sleep as anaesthetics do. A combination of barbiturates and alcohol can be fatal. Act like tranquillisers	Reduce anxiety and inhibitions. Can make you sleepy. Large amounts can lead to disorientation, confusion and abusive behaviour
Opiates	Codeine, morphine and heroin are opiates. Heroin is the strongest. Neurons are damaged with prolonged use of heroin.	Firstly gives pleasure. Then tolerance means need more and more. Dependence leads to addiction. Cannot stop – avoid withdrawal symptoms

Table 8.7 (cont.)

Drug(s)	Neurotransmitter	Effect on behaviour
Major tranquillisers (e.g. chlorpromazine – an anti-schizophrenic drug)	Mimic dopamine and bind to dopamine receptors so that dopamine cannot be effective (some sites remain to receive some dopamine)	Reduce schizophrenic symptoms, so it seems as if one cause of schizophrenia may be too much dopamine
Minor tranquillisers (e.g. anti-anxiety drugs such as diazepam)	These drugs bind to inosine receptor sites (so inosine might be our natural anti-anxiety neurotransmitter)	Calming, reduce anxiety, while remaining alert. Not anti-depressant, but anti-anxiety
Tricyclic antidepressants (e.g. imipramine)	Stop noradrenaline and serotonin from breaking down	Bring euphoria and block rapid eye movement
Monoamine oxidase antidepressants	Inhibit the enzyme monoamine oxidase and stop the breakdown of monoamine transmitters	Bring euphoria and block rapid eye movement
L-dopa	L-dopa is converted into dopamine	Used to treat Parkinson's disease, but can produce schizophrenia-like effects

Source: Adapted from Gross (1996)

Although the way drugs work is more complex than appears in this summary, basically some inhibit the effect of the neurotransmitter (some hallucinogens), and some act in the same way as the neurotransmitter (some tranquillisers). Others prevent specific neurotransmitters from dispersing, and maintain the effect (anti-depressants). Some drugs are converted by the body into a specific neurotransmitter (L-dopa and some tranquillisers).

Antagonists and agonists

Drugs that block the effect of a neurotransmitter are called **antagonists**. Drugs that mimic or increase the effect of a neurotransmitter are called **agonists**. The specific effects of some particular drugs are considered below.

Consequences of drug abuse

Different drugs have different consequences.

Alcohol

Alcohol is probably the most widely abused drug. It increases the effect of social influences on people – for example, you are more likely to be less inhibited after drinking alcohol at a party than if drinking at home.

Drinking too much alcohol is also likely to bring cognitive deficits such as lack of reasoning ability and poor memory. However, if problem drinkers stop before the age of 40, their performance on cognitive tasks does improve (Goldman, 1983). Alcohol also affects movements.

How alcohol affects us

Alcohol inhibits the flow of sodium and so interferes with neuronal activity. It also makes the GABA receptors on the cell membrane more responsive (GABA is a neuro-transmitter; its effects are usually inhibitory). When GABA receptors are triggered chloride ions, which are negatively charged, can cross into the cell more quickly and affect the balance between action and resting potential. GABA transmission tends to prevent action potentials, and leads to relaxation and reduction of anxiety. Other effects of alcohol include the withdrawal symptoms that are felt after a period of intense drinking. These include sickness, fever and hallucinations. Drinking alcohol during pregnancy can affect the developing fetus.

Why do some people develop a drink 'problem'?

The social stituation affects how much people drink, but why do some people develop a drink 'problem' and others do not? There could be genetic predispositions to becoming an alcoholic – inherited factors might make developing a drink problem more likely. Anyone closely related to an alcoholic is more likely to develop a drink problem, even if they were adopted and brought up in a family without drink problems (Gabrielli and Plomin, 1985). One particular gene has been found in 69% of alcoholics, but in only 20% of non-alcoholics, which is quite good evidence for a genetic involvement in alcoholism. This gene is also more common in drug abusers than in non-drug abusers (Smith *et al.*, 1992). Some people do seem to have an addictive 'personality' and this gene, which is associated with a visible marker on a human chromosome, seems to be involved. How it works is not yet known.

Other genes seem more specific to alcohol abuse than general addiction, for example there are genes that affect how alcohol is metabolised. Ethanol is metabolised in the liver to acetaldehyde (which is poisonous). This is then converted into **acetic acid**, which is used as energy by the body. Acetaldehyde can cause cirrhosis of the liver and damage to other organs. People of Asian origin have different amounts of acetaldehyde dehydrogenase (the enzyme that converts acetaldehyde into acetic acid) than other racial groups (Helzer *et al.*, 1990). This means that Asians are more likely to feel ill after drinking alcohol, which could help to explain why alcohol abuse is less common amongst certain groups than others.

Antabuse (a drug used to treat alcoholism) decreases the level of acetaldehyde dehydrogenase and inactivates the enzyme that converts the alcohol into acetic acid. People who take Antabuse must avoid all alcohol (at least at first), or will become seriously ill. Antabuse is supposed to work by making a person feel ill when they take any alcohol, so they learn an aversion to the taste of alcohol. This aversion can be explained in terms of classical conditioning.

ACTIVITY

Recall AS material and the principles of classical conditioning, and then use these principles to explain how the use of Antabuse would lead to an aversion to the taste of alcohol.

Evaluation

- Many people using Antabuse do not give up drinking alcohol because they associate it with feeling ill – they give up immediately, due to the threat of feeling ill. They don't actually get to the stage of associating illness with drinking alcohol (Fuller and Roth, 1979).

- We could argue that therapists have power, and they might be using that power when persuading people to undertake such therapies. This issue would be useful when considering synoptic issues for Unit 6, where you

could be asked about ethical issues involved in changing behaviour. Treatments such as aversion therapy would be useful examples of such issues. This is about social control, an issue that is returned to in Chapter 10.

The long-term effects of alcohol

If a pregnant woman drinks, the alcohol can affect her fetus, not only before birth by causing physical defects but also later, by affecting the learning ability of the child. Drinking also leads to accidents, for example, drink driving is a major cause of death. People are affected differently by drinking, but cognitive impairment and problems with motor performance are common. There are many misconceptions about the effects of alcohol. Jaccard and Turrisi (1987) found that college students underestimated the effects of drinking, thinking that later drinks had less impact, that beer was less of a problem than wine and that mixing drinks was the worst thing to do.

Long-term drinking can lead to cirrhosis – liver cells die and are replaced by scar tissue, so the liver cannot cleanse the blood as it should. Heavy drinking has also been linked to cancer, high blood pressure, heart disease and brain damage. People who continue to drink die earlier on average than those who stop; however, some problems caused by drinking do not disappear if the individual stops, and there can be permanent damage.

ACTIVITY

Research the effects of alcohol, making use of the Internet. For example, find out the facts about drink driving, and find out which types of drink make people most drunk. Then prepare a questionnaire to research these effects. You could formulate questions from the answers Jaccard and Turrisi (1987) found (such as whether beer is worse than wine), or you could generate questions of your own. Remember to be guided by ethical principles – ask people about their knowledge of the effects of alcohol, rather than about their own drinking habits.

Drinking in moderation is good for you

It was suggested earlier that drinking in moderation is good for us. Longitudinal studies such as that of Rimm *et al.* (1991) show this to be true. The most benefit seems to be in reducing heart disease, although in such studies it is hard to control for all factors. Alcohol could help to reduce stress, and so reduce heart disease, or it could promote the production of substances in the blood that reduce cholesterol. Not enough is known about this yet.

Cocaine

Cocaine is a strong stimulant. It has medical uses – for example, it is used as an anaesthetic drug, especially for eye surgery. It is also addictive, because it provides a sense of well-being and gives pleasure. The stimulant effect is produced because cocaine increases dopamine and noradrenaline activity at synapses. It is well known that Freud took cocaine because of his depression. Cocaine was originally an ingredient in Coca-Cola, but no longer.

Addiction

Drugs that activate dopamine synapses or increase dopamine activity tend to be habit-forming (Harris *et al.*, 1992). Some dopamine receptors (D2 and D3) seem to be important for addiction (Caine and Koob, 1993). It seems that decrease of acetylcholine release or increase of dopamine release is the most likely combination for addiction (acetylcholine seems to have the opposite effect to dopamine). Morphine increases the release of dopamine and decreases the release of acetylcholine, and when a morphine user goes into withdrawal, dopamine release is decreased, and acetylcholine is increased (Rada *et al.*, 1991).

How does cocaine work?

Cocaine acts like amphetamine – a stimulant that stimulates dopamine synapses by increasing the release of dopamine and blocking its re-uptake. So the dopamine remains in the synaptic gap for longer and continues to stimulate the receptors. Cocaine also stops the re-uptake of dopamine and noradrenaline, so their effects last longer. A small amount of cocaine stimulates mainly D1 dopamine receptors, which inhibit dopamine activity, so cocaine decreases brain activity (London *et al.*, 1990). Although cocaine decreases brain activity the drug is also a stimulant, and so there is arousal, activity and a sense of well-being. There seems to be a contradiction here – but decreased brain activity may lead to less inhibition of muscle activity, increasing muscle activity, so the behaviour of the individual might be described as 'uninhibited'. Because the neurotransmitters are not taken back up and reused by the neuron they remain at the synapse longer and therefore their effect lasts longer before they dissipate. This means it takes longer for the neuron to build up more supplies. So users often report a 'crash', or depressed state, after use of the drug.

Crack cocaine

Cocaine abuse was not too much of a problem compared with other drugs. However, development of crack cocaine led to much more severe drug abuse. In crack cocaine the hydrochloride group has been converted to a free base. Crack cocaine can be smoked, giving a 'rush' to the brain in seconds. The faster any drug gets to the brain, the greater its effect, and the more likely addiction is to follow. It was this change to allow cocaine to be smoked that led to the seriousness of cocaine abuse.

Effects of taking cocaine

Cocaine can also be taken by rubbing it on the gums, or inhaling it through the nose. The nose can become damaged, and cosmetic surgery may be needed to repair damage. Taking cocaine can lead to cocaine psychosis, convulsions and bleeding in the brain. Formication is also an effect. This is the feeling that insects are crawling under the skin, and seems to come from neural activity in the brain. Some users try to remove the 'insects' by cutting themselves. Cocaine taken during pregnancy can affect the developing fetus.

Long-term effects of using cocaine

Babies born to addicted mothers are likely to also be addicted. Cocaine causes blood vessels to constrict, speeds up the heart rate and suddenly increases blood pressure, which can cause a stroke or a heart attack, and some cocaine users have permanent damage to the heart muscle. Cocaine also destroys cells in the liver, causes brain seizures and can damage cells in the nose, as outlined above.

Smoking and nicotine

Nicotine has complicated effects. It stimulates heart rate and blood pressure, but many people say it relaxes them. This may be because nicotine increases the breathing rate for some people, but decreases it for others, so some would find it relaxing, and others would not (Jones, 1987). It is not known how nicotine affects breathing rate.

How does nicotine work?

Nicotine stimulates one type of acetylcholine receptor found in the central nervous system and at the nerve–muscle junction of skeletal muscles. Nicotine can stimulate the nerve–muscle junction, and sometimes causes twitching because it substitutes for acetylcholine. Drugs that block this particular acetylcholine receptor, which is called the nicotinic receptor, can cause paralysis (curare does this, and South American Indians use curare on the tips of their arrows to paralyse their prey). Nicotine stimulates dopamine receptors. It also has other effects, and this probably explains the different behavioural effects it can have on different people. Nicotine is the addictive chemical in cigarettes. It causes changes in brain chemicals that arouse the body, and increase alertness, heart rate and blood pressure.

In 1964 the health effects associated with smoking tobacco were made public and warnings against smoking appeared on packets of cigarettes. About 30% of American men and 26% of women smoke regularly, compared with 60% of men and 40% of women in the mid-1960s (Johnston *et al.*, 1991b).

Cigarette smoke contains a lot of carbon monoxide, which is easily absorbed into the bloodstream, affecting the individual's physiological functioning by reducing the oxygen-carrying capacity of the blood. Tars in the smoke have important health effects, but do not seem to affect a person's desire to smoke.

The nicotine regulation model

Established smokers continue to smoke to avoid withdrawal symptoms. Schacter *et al.* (1977) did experiments to demonstrate this. Smokers were asked to smoke low-nicotine cigarettes one week and high-nicotine cigarettes another week. They smoked more low-nicotine cigarettes, which suggests that they smoked to maintain levels of nicotine in their bodies.

The behavioural model

Some people do not become addicted (they don't show tolerance or withdrawal symptoms) and may smoke simply to regulate their cognitive and emotional state. Smoking triggers the release of acetylcholine and noradrenaline, which increase alertness and feelings of pleasure and decrease withdrawal symptoms. The feelings of pleasure can be seen as reinforcing. Some of the factors involved in addiction, including the role of reinforcement, are considered below.

The long-term effects of smoking – cancer

Many diseases have been linked to smoking. Ashton and Stepney (1982) describe two studies that link it with cancer: one study showed that non-smokers live longer than smokers, and the other showed that animals given cigarette tar developed cancer. It is now accepted that there are chemicals in tobacco that cause cancers of many different sorts. One cancer strongly linked to smoking is lung cancer – as smoking has increased, so has the incidence of lung cancer, which demonstrates at least a correlation. It is interesting that at first the link was mainly in males, but since the 1960s the incidence of smoking in females has grown, whereas smoking in males has decreased. Corresponding changes can also be seen in the incidence of lung cancer, again strengthening the link between smoking and the disease (American Cancer Society, 1992, cited in Sarafino, 1994).

The effects of passive smoking

Breathing in smoke from someone else's cigarette is called passive smoking. Passive smoking can cause lung cancer and other diseases: children of smokers have more respiratory infections, for example. The problems of passive smoking are greater for those who already have asthma, heart disease or other problems such as hay fever.

Smoking and heart disease/stroke

The risk of developing heart disease before the age of 65 is about twice as high for smokers as for non-smokers (American Heart Association, cited in Sarafino, 1994). The risks are greater for men between 45 and 55, who have

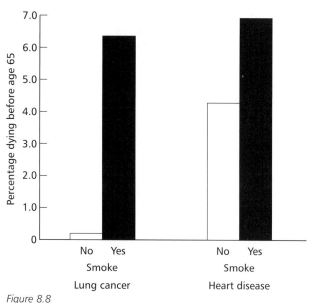

Figure 8.8
Probability of a 35-year-old man dying of lung cancer or heart disease before age 65 as a function of smoking heavily or not smoking. Data for women were less complete but would probably reveal similar increases in risk (Source: Sarafino, 1994; data from Mattson, Pollack and Cullen, 1987)

high levels of cholesterol in their blood, high blood pressure, and who have a family history of heart disease. Lifestyle and level of stress are also factors.

Nicotine as a cure

As with other drugs, it is thought that nicotine can have good effects as well as bad.

Some other drugs

MDMA (Ecstasy)

Ecstasy is related to amphetamine and was originally developed as an appetite reducer. Ecstasy in small amounts gives a feeling of euphoria, increases self-confidence and sexual confidence. Larger amounts can cause hallucinations. Ecstasy affects serotonin and dopamine. It causes dehydration, so users need to drink a lot of water. Blood pressure also rises, and a user can have a stroke, which can lead to permanent brain damage. Ecstasy is linked to Britain's 'rave' scene, and the high temperatures in the environment would increase the hyperthermia that comes from the drug itself. Green (1996) also reports depression, panic attacks, kidney and liver failure as being associated with the long-term use of the drug.

Heroin

Heroin is an opiate. It is derived from morphine, and morphine is found in opium, which comes from the poppy.

How opiates work

Opiates depress neural activity and reduce physical sensations, and are used in reducing severe pain.

However, morphine and heroin bring physiological dependence. Heroin can be smoked, inhaled or injected. It gives the user an overwhelming feeling of pleasure, and this feeling overrides all others. The heroin is converted into morphine in the body, which causes feelings of euphoria and relaxation. If used for a long time, heroin appears to damage the body's immune system. Long-term users also tend to become aggressive and socially isolated. Health is also endangered because of the use of needles, which can be contaminated, and because users tend to eat a poor diet. Tolerance develops quickly to heroin, and both physical and psychological dependence occur.

Withdrawal symptoms progress from flu-like symptoms to tremors, sweating, high blood pressure, insomnia and diarrhoea. The 'goose bumps' that develop have given rise to the term 'cold turkey', which used to refer to someone trying to give up the use of heroin. The term 'kicking the habit' comes from the leg jerks that often accompany withdrawal. Withdrawal symptoms last about a week. The pain of the withdrawal symptoms could be because the use of opiates overloads the endorphin sites in the brain. Endorphin is the brain's natural painkiller, and if these sites are not responding to endorphin, a person might feel more pain.

Methadone
Methadone is a synthetic opiate that is prescribed as a substitute for heroin for people trying to give up using the drug. Methadone does not give the accompanying 'rush' that heroin gives, and acts more slowly.

Cannabis
Cannabis is widely used and comes from the plant *Cannabis sativa*. Dekta-9-tetrahydrocannabinol (THC) is the psychoactive ingredient in the plant. It seems to influence serotonin and noradrenaline. The sticky resin of the plant, where THC is highly concentrated, is made into hashish. Marijuana comes from the branches and leaves, and is less potent than hashish.

Cannabis is usually smoked or eaten. The smoked cannabis gets to the brain very quickly and brings a mild 'high' giving relaxation and good humour. Heart rate is increased, co-ordination is affected and short-term memory is impaired. Some users have negative emotions. The effects of cannabis are affected by the social situation. If large amounts are taken the user might hallucinate, and time might seem to go more slowly. Cannabis damages the lungs more than normal smoking does, and in pregnancy, cannabis can damage the fetus. It also disrupts sex hormones.

Cannabis is used by people with multiple sclerosis to help reduce muscle spasm, and by cancer patients receiving chemotherapy, as it can reduce feelings of sickness. It is

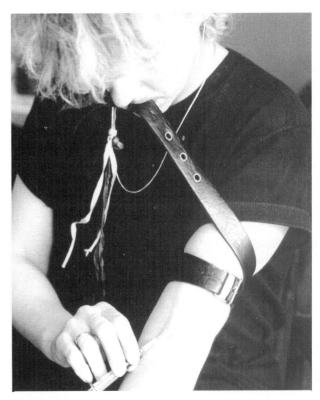

Figure 8.9

Drug use can bring euphoria early on, but the need to cope with loss of drugs then takes over. Tolerance to drugs often develops, and taking the drug no longer gives a 'high'

also used to reduce fluid pressure in the eye as a treatment for glaucoma.

Factors of addiction

↺ Recall AS material
Recall the main assumptions of the learning approach, the social approach and the cognitive approach, or look them up. It is useful to keep these main approaches in mind for what follows, and you will need the material also for the synoptic questions in Unit 6.

Learning theory

Social learning theory
It has already been suggested that modelling on others affects behaviour, certainly in adolescents. Social learning theory suggests that we imitate certain role models, and this is discussed below, as these roles concern social factors.

Operant conditioning
In learning theory, the law of effect suggests that if some behaviour has a pleasant outcome it will be repeated. In many cases drug taking does have a pleasant effect, as has

been outlined above. Recreational drugs bring a feeling of euphoria, and learning theory can be used to explain addiction. There is positive reinforcement from taking the drug, and so the behaviour is repeated. Addiction – finding it necessary to continue taking the drug – can be explained by both positive and negative reinforcement. The positive reinforcement is the pleasurable feeling; the negative reinforcement comes from the wish to avoid withdrawal symptoms. For example, stopping taking heroin leads to strong and very unpleasant withdrawal symptoms. The individual must keep taking the drug to avoid these unpleasant symptoms – and negative reinforcement is the motivating factor.

Evaluation

- Many people report that their first taste of alcohol is not a pleasant experience, and neither is their first cigarette. So there must be other reasons for addiction, such as imitation and social factors.

Classical conditioning

Principles of classical conditioning can be used to help in the treatment of addiction, although principles of operant conditioning are perhaps more useful in explaining addiction.

Aversion therapy is used to help in cases of alcoholism. Alcohol (such as whisky) is paired with an emetic drug (which gives feelings of nausea) and the feeling of sickness becomes the conditioned response instead of the pleasurable feeling.

ACTIVITY

Try this as a group activity. For each approach, consider how addiction would be explained. Use the main concepts of each approach, and think of how these concepts would be used to help to explain someone's addiction to a particular drug, before reading on.

↻ Recall AS material

Recall from your AS material how aversion therapy works.

Psychological factors (including salience and euphoria)

Psychological factors here refer to those that lead to addiction, other than learning by reinforcement or obeying social norms and rules. However, it is hard to separate psychological and social factors, so the reasons given here are psychosocial ones. One obvious reason for addiction is the feeling that taking the drug gives. Many drugs, at least at first, produce feelings of disinhibition and euphoria, which are pleasurable, and the individual takes the drug again to repeat them. You could argue that these feelings involve physiological factors, and this is

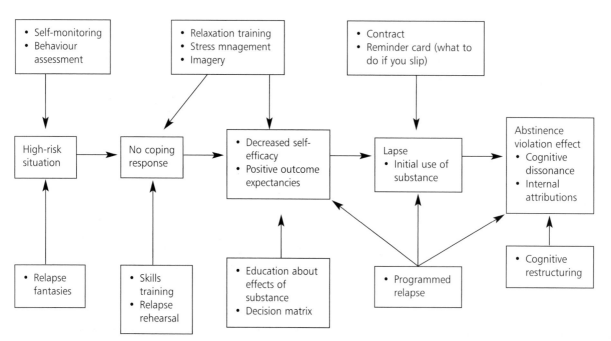

Figure 8.10
Strategies for preventing relapse (Source: Ogden, 2000)

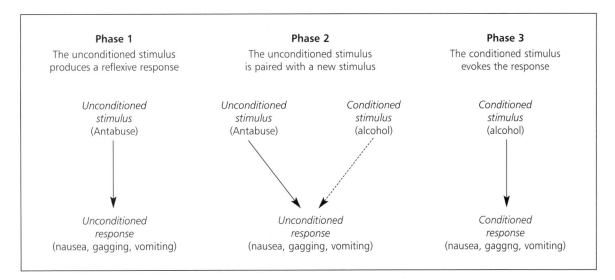

Figure 8.11
A classical conditioning approach to the treatment of alcoholism (Source: Taylor, 1999)

indeed the case, but psychological addiction is also a factor, and 'good' feelings that do not have a physiological base can come from taking a drug. Smoking, drinking alcohol or taking Ecstasy, for example, can boost self-esteem, and bring pleasurable feelings for that reason. If we see ourselves as a certain sort of person, and drug taking goes with this image, then addiction to that drug might follow.

Tomkins (1966,1968, in Sarafino, 1994) suggests four psychological reasons why people smoke.
- To achieve a positive effect, as explained by principles of positive reinforcement. Positive effects include stimulation, relaxation and pleasure.
- To reduce negative effects such as anxiety and tension, as explained by principles of negative reinforcement.
- Because the behaviour is habitual, automatic and occurs without awareness (this could also be seen as a physiological explanation).
- To control the positive and negative effects of addiction or a psychological dependence.

Recall AS material

Recall your AS material on ethical principles (or look it up). There are problems in researching in this area. For example, we are not supposed to cause anyone distress, but by asking questions about why people take drugs, we could cause distress or be intrusive. However, it might be possible to ask about smoking and drinking habits in general.

ACTIVITY

Carry out a questionnaire to examine smoking and/or drinking habits. If you choose to ask individuals about their own habits, then you need to get informed consent – you need to be sure that they do not mind disclosing personal details. You could avoid this by asking impersonal questions such as 'why do you think people smoke?' To avoid personal questions your questionnaire could include questions such as 'smoking is dangerous only to older people' and 'smoking can help people when they feel nervous and embarrassed', which people would assess on a Likert scale (recall this from AS material).

The data you collect can be analysed, and you could divide reasons up into those that learning theory could be applied to, as well as psychological, social and cognitive factors.

There has been some interesting evidence to show that Tomkins is correct in saying that people smoke for different reasons. Studies showed that 'positive-effect' smokers consumed fewer cigarettes that had been dipped in vinegar (for the purposes of the study) than other types of smoker, which suggests they smoke because of the positive effect that occurs. 'Negative-effect' smokers smoked more after watching a 'frightening' film than did other types of smoker, and this also suggests that they are smoking for a different reason (to reduce anxiety). Wills (1986) found that people do smoke to relieve stress, which could be either a physiological or a psychological cause.

Social factors (e.g. availability, cultural norms and attitudes)

Social factors can affect whether someone takes drugs. As has been discussed, adolescents seem to be affected by parents and peers: they are, for example, more likely to smoke if their parents and friends smoke (Hansen *et al.*, 1987). Leventhal *et al.* (1985) have shown that a young person's first cigarette is usually smoked in front of peers. Modelling and peer pressure seem to be important factors in such habits. Peer pressure involves norms and attitudes.

Evaluation

• If smoking runs in families, and studies suggest that it does, then there could be biological reasons. Hughes (1986) reports genetic factors in smoking from twin and adoption studies. Genes could affect addictive behaviour, by giving certain personality traits such as rebelliousness, by influencing whether the experience is found to be pleasant or unpleasant or by affecting the likelihood of dependence.

↺ Recall AS material

Recall or look up your AS material on twin and adoption studies, to help you understand the above claim. This material is also useful for the synoptic questions in Unit 6.

Cognitive factors (e.g. expectation)

Just as psychological addiction can arise from increase in self-esteem from taking a drug or smoking, so cognitive factors can be seen in whether a person takes a drug in the first place (which could then lead to addiction). Studies have been done asking people about their smoking habits, and answers show cognitive factors. Two such longitudinal studies asked adolescents about their habits (Chassin *et al.*, 1991: Murray *et al.*, 1983, cited in Sarafino, 1994). It was found that smoking tended to continue or increase

• if parents smoked or were unconcerned about smoking;
• if siblings or friends smoked;
• if there was peer pressure to smoke;
• if the individual had positive attitudes about smoking;
• if they did not feel smoking would endanger their health.

It can be seen here that expectations about smoking (whether it would enhance their standing with friends, or whether it was harmful, for example) affected behaviour.

Self-test

Write a timed essay, under exam conditions (or as close as you can manage) using the title 'Discuss the physiological and psychological effects and consequences of the use of two drugs'.

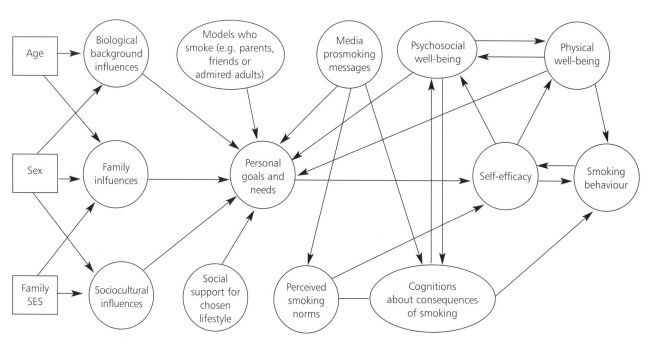

Figure 8.12
Factors influencing whether an adolescent begins to smoke (Source: Taylor, 1999)

Stress

Concept of stress

There are three ways of defining stress.

- Things that we see as threatening or harmful are called **stressors**, and stress is a stimulus, leading to a physiological response. Major life events, traumatic single events or chronic circumstances can all be seen as stressors.
- Stress is a person's state in response to a stressor. For example, we can become stressed when having to give a performance in public. The response can involve both physiological and psychological factors, and this response is called **strain**.
- Stress refers to the process, which includes both stressors and strain, but also involves transactions between the individual and the environment. Here the individual is active in the process and can influence the impact of the stress.

When the demands of a situation go beyond the resources the individual has to cope with it, **stress** is the result. Individuals have different resources to cope with demands, and so different people will experience different levels of stress in a given situation. Our first assessment is a primary appraisal. We judge the amount of harm or loss that has occurred, we look at what future harm or loss is likely, and we appraise the challenge that tackling the situation will bring. For example, a new job might bring loss (from the present job, or if we don't succeed), threat (in that we might not succeed at the new job or might not like it), and a challenge (we might be good at the new job and make more money). We also make secondary appraisals, and ongoing appraisals, and these affect our first judgements. Examples of secondary appraisals include the idea that if a job is too difficult we can turn to another option, or if there is a particular problem we can ask someone for help. These are cognitive appraisals, and if the demands of the situation go beyond the resources we have for coping, we then experience **strain**.

Cohen and Lazarus (1983) and Lazarus and Folkman (1984) have studied factors leading to stressful appraisals, and identify internal and external factors.

Internal factors

Internal or personal factors involve motivation and personality. For example, people with high self-esteem are likely to think that they have the required resources, whereas those with low self-esteem are more likely to see a situation as a threat than a challenge. Also, the more important a goal is (the more motivated a person is to achieve that goal) the more he or she is likely to experience threat, and to see their resources as not equalling the demands.

Belief systems are also important, as irrational beliefs can increase stress. For example, anyone who thinks they must be liked by everyone at all times is often going to believe that they have insufficient resources to meet the demands of tasks.

External factors

External factors involve the type of situation, and the effect of the environment. Some situations are going to be more stressful than others.

- Likely stressful situations are those with strong urgent demands, where there is little time for appraisal. For example, finding that you need urgent surgery is likely to be more stressful than if you have time to appraise a less dramatic situation such as a visit to the dentist for a check-up next week. The demands of the situation involve external factors.
- Major life events (called **transitions**) are also stressful. Examples are starting a new school, getting married, moving house, becoming a parent, retiring from a career. Not only are these life events stressful, but their timing can add to the stress of the experience. These transitions are external factors – however, how we perceive them involves internal factors.
- There is an expected timetable for such events in a culture, and deviating from it can deprive the person of friends and peers in the same situation. This in itself can make the situation more stressful. If the timing is wrong, the individual can be seen as a failure, for example, which adds to their judgement that their resources won't meet the demands of the situations. This expected timetable is an external factor, given by our culture.
- Lack of clarity in a situation can also lead to more stress being experienced. **Role ambiguity** means a more difficult appraisal of the situation, for example. Unclear guidelines about a job can lead to such ambiguity at work. **Harm ambiguity** means that it is hard to appraise the amount of harm that might occur, or when we don't know what resources we will need to meet the demands of the situation. For example, someone who is seriously ill needs information to help them make appropriate judgements. Ambiguity can be external or internal: the situation (for example, a poor job description) is external but our view of the situation is internal.
- The desirability of the situation is also a factor in the amount of stress experienced. Some events are always undesirable – such as losing all your possessions in a fire. However, some situations, such as moving house, can be desirable. Undesirable situations are usually more stressful, but desirable ones can also be stressful, depending on how the individual perceives the resources they have for coping with the demands. Whether we view a situation as desirable or undesirable tends to be an internal decision, although some

environmental events (such as a house fire) are external, and obviously undesirable.

• How far the situation is controllable is another factor. You have **behavioural control** if you can do something to affect the stress of the situation. For example, if your job is stressful, and you are in a position to find another job, you should experience less stress than if you had no control over the situation. **Cognitive control** means we can use mental strategies to improve the situation – for example, secondary appraisals such as planning a second strategy if the first does not work. The amount of control can be viewed as internal, depending on our attitudes, although sometimes we have little behavioural control (for example, over a serious illness) and this would be an external factor.

Interactional factors involved in experiencing stress

It can be seen by the above analysis that generally there is an interaction between an individual's attitude to the situation and the external pressures of the situation. A factor is rarely completely external or completely internal. Reactions to stress tend to be best understood within the biopsychosocial model discussed earlier in this chapter, as are the causes of stress.

Physiological response to stress

Biological aspects of stress

Stress has been defined as both a stimulus and a response to certain situations. Some things are stressors, and the response is strain. Biological aspects of stress focus on strain on the body. Physiological reactions to stressors are quite well known. Think of a time when you experienced a frightening event, perhaps a near miss when driving, or nearly falling down some stairs. You will have experienced quite a 'jolt', and your heartbeat and breathing rate will have increased immediately. After the danger had passed, you may have experienced shaking, and had to sit down quickly. This is not stress, but a normal reaction. Stress is when this reaction continues instead of calming down.

The fight-or-flight response

Cannon (1929) described how the body reacts to an emergency, and the fight-or-flight response is often called the emergency reaction or alarm reaction. An organism seems to be biologically prepared in an emergency to fight or to flee – a useful survival trait.

An organism that is the most fitting for a particular environment will survive. So an organism that had a fight response, and was able to fight its way out of trouble, might have survived – as might one that could flee to get out of trouble. Perhaps those who could fight when needed, and flee on other occasions – and made the right choices – were those most likely to survive. So the genes for this emergency reaction are passed on, as those with such genes would have survived to reproduce.

↻ Recall AS material

Recall, from your studies of the physiological approach, information about the fight-or-flight response, which you may have studied. This response occurs in the peripheral nervous system. Recall also the theory of natural selection – or look this up.

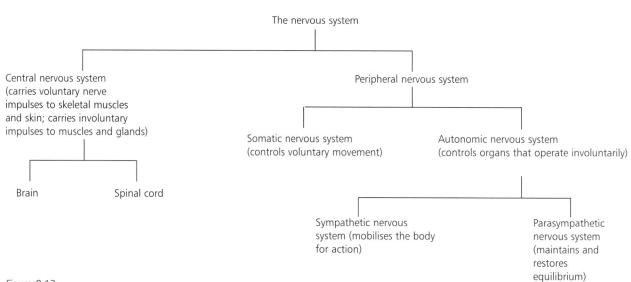

Figure 8.13
The components of the nervous system (Source: Taylor, 1999)

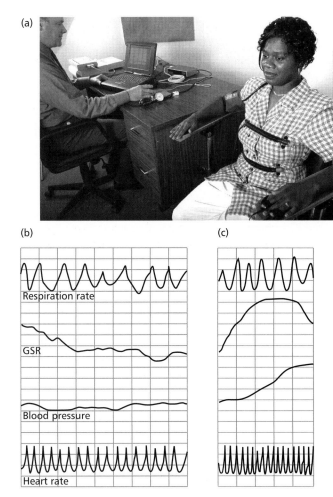

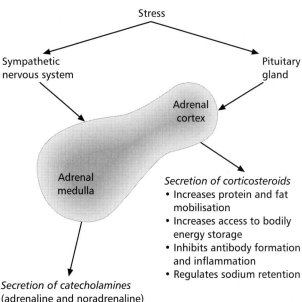

Figure 8.15
Adrenal gland activity in response to stress (Source: Taylor, 1999)

Figure 8.14
A typical polygraph (a) makes a graphical record of several factors affecting arousal, including blood pressure, heart and respiration rates, and the galvanic skin response (this measures skin conductance, which is affected by sweating). A comparison of the two graphs depicts the difference in arousal between someone who is calm (b) and someone who is under stress (c) (Source: Sarafino, 1994)

In the fight-or-flight response the sympathetic part of the peripheral nervous system is activated, and when the emergency is over, the parasympathetic part of the peripheral nervous system acts to take us back to our normal state. The sympathetic system is properly called the sympathetic adrenomedullary (SAM) system, and the hypothalamic-pituitary-adrenocortical (HPA) system is also involved in stress.

HPA system

The SAM system stimulates the adrenal glands to secrete adrenaline, which arouses the body. Information from the cortex (when something is perceived as threatening, for example) is sent to the hypothalamus, and this triggers the sympathetic nervous system into the alarm reaction. The alarm reaction first causes arousal to drop below normal and then to rise above normal. Arousal is measured by physiological measures such as blood

pressure, breathing rate and heart rate. Arousal leads, amongst other things, to increased blood pressure, increased heart rate, increased sweating and constriction of peripheral blood vessels. The endocrine system releases hormones to give this quick increase in arousal. The hypothalamus releases corticotrophin-releasing factor, which influences the pituitary gland. The pituitary gland secretes adrenocorticotrophic hormone, which causes the adrenal glands to release adrenaline and noradrenaline (catecholamines), and cortisol (a corticosteroid) into the bloodstream. Cortisol helps to reduce inflammation from injuries, and is important in returning the body to a steady state after the alarm reaction. The body cannot maintain a high level of arousal for long.

HPA activity raises rates of growth hormone and prolactin, both secreted by the pituitary gland, and raised amounts of the opioids beta-endorphin and enkephalin are found in the brain in response to stress.

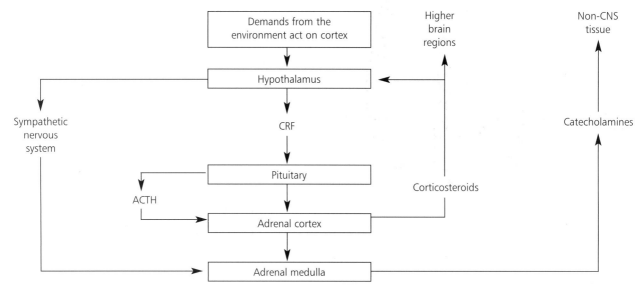

Figure 8.16
How stress affects our health (Source: Taylor, 1999)

Many stressors increase secretion of hormones by the adrenal glands (Baum *et al.*, 1982). Examples include cold temperatures, noise, pain, failure, taking exams, and being in crowds (Sarafino, 1994).

Evaluation

• There are other factors that affect the amount of strain experienced, and some of these have been outlined above (for example, the type of person, or the exact stressor). These other factors can affect the amount of hormone released. For example, a reaction that involves a high emotional response leads to a different amount of hormone being released than one causing less intense emotions. It does not seem that one hormone is released no matter what the situation (Mason, 1975) – it has been claimed that adrenaline, noradrenaline and cortisol are released but sometimes only two of these are found (all three are likely if there is a highly emotional response). Cognitive factors are also important. Tennes and Kreye (1985) tested the cortisol levels of children before and after taking a test. Those with higher intelligence scores had higher levels of cortisol on the day of the test. The researchers thought that the exams might have been more important for those with higher intelligence, as they were more concerned about academic achievement. Therefore, those children saw the tests as more threatening, and had higher arousal as a result. These two examples show the importance of looking at the interaction between physiological and other factors.

Effects on the immune system

A problem with the fight-or-flight response is that, although it is a useful mechanism for getting us out of danger, a continued state of high arousal can be harmful. Over a long period, excessive amounts of adrenaline and noradrenaline can suppress the immune function, increase

blood pressure and heart rate, break up the normal rhythm of the heart and give neurochemical changes that can lead to psychiatric disorders. Increases in cortisol have been related to lymphocyte functioning (they affect the immune system adversely). Neurons in the hippocampus can be destroyed by increased levels of cortisol, which can lead to memory deficits. HPA activation can also lead to fat being stored near the waist rather than at the hips (and a measure of stress is the waist–hip ratio – Bjorntorp, 1996). Depressed people often have high levels of cortisol.

The immune system is there to protect the body from foreign substances (called antigens), which include bacteria, viruses, tumour cells and toxins. Lymphocytes (white blood cells) identify and eliminate antigens. Immune cells such as T-helper cells and natural killer (NK) cells can be counted to test the immune system. Another measure of the immune system is to see how lymphocytes proliferate (divide), because this is a necessary immune response. Glaser and Kiecolt-Glaser (1994) and Cohen and Herbert (1996) have both shown that psychosocial stress is associated with a weakening of the immune system. Studies have shown that bereaved people, divorced people, carers of those with Alzheimer's disease, and those with major depression all have a weakened immune system.

General adaptation syndrome

Selye (1956) talked about the general adaptation syndrome (GAS). This is what happens to an organism when the fight-or-flight response is continued, and the state of arousal is not 'cancelled' by the parasympathetic nervous system. There are three stages in the general adaptation syndrome.

1 The alarm reaction outlined above.
2 The stage of resistance. As the strong stressor continues

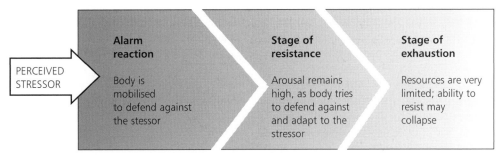

Figure 8.17
The general adaptation syndrome (Source: Sarafino, 1994)

the physiological response continues but at a slightly reduced level. The body has to renew the hormones released by the adrenal glands. The organism does not appear outwardly to be suffering from stress, although it will not cope well with new stressors. The body will be more vulnerable, and health problems that might occur at this stage are described as diseases of adaptation (Selye, 1956). Examples of such problems are ulcers, high blood pressure, asthma and illnesses that relate to a weakened immune system.

3 The stage of exhaustion. The immune system is very weak at this stage, and physiological resources are low.

Causes of stress

We cannot say that there is *one* cause for stress, as the stimulus, the response and the appraisal of the individual are all factors in whether stress is experienced or not.

Biological factors

Selye explains stress by means of the GAS, and shows how continuous release of hormones for 'fight-or-flight' purposes can lead to illness and even death as the body tries to maintain the alarm reaction. Stressors produce physiological changes. Biological factors are involved in stress, and in this way can be said to cause stress. However, you could argue that they are the result of a stressor, and the response of the body, rather than a cause of stress.

One biological factor that is said to cause stress is disruption of bodily rhythms.

↻ Recall AS material

Recall your AS material relating to disruption of bodily rhythms (or look it up), in particular discussions about the 24-hour society, shift work and jet lag.

Social factors

Causes of stress are often social factors, such as the life events discussed above. Unemployment, retirement, examinations and holidays are all life events that can cause stress. However, the reaction of others can also be a factor in whether stress is felt following such life events.

Lack of social support

An important social factor when looking at causes of stress is social support – comfort, caring and help given by others. Evidence for this is that married people, who support one another, are said to live longer (Lynch, 1977) and social support is supposed to reduce birth complications (Oakley, 1992). Arnetz *et al.* (1987) compared unemployed people on benefits with those who had a psychosocial support programme as well as receiving benefits. Those with social support showed better immune functioning, so it seems that social support is an important factor in alleviating stress. Perhaps people with social support experience less stress, so lack of social support is a cause of stress.

Figure 8.18
The Amish people provide social support for one another

The 'main effect' hypothesis suggests that lack of social support is in itself stressful, and lack of social support is itself a stressor. The 'stress buffering' hypothesis suggests that social support helps in coping with stress, and lack of it is not a cause of stress. It should be noted that other people affect the individual's appraisal of the situation, and it is clear that social factors affect whether stress is experienced.

Schwarzer *et al.* (1994) tested the relationship between social support and health in a longitudinal study where data were collected at three points. The participants were 235 East German migrants living in West Berlin: 62% were refugees who arrived before the wall was opened, 38% were legal immigrants (after the opening of the wall). The participants' job status, level of social support and level of ill health were all recorded at three times. People who were unemployed reported more ill health, and men in this group reported more ill health than women. Social support did not affect the 'employed' group, but had a great effect on the unemployed group: those who were unemployed but with social support reported far fewer ill-health symptoms than those who had no social support. It did appear that employment affected social support and vice versa – those with jobs had more social support, and those with more social support were more likely to get jobs.

Figure 8.19
Many elderly people are isolated and do not receive the social support they need

Psychological factors

Cognition and emotion have already been linked to how we experience stress in a physiological sense. Levels of cortisol are affected by motivation, and emotion affects which hormones are released, so cognitive and emotional factors can be said to be causes of stress (or at least to affect whether stress is felt or not). High levels of stress can also affect cognitive functions. For example, your memory can be impaired by the stress of examinations.

Noise and cognition

Noise can be a stressor, especially if it is chronic (always there). Noise is an environmental factor, but becomes a psychological factor when it affects our attention and cognitive functioning. People tend to cope by 'tuning out' noise – by not paying attention to it. Cohen (1980) suggests that children who generally tune out chronic noise – if they live by a railway track, for example – may have problems in knowing what to attend to and what to tune out, which may affect their learning. Cohen *et al.* (1973) showed that children living in noisier environments (living on a bridge over a busy road) had more difficulty in discriminating between pairs of words (e.g. house and mouse) than did children in a quieter environment.

Baum (1990) points out not only that stressors can affect our cognitive functioning but also that our thinking affects the amount of stress felt. If we carry on thinking about a problem, the stress is more likely to continue than if we manage to put it out of our minds.

ACTIVITY

Think of two groups you know of, where one experiences chronic noise and the other does not. If there is an obvious group of participants in your area that is fine, although remember ethical principles. You could arrange for people from each group to do an experiment in a noisy environment and one in quiet surroundings This is not testing the effect of chronic noise (as the noise will not be 'always there') but it might be an interesting test. The noisy surroundings must be natural and fair (a school dining room?), and the noise must be something the participants would normally encounter – remember ethical principles and be guided by your teacher.

Although Cohen et al.'s study involved children, you should use adults in your sample, even if you cannot then exactly replicate what Cohen found. Your aim is to see if noise affects cognitive functioning.

When you have chosen your sample, devise a simple test like the one suggested above, where people have to discriminate between word pairs, perhaps separating those that sound alike from those that do not (e.g. house/mouse, bed/chair). Time them and see how successful they have been. Your score could be number of word pairs correctly discriminated, time taken, or a combination of both.

Emotion

Emotion can also affect the amount of stress felt. The same situation can give us different emotions, and the different emotions, though each bringing stress, can affect the amount of stress felt. Fear is an emotional reaction that gives stress. An intense, irrational fear directly associated with specific events is called a phobia. Anxiety is more a vague feeling of unease to a generally fairly unspecific threat. As we get older we experience more anxiety, as our fears tend to become less specific (Sarafino, 1986). Another emotion linked to stress is depression. Everyone feels depressed sometimes, but depression becomes a disorder when it becomes more serious. For example, if people are generally unhappy, feel hopeless about the future, are listless and passive, have problems with eating and sleeping and have low self-esteem, then depression is becoming a disorder. Chapter 1 discusses depression, anxiety and phobias.

Other psychological factors involved in stress are self-efficacy (the individual's level of confidence that they can do something) and hardiness (level of commitment and desire to accept challenges). So psychological factors, including cognitive and emotional ones, can affect whether stress is felt or not, and can contribute to stress.

Personality type

It has been shown that certain clusters of behaviour are more likely to lead to experiences of stress. Friedman and Rosenman (1974), amongst others, have discussed two different personality types: Type A and Type B. Type A people are competitive and achievement oriented. They tend to be self-critical and move towards a goal without enjoying their accomplishments. They struggle against the clock and become impatient at delays. They try to do more than one thing at a time, and are easily aroused to anger. 'Type B' people, however, have low levels of competitiveness, and are less hostile. They take their time, and take time out. Type A individuals react more quickly and more strongly to stressors, and are more likely to see them as threats to their overall control. They might even be more likely to encounter stressors, given their competitiveness. Type A people show more reactivity – reactivity is their arousal when experiencing stressors as measured against their resting, non-aroused state. Structured interviews are used to measure these personality types, and then health patterns are looked at.

Locus of control and self-efficacy

A sense of control makes a difference when appraising a situation. The importance of controllability of the situation has already been mentioned. Those with a strong sense of control may experience less strain from a stressor (Suls and Mullen, 1981).

There are different types of control:

- **Behavioural control** – the ability to do something active about the situation.
- **Cognitive control** – being able to use strategies, including thinking positive thoughts.
- **Decisional control** – being able to choose different courses of action.
- **Informational control** – being able to get information, on which to base decisions.
- **Retrospective control** – finding a sense of meaning about what has happened.

All these types of control can reduce stress, but cognitive control seems to be very important (Cohen *et al.*, 1986).

People who think they have control over their successes and failures are said to have an **internal locus of control**. Those who think events lie outside themselves have an **external locus of control** (Rotter, 1966). Rotter has developed an I–E scale, which is how far someone has internal or external locus of control (think of 'locus' as being 'place'). Most people have a belief mid-way between internal and external locus of control.

ACTIVITY

Generate some statements about locus of control and measure replies using a Likert scale. Statements such as 'usually people have some say in government decisions', if agreed with, show a belief in an internal locus of control; 'we can't do much in influencing decisions, as those in power tell us what to do', if agreed with, would show a belief in an external locus of control. You need to think of other such statements, and then score the questionnaire. Make sure you adjust the scoring to suit the statement. For example, the first statement has a scoring of strongly agree = 5, agree = 4, not sure = 3, disagree = 2 and strongly disagree = 1. However, the second statement would be scored as strongly agree = 1, agree = 2, not sure = 3, disagree = 4 and strongly disagree = 5 (for this way of scoring, a high score shows a belief in an internal locus of control).

You can test whether people generally have a mid-way score. You could also look at gender or age differences, and for this you must collect relevant personal data – remember ethical principles, however.

Another factor involved in whether we believe we have internal or external locus of control is **self-efficacy**, which is the belief that we can succeed at something we want to do (Bandura, 1977b). People use their past experiences to decide firstly on whether something is going to lead to a positive outcome, and, secondly, whether they think they can do it. Those with a strong sense of self-efficacy show less psychological and physiological strain in response to stressors than do those with a weak sense of self-efficacy (Bandura *et al.*, 1985).

Self-test

Write a timed essay, under exam conditions (or as close as you can manage), using the title 'Discuss one biological, one social and one psychological factor that may cause stress'.

Management and coping strategies

From what is suggested above, you will see that there is probably rarely one cause of stress, and that there is more than one way of coping with stress.

Coping is the way people try to manage the difference they perceive between their resources and the demands of the situation. They make primary and secondary appraisals of the situation, including their resources and the demands, and have different choices about how to manage the situation. If they manage it, they are coping – or at least there is an extent to which they can manage, and an extent to which they cannot. Of course, it depends what we mean by coping. You might manage a stressful situation at work by staying away with illness; someone else could manage by moving to another job. There is doubt as to what extent this is coping, but both people would be managing the situation. Coping is an ongoing process of continuous appraisal and reappraisal as the situation changes.

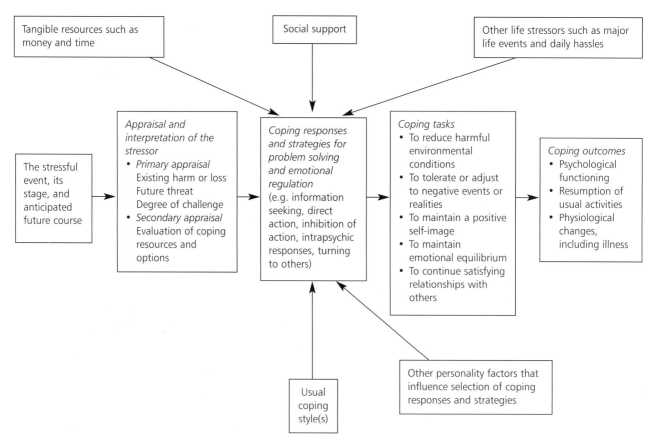

Figure 8.20
The coping process (Source: Taylor, 1999; from Cohen and Lazarus, 1979; Hamburg and Adams, 1967; Lazarus and Folkman, 1984; Moos, 1988; Taylor, 1983)

Defence mechanisms

One way of coping is to use defence mechanisms. However, saying that we 'use' them might not be quite accurate, because the whole point is that our unconscious defends us by means of such mechanisms, and it is not a conscious process.

↻ Recall AS material

Recall your AS material about defence mechanisms, as outlined in Freud's psychoanalytic theory. Look it up if you can't remember.

Defence mechanisms on the face of it protect us from stressful situations. Defence mechanisms are cognitive strategies and mean distorting memory or reality.

- Something that is too painful can be denied – this defence mechanism is called **denial**.
- **Intellectualisation** is also a defence mechanism, and means dealing with a stressor at an intellectual level, in an abstract fashion (so it does not 'touch' you).
- **Suppression** is a defence mechanism, where someone puts the problem out of their mind.

Defence mechanisms can be useful strategies if there is nothing that can be done about the problem, and when problem-focused strategies are unlikely to be useful. However, they are not useful if something can be done about the problem. At first avoidance strategies, like using defence mechanisms can be useful, but the attention strategies, such as problem-focusing are more useful in coping with stress (Suls and Fletcher, 1985).

Problem-focusing

One way of sorting out different coping strategies has been to label them either **problem-focusing** or emotion-focusing.

Coping can do two things – either alter the problem or change the emotional response to the problem. Problem-focused coping aims to reduce the demands of the situation and increase resources to cope with it (you can leave a stressful job, or put together a new revision plan when an examination is looming). If the resources and/or the demands of the situation are changeable, then it is best to use problem-focused coping.

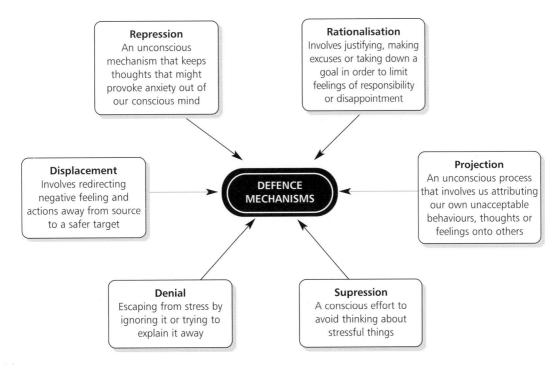

Figure 8.21
Defence mechanisms that protect us from anxiety by distorting or denying reality (Source: Banyard, 1996)

ACTIVITY

To find out whether you tend to use problem-focusing or emotion focusing, think of a stressful situation you have recently encountered – or one you have encountered at some stage. Go through the following list and tick the statements that applied at the time.

1 *Talked with someone about the problem*
2 *Tried to see the positive side*
3 *Did something to improve the situation*
4 *Took it out on others a bit*
5 *Decided not to worry and let it sort itself out*
6 *Drew on previous similar experience*
7 *Thought of several possibilities to sort things*
8 *Got busy with something else*
9 *Prayed for strength or guidance*
10 *Took one step at a time*
11 *Tried to step back and be objective*
12 *Talked with a professional person*

(adapted from Sarafino (1994, p140)

Statements 1, 3, 6, 7, 10, 12 are problem-focusing strategies and statements 2, 4, 5, 8, 9, 11 are emotion-focusing strategies. Work out your main style.

Emotion-focusing

Emotion-focused coping is when the emotional response is controlled, or at least that it is the aim. Behavioural approaches to emotion-focusing include taking drugs (including alcohol), looking for social support from others, or involving oneself in other activities 'to take your mind off the problem'. Cognitive approaches to emotion-focusing include altering the way the situation is perceived. For example, you can think of worse things, or think of the positive side. You could deny that the situation is happening (this is using defence mechanisms, as outlined above). Lazarus and Folkman (1984b) suggest that emotion-focusing is used when the situation cannot be changed.

Studies have looked at situations to see when problem-focused coping is used, and when emotion-focused coping is used. Billings and Moos (1981) did a survey involving around 200 married couples. The participants answered questions about a recent negative life event or

Table 8.8 The coping strategies identified by Folkman and colleagues

Scale 1: Confrontive coping
• Stood my ground and fought for what I wanted
• Tried to get the person responsible to change his or her mind
• I expressed anger to the person(s) who caused the problem
• I let my feelings out somehow

Scale 2: Distancing
• Made light of the situation; refused to get too serious about it
• Went on as if nothing had happened
• Didn't let it get to me; refused to think about it too much
• Tried to forget the whole thing

Scale 3: Self-controlling
• I tried to keep my feelings to myself
• Kept others from knowing how bad things were
• I tried to keep my feelings from interfering with other things too much

Scale 4: Seeking social support
• Talked to someone to find out more about the situation
• Talked to someone who could do something concrete about the problem
• I asked a relative or friend I respected for advice
• Talked to someone about how I was feeling

Scale 5: Accepting responsibility
• Criticised or lectured myself
• Realised I brought the problem on myself
• I made a promise to myself that things would be different next time

Scale 6: Escape–avoidance
• Wished that the situation would go away or somehow be over with
• Hoped a miracle would happen
• Had fantasies about how things might turn out
• Tried to make myself feel better by eating, drinking, smoking, using drugs or medication, and so forth

Scale 7: Planful problem solving
• I knew what had to be done, so I doubled my efforts to make things work
• I made a plan of action and followed it
• Changed something so things would turn out all right
• Drew on my past experiences; I was in a similar position before

Scale 8: Positive reappraisal
• Changed or grew as a person in a good way
• I came out of the experience better than when I went in
• Found new faith
• Rediscovered what is important in life

Source: Stroebe (2000)

personal crisis. Both husbands and wives used more problem-focused strategies for coping but wives reported using more emotion-focused strategies than did husbands. Low income and low education meant more emotion-focusing, there was less problem-focusing when the crisis was a death in the family and more problem-focused coping when problems were illness or financial difficulties.

Clearly the type of situation affects the type of coping, although in general more problem-focused strategies are used. People do use both problem-focused and emotion-focused strategies together. For example, you might react to stress at work by resigning and looking for a new job (problem-focusing) and at the same time control your impulse to lose your temper (emotion-focusing).

Some mixed strategies – problem-focused and emotion-focused

Here are some examples of using different strategies in response to being stressed at work:
- Direct action – directly dealing with the stressor. A problem-focused approach would be to negotiate less work, and an emotion-focused approach would be to argue with someone about the level of work.
- Seek information – which might help in dealing with the stressor. A problem-focused approach would be to find out your rights by contacting a Union.
- Turn to others – talk to family and friends. A problem-focused approach would be to seek a loan from a family member to enable you to give up the job for a short while and look for another. An emotion-focused approach would be to seek emotional support.

Some emotion-focused strategies
- Come to terms with the problem. This strategy is used when a situation cannot be changed.
- Release emotions. Using jokes, shouting or crying can be ways of releasing emotions.
- Cognitive strategies to change the way of thinking about the situation, and possibly distorting it, can be emotion-focusing.

Not releasing emotions can mean that stress continues. Some people have intrusive thoughts (Baum, 1990) and keep reliving the problem, therefore maintaining the stress. For example, they might keep thinking about how they are to blame for the problem, or they might have flashbacks of traumatic events. These individuals are likely to have poorer health. Talking and/or writing about the problems can help to release emotions (Pennebaker, 1990).

Resources in coping

In general, people use more than one coping strategy, although they tend to be consistent. Avoidance strategies (whether defence mechanisms or emotion-focusing) tend to lead to more ill health.

Evaluation
- You could argue that, if avoidance strategies tend to be used when nothing can be done about a problem, then this is the more serious situation, causing greater stress, and so more ill-health is likely.

Social

When looking at social factors involved in causes of stress, social support was mentioned. It was claimed, for example, that even when unemployed and with problems that might cause stress, people with social support exhibited fewer signs of stress than those without social support. So social resources in coping are important. Use the material outlined above about the importance of social support when considering social resources in coping.

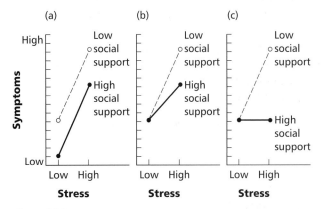

Figure 8.22
Social support is assumed to benefit health in two ways. In the direct effect hypothesis (a) social support is beneficial regardless of the level of stress. The buffering effect hypothesis proposes that social support protects individuals against the negative impact of stress to some extent (b) or totally (c) (Source: Stroebe, 2000)

Some parts of society have less social support than others (Ratliff-Crain and Baum, 1990): men tend to have larger social networks, but women seem to use their support more effectively; elderly people have less social support and fewer means to get it; social networks are smaller if income and education levels are lower.

Educational

Billings and Moos (1981) showed that people with a higher income and better education used more problem-focused strategies for coping, so it seems that resources when coping included educational ones. Social networks are larger for these people.

Figure 8.23
Social support from family and friends helps keep people healthy and may help them recover faster when they are ill

Figure 8.24
Religion promotes psychological well-being, and people with religious faith may be better able to cope with adverse events

Self-test

Write a timed essay under exam conditions (or as close as you can manage), using the title 'Discuss various management/coping strategies used when dealing with stress'.

Health promotion

Treatments and therapies

Health promotion can refer to treatments and therapies – for example, teaching someone to use stress management can promote good health. Some factors involved in stress cannot be changed (such as age or family history) but other factors can be changed by the individual – cognitive/behavioural interventions can, for example, modify the Type A personality. Relaxation can alter a person's physical response to a stressful situation, and rational–emotive therapy (RET) can lead to this more relaxed approach. RET involves a person in examining their responses to situations, and changing them. Ellis (1977) discussed the ABCDE paradigm. A stands for the activating experience (the situation causing the stress). B stands for the beliefs in the person's mind at the time. C stands for the consequences. D stands for the disputing of irrational beliefs, and this is the key to the therapy. E stands for the effect of the therapy, which is a restructured belief system. RET is discussed in Chapter 1.

Preventing problems

Health promotion mainly refers to work before there is a health problem. The idea, as outlined in the introduction of this chapter, is that once something is identified as a health risk or a health problem steps should be taken to prevent this problem from developing. For example, if we find out that smoking is bad for our health, then a health promotion campaign to stop people from smoking is going to be a useful way of improving health in general (and the health of particular individuals).

Harris and Guten (1979) carried out a survey to see what health-protective behaviours people used. They found that around two-thirds of the people asked did admit to eating sensibly, getting enough sleep and keeping emergency phone numbers near the phone (these were the top three health-protecting actions); about half said they got enough relaxation, had a first aid kit in the home and saw a doctor for a regular check-up; just under half said they prayed, avoided getting chilled and watched their weight; 46% said they did things in moderation and took enough exercise; 41% avoided parts of the city where there was a lot of crime, and 41% did not smoke.

Turk *et al.* (1986) used a similar study, and found that nurses were more likely to keep emergency phone numbers handy, teachers had watching their weight as the top answer for health-protecting actions, and students gave their highest answer as getting enough exercise.

Some of these health-protective behaviours are there to promote health, and others are there to avoid risk (getting enough sleep and enough exercise promote health, whereas keeping your weight down avoids risk). Similarly, health promotion acts to avoid problems, and disease prevention does the same from a different direction. Both of these are needed to advance health in general. For example, to protect against tooth decay we encourage good practice regarding care of teeth (e.g. regular brushing), we use environmental measures (e.g. fluoride in the water supply) and use medical interventions (e.g. repairing cavities). Breslow (1983) says that in industrialised nations the best health promotion seems to be in influencing behaviour. There are three levels of prevention: primary, secondary and tertiary. The individual can be involved in these preventative measures, as can their social network and professionals working to promote health.

↺ Recall AS material

Recall your AS material about the physiological approach and about genetic counselling, including how understanding of genes and related issues can lead parents to have to make difficult decisions about the unborn child.

One way of tackling primary prevention is to use questionnaires to ask people to assess their risk factors, as you might have done if you completed the questionnaire given earlier in this chapter. Questions used in such questionnaires include those about age, gender, race, height, weight, drinking and smoking habits, and physical activity.

ACTIVITY

Try this as a group activity. Ask the age, occupation and gender of a group of people, then make a list of likely health-promoting behaviours and ask participants to tick those behaviours that apply to them. The more people you ask, the more varied the answers are likely to be, although you don't need too many participants. Remember ethical principles. You could compare your answers with those of Harris and Guten. It would be interesting to see what differences you find given that their study was done quite a long time ago.

ACTIVITY

1 Health promotion campaigns involve media coverage. There tends to be a cycle of such campaigns (as is often the pattern with media topics), and one issue that recurs is that of vaccinating children. Use a CD-ROM or the Internet to research such issues, by checking through back editions of newspapers. Write a brief report giving the arguments for and against vaccination programmes. Then draw three conclusions, one from the point of view of the government health campaign (pro-vaccination), another from an anti-vaccination parent's viewpoint, and a third from a parent who is pro-vaccination.

2 Construct a questionnaire to gather information about trends in health behaviours, using some of the ideas and factors given above. Then analyse the data, and write a report suggesting primary prevention measures that could be carried out. You could include a recommendation regarding a health promotion campaign. The results and report would make a good presentation.

Primary prevention

Primary prevention involves taking actions to avoid disease or injury – for example, using a seat belt when riding in a car. Promoting primary prevention can involve a government campaign. Primary prevention can start before a child is born – a mother might decide to stop smoking, for instance; for some inherited diseases or problems a genetic counsellor can give parents information that may help them in assessing any risks (there is often an increased risk as parental age increases) and genetic tests can reveal problems with the unborn child. Sickle-cell anaemia and Duchenne muscular dystrophy are disorders that can be discovered by such procedures.

Primary prevention also includes following immunisation programmes for children. Diseases controlled in this way include diphtheria, tetanus, whooping cough, measles, rubella, mumps and polio. However, many children are not immunised.

Secondary prevention

Secondary prevention involves treating a problem early enough to stop it becoming more serious. Blood pressure checks, for example, mean that early intervention can be used to prevent a serious problem developing. Eye checks for glaucoma can control a potential problem, and people whose parents have glaucoma are given free eye checks. Another example of secondary prevention is that mammograms are recommended for women over 50 to test for breast cancer.

Tertiary prevention

Tertiary prevention is what happens after a disease or problem has passed the early stages – when something could still be done to prevent further damage. Tertiary prevention involves helping people to live with their problems or helping to prevent further problems arising. For example, someone with severe arthritis might be given exercises or some medication to relieve the pain. There might be something that can be done to keep incurable cancer in remission, or to make sufferers more comfortable.

Hygiene as health promotion

Good hygiene is essential in hospitals, but hospitals themselves have health hazards, including use of chemicals (Clever and Omenn, 1988). For example, someone is exposed to the sterilising agent ethylene oxide for a long time risks developing cancer.

Micro-organisms can cause disease, and diseases can easily be spread through hospitals, so many steps have been introduced to try to prevent patients from developing illnesses during their hospital stay. An infection that a patient contracts while in a hospital setting is called a **nosocomial infection**. Steps to prevent diseases of infections from spreading including washing hands and wearing masks.

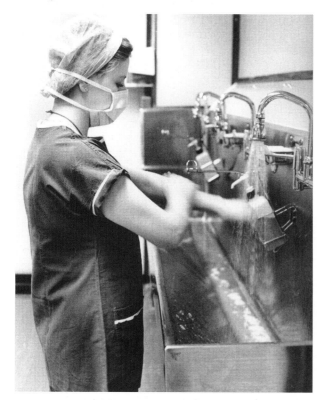

Figure 8.25
Hospitals try to reduce the spread of infection using rules about medical staff wearing clean masks, clothing and gloves

The idea of washing to prevent the spread of germs is something that most people understand, and there are basic rules regarding hygiene. These days, for example, people who work in kitchens or with food have to hold hygiene certificates, and there are strict health regulations regarding hygiene.

Nutrition as health promotion

One problem with maintaining good health is that many of the behaviours promoted in our society do not lead to good health. These behaviours can include poor nutrition habits. A 'wellness' lifestyle is one that includes as many 'good' habits as possible, with regard to health behaviours, but a problem in adopting such a lifestyle is that some behaviours (for example, smoking) may have led to addiction, and may be hard to control. Also, someone who is healthy may not focus on wellness behaviours because they do not think about their health. Research also shows that even when people are ill they continue with poor habits, or don't take recommended medicine (Rosenstock and Kirscht, 1979).

One way of promoting good health is to focus on diet. A healthy diet is good for everyone, especially those at risk of developing a chronic disease. Dietary habits may contribute to the development of some cancers (Steinmetz *et al.*, 1994); salt is linked to hypertension and heart disease; changing a diet can reduce cholesterol. One problem in recommending changes to a person's diet is that it needs to be maintained, which can be difficult. Shopping habits, meal planning, cooking methods and eating habits all need to alter, and new habits may be difficult to maintain. Poor diet is associated with low self-efficacy, a preference for meat, a low interest in exploring new foods and a low awareness of the link between diet and illness (Hollis *et al.*, 1986). Mass media campaigns are used to raise awareness of the importance of a good diet, but may not be successful in producing long-term behaviour change.

Social skills in health promotion

Efforts to improve the dietary habits of high-risk individuals have recently focused on the family, because if all family members are committed to the changes, the target seems easier to achieve. For example, someone in a family that eats together will find a low cholesterol diet difficult to follow if no one else wants to. Social skills in going your own way, against the habits and customs of those around you need nurturing. Usually we follow the norms and customs of our in-groups.

Social factors also tend to determine what is expected. Boys are expected to be more physical than girls, for example. Rubin *et al.* (1974) found that parents of newborn girls rated their children as smaller, softer and less attentive, whereas sons were seen as firmer, stronger, better co-ordinated and more alert. These perceptions tend to affect how the children are treated, which can affect their health.

Health education programmes

Programmes promoting health attempt to encourage behaviours related to good health. They might teach individuals what these behaviours are, or how to perform them; they might focus on changing poor behaviour or on motivating individuals to change their behaviour and modify their attitudes.

AIDS

The campaigns to raise awareness about acquired immune deficiency syndrome (AIDS) are good to investigate. Some focus entirely on changing attitudes, some on changing habits, some on the negative consequences of not changing health-related behaviour, and some on the positive consequences of good-health-related behaviour. Perhaps the best promotional campaigns focus on as many factors as possible. Some campaigns involve learning theory, as they use 'models' to deliver the message (a message for young girls would be best delivered by another young girl, for instance).

AIDS is a major health problem world-wide, with over 160 countries reporting cases. The World Health Organization estimated that 10,000,000 people had been infected with the human immunodeficiency virus (HIV) by 1990, and that 40,000,000 would be infected by 2000 (Altman, 1991). There are a huge number of cases in Africa, Asia and South America. In the USA, and other developing countries, the rate of infection is slowing, although AIDS is the fourth leading cause of death among 25–44 year olds in the USA. It seems likely that between 75% and 99% of people infected with HIV will die from AIDS. There is no vaccine against HIV, which spreads via body fluids (only) – the main ways are through sexual practices or infected needles but infected mothers can spread the virus to their babies. Changing people's behaviour is the only way of preventing the virus from spreading, as there is no vaccination and no cure. Promotional campaigns have focused on three main messages:

- Use safer sex practices by careful selection of partners and by using condoms.
- Make sure needles or syringes are sterile, and do not share them.
- Avoid pregnancy if infected with HIV.

Raising awareness is also a large part of the campaigns. Information can help in changing behaviour and correcting misconceptions. For example, if people think AIDS happens only to homosexuals, they will not change their behaviour if they are not homosexual themselves. Some studies have found that the fear-arousing messages have worked (Vener and Krupka, 1990), whereas others suggest that misinformation (such as that 'it only happens to homosexual men') has led to insufficient changes of behaviour amongst certain groups (such as heterosexual men) (Hernandez and Smith, 1990).

Campaigns need to deal with coping skills, beliefs and cultural issues, as well as the issues raised above, if they are to be more successful. Giving information and arousing fear are two successful strategies, but other factors must also be considered. Some of these other factors are considered below.

Figure 8.26
Efforts to prevent the spread of AIDS include using billboards

ACTIVITY

The following statements are adapted from a list by Sarafino (1994, p.200), and are based on various other surveys.

Tick whether you think the statement is true or not, and then mark your answers to see how much you know about AIDS.

1 *People with AIDS usually die within a few years*   T/F
2 *Blood tests can usually tell within a week after infection whether someone has the AIDS virus or not*   T/F
3 *People do not get AIDS from swimming pools after someone with AIDS has swum in them*   T/F
4 *AIDS can be prevented by a vaccine and cured if discovered early enough*   T/F
5 *People with AIDS usually look and feel well*   T/F
6 *People have got AIDS from insects or mosquitoes that have previously bitten someone with AIDS*   T/F
7 *Lesbians get AIDS more than heterosexual women, but not as often as gay men*   T/F
8 *Health workers have a high risk of getting AIDS or of spreading the virus to their patients*   T/F
9 *Kissing or touching someone with AIDS can give you the disease*   T/F
10 *AIDS is less contagious than measles*   T/F

(Answers: 1:T; 2:F; 3:T; 4:F; 5:T; 6:F; 7:F; 8:F; 9:F; 10:T)

Changing attitudes

One way of motivating people to change their behaviour is to change their attitudes. The health belief model (outlined below) suggests that people carry out good-health-related behaviour according to how far they believe they will become ill, and how they weigh up the costs and benefits of such behaviour. A message giving fear about a certain disease or about behaviour that is not good for one's health can affect beliefs and (according to the health belief model) behaviour. Giving warnings about poor-health-related behaviour does seem to be effective (although the health warning on cigarettes has not stopped everyone from smoking).

It has been claimed that arousing too much fear can mean the warning does not work (Janis, 1967, 1984). Self and Rogers (1990) found that self-efficacy is an important factor. A strong 'fear' message with no accompanying message that something could be done about the problem did not seem to work. If people knew that they could put a new behaviour into practice and thus succeed in avoiding the health problem, then strong fear-arousing messages did work. For example, a newspaper article repeatedly asserting that giving up smoking at any stage would improve a person's health is more likely to lead to someone giving up smoking.

Evaluation

• A problem with focusing on changing attitudes is that a change in attitude does not always lead to a change in behaviour. It is important also to improve someone's self-confidence and persuade them that they can change.

Raising awareness

To change someone's attitude it is necessary to raise their awareness of the problem. People need information. For example, there is information at the moment about the need to reduce cholesterol, but people need to know what cholesterol is, and what damage 'high cholesterol' can do (it can clog blood vessels and lead to heart disease).

One method that has been found to be useful in promoting good-health-related behaviour is to ask people to change their habits for one day. This is a manageable target, and people feel able to achieve it. These campaigns (such as having a 'no smoking day') are apparently more successful than messages that simply spell out the negative consequences of the behaviour (Flay, 1987). Information is often found in medical settings such as a hospital waiting room or doctor's surgery. The advantages of using medical settings are that people are likely to go there, and they respect the expert opinion. However, the disadvantages are that maintaining levels of such information takes time in busy practices, and the suggested health-related behaviours need to be followed up. Even if leaflets in a surgery promote the advantages of stopping smoking, doctors rarely have time (or take time) to suggest that their patients give up smoking (Frank *et al.*, 1991).

ACTIVITY

It might be interesting to try asking some people if they know what cholesterol is and what damage it can do. A brief survey might show that those who know little about what cholesterol is have done less about it than those who do. You could ask a participant if they have had their cholesterol level measured by a doctor. You could also ask what they know about cholesterol. Find out if they think high or low levels are a problem. Ask what sort of levels are problematic – you could list some numbers (perhaps getting information from an Internet source), and see what people tick. You could ask what health risks there are. You should find that those who know about cholesterol have had their own levels checked (or those who have had their levels checked know about cholesterol).

Self-test

Write a timed essay under exam conditions (or as close as you can manage), using the title 'Discuss the value of health promotion when attempting to alleviate one illness or disease'.

Health belief model

Another factor of interest is the individual's own belief system, which may in part stem from the person's family and how they were brought up. For example, Livermore (1991) explains the beliefs behind reflexology, where it is held that each area of the foot connects to a specific area of the body. If you believe in reflexology, and have, for example, a back injury, you might believe that massaging a certain area of your foot would help – however, if you do not have this belief, you are unlikely to believe in this course of action. Fradkin and Firestone (1986) tested the effects of a person's beliefs on premenstrual tension (PMT). A control group of women were given no information about PMT, another group were given 'biological' information, and a third group was given 'psychological' information (that PMT is an illusion). The participants all completed questionnaires before and after the test (which consisted of giving the information). The participants' beliefs about PMT before the test were very similar. The results showed that after the test, the control group and those who had been given 'biological' information about PMT still had very similar beliefs. However, those given 'psychological' information that suggested that there was no such thing as PMT showed that their beliefs about experiencing symptoms of PMT had reduced. The **health belief model** looks at why people have certain beliefs about their own health and illnesses.

The model holds that the likelihood of someone taking preventative action regarding their health depends on two assessments they make: how far they think they will develop a health problem and the pros and cons of taking action.

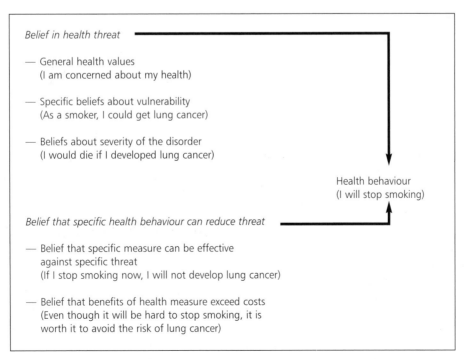

Figure 8.27
The health belief model applied to the health behaviour of stopping smoking (Source: Taylor, 1999)

How far a person thinks they will develop a problem depends on several factors:

- The seriousness of the health problem – the more serious they think the problem is, the more likely they are to take action.
- How likely they think they are to develop the problem – the more vulnerable they feel, the more likely they are to take action.
- Whether they are reminded about the problem, for example, by means of a promotional campaign. The more cues they receive about a problem, the more likely they are to take action.

Three factors involved in whether someone takes preventative action are:

- Demographic variables (age, gender, race, background, etc.).
- Sociopsychological factors like personality traits, social class and social pressure.
- Structural variables such as previous knowledge of the problem.

The pros and cons of taking action also depend on several factors. The decision has to be made as to whether the perceived benefits, such as being healthier, outweigh the perceived costs. For example, regular health checks might cost money (in some circumstances) or time. These decisions are in turn, of course, affected by how likely someone thinks a problem is to develop. All the factors are linked. For example, someone with a lower economic status might give a higher consideration to the cost of a health check, as they have to take bus or taxi fare into account as well: older people might consider the 'cost' of feeling they need a health check to be appearing to be getting old.

The above discussion of the health belief model looks at decisions regarding primary prevention, but the same factors are involved in decisions about secondary prevention – for example, whether to take medication or not. Some people find the cost of taking medication is simply too great. Tertiary prevention is similarly affected by the health belief model – for example, people have to decide to stick to an exercise routine. Those involved in researching the health belief model include Becker (1979), Kirscht (1983) and Rosenstock (Becker and Rosenstock, 1984; Rosenstock and Kirscht, 1979). Some conclusions from these studies show that, for example, people who do not have vaccinations (which they presumably see as a risk), visit the dentist regularly, have regular breast cancer checks, and take part in exercise programmes believe that they are susceptible to particular health problems. These people also believe that the problem would have serious effects, and that the benefits of preventative action are

worth more than the costs involved in undertaking the action.

ACTIVITY

Conduct a survey about health-related behaviour. Generate some statements (such as 'I am concerned about my health' or 'I will worry about my health later') that participants could use a Likert scale to answer. Include questions about the costs or benefits of taking health-related action (for example, 'I regularly visit the dentist' or 'I take exercise every day'). You should be able to generate a score regarding each person's health-related behaviour, and then one about their health-related beliefs. You should see whether high health-related behaviour scores are related to the likelihood that the respondent believes they are at risk of developing a health problem. This would be evidence for the claims of the health belief model.

As with all surveys, remember ethical principles. You must ask health-related questions sensitively. It is best to stick to general questions as the more specific a question is, the more sensitive it is likely to be. For example, you can ask people to rate their concerns about developing a health problem, but it would be unethical to ask about their concerns about developing cancer, especially if you then ask if anyone close to them has died of cancer. A pilot study using other students in the class might be a good way of checking that your questions are general enough.

Theory of reasoned action

The **theory of reasoned action** holds that people decide what to do, and that intentions are the best way to predict what people will do (Ajzen and Fishbein, 1980). This theory suggests that intentions are determined by two main attitudes:

1 The attitude regarding the behaviour. This attitude is based on the belief about the outcome of the behaviour, and the beliefs about whether the behaviour would be rewarding.

2 The attitude about other people's responses to the behaviour. Questions such as whether it is a socially acceptable thing to do are asked. This attitude is based on beliefs about other people's opinions and the individual's motivation to comply with other people's opinions.

According to the theory of reasoned action these two attitudes are put together and produce an intention (to act or not to act). For example, if you believed that exercising was too much like hard work, that you are doing enough in any case, that other people don't exercise either and that you value the opinions of other people, you probably would not take much exercise. This is the theory of reasoned action in practice.

Bagozzi (1981) carried out a study to test the theory of reasoned action. The study looked at people's willingness to give blood after a promotional campaign asking people to 'give blood'. The participants completed a questionnaire before the campaign and their intentions were recorded. They were asked questions such as the pleasantness of giving blood. Information was then elicited as to whether participants gave blood or not. Attitudes about giving blood did predict their behaviour as to whether they gave blood or not.

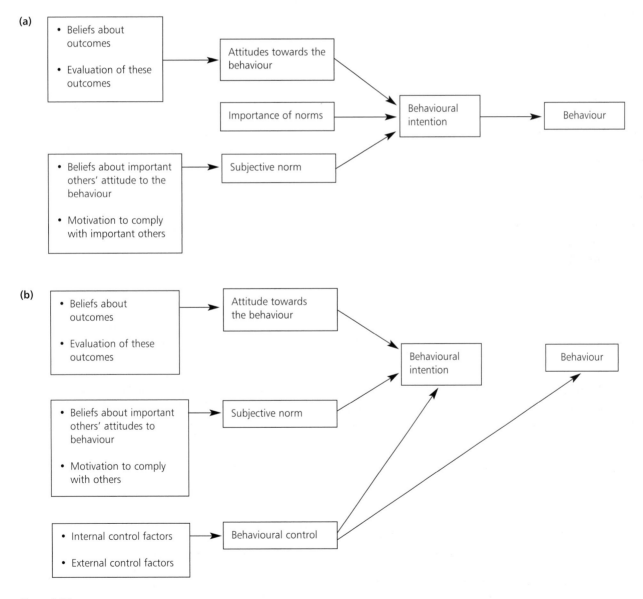

Figure 8.28
Basics of the theory of reasoned action (a) and the theory of planned behaviour (b) (Source: Ogden, 2000)

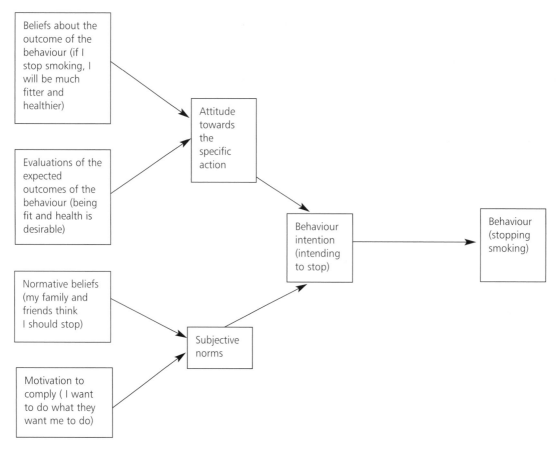

Figure 8.29
The theory of reasoned action applied to the decision to give up smoking (Source: Stroebe, 2000)

Evaluation

- One problem is that intentions do not always predict actions.

- There is no mention of a person's previous experiences, which might affect their attitudes and actions. It is usually found that those who have exercised in the past are those who are more likely to exercise in the future, for example.

ACTIVITY

Use a questionnaire to test a theory. Generate some statements and questions based on the information given above about people's attitudes and intentions – for example, towards smoking and giving up. Remember ethical principles, of course. You will need to find out some behaviour, for example, whether they have given up smoking or not, because you need to measure people's intentions and beliefs against their action.

Social action theory

A different theory as to why people carry out health-protective behaviour (or not) is the **social action theory** (Ewart, 1991). This theory suggests that health protective behaviour occurs within a system with three spheres:

- The sphere of 'self-change processes' looks at the factors involved directly when someone changes their habits or adopts new habits.
- The sphere of 'action states' refers to existing habits, how these connect to actions, and the habits of others around the individual. The models surrounding a person, as well as the cues that lead them to certain actions, are important.
- The sphere of 'biopsychosocial contexts' involves the situations within which the other spheres operate. These situations involve the environmental, biological and social factors that lead to a change in someone's behaviour (or no change).

Table 8.9 Social action theory's three spheres and included factors that determine people's health-related behaviour

Biopsychosocial contexts

Environment
- Physical features (e.g. places to exercise)
- Societal models of behaviour
- Organisation of institutions (e.g. health care system)

Biophysical characteristics of the person
- Biological condition (e.g. medications taken)
- Temperament

Mood/arousal of the person
- Stress
- Energy versus fatigue

Self-change processes

Social support
- Tangible or instrumental support
- Instrumental support
- Esteem support

Cognitive resources
- Existing knowledge
- Skills to focus attention and process information

Motivation
- Self-efficacy
- Outcome expectancies (e.g. barriers and benefits)

Problem solving
- Planning for change
- Dealing with obstacles

Action states

Health routines
- 'Automatic' habits (e.g. smoking, eating)
- Non-automatic routine behaviour (e.g. exercising)

Social interdependence
- Daily routines of other people
- Shared routines (e.g. eating meals together)

Outcomes (immediate and delayed)
- Reinforcement
- Punishment

Source: Sarafino (1994), based on Ewart (1991)

An example of the theory in action is to look at an individual's exercise behaviours. The 'action states' sphere shows that this person exercises regularly, which means they look and feel good. This exercise behaviour disrupts the routine of another family member, however. In the 'biopsychosocial contexts' sphere, the individual is affected by medication they take, which sometimes affects their mood. So sometimes they feel less happy about exercising because of a particular mood, and sometimes they enjoy it less because of upsetting the family member. The spheres interact with one another. The whole is a system, and factors from one sphere can affect factors in another, so that behaviour and habits change.

Suggested reading

Banyard, P. (1996) *Applying Psychology to Health*. London: Hodder & Stoughton.
Curtis, A.J. (2000) *Health Psychology*. London: Routledge Modular Series.
Kalat, J.W. (1995) *Biological Psychology, Fifth Edition*. Pacific Grove, Ca.: Brooks/Cole.
Ogden, J. (2000) *Health Psychology: A Textbook,* Second Edition. Buckingham: Open University.

Self-test

1 Write a timed essay under exam conditions (or as close as you can manage), using the title 'Discuss the health belief model as an explanation of why some people do not make use of disease prevention or screening tests'.

2 Write a timed essay under exam conditions (or as close as you can manage), using the title 'Discuss the theory of reasoned action in explaining behavioural intentions – with relevance to health'.

Sarafino, E.P. (1994) *Health Psychology, Biopsychosocial Interaction,* Second Edition. New York: John Wiley & Sons, Inc.
Stroebe, W. (2000) *Social Psychology and Health,* Second Edition. Buckingham: Open University Press.
Taylor, S.E. (1999) *Health Psychology,* Fourth Edition. New York: McGraw-Hill.

9

Methods in psychology

The aims of this chapter

The aims of this chapter are to enable the reader to:

- *outline research methods used in psychology (including experiments, case studies, questionnaires, observations, interviews and content analysis)*
- *evaluate methods by means of advantages and disadvantages*
- *demonstrate an understanding of important methodological issues (such as hypotheses, designs, levels of measurement, variables, sampling, correlational designs, descriptive statistics and issues of validity, reliability and generalisability)*
- *understand issues concerning the use of inferential statistics, including levels of significance, direction of hypotheses, reasons for choice of tests, tests themselves, critical values, standard deviation and variance, and normal distribution*
- *understand issues of subjectivity and objectivity, and how to analyse qualitative data.*

STUDY AID

When you have finished working through this chapter you should test yourself on each of the above points. This will help you to see how good your knowledge and understanding of methodological issues is.

This chapter covers

The A2 part of the Edexcel course includes questions on method in Unit 5b. You must be able to recall your AS material on method, and this is only briefly reviewed in this chapter. Questions can also be asked about inferential statistics and about the analysis of qualitative data. The aim of this chapter is to review all that is needed, although other sources can provide more depth. Understanding of method is useful throughout the course, because evaluation of the method used in a study is often a good way of evaluating the study itself. You will already have a good understanding of many – if not all – the issues presented here. With this in mind this chapter often presents only outlines of what is needed.

Reviewing AS material

Some of the main terms used

Validity

A study is **valid** if it measures what it is said to measure. For example, Bandura *et al.*'s 'Bobo doll' study (1983) has been criticised for lack of validity. Children observed an adult hitting a Bobo doll, and were then left in a room where there were toys including a Bobo doll. The children were observed to see if they hit the Bobo doll – to see if they copied the adult behaviour. They did, and it was concluded that children are more aggressive if they have observed aggression. However, if a study claims to be measuring aggression, it should not be measuring 'copying adult behaviour'. Is copying an adult hitting a plastic doll really 'aggression'? It could be said that this study is not valid as it has not measured what it claims to measure.

Experiments are not usually valid. There is much about an experiment that is artificial, including the setting and the task, so it often cannot be said to be about 'reality'. Naturalistic observations are much more likely to be valid because they are in a natural setting, and usually mean observing 'real' behaviour.

Types of validity
- **Ecological validity** – measuring what you are claiming to measure with regards to the setting. If aggression in children is studied in a school playground, by observation, then the study is likely to have ecological validity, because the children are observed in their natural setting.
- **Face validity** – on the face of it, the results do appear to be a 'true' measure. So if you ask someone the way to the post office, and record whether they smile and/or point, on the face of it this is a good measure of helpfulness. Of course, they could smile and point you in the wrong direction, so it might not be a valid measure after all.

- **Construct validity** – measures are good measures of some personality trait or some other construct. This means, for example, that you have to look at the sorts of things involved in being an extrovert, and check whether they go together to make such a trait after all. For example, if we say an extrovert is outgoing and a party animal, then these two things will go together if the construct is valid – outgoing people must tend to be party animals, otherwise we could say there is no such thing as an extrovert. In this example, extroversion is a construct.
- **Predictive validity** *t*ends to refer to therapies and diagnoses, rather than research methods. A therapy or diagnosis might be valid if what it predicts does happen – if schizophrenics are said to hear voices, then it is a valid measure of schizophrenia if someone diagnosed as being schizophrenic hears voices as one of their symptoms.

Reliability

A study is **reliable** if, when repeated, the same results are found. If a carefully planned and controlled study is repeated with the same care, the design is reliable if the same (or very similar) results are found.

Experiments are carefully planned and controlled, so tend to be reliable. Naturalistic observations happen at a particular moment in time, and looking at a particular situation. Often that situation cannot be repeated, so naturalistic observations tend to be less reliable.

If a study is not reliable often this means it is more valid, and less valid usually means more reliable. The more natural the setting, the more valid the study. However, the more natural a setting, the less reliable the study. Similarly, the more you control the various factors in a study, the more reliable it will be, because you can do it again and get the same results. However, the more controlled the study is, the less natural, and so the less valid, it is.

Observations can be tested for reliability. The observations of more than one observer can be tested to see if they agree with one another. If they do this is called **inter-observer reliability**. If the observers are rating participants in some way – perhaps to see how aggressive they are on a scale of 0 to 5 – then their ratings can be compared, and this is called testing for **inter-rater reliability**.

Sampling

Your **target population** is all those you are interested in. If comparing male and female driving behaviour, your target population would be all male and female drivers. Sometimes you can study all the people in your target population but it is rare that you have access to everyone. Researchers use a **sample** to make the study manageable.

There are a number of different ways of choosing a sample, depending on what you need to know, and on constraints such as time, cost and availability.

Random sampling

This is probably the fairest way of choosing a sample from your target population. All those in the target population have to have an equal chance of being chosen each time. The idea of a **random sample** is that if everyone has had an equal chance of being picked, then the sample itself should be representative of the target population. You should have someone from each category, and in the right proportion. For example, if there were twice as many women as men in your target population, then twice as many women have a chance of being picked each time, so things should work out fairly evenly. Even if they don't, at least you cannot have shown any bias when picking the sample. It is very difficult to do truly random sampling.

Quota sampling

With random sampling you don't know what the chosen sample will be like. You know it should represent the target population, but you don't know how it will be made up. Sometimes you have to have representatives from certain groups – young middle-class men, young middle-class women, older middle-class men, older middle-class women, and so on. **Quota sampling** means having a set number of people in each group or category.

Stratified sampling

Stratified sampling is difficult to distinguish from quota sampling, because it involves making sure that certain groups are represented in the sample. It is different, however, because the number of people in each group is in the same proportion as it is in the whole population. This means, for example, that if 30% of all drivers drive small cars, you will want 30% of your sample to be drivers of small cars. Then, when you are choosing the sample of drivers of small cars (to continue with the example), you would choose randomly from all the drivers of small cars. Quota sampling does not use random sampling.

Systematic sampling

Systematic sampling means taking, for example, the third or fifth person you meet, and giving them a questionnaire. You are systematically choosing your sample. This is not random sampling. It is often taken to be random (and is sometimes called quasi random), but actually not everyone has an equal chance of being chosen. If you choose every third person, then the second, fourth person, and so on, never gets the chance to be picked.

Opportunity sampling

Many students doing GCSE and advanced courses use **opportunity sampling**. The researcher takes whoever they can get – sticking to ethical guidelines of course. This sort of sampling is usually quicker and more ethical but it will be a biased sample. If researchers choose whoever is available, this is bound not to be representative of the target population. For example, if you ask anyone in your local town market on a Tuesday morning, this will be a particular group of people, and everyone else will be excluded – for instance people who are at work on Tuesday mornings.

Volunteer or self-selected sampling

Volunteer sampling is where your participants have volunteered to carry out the study. The problem here is that participants are **self-selected**. The participants will be similar in that, for example, they have all read an advertisement that was placed, have all had access to the same publication, all have time or inclination to do the study, and all have similar interests, perhaps. So this type of sampling is biased. On the other hand, it is in a way more ethical. At least the participants have chosen to give up their time, and to take part in the study.

Generalisability

Generalisation refers to being able to transfer results of one study to other people. A study can be generalised to the target population, but only if the sampling is good. A study has generalisability if it involves careful sampling from the target population and careful controls. In these circumstances, you can say that what you found from your study is true of everyone in the area of interest. Whenever there is careful sampling, a study's results are likely to be generalisable.

Case studies, however, involve looking at individuals or small groups in depth, so the results are very unlikely to be generalisable to any other individual or small group. Even in an experiment where careful sampling is carried out, the study will almost certainly be in one area or one country. So findings should only be generalised within that area or country. Often, when studies are done in one country, the findings are said to be true of all countries, and this is where you need to be very critical when studying psychology. There are differences between cultures and you cannot really generalise from a target population in one culture to a different culture, although this is often done.

Qualitative or quantitative data

Data are what are gathered from any study. The data are the findings; what we are interested in. One way of distinguishing between types of data is to see if the data are **quantitative** or **qualitative**. This distinction is referred to again in Chapter 10.

Quantitative data

Data are called quantitative if they are collected using a measure. You cannot easily measure the content of your dreams, for instance, but you can count the number of times a child hits a doll, and counting is a measure. In what follows you will see that some measures are more 'mathematical' than others. Reaction time is a very clear measure, but rating someone on a scale of attractiveness is not. Both, however, are quantitative data, which tend to include numbers.

Qualitative data

Any data that are not quantitative are called qualitative. If a questionnaire asked you to write a short sentence about your attitudes to male drivers, then the data gathered would not be measurable. Such data are qualitative data. If, however, we scored our attitudes on a scale of 1 ('male drivers are terrible') to 10 ('male drivers are great'), then we are gathering quantitative data. Testing memory by counting the number of words recalled means gathering quantitative data. Testing memory by interviewing someone and asking them to recall occasions throughout their life means gathering qualitative data.

Types of quantitative data – levels of measurement

Within quantitative, measurable data, there are different types of data, which are called levels of measurement. Data are collected in lots of ways when doing psychological research. The way the data are collected affects the conclusions that can be drawn. There are three levels or measurement, or types of data, for the purposes of research in psychology.

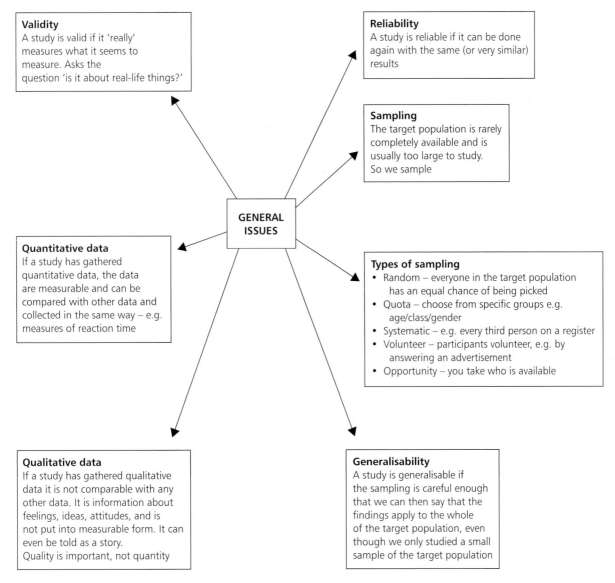

Validity
A study is valid if it 'really' measures what it seems to measure. Asks the question 'is it about real-life things?'

Reliability
A study is reliable if it can be done again with the same (or very similar) results

Sampling
The target population is rarely completely available and is usually too large to study. So we sample

GENERAL ISSUES

Quantitative data
If a study has gathered quantitative data, the data are measurable and can be compared with other data and collected in the same way – e.g. measures of reaction time

Types of sampling
• Random – everyone in the target population has an equal chance of being picked
• Quota – choose from specific groups e.g. age/class/gender
• Systematic – e.g. every third person on a register
• Volunteer – participants volunteer, e.g. by answering an advertisement
• Opportunity – you take who is available

Qualitative data
If a study has gathered qualitative data it is not comparable with any other data. It is information about feelings, ideas, attitudes, and is not put into measurable form. It can even be told as a story. Quality is important, not quantity

Generalisability
A study is generalisable if the sampling is careful enough that we can then say that the findings apply to the whole of the target population, even though we only studied a small sample of the target population

Figure 9.1
Summary of some main terms

- **Nominal data** – putting things into groups or categories
- **Ordinal data** – ranking data
- **Interval or ratio data** – assigning real mathematical measures

Sometimes data are called interval data when the measure is not actually mathematical. For example, you may have done some memory studies such as count the number of words recalled from a list. Although this is not really a mathematical measure like time or height, if you recall 20 out of 20, and I recall 10 out of 20, you have remembered twice as many as I have. This sort of data is called **quasi interval**, and it is treated as interval/ratio. It is 'sort of' interval (quasi means 'sort of and treated as such'). Earlier it was said that a stratified sample is sometimes called quasi random, which means 'sort of random and treated as such'.

Why do we need to know about the level of measurement?

It is not possible to work out what inferential statistical test is needed to test whether results of a study are significant without knowing what the level of measurement is. Knowing this also helps in deciding which **measures of central tendency** to use. Some inferential tests use mathematical calculations such as squares and square roots of numbers. If you don't have interval/ratio data in the first place then you cannot square root or square the numbers. So to choose which statistical test you need you must be able to decide what level of measurement is being used.

Summary of main methods

Main methods used in research in psychology are:
- laboratory experiment
- field experiment
- natural experiment
- participant observation
- non-participant observation
- structured interview
- unstructured interview
- case study
- discourse analysis
- content analysis
- questionnaire
- free association
- clinical interview
- dream analysis
- longitudinal study
- cross-sectional study
- cross-cultural study.

Self-test

You probably know quite a lot about each of these methods from your AS material. Test yourself by writing down a brief description of each.

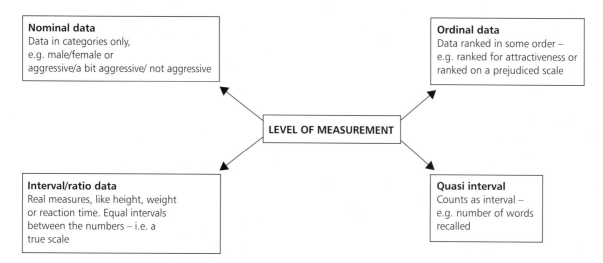

Figure 9.2
Summary of levels of measurement

Experiments

Here is a list of terms connected with methods in psychology. You may already know a lot of this so, instead of going over it all again, you could tick what you already know. If you don't know many of the following terms, read on, then return to this task at the end of the section to check that you now understand.

Control group	☐	Alternative hypothesis	☐
Null hypothesis	☐	Independent variable	☐
Dependent variable	☐	Situational variable	☐
Participant variable	☐	Repeated measures design	☐
Matched pairs design	☐	Independent groups design	☐
Confounding variable	☐	Counterbalancing	☐
Order effects	☐	Fatigue effect	☐
Practice effect	☐	Demand characteristics	☐

Research in psychology has many purposes, and the reasons for doing a study often lead to the choice of method. Experiments are chosen because they are 'scientific'. If we control everything and only look at one thing, then we can perhaps come to some conclusions about it.

Hypotheses – alternative, experimental and null

When doing research, first, the researcher starts with a vague **theory** (often developed from other people's studies). From this theory, the researcher forms **hypotheses** (statements of what is expected). There are many ways of making this statement, but it must be in a formal way.

Here are some examples of different types of hypotheses, using the example of a study to look at gender differences in driving behaviour, in which the researcher counts the number of cones knocked down when the participant drives round a specially designed course.

- **Alternative hypothesis** – An example of an alternative (or alternate) hypothesis is: 'there is a meaningful difference in the driving behaviour of men and women'. There is bound to be some difference, but it has to be big enough to be worth talking about, so I have called it 'meaningful'. More correctly, we ought to say there will be a meaningful difference in the number of cones knocked down, as that is what we are measuring. The alternative hypothesis is the statement of what is expected.
- **Experimental hypothesis** – If the study uses experimental method, *and only then*, the alternative hypothesis is called an experimental hypothesis. This is true in the example used here: the experimental

hypothesis is 'there is a meaningful difference in driving behaviour (number of cones knocked down) between men and women'. (The difference has to be big enough to be meaningful.)
- **Null hypothesis** – The null hypothesis is where a statement is made that is the opposite of what is expected. In this case the null hypothesis for the driving behaviour study would be: 'there is no meaningful difference in driving behaviour (number of cones knocked down) between men and women'. You should add that any difference there is (you are sure to find some difference) is due to chance factors or some other variable that has not been considered.

Operationalising concepts

In the above example, the hypotheses ought to say 'number of cones knocked down', not 'driving behaviour', because what is being measured is the number of cones knocked down. Driving behaviour involves much more than number of cones knocked down, and the hypotheses should always say exactly what is being measured. When we make sure that we have made something measurable, we have **operationalised** the concept. For example, helpfulness is not really measurable, but we can operationalise it by measuring how many of the people we ask to show us the way to the post office do so.

Why have a null hypothesis?

The null hypothesis is the important one. This has to do with testing whether the expected difference is meaningful or not, and when testing people there will nearly always be a difference. For example, if the task is difficult, we would not expect every driver to knock down the same number of cones. The important thing is, is the

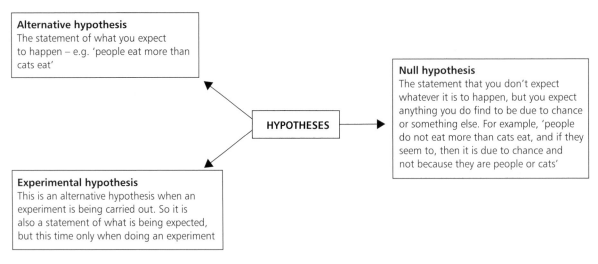

Figure 9.3
Summary of hypotheses

difference big enough to be important? The null hypothesis states that any difference (for example, in number of cones knocked over by male and female drivers) is no more than we would have found by chance. Inferential statistical tests are used to see if the difference is larger than we would expect to find by chance; to see if the null hypothesis can be rejected (the difference is bigger than we would find by chance) or retained (the difference is no larger than we would expect to find by chance). As it is the null hypothesis that is being tested, the null hypothesis is the important one.

Variables and controls

Each time you make a statement about what you expect, in the form of a hypothesis, you are saying that you will measure **variables**. A variable is something that you are measuring or interested in, and is something that varies. So if you are expecting to see a difference in the play behaviour of boys and girls you are interested in the variables 'play behaviour', and 'boys and girls'.

Situational variables

In an experiment the researcher will be controlling lots of variables, such as heat, noise, place, light and time of day, depending on what is of interest. Variables to do with the situation are called **situational variables**. These must be controlled (kept the same for all participants).

Participant variables

Differences between or within participants also affect conclusions. These are **participant** variables, which are factors to do with the individuals taking part.

Extraneous variables

Extraneous variables get in the way of the study. These variables have made it look as though we found what we expected, even though we did not, and have confounded

the results. Examples might be the room temperature, or the person's emotional state. We try to control all the variables, but we can only control those we know about. Good sampling and well chosen controls should stop extraneous variables from affecting the results.

Confounding variables

Extraneous variables, whether situational or participant, are called **confounding variables** when they can be interpreted as causing the result. Either the variable we manipulate has caused the result (whether in a memory experiment a word list is categorised or not, for example) or some other variable has done so (perhaps participants remembered more categorised words because the words were shorter, for example). In this case we don't know whether participants learnt more of the first list because it was categorised or because the words were shorter. The difference in word length becomes a confounding variable.

Independent and dependent variables

All variables need to be controlled for so that the variables you are actually interested in (for example, gender and play behaviour) are the ones that change or vary, and everything else stays the same. Once all possible variables are controlled for, the researcher can concentrate on the original hypothesis. The **independent variable** (**IV**) is what you are interested in, and what you vary. The **dependent variable** (**DV**) is what you measure as a result of varying (or manipulating) the IV. In the example of a study on driving behaviour, the IV is gender and the DV is the number of cones knocked down.

Controls

Controls are used to keep everything the same except for what is manipulated by the researcher. Many controls involve the above variables.

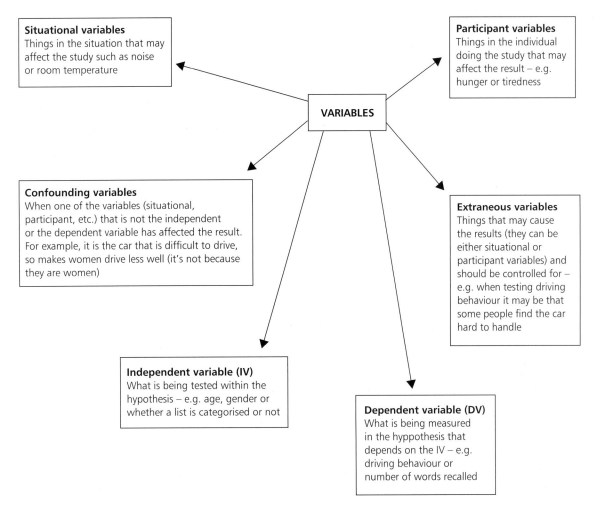

Figure 9.4
Summary of variables

Standardised instructions

An important control in an experiment is what is said to the participant: each participant must be given the same instructions, so that none has an unfair advantage. So instructions are standardised: everything said to the participants must be written down beforehand in order to control for any differences in instructions.

Ethics

Standardised instructions are useful, as they can include advice to participants about their rights (ethical guidelines are outlined in Chapter 10). Important issues include confidentiality, consent and the right to withdraw. Standardised instructions read out before the study can include important information about ethical issues, such as giving the participant the right to withdraw, information about how the results of the study will be used, and how confidentiality is assured. The participant should be told as much as possible about the study, so that the consent obtained from them to take part is informed consent.

Types of experimental design

There are three types of experimental design, ways that participants can be used to do the experiment: one person does all the conditions (parts of the study), or different people are used for each condition. Or there is a compromise, where different people are used, but matched in important ways.

Order effects

The main problem in choosing a design is whether to use the same people to do all the conditions, or whether to use different people. If the same people are used, after they have completed the first condition they will already have practised doing whatever is being asked when they come to the second, so they might always do the second condition better. Alternatively, participants may be tired or affected by the first condition in some way, and so might always perform the second condition less well. These effects are called **order effects**, because the problems arise from the order in which conditions are carried out. The **fatigue effect** is that a participant may do less well in the second condition because of being tired or bored after the first condition. With a **practice effect** the participant does better in the second condition because they have practised the task.

Counterbalancing or randomising the order of presenting the conditions

To counteract order effects, the researcher can toss a coin to decide in each case whether the participant does condition one or two first. This is **randomising** the order. Alternatively, the researcher can use **counterbalancing**.

This means alternating the order in which the tasks are done – the first participant does condition 1 and then condition 2, the second participant does condition 2 and then condition 1, and so on.

Repeated measures design

A **repeated measures** design means asking one person to repeat all parts of the study. It is in repeated measures designs that order effects can be a problem so counterbalancing or randomising is needed.

Table 9.1 *Advantages and disadvantages of a repeated measures design*

Advantages	Disadvantages
Using the same person across all conditions of the experiment means there are no problems with individual differences. He or she will have the same abilities, mood and so on. Therefore participant variables are controlled for As one person does all the conditions, the researcher can carry out the study using fewer people than for an independent groups design. This makes the study more ethical and more manageable	There are likely to be order effects unless counterbalancing is used. Even then, having done one condition can affect how a person does the other one The person could guess what the study was about. If he or she receives clues from the study and can guess what they are meant to do, there are said to be **demand characteristics** (see p 308)

Independent groups design

If the same person does not do all the conditions, then different people must be used in each condition: this is an **independent groups design**. For example, in a memory

study the group learning a categorised list might be independent from the group learning a randomised list. They are different people.

Table 9.2 *Advantages and disadvantages of an independent groups design*

Advantages	Disadvantages
There are no order effects. You simply have different people, so they don't even know what the other condition is There are no demand characteristics. They can't compare the different parts of the study and use their knowledge to guess what is required	When you are comparing the two sets of results, you are comparing different people. You are saying that for one participant 18 out of 20 words were recalled when the words were in categories compared with another participant who got 14 out of 20 when they are given a random list. The person getting 18 and the person getting 14 are different people. One of them might have a better memory. You have to use careful sampling, and enough people, before you can be reasonably sure that the difference you found was not just due to different people having done the different parts of the study You have to find twice as many participants to do the study

Matched pairs design

In a **matched pairs design** different people are used for the different conditions, but they are matched so that they are similar in many ways. A matched pairs design can appear to solve problems with repeated measures and independent groups designs. One way that researchers have used a matched pairs design is to use identical twins in studies. An alternative is to look at what factors are important and make sure that the participants are similar in these important ways.

Table 9.3 Advantages and disadvantages of matched pairs design

Advantages	Disadvantages
Using different people means there are no order effects, and there is less likely to be demand characteristics. In other words, there are all the advantages of an independent groups design Similarly there are the advantages of a repeated measures design. The paired individuals are treated as if they are the same people, so comparisons can be made between them	A matched pairs design does mean using different people, however hard we try to match them up on important variables. So there will be individual differences and participant variables. Even identical twins are not the same people and are subject to different moods and different experiences

Types of experiment

- **Laboratory experiment** – takes place in an unnatural setting but means there can be good controls.
- **Field experiment** – takes place 'in the field', which is a more natural setting. However, this does affect the controls. The independent variable is still manipulated as it is in a laboratory experiment.
- **Naturalistic or natural experiment** – takes place 'in the field' using a naturally occurring independent variable. So the researcher does not have to set the independent variable up. This is a more valid measure (because it really occurs), but controls can be difficult (because there are sure to be other things in the environment that happen with or alongside the independent variable).
- **Quasi experiment** – the participants are not allocated to the conditions, but naturally fall into the different groups. A naturalistic experiment is a quasi experiment because the participants naturally fall into the separate groups.

Table 9.4 Advantages and disadvantages of experiments

Advantages	Disadvantages
Laboratory experiments Good controls, so reliable IV can be manipulated clearly Cause and effect can be suggested Findings can be repeated by others	Lots of controls, so not valid IV is not naturally occurring so not valid Tasks are not natural, so not worth doing?
Field experiments More natural than laboratory experiments Still have control over some variables A bit more ethical for participants	Lose control over some variables Less reliable than laboratory experiments
Natural experiments More natural than laboratory or field experiments Measuring naturally occurring events More ethical for participants	Lose even more control over variables Less reliable than laboratory or field experiments

Correlational design

A **correlation** is a co-relationship. Two things change together. An example is age and reaction time: the older you get, the slower your reactions; age and reactions co-vary.

A correlation is more like a type of design than a method in itself; for example, you might do a questionnaire and find a correlation. The main thing about a correlation is that you are looking only at things that go together, not cause one another. For instance, it used to be said that the more you smoke the more likely you were to have an illness, which was a correlation. Now we would say that smoking *causes* illness – it is not that smoking correlates with illnesses like cancer and heart disease, it causes these diseases.

Positive and negative correlations

When two variables both rise together, they are said to be **positively correlated**. For example, the higher the temperature the higher the sales of ice creams – there is a positive correlation between them.

If, however, one score of a variable falls as the other rises, this is a **negative correlation**. Age and hours of sleep are negatively correlated – the older someone is, the lower the number of hours they are likely to sleep at night. A perfect positive correlation (when one variable varies perfectly with another) is +1 and a perfect negative correlation is –1. So if, for everyone asked, the older they were the less they slept, this would be a perfect negative correlation – or if, for each hotter and hotter day, sales of ice creams rose and rose, then this would be a perfect positive correlation. There would have to be no hot day when ice cream sales fell below those of a colder day. A correlation of +0.76 is quite a high positive correlation (being near +1), and –0.52 is a reasonable, but not very high negative correlation (being mid way between 0 and –1). One way of knowing if there is a correlation is to draw a **scattergram** – the direction of any slope in the points will give you an idea of what sort of correlation there is.

Surveys by questionnaire

Questionnaires are good ways of finding things out, although there are drawbacks, as with every method.

Open and closed questions

Closed questions require a fixed response, for example the participant ticks whether they are male or female. There is a choice, but no opportunity to say anything else or to expand with closed questions. It is usually a good idea to include a 'don't know' or 'neither' option, so that the participant is not forced too much into inaccurate responses.

Open questions give an opportunity for the participant to expand and answer in their own words.

Closed questions give quantitative data, and open questions give qualitative data.

Personal data

A questionnaire involves asking questions around a particular area of interest to the researcher. However, at the same time, the researcher needs to know personal data – the participant's age, gender, occupation, etc.

Standardised instructions

Participants in experiments should be given standardised instructions as a control, and to make things fair. Standardised instructions are also included for ethical reasons.

Pilot study

One way of making sure that your questions are understood is to carry out a **pilot study**. This means testing your questionnaire out on a small group to find out any problems before the main study. You can make sure your questions are clear, and that they do not give offence. You can also discover problems such as a category missing.

Demand characteristics

In questionnaires as well as experiments you can ask questions that give participants a clue about what you expect, which can bias the results. If the participant can guess from the questions what they are supposed to say, they could alter the answer to help you (or to go against what is expected). The characteristics of the question demand a certain answer.

Take the example of an experiment where the hypothesis is that hungry people recall more words that are related to food than less hungry people. If half the participants are offered food, but the other half are not, before a study that includes learning food-related words and those participants who did not eat lunch know that the others have been offered food, they might guess that hunger is important in the study, and this knowledge could affect the results. The characteristics of the study might demand a particular answer, and the study is said to have been affected by demand characteristics.

Social desirability

Participants may say what they think they ought to say (this is called **social desirability**). Few people on being asked 'are you a racist?' would say they are. Questions need to be carefully written, so that 'real' answers are obtained, rather than social norms. One way to measure social desirability is to include a question to which the answer is clear – for example, asking whether someone talks about other people. They almost certainly do talk about others, so if they answer that they don't, it might be concluded they are not answering the other questions honestly.

Table 9.5 Advantages and disadvantages of using a questionnaire

Advantages	Disadvantages
Participants can see what is asked so can give informed consent	Participants may not be truthful, so validity lacking
Closed questions are quite easily analysed	Closed questions mean participants cannot give all information so data may be lost
Can be reliable, because can easily be repeated	If repeated on a different day, different answers might be given
Quite quick and cheap to administer	Poor response rate, especially if sent by post
	Questionnaires only find out about attitudes towards something, not about how a person would actually behave

Interviews

Surveys can be carried out by interview, instead of by questionnaire. Interviews can also be used as part of a case study. Structured interviews seem like questionnaires; however, questionnaires can be completed in the researcher's absence, whereas interviews must be conducted by someone asking the participant questions. Also, you might ask a great many participants to complete a questionnaire but you might interview only a few people.

Structured interviews

In a **structured interview** everyone is asked the same questions. In this way data can be compared. The problem is that the interviewer does not have the freedom to explore any issues that arise. Structured interviews usually yield qualitative data, because the questions are usually designed so that the participant can give quite a full verbal answer. However, sometime, tick boxes are used, and this means that quantitative data can be analysed and compared.

Unstructured interviews

An **unstructured interview** involves exploring an issue by allowing the participant to impose their own structure on what is being asked. The participant's comments are pursued. The data from an unstructured interview has more quality, in the sense that the participant has more of an opportunity to say what they like.

Objectivity v. subjectivity

In the unstructured interview a problem is that it is not only the participant who can decide the course of the interview. It is the researcher who decides what questions to pursue, and these questions may reflect the researcher's own interests. The researcher's objectivity can be questioned. Subjectivity is an important factor in methods used in psychology. Researchers have to somehow separate themselves from the situation. Researchers must be objective – they must not let their own thoughts and feelings affect the results. In practice, this is probably almost impossible.

Table 9.6 Some advantages and disadvantages of using interviews to collect data

Advantages	Disadvantages
Researcher can explore in more depth	Objectivity is difficult to achieve
Participant can expand on areas they see as important	Difficult to analyse the data
Gives rich and in-depth information that other methods may not uncover	Unique to one person, so not generalisable to others

Observations

Observations can give useful information about people and about interactions between people. From an ethics point of view observing people in a public place is usually accepted as it could be reasonably claimed that they could expect to be watched. So usually observations are acceptable if they take place in 'public'.

Some experiments involve observation. For example, Bandura's Bobo doll study involved observing children playing after watching a film. However, this is still an experiment, even though observation was used. Observations are usually naturalistic, in that they take place in a natural setting.

Overt v. covert observations

Overt observations are ones where the participants know they are being observed. Overt really means that the observation is done openly. **Covert observations** are done secretly. The participants do not know they are being watched. Overt observations are more ethical, but the people being watched are less likely to behave naturally. Covert observations are more likely to give natural behaviour, but they are not very ethical. Also it is easier to observe overtly, as you don't have to pretend to be doing something else. With covert observations you will have to either pretend to play a different role or actually hide. This can be difficult. Covert observations are more valid, because they are less likely to affect the participants' natural behaviour, and what is observed is more like real life.

Participant v. non-participant observations

Participant observations are where the researcher is also a participant in the group. For example, you could observe children's behaviour in the classroom, and you would be a participant observer if you were also the teacher or a classroom helper. **Non-participant observations** are when the researcher is not part of the group – a non-participant observer would sit at the back of the class, not taking part in any activities. Non-participant observations can affect what is happening.

The participants usually know the observer is there, and the presence of the researcher alone can affect the participants' behaviour. So non-participant observation does not yield very valid data unless it is covert: overt non-participant observation is likely to affect results. Participant observation does affect results in one way, because the researcher is a participant in what is happening, but if the researcher is, for example, the teacher, then they would be present anyway, so the behaviour is natural. However, with participant observation the observer is involved in more than one role and may find it difficult to record all the information.

Inter-observer and inter-rater reliability

One observer can be biased in what is recorded. For one thing, he or she can only watch one thing at a time and might miss something of interest. If a study is reliable, we get the same results if we do it again, but if we have bias in observation another observer is unlikely to find the same results. So observations can be said to be unreliable. In order to overcome this unreliability, more than one observer can be used. If more than one observer is trained to observe in the same way, and they observe the same situation, we should be able to compare their results and claim reliability for the study (if their results match). This sort of reliability is called **inter-observer reliability**. If the observers are rating behaviour, for example, as aggressive or not, then instead of saying we have inter-observer reliability, we say we have **inter-rater reliability**. We would have to test for this reliability by looking at the results of each observer and seeing if they were the same.

Case studies

Case studies involve in-depth study of an individual or small group. Where experiments aim for strict controls, leading to an examination of cause and effect, case studies aim for rich examination of all sorts of issues. Case studies are useful at the start of a study. Until we know what variables to control, and what to manipulate, we can't do experiments in any case. A case study will

Table 9.7 Advantages and disadvantages of observations as a method

Advantages	Disadvantages
Observing a natural situation gives natural behaviour (valid)	No controls over variables, so hard to draw conclusions
	Observer bias is possible
Actual behaviour itself is natural, and there are no demand characteristics	Observer can create an unnatural situation
Rich data can be collected	Might miss some information

examine every aspect of a situation, and might highlight areas for further study.

In some ways a case study is not a method. To carry out a case study lots of methods can be used. Researchers use interviews, questionnaires and observations. They can examine documents, or ask people to keep diaries. Anything can be of interest in a case study.

Ethnography

Some studies are called **ethnographic**. These are studies of a culture or small group, and involve describing the subject matter in great detail. In an ethnographic study you can expect to find every issue documented and examined. Researchers will immerse themselves in the area of interest. There might be participant observation, non-participant observation, interviews or questionnaires. It is unlikely that experiments will be used, as the researcher is concentrating on validity. There is a stated intention of finding out what is really going on.

Triangulation

Although you could say that case studies look at real data, and are high in validity, there is a problem in knowing how much to believe what is claimed. It is hard for a single researcher to be objective, and usually case studies are carried out by one person. It is necessary to give evidence for any claims.

This is done by **triangulation**. One piece of evidence gathered in one way is not sufficient. However, if the same piece of evidence is gathered by more than one means, then it is 'harder' evidence. Triangulation means taking evidence from different methods and putting it together to form the story or the picture. Figure 9.5 gives an idea of what triangulation means.

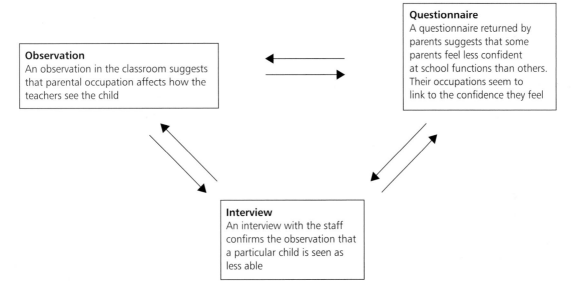

Observation
An observation in the classroom suggests that parental occupation affects how the teachers see the child

Questionnaire
A questionnaire returned by parents suggests that some parents feel less confident at school functions than others. Their occupations seem to link to the confidence they feel

Interview
An interview with the staff confirms the observation that a particular child is seen as less able

Figure 9.5
Triangulation

Table 9.8 Some advantages and disadvantages of case studies

Advantages	Disadvantages
Valid data is gathered	One person or small group, so cannot generalise from the findings
Can generate a lot of other research	
Rich data can be collected	Not reliable, as a different situation another time, and a different researcher, may yield different results
Can generate a lot of data	An element of subjectivity from the researcher
Can test a theory and gather in-depth evidence	

Discourse analyses, content analyses and analyses of diaries

The main methods used when studying psychology have been outlined. However, there are other interesting methods.

Researchers use methods that tell them about interactions between people, and that give in-depth information. If you are studying sociology, you will know about the interactionist approach. Sociologists use case studies, ethnography and observations in real-life settings to find more about interactions between people. Many researchers in psychology have realised that people cannot be studied in isolation, as they tend to be in experiments: the interactions between people themselves have importance. Similarly, questionnaires and experiments uncover only small, and perhaps insignificant, issues about people. There are other methods that look more directly at real people in real situations.

Diary methods

Researchers sometimes analyse historical documents and diaries of individuals to study aspects of their behaviour and beliefs. In psychology, however, usually the diary method means asking someone to keep a diary. From a therapy point of view, you can find out quite a lot of what leads to problems in a person's life, such as sleeplessness or panic attacks, by asking them to keep a detailed diary. Researchers have turned to such methods in order to get rich and valid data.

Table 9.9 Advantages and disadvantages of diary methods

Advantages	Disadvantages
Gathers real data in the sense that the participant is recording their feelings and actions	Depend on the participant to tell the truth
Gather rich data as the participant is free to record whatever they wish to record	The participant may forget to record something
	Not reliable, because each individual situation is unlikely to happen again

Content analysis

Content analysis involves going directly to a source of data – a newspaper or the television, for example. The content is then analysed closely. Patterns are looked for. Content analysis needs careful planning.

Table 9.10 Advantages and disadvantages of using content analysis

Advantages	Disadvantages
Valid becuse collects direct data	Only looks at a particular situation, so may not be able to repeat the study
Ethical because there are no participants and the situation is already present	Uses media as sources, and the facts are often biased in the media
The researcher can do content analysis in their own time and without disturbing others so relatively easy	Need to use careful sampling of items to analyse – each newspaper has its own bias for example

Discourse analysis

Discourse analysis involves collecting qualitative data in the form of other people's 'discourses' or conversations and analysing them. These conversations can be in written form, and can include texts, and discourse analysis is similar to content analysis as a method.

However, discourse analysis is interested in people talking, and in interactions between them, rather than the more sociological content of content analysis. Also it goes beyond 'just' conversations (and is more complex than this brief explanation can show). Content analysis focuses on issues such as gender roles, or helping behaviour; it looks at social behaviour in general. Discourse analysis looks more specifically at conversations and the effect of culture. One of the main features is examination of the way we understand language, and how it can be interpreted differently by different people in different situations. The idea is that issues examined in psychology, especially within social psychology, are not real things that can be looked at. They arise from one person's interactions with another, and can only be studied with that in mind. It is not that we can measure self, or gender, but we can only study these sorts of issues by looking at what they mean to people. The way to study this is to look at interactions between people, especially interactions using language.

Table 9.11 Some advantages and disadvantages of using discourse analysis

Advantages	Disadvantages
Just as content analysis looks at 'real' data, so discourse analysis looks at real conversations – so it is a valid method	There is almost bound to be subjectivity since the discourse between the researcher and the participant can be part of what is studied, so there is bias
The researcher can arrive at a novel way of categorising social issues	Any analysis even of the same material is likely to be different, so the method is not reliable
Tends to use a small number of participants and this can be easier and more ethical	It is hard to do – the researcher starts with a clean sheet and has to build categories
	Tends to use a small number of participants and analyse in depth, so results are not generalisable

Longitudinal, cross-sectional and cross-cultural methods

Longitudinal method

A longitudinal study is a study is carried out on the same group of people over a length of time. Even a study of babies over a few months can be a longitudinal study, if each baby's ability at one stage is to be compared with their ability a few months later. The same baby is used at each stage, so this is a longitudinal study. Some longitudinal studies carry on for years.

Table 9.12 Advantages and disadvantages of longitudinal studies

Advantages	Disadvantages
You are studying the same person, so there are no individual differences	So much will change over the period of time that it will be hard to know what is causing any effect you are looking at
	Participants will drop out or move away
	Even the researcher might move on, leaving someone else to continue the work

Cross-sectional method

A cross-sectional study is a study carried out at one moment in time using different groups. For instance, babies of 3 months can be compared with babies of 6 months – but two different groups of babies would be needed. With the longitudinal study, the researcher would have waited 3 months for the same babies to grow before testing them again.

Table 9.13 Advantages and disadvantages of cross-sectional methods

Advantages	Disadvantages
The researcher can gather all the data straight away There is less likelihood of people dropping out of the study, or the researcher leaving than when using a longitudinal method	There is still a problem of individual differences because the researcher is comparing different people The older group will have been through different events, and there are too many variables for good controls to be possible

Cross-cultural designs

Cross-cultural studies are those done between cultures. If something is found to be true of all participants, in more than one culture, then we assume that the ability is innate (inborn). If differences are found between participants in different cultures, we tend to say the ability is learnt.

Table 9.14 Advantages and disadvantages of cross-cultural designs

Advantages	Disadvantages
Useful for finding out whether something is innate or learnt through experience	The researcher might not know the culture, so might easily misunderstand what is going on The researcher might use inappropriate materials, for example, that those in another culture are not familiar with. If they use the same materials in both cultures, they might be spoiling the study because one culture is unfamiliar with the materials and this affects the results. If they don't use the same materials, they have lost some of the control There may be language problems

Inferential statistics and analysis of data

The results of any study must be analysed to see what has been found. Firstly, when using quantitative measures, a researcher would see whether there was a difference or a relationship between the scores of two sets of participants, and then whether that difference or relationship is large enough to be meaningful. In order to analyse quantitative data, firstly **descriptive statistics** are used to give a picture of the situation. Secondly, **inferential statistics** test to see how far the findings might be due to chance or some other variable, rather than being because of the manipulation of the independent variable. Analysis of qualitative data is briefly looked at in the final section of this chapter.

Measures of central tendency

For quantitative data the **mean**, **median**, **mode**, and **range** need to be calculated – or whichever of these is suitable for the given level of measurement (whether the data are nominal, ordinal or interval/ratio). The mean, median and mode are measures of central tendency and are also descriptive statistics (which also include the range, bar charts and line graphs). The mean, median, mode and range cannot all be calculated for all levels of measurement – for example, if the data are nominal. You can only calculate the median and mode if you have ordinal data. However, you can calculate them all if you have interval data.

Calculating the mean average

For any set of scores, to calculate the mean average total up the scores themselves and then divide by the number of scores there are in the set.

Calculating the median

Calculating the median means finding the middle score. Scores are put in ascending order, from the lowest to the highest, then the middle score is identified. If there is not an exact middle score, because there is an even number of results, then the median will be mid way between the middle two numbers. For example, the list

11, 12, 12, 14, 14, 15, 16, 16, 17, 17, 18, 18, 18, 20, 20

has 15 numbers, so the middle is the eighth one, and the median is 16. In this list

12, 12, 14, 14, 15, 16, 16, 17, 17, 18, 18, 18, 20, 20

there are 14 numbers, so the middle lies between the seventh (16) and eighth (17) – 16.5.

Calculating the mode

The mode is the most usual score (the 'fashionable' one) in a list. For example, in this list of scores

11, 12, 12, 14, 14, 15, 16, 16, 17, 17, 18, 18, 18, 20, 20

18 appears most often (three times), so the mode is 18. If two numbers appear most often – for example, here

11, 12, 12, 12, 12, 14, 14, 16, 16, 17, 17, 18, 18, 18, 18, 20, 20

both 12 and 18 appear four times – there are two different modes and the set is **bi-modal**. This is important when choosing a statistical test, as is explained below. If, when drawing up a table of descriptive statistics, you find more than one mode, either leave that section blank or put in all the 'modes'.

Calculating the range

The range (spread of scores) is basically the top score minus the bottom score, although there are two ways of working out the range.
- If the set of scores involves numbers where both the bottom and the top score can be reached, then the range is the top score minus the bottom score plus 1.
- If the set of scores involves numbers where the bottom score is the starting point, but the top score cannot be achieved, then the range is the top score minus the bottom score, without adding 1.

For example, if the number of words recalled from a list of 20 by 16 participants are

11, 12, 12, 12, 12, 14, 14, 16, 16, 17, 17, 18, 18, 18 18, 20, 20

the range is 20 – 11 + 1, which is 10. The scores range between 11 and 20 and there are 10 scores in that range.

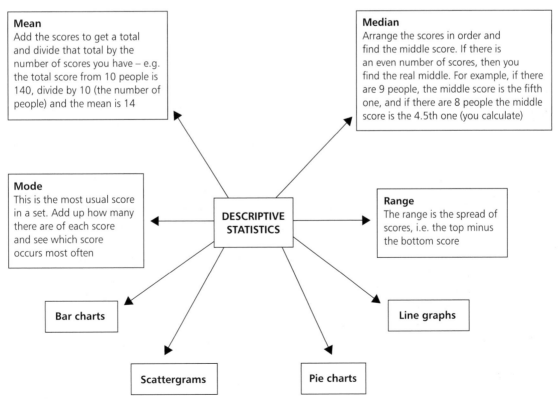

Figure 9.6
Descriptive statistics

However, in some cases the top score possible is not achieved – for example, in a series of voltage measurements levels between 11.0 and 19.999 are obtained, and the highest possible voltage of 20 V was not reached. In this case 1 is not added – the range is from 11 to 20, which is 9. Usually in psychology the range measures the top score actually achieved minus the lowest score actually achieved, so 1 should be added (although often it is not).

Levels of measurement

There are three levels of measurement as far as psychology is concerned – nominal, ordinal or interval/ratio (these have already been described in this chapter). Not all levels of measurement allow calculation of all measures of central tendency. We get in the habit of saying calculate the mean, median, mode and range, but in fact this cannot always be done.

Measures of central tendency, normal distribution and similarity of variance

Measures of central tendency can give a good picture of the results, although how far each measure is useful depends on the level of measurement.

- **Nominal data**, where categories are recorded, do not involve measuring on a numerical scale, so the descriptive statistics that can be done are limited. An inferential test can be carried out (as is explained later), but the data can only be displayed visually in a table.
- **Ordinal data** are not numbers used in a mathematical way so the mean average is not useful. However, numbers are used when ranking, and the median, mode and range do help to describe the data, and are useful. Graphs and charts can also be used. Inferential testing can be carried out, using specific tests.
- **Interval/ratio data** require the mean, median, mode and range to be calculated and displayed to describe the data, and charts and graphs are also needed. Inferential tests can be carried out, although as explained below certain tests can only be used if the data are gathered using a mathematical scale, there is normal distribution, and similarity of variance. When the data gathered are on an interval/ratio scale, the researcher must check to see, firstly, if there is normal distribution and, secondly, if the variance is similar.
- **Normal distribution** can be checked for by comparing the mean, median and mode. If these three measures are very similar, then the scores are likely to be normally distributed. A frequency chart can be drawn up to see if there is a normal distribution curve. Chapter 4 has a section on IQ, which gives a more detailed example about normal distribution curves. If there is no mode, or if the set of scores is bi-modal, then the scores are not

normally distributed – and they are not normally distributed if the measures of central tendency (mean, median and mode) are not very close. If scores are not normally distributed there might be something wrong with the sample of people chosen (or the independent variable is not normally distributed in the target population), and care should be taken in interpreting the results.

Similarity of variance can be checked for by comparing ranges and by calculating **standard deviation**. Similar ranges in two sets of scores suggest a similar spread of scores. If a set of scores is bi-modal, then this means that the scores are not normally distributed.

Standard deviation

Standard deviation is a way of calculating how far scores vary from the mean. A large standard deviation means scores vary quite a lot, a small standard deviation means scores cluster more around the mean. Standard deviation can show the spread of scores. If a researcher is comparing two sets of scores and wants to check for similarity of variance (sometimes called 'homogeneity of variance') he or she calculates the standard deviation, which must be very similar in both sets of scores. It is hard to say what 'similar' means when comparing two standard deviations as it depends on the measure being used. For example, IQ measures can vary between 70 and 130 or more, whereas reaction time might only vary between 6 and 11 seconds. Where the possible spread of scores is large, we could say that two standard deviations are similar even if they have fairly different values; however, where the possible spread of scores is small, similarity of standard deviation must mean almost the same.

Variance is the standard deviation squared. If two sets of scores to be compared have similar standard deviations and similar variances then the spread of the scores is similar.

Calculating variance and standard deviation

Standard deviation is a calculation of how far each score deviates from the mean of a set of scores. To calculate standard deviation:

1 Take the difference of each score from the mean.
2 Square that difference in each case.
3 Add up all the squared differences in the set of scores.
4 Take the number of scores in the set and subtract one.
5 Divide the total of the squared differences is divided by the answer found for **4**.
6 The answer at this stage is the variance. To get the standard deviation, take the square root of the variance:

$$S = \sqrt{\frac{\Sigma_N d^2}{(N-1)}}$$

This way of calculating standard deviation is one of two possible formulae, and is the one usually for psychology studies. It is the one used where a *sample* of the population is measured, not the whole group. In psychology, the actual group tested is almost always only a sample of the target population, rather than the whole group. As the sample scores are not those of the whole group or population, the equation used involves (N – 1) to take some account of this fact.

Sampling error

Another problem with using a sample of the population rather than the whole population is that it is assumed that the mean of those tested is the same as the mean of the whole population, although, depending on the success of the sampling, this may not actually be the case. The **sampling error** is how far the mean of the sample studied differs from the actual mean of the target population, which cannot be known accurately. However, in general, the larger the sample size, the smaller the sampling error is likely to be.

Why calculate the standard deviation and variance?

When a standard deviation is known, then, if the scores are normally distributed, we know where certain scores will fall in relation to other scores, which can be useful. Look at Figure 9.7: around 68% of all scores fall within one standard deviation either side of the mean, and around 96% fall within two standard deviations either side of the mean. If we know the mean and the standard deviation of a set of scores, we can tell where a particular score falls as a percentage of other scores.

For example, if on a memory test I recall 20 words out of 30, I may not know whether this is a good score or a bad score. However, if I know that the mean of the scores of a whole group doing the test was 15, and that the standard deviation was 2.5, then I know that my score is just about in the top 2% of all scores – I have done very well. On the other hand, if the mean is 15 and the standard deviation 5 my score of 20 is just within the top 16% of all the scores, and I have not done quite so well. Knowing the mean and the standard deviation researchers could work out whether a score is good or bad, because if the scores are normally distributed, the percentages of scores within one and two standard deviations remains the same in every set of scores. If the normal distribution curve of a set of scores has a fairly flat curve, then the standard deviation is likely to be large (as around 68% of the scores will be quite widely spread around the mean). If the normal distribution curve of a set of scores has a tall curve, then the standard deviation is likely to be small (as around 68% of the scores will be clustered around the mean). Standard deviation measures the width of the distance that around 68% of scores lies either side of the mean (and two standard deviations gives around 96% either side of the mean).

Another reason for calculating standard deviation and variance (the standard deviation squared) is that some inferential tests can be used only under certain conditions, one of which involves variance. To compare two sets of scores using some of the tests being considered here, the scores must be normally distributed and have similar variance because some of the tests used involve using mathematical calculations such as squares and square roots. These calculations cannot meaningfully be done on data that are not of interval or ratio status because with interval/ratio data the intervals between the numbers are assumed to be equal. If they are not equal the mathematical calculations cannot be done. For both these calculations, the scores must be interval/ratio in any case – the score must involve numbers that have equal intervals between them – otherwise the tests will not be useful. Also, the mean can only be usefully calculated if the data are interval/ratio. For example, if I score 10 out of 20 on a memory test, and you score 20 out of 20, you have twice as many correct as me – we can do mathematical calculations on the data, and say I am 50% as good at the test as you, and you have scored 100% more than I have. However, I might give someone 5 on an attractiveness scale of 0–10 and you might give them 10, but that doesn't mean I think they are 50% less attractive than you do. I might not have given more than 6 to anyone, so my scale may be different to yours. So mathematical calculations can only be done if the data are interval or ratio.

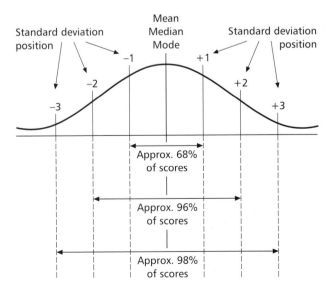

Figure 9.7
Standard deviation positions

In Table 9.15 three of the tests require interval/ratio data – related *t*, unrelated *t*, and Pearson's Product Moment Correlation Coefficient. These three tests cannot be used (1) if the data are not interval/ratio, (2) if the data are not normally distributed, and (3) if there is not similar variance between the two sets of scores of interest. If one of these three conditions is missing, then the appropriate test for use with ordinal data must be used. For example, if a related *t* test seems appropriate because the data are interval/ratio, but the data are not normally distributed (perhaps bi-modal), then the Wilcoxon test must be used instead.

Statistical analysis – inferential statistics

Displaying data in tables and using graphs and charts means that someone can begin to assess the findings of a study. Using the mean, median and mode it can be seen if scores are normally distributed, and using the range and standard deviation it can be seen if scores are similarly spread. The means of the two sets of scores can be compared to see if one is larger than the other, which helps to see if any difference between scores is large enough for the alternate hypothesis to be accepted.

However, if you really wanted to know if the difference between two sets of scores was big enough to accept the alternative hypothesis, or whether the null hypothesis should be accepted, you would do a statistical test. There is a choice of tests. Usually at 'A' level only eight main tests

are used (outlined in Table 9.15). Details about how to do the test are not given here, since step-by-step instructions are easy enough to follow, and can be found in textbooks about statistics. You do need to know how to choose a test, and why a test is needed.

Statistical tests are used to answer the question 'to what extent would these results occur by chance?' The null hypothesis claims that any difference between two sets of results will be due to chance, and the test looks at how far it is the case that the results are due to chance. If the result is significant (how to find this out is explained below), then the null hypothesis is rejected; however, if the result is not significant, then the null hypothesis cannot be rejected.

Different tests are available for different designs, and for different levels of measurement. Once the test is chosen, the calculations are worked through, a result is arrived at and special tables are used to look up whether the result is significant or not.

Interpreting the results of the test

Each statistical test gives a result (for example, $t = 3.45$ or rho $= +0.67$). At this stage you will need to know what to do with the result.

One or two tailed?

In order to interpret the result of a statistical test, it is necessary to know if the alternative hypothesis needs a one or two-tailed test.

Table 9.15 Choosing a statistical test

		Experiment			Correlation
	Nominal data	**Ordinal data**	**Interval/ratio data**		
Repeated measures or matched pairs design	Sign test	Wilcoxon matched pairs sign ranks test	Related *t* test (only if normal distribution and similar variance, else Wilcoxon)		For ordinal data Spearmans rank order correlation coefficient
Independent groups design	Chi squared test for independent samples	Mann–Whitney U test	Unrelated *t* test (only if normal distribution and similar variance, else Mann–Whitney U)		For interval/ratio data Pearson's product moment coefficient (only if normal distribution and similar variance, else Spearman)

- **One tailed** means the direction of the result is predicted in the hypothesis – a directional word like 'more' or 'better' will be used. For example, if the alternative hypothesis says that there is a meaningful difference in that more words are recalled when the list is categorised than when it is randomised, this is one-tailed.
- **Two tailed** means there is no predicted direction. If the alternative hypothesis is that there is a meaningful difference in the number of words recalled depending on whether the list is categorised or randomised, this is two tailed.

Level of significance

To interpret whether the result of a statistical test is significant, a level of significance must be chosen. The level of significance is the measure of what percentage of results the researcher is willing to allow to be due to chance, whilst still rejecting the null hypothesis. It is the probability that the results are due to chance (p). If a null hypothesis is to be rejected (the study 'worked') then any difference or relationship between scores must be bigger than would be expected by chance. The level of significance is the level chosen that could be due to chance, and at which level the alternative hypothesis would still be accepted, and the null hypothesis rejected.

For example, if the study is exploratory, it might be accepted from the start that 5% of the results are likely to be due to chance factors ($p \leq 0.05$), but 95% would then be due to the manipulation of the independent variable (what was done in the study). In this case, the level of significance is 5% – the level at which the null will still be rejected, even though (in this case) 5% of the results could be due to chance.

In another study, where the findings are perhaps going to be used to make important policy such as choosing a reading scheme in all primary schools, the researchers might not be willing to accept that as many as 5% of the findings could be due to chance. They might look for a 1% level of significance ($p \leq 0.01$), where 99% of the results are likely to be due to the IV. This means that 99 out of 100 should do what is expected, and is a stricter level of significance than 5%, where 95 out of 100 would do what is expected. When looking up whether the result of a test is significant, the number of participants is important, and the tables that show the critical values (against which the result is measured) allow for the fact that very few studies will ask 100 people. The tables allow for asking any number of participants, and yet still the level of significance (such as 1 in 100) can be used.

Choosing the level of significance

The level of significance should be chosen before the study is carried out. If the area is well tested, it might be thought that only 1 in 100 of the results should be due to

chance. If the area is new, a 5% level might be accepted in order to move the research forward. If the choice is left until after the results have been gathered, it will be tempting for the researcher to choose the level that makes the study 'work' (the level at which the result is significant), rather than choosing for the right reasons. A 5% level is expressed as $p \leq 0.05$, which means that the probability of the results being due to chance (p) is less than or equal to ($\leq$) 5% (0.05).

Testing the null hypothesis

The null hypothesis says that what is predicted is not the case and that any difference found will be due to chance. The statistical test checks how much is due to chance. If 1% is due to chance, the researcher will probably accept that, and say that the study 'worked'. If 10% is due to chance (10 people out of every 100 did not do what was predicted ($p \leq 0.10$)), then the alternative hypothesis cannot be accepted (5% is the most generous that is accepted in psychology ($p \leq 0.05$)).

If you find 10% is due to chance (and how you find this is explained below), then you have to reject the alternative hypothesis and accept the null hypothesis that 'there is no meaningful difference, and that any difference between two scores that are being measured is due to chance'. Another way of putting this is to say $p > 0.05$, which means that the probability of the results being due to chance (p) is greater than ($>$) 5% (0.05).

Degrees of freedom (df) and number of participants

You have nearly all the information you need now to see if a result from a statistical test is significant or not. However, when you look up the results of the test to see what it means, you will need to know either the number of participants (which is the easy part, and is usually represented by N) or the number of degrees of freedom. You are not expected to explain what 'degrees of freedom' means in the AS or A2 examination, simply what 'df' means and how to calculate it.

The degrees of freedom in a trial have to do with the number of participants. If you are using a repeated measures design, with 10 participants, df $= N - 1 = 9$. This is loosely because when 9 of the scores are in the table of 10 scores, the last score has no degree of freedom to go anywhere else in the table. If you are using an independent groups design, with 20 participants (10 in each group), then df $= 18$. This is loosely because this time, with each set of 10, the last one has to go in the last slot, so in each case there is one score which has no choice as to where it goes. So here df $= N - 2 = 18$. For each test, the degrees of freedom will be calculated differently.

Using critical values

At this stage you need to turn to a book to find out how to use the various tests, although you will not need to do any calculations for the Edexcel 'A' level examination. In order to learn more it is a good idea to use a set of scores that you have generated (perhaps from your coursework for Unit 3) and to do the correct statistical test. Once you have the result of the test, find the appropriate table of critical values. You will see, depending on the table, that you need to know:

• level of significance
• whether your alternative hypothesis is one or two tailed
• df and/or N
• the result you found from doing the test.

Using the table look down the columns using the appropriate information; you will find a critical value. Write that down. Then read at the top of the table to find out if your result should be more than the critical value or less than the critical value.

• If it should be greater than the critical value, and is greater, then you can reject the null hypothesis, and the study worked.
• If it should be lower than the critical value, and is lower, then you can reject the null hypothesis.
• In all other cases you must retain the null hypothesis and conclude that the findings could be due to chance or some other variable.

Analysis of qualitative data

Analysis of qualitative data is different in important ways from analysis of quantitative data. Qualitative data involve opinions and attitudes, which can not be easily categorised or summarised. Often researchers convert qualitative data into quantitative data for the purposes of analysis. For example, when doing content analysis, a researcher tends to use tallying, so that categories can be counted and compared, such as how many females appear in stereotypical roles in adverts. However, an advantage of qualitative data is that information is gathered that is rich and interesting, and this richness can be lost if qualitative data is converted into quantitative data for the purposes of statistical analysis.

Categorising the results of a qualitative study

Qualitative data often take the form of a story, and the results are the story itself. In a case study, for example, the researcher may have taped many hours of conversation; in a diary study, there may be pages of information to be presented. The researcher must choose what is to be presented to the reader, and the researcher's subjective interpretation must be noted. A transcript of a conversation or tape recording is important and must be complete, so that the researcher starts with the whole picture. Then he or she can look for repetitions in what is being said, or can look for common patterns, in order to build categories and present the data more clearly.

This is not the same as using categories when analysing quantitative data, however, as with qualitative research the data will be categorised using the meanings of the participant, rather than being grouped using the researcher's categories. For example, if aggression is studied by observing behaviour and tallying, the researcher will use pre-selected categories of what is aggressive and what is not. However, if a case study is carried out using a participant who is known to be aggressive, then the participant's own categories will be analysed, such as 'I thought he was going to attack me' or 'I was not letting him get away with that'. In this example, a researcher might conclude that aggressive people sometimes attack because they see others as a threat, or sometimes attack to protect their self-image.

A researcher might impose the categories as similar statements and comments emerge. Sometimes the participant imposes the categories as they naturally refer to different people in particular ways – for example, someone might refer to 'them' and 'us' using particular terms. Types can emerge – for example, the participant who is being studied to look at aggression might group people into 'those looking at me', 'those asking for it', and 'those taking a liberty…with what is mine'.

Collaborative research to improve validity

Collaborative research is where a researcher and a participant collaborate – for example, the data are written up and then read by the participant, who can agree that the information is correct. This is a way of giving validity to the data. Collaborative research can also improve reliability, as if another researcher were to use the same participant in the same way, then in theory he or she should discover the same findings.

Triangulation to improve validity

Triangulation was mentioned earlier in this chapter when case studies were discussed (p. 311). Triangulation is a way of testing the validity of qualitative data, and involves gathering data from different sources and methods. The idea is that if the same piece of information is found using different methods and sources the findings are more valid. Triangulation can also improve reliability, as another researcher should discover the same findings if the study was replicated, and triangulation has been used.

Grounded theory

Grounded theory refers to the way that theory can come from the analysis, rather than preceding it. For example, compare quantitative and qualitative research. People gather quantitative data, usually develop a hypothesis derived from a theory, and then test it in some way. For example, it might be thought that older people recall early events in their lives better than they recall what happened the previous day. A hypothesis might be that older people remember people they knew at school better than they recall people they met yesterday. A situation might be set up where the participants meet new people. Then the next day researchers ask questions about the people the participant met yesterday, and ask questions about their school friends. Findings should show that more detail is recalled about school friends. If a qualitative study were done to look at the memory of an older person, the researcher might spend time talking with a single participant, and might tape record several hours of conversation. Although the researcher might have the general aim of exploring past memories and current memories, an interview would be unstructured, and the participant would be encouraged to talk freely rather than to respond to particular questions. Conversations could be transcribed, quotations used and checked with the participant, categories suggested to the participant to check validity (as is done in collaborative research), and finally a theory might be suggested. In this way the theory comes from the data, rather than being imposed from the beginning – this is grounded theory. The researcher is likely to begin with some general aim, and then early analysis takes place. However, the final theory has been grounded in the data that has been gathered. From early analysis, the researcher is likely to visit the participant more than once to keep checking that they are working within the meanings of the participant, rather than within the researcher's own subjective interpretation of the data.

Qualitative data give validity

A scientific approach to psychology involves gathering quantitative data so that statistical tests can show how far findings are likely to be due to chance, and so that some measure of reliability can be assured. Those working within this positivist approach would accept the value of qualitative data, but only in so far as it adds to what is found 'scientifically'. Qualitative methods would be secondary to quantitative ones, and qualitative data would be of interest for what is found that is unusual, and what would inform more scientific study. However, many researchers see qualitative methods as more useful than more scientific ones, as validity is hard to achieve using scientific methods, whereas a strength of qualitative methods is their validity.

Content analysis, discourse analysis, diary methods

Content analysis, discourse analysis and diary methods were outlined earlier (p. 312). Content analysis can involve tallying and can yield quantitative data, as can discourse analysis and the analysis of diary data. However, all three also give valuable qualitative data, and reducing what is gathered to quantitative categories will lose some of the richness and individuality that characterises such data. This richness and depth of information is just what is interesting in qualitative data. Categories will be looked for by analysing particular statements, or clustering comments that seem to have similar meanings.

Objectivity and subjectivity

Where a researcher becomes as immersed in the situation (as they usually do when gathering qualitative data) they could be accused of bringing subjective interpretation into their account. Scientific study should be objective, and there should be no influence from the researcher. When doing a qualitative study, however, the researcher is closely involved in gathering the data, and should note where subjectivity is likely to have affected results. If the researcher influences the results, they are less valid. Ways of ensuring validity (outlined above) include collaborative research, triangulation and grounded theory – and can guard against subjectivity. If the researcher checks back with the participant as the research progresses, then the study is more objective, and the researcher's influence should be minimised. Interpretation is useful, in that categories must be developed, and this interpretation should be made clear so that it is not subjective. For example, exact quotations can be listed to justify the choice of a particular category, and evidence can be presented just as it would if quantitative data were being presented.

Conclusion

It might be thought that a study gathering qualitative data is easier because there is no need for statistical analysis, and writing a story sounds easier than measuring variables. However, since there is no clear structure for analysing qualitative data, since gathering data is very time-consuming, and since it is so important to present evidence for conclusions, it is usually accepted that qualitative methods are in many ways more difficult to use. Some researchers would claim that it is so difficult to ensure validity, objectivity or reliability that such research is not useful. Others would claim that the richness of information – which often could not be collected in any other way – is precisely what is of interest to psychologists, and that qualitative methods are the only ones worth using.

Suggested reading

Cardwell, M., Clark, L. and Meldrun, C. (1996) *Psychology for A level*. Hammersmith: Collins Educational.

Clegg, F. (1991) *Simple Statistics*. Cambridge: Cambridge University Press.

Coolican, J. (1994) *Research Methods and Statistics in Psychology*, Second Edition. London: Hodder and Stoughton.

10 Issues, perspectives and debates in psychology

The aims of this chapter

The aims of this chapter are to help the reader draw on previously learnt material in order to:

- *distinguish between approaches/perspectives in psychology*
- *discuss contributions of approaches/perspectives to the study of psychology and to society*
- *discuss social and moral implications of psychological research, including the issue of social control*
- *discuss the nature/nurture debate in psychology*
- *discuss the question of whether psychology should/could be called a science*
- *discuss methods used in psychological research, including qualitative and quantitative methods*
- *discuss ethical issues involved in the use of humans and animals in psychological research.*

STUDY AID

When you have finished working through this chapter you should write an essay about, or at least test yourself on, each of the above points. This would help you to see how good your knowledge and understanding of these issues is.

This chapter covers

science
Should psychology be a science? Is it important? Why?

METHODS, SCIENCE AND PSYCHOLOGY
Qualitative and quantitative methods

Scientific and non-scientific methods
Ethical issues in psychological research

Introduction to issues, perspectives and debates in psychology

This chapter deals with the synoptic part of the Edexcel A2 course, focusing on Unit 6, and so there should be very little subject matter here that you don't already know. You must re-read various parts of your course to cover what is needed. Rather than giving you all the material – which is not necessary, as you have already studied much of it – this chapter focuses on some overall issues that are important, and that help in understanding psychology, including:

• The contributions of particular approaches and perspectives. These are useful when evaluating an approach or perspective. For example, we can say that a certain approach is useful because it leads to useful consequences. It is also interesting to look at the contributions of psychology for themselves.
• Social and moral implications of psychological research. Implications are important, as psychologists need to be aware of the consequences of any research. Consider an example – if it is found that there is a gene for intelligence, it might be thought that those without it need not be educated, so a whole section of society could be disadvantaged.
• The use of psychology in social control. Examining issues of social control helps us to focus on how the findings of research in psychology are used. For example, conditioning can be called brainwashing, or treatment for a mental disorder could be seen as controlling behaviour to suit society.
• Whether an ability or behaviour comes from our genes (our nature) or whether it is learnt from our environment (our nurture). This question has been raised very often in psychology, and is still of interest. Genes are still being researched, and specific genes for specific abilities or behaviours are still being discovered.
• The question of whether psychology is a science. The answer to this question is less important than the issues raised. Studying the question of whether psychology is a science helps us to focus on the many different paradigms or approaches within psychology, and also

helps us to look carefully at the methods we use to build a body of knowledge. These issues are useful when evaluating psychology and its findings.
• Methodological issues. Researchers must ensure that conclusions are as fair as possible, do not mislead, do not lead to harmful consequences for individuals, and help to build a firm body of knowledge from which to draw conclusions. For example, offender profiling is used to try to catch criminals, and leads to serious consequences. Any research carried out to give information about offenders must be undertaken very carefully indeed, given the possible consequences of findings.
• Ethical issues. Researchers need to use care and consideration when dealing with participants (both human and other animal).

Psychological perspectives and approaches

Introduction

In this section you need to:
• Recall the assumptions and basic principles involved in all the six main approaches that you have studied for the AS. Whilst you can focus on the six main approaches given for the AS course, a few more approaches will be briefly outlined here. The terms 'approach' and 'perspective' are both found in textbooks, and are used interchangeably here.
• Discuss how these approaches have contributed to the study of psychology, for example, how Freud's views led Erikson to develop his slightly different psychosocial theory.
• Discuss how these approaches have contributed to society. Consider the applications of psychology to society: in education, work, health, child development, sport, environment, and crime for instance. It is a good idea to work through these different applied areas, to help you to list where a particular approach has made a contribution.

Table 10.1 *Contributions of approaches to psychology and society*

Contributions to psychology	Contributions to society
The cognitive approach enables experimental testing of the way we process information, and helps link findings from different approaches (e.g. linking physiological and psychological information about memory)	Behaviourism has led to behaviour modification techniques and behaviour therapies
	The psychodynamic approach has led to psychotherapies
The physiological approach, by using information from genes etc., provides a scientific footing for psychology	The physiological approach has helped in many areas e.g. sleep, jet lag, IQ and mental illness
The psychodynamic approach has led to an emphasis on 'talking cures' and further research looking at emotions and underlying motivation	The cognitive approach has helped people with memory loss, and has helped in education
	The cognitive–developmental approach has helped to construct classroom learning techniques
Behaviourism has led to more theories of learning – e.g. social learning theory	The social approach has helped in understanding crowds, environmental issues, helping behaviour, and why we obey
The cognitive–developmental approach has led to research into education	The humanistic approach has led to an emphasis on self-actualisation and unconditional positive regard
The social approach has linked to sociology and enabled studies of interactions between people, as well as leading to new methods such as discourse analysis	The cognitive approach has led to therapies, and turned our attention to positive thinking

Contributions of the behaviourist approach

Refer back to your AS notes to review the main principles of the behaviourist approach. Note that social learning theory comes into the learning approach, and draws on behaviourist principles, although it is not strictly speaking a theory within the behaviourist approach.

ACTIVITY

List how you think the learning approach has contributed to the study of psychology and to society.

To psychology

The behaviourist approach:
- When developed, focused on what was measurable and turned to scientific methods.
- Was a science, which raised the profile of psychology at the time.
- Used a strict experimental approach, which led to some firm conclusions about cause and effect.
- Focused on measurable behaviour, and so its principles can be applied to observable behaviour, which is behaviour we are interested in.

- Gave a method (experiment) that was extended for use in other areas, such as social psychology (for example, Asch's (1956) study on conformity, and Milgram's well-known studies).
- Led to the development of social learning theory, which has been used to explain many behaviours.
- Has provided principles of learning that are still used in studies today.

However, it:
- Did not look at thought processes or emotions, so the findings are limited.
- Used animals in experiments, so the findings cannot always be generalised to humans.
- Used animals in experiments, which has been criticised as unethical.
- Assumed that there are general laws of behaviour to be found, which is disputed by some.
- Treated humans as the same, and as behaving in the same way in a given situation – and this is disputed.

To society

The behaviourist approach:
- Led to the development of learning techniques to improve learning in schools.
- Led to the development of learning techniques to train

animals (for example, dogs to help the blind).

- Has been used to develop behaviour modification techniques such as systematic desensitisation, which helps people with phobias.
- Has been used to help in overcoming alcoholism and addictions, through aversion therapy.

However, there are problems with this approach:

- It focuses on desirable behaviour, but this is what is desirable for society, not what is desirable for the individual.
- It focuses on the problem behaviour, and not the underlying cause of the behaviour, so might not be a 'cure'.
- Treatments and modification might work only in the situation the person is in under treatment, and improved behaviour might not be transferred to a different situation (e.g. the person's behaviour might improve in hospital, but not when he or she returns home).

Contributions of the psychodynamic approach

Refer back to your AS notes to review the main principles of the psychodynamic approach.

ACTIVITY

List how you think the psychodynamic approach has contributed to the study of psychology and to society.

To psychology

The psychodynamic approach:

- Has led to the development of lifespan theories such as Erikson's.
- Has led to other approaches such as Humanism, and other types of therapy.
- Has given some novel methods to help to uncover motives, such as free association and dream analysis.
- Has focused on emotions and underlying motivation, rather than on behaviour or cognition.
- Gives alternative explanations for many neuroses, so helps in drawing conclusions about them.

However, it:

- Has been criticised as being unscientific since the ideas are difficult to operationalise and so hard to test empirically.
- Has been criticised as focusing too much on sexual matters, and might have adversely affected people's perception of psychology.

- Ignores other causes for behaviour, and does not fit in well with other approaches (except those that arose from the psychodynamic view, such as the humanistic approach), so builds its own unique body of knowledge.

To society

The psychodynamic approach:

- Has led to many different ways of doing psychotherapy, including counselling techniques.
- Has brought ideas such as the importance of unconscious desires into everyday thinking.
- Has emphasised that dreams have meanings, and alerted individuals to the need to attend to unconscious forces.
- Has focused on the first five years of life, and emphasised the importance of early upbringing – e.g. leading Bowlby to stress the importance of attachments, and helping children in many ways.
- Has turned focus towards looking at emotions in problems, and away from medicines as cures.
- Has led to other theories such as Erikson's, which has focused on lifespan, looking at the experiences of older people.

However, it:

- Has been accused of leading to false memories and causing problems.
- Can lead away from medical intervention, if it is assumed that all neuroses have a hidden cause in the unconscious.
- Has led to an expensive cure that certain groups miss out on.
- Has perhaps led to an overemphasis on sexual problems.
- As a theory has no real empirical evidence to support it, so the contributions might not rest on firm theoretical foundations.

Contributions of the cognitive approach

Refer back to your AS notes to review the main principles of the cognitive approach.

ACTIVITY

List how you think the cognitive approach has contributed to the study of psychology and to society.

To psychology

The cognitive approach:

- Has discovered information about what goes on between the stimulus and the response, helping to build a body of knowledge.

- Has provided evidence for functions of some areas of the brain – for example, areas used in language.
- Has advocated the use of new technologies, such as scanning, to help to discover more about the brain and behaviour.
- Has helped link knowledge of the physiology of the nervous system to cognitive functions, so linking approaches and moving towards a new paradigm.
- Has used the computer analogy to help to understand cognition, and also been of use to those working in computers, to help in their development, again helping to link different approaches and fields.

However:

- It is difficult to separate thinking processes – for example, it is hard to separate memory and attention – so it is hard to isolate variables for study.
- The workings of the brain are very complex, and it is hard through introspection or experimentation to find out what particular parts of the brain are for – although scanning is leading to some interesting discoveries.
- The approach will probably merge with physiological measures at some stage, becoming a neuroscience, as physiological knowledge becomes more certain.

To society

The cognitive approach:

- Has given many ideas about study skills, how to learn, how to make good use of memory, note taking, using different learning styles and so on, and so has aided educational processes.
- Has led to more understanding of age-related memory impairment, and has led to different therapies and techniques for discovering (and helping with) problems.
- Has helped people to improve their attention span, or to improve their memory, so helping with quality of life for those with difficulties.
- Has led to the development of therapies for difficulties – for example, use of positive thinking, or strategies for relieving symptoms of stress.
- Has led to useful techniques for police interviewing, as well as useful information about possible bias in eyewitness testimony and related areas.

However:

- Therapies using cognitive psychology, such as using positive thinking, work best with those who can reason and control their thinking in some way. Not everyone is able to do this.
- As there are many theories about how memory works, using knowledge from a particular theory might not be useful, if the theory is not correct

Contributions of the physiological approach

Refer back to your AS notes to review the main principles of the physiological approach.

ACTIVITY

List how you think the physiological approach has contributed to the study of psychology and to society.

To psychology

The physiological approach:

- Relies on biological findings, which are considered to be more reliable than findings from psychology experiments, so gives results scientific backing, making them more acceptable.
- Supports findings from other areas such as cognitive psychology, and this is more likely to lead to one overall paradigm for psychology.
- Helps in areas such as jet lag, shift work and sleep. These are areas of interest in more than one applied area, for example, in the field of health, clinical and occupational psychology.
- Gives support to theories by helping to identify genes for certain behaviours and attributes.
- Provides methods for studying the subject matter of psychology, for example, scanning techniques and the use of animals.

However, it:

- Gives biological information, but this is not easy to translate into information about emotions or motives.
- Needs subject matter that can be measured, whereas psychology is interested in qualitative data too.

To society

The physiological approach has led:

- To drug therapies – for example, to help to control the symptoms of schizophrenia, or to help with jet lag.
- To greater understanding of the functions of the brain and nervous system, so that damage to certain areas can be linked to particular behavioural or emotional problems.

However, this approach:

- Focuses on biological processes so looks for physiological causes of any difficulties, rather than looking at emotional difficulties, and suggesting alternatives like a 'talking cure'.
- Is reductionist, and looks at a problem by breaking it into parts, whereas some problems need to be tackled

as a whole – including the physiology of a person and their cultural background or environmental situation.

Social and moral issues in the application of psychology

Research in psychology uses humans and animals as participants and then draws conclusions about their behaviour. From such conclusions a body of knowledge is built, which is then made use of in some way. For example, studies have looked at helping behaviour, and more is now known about who would be expected to help in a given situation. Conclusions like these can have implications for others, and these implications should be understood and noted. Some issues have social consequences, for example, policy decisions about education can be made from research such as Piaget's. Some issues have moral implications, for example, decisions about using behavioural therapies to 'cure' homosexuality. Some of the implications are to do with research, and suggest that such research might not be acceptable. Some of the implications are to do with social control, and suggest that we should be careful in how we use understanding to control people's behaviour.

Social and moral implications of psychological research

ACTIVITY

Consider Milgram's well-known study, which led to the conclusion that it was not that the Germans were different in what they did to Jews, but that it is likely that anyone would obey under certain circumstances. Note down some social implications of Milgram's study, and some moral implications. Choose one other study, and carry out the same task.

Very many studies within psychology have social and/or moral implications, and only some examples can be outlined here. If a study is carried out unethically, this itself has moral implications, and we should ask whether the study should be done at all. As studies are of people, often in specific social situations, most (if not all) studies could be cited as having social and/or moral implications.

Here are some examples from criminal psychology.

Study 1: Adlam (1985), a replication of Hanewicz (1978) (adapted from Brewer, 2000)

• Aimed to see if British police officers show particular personality types.

• Used the Myers Briggs Type Indicator (MBTI).
• MBTI gives four dimensions: extravert/introvert (EI); thinking/feeling (TF); sensing/intuition (SN); judging/perceiving (JP). For example, a test would produce a type such as EFNP or ITSJ.
• 304 British police officers were tested (ranking officers). Hanewicz had tested patrolmen in the USA.
• Hanewicz found 20.7% ETSJ and 14% ITSJ; Adlam found 22.04% ETSJ and 37.82% ITSJ.
• Both types tend to be organised, practical, realistic with good administration skills.
• It was concluded that police are more sensing and thinking, and good at routine, unemotional tasks.

Implications of Study 1

• It is possible that someone joining the police force would be given such a test, and if they did not have the 'right' personality they might not be accepted. This has implications for individuals, as they might not be accepted into their chosen profession. It might also have social consequences – for example, if people from a certain culture were discriminated against by the test, then recruitment would reflect this bias. Chapter 4 examines the issue of bias in testing.

• From an ethical viewpoint, the study could be questioned as it is possible that the participants felt that they had to consent to taking part and might not have felt that they had the right to withdraw: true consent may not have been given. The right to withdraw and giving consent are two main ethical principles, which might have been broken in this study.

Study 2: Kassin and Kiechel (1996) (adapted from Brewer, 2000)

• Aimed to create a coercive-internalisation situation in an experiment.
• Participants were given a reaction time (RT) test, and were told not to touch the ALT key on the keyboard.
• There were 'witnesses' who falsely accused the participants of touching the key.
• The question was, would the participants admit to touching the key, when they had not?
• 69% (average) admitted touching the key and 10% even pictured themselves doing so.
• It was concluded that the participants had internalised the false claims.

Implications of Study 2

• *Social implications* – If it is said that we do adopt false memories, then our memories should not be relied upon, for example, as evidence in a court case. Many studies have demonstrated that we do seem to internalise false memories, so we may now start to question memory in all situations. However, a further social implication is that criminals may be released when they should be convicted, just because we no longer rely on witness testimony to the same extent. In either case, showing that memory can be unreliable has important consequences in areas such as criminal psychology.

- *Ethical implications* – The participants in this study are made anxious by being falsely accused. They are also deceived.
- *Moral implications* – After the studies the participants might consider themselves to be unreliable and gullible, and this could affect their self-esteem.

Study 3: Farrington and West (1990) (adapted from Brewer, 2000)

- This was the Cambridge study in the development of delinquency.
- Aimed to see if teenage delinquents become adult offenders.
- 411 white working-class boys from Camberwell took part in the study, and were followed from the age of 8–9 years for 30 years (from 1961).
- 75% of those who were convicted of an offence between 10 and 16 years old were also convicted of an offence when they were between 17 and 24.
- 50% were re-convicted between the ages of 25 and 32.
- The most serious offenders were deviant at aged 18 in more than one way – they drank, smoke and were involved in more fights.
- It was concluded that being a difficult child in primary school, having a poor, large family, living in poor housing, and experiencing parental neglect were important factors in the development of delinquency.
- Low social class and working mothers were not significant factors.

Implications of Study 3

- *Moral implications* – From these findings it might be assumed that young offenders are going to re-offend and should be treated accordingly. The self-fulfilling prophecy suggests that we fulfil the expectations of others, so if it is thought that 'once a criminal, always a criminal', then this is likely to become true. The self-fulfilling prophecy is outlined in more detail in Chapter 2.
- *Social implications* – Poor, large families, for example, might be targeted for special attention, and their children might be discriminated against in some way. Also it is clear that not all children from poor, large families become juvenile delinquents. On the positive side, it could be claimed that findings such as these help to highlight those who might become offenders, so they can be helped.
- *Ethical implications* – Include such issues as whether a longitudinal study such as this one affects the participants and their development. It is important to see whether the young people had the opportunity to refuse to take part in the study in the first place, and

also to consider if they had the right to withdraw as the study progressed.

Study 4: Palmer and Hollin (1998) (adapted from Brewer, 2000)

- Aimed to compare moral reasoning in male delinquents and male and female non-delinquents.
- 126 offenders from a young offenders institution were studied, and 122 male and 210 female non-offenders.
- Participants were given the Socio-Moral Reflection Measure – Short Form (SRM-SF), and items included moral dilemma-related questions (such as keeping a promise to a friend).
- The delinquent group showed less mature moral reasoning.

Implications of Study 4

- *Social implications* – We might label delinquents as having lower moral reasoning ability, and therefore expect them to reoffend. Labelling can lead to the self-fulfilling prophecy, and so this would not be giving individuals a fair chance.
- *Moral implications* – The individuals being tested may see themselves as less moral after having taken part in the study, and this might affect their future development. There is also the possibility that, having been labelled as 'less mature' in one type of reasoning, they may be considered 'less mature' in other ways, which might lead to more discrimination.
- *Ethical implications* include the question of whether people in institutions are free to withdraw their consent when asked to take part in a study. It is possible that their full consent is not obtained, as they feel obliged to be participants.

Study 5: Riordan (1999) (adapted from Brewer, 2000)

- Aimed to understand how female victims experience indecent exposure, and how it relates to their general fears of sexual crime.
- 72 questionnaires were distributed. Participants were postgraduate students, council employees, university administration staff and women living on an estate – all in the East Midlands.
- 35 respondents had been victims of indecent exposure once, seven had experienced indecent exposure twice, and one five times.
- 48.6% reacted with shock, 34.3% reacted with amusement, 25.7% reacted with fear, 5.7% felt disgust and 2.9% felt annoyance.
- 23 victims and 26 non-victims thought that the exposers were dangerous.
- 80% of the victims were concerned about what the exposers would do following the exposure.
- Ten victims had increased fear about sexual crime following the exposure.

- Ten victims changed their behaviours after the exposure.
- It was concluded that exposure is not a trivial offence, and can reinforce fears of sexual crime.

Implications of Study 6

- *Social implications* – It is useful to know how victims of indecent exposure react, as this can reveal what help is needed after the event – in terms of victim support, for example. Issues such as this are important, but are difficult to study, and are, therefore, not explored in many studies.
- *Moral implications* include consideration of whether calling to mind an unpleasant or upsetting experience is acceptable, and this is also an ethical consideration.
- *Ethical considerations* include asking how much the participants are going to be made anxious by being asked to review such experiences. Also, even those who have not been victims of indecent exposure might be upset by the questions, and might start to fear encounters, when previously they would not have been afraid.

Study 6: Ceci et al. (1994) – adapted from Gross (1999)

- Aimed to see if children's memories are altered by questioning.
- Over a 10-week period they asked children to think about events – some events were real, and others were suggested to the children by the researchers. For example, they said things like 'think hard, and tell me if this ever happened to you. Do you remember going to hospital with a mousetrap on your finger?'
- 58% of the children under school age described false events or gave false stories.
- 25% replied with memories of most of the false events, and not just one or two.
- It was concluded that even exposure to an adult telling a child about events that did not take place was enough for the child to develop false memories.

Implications of Study 6

- *Social implications* – Adults should take care not to suggest false events to children, as they are likely to internalise them, and to remember them as having occurred. If children are suggestible, then adults in positions of responsibility – for example, teachers – must take care with what is being suggested to a child.
- *Moral implications* include the responsibility of shaping a child's memory.
- *Ethical implications* concern the use of children as participants, and the special permission that is needed. Also false memories were implanted in this study. Several children remembered having had a mousetrap on their finger – perhaps a harmless memory, but one that is false (which involves deceit) and involving the

suggestion of pain and a hospital visit, which might alarm a child and have future implications.

Social and moral implications regarding social control

The above studies show how psychologists have an effect on participants when doing research; they also affect their patients and clients. Psychological findings can be used to develop ways of social control, and the implications of psychologists and others using such power to control others are considered in this section. Social implications concern any effect on society, and moral implications examine the issue of whether we should take certain actions that affect other individuals. Moral implications can involve what is right for the individual, and also what is right for society.

Therapists influence patients

Psychologists working as therapists clearly want to influence their patients, in that their patients usually come to them desiring some change and the therapist's job is to help to effect this change. Therapists work within different approaches – as outlined in Chapter 1. Often a therapist will vary their approach, depending on which they consider the most suitable for a particular problem. However, some therapists prefer one particular approach to therapy, claiming that they do not influence their clients, and they criticise other approaches as being too influential. For example, it could be claimed that psychotherapists working within a humanistic approach do not influence their patients but simply provide a listening service; behaviourists, however, might be said to deliberately alter behaviour by means of reinforcements. Wachtel (1977) says psychotherapists consider that behaviour therapy demeans people, but think that their own methods help people to find a client's true potential. However, Wachtel also points out that psychotherapists also influence their clients – for example, giving unconditional positive regard could be called giving positive reinforcement. Wachtel goes on to say that behaviourists have a co-operative relationship with their patients, just as psychotherapists do. Therefore, separating the different types of therapy in terms of how far the therapist influences the client is not easy.

Wachtel claims that all therapists influence their patients, because they aim to change the patient in some way. Davison and Neale (1994) make a similar point when they say that psychiatrists impose their own values on patients. So the psychologist has some control over a patient, and there are moral implications here. It could be argued that therapists are using their power for the good of the patient; however, there is often an element of control on behalf of society (social control), and this has moral implications. Some questions should be asked – for example: What happens if the needs of the individual and the needs of society conflict? How far is the patient influenced by wanting to please the therapist?

Therapy can involve behavioural control (the learning approach)

> **ACTIVITY**
>
> *Make a list of behavioural therapies. Then write down ways in which each one could be seen as social control – this is looking at social implications. Finally, note down some moral implications for each one.*

Therapy using behavioural techniques is carried out to help the patient. Conditioning principles can be used, for example, in aversion therapy. However, conditioning principles can also be seen as brainwashing, and brainwashing is a form of social control. Here some examples of behavioural control are examined to look at social and moral implications.

Aversion therapy

Aversion therapy is used to help someone to defeat an addiction, for example. Classical conditioning principles are used and a previously desired stimulus (such as alcohol) is paired with something that gives an undesired response (such as a drug that makes people feel ill). Soon the desired stimulus will make the person feel ill, and an aversion is developed. If a patient consents to such a treatment, then they are being helped. However, doctors and therapists, due to their roles, are in a position of power, and a patient may not feel able to withdraw. Another point is that the patient may undergo aversion therapy because of desiring something a society disapproves of, so the therapy is itself a form of social control. For example, homosexuality used to be considered an illness, and so a treatment was proposed in which a man received an electric shock if, when switching from slide to slide in a display, he lingered too long on a picture of a naked man. Here is an example of aversion therapy being used as a form of social control. If someone has desires that are outside what society approves of, they may well desire treatment, in order to conform. In some cases the individual might be in an institution where the person has no 'real' power to refuse such treatment, even if their consent is obtained.

↻ *Recall AS material*

Recall your AS material from the social approach, in particular agency theory and the idea that we obey and act as an agent of someone, rather than acting in an autonomous way. When undergoing therapy, the patient may feel obliged to carry out the wishes of the therapist, who then has the power.

Systematic desensitisation

↻ *Recall AS material*

Recall your AS material on the learning approach, where it is likely that you studied how systematic desensitisation is a way of helping when someone has a phobia. Note down what systematic desensitisation is and how it is carried out. Link your account to the principles of classical conditioning. Then note down how there might be social or moral implications in carrying out systematic desensitisation. Is it used as a form of social control?

Systematic desensitisation is used to help reduce anxiety, especially when dealing with phobias. A person is gradually introduced to a feared object or situation, in a series of steps. At each stage, the individual must stay relaxed. Gradually it is hoped that this relaxed response will replace the fear response to the object or situation. Moral implications are that an individual should be freed from the anxiety. Usually phobias restrict an individual, so systematic desensitisation would be seen as a good thing and unlikely to be used as a form of social control.

A token economy programme

Token economy programmes involve the principles of operant conditioning. Basically, a token of some kind, usually something which is currency in the institution, is given for desired behaviour. This is similar to a 'gold star' system in a school – a reward is given for good behaviour, and undesirable behaviour is ignored (or punished). Tokens can be given for tidying a bed, or keeping a room tidy, or for good table manners. It depends on what behaviour is to be changed.

Although it can be argued that if a person's behaviour is shaped in this way to be more acceptable he or she may be happier, it could also be argued that this type of conditioning is a form of social control. 'Desired' behaviour is usually behaviour that is socially acceptable, and 'undesired' behaviour is usually behaviour that is socially unacceptable. Moral implications are that someone's rights as an individual may be diminished, if they are encouraged to conform by use of a token economy programme. Social implications are that society would presumably be more cohesive, if behaviour is more predictable, and, therefore, more comfortable for others.

Token economy programmes, or other similar reward systems, are used within social institutions such as schools, hospitals and prisons. This in itself suggests a strong element of social control. For instance, Laing has argued that people with schizophrenia should not be treated at all, but left alone to act as individuals. His idea underlines how behaviour programmes have an element of social control. People with schizophrenia may well be trained to act more 'normally' by means of a reward system such as a token economy programme, although it could be argued that this is not 'right'.

Wachtel (1977) raises the ethical questions, and says that the token economy programme is subject to abuse. One problem is that staff may administer the system unfairly, and the patient has no power: the staff have the power. Often, alongside the giving of rewards, there is also a withdrawal of privileges, and this type of power can have serious moral implications.

Therapy can involve control by drugs (the physiological approach)

One type of therapy is chemotherapy – the use of drugs. For example, although people with schizophrenia can receive training in an institution to behave in a desired way, they may also be given a drug such as chlorpromazine to help calm them. Laing may claim that this is not to help the patient but to control his or her behaviour so that it is more acceptable to those around. In this example, drug therapy can be seen as a form of social control. It could be argued that other drug therapies are forms of social control – see chapters 1 and 8.

Psychotherapy as social control (the psychodynamic approach)

'Psychotherapy' is a term used to refer to all forms of therapy that employ 'listening' or psychological therapies and to contrast these types of therapy with any treatments or physiological therapies. However, psychotherapy often refers to psychoanalysis, which is a form of psychotherapy that has been criticised on ethical grounds.

Masson (1992) was a psychoanalyst who then criticised the psychodynamic approach to therapy. Masson's main criticism is the amount of power the therapist has over the patient. Masson goes so far as to claim that patients suffer emotional, sexual and financial abuse from the therapist. Holmes (1994), cited in Gross (1995), agrees with Masson in general and asks that all therapists be supervised. Psychoanalysis and other forms of psychotherapy are intended to help patients gain control over their lives, but if the therapist has the control and the power, the patient

is likely to act as an agent rather than acting in an autonomous fashion. Since the therapist is likely to encourage desirable and 'normal' behaviour in the client, there can be an element of social control. Moral implications concern the rights of the individual, and these rights may be affected if the power in the situation is with the therapist. In order to address some of these issues, 'patients' are usually called 'clients' as then they may be seen as having an element of power in the situation.

Debates within the study of psychology

The nature/nurture debate

The nature/nurture debate is often mentioned in the study of psychology. Our nature comes from our genetic make-up (we get 50% of our genes from our father and 50% from our mother; our parents in turn received 50% of their genes from each parent). Our nurture is our environment when we are growing up, and includes the people around us, the physical setting, social structures such as school and family structure, and all the other influences around us that we can learn from. The 'debate' is the problem of finding out which part of a particular behaviour or attribute (if any) comes from our genetic make-up and which comes from our experiences. For example, if we knew that language ability was innate, coming from our nature, then anyone with poor language ability could not be helped, because we cannot change our nature. If, however, we knew that language ability developed through stimulation within our environment, then we could help anyone with poor language development by improving their environment. Usually an issue has both 'nature' and 'nurture' aspects, and the problem is to find out what help can be given, and how much cannot be helped.

ACTIVITY

Amongst the psychology that you have studied there will have been many areas where the nature/nurture debate has arisen. Make a list of the areas that you can think of, and note down what the issue was.

Table 10.2 lists areas where the nature/nurture debate has been mentioned.

Table 10.2

Area of study	Discussion	AS/A2
The cognitive approach	Brain-damaged patients are often studied to discover the functions of certain areas of the brain. However, it is rare that only one area of the brain is damaged, and so it is hard to draw conclusions that one particular area has one particular function. Also it is not known what normal functioning was like for that person. Although brain damage suggests a cause for a problem, there may be nurture issues involved	AS
The social approach	One theory suggests that some people are more suggestible to hypnosis than others. This suggestibility could be due to their genes, or could be due to their experiences and learning	AS
The cognitive–developmental approach	Piaget assumes that we all go through the same stages of cognitive development, through a process of maturation. These stages are programmed, and in our nature. However, others have claimed that we can reach stages sooner by being stimulated or taught, and so there must be more to it than a natural progression, and learning (nurture) must be important	AS/A2 (education)
	The whole idea of education – including scaffolding, the spiral curriculum, and co-operative learning – involves an underlying assumption that learning is important, and that teaching can affect learning. This assumes that nurture is important, and that nature is less so. For example, we do not focus on people who might be 'naturally' more intelligent, but emphasise how hard work brings rewards	AS/A2 (education)
The learning approach	Includes classical conditioning, operant conditioning and social learning theory. Focuses on nurture and not on nature. Any 'natural' abilities are not considered	AS
The psychodynamic approach	Within the psychodynamic approach emphasis is partly on nature, as it proposes that we have an inbuilt personality structure, for example. However, the psychodynamic approach also emphasises nurture, for example in stressing the important role of the father in the development of the son	AS
The physiological approach	Emphasises the importance of genetic influences on our behaviour. Methods of studying genetic influences on individual differences are discussed. Twin studies, family and adoption studies are outlined, and the nature/nurture debate itself is examined	AS
	The topics of sleep and dreaming are studied. Some theories propose that sleep has evolved because it leads to survival. According to these theories, sleep would therefore have a genetic basis	AS

Table 10.2 (cont.)

Clinical psychology	Includes the study of different disorders, including schizophrenia and mood disorders. It is suggested that many disorders might have some genetic basis, as in many cases identical twins tend to both have the disorder more than non-identical twins. However, as identical twins share 100% of their genes, but by no means all non-identical twins have the same mental disorder, the cause cannot wholly be genetic	A2 Clinical Psychology
Criminal psychology	Includes the study of the effect of the media on aggressive behaviour. Social learning theory predicts that our environment, including media images, affects our behaviour. However, there is an alternative view that aggression is in our nature, and arises from a balance of hormones, or from neurotransmitter reactions. Suggestions for controlling aggression depend on what the perceived cause is. If we think aggression comes from media violence, we can suggest removing images of violence. If we think aggression comes from hormones, we can suggest altering the balance of hormones	A2 Criminal Psychology
The psychology of education	Much of what we propose in education rests on the idea that environment can affect learning, and a good environment can improve learning. If we thought that intelligence was innate, and that the environment had no effect, this would change our education policies	A2 Education
	It is suggested that gifted children might have exceptional abilities because of their 'nature'. For example, autism could have a genetic cause, and some of those with autism have exceptional abilities, which could, therefore, have a genetic basis	A2 Education
The psychology of work	Personality testing, including its use in personnel selection, could be said to be measuring innate aptitudes for certain jobs. This suggests that some people are innately better equipped for particular work, and that our genes are important in predicting our behaviour and abilities	A2 Work
	It has been claimed that leaders are born, and that some people have the necessary qualities and others do not. Some studies, however, suggest that anyone can be a leader if put in that position. So there is a question of whether leadership is natural or learned	A2 Work
	Stress at work is a common phenomenon. Studies show that some people are more able to deal with some situations than others. Stress occurs when the demands of a situation exceed a person's ability to cope – and people have different abilities to cope. It is suggested that these abilities could be partly genetic	A2 Work

Table 10.2 (cont.)

Sport psychology	Socialising influences are thought to be very important when it comes to sporting behaviour; however, it can also be suggested that some people are naturally better able to perform under stressful conditions than others	A2 Sports
	Anxiety and arousal are important concepts in sports psychology, as some arousal seems to improve performance, but too much anxiety can impair performance. It is possible that some people have different levels of arousal than others, and that some might therefore do better under arousing conditions than others	A2 Sports
Clinical psychology	It is thought that there is an evolutionary basis to attachment, and that babies naturally have the tendency to form attachments. However, their environment (for example, the availability of an attachment figure) will affect their attachments, and their development	A2 Child
	Some children are more popular than others, which could be because of the sort of person they are due to their upbringing and experiences, or because of the sort of person they are due to an inherited temperament	A2 Child
Environmental psychology	It appears that we all have specific distances that we like to maintain between ourselves and others. The precise distances depend on the relationship we have with the other person, but it seems that we naturally have a personal space that we wish to defend. The size of the personal space can vary between cultures, so it seems that we might learn these distances, rather than them being in our nature	A2 Environmental
Health psychology	Health psychology focuses on stress, amongst other areas. It is thought that some personality types cope with stressful situations better than others, and so our genetic make-up can be a factor in whether we 'suffer' due to stress or not	A2 Health

Genetically determined human behaviour or attributes

Examples of human behaviour or attributes that may be genetically given include intelligence, the potential to develop schizophrenia, a tendency towards developing mood disorders and addictions such as alcoholism.

Intelligence

The topic of intelligence is covered in more detail in Chapter 4, which looks at the psychology of education. Intelligence is measured in IQ ('intelligence quotient') tests by dividing a child's actual age (chronological age) by their mental age, and multiplying by 100. 'Mental age' refers to the IQ tests that a child can master. IQ tests are standardised to match particular ages. For example, a test that measures what 9 year olds can usually do has been developed by carrying it out with enough 9 year olds to find a norm. If a 9-year-old child achieves a certain score on an IQ test for 9 year olds, he or she has a mental age of 9. Nine divided by nine and multiplied by 100 gives 100, which is the 'normal' IQ.

A child of parents who have a high IQ is likely to have a high IQ too, and it has been suggested that this means IQ has a genetic basis. However, children share the environment of their parents, and we cannot easily separate genes from environment. Children of parents with high intelligence may have high IQ because of a stimulating environment, or because they imitate their parents' behaviour.

Schizophrenia

The topic of schizophrenia is covered in more detail in Chapter 1. Genetically identical twins (MZ twins) are more likely to both have schizophrenia than non-identical (DZ) twins. Heritability estimates (how far it is thought that a behaviour or attribute is caused by gene structure) vary in different studies, although there does seem to be evidence for a genetic basis – for schizophrenia itself to develop, or for a propensity for schizophrenia to develop. It may be that some environmental factors are needed to trigger this propensity. If schizophrenia were entirely genetically given, then every time one MZ twin had schizophrenia, the other one would have it too, which is not the case. When looking at MZ and DZ twins, an average estimate is that MZ twins have a 50% concordance rate – in 50% of cases where one MZ twin has schizophrenia, the other does too, and in 50% of cases this does not happen. If genetically identical people do not share an attribute or behaviour every time, then this attribute or behaviour is unlikely to have a wholly genetic cause. However, DZ twins have a much lower concordance rate for schizophrenia (15%) than MZ twins, so there is at least some genetic element in whatever causes schizophrenia.

A problem with using MZ twins is that, although they share genes, they also usually share their environment. However, DZ twins usually share their environment too, so the evidence for there being a genetic basis as outlined above is usually accepted. It could be argued that identical twins are treated more alike than non-identical twins, because they look alike and are always the same gender, and this could be used to criticise the above conclusions.

Mood disorders

Mood disorders are examined in more detail in Chapter 1. Mood disorders also seem to 'run in families' and so have a genetic cause. Again evidence from MZ and DZ twins and family studies is presented. Where there is some mood disorder in a family, it seems more likely that others in the family will suffer from mood disorders, although not always from the same disorder. Some evidence comes from adoption studies. Children who have been adopted into a family without mood disorders, but who have a biological family with mood disorders, seem more likely to develop some disorder. Since they have been away from their biological family, and so not in the same environment, this evidence suggests at least some genetic basis to mood disorders.

The complexity of the nature/nurture debate

Although nature has been described as a person's inherited characteristics, and nurture as their upbringing, it has been argued that it is only at the moment of conception that a pure investigation of genes can occur. Immediately afterwards, environmental factors start to shape the individual in conjunction with their genes. Nativists suggest that our inherited characteristics determine what we can do. Empiricists suggest that we are born ready to receive information, but like a 'blank slate' ready to be written on. However, it is quite clear that it is the interaction between nature and nurture that we wish to study, and the question is not whether something comes from our nature or from our nurture, but how much each contributes (Plomin, 1994).

McGurk (1975) points out that gene–environment interactions start before birth. Cells themselves have environments that affect their development, such as the number of other cells around them. Also the mother's diet, including whether she smokes, drinks alcohol, or takes drugs, can affect the developing fetus. Rutter and Rutter (1992) discuss fetal alcohol syndrome, which is characterised by problems in intellectual functioning and hyperactivity, and is caused by the mother drinking high levels of alcohol.

So we might claim that our nurture begins from conception, and separating nature from nurture is not useful in trying to understand human behaviours. We are affected by environmental factors from the start. Also we make our own environment, in that we act on the environment (Scarr, 1992). Arguments about whether a behaviour or attribute comes from our nature or our nurture tend to suggest that we are passively affected by our environment; however, we actively construct our reality from the environment that we are in. The self-fulfilling prophecy is an example of how the effect of our environment is a two-way process, and studies in other areas (e.g. Smith and Lloyd, 1978) have shown that our reactions to others help to shape what they become. Smith and Lloyd found that participants reacted differently to a baby they thought was a boy than when they thought the baby was female. When we stereotype people we tend to elicit particular reactions from others, and so to an extent we shape our own environment.

The status of psychology as a science

The main approaches in psychology have been covered in the AS part of the Edexcel course. In general, main approaches can be sorted into those that tend to be scientific, having scientific methods and aims, and those that are not scientific, as they do not have scientific aims or use scientific methods (Figure 10.1).

Table 10.3 The nature/nurture debate

- We are the product of our nature and our environment, and the two cannot be meaningfully separated
- Not only are we affected by our environment, but we affect our environment and can be said to make our own environments
- We should not ask *whether* a characteristic or behaviour comes from our nature or our nurture (e.g. mood disorders, IQ or schizophrenia), but *how much* of the cause of the behaviour might be from each

- We receive 50% of our genes from each biological parent; however, usually we share our environment with our biological parents, so to find out about nature/nurture influences we often compare MZ and DZ twins, and use adoption studies
- Within our family and shared environment, there are many environmental differences, for example, position in the family, and our own influence on our environment, via the self-fulfilling prophecy

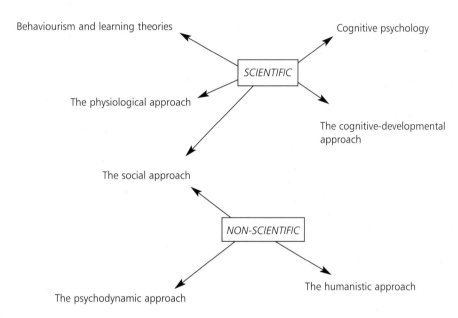

Figure 10.1
Scientific and non-scientific approaches

Synoptic Note

Throughout the chapters of this book, where the debate about whether psychology is a science arises, it has been mentioned in one of the Synoptic note boxes. Relevant boxes are found in chapters 1, 3 and 7.

Introduction

A generalised view of science is used when discussing the status of psychology as a 'science'. The measure of whether psychology is a science usually takes place by looking at a general view of 'science', but it should be noted that this general view is open to criticism.

Science is meant to be objective and unbiased. It should be free of values and should discover truths about the world. **Positivism** is the view that science is objective and a study of what is real and 'out there'. For example, schizophrenia, when diagnosed as being caused by excess dopamine (see Chapter 1), is being studied in a scientific manner. The explanation does not take into account any cultural customs or individual differences that might lead to behaviour we might call schizophrenic. However, even in scientific research like this the person doing the diagnosis has his or her own views, and may misinterpret behaviour because of his or her own subjective biases. For example, if someone talks about hearing voices, they may be referring to a spiritual experience, but a medical practitioner unfamiliar with such experiences might well diagnose schizophrenia. So objective, value-free study is not easy, because the scientist has views and biases, and cultural or other issues are perhaps important. Some say that truly objective study is not possible, and that a scientific approach to the study of people is not desirable.

Questions to be answered

- What is science?
- Can there be scientific and objective study of issues within psychology?
- Should there be scientific and objective study of issues within psychology?
- What is psychology?
- Is psychology sufficiently one 'thing' that we can talk about its issues in a general way?
- Are there issues within psychology that can be studied scientifically, and some that cannot?
- Why are we interested in whether we can call psychology a science?

ACTIVITY

Try answering each of these questions in turn, ready for what follows. You are probably now at the end of the course, and should have enough information to give answers. This would make a good group exercise, and you could pool ideas.

Psychology as a science – defining terms

Positivism

Science involves a search for understanding and knowledge, and it gives power over the forces of nature. Science is to an extent the search for power. When Descartes (1596–1650) divided the world into two realities – physical matter and non-material mind – this led people to see matter as inactive and separate from mind. This idea in turn led to the view that matter could be objectively observed and studied. Science became the objective study of matter. This is the **positivist** view.

Mechanistic

Descartes thought of all matter as being connected, and as having mechanical laws that explain how objects in the world interact. This is a **mechanistic** view. When Descartes suggested that this mechanistic view could be extended to animals, and that the human body is like a machine, he was setting up the positivist view of the study of people that is still found today. It was thought that the body was made up of connected matter, with mechanical laws to explain its functions and behaviour.

Reductionism

Descartes also believed that the 'machine' could be studied by examining the parts that make up the machine. The view that something can be understood by examining its parts is called **reductionism**. For example, if schizophrenic behaviour is seen as being caused by excess dopamine, then the brain of the schizophrenic is being studied, which is part of the person. Also certain symptoms are being studied, which are part of the 'disease'. The opposite of a reductionist approach would be to study the person and their behaviour as a whole, rather than looking at separate symptoms.

Introspectionism

Descartes also thought that the mind could only be understood by looking at one's own thoughts 'inside' our heads. The term for studying the mind by examining what goes on within one's head is called **introspectionism**.

Empiricism

This mechanistic view of the world underlines the idea that there can be an objective unbiased study of things in the world – in other words a scientific approach. In order to study things 'out there' evidence must be gathered via our senses. We see, hear, feel, taste, touch and smell, and are limited to these sources of evidence. The idea of only being able to gather knowledge by means of sense data is called **empiricism**. Science and empiricism go together, as things are studied in an objective and unbiased manner by gathering information through our senses.

Deductive v. inductive reasoning

The only form of knowledge, other than that gathered through our senses, is knowledge that we can work out rationally. For example, if we know that all animals breathe, and we know a fox is an animal, we don't need our senses to tell us that a fox can breathe. We can deduce this from the statements 'all animals breathe' and 'a fox is an animal'. When knowledge is arrived at in this way, the reasoning is called **deductive**. When we arrive at knowledge from our senses, the reasoning is called **inductive**.

Nomothetic research

Early in the development of psychology as a discipline it was recognised that there could be problems in studying human behaviour, for reasons like the complexity of the subject matter. Those working within the behaviourist approach wanted to discover scientific laws partly because in the early 1900s 'science' was the aim, and Western culture valued scientific discoveries. People looked for general laws that could be applied to human behaviour. If laws could be discovered by isolating variables for study, and then finding cause and effect relationships (for example, Pavlov's discovery that dogs can be conditioned to salivate under certain conditions) then laws could be generalised to cover all human behaviour. An approach that looks for general laws is called **nomothetic**. Nomothetic approaches follow scientific traditions.

Psychology is not a science – defining terms

Holism, not reductionism

A scientific approach to understanding the world largely comes from the Western world. Within this scientific approach, for example, schizophrenia is seen as an illness, caused by a problem with some part of the body, and needing to be put right or cured so that behaviour can become normal again. Another view, however, is that behaviour must be seen in the context of the whole person. For example, behaviour that is labelled schizophrenic could just be a different way of behaving with some cultural or spiritual significance. Science is reductionist in that parts are examined to try to discover things about the whole. An opposing view is **holism**, and holists claim that when looking at parts, the whole can never be understood because some relationship between the parts is overlooked. They say that something can only be understood by looking at it as a whole, which is more than the sum of its parts.

Humanistic psychology, not the mechanistic view

Humanistic psychology emerged as a reaction against the mechanistic view of a person. Maslow referred to humanistic psychology as the 'third force', behind behaviourism and the psychodynamic approach. A holistic view of psychology meant the behaviourist and psychodynamic views had to be merged, because the whole person should be studied. The humanistic approach was seen as the way to unify other theories. The humanistic view is **idiographic**, since it looks at the individual; it is also holistic, as it looks at the whole person. For Maslow, and others who took a humanistic stance, an individual *must* be seen as a whole person, and the way that person views their world is part of them. People interact with their environments, and are free to make choices and decisions. A scientific objective search for general laws will not capture this active interacting individual, and so the humanistic approach uses methods that are not scientific. For Maslow, an individual's goal is to self-actualise, and to fulfil his or her own potential. Rogers had a similar view but focused more on the processes used to self-actualise than on what a person becomes. As each person finds their own unique fulfilment, he or she must be examined as a complete individual and a scientific approach is not useful.

Evaluation

- Rogers did use methods such as a Q-sort to examine an individual's ideas and thought processes, so empirical methods are found within the humanistic approach, and scientific methods are not completely discounted. The Q-sort asks people to sort statements about themselves (for example, 'I am ambitious') into 'true' or 'false' piles. This method examines individual preferences, but allows for measurable objective data.

Social representation theory, not positivism

Social representation theory suggests that we cannot study behaviour away from a cultural setting, because we cannot understand behaviour without its setting. To continue with the example of schizophrenic behaviour, in Western culture we measure such behaviour against a norm, and we say such behaviour is 'not normal'. However, in saying this, we are possibly ignoring the cultural setting.

Synoptic Note

A discussion of definitions of abnormality can be found early in Chapter 1.

↻ *Recall AS material*

When studying your material for the AS exam you may have looked at social representation theory. If you have, recall the main principles.

Social representation theory suggests strongly that human behaviour cannot be studied outside the social context. This view is far away from the 'scientific' idea that we can isolate parts of behaviour, such as memory for words, and then build a picture of the behaviour, such as how memory works. Social representation theory puts forward the idea that there is no such thing as a reality to be measured that is set outside our experiences. For example, memory is not a thing that can be split up into short-term, long-term, articulatory loop and so on, but is 'memory of a bank robbery on Saturday' or 'memory of a birthday party'. Evidence shows that eyewitness testimony is in many ways unreliable because other factors are involved – such as the way questions are asked or the effect of expectations. Those focusing on overall experiences in this way do not aim for a scientific study of phenomena that are 'out there', and from this view psychology could be said to be non-scientific.

Idiographic, not nomothetic

As outlined above, some theorists are interested in the individual as a whole person. Applying general laws of behaviour is not useful for those who want to focus on individuals. As general laws are not sought, variables are not separated for study, and parts are not isolated from the whole. This is the idiographic approach and is not scientific.

Evaluation

- Although it seems simple to say some views of psychology focus on the individual and some look at generalisations about people, this differentiation may not be simple. Is each person unique? Many areas of psychology have developed complex theories about people based on general laws, and on generalised findings from 'scientifically designed' studies.

These theories are then applied to individuals. For example, if you sit close to a stranger on a park bench, it is predicted that the stranger will move. So a general law about personal space has been used to predict a unique individual's behaviour. When Maslow claims that it is the goal of the individual to self-actualise, he is making a generalised claim. We could claim that individuals all have different goals, although patterns can be found. For example, children of prejudiced parents are more likely to be prejudiced themselves, so we can suggest a pattern in that a unique individual will have many of the views of their parents. Symbolic interactionists suggest we can learn about social roles by taking the role of others, and that our goals can come from what we learn in our culture about social roles. Therefore, we can suggest a pattern in that a unique individual will be acting out many social roles in ways that we can recognise and predict. This distinction between an idiographic and nomothetic approach is not as clear-cut as it may seem.

Both the idiographic and the nomothetic researcher look for general laws, or at least a theoretical framework to explain behaviour. An idiographic approach then applies the framework to one individual; however, a scientific aim is still evident. Researchers aim to explain something and wish to do so using evidence in some form, and then drawing conclusions. This is the case whether the approach is idiographic or nomothetic.

Symbolic interactionism

Following the humanists' idea that the subject matter of psychology is people as individuals, new methods were found that would be more useful than scientific methods where variables are controlled, and measurable parts of behaviour are studied. To look at the whole person, different methods were needed. Sociology also moved into a new paradigm at the same time, moving away from scientific methods and positivism for the same reasons.

Symbolic interactionism is a view put forward by Mead and Blumer, amongst others.

1 In order to study people we need to study interactions between them, and how these interactions affect the whole situation. People cannot be studied in isolation, because they react to others, and how others react to them affects the transactions.

2 In these interactions shared symbols are very important, as we reach shared meanings. Language is the main set of symbols used.

STUDY AID

If you are studying sociology, you will be very familiar with symbolic interactionism, phenomenology and post modernism. Recall the meaning of these terms.

New paradigms, new methods

As it became clear that watching and asking would gain useful insights into real interactions between people, some way of making sure the data were reliable and valid was needed in order to draw conclusions from apparently casual observations.

There are ways of turning casual observation into an 'acceptable' method:

- Researchers should be very clear about their own views and should analyse their own conclusions, drawing attention to where biases may have occurred.
- The participant could help in planning and summarising the research. By collaborating, the researcher and the participant can validate the data. This is called doing collaborative research.
- Discourse analysis can be used to study discourse (conversation) itself. The idea links to the humanistic view, as discourse is seen as a major way in which we achieve our goals. Discourse analysis has been used to examine psychological theories, to show how the way the theory is presented can help to persuade us of its power. One example is given by Soyland (1994), who discusses how a metaphor can be used and then taken as 'true'. For example, if we say that animals act like humans in using tools, this is using a metaphor. Then we might conclude that the tool use of the animal is done with the same purpose and intent in mind as humans have. This might be using a metaphor and then taking it as true (that animals use tools with the same thinking in mind as humans do). Another example of how language must be part of what we study is found in memory theories. Bartlett (1932) suggested that we reconstruct our memories, and this is similar to saying that we use memories either to prove our point or argue in our defence (Coolican, 1994). Memories are not, therefore, things 'out there' that can be measured. What people say is part of what must be studied.

Evaluation

- These ideas about how we can study 'real' people underline how different the new paradigm is from the 'old' scientific method.

- However, it is important to note that casual observation has not been accepted as a method without some attempt to turn any subjectivity on the part of the researcher into objectivity. In aiming for objectivity, by using collaborative research, or by using discourse analysis, the researcher appears to desire scientific methods, where general laws can be generated, and cause and effect relationships discovered.

Conclusion 1 – Psychology is a science

On the one hand psychology *is* a science. The subject matter is behaviour, including mental aspects of behaviour such as memory, and the subject matter is divided up for study. Variables are isolated to be measured. There is an independent variable (IV), which is the one being manipulated, and a dependent variable (DV), which is the one where change is measured to see what effect the manipulation of the independent variable has had. Everything but the IV and the DV is controlled as far as possible, and from a carefully controlled study of isolated variables to see what effect one has on another, cause and effect conclusions can be drawn. Laboratories are often used in an effort to improve controls, and even where studies are done in the field because it makes a variable (such as play behaviour) more accessible, controls are as thorough as possible, so general laws of behaviour can be built.

ACTIVITY

List as many areas of psychology and approaches to psychology you can think of that fit this 'scientific' definition of psychology.

Some areas that usually fit this scientific explanation are:
- behaviourism
- many areas within cognitive psychology
- many areas in sport psychology
- studies of jury decision-making
- many areas within clinical psychology
- the physiological approach
- cognitive–developmental studies
- leadership studies
- social learning theory.

Table 10.4 Psychology as a science – list of terms

• Reductionism
• Nomothetic
• Postivitism
• Mechanistic
• Objective
• Controls
• Cause and effect
• General laws
• Quantitative data

Conclusion 2 – psychology is not a science

On the other hand psychology is *not* a science and does not aim at scientific principles to measure a world 'out there'. In many areas of psychology there is no attempt to generalise from some human behaviour to all human behaviour. Social representation theory focuses on interactions. The humanistic view focuses on self-actualisation and the individual's experiences and actions. Where there is focus on interactions between people, and on the individual's experiences, scientific methods are not useful. 'Non-scientific' methods include case studies, unstructured interviews, some forms of observation, and diary methods. If a method is 'not scientific' it aims for good validity, in-depth material about someone or a small group, qualitative data, and a richness of data that is not found by isolating variables for study.

Some areas that fit this 'non-scientific' explanation are:
- humanistic psychology
- some areas of social psychology
- some psychodynamic approaches
- some parts of the psychology of work, for example, when looking at motivation.

Table 10.5 Psychology as not scientific – list of terms

• Idiographic
• Holistic
• Subjective
• Qualitative data
• Interactionist

Should psychology be a science? Is it important? Why?

If you are asked to answer a question about whether psychology is a science, you will probably explain that in some ways it is a science, and in some ways it is not. You may be asking why it is important to find out whether psychology is a science, which is a good question. Some researchers do like psychology to be treated as a science, partly because more funding is often available for scientific research, and partly because scientific research is seen by some to have more credibility. If a body of knowledge can be built because general laws are claimed, then this body of knowledge can, like sciences, be thought of as 'true'. Many researchers test hypotheses and examine behaviour because they want to find out the truth about human actions and interactions. They want to prove something. It could be argued that psychology should be a science, and that what is not scientific should be ignored. However, the arguments outlined above about the importance of studying the individual should have shown that the argument that psychology should not be a science is also valuable.

Science and falsifiability

Popper has discussed scientific method, and has claimed that there is no such thing as proof in any case. At least, he claims that we cannot prove that something is true, although we can prove that something is false. Popper argues that what is important is **falsifiability**. We should seek to falsify things, rather than to prove them true. Usually, we seek to prove things true, and this is a problem, according to Popper. A well-known example concerns swans: the claim that 'all swans are white' can be disproved quite easily by finding a black swan; however, the claim cannot be proved because every swan would have to be considered (to see if it is black), which would not be possible. Scientific truths should be looked for by trying to falsify hypotheses, rather than trying to prove them true.

In psychology, however, usually we look for confirming instances, and then conclude that something is true. For example, we suggest that if we sit close to a stranger he or she will move away, and then we try sitting close to see what happens. This is an attempt to prove the truth of the claim that we value our personal space. However, we should find out if some people do not move away when their personal space is invaded in this way. If this happens, then we should say that we have disproved the claim that people value their personal space. However, in psychology, it is rare to make claims about 'all people': usually hypotheses are more general, and claim only that some difference or relationship is expected, and that this difference or relationship is more than would be expected by chance.

In psychology, it is rare for all participants to behave as a hypothesis predicts they will behave and if we took one instance that went against the prediction as falsifying the whole claim there would be few theories left. So, instead of taking one instance that goes against a prediction as meaning we have to reject the prediction, we accept that there will usually be some contradicting results, but that the prediction can still be upheld as a general principle. As there are nearly always some contradicting results, we use inferential statistical tests to show if a prediction is sufficiently supported by the results – in other words if any difference or relationship found is more than would be expected by chance.

Use of inferential statistical tests is a way of putting psychology into the category of a science.

Science and paradigms

Science usually works within a **paradigm** (a body of knowledge that is accepted), and any testing or investigating is carried out within the assumptions of that body of knowledge. One important thing about psychology is that there is more than one paradigm within which psychologists research. For example, some research is done within the psychodynamic or humanistic

approach, and other research takes place within the cognitive approach. The assumptions of the approach guide the type of questions asked, as well as the methods likely to be chosen. As psychology does not have a single paradigm, it is possible to claim that some approaches within psychology can be called 'science' whereas others cannot.

Why is it important whether psychology is a science or not?

The discussion of whether psychology is a science or not has been included in the specification because it raises interesting issues, rather than because the answer is important. When studying psychology, it is important to focus on problems with studies because any conclusions drawn from a study can only be within a particular setting and culture. It is important to be aware of issues such as to what extent generalisation from findings can be made, and how sure findings are. If we want to understand human behaviour, then we need to build some body of knowledge. However, we need this knowledge to be set within its boundaries, otherwise findings that belong to one situation at one moment in time will be extended to apply to all situations, and false conclusions may be drawn. These false conclusions may be acted upon, and consequences may be harmful to someone. For example, if someone is wrongly diagnosed as being schizophrenic, because of some misunderstanding of cultural issues that affect their behaviour, this can have serious consequences for them.

Freud's theories have been criticised because they are 'not scientific'. His ideas are not falsifiable, because the subject matter of interest – for example, dreams – is not measurable. Popper claims that as Freud's ideas are not falsifiable, they cannot be properly tested, and so his theories cannot be called scientific. Freud carried out case studies, using an idiographic approach, employing subjective interpretation as his method, and yet used his findings to build general laws about everyone's behaviour. This is not 'doing science'. However, although this is a useful criticism of Freud's claims, it does not make them wrong. The question of whether psychology is a science raises many useful points that can be used to evaluate research findings, but the answer itself is not perhaps so important.

Methods, science and psychology

This chapter deals with the A2 part of the Edexcel psychology course, and the AS covers methodology in a great deal of detail. Your AS textbook will give you the information you need for this part of the Edexcel course, and you should re-read your AS material on method as well as Chapter 9 of this book. Some methodological issues link to the question of whether psychology is a science or not, and those are reviewed here.

Qualitative and quantitative methods

↻ Recall AS material

Recall your AS material concerning methods, and give definitions of what qualitative and quantitative data are.

The way to distinguish quantitative from qualitative research is to consider the type of data gathered by the researcher. If the data are measurable, and quantities are measured, then the data are quantitative. If the data gather information about quality, then they are qualitative data. In general it can be claimed that scientific methods gather quantitative data, and non-scientific methods gather qualitative data, and one way of telling whether a scientific method is likely to be called scientific or not is to consider whether the data are quantitative or qualitative.

Scientific and non-scientific methods

It is not really true that psychology is either scientific or not scientific – sometimes in psychology scientific methods are used, and sometimes they are not. It is not easy to say that a method is either scientific or not, because it depends on how the study is carried out. For example, a survey can be carried out in a scientific manner, when an IV and a DV is identified, controls are carefully used, quantitative data are gathered, and objectivity is achieved. However, a survey can use an unstructured interview, and an unstructured interview is not completely 'scientific'. In an unstructured interview objectivity is aimed for, and an IV is often being manipulated, however, qualitative data are gathered, and subjectivity is often present because the researcher interprets the data.

Laboratory experiments

Laboratory experiments could be called the most scientific because:
- Variables (anything that can affect the study) are controlled.
- Samples of participants are carefully chosen.
- What is being tested is operationalised so that it is measurable.
- One possible cause is tested and all other possible causes are controlled for.
- It is then claimed that one effect comes from one cause.
- General laws are sought.
- Objectivity is required.

ACTIVITY

Here are some examples of data gathered in psychological studies. Note down in each case whether the data are quantitative or qualitative.

1 The level of aggression of boys when playing, as rated by the observer (e.g. very aggressive, moderately aggressive and not aggressive).

2 Whether boys and girls in the playground are aggressive or not (e.g. noting down a tick if they are aggressive, and a cross if they are not).

3 Attitudes to aggression in society (e.g. doing a survey and asking what people think about aggression in society, using open questions).

4 Reaction time of participants, by measuring how long they take to catch a falling ruler.

5 The level of electric shock that participants 'give' when hearing a wrong answer.

6 The number of times a child hits a bobo doll.

7 Attitudes people have to overcrowding, as measured by asking them to write down an account of their opinions.

8 The levels of attractiveness of pupils who are considered intelligent, as measured by an independent person giving a rating out of 10.

Case studies

Case studies could be called the least scientific because:
- Individuals or small groups are studied so results cannot be generalised easily to other groups or situations.
- Variables are not controlled, because the whole setting, situation and interactions are studied as they occur.
- Many different methods are used when doing a case study to try to get rich in-depth data.
- Subjective assessment by the researcher can be part of the data.
- The aim is to discover in-depth information about a whole group or individuals, so a reductionist approach (breaking aspects of something into parts that can be measured and studied) would not be suitable.
- Qualitative data are gathered.

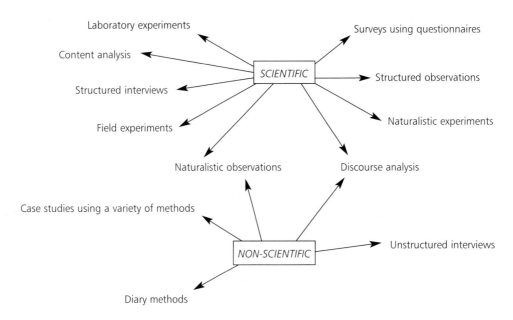

Figure 10.2
Scientific and non-scientific methods

Table 10.6 *Whether methods are scientific or not*

Experiment (scientific)	Structured questionnaire (scientific)	Unstructured interview (not scientific)	Case study (not scientific)
Control of variables	Control of variables	Careful but limited sampling	Does not control variables
Isolation of IV and DV	Isolation of IV and DV	Good validity	Does not isolate an IV and a DV
Careful sampling	Careful sampling	In-depth data	Sampling can be difficult
Operationalisation of variables	Operationalisation of variables	Has aims not hypotheses	Variables not operationalised
Avoidance of experimenter bias	Avoidance of researcher bias	Involves participants more	Researcher bias is possible
Careful generalising	Careful generalising	Explores areas in depth	Generalising is not possible
Statistical analysis	Statistical analysis	Idiographic approach	Statistical analysis is not used
Good reliability	Reasonably good reliability	Subjective analysis	Poor reliability
Tests a hypothesis	Tests a hypothesis	Tests aims	
Nomothetic approach	Nomothetic approach	Subjectivity is revealed	
Objectivity required	Objectivity required	Qualitative data	
Poor validity	Poor validity	Uses many methods/triangulation	
Quantitative data	Quantitative data	Looks at all aspects	
	Avoidance of demand characteristics	Explores areas	
	Avoidance of social desirability		

Ethical issues in psychological research

Using human participants

⟲ **Recall AS material**

Recall your AS material concerning ethical issues when doing psychological research. Recall the main ethical principles that must be adhered to when carrying out research with human participants.

The AS part of the Edexcel psychology course covers ethics in a great deal of detail. You should re-read your AS material on ethics, especially the material relating to the use of humans in research.

Gross (1999) says we should see every psychological investigation as an ethical situation. This means that ethical issues should always be considered. In 1983, the BPS published their Code of Conduct for Psychologists and in 1990 (revised in 1993) the BPS published the Ethical Principles for Conducting Research with Human Participants. In 1983, the BPS produced Guidelines for the Professional Practice of Clinical Psychology – which were for those in practice, rather than researchers.

Consent

Participants must give their consent to the study taking place. However, this is not always possible. Consider an observation in a busy shopping centre, where the aim is to see who helps people. It would not be possible to ask their consent. Then there are other ethical principles to cover this difficulty, and these are outlined below. In general, wherever possible, consent must be obtained. Sometimes consent should be in writing, for example, when children are participants.

Informed consent

Consent is important, but it should be *informed* consent. Before giving consent, the participant must be fully informed about the investigation. This is very difficult to achieve in many cases, because if the participant is told everything they will know what to expect, and possibly how to behave, which will probably spoil the study. There are other guidelines that tell a researcher what to do if they cannot get informed consent.

Right to withdraw

It is difficult to get consent or informed consent, but right to withdraw is usually possible. Where possible the participant must be informed that they can stop taking part at any time. However, if the study involves observation in a public place, it may not be possible to give participants the right to withdraw. Another problem is that the researcher might know the participants, who might not then feel able to withdraw – they *must* be assured that they do have that right. Some participants are paid to take part (for example, Milgram and Zimbardo both paid their participants), and this too could be a problem, as they then might not feel they have the right to withdraw. Any problems should be put in front of others who can act as judges for the researcher.

Consent and right to withdraw in special cases

There are special cases where consent and the right to withdraw may not be properly given. The special case of research with children is examined below; however, there are others who may need special protection. For example, prisoners may feel they have to take part in a study when asked. To illustrate this point, consider Perrin and Spencer's (1981) conformity study of young offenders. Young offenders in an institution are likely to conform more, and may have felt they had to take part in the study. There is also a problem when the participant perceives the researcher as having power (which is often the case); this affects how they see their right to withdraw. Milgram had power in his well-known study, and this affected the ethics of it. Those without the power hardly have the right to withdraw, and also may not be giving consent freely.

Deception

Researchers must not deceive the participants, although many studies do involve deception. For example, most memory studies require participants to be deceived. If you are testing to see if categorised lists are better recalled than random lists, you can't very well tell the participants this, or they might try harder for the categorised list. Studies involving deception in this way are unethical, but deception is often necessary. So other guidelines are used to 'offset' the poor ethics involved in using deception.

Debriefing

A useful way of overcoming some of the problems mentioned above is by using debriefing. The idea is that the participants are told exactly what they have been doing, and why, and then they are asked whether the results can be included in the study. They still have the right to withdraw from the study, and this must be made clear. Although nothing should have been done that at the end of the study will make the participant regret taking part, debriefing can still be a useful way of making sure that the participant has not been affected by the study. Debriefing can help in cases of necessary deception. Debriefing can also help where it has not been possible to get informed consent.

Protection of participants

The participant must leave the situation in the same frame of mind that they brought to the situation. They must be protected from both physical and psychological harm. Debriefing can help here too, as the researcher can make sure that everything has been understood by the participant and that the participant has not come to any harm.

In some cases there are follow-up sessions. Milgram has been criticised for his research, as you will have learnt, but he did use a questionnaire to follow up on the participants, and to see if they felt the study (and the deception) was justified. Many did indeed think the research was justified. Haney *et al.*, in their study of the roles of prisoners and guards, also debriefed their participants fully and followed up after a few months, and again after a year.

Some studies do not protect participants, however, and the Little Albert study could be put into this group. Some reports say that Little Albert's fear was not extinguished, so he did come to harm.

Competence and conduct
Researchers must be competent to carry out the study. If in any doubt, they must ask others for their opinion. This is quite usual practice. Milgram, for example, in his well-known study, asked others if they thought the participants would give such high 'shocks'. If the answers had been that the participants would do that, he might have reconsidered the study; however, they decided that this would not happen so he continued with the study.

Researchers must also conduct themselves properly. They must stick to all these guidelines for a start, and never tackle anything they are not competent to do. Researchers should not claim to know more than they do know, or to be able to do more than they can.

Confidentiality
It is usually quite easy to maintain confidentiality. The participant's actual name must not be used, the area in which the study was carried out must be disguised. Participants must know that they will not be identified by anyone. Most of the time researchers maintain confidentiality.

Observing in a public place
Observations are particularly difficult because permission to observe someone is hard to obtain. Sometimes permission can be obtained, but often that would upset the behaviour to be studied. Often you would not know who was going to be a participant until after the event, for example, when observing helping behaviour. The participant would need to be a helper first to select themselves as a participant. The problems of informed consent and right to withdraw are overcome if the observation is in a public place. The general idea is that in a public place you might reasonably expect to be watched. You are not likely to be doing something that you would not want watched, so it seems reasonable to observe someone on that basis.

You should not observe someone if you think they would not want to be observed, and you should be aware of cultural differences. When someone is a participant in a study and they don't know they are taking part in a study at all is an occasion when debriefing is needed, although this is just the occasion when there is no debriefing. For example, some of the social psychology experiments involve situations such as someone pretending to be drunk to see what help they get. An individual might help, and, therefore, become a participant in an experiment. They will not have volunteered to be a participant. You should at least go after them, after they have helped, and explain what the study is about, and ask their permission for the results to be included. It is understandable if a researcher thinks that debriefing will cause more anxiety than not debriefing, but these sorts of issues must be carefully considered.

Ethical standards for research with children
There are special problems when it comes to using children in psychology studies. They may be too young to give consent – or, if they are old enough to give consent, it may not be informed consent. They may feel forced to agree to take part. The Ethical Standards for Research with Children have been issued by the Society for Research in Child Development.

Children could be more vulnerable and are likely to be more stressed by studies than adults. Also, they don't have the experience to know what is being asked of them. Parents must give their consent, as well as the children. Here is a summary of some of the rules when using children in research.

- The child's rights come first, no matter what their age.
- The researcher has the responsibility for the ethics of a study.
- The researcher is responsible for everyone else taking part in the study.
- The researcher should answer the child's questions and give them full information.
- The child must be allowed to stop taking part at any time.
- Informed consent of parents and others (e.g. head teachers) must be obtained, preferably in writing.
- No research operation can be used that will physically or psychologically harm the child.
- If deception is essential (as sometimes it is), then a committee of peers of the researcher must be consulted.

- All information must be confidential.
- After data collection, the researcher must report the findings to the participants, unless it is more humane to withhold the information – when doing so does not harm the participant.
- If the researcher finds information that affects the child's well-being, this must be discussed with an expert in the field so that parents can be informed.
- If the experiment will lead to undesirable consequences, as soon as this is known, these consequences should be corrected.
- The social, political and human implications of the research must be considered, and reporting must take this into account.
- If an experimental treatment is thought to be of benefit, the control group must be offered other beneficial treatments if available, not just 'no treatment'.

Access to data

Although it is not mentioned much in psychology, the Data Protection Act (1984) is very important. Data cannot be stored about someone without their knowledge and without permission.

Prior consent and presumptive consent

To overcome problems with informed consent and not deceiving participants, sometimes prior consent is obtained. You can ask people if they would consent in general, in other words they would be in a pool of volunteers. You could explain that sometimes deception might be necessary, and they would agree to this. The problem is the individuals would not know precisely what they were agreeing to, but it is better to get prior consent than no consent at all.

Presumptive consent refers to asking others if the study is ethical. You can explain the whole thing to people who are not going to be participants, and see if they say they would have agreed to take part. This suggests that 'normally' people would not mind taking part, so you hope your participants would not mind either.

Using non-human participants

⟳ *Recall AS material*

Recall your AS material concerning ethical issues when doing psychological research. Recall the main ethical principles that must be adhered to when carrying out research with animal participants.

The AS part of the course covers ethics in a great deal of detail. Your AS textbook will give you the information you need for this part of the Edexcel course, and you should re-read your material on ethics, especially the material relating to the use of non-humans in research

Guidelines when using animals in research

Guidelines focus on the use of non-human animals rather than on the question of whether they should be used at all. The guidelines assume that animals are being used, and then look at rules for safeguarding them to an extent. The research must be carefully designed and the use of animals justified.

Gray (1987) investigates the use of animals in experiments and draws conclusions by considering the use of rats. Firstly, he looks at when they are deprived of food to see if this is causing them distress. He claims that this does not cause distress. They are often fed after the experiments, that is once a day. If not, their body weight is maintained at 85% of what they would be if they fed normally, and this is actually healthy. Secondly, he looked at when they are given shocks. The average shock allowed is one that would cause a tickling sensation in humans. So he concludes that this is not real suffering. Everyone who uses animals in research needs a Home Office licence, and has to obey Home Office rules.

Some important rules (these are taken from the Society for Neuroscience Guidelines for Animal Research):
- Researchers must have a Home Office licence and certificates.
- Experimenters must be familiar with the use of anaesthetics, and use them.
- Senior staff must be available to supervise studies.
- Caging and social environment must suit the particular species.
- Marking of wild animals or attachment of transmitters must be done with regard to stress involved.
- If the animal is to be deprived (for example, of food or drink) then this must be monitored according to the species and suffering minimised.
- Field workers should disturb animals as little as possible (for example, when observing in the wild).
- Animals must not be subjected to avoidable distress or discomfort.
- Anaesthetic must be given if at all possible if any surgical procedures are involved.
- If no anaesthetic is given, blood pressure and heart rate must be monitored to understand the pain involved and then researchers must take action to alleviate the pain (or end the experiment).
- No more animals must be used than is necessary.
- Living animals should be used only if necessary.
- Alternatives should always be sought.
- Research animals must be acquired and cared for according to guidelines published in the NIH Guide for

the Care and Use of Laboratory Animals (National Institute of Health Publications, NO. 85-23, Revised 1985).

- Researchers should take care after operations with animals, and should guard against infections and so on in the usual way.
- Restraints that the animal cannot easily adapt to should be used only if there is no alternative.
- There should be a reasonable time between studies where the animal can recover and rest.

Should non-human animals be used at all?

Mnay people feel that we should never use non-human animals in research. As far as I know nobody thinks that non-human animals should suffer pain just for the purposes of research. Some, however, think that non-human animal suffering is acceptable if the result is worthwhile – to humans, although sometimes non-human animals gain too. The argument is not really whether we should inflict pain on non-human animals, but whether it is ever justified. Many researchers claim that the end results do justify the means of getting the results.

You need to read this section and then decide for yourself. You may be very clear in your mind that non-human animals should never be used. However, sometimes humans benefit from treatments that would not have been available without the use of animals. It is much harder to make the decision that non-human animals should never be used when you start considering how you yourself have benefited from their use – even if you have only had paracetamol, or been grateful for a dentist's knowledge.

The above argument has mainly been about medicines, and we are considering research in psychology here. However, again you have to stop to think about what research in psychology has offered to people. There is a much better understanding of stress and depression now. We know more about the nervous system, and how mental processes affect our physiology and vice versa. We know that stress can contribute to physical illnesses, as well as that illnesses lead to stress (see Chapter 8). We know more about the effects of overcrowding, for example, and how it can lead to violent behaviour (see Chapter 7). We have learnt how to help when someone has a phobia (see Chapter 1). Research in psychology leads to improvements in the quality of our lives, and such knowledge is often gained from animal studies.

One reason for using animals is to avoid doing to humans what we consider unacceptable. The implication is that we can study animals and then generalise from results to draw conclusions that apply to humans. This is all because

of Darwin's idea – that through survival of the fittest we have evolved into the species that we are. Since different capabilities are needed for survival in different surroundings, life has evolved from basic life forms into lots of different species. The basic idea is that what is useful leads an organism to survive. The organisms without useful capabilities cannot reproduce, die out and so those 'not useful' capabilities are not passed on. Therefore mainly useful capabilities survive.

In one example, Darwin looked at finches. If their surroundings meant that there were a lot of trees, and insects needed to be dug out of bark, then those finches with beaks capable of digging insects out of bark survived better than those with blunt beaks. Those with blunt beaks would die out in those surroundings, and finches there would have sharp beaks.

Humans are animals too, and have evolved through the same processes. If people thought that humans were completely different from animals, we may never have started to experiment using animals. Some people (creationists) still think that humans were separately created. You need to be aware of the different views when considering arguments about using animals in research. The main point is that without the underlying assumption that humans are animals, it is doubtful that we would have been so interested in studying non-human animals as a way of learning about ourselves.

The case for using non-human animals

Research using non-human animals has led to improved knowledge about the way animal (and human) systems work. Improvements have been made in the quality of life of both non-human animals and humans, mainly because of advances in medical knowledge. In order to continue to study the complexities of living organisms, some say that living non-human animals must be used. Green (1994) says that many drugs could not have been developed without the use of non-human animals.

It is claimed that there are few alternatives. Some humans with life-threatening diseases do take drugs to test them. However, this is almost always only when all other medication has failed, so the individual has more to gain than to lose. Also, this is only done after the drugs have first been tested extensively on non-human animals. Various scanning techniques are now used on humans much more widely, and much is being learnt from this technique so experiments on animals may not be needed. However, scanning simply involves looking rather than touching and altering, whereas planned experimental testing is done on non-human animals. Progress towards curing various diseases, and towards improving the quality of life for humans, cannot be made without the use of living non-human animals in research. If you accept this argument, then the use of non-human animals in research is both ethical and appropriate. Gray (1991) goes so far as to say that it is our duty to our species to improve our own quality of life, even if this means 'using' other species to do so. This argument is called 'pro-speciesism'.

Although psychology is not directly involved in developing drugs as cures for diseases, the same arguments apply to the use of treatments and therapies in psychology. By studying animals, we can find a lot out about the workings of the human nervous system. We can test non-human animal reactions to stressors, for example. We can test the memory of non-human animals and use the results to draw conclusions about our own memory and forgetting processes. Experiments can be done using non-human animals that cannot be done using humans. We can learn a great deal from such experiments, and can use the findings to improve conditions for humans.

While the aims of the studies are almost always to look at human behaviour, and to improve things for humans, some argue that animals too have benefited. For example, we know more now about the effects of overcrowding on animals, so zoos can take this knowledge into account. Most of the above argument has been discussing the use of non-human animals in experiments. Psychology also involves studying animals in a more natural setting. Ethology is the study of animals in their natural setting. Usually, ethology as a method is less criticised than laboratory studies. However, there are many reasons why using non-human animals in the laboratory is helpful. Many species have a much shorter reproductive cycle, and therefore many generations can quickly be studied. This is helpful in the study of genetics. Similarly, many species are small and easy to handle, which again makes things easier for the researcher.

The case against using non-human animals

Non-human animals are different from humans. Is it useful to carry out research on non-human animals when there are these important differences? What can be learnt from studying stress in non-human animals that can be generalised to humans? Although it is the case that many non-human animals share aspects of the human nervous system and brain structure, animals are different from one another, and different from humans. It may be that no generalisations should be made because of these differences.

Another issue that is widely supported is that non-human animals should not be experimented upon at all for ethical reasons. Non-human animals cannot answer back, and cannot refuse to take part. It is widely accepted that non-human animals feel pain (although there is some debate about this in the case of some creatures), and should we be allowed to cause pain in another being just to improve the quality of our own lives?

The argument that we should do all we can for our own species was put forward above as a reason for using non-human animals in research. However, the problem is that we only know the value of the research after it has taken place. There may be many experiments that eventually lead nowhere, and so the animal suffered for no benefit in the end. It is difficult to say that we need to balance the benefit of the research against the non-human animal suffering, if we only know the benefit much later. Some people use this argument as another reason why non-human animals should not be used.

Many think that studying animals in their natural setting is more acceptable, and that a great deal can still be learnt. Perhaps this is less of an ethical issue, although it could still be argued that we are disturbing their natural setting simply by being there and observing. The argument against the use of non-human animals is sometimes extended to their use in the 'wild', but in practice most people find the study of animals in their own environment is acceptable.

Suggested reading

Gross, R. (1995) *Themes, Issues and Debates in Psychology*. London: Hodder & Stoughton.

Gross, R. (1996) *Psychology The Science of Mind and Behaviour, Third Edition*. London: Hodder & Stoughton.

Appendix A

A2 Suggested questions and revision ideas

Here are some suggestions about revision, and some guidance on the format of the exams for the A2. Also here are some suggested questions that can be used to prepare for the A2 examinations. However, they are only suggestions, and are not precisely in the format you would expect in the examination.

General guidance on exam format

Remember Units 1, 2 and 3 form the AS part of the overall A-level examination.

Units 4 and 5a – applications

Each application has one compulsory main question, and within it there are three sub-sections that follow the specification (a, b and c). The overall question is worth 36 marks, which are usually spread fairly evenly between the three sub-sections. There may be essay questions worth between 12 and 16 marks.

For Unit 4, students must answer two 'application' questions, and will have 45 minutes for each 'application' question (the paper is worth 72 marks and lasts 1.5 hours).

For Unit 5a students must answer one application question worth 36 marks in 45 minutes.

Unit 5b – method

Unit 5b consists of method questions worth 36 marks in 45 minutes (the paper – Unit 5a and Unit 5b – is thus worth 72 marks and lasts 1.5 hours).

Unit 6 – perspectives, ethics, method and issues

Unit 6 consists of three main questions, and the student must choose two of these to answer in 1.5 hours – 45 minutes per question. Each of the three main questions will be broken down into smaller parts, and within these there may be an essay question for up to 20 marks. The three main questions will be on different topics, and the intention is that a range of topics will be covered.

Preparing for the A2 examination

Write in-depth essays

A good way to prepare for the A2 examination, after having chosen three applications out of the eight, is to write essays. Although the questions will be 'broken essays', which means that there will be some short-answer questions leading to longer answers, a good way to prepare is to write an extended essay on each given topic. In this way, if a question is asked about defining a term, you will know and your essays will have the necessary depth and detail.

Prepare descriptions and evaluations of studies

However, essays do not usually include long descriptions and evaluations of studies, so another way to prepare is to write descriptions and evaluations of at least one study per small topic on the specification. Assume about 5 marks for the description and 5 for the evaluation.

Use the specification wording as if it is an exam question

The specification is worded as if it was a question – for example, 'describe examples of good and bad practice in architectural design' (environmental psychology), or 'discuss possible effects of parental separation/divorce and parental death' (child psychology). Make each of these 'injunctions' into a question and prepare an answer. This is what has been done for you below, so that you have some suggested questions to work on.

Define key terms

Make a list of all the key words used in the specification and write out definitions for them.

Nearer the exam, practise keeping to time

When preparing answers, take as long as is necessary to write a full answer. Nearer the time of the examination practise writing the answer (e.g. describing a study for 5 marks) in the right length of time. There are 72 marks on the paper, and 90 minutes available, so given reading and thinking time, take 1 mark per minute.

Nearer the exam, practise giving enough for the marks available

When preparing answers, write as much as is needed to be as thorough as possible. However, nearer the time of the examination, practise writing enough to get the available marks. For example, if 5 marks are available for description, then give 5 clear points only. There will not be time to finish the paper otherwise.

Suggested questions

The questions that follow are suggestions to help with your study, but they are not modelled on the style of the exam papers themselves. These questions are set so that you can test yourself, practise essay skills, and make sure you have covered the right material. They will not test absolutely everything you need to know, or always offer the right depth, but they will help you a lot in your studies. You will need to obtain specimen papers either from your teacher or from the awarding body, and past papers would also be useful.

Paper 4

Clinical psychology

Section a

1. Give two psychological definitions of abnormality. 4 marks
2. Describe the DSM classification system. 4 marks
3. What is meant by 'multi-axial tool'? 2 marks
4. Discuss implications of diagnosis regarding mental health issues. 10 marks
5. What is meant by 'validity' with regard to mental health issues? 2 marks
6. What is meant by 'reliability' with regard to mental health issues? 2 marks
7. Discuss cultural factors affecting diagnosis of mental health issues. 8 marks

Section b

1. Describe two different therapeutic approaches to mental disorders. 6 marks
2. Distinguish between two therapeutic approaches to mental disorders. 6 marks
3. Discuss the medical/biological approach and one therapy from the approach. 8 marks
4. Discuss the psychodynamic approach and one therapy from the approach. 8 marks
5. Discuss the behavioural approach and one therapy from the approach. 8 marks
6. Discuss the cognitive approach and one therapy from the approach. 8 marks
7. Discuss the humanistic approach and one therapy from the approach. 8 marks
8. Discuss recent developments regarding social approaches to mental health issues. 8 marks

Section c

1. Describe the main symptoms of two disorders from schizophrenia, mood disorders, anxiety disorders and eating disorders. 10 marks
2. Discuss possible causes of two of the above disorders. 14 marks
3. Compare biological explanations with social and psychological explanations for one of the above disorders. 14 marks
4. What is meant by physiological factors when talking about causes for disorders such as those above? 8 marks
5. What is meant by social factors when talking about causes for disorders such as those above? 8 marks
6. What is meant by psychological factors when talking about causes for disorders such as those above? 8 marks

Criminological psychology

Section a

1. Describe two studies of eyewitness testimony. 10 marks
2. Evaluate each of the two studies you described above. 10 marks
3. Discuss how recall is affected by attributional biases. 14 marks
4. How useful is hypnosis in helping victims and witnesses to recall information? 10 marks
5. Compare the British approach to offender profiling with the US approach. 10 marks

6 Discuss influences on decision making processes as they relate to juries.   12 marks

7 Describe one study that looks at decision making amongst jurors.   6 marks

8 Evaluate the study you described above.   5 marks

9 Discuss possible effects of social pressure and conformity on jurors.   8 marks

10 Describe one study of the effects of defendant characteristics on the jury.   5 marks

11 Evaluate the study you described above.   4 marks

Section b

1 What is meant by the 'just world hypothesis'?   4 marks

2 Evaluate what is claimed about the 'just world' hypothesis.   6 marks

3 Discuss the effects of the media on aggressive behaviour, using at least two studies.   10 marks

4 Discuss limitations of research methods used when looking at the effect of the media on aggressive behaviour.   12 marks

Section c

1 Outline two means of controlling aggression.   6 marks

2 Discuss two means of controlling aggression.   14 marks

3 What is meant by zero tolerance?   2 marks

4 How effective is zero tolerance as a means of controlling crime?   10 marks

The psychology of education

Section a

1 Describe the use of behavioural principles in the delivery of education.   6 marks

2 Outline the use of one behavioural principle to reduce problem behaviour in the classroom.   3 marks

3 Evaluate the usefulness of the behavioural approach to learning.   10 marks

4 What are some educational implications of Piaget's theory?   6 marks

5 Describe what is meant by 'discovery learning'.   4 marks

6 According to cognitive-developmental theorists why should we pay attention to the ways children think?   6 marks

7 Outline one key assumption of the cognitive approach to psychology.   3 marks

8 Discuss the application of information-processing principles to education.   8 marks

9 Outline Ausubel's ideas about education.   5 marks

10 Outline Gagne's ideas about education.   5 marks

11 Evaluate the usefulness of the cognitive approach to education.   10 marks

Section b

1 Describe two teaching styles.   6 marks

2 Discuss the possible effects of the teaching styles you described above on student performance.   12 marks

3 What are possible effects of teacher attitudes and expectations on performance?   8 marks

4 What is meant by labelling?   2 marks

5 What is meant by stereotyping?   2 marks

6 Discuss the differences between individual, co-operative and competitive learning.   12 marks

7 Discuss some individual differences in learning/cognitive styles.   8 marks

8 Discuss the effectiveness of two cognitive/learning styles.   10 marks

Section c

1 Discuss factors such as reliability and validity when measuring IQ.   12 marks

2 What is meant by bias in educational assessment?   6 marks

3 Discuss research into how assessment can discriminate (with reference to education).   10 marks

4 How can educational assessment discriminate by gender and by culture?   8 marks

5 Discuss the process of identifying, categorising and assessing students with special educational needs.   14 marks

6 What are difficulties in identifying special needs?   8 marks

7 What are the problems of labelling and underestimating abilities, with regard to special educational needs?   8 marks

8 Discuss issues surrounding the identification and assessment of gifted children.   12 marks

The psychology of work

Section a

1 Discuss the concept of work and its importance in adult life.   12 marks

2 How are factors such as social roles and self-actualisation important to the adult with regard to their work role?   10 marks

3 Discuss one theory of work motivation.   10 marks
4 Discuss two methods used to select personnel.   12 marks
5 Discuss the use of psychometric tests for recruitment, promotion and demotion.   10 marks
6 Give two examples of aptitude tests.   2 marks

Section b
1 Discuss different styles of leadership.   10 marks
2 What is meant by autocratic, democratic and laissez-faire leadership styles?   6 marks
3 Discuss one theory of leadership effectiveness.   12 marks
4 In the context of leadership discuss group dynamics and decision making.   10 marks
5 What are possible effects of the mere presence of others and conformity to a group, with regard to leadership?   10 marks
6 Outline two types of group influence.   4 marks
7 What is group cohesiveness?   3 marks
8 Describe what is known about minority influences with regard to leadership.   5 marks
9 Discuss two factors affecting group decisions.   8 marks

Section c
1 Discuss psychological implications for the individual of unemployment and retirement.   10 marks
2 Discuss psychological implications for the individual of redundancy and increased leisure time.   10 marks
3 Discuss two factors that produce stress at work.   14 marks
4 Discuss research looking at specific stressful occupations.   12 marks

Sport psychology

Section a
1 Discuss the usefulness of the trait approach to sport psychology.   12 marks
2 Discuss research linking personality traits to choice of sport and sporting success.   14 marks
3 Discuss individual differences in behaviour as explained by social learning theory.   10 marks
4 Give examples of socialising influences with regard to sporting behaviour, and describe a little.   6 marks
5 Discuss sport as an influence of social development.   10 marks

Section b
1 Define the terms 'extrinsic' and 'intrinsic' motivation.   6 marks
2 Discuss how both intrinsic and extrinsic motivation can be related to sport psychology.   14 marks
3 Describe achievement motivation and discuss its application to sport psychology.   16 marks
4 Define the term 'self-efficacy'.   5 marks
5 Discuss how self-efficacy can be used to boost motivation in sport.   10 marks
6 Describe Weiner's (1972) attribution theory.   5 marks
7 Discuss how attribution has been applied to improving motivation in sport.   10 marks

Section c
1 What is meant by 'social facilitation'?   4 marks
2 Discuss Zajonc's drive theory and Cottrell's evaluation apprehension theory as explanations of social facilitation.   12 marks
3 Discuss the relationship between team cohesion and performance.   10 marks
4 What is meant by 'social loafing'?   4 marks
5 Discuss possible negative effect of team membership on individual performance, including social loafing.   14 marks
6 What is meant by the 'inverted U hypothesis'?   4 marks
7 Discuss the effects of anxiety and arousal on sporting performance.   14 marks

Paper 5a

Child psychology

Section a
1 Define what is meant by 'attachment'.   2 marks
2 Outline what is meant by 'the evolutionary basis of attachment'.   3 marks
3 What is meant by 'the strange situation' in psychology?   3 marks
4 Discuss research involving the strange situation.   10 marks
5 Describe one cross-cultural study using the strange situation.   4 marks
6 Discuss the relationship between attachment types and caring style.   10 marks

Section b
1 Outline two possible effects of short-term deprivation.   4 marks

2 What is meant by 'short-term
deprivation'? 2 marks

3 Describe one study that looks at the
effects of day care and intellectual
development. 4 marks

4 Discuss research findings into the effects
of day care. 12 marks

5 Describe one study that looks into the
effects of family reordering on children 4 marks

6 Evaluate the study described in the
question above. 4 marks

7 Discuss possible effects of parental
separation/divorce on children. 8 marks

8 Describe one study that looks at the
possible effects of institutional care and/or
adoption on children. 5 marks

9 Define what is meant by 'privation'. 2 marks

10 Describe Koluchova's (1972) study of
the 'Czech twins'. 5 marks

11 Evaluate the study described in the
question above. 4 marks

12 Describe the case study by Curtiss (1977)
of Genie. 5 marks

13 Evaluate the study you described in the
question above. 4 marks

14 Discuss the issue of reversibility of
privation. 12 marks

Section c

1 Give an example of each of the following
categories of play: solitary, parallel,
co-operative. 3 marks

2 Discuss possible factors affecting
children's play. 10 marks

3 Describe the cognitive–developmental
theoretical perspective on play. 5 marks

4 Discuss the therapeutic value of play. 8 marks

5 Describe developmental trends in peer
relationships. 5 marks

6 Describe one study looking at popularity
of individual children. 4 marks

7 Evaluate the study described in the
question above. 4 marks

8 Discuss cultural differences in peer
elationships. 8 marks

Environmental psychology

Section a

1 What is meant by 'personal space'? 3 marks

2 Discuss individual and cultural differences
in personal space. 10 marks

3 Discuss the importance of territory. 12 marks

4 Outline two functions of territory. 6 marks

5 Discuss the effect of architecture on
communication and on residential
satisfaction. 14 marks

6 Outline Oscar Newman's ideas about
defensible space. 8 marks

7 Discuss the concept of defensible space
and the effect on vandalism, other
crimes and residential satisfaction. 12 marks

8 Describe one example each of good
and bad practice in architectural design
with respect to defensible space. 10 marks

Section b

1 Outline three sources of environmental
stressors. 9 marks

2 Describe and evaluate one study of the
effects of environmental stress. 10 marks

3 Discuss the effects of three environmental
stressors on behaviour. 12 marks

4 Describe and evaluate two strategies for
coping with environmental stressors. 10 marks

5 Describe and evaluate one study of the
effect of crowding in animals. 8 marks

6 Discuss the effects of high-density living
on humans. 14 marks

7 Describe and evaluate two theories of
crowding. 12 marks

Section c

1 Discuss reasons why behaviour is often not
environmentally friendly in terms of
recycling. 12 marks

2 Describe and evaluate two ways of
changing attitudes with regard to
environmental issues such as recycling. 12 marks

Health psychology

Section a

1 Define the terms 'tolerance', 'withdrawal',
'relapse', 'psychological dependence', and
'physiological dependence'. 10 marks

2 Describe ways in which two drugs might
affect neurotransmitters and synaptic
functioning. 10 marks

3 Discuss the physiological and
psychological effect of two drugs 8 marks

4 Discuss the long-term consequences of
the use of two drugs. 8 marks

5 Discuss the effects of abstinence from
two drugs. 6 marks

6 Discuss psychological, cognitive and
social factors of addiction. 8 marks

7 Discuss how the learning theory helps to
explain addiction. 6 marks

Section b

1 Discuss the concept of stress including
internal, external and interactional
factors. 12 marks

2 Describe the physiological response to stress. 8 marks

3 Discuss effects of stress on the immune system. 8 marks

4 Discuss one biological, one social and one psychological factor which may cause stress. 14 marks

5 Discuss the various management/coping strategies for dealing with stress, including problem-focusing and emotion-focusing. 12 marks

6 Discuss the importance of two resources in coping. 8 marks

Section c

1 Discuss primary prevention with regard to health care. 6 marks

2 Discuss health education programmes aimed at AIDS and smoking and their use in raising awareness and changing attitudes. 12 marks

3 Discuss the health belief model as an explanation of why some people do not make use of disease prevention or screening tests. 10 marks

4 Discuss the theory of reasoned action in explaining behavioural intentions. 10 marks

Paper 5b

1 Discuss ways in which qualitative data may be analysed. 10 marks

2 Discuss issues of objectivity and subjectivity with regard to the analysis of data in psychological research. 10 marks

3 Discuss the use of animals in psychological research, with regard to ethical issues. 10 marks

4 Define the terms:
  (a) level of significance 3 marks
  (b) inferential test 2 marks
  (c) one/two-tailed 2 marks
  (d) standard deviation 2 marks
  (e) variance 1 mark
  (f) normal distribution 2 marks
  (g) critical value 1 mark
  (h) repeated measures design 1 mark
  (i) counterbalancing 1 mark
  (j) correlational design 2 marks
  (k) random sample 1 mark
  (l) target population 1 marks
  (m) level of measurement 2 marks
  (n) measure of central tendency 2 marks

5 Give an example of:
  (a) a null hypothesis 2 marks
  (b) an alternative hypothesis 2 marks

  (c) an inferential test 1 mark
  (d) a level of significance 1 mark
  (e) an experimental design 1 mark
  (f) a sampling technique 1 mark
  (g) a level of measurement 1 mark
  (h) a measure of central tendency 1 mark

6 Outline what is meant when a variable is said to have been operationalised. 3 marks

7 Discuss issues of reliability, validity and generalisability with regard to psychological research. 10 marks

8 Which measure of central tendency is best for a) ordinal data and b) interval data? 2 marks

9 Identify the independent variable and the dependent variable in the following alternative hypotheses:
  (a) There is a difference in average hours slept, and older people sleep fewer hours than younger people. 2 marks
  (b) There is a difference in helping behaviour according to whether a person needing help appears to be drunk or not. 2 marks
  (c) There is a difference in number of words recalled depending on whether the participant has to consider the meaning of the word when learning it, or the sound of the word. 2 marks

10 Taking the three hypothesis given in the previous question, in each case identify whether a test would be one or two tailed. 3 marks

11 When considering which inferential test to use, if an experiment uses a matched pairs design, would you choose the test for repeated measures or the test for independent groups? 1 mark

12 Give three possible reasons for choosing a Wilcoxon test. 3 marks

13 Give three possible reasons for choosing a related *t* test. 3 marks

14 What does df stand for? 1 mark

15 If a variable is measured by hours of sleep, what level of measurement is this? 1 mark

16 If a variable is measured by whether a person is aggressive or not, but without giving a score, what level of measurement is this? 1 mark

17 If a variable is measured when a participant rates behaviour on a scale of 0–10 for aggression, what level of measurement is this? 1 mark

18 Define what is meant by a) systematic sampling and b) quota sampling. 4 marks

19 What two inferential tests can be used for correlations? 2 marks

20 Give one advantage and one disadvantage of using a correlational design. 2 marks

21 Give one advantage and one disadvantage of using a repeated measures design. 2 marks

22 Give one advantage and one disadvantage of using an independent groups design. 2 marks

23 Discuss the role of participant and situational variables in psychological research, and how these might be controlled. 8 marks

24 Discuss reasons for using inferential tests when using quantitative data in psychological research. 10 marks

Paper 6

1 Distinguish between two approaches/perspectives in psychology, choosing two from behaviourism, the psychodynamic approach, the cognitive approach, and the physiological approach. 12 marks

2 Describe contributions of the psychodynamic approach to psychology and to society. 10 marks

3 Discuss contributions of the behaviourist approach to psychology and to society. 10 marks

4 Compare and contrast the cognitive approach with the physiological approach to psychology. 8 marks

5 Discuss contributions of the physiological approach to psychology and to society. 10 marks

6 Discuss contributions of the cognitive approach to psychology and to society. 10 marks

7 Discuss similarities and differences between the psychodynamic approach and the physiological approach. 8 marks

8 Discuss social implications of psychological research. 14 marks

9 Discuss moral implications of psychological research. 14 marks

10 Outline two examples where psychological research might be said to be involved in social control. 6 marks

11 Discuss issues regarding social control when considering psychological research. 14 marks

12 Discuss the nature/nurture debate in psychology. 20 marks

13 Describe an example of the nature/nurture debate in psychology. 4 marks

14 Outline two approaches that might be called 'scientific' and say why. 8 marks

15 Outline two approaches that might be called 'not scientific' and say why. 8 marks

16 Discuss the question of whether psychology should be called a science. 20 marks

17 Describe three ethical principles that should be adhered to when doing psychological research with human participants. 6 marks

18 Outline a study using human participants where at least one ethical principle appears to have been broken, and say why. 6 marks

19 Outline a study using human participants where at least one ethical principle appears to have been adhered to, and say why. 6 marks

20 Describe three ethical principles that should be adhered to when doing psychological research with animal participants. 6 marks

21 Outline a study using animal participants where at least one ethical principle appears to have been broken, and say why. 6 marks

22 Outline a study using animal participants where at least one ethical principle appears to have been adhered to, and say why. 6 marks

23 Discuss ethical issues involved in the use of human participants in psychological research. 20 marks

24 Discuss ethical issues involved in the use of animal participants in psychological research. 20 marks

25 Discuss two methods used in psychological research, including a discussion of their relative strengths and weaknesses. 20 marks

26 What is meant by 'quantitative data'? 4 marks

27 What is meant by 'qualitative data'? 4 marks

28 Discuss problems in using qualitative data in psychological research. 14 marks

29 Discuss problems in using quantitative data in psychological research. 14 marks

Appendix B

An outline plan for covering the A2 over one year

Notes:
- Based on a 30-week teaching year and three sessions per week of around 1.5 hours per session.
- Adjust according to your own schedule.
- Depending on what application you have chosen, please use the outline plan and 'insert' the relevant plan from the 7-week ones below.
- For homework time do at least as much a week as you get in teaching time.

Outline plan

Month	Week	Topic area
June/July	3 weeks (9 sessions)	Suggestions: Review Unit 6 issues and relate to AS material Cover method for Unit 5b and 6 and include inferential statistics. Plan and carry out a study based on a chosen application, gather data, carry out a thorough analysis to learn about method issues Overview what is to come in each of the applications (one week each) to check students' commitment Start the first application – note 14 weeks allocated, and if the first term is shorter, start on the first application
END OF TERM		
Sept/Oct Nov/Dec	7 weeks (21 sessions) 7 weeks (21 sessions)	Application One for Unit 4 (see separate scheme of work) Application Two for Unit 4 (see separate scheme of work)
END OF TERM		
January	2 weeks (6 sessions)	Revise and (a) do January modules or (b) do mock exams Time allowed here as some students may be resitting or taking a new module. If not, then revision of Unit 4 would be useful.
Jan/Feb/March March	7 weeks (21 sessions) 1 week (3 sessions) Session 1 Session 2 Session 3	Application One for Unit 5a (see separate scheme of work) Method – Unit 5b and 6 Revise method from AS – use list of terms and match definitions (group work) Revise method from AS – descriptive statistics and levels of measurement – use scores from an experiment and keep ready for next session. Standard deviation and normal distribution Inferential statistics – use scores from last session to do a statistical test. Justify the test in terms of levels of measurement and design
March	1 week (3 sessions) Session 4 Session 5 Session 6	Method – Unit 5b and 6 Inferential statistics – deciding about significance, one or two tailed, choosing level of probability, choosing a test Inferential statistics – correlations. Practise choosing a test Quantitative v qualitative data – analysing qualitative data
END OF TERM		
April	1 week 1 week 1 week	Unit 6 Review approaches and study contributions (brainstorm in groups) Review ethics, and social and moral implications of research Review social and moral implications – social control Nature/nurture issues Is psychology a science?
May	2 weeks	Revise and practise questions/papers

Seven-week plans for each application

Clinical psychology

Week	Session	Topic area
1	1	What is clinical psychology?
	2	Abnormality and definitions
	3	Classifying including DSM
2	4	Reliability and validity of diagnosis
	5	Cultural factors in diagnosis
	6	Questions to review
3	7	Review AS material – psychodynamic and learning approaches, and mental health
	8	Medical approach and one therapy
	9	Cognitive approach and one therapy
4	10	Humanistic approach and one therapy
	11	Social approaches e.g. care in the community
	12	Questions to review
5	13	Review AS material – learning approach and phobias
	14	Anxiety and causes
	15	Review AS material – physiological approach and methods (e.g. twin studies)
6	16	Schizophrenia and causes
	17	Schizophrenia and causes
	18	Schizophrenia and causes
7	19	Mood disorders and causes
	20	Mood disorders and causes
	21	Questions to review

Criminological psychology

Week	Session	Topic area
1	1	What is criminal psychology?
	2	Review AS material – cognitive approach and eye witness testimony
	3	Attribution errors and recall
2	4	Attribution errors and recall
	5	Hypnosis and recall
	6	Offender profiling – US approach
3	7	Offender profiling – British approach
	8	Jury decision making
	9	Jury decision making
4	10	Defendant characteristics
	11	Questions to review
	12	Review AS material – learning theory, social learning and the work of Bandura
5	11	Just world hypothesis
	14	Self-fulfilling prophecy
	15	Media violence and real-life aggression
6	16	Media violence and real-life aggression
	17	Questions to review
	18	Controlling aggression – one way
7	19	Controlling aggression – second way
	20	Zero tolerance and its effectiveness
	21	Questions to review

The psychology of education

Week	Session	Topic Area
1	1	What is the psychology of education?
	2	Review AS material – learning theory and programmed learning
	3	Reinforcement and punishment
2	4	Evaluate the usefulness of the behavioural approach
	5	Review AS material – cognitive development and discovery learning
	6	Information processing and education
3	7	Ausubel and Gagné
	8	Evaluate the usefulness of the cognitive approach
	9	Questions to review
4	10	Teaching styles
	11	Teacher attitude, expectations and labelling
	12	Learning/cognitive styles
5	13	Questions to review
	14	IQ, reliability and validity
	15	IQ, reliability and validity
6	16	Bias in assessment
	17	Identifying, categorising and assessing special needs
	18	Identifying, categorising and assessing special needs
7	19	Gifted children
	20	Gifted children
	21	Questions to review

The psychology of work

Week	Session	Topic area
1	1	What is the psychology of work?
	2	The importance of work in adult life
	3	Theories of work motivation, e.g. Herzberg
2	4	Theories of work motivation, e.g. goal setting theory
	5	Methods of personnel selection
	6	Methods of personnel selection
3	7	Use of psychometric testing
	8	Questions to review
	9	Leadership styles and one leadership theory
4	10	Group dynamics, decision making
	11	Conformity, mere presence of others
	12	Minority influence, group cohesiveness and roles
5	13	Factors affecting group decisions
	14	Questions to review

	15	Unemployment
6	16	Redundancy
	17	Retirement, leisure
	18	Factors affecting stress at work
7	19	Factors affecting stress at work
	20	Specific stressful occupations
	21	Questions to review

Sport psychology

Week	Session	Topic area
1	1	What is sport psychology?
	2	Trait approach to personality – Eysenck
	3	Trait approach to personality – Cattell
2	4	Personality and choice of sport – and sporting success
	5	Evaluate usefulness of trait approach
	6	Review AS material – social learning theory and relate to sport
3	7	Social learning theory and individual differences in behaviour
	8	Socialising influences on sport, and sport influencing socialisation
	9	Questions to review
4	10	Intrinsic and extrinsic motivation
	11	Relate intrinsic and extrinsic motivation to Sport Psychology
	12	Achievement motivation
5	13	Self-efficacy and motivation
	14	Weiner (1972) and attribution
	15	Attribution and sport
6	16	Questions to review
	17	Social facilitation – Zajonc's drive theory
	18	Cottrell's evaluation/apprehension theory
7	19	Team cohesion and team membership (social loafing)
	20	Anxiety and arousal
	21	Questions to review

Child psychology

Week	Session	Topic area
1	1	What is child psychology?
	2	Attachment and evolutionary basis
	3	Bowlby's theory
2	4	Strange situation
	5	Strange situation and cross-cultural studies
	6	Attachment types and styles
3	7	Questions to review
	8	Short term deprivation
	9	Day care and studies of intellectual and social/emotional development
4	10	Family ordering, parental separation (divorce, death)
	11	Institutional care, adoption, including Tizard and Hodges (1989b)

	12	Privation - Genie (Curtiss, 1977)
5	13	Privation - Czech twins and reversibility (Koluchova, 1972)
	14	Questions to review
	15	Types of play and theories of play
6	16	Recall AS material – cognitive developmental approach and link to types of play
	17	Recall AS material – psychodynamic principles. Axline and play therapy
	18	Peer relationships – developmental trends
7	19	Peer relationships – cultural differences
	20	Popularity of individual children
	21	Questions to review

Environmental psychology

Week	Session	Topic area
1	1	What is environmental psychology?
	2	Personal space
	3	Personal space
2	4	Importance of territory including concept of territory
	5	Two functions of territory
	6	Effect of architecture on communication and resident satisfaction
3	7	Oscar Newman – defensible space
	8	Architectural design and defensible space
	9	Questions to review
4	10	Environmental stressors – e.g. Noise
	11	Environmental stressors – e.g. Heat
	12	Crowding in animals (Calhoun)
5	13	High density living in humans
	14	Theories of crowding
	15	Theories of crowd behaviour
6	16	Questions to review
	17	Why is behaviour often not environmentally friendly?
	18	Ways of changing behaviour – reinforcement and punishment
7	19	Ways of changing behaviour – changing attitudes (Yale model)
	20	Recycling as a case study
	21	Questions to review

Health psychology

Week	Session	Topic area
1	1	What is health psychology?
	2	Physiological and psychological dependence – define the terms
	3	Recall AS material – the physiological approach and the nervous system. Drugs and synaptic functioning
2	4	Drugs and synaptic functioning
	5	Physiological and psychological effects of abstinence – one drug

Appendix C

Useful Web sites

Web address	Comments
http://www.psychology.ltsn.ac.uk	Teaching tips including icebreakers, study skills, etc.
http://www.link.bubl.ac.uk/psychology	Links to others – e.g. school psychology, giving information on learning disabilities, gifted children etc. Exam questions too.
http://psychology.psy.bris.ac.uk/psybris	About Bristol University
http://www.sportpsychology.co.uk	From professional sports people (advice)
http://www.psychologyatwork.co.uk	workplace behaviour and psychometrics
http://devpsy.lboro.ac.uk/eurodev	Developmental psychology – European
http://www.businesspsychologist.com/news.html	Successful management etc.
http://academyofabpps.org	Counselling psychology
http://www.hp-add.com	Health psychology
http://www.psych.bangor.ac.uk	Interesting to see what research is going on
http://www.hypnosis.demon.co.uk	About self-help really
http://members.tripod.co.uk	Useful information on psychology degree for students – courses, academic information etc. Links to other sites too, such as healthweb.org
http://www.psychcrawler.com	Searches in general
http://www.bps.org.uk	BPS site
http://www.psychology.plymouth.ac.uk	Not available when tried, but SALMON study has learning materials on line
http://psychpages.com	Lots of articles by Dr Debra Moore
http://www.voicelessness.com/essay.html	Richard Grossman essays on problems in living e.g. depression
http://psychematters.com	Psychoanalytic resources
http://www.s-cool.co.uk	Teacher resources
http://www.psychsite.com	
http://www.academicinfo.net/psych	
http://www.psych.co.uk	
http://www.socialpsychology.com	
http://www.bubbl.ac.uk	
http://www.niss.ac.uk	

Web address	Comments
http://www.socialpsychology.org	
http://www.boxmind.com	Academic
http://www.apa.org	
http://www.sciam.com	*Scientific American* site
http://www.liv.ac.uk	
http://www.sleepnet.com	Good for 'sleep' as a topic. Some interesting research can be found

Glossary of terms

Acetic acid – A chemical that gives energy.

Achieved privacy – What people manage to get in the way of protecting themselves from others. People are dissatisfied if achieved privacy falls short of desired privacy.

Achievement motivation theory – A motivation theory proposed by McClelland, in which some people are said to have a greater need for power than others. Some prize power as a goal more than they prize other achievements, and this is why some strive to move up an organisational ladder more than others.

Actor–observer effect – Can lead to an attribution error. If we are the actor, then we emphasise an external cause for our behaviour. However, if we are observing another actor, then we emphasise an internal cause for their behaviour, even if the behaviour is the same.

Acute illness – A short-term illness.

Addiction – When someone is either physiologically or psychologically dependent (or both) on a substance they have been using over a period of time.

Advance organiser – A term used by Ausubel, which means that the teacher should outline material before the lesson starts so that it can be meaningful for the student. There are two types of advance organiser – comparative organiser and expository organiser.

Agonists – Drugs that increase the effect of or mimic a neurotransmitter.

Alpha personal space – The actual distance between people. Compare it with beta personal space, which is the subjective estimate of the distance.

Ambient conditions – Physical aspects such as light, noise, and temperature (compared with architectural features such as layout or size).

Antabuse – A drug that helps break the habit of drinking alcohol.

Antagonists – Drugs that block the effects of a neurotransmitter.

Anxiety – The emotional state, usually negative, that comes with arousal. Cognitive anxiety refers to the negative thoughts a person might have about achievement or expectations. Somatic anxiety refers to the worry given by the physiological state that is arousal – a person becomes anxious because they are sweating, feel queasy, etc.

Anxious/avoidant – A form of attachment (from Ainsworth) in which a child does not approach its mother when she comes back into a room (after leaving them). The child actively avoids the mother.

Anxious/resistant – A form of attachment (from Ainsworth); children go to their mothers when they return to a room (after leaving the child). They cry to be picked up, and also struggle to be put back down.

Architectural determinism – Suggests that building design can itself affect behaviour – for example, a building design can be linked to crime.

Architectural features – More permanent physical conditions than ambient conditions, such as colour, size and layout.

Arousal – The physiological response that the sympathetic part of the autonomic nervous system produces when we are getting ready for action in some way. The parasympathetic part reduces the physical response when it is time to calm down.

Associative network model of memory – Nodes or ideas are connected by association/links that make a route for cognitive activity to spread along.

Associative play – A type of play in which children share with one another.

Atomisation – A term used in environmental psychology that means that friendships do not build, and everyone has to look out for themselves.

Attachment – A two-way process in which an infant and a caregiver become dependent on one another. Attachment can be seen when the infant cries on being separated from the caregiver, or clings when a stranger is present. There are other factors too, such as interactional synchrony, where an infant mirrors the actions of the attachment figure.

Autonomous competence stage – One of Veroff's stages: aged between 3 and 4 years the child focuses on mastering skills in the environment and testing themselves. As personal competence grows, autonomous evaluation builds. 'Autonomous' means under one's own power.

Behaviour settings – Include the physical settings that surround an individual. An example of a behaviour setting would be a classroom. Social rules are part of a person's behaviour settings.

Beta personal space – A subjective estimate of the distance between people, compared with alpha personal space, which is the actual distance.

Biodata – Biographical information about a candidate for a job – including past work experience.

Biomedical model – Looks at physical causes for illnesses. Uses diagnoses, examines symptoms and suggests physical cures.

Biopsychosocial model – Looks at complex causes for illnesses, including biological, social and psychological factors.

Bipolar scale – A scale with two opposing criteria or adjectives. For example 'pleasant/unpleasant'. Contrast with a continuum, which refers to (for example) pleasant and unpleasant as two ends of a sliding scale, where the person can rate something along the scale. With a bipolar scale, only one of the criteria can be chosen.

Body buffer zone – The area of personal space surrounding an individual.

Body territory – The physical self; the boundary is one's self. This is not the same as personal space, where the boundary is some distance away.

Bonding – Forming an important relationship with those around.

'Bottom-up' processing – Information is gathered via the senses and then from such evidence conclusions are drawn. Previous knowledge and information is not used, as it is in 'top-down' reasoning.

Branch programmed learning – Presenting material in multiple choice format and then, if the answer is wrong, moving to a 'branch' where more of the same questions can be asked to help the learner practice.

Burnout – The stage of becoming less committed to a job and gradually withdrawing from the work.

Central nervous system – The brain and spinal column.

Chronic illnesses – Develop slowly. People with these diseases can live for quite some time after contracting them.

Coactive teams – Teams like rowing and swimming teams, in which members rely less on each other, and have to do only their own task successfully.

Coactors – Those who are present and affecting a performance, but who are not in the audience.

Cocaine – A strong stimulant drug that prevents reuptake of dopamine, so the effects of dopamine last longer.

Cohesion – A continuously changing or dynamic process demonstrated by the tendency of a group to stay together to achieve goals.

Collectivism – A collaborative socialisation, where the good of others is more important than individual achievement. There is co-operation rather than competition. Some societies have a collectivist approach.

Commons dilemma – A term used in environmental psychology to refer to the way natural resources are overused because there is a conflict between individual interests and group interests.

Commons – A term used in environmental psychology to describe any resource held by a group of individuals, rather than owned by one individual.

Comparative organiser – A term used by Ausubel – the introduction at the start of a lesson (the advance organiser) compares the material to be learned with previously learned information or concepts.

Competitive trait anxiety – The motive to avoid failure.

Competitiveness – The motive to gain success. It is made up of three parts – competitiveness, win orientation and goal orientation.

Concurrent validity – A type of criterion-related validity. The test result compares well with another score arrived at differently at the same time or earlier.

Consensus view of crime – Suggests that crime is an act that is against the law, which is arrived at by consensus of the people in the society.

Content validity – The content of an item is what it is supposed to be.

Continuum – When we think of something as having a range from one end or dimension to another. For example, we might think of cars as ranging along a continuum from slow to fast.

Co-operative learning – Can refer to group work in which pupils co-operate to learn, or to a cultural style in which the emphasis is on the success of the group rather than on individuals.

Co-operative play – A type of play in which children play structured games involving rules with other children.

Cost-benefit model – Term used in environmental psychology. The costs and benefits of defending territory are weighed up. If there are sufficient resources to make defending territory worthwhile, then it is defended – the cost in terms of energy spent is worth the benefits from the resources. When resources are low, any territory would have to be large so it is not defended because the cost of defending is more than the benefit gained.

Countertransference – A psychoanalytic term: the therapist may transfer feelings on to the analysand (the person undergoing therapy).

Craving – The very strong desire to consume a substance.

Credulous view – When an idea seems right when looking at real-life evidence. It is a believable view.

Criterion-related validity – A test result is compared with some other result to see if they match. Concurrent validity means the test score matches a different score arrived at at the same time (or earlier). Predictive validity means the test score matches a different score arrived at later.

Critical period – The time when a behaviour must develop, or it never will.

Crowding – Feeling depending on an individual's perception of the density – does a space *feel* crowded?

Deductive reasoning – Drawing conclusions from statements that are true. For example, if all animals breathe, and if a fox is an animal, then we can logically conclude that a fox breathes. In deductive reasoning the conclusion is bound to be true if the first statement is true. Deductive reasoning involves a certainty that is not there in inductive reasoning.

Defensible space – An area that residents place value on.

Deficiency needs – According to Maslow these are needs that are lower order and must be met before higher order needs can be met. Examples are physiological needs (such as hunger), safety needs and social needs.

Deindividuation – Loss of identity, and means that behaviour becomes impulsive, irrational and disinhibited. In a crowd people no longer act as individuals.

Density – The measure of physical space per person. Within a dwelling it is household density; within an area it is neighbourhood density or population density.

Deprivation – When an attachment that has been formed is broken. This is often a short-term situation.

Desensitisation – Refers to the way someone might get so used to watching violence that they cease to be offended or moved by it.

Desired privacy – What someone wants in the way of interaction with others.

Didactic teaching – Direct teaching, in which a teacher delivers some part of the curriculum (a body of knowledge to be covered) to students, who listen.

Disattachment – According to Bowlby this is the third stage that a child who has been separated from its mother goes through – the child becomes indifferent to other people.

Disinhibition – A reduction in social forces that might normally prevent certain acts. It means losing one's normal inhibitions.

Dispositional attribution – When we give something inside the person as the reason for an action. This contrasts with situational attribution.

Dispositional characteristics – Characteristics within a person, to do with their character or personality (as opposed to situational characteristics, which are to do with the situation).

Dispositional stress – The source of stress comes from the individual – for example, from their personality.

Distress – A term sometimes applied to stress involving negative feelings (as opposed to eustress).

Distribution of illness – Whether the number of cases is going up or down.

Distributive justice – Whether a trial, for example, has a just outcome. Some of the errors in justice are to do with errors in eyewitness testimony, and some are attribution errors.

DSM-IV – The Diagnostic and Statistical Manual of Mental Disorders, version IV, updated and revised. DSM-IV is published by the American Psychiatric Association.

Emotion-focused strategies – Strategies focusing on thoughts and emotions rather than on practical actions to avoid stress.

Empiricism – Gathering data by means of our senses.

Environmental after-effect – Where performance is affected by earlier environmental disturbance, such as noise.

Environmental possibilism – Suggests that the environment sets limits to our behaviour and sets the possibilities. The individual helps to shape his or her own behaviour, but within a physical environment.

Environmental probabilism – We can look at both the design of the physical environment and psychological factors and predict likely behaviour that will come from mixing the two.

Environmental stressors – Factors in our environment, often in the background, that can lead to stress, and can affect performance.

Epidemiology – The study of the incidence of diseases – how often they occur, and where.

Ethology – The study of behaviour of animals in their natural settings.

Eustress – A term sometimes applied to stress involving positive feelings (as opposed to distress).

Exploration–Play–Application sequence – An ethological approach suggesting that play links exploration of the unfamiliar with an application of what is learnt to help control the organism's environment.

Expository organiser – A term used by Ausubel: the introduction at the start of a lesson (the advance organiser) outlines the material in brief form. This is important if the topic is completely new.

External locus of control – Thinking that the cause of what happens to you lies outside yourself.

External validity – A study's findings can be extended to other settings.

Extinction – A term used in operant and classical conditioning, referring to when undesired behaviour or responses have stopped.

Extrinsic motivation – Motivation linked to external factors – for example, when a worker is motivated by something outside the work itself, such as pay.

Face validity – When a test measures what people think it should. For instance, if people are asked if items on a test measure IQ, and they agree that they do, the test has face validity.

Fantasy play – A type of play in which an object or person is used to represent something other than it is.

Friendship – Close ties with another person, through a mutual interest and a shared positive feeling for doing the same things.

Functional distance – The way the design of a building makes some people more likely to interact – for example, people living near the stairs are more likely to meet those using the stairs.

Fundamental attribution error – The tendency we have to overemphasise internal factors as causing the behaviour of others, but to overemphasise external factors when we consider the reasons for our own behaviour.

Geo-behavioural environment – The whole environment, including the individual and physical surroundings.

Giving – A term used in environmental psychology to refer to adding to pollution or environmental problems, for example, by dumping rubbish on the side of a road (as opposed to 'taking' or 'harvesting').

Goal orientation – The desire to reach personal goals.

Group polarisation – Term used for the tendency for groups to make decisions that are more extreme than decisions made by individuals. Decisions don't have to be riskier, as the risky shift idea claims, but they are different from the individual decisions in that they are either riskier (one pole) or more cautious (another pole).

Group – Two or more people achieving some goal by means of social interaction.

Group work – Small groups working on a topic. In teaching can be linked to a progressive style.

Groupthink – Where a group does not go through the evaluative process of considering alternatives when coming to a decision, but acts hastily and without discussion.

Growth needs – According to Maslow, higher order needs, including esteem and self-actualisation. However, lower order needs must be met before growth needs – if you are hungry you cannot hope to self-actualise.

Harvesting and taking – Terms used in environmental psychology to refer to plundering resources, for example, by cutting down a protected tree (as opposed to 'giving').

Hawthorne effect – Effect found by Mayo in a factory in Hawthorne. No matter how he varied the lighting or the environment the participants were working in, the productivity rose. It was thought that the increase in productivity was an effect of being observed.

Health belief model – Whether people follow health-related behaviours depends on how far they think they will develop a health problem, how serious they think the problem will be, and how they weigh up the costs and benefits of taking such action. Other variables include social class and age. The beliefs a person has affect their decisions regarding health-related behaviour.

Hedonic relevance – An event has meaning for us. This can lead to an attribution error.

Holists – Claim that, when looking at parts, the whole can never be understood because some relationship between the parts is overlooked. The view that something can only be understood by looking at it as a whole, which is more than the sum of its parts, is called **holism**.

Hyperactivity – Behaviour lacking in control and very active. The individual cannot concentrate.

Hypothetical construct – Something that cannot be directly measured, but only inferred or guessed at from watching someone's behaviour or listening to what they say. Personality is said to be a hypothetical construct.

Idiographic – Looking at individual differences, rather than for general laws.

Imprinting – Precocial animals follow the first moving object they see after they are born. This is usually the mother.

Incidence of crime – The amount of crime as a percentage of a population.

Incidence of illness – How many new cases developed in a given time period.

Independent learning – The individual learns alone, rather than co-operatively.

Individual learning – Can refer to a cultural style, where the emphasis is on the success of the individual, or to the opposite of co-operative learning (an individual learns independently).

Individualism – A type of socialisation in which the achievement of an individual is most important, and there is competition rather than co-operation. Some societies have a competitive approach.

Individuation – Differentiating between individuals in order for their individual personality to develop.

Inductive reasoning – Reasoning from sense data. For example, 'I see lots of white swans. I have never seen a black swan. Therefore all swans are white.'. The problem here is that I only need to see one black swan to make my conclusion incorrect. In inductive reasoning the conclusion will only be true according to our current experiences, and any new experience can change the conclusion.

Innate – Something that is inborn, rather than learnt through interaction in the environment.

Integrated stage – One of Veroff's stages. In the integrated stage a person has autonomous competence and uses social comparison. Although some people may not reach this stage, those who do can be at any age.

Interactional territories – Where a group of interacting people temporarily have control, for example, classrooms or football pitches.

Interactionism – In relation to environmental psychology this holds that the person and the environment are separate but constantly interact.

Interactive teams – Teams such as basketball and hockey teams, where there is a high division of labour. Individuals in the team have specialist roles.

Internal locus of control – The belief of having control over one's successes and failures.

Intrinsic motivation – Motivation linked to a person's internal mechanisms (like hunger). In work psychology it can mean a worker is motivated by something within the work itself, from which satisfaction is drawn.

Introspectionism – The view that the mind can be studied by looking inside one's head and examining thought processes.

Job analysis – Systematic study of the duties, responsibilities and tasks involved in a job.

Job description – A list of what tasks a job entails, including what is done, what equipment is needed and what output is aimed for.

Job evaluation – Analysis of the worth of the job for the organisation.

Job specification – Information about the sort of person needed for a job, including education, experience, and personality characteristics.

Just-world hypothesis – Seeing someone suffer arouses selfish feelings, so that we can preserve our belief that our world is 'just'. Therefore, if we cannot help, we are likely to derogate a victim of misfortune as one who must have deserved the suffering (because the world is a just one).

Kibbutz – Israeli farm or collective. Children are often reared in groups, having guidance from many adults and children. Co-operation is emphasised. Plural kibbutzim.

Leadership – Ability to lead a group towards the attainment of its goals.

Linear programmed learning – Learning material, usually presented on a computer in such a way that the pupil moves from one question to another, either getting the answer right and moving on or getting it wrong and doing the question again.

Longitudinal study – Where a group of people are studied over a period of time.

LPC – 'Least preferred co-worker'. A measure of someone's opinion of the person with whom they had the most difficulty in getting a job done. It is a measure used by Fiedler in his contingency model.

Meaningful verbal learning – A concept of Ausubel's. To learn something it must be meaningful and must relate to previously learned information.

Mechanistic – Descartes thought of matter as being connected, and as having mechanical laws that explain how objects in the world interact. This is a mechanistic view.

Meta-analysis – Considering many studies and drawing together their conclusions to give an overview or overall conclusion.

Monotropy – Tendency to attach to one particular individual.

Morbidity – How many people have a particular disease at a certain point in time. Can refer to the instances of the disease (how many new cases there are) or the prevalence of the disease (how many have it).

Mortality – How many people have died from a particular cause.

Multiaxial system – A system in which the individual is assessed on more than one criterion.

Need hierarchy theory – Maslow's theory that we have a hierarchy of needs that have to be met in order. The lowest level contains physiological needs and the highest level contains self-actualisation needs.

Negative correlation – A relationship between two variables where one variable (for example, age) increases but the other (for example, driving speed) decreases.

Neuromodulator – A substance that acts 'in front' of a neurotransmitter, setting the scene so that the neurotransmitter will act in a certain way.

Neuroses – Tend to be mental disorders where the person is different from normal only in there being an exaggeration of certain symptoms. The person is still in touch with reality, and knows he or she has a problem.

Neurotransmitters – Act at the synapse to inhibit it (stop action) or excite it (start action), and stop or send a message on.

Nicotine – A drug that stimulates certain acetylcholine receptors. Also has other effects.

Nomothetic – Looking for general laws about people, rather than individual differences.

Onlooker play – A type of play in which a child looks on but does not take part.

Outcome goal oriented – Focusing on winning, and the outcome, rather than on performance.

Paradigm – A set of basic assumptions about how something is thought about, how data is gathered, and what influences there might be.

Parallel forms – A way of testing for reliability. Means doing two different forms of the same test and correlating the results. A correlation of around 0.9 would be expected if the test is said to be reliable.

Parallel play – A type of play in which children play alongside others, but do not involve each other in the play.

Parsimony – Choosing the most elegant and simple solution or theory. This is often thought to be the most likely to be 'true'.

Peer groups – Groups that develop their own values and goals and have strong social relationships.

Peers – Equals – people who are developmentally similar and interact at the same level.

Performance criteria – Used to see how well a person is doing in their job.

Personal space – The area around us into which other people may not enter. The size of your personal space depends on factors such as how well you know the person entering your 'space'. Personal space is really interpersonal space, as it involves interactions with others.

Physical dependency – The state when a body has got used to a substance and its use has become part of the normal functioning of the body.

Play – An activity done for its own sake, not for a serious reason. Usually the means are more important than the ends.

Positive correlation – A relationship between two variables in which as one variable (for example, age) increases the other also increases (for example, number of wrinkles).

Positivism – The view that science is objective and a study of what is real and 'out there'.

Precocial – The young of a precocial species can move about very young and have well developed sense organs.

Predictive validity – A type of criterion-related validity. The test results compares well with another score arrived at later.

Premack principle – Positive reinforcement that includes a 'bribe'. For example, a parent might say to a child 'eat your tea and then we will go to the park'.

Prevalence of crime – The number of individuals who have experienced crime.

Prevalence of illness – The overall number of cases of an illness.

Primary motives – An organism is motivated to get what it needs for survival. Secondary motives are drives that are learned.

Primary prevention – Preventing health problems in the first place. For example, promotional campaigns might lead to children being vaccinated.

Primary spectators – People actually at an event.

Primary territory – The area of territory associated with a primary group such as the family – a group that is central to us with regard to protecting our privacy. Primary territory is the most hotly defended.

Privacy – The way a person makes himself or herself available to others. Personal space and territory are important in determining levels of privacy.

Privacy regulation – The way people make themselves more or less available to others.

Privation – When no attachment has been formed between an infant and a caregiver. This usually has long-term effects.

Problem-focused strategies – Focus on practical actions, rather than on emotions and feelings, to reduce stress.

Procedural justice – The procedures we use to try to make sure that justice is done. Procedural justice is to do with trying to avoid errors, so that we can achieve distributive justice.

Progressive style – The idea of working in small groups, opposed to didactic or whole-class teaching. It is linked to discovery learning.

Prosocial behaviour – Behaviour in a group that is helpful and goes beyond the role expectations, so the individual may not benefit.

Prospective research – Looking forward to see how a relationship between two variables changes over time. This adds to information gained from correlational analysis. If we say that personality is related to heart disease, but it is hard to know whether the disease causes the personality trait or the trait causes the disease, we can look forward from early years to see what developed first. If the trait was present in childhood, and the heart disease developed later, it is likely that the trait caused the disease, not the other way around.

Psychological dependence – Compulsion to take a substance even when not physically dependent upon it. When psychologically dependent on a substance, someone will rely on it to help them to feel good, and to help them in their life.

Psychoses – Mental disorders in which the individual is not in touch with reality.

Public territory – An area that anyone can access. Territorial markers such as hedges and fences are used to deter intruders. For example, people can leave a bag on a chair in a restaurant as a marker.

Qualitative data – Data that involve asking about a person's attitudes, emotions, feelings or characteristics in an in-depth way that does not involve a measurement scale.

Quantitative data – Data that involve measurements of some sort, so that comparisons between data gathered using the same measures can be made.

Reality play – A type of play.

Recidivism – A criminal reverts to criminal behaviour after treatment or punishment has taken place.

Reciprocity rule – Co-operation within a work group happens because individuals want to give help but expect help in return.

Reclamation – Waste material is used again to make a different product.

Recycling – Rubbish is processed back into the original product, using the same resources.

Reductionism – The view that something can be studied by examining the parts that make it up, rather than looking at the whole thing.

Reductionist – Breaking a problem down into parts, to study the parts, then putting the findings back together to claim knowledge of the whole. For example, headaches could be studied by looking at eyesight or by taking a brain scan to look for abnormalities.

Relationship oriented – Focusing on individuals within a group and relating to them to help to get a job done, by getting the most out of the individuals.

Reliability – The same results are found when a test is repeated. In the case of diagnosis, it means that more than one psychiatrist or clinical psychologist would give the same diagnosis to the same patient if interviewed separately.

Resource recovery – Involves recycling and reclamation.

Response burst – When bad behaviour is ignored by the teacher, at first the child is likely to increase their bad behaviour to try to get the attention that has been withdrawn.

Retrospective research – Looking back in the lives of sufferers of a certain illness to see if there were any common factors.

Reuptake – Reabsorption of a neurotransmitter so that it can be used again.

Risky shift phenomenon – A group makes a more risky decision than the decision of the individuals that make up the group (using the same dilemma or problem).

Sceptical view – Doubt that an idea has real-life application.

Secondary motives – Drives that are learned, as opposed to primary motives, which are what drive us to get what we need to survive.

Secondary prevention – Attempts to prevent a problem becoming worse. For example, prescription of medicine, or an exercise regime.

Secondary spectators – People watching an event on television or reading about it.

Secondary territory – The area that is not personally owned, but which is not public either. It can be a bar in a pub, where locals usually gather.

Secure attachment – According to Mary Ainsworth, a form of attachment in which a child is happy when the mother returns (having left the child), and wants to reach the mother straight away on her return.

Self-actualisation – The fifth goal in Maslow's hierarchy of needs. It is the final need, and refers to a feeling of fulfilment and achieving one's fullest potential. This state cannot be reached until all the other four needs have been met (physiological, safety, social, and esteem needs).

Self-efficacy – The belief that you can succeed at something you want to do. It means that a person expects to do well in a task. Self-confidence is an overall term for feeling comfortable about one's performance, but self-efficacy refers to doing well in a particular task or at a particular skill.

Self-serving bias – When we use internal causes and internal control factors as reasons for our successes but use external causes and external control factors as reasons for our failures.

Sensitive period – Time when a behaviour is likely to develop and normally develops. However, the behaviour can happen at a different time.

Separation anxiety – A young child becomes very distressed after a separation, because they fear another separation.

Situational attribution – Giving something in the situation as the reason for an action. This contrasts with dispositional attribution.

Situational characteristics – External characteristics to do with the situation, compared with dispositional characteristics, which are those within a person.

Situational stress – Where the source of the stress comes from the situation.

Social cohesion – How much team members like one another.

Social comparison stage – One of Veroff's stages. By 5 years old a child starts to compare itself with others of the same age, and starts to want to be better than others. Normative comparisons mean focusing on winning (being above the norm), whereas the informative value of comparisons means evaluating your own skills.

Social density – The number of people in an area. An increase in social density means more people for the space.

Social desirability – On a questionnaire the respondent gives the answers they think they ought to give, and those that are socially acceptable. This can be a source of bias.

Social dilemma – Something is a social dilemma when (a) a person gets more for choosing self-interest over public interest; (b) a group of people benefit more if they act in the public interest than in self-interest. This is a dilemma in that an individual benefits by being selfish, but when that same individual is part of a group, he or she benefits more by acting in the public interest.

Social facilitation – The effects of the presence of others on performance.

Social fantasy play – A type of play in which a child (often of around 5 years old) pretends to be someone else or adopts a role.

Social loafing – The way an individual can refuse to co-operate in a group, and contributes less when in a group than when acting as an individual.

Social trap – A term used in environmental psychology. The time trap, where, when people act in order to get immediate rewards, there is some gradually building cost rather than an immediate large cost due to their behaviour.

Socialisation – The process of learning social rules and norms, and of becoming part of a particular culture or of society.

Sociometric choices – Measured by asking people who they like most, for example, and who they interact with.

Solitary play – The type of play that children engage in when alone.

Spatial density – The size of an area. An increase in spatial density means less space for the people in the area. Someone living alone in a small room is in high-density conditions, but this would be called cramped, rather than crowded.

Special educational needs – Having difficulties that prevent normal progress in school.

Split-half reliability – A way of testing for reliability. Splitting a test into two halves and comparing a person's score on each half. It can only be done if the items on the test are similar in both halves. If the test is reliable a high correlation between the results from the two halves would be expected.

Standardisation of a test – A test is carried out on enough people within a population that, when an individual is tested, their results can be compared with a norm (what is normal) and so interpreted taking into account the whole population. For example, IQ tests measure what the norm is for a particular age group – and this is found out by testing lots of people of that age. Once we know what someone of that age would normally be expected to do, we have a standard against which others can be measured. Then we can say if they have a high or a low IQ for their age.

Stigmata – Visible or non-visible difficulties – such as amputation, mental illness, or epilepsy.

Stimulant drugs – Drugs that tend to increase activity and arousal.

Strain – The physiological and psychological response to a stressor.

Stranger fear – A young child clings to its attachment figure when a stranger appears.

Street-gang theory of territory development – Territory is owned by units such as families. When two units owned by different families are next to each other conflict can occur and the territory can change hands. If this process continued, one gang would control most of one territory, and another gang would control most of another. Fewer units owned by different gangs would be next to one another so fewer conflicts would occur. In this way territory can be a social organiser.

Stress – Being in a state of physiological arousal, which has arisen because we don't think we have the resources to cope with the demands of the situation. In occupational psychology stress refers to a physiological or psychological response when the skills and abilities of a person do not match the demands of the job.

Stressor – Something in the environment that acts as a stimulus and causes stress.

Subjectivity – The attitudes or beliefs of an individual making a judgement or carrying out a test affect the conclusions drawn from data gathered, or even the data themselves.

Synaptic functioning – What happens at a synapse when neurotransmitters are released on one side of the synaptic cleft, and are received by the receptors of the opposite neuron.

Taking and harvesting – Terms used in environmental psychology to refer to plundering resources – for example, by cutting down a protected tree (as opposed to 'giving').

Task cohesion – How well a team works together to achieve the required goal.

Task goal oriented – An individual focuses on their own performance. They examine their own achievement, without reference to others.

Task oriented – People who focus on getting the job done, rather than focusing on relationships between group members.

Territoriality – The way an owner of territory controls what happens on or near that territory.

Tertiary prevention – Activities that happen after a problem has developed. For example, a person may be given medication to stop a disease from getting worse, even though it has developed beyond the stage of reversing it. Exercise programmes to alleviate pain are categorised as tertiary prevention, as is keeping someone who has a terminal illness more comfortable.

Test–retest – A way of testing for reliability. Repeating a test after an interval and looking for a correlation between results. If the test is reliable there should be a correlation of around 0.9 (which is high).

Third-person effect – How many people think that, whereas other people are persuaded by advertising and other sorts of persuasive communication, they are not.

Tolerance – The way the body continues to adapt to a substance. To have the same effect, more and more of the substance is needed, although a plateau is eventually reached.

'Top-down' processing – Using previous knowledge and information to draw conclusions about a current situation. It is not that 'pure' information comes in via the senses and is interpreted. Previously stored knowledge is used when making judgements.

Transactionalism – In relation to environmental psychology this suggests that a person and their environment are one entity.

Transference – A psychoanalytic term; a person undergoing therapy transfers feelings onto the therapist.

Validity – A test measures what it claims to measure, and can be used in a real-life situation. For example, a test to measure helpfulness might not be valid if it measured someone seeming to help, but actually not helping at all.

Weapon focus effect – When a witness focuses attention on a weapon, rather than on facial features of the offender. Memory can be affected by the presence of a weapon.

White-collar crime – Crimes such as fraud, that are committed by those in business (white-collar workers).

Whole-class teaching – A formal teaching style, in which a whole class is introduced to a topic and where they do not work in groups.

Win orientation – Wanting to win competitions between individuals.

Withdrawal – The miserable symptoms that are experienced when people stop using a substance on which they have become physically or psychologically dependent.

Zero tolerance – Not accepting any criminal behaviour, and not 'turning a blind eye' to any misbehaviour.

References

Aamodt, M.G. (1999) *Applied Industrial/Organisational Psychology*, 3rd edition. Belmont, CA: Wadsworth Publishing Company.

Abelson, J.L. and Curtis, G.C. (1993) Discontinuation of alprazolam after successful treatment of panic disorder: A naturalistic follow-up study. *Journal of Anxiety Disorders*, 7, pp. 107–117.

Ackerman, P.L. and Kanfer, R. (1993) Integrating laboratory and field study for improving selection: Development of a battery for predicting air traffic controller success. *Journal of Applied Psychology*, 78, pp. 413–432.

Adams, G.A., King, L.A. and King, D.W. (1996) Relationships of job and family involvement, family social support, and work–family conflict with job and life satisfaction. *Journal of Applied Psychology*, 81, pp. 411–420.

Adams, L. and Zuckerman, D. (1991) The effect of lighting conditions on personal space requirements. *Journal of General Psychology*, 118, pp. 335–340.

Adlam, K.R.C. (1985) The psychological characteristics of police officers. In Thackrah, J.R. (ed.) *Contemporary Policing*. London: Sphere Reference.

Ahlstrom, W.M. and Havinghurst, R.J. (1971) *400 Losers*. San Francisco, CA: Jossey-Bass.

Aichorn, A. (1955) *Wayward Youth* (translation). New York: Meridian Books.

Aiello, J.R. and Pagan, G. (1982) Development of personal space among Puerto Ricans. *Journal of Nonverbal Behaviour*, 7, pp. 59–80.

Aiello, J.R. and Thompson, D.E. (1980) Personal space, crowding and spatial behaviour in a cultural context. In Altman, I, Wohlwill, J.F. and Rapoport A. (eds) *Human Behaviour and Environment*, volume 4. New York: Plenum.

Ainsworth, M.D.S. (1967) *Infancy in Uganda: Infant care and the growth of love*. Baltimore: Johns Hopkins Press.

Ainsworth, M.D.S. (1993) Attachment as related to the mother–infant interaction. In Rovee-Collier, C. and Lipsett, L.P. (eds) *Advances in Infancy Research* (Vol. 8). Norwood, NJ: Ablex.

Ainsworth, M.D.S. and Bell, S.M. (1969) Some contemporary patterns of mother-infant interaction in the feeding situation. In Ambrose, A. (ed.) *Stimulation in Early Infancy*. New York: Academic Press.

Ainsworth, M.D.S., Blehar, M.C., Waters, E. and Wall, S. (1978) *Patterns of Attachment: A Psychological Study of the Strange Situation*. Hillsdale, NJ: Lawrence Erlbaum.

Airasian, P. and Bart, W. (1975) Validating a priori instructional hierarchies. *Journal of Educational Measurement*, 12, pp. 163–173.

Aitkin, M., Bennett, S. and Hesketh, J. (1981) Teaching styles and pupil progress: A re-analysis. *British Journal of Educational Psychology*, 51, pp. 170–186.

Ajzen, I. and Fishbein, M. (1980) *Understanding Attitudes and Predicting Social Behaviour*. Englewood Cliffs, NJ: Prentice-Hall.

Albert, S. and Dabbs, J.M. Jr (1970) Physical distance and persuasion. *Journal of Personality*, 15, pp. 265–270.

Aldag, R.J. and Fuller, S.R. (1993) Beyond fiasco: A reappraisal of the groupthink phenomenon and a new model of group decision processes. *Psychological Bulletin*, 13, 533–552.

Alderfer, C.E. (1972) *Existence, Relatedness and Growth: Human Needs in Organisational Settings*. New York: Free Press.

Alexander, K. (1991) Seeking change in school physical education: Learning from a negative result. *The ACHPER National Journal*, Summer.

Alexander, R., Rose, J. and Woodhead, C. (1992) *Curriculum Organisation and Classroom Practice in Primary Schools: A Discussion Paper*. London: Department of Education and Science.

Allison, S.T. and Messick, D.M. (1985) Effects of experience in a replenishable resource trap. *Journal of Personality and Social Psychology*, 49, pp. 943–948.

Allison, S.T. and Messick, D.M. (1990) Social decision heuristics in the use of shared resources. *Journal of Behavioural Decision Making*, 3, pp. 195–204.

Allport, G.W. (1961) *Pattern and growth in personality*. New York: Rinehart and Winston.

Allyn, J. and Festinger, L. (1961) The effectiveness of unanticipated persuasive communications. *Journal of Abnormal and Social Psychology*, 62, pp. 35–40.

Alper, A., Buckhout, R., Chern, S., Harwood, R. and Slomovits, M. (1976) Eyewitness identification: Accuracy of individual vs. composite recollection of a crime. *Bulletin of the Psychonomic Society*, 8, pp. 147–149.

Altman, I. (1975) *Environment and Social Behaviour: Privacy, Personal Space, Territory and Crowding*. Pacific Grove, CA: Brooks/Cole.

Altman, I. (1993) Dialectics, physical environments and personal relationships. *Communication Monographs*, 60, pp. 26–34.

Altman, L.K. (1991) W.H.O. says 40 million will be infected with AIDS virus by 2000. *New York Times*, p.C3.

Altman, I. and Chemers, M.M. (1984) *Culture and Environment*. Monterey, CA: Brooks and Cole Publishing.

Amato, P.R. (1993) Children's adjustment to divorce: theories, hypotheses and empirical support. *Journal of Marriage and Family*, 55, pp. 23–38.

Ames, E.W. *et al.* (1990) cited in Goldberg, S. (2000) *Attachment and development*. London: Arnold, p.124.

Ammerman, H.L. (1965) *A Model of Junior Officer Jobs for use in Developing Task Inventories* (HumPRO Tech. Rep. 65–10). Alexandria, VA: Human Resources, Research Organisation.

Anderson, J.R. (1990) *Cognitive Psychology and its Implications*, 3rd edition. New York: Freeman.

Anderson, N. (1997) The validity and adverse impact of selection interviews: a rejoinder to Wood. *Selection and Development Review*, 13, pp. 13–17.

Anderson, N. and Ostroff, C. (1997) Selection as socialisation. In Anderson, N. and Herriot, P. (eds) *International Handbook of Selection and Assessment*. Chichester: Wiley.

Andreasen, N.C., Swayze, V.W., Flaum, M., Yates, W.R., Arndt, S. and McChesney, C. (1990) Ventricular enlargement in schizophrenia evaluated with computed tomographic scanning: Effects of gender, age, and stage of illness. *Archives of General Psychiatry*, 47, pp. 1008–1015.

Appleyard, D. and Linteli, M. (1972) The environmental quality of city streets: the residents' viewpoint. *Journal of the American Institute of Planners*, 38, pp. 84–101.

Argyle, M. (1989) *The Social Psychology of Work*, 2nd edition. Harmondsworth, Middlesex: Penguin.

Arnetz, B.B., Wasserman, J., Petrini, B. *et al.* (1987) Immune function in unemployed women. *Psychosomatic Medicine*, 49, pp. 3–12.

Arnold, J., Cooper, C.L. and Robertson, I.T. (1995) *Work Psychology*, 2nd edition. London: Pitman.

Arnot, M., Gray, J., James, M., Rudduck, J. and Duveen, G. (1998) *Recent Research on Gender and Educational Performance*. London: HMSO.

Aronson, E., Blaney, N., Stephen, C., Sikes, J. and Snapp, M. (1978) *The Jigsaw Classroom*. Beverly Hills, CA: Sage Publications.

Asch, S.E. (1956) Studies of independence and submission to group pressure: 1: A minority of one against a unanimous majority. *Psychological Monographs*, 70 (Whole No. 416).

Ashour, A.A. (1973) The contingency model of leadership effectiveness: An evaluation. *Organisational Behaviour and Human Performance*, 9, pp. 339–355.

Ashton, H. and Stepney, R. (1982) *Smoking: Psychology and Pharmacology*. London: Tavistock.

Atchley, R.C. (1976) Selected social and psychological differences between men and women in later life. *Journal of Gerontology*, 31, pp. 204–211.

Atchley, R.C. and Robinson, J.L. (1982) Attitudes towards retirement and distance from the event. *Research on Ageing*, 4, pp. 288–313.

Atkinson, J.W. (1964) *An Introduction to Motivation*. Princeton, NJ: Van Norstrand.

Austin, J., Hatfield, D.B., Grindle, A.C. and Bailey, J.S. (1993) Increasing recycling in office environments: the effects of specific, informative cues. *Journal of Applied Behaviour Analysis*, 26, pp. 247–253.

Ausubel, D.P. (1968) *Educational Psychology: A Cognitive View*. New York: Holt, Reinhart and Winston.

Axline, V. (1971) *Dibs: In Search of Self*. Harmondsworth: Penguin.

Ayman, R., Chemers, M.M. and Fiedler, F. (1995) The contingency model of leadership effectiveness: Its levels of analysis. *Leadership Quarterly*, 6, pp. 147–167.

Baddeley, A. (1995) Memory. In French, C.C. and Coleman, A.M. (eds) *Cognitive Psychology*. London: Longman.

Bagozzi, R.P. (1981) Attitudes, intentions, and behaviour. A test of some key hypotheses. *Journal of Personality and Social Psychology*, 41, pp. 606–627.

Baker, E. and Shaw, M.E. (1980) Reactions to interpersonal distance and topic intimacy: A comparison of strangers and friends. *Journal of Nonverbal Behaviour*, 5, pp. 80–91.

Baker, J. and Crist, J. (1971) Teacher expectancies: a review of the literature. In Elashoff, J. and Snow, E. (eds) *Pygmalion Reconsidered*. Worthington, OH: Jones.

Ballenger, J.C., Burrows, G.D. and Dupont, R.L. (1988) Alprazolam in panic disorder and agoraphobia: Results from a multicenter trial: Efficacy in short-term treatment. *Archives of General Psychiatry*, 45, pp. 413–422.

Balogun, S.K. (1991) The influence of sex and religion on personal space among undergraduate students. *Indian Journal of Behaviour*, 15, pp. 13–20.

Bandura. A. (1973a) *Aggression: A social learning analysis*. Englewood Cliffs, NJ: Prentice-Hall.

Bandura, A. (1973b) Social learning theory of aggression. In Kautson, J.F. (ed.) *The Control of Aggression: Implications From Basic Research*. Chicago, IL: Aldine.

Bandura, A. (1976) Social learning analysis of aggression. In Ribes-Inesta, E. and Bandura, A. (eds) *Analysis of Delinquency and Aggression*. Hillsdale, NJ: Lawrence Erlbaum.

Bandura, A. (1977a) *Social Learning Theory*. Englewood Cliffs, NJ: Prentice-Hall.

Bandura, A. (1977b) Self-efficacy: Towards a unifying theory of behavioural change. *Psychological Review*, 84, pp. 191–215.

Bandura, A. (1982) Self-efficacy: Mechanisms in human agency. *American Psychologist*, 37, pp. 122–147.

Bandura, A. (1986) *Social Foundations of Thought and Action*. Englewood Cliffs, NJ: Prentice-Hall.

Bandura, A. (1997) *Self-efficacy: The Exercise of Control*. San Francisco: W.H.Freeman.

Bandura, A., Ross, D. and Ross, S.A. (1963) Imitation of film-mediated aggressive models. *Journal of Abnormal and Social Psychology*, 66, pp. 3–11.

Bandura, A., Taylor, C.B., Williams, S.L., Mefford, I.N. and Barchas, J.D. (1985) Catecholamine secretion as a function of perceived coping self-efficacy. *Journal of Consulting and Clinical Psychology*, 53, pp. 406–414.

Banyard, P. (1996) *Applying Psychology to Health*. London: Hodder & Stoughton.

Barash, D.P. (1973) Human ethology: personal space reiterated. *Environment and Behaviour*, 5, pp. 67–73.

Barker, R.G. (1968) *Ecological psychology: Concepts and Methods for Studying the Environment of Human Behaviour*. Stanford, CA: Stanford University Press.

Barker, R. and Wright, H. (1955) *Midwest and its Children: The Psychological Ecology of an American Town*. New York: Harper and Row.

Barlow, D.H. (1988) *Anxiety and its Disorders: The Nature and Treatment of Anxiety and Panic*. New York: Guilford.

Barnard, W.A. and Bell, P.B. (1982) An unobtrusive apparatus for measuring interpersonal distance. *Journal of General Psychology*, 107, pp. 85–90.

Barnett, W. (1995) Long-term effects of early childhood programs on cognitive and school outcomes. *The Future of Children*, 5, pp. 25–50.

Baron, R.A. (1977) *Human Aggression*. New York: Plenum.

Baron, R.A. (1978) Invasion of personal space and helping: Mediating effects of invader's apparent need. *Journal of Experimental Social Psychology*, 14, pp. 304–312.

Baron, R.A. (1990) Environmentally induced positive affect: its impact on self-efficacy, task performance, negotiation and conflict. *Journal of Applied Social Psychology*, 20, pp. 368–384.

Baron, R.A. and Bell, P.A. (1976) Aggression and heat: the influence of ambient temperature, negative affect, and a cooling drink on physical aggression. *Journal of Personality and Social Psychology*, 33, pp. 245–255.

Barrick, M.R. and Mount, M.K. (1993) Autonomy as a moderator of the relationship between the Big Five personality dimensions and job performance. *Journal of Applied Psychology*, 78, pp. 111–118.

Barrick, M.R., Mount, M.K. and Strauss, J.P. (1994) Antecedents of involuntary turnover due to reduction in force. *Personnel Psychology*, 47, pp. 515–535.

Bartlett, F.C. (1932) *Remembering*. Cambridge: Cambridge University Press.

Bartram, D., Burke, E., Kandola, R., Lindley, P., Marshall, L. and Rasch, P. (1997) *Review of Ability and Aptitude Tests (Level A) for Use in Occupational Settings*. Leicester: BPS books.

Bateman, T.S. and Organ, D.W. (1983) Job satisfaction and the good soldier: The relationship between affect and employee 'citizenship'. *Academy of Management Journal*, 26, pp. 587–595.

Bateson, G., Jackson, D.D., Haley, J. and Weakland, J.H. (1956) Toward a theory of schizophrenia. *Behavioural Science*, 1, pp. 251–264.

Baum, A. (1990) Stress, intrusive imagery, and chronic distress. *Health Psychology*, 9, pp. 653–675.

Baum, A., Fisher, J.D. and Solomon, S. (1981) Type of information, familiarity and the reduction of crowding stress. *Journal of Personality and Social Psychology*, 40, pp. 11–23.

Baum, A., Grunberg, N.E. and Singer, J.E. (1982) The use of physiological and neuroendocrinological measurements in the study of stress. *Health Psychology*, 1, pp. 217–236.

Baxter, J.C. (1970) Interpersonal spacing in natural settings. *Sociometry, 33*, pp. 444–456.

Beck, A.T. (1967) *Depression: Clinical, Experimental, and Theoretical Aspects*. New York: Harper Row.

Beck, A.T. and Emery, G. (1985) *Anxiety Disorders and Phobias: A Cognitive Perspective*. New York: Basic Books.

Beck, A.T., Ward, C.H., Mendelson, N., Mock, J. and Erbaugh, J. (1961) An inventory for measuring depression. *Archives of General Psychiatry, 4*, p.5363.

Becker, F.D. and Poe, D.B. (1980) The effects of user-generated design modifications in a general hospital. *Journal of Nonverbal Behaviour, 4*, pp. 195–218.

Becker, J.L. (1963) *A Programmed Guide to Writing Auto-instructional Programmes*. RCA Service, NJ.

Becker, M.H. (1979) Understanding patient compliance: The contributions of attitudes and other psychosocial factors. In Cohen, S.J. (ed.) *New Directions in Patient Compliance*. Lexington, MA: Heath.

Becker, M.H. and Rosenstock, I.M. (1984) Compliance with medical advice. In Steptoe, A. and Mathews, A. (eds) *Health Care and Human Behaviour*. London: Academic Press.

Bee, H. (1992) *The Developing Child*. New York: Harper Collins.

Beehr, T.A. (1985) Organisational stress and employee effectiveness: A job characteristics approach. In Beehr, T.A. and Bhagat, R.S. (eds) *Human Stress and Cognition in Organisations: An Integrated Perspective*. New York: John Wiley and Sons.

Belar, C.D. and Deardorff, W.W. (1995) *Clinical Health Psychology in Medical Settings: A Practitioner's Guidebook*. Hyattsville, MD: APA.

Bell, P.A. and Fusco, M.E. (1989) Heat and violence in the Dallas field data: linearity, curvilinearity, and heteroscedasticity. *Journal of Applied Social Psychology, 19*, pp. 1479–1482.

Bell, P.A. and Greene, T.C. (1982) Thermal stress: physiological, comfort, performance and social effects of hot and cold environments. In Evans, G.W. (ed.) *Environmental stress*. New York: Cambridge University Press.

Bellack, A.S. (1992) Cognitive rehabilitation for schizophrenia: Is it possible? Is it necessary? *Schizophrenia Bulletin, 18*, pp. 43–50.

Belson, W. (1975) *Juvenile Theft: The Causal Factors*. New York: Harper and Row.

Benne, K.D. and Sheats, P. (1948) Functional roles of group members. *Journal of Social Issues, 4*, pp. 41–49.

Bennett, G.K. (1980) *Bennett Mechanical Comprehension Test*. San Antonio, TX: The Psychological Corporation.

Bennett, N. (1976) *Teaching Styles and Pupil Progress*. London: Open Books.

Bennett, N. and Dunne, E. (1989) *Implementing Cooperative Group Work in Classrooms*. Exeter: University of Exeter Department of Education.

Berglas, S. (1987) The self-handicapping model of alcohol abuse. In Blane, H.T. and Leonard, K.E. (eds) *Psychological Theories of Drinking and Alcoholism*. New York: Guilford Press.

Berkowitz, L. (1984) Some effects of thoughts on anti- and pro-social influences of media events: A cognitive-neoassociation analysis. *Psychological Bulletin, 95*, pp. 410–427.

Berkowitz, L. and Le Page, A. (1967) Weapons as aggression-eliciting stimuli. *Journal of Personality and Social Psychology, 7*, pp. 202–207.

Bernstein, B. (1961) Social class and linguistic development. In Halsey, A., Flaud, J. and Anderson, C. (eds) *Education, Economy and Society*. London: Collier-Macmillan.

Bernthal, P.R. and Insko, C.A. (1993) Cohesiveness without groupthink: The interactive effects of social and task cohesion. *Group and Organisational Management, 18*, pp. 66–87.

Best, A. (1992) *Teaching Children with Visual Impairments*. Buckingham: Open University Press.

Bifulco, A., Harris, T. and Brown, G.W. (1992) Mourning or early inadequate care? Re-examining the relationship of maternal loss in childhood with adult depression and anxiety. *Development and Psychopathology, 4*, pp. 433–449.

Billings, A.G. and Moos, R.H. (1981) The role of coping responses and social resources in attenuating the stress of life events. *Journal of Behavioural Medicine, 4*, pp. 139–157.

Bilton, T., Bonnett, K., Joines, P., Skinner, D., Stanworth, M. and Webster, A. (1996) *Introductory Sociology*, 3rd edition. London: Macmillan.

Binet, A. (1905) cited in Childs, D. (1999) *Psychology and the Teacher*, 6th edition (pp. 248–249). London: Cassell Education.

Binet, A. and Henri, V. (1896) Psychologie individuelle. *Annee Psychologie, 3*, pp. 296–332. In Phares, E.J. and Trull, T.J. (1996) *Clinical Psychology*, 5th edition. Pacific Grove, California: Brooks/Cole.

Birch, H.G. (1945) The role of motivational factors in insightful problem-solving. *Journal of Comparative Psychology, 38*, pp. 295–317.

Bird, A.M. and Williams, J.M. (1980) A developmental-attribution analysis of sex-role stereotypes for sport performance. *Developmental Psychology, 16*, pp. 319–322.

Bixenstein, V.E. and Douglas, J. (1967) Effects of psychopathology on group consensus and cooperative choice in a six person game. *Journal of Personality and Social Psychology, 5*, pp. 32–37.

Bjorntorp, P. (1996) Behavior and metabolic disease. *International Journal of Behavioral Medicine, 3*, pp. 285–302.

Black, S.L. and Bevan, S. (1992) At the movies with Buss and Durkee: A natural experiment on film violence. *Aggressive Behaviour, 18*, pp. 37–45.

Black, B. and Hazen, N.L. (1990) Social status and patterns of communication in acquainted and unacquainted preschool children. *Developmental Psychology, 26*, pp. 379–385.

Blackmore, J. (1974) The relationship between self-reported delinquency and official convictions amongst adolescent boys. *British Journal of Criminology, 14*, pp. 172–176.

Blake, R. and Mouton, J. (1964) *The Managerial Grid*. Houston, TX: Gulf Publishing.

Blake, R.R. and McCanse, A.A. (1991) *Leadership dilemmas – Grid Solutions*. Houston, TX: Gulf Publishing.

Blake, W. (1973) The influence of race on diagnosis. *Smith College Studies in Social Work, 43*, pp. 184–192.

Bleuler, E. (1911) *Dementia Praecox of the Group of Schizophrenias*. (Translated 1950 by J. Zinkin). New York: International Universities Press.

Bliese, P.D. and Halverson, R.R. (1996) Individual and nomothetic models of job stress: An examination of work hours, cohesion, and well-being. *Journal of Applied Social Psychology, 26*, pp. 1171–1189.

Bloom, B. (ed.) (1956) *Taxonomy of educational objectives. Handbook 1: Cognitive Domain*. New York: David McKay.

Bodenhauser, G.V. and Lichtenstein, M. (1987) Social stereotypes and information-processing strategies: The impact of task complexity. *Journal of Personality and Social Psychology, 52*, pp. 871–880.

Boggiano, A.K., Klinger, C.A. and Main, D.S. (1986) Enhancing interest in peer interaction: A developmental analysis. *Child Development, 57*, pp. 852–861.

Bohman, M. (1978) Some genetic aspects of alcoholism and criminality. *Archives of General Psychiatry, 35*, pp. 269–276.

Bonnes, M. and Secchiaroli, G. (1995) *Environmental Psychology: A Psycho-Social Introduction*. London: Sage.

Boon, J. and Davies, G. (1992) Fact and fiction in offender profiling issues. *Legal and Criminological Psychology, 32*, pp. 3–9.

Booth, A. and Edwards, J.N. (1976) Crowding and family relations. *American Sociological Review, 41*, pp. 308–321.

Borkovec T.D. and Mathews, A.M. (1988) Treatment of nonphobic anxiety disorders: A comparison of nondirective, cognitive, and coping desensitisation therapy. *Journal of Consulting and Clinical Psychology*, 56, pp. 877–884.

Borkovec, T.D. and Costello, E. (1993) Efficacy of applied relaxation and cognitive-behavioural therapy in the treatment of generalised anxiety disorder. *Journal of Consulting and Clinical Psychology*, 61, pp. 611–619.

Bowlby, J. (1946) *Forty-Four Juvenile Thieves*. London: Baillière, Tindall and Cox.

Bowlby, J. (1956) The effects of mother–child separation: A follow-up study. *British Journal of Medical Psychology*, 29, pp. 211–47. (Cited in N. Hayes, *Foundations of Psychology*, 3rd edition, Thomson Learning.)

Bowlby, J. (1969) *Attachment and loss: Vol. 1: Attachment*. London: Hogarth Press.

Bowling, B. (1999) The rise and fall of New York murder: Zero tolerance or crack's decline? *British Journal of Criminology*, 39, pp. 531–554.

Brann, P. and Foddy, M. (1987) Trust and the consumption of a deteriorating common resource. *Journal of Conflict Resolution*, 31, pp. 615–630.

Brannon, L. (1996) *Gender: Psychological Perspectives*. Boston: Allyn and Bacon.

Brattesanti, K., Weinstein, R. and Marshall, H. (1984) Student perceptions of differential teacher treatment as moderators of teacher expectation effects. *Journal of Educational Psychology*, 76, pp. 236–247.

Brechner, K.C. (1976) An experimental analysis of social traps. *Journal of Experimental Social Psychology*, 13, pp. 552–564.

Breslow, L. (1983) The potential of health promotion. In Mechanic, D. (ed.) *Handbook of Health, Health Care and The Health Professions*. New York: Free Press.

Brewer, K. (2000) *Psychology and Crime*. Heinemann.

Briere, J., Downes, A. and Spensley, J. (1983) Summer in the city: urban weather conditions and psychiatric emergency room visits. *Journal of Abnormal Psychology*, 92, pp. 77–80.

Broadbent, D.E. (1979) Human performance and noise. In Harris, C.M. (ed.) *Handbook of Noise Control*. New York: McGraw-Hill.

Bronzaft, A.L. and McCarthy, D.P. (1975) The effects of elevated train noise on reading ability. *Environment and Behaviour*, 7, pp. 517–527.

Brophy, J. and Evertson, C. (1976) *Learning From Teaching: A Developmental Perspective*. Boston: Allyn and Bacon.

Brophy, J. and Good, T. (1974) *Teacher–Student Relationships*. New York: Holt, Rinehart and Winston.

Brown, G.W. and Harris, T.O. (1978) *Social Origins of Depression*. London: Tavistock.

Brown, H. (1985) *People, Groups and Society*. Milton Keynes: Open University Press.

Brown, J., Cooper, C. and Kircaldy, B. (1996) Occupational stress among senior police officers. *British Journal of Psychology*, 87, pp. 31–41.

Brown, P. and Elliott, R. (1965) Control of aggression in a nursery school class. *Journal of Experimental Child Psychology*, 2, pp. 103–107.

Brown, R.B. (1971) Personality characteristics related to injury in football. *Research Quarterly*, 42, pp. 133–138.

Bruner, J. (1961a) *The Process of Education*. Cambridge, MA: Harvard University Press.

Bruner, J. (1961b) The act of discovery. *Harvard Educational Review*, 31, pp. 21–32.

Bruner, J.S., Goodnow, J.J. and Austin, G.A. (1956) *A Study of Thinking*. New York: Wiley.

Brunswik, E. (1943) Organismic achievement and environmental probability. *Psychological Review*, 50, pp. 255–272.

Buckhout, R. (1974) Eyewitness testimony. *Scientific American* 231, pp. 23–31.

Buckhout, R. (1980) Nearly 2,000 witnesses can be wrong. *Bulletin of the Psychonomic Society*, 16, pp. 307–310.

Bullinger, M. (1989) Psychological effects of air pollution on healthy residents – a time-series approach. *Journal of Environmental Psychology*, 9, pp. 103–118.

Burke, M.J. (1992) Computerised psychological testing. In Schmitt, N. and. Borman, W.C. (eds) *Personnel Selection*. San Fransisco: Jossey-Bass.

Burn, S. (1991) Loss of control, attributions and helplessness in the homeless. *Journal of Applied Social Psychology*, 22, pp. 1161–1174.

Burn, S.M. and Oskamp, S. (1986) Increasing community recycling with persuasive communication and public commitment. *Journal of Applied Social Psychology*, 16, pp. 29–41.

Bynner, J. and Parsons, S. (1997) *Does Numeracy Matter? Evidence From The National Child Development Study on The Impact of Poor Numeracy on Adult Life*. London: Basic Skills Agency.

Byrne. B.M. (1993) The Maslach Burnout Inventory: Testing for factorial validity and invariance across elementary, intermediate, and secondary teachers. *Journal of Occupational and Organisational Psychology*, 62, pp. 123–134.

Cadoret, R.J. and Cain, C. (1980) Sex differences in predictors of antisocial behaviour in adoptees. *Archives of General Psychiatry*, 37, pp. 171–175.

Caine, S.B. and Koob, G.F. (1993) Modulation of cocaine self-administration in the rat through D-3 dopamine receptors. *Science*, 260, pp. 1814–1816.

Calhoun, J.B. (1962) Population density and social pathology. *Scientific American*, 206, pp. 139–148.

Calhoun, J.B. (1971) Space and the strategy of life. In Esser, A.H. (ed.) *Environment and Behaviour: The Use of Space by Animals and Men*. New York: Plenum.

Calhoun, J.B. (1973) Death squared: the explosive growth and demise of a mouse population. *Proceedings of the Royal Society of Medicine*, 66, pp. 80–88.

Campbell, D.J. and Furrer, D.M. (1995) Goal setting and competition as determinants of task performance. *Journal of Organisational Behaviour*, 16, pp. 377–389.

Cannon, W.B. (1929) *Bodily Changes in Pain, Hunger, Fear and Rage*, 2nd edition. New York: Appleton.

Canter, D. (1994) *Criminal Shadows*. London: Harper Collins.

Canter, D. (1998) New developments in investigative psychology. *The Fifth International Investigative Psychology Conference, September*, pp. 14–16.

Caplan, N., Choy, M. and Whitmore, J. (1992) Indochinese refugee families and academic achievement. *Scientific American*, 266, pp. 18–24.

Carayon, P. (1994) Stressful jobs and non-stressful jobs: A cluster analysis of office jobs. *Ergonomics*, 37, pp. 311–323.

Carr, A. (1999) *The Handbook of Child and Adolescent Clinical Psychology*. London: Routledge.

Carron, A.V. (1982) Cohesiveness in sports groups: Interpretations and considerations. *Journal of Sport Psychology*, 4, pp. 123–138.

Cattell, R.B. (1965) *The Scientific Analysis of Personality*. Baltimore: Penguin.

Caughy, M.O., DiPietro, J.A. and Strobino, D.M. (1994) Daycare participation as a protective factor in the cognitive development of young children. *Child Development*, 65, pp. 457–471.

Cavan, S. (1963) Interaction in home territories. *Berkeley Journal of Sociology*, 8, pp. 17–32.

Ceci, S.J., Huffman, M.L.C., Smith, E. and Loftus, E.F. (1994) Repeatedly thinking about a non-event: Source misattributions among preschoolers. *Consciousness and Cognition*, 3, pp. 388–407.

Chan, D., Schmitt, N., DeShon, P., Clause, C.S. and Delbridge, K. (1997) Reactions to cognitive ability tests: the relationships between race, test performance, face validity perceptions, and test-taking motivation. *Journal of Applied Psychology*, 82, pp. 300–310.

Chandler, M.J. (1973) Egocentrism and anti-social behaviour: the assessment and training of social perspective-taking skills. *Developmental Psychology*, 9, pp. 326–332.

Chassin, L., Presson, C.C., Sherman, S.J. and Edwards, D.A. (1991) Four pathways to young-adult smoking status: Adolescent social-psychological antecedents in a Midwestern community sample. *Health Psychology*, 10, pp. 409–418.

Chein, I. (1954) The environment as a determinant of behaviour. *Journal of Social Psychology*, 39, pp. 115–127.

Chen, X., Rubin, K.H. and Sun, Y. (1992) Social reputation and peer relationships in Chinese and Canadian children: A cross-cultural study. *Child Development*, 63, pp. 1336–1343.

Cherniss, C. (1980) *Staff Burnout: Job Stress in Human Services*. Beverley Hills, CA: Sage Publications.

Child, D. (1999) *Psychology and the Teacher*, 6th edition. London: Cassell Education.

Chisholm, K., Carter, M., Ames, E.W. and Morrison, S.J. (1995) Attachment security and indiscriminately friendly behaviour in children adopted from Romanian orphanages. *Development and Psychopathology*, 7, pp. 283–294.

Chmiel, N. (ed.) (2000) *Introduction to Work and Organisational Psychology*. Oxford: Blackwell.

Christian, J.J., Flyger, V. and Davis, D.E. (1960) Factors in the mass mortality of a herd of sika deer, *Cervus nippon*. *Chesapeake Science*, 1, pp. 79–95.

Christianson *et al.* (1998) cited in Brewer, K. (2000) *Psychology and Crime* (p. 45). Oxford: Heinemann.

Churchman, A. and Ginsburg, Y. (1984) The image and experience of high-rise housing in Israel. *Journal of Environmental Psychology*, 4, pp. 27–41.

Cialdini, R.B., Kenrick, D.T. and Hoerig, J.H. (1976) Victim derogation in the Lerner paradigm: Just world or just justification? *Journal of Personality and Social Psychology*, 33, pp. 719–724.

Claiborn, W. (1969) Expectancy effects in the classroom: a failure to replicate. *Journal of Educational Psychology*, 60, pp. 377–383.

Claridge and Herrington (1963) cited in Claridge, G.S. (1967) *Personality and Arousal*. Oxford: Pergammon Press.

Clark D.M. and Beck, A. T. (1988) Cognitive Approaches. In Last, C.G. and Hersen, M. (eds) *Handbook of Anxiety Disorder*. New York: Pergammon Press.

Clark, N.K. and Stephenson, G.M. (1995) Social remembering: Individual and collaborative memory for social information. *European Review of Social Psychology*, 6, pp. 127–160.

Clarke-Stewart, A. (1989) Infant day care: Maligned or malignant? *American Psychologist*, 44, pp. 266–273.

Clarke-Stewart, A. (1993) *Daycare* (revised edition), Cambridge, MA: Harvard University Press.

Clever, L.H. and Omenn, G.S. (1988) Hazards for health care workers. In Breslow, L., Fielding, J.E. and Lave, L.B. (eds) *Annual Review of Public Health, Vol. 9*. Palo Alto, CA: Annual Reviews.

Clifford, B.R. (1979) The relevance of psychological investigation to legal issues in testimony and identification, *Criminal Law Review*, pp. 153–163.

Clifford, B.R. and Hollin, C.R. (1981) Effects of the type of incident and the number of perpetrators on eyewitness memory. *Journal of Applied Psychology*, 66, pp. 364–370.

Clifford, B.R. and Richards, V.J. (1977) Comparison of recall of policemen and civilians under conditions of long and short durations of exposure. *Perceptual and Motor Skills*, 45, pp. 503–512.

Clough, J., McCormack, C. and Traill, R. (1993) A mapping of participation rates in junior sport. *The ACHPER National Journal*, winter, pp. 4–7.

Cobb, S. and Rose, R.M. (1973) Hypertension, peptic ulcer, and diabetes in air traffic controllers. *Journal of the American Medical Association*, 224, pp. 489–492.

Cochrane, R. (1974) Circadian variations in mental efficiency. In Colquhoun, W.P. (ed.) *Biological Rhythms and Human Performance*. London: Academic Press.

Cockett, M. and Tripp, J. (1994) Children living in disordered families. *Social Policy Research Findings, No. 45*, Joseph Rowntree Foundation.

Cohen, D. (1987) *The Development of Play*. London: Croom Helm.

Cohen, D. (1993) *The Development of Play*, 2nd edition. London: Routledge.

Cohen, F. and Lazarus, R. (1979) Coping with the stresses of illness. In Stone, G.C., Cohen, F. and Adler, N.E. (eds) *Health Psychology: A Handbook*. San Francisco: Jossey-Bass.

Cohen, F. and Lazarus, R.S. (1983) Coping and adaptation in health and illness. In Mechanic, D. (ed.) *Handbook of Health, Health Care and the Health Professions*. New York: Free Press.

Cohen, S.A. (1978) Environmental load and the allocation of attention. In Baum, A., Singer, J.E. and Valins, S. (eds) *Advances in Environmental Psychology, Volume 1*. Hillsdale, NJ: Erlbaum.

Cohen, S. (1980) Aftereffects of stress on human performance and social behaviour. A review of research and theory. *Psychological Bulletin*, 88, pp. 81–108.

Cohen, S., Evans, G.W., Stokols, D. and Krantz, D.S. (1986) *Behaviour, Health and Environmental Stress*. New York: Plenum.

Cohen, S.A., Glass, D.C. and Singer, J.E. (1973) Apartment noise, auditory discrimination, and reading ability in children. *Journal of Experimental Social Psychology*, 9, pp. 407–422.

Cohen, S. and Herbert, T.B. (1996) Health psychology: psychological factors and physical disease from the perspective of human psychneuroimmunology. *Annual Review of Psychology*, 47, pp. 113–142.

Cole, M. and Cole, S.R. (1996) *The Development of Children*, 3rd Edition. New York: W.H. Freeman and Company.

Comer, D.R. (1995) A model of social loafing in real work groups. *Human Relations*, 48, pp. 647–667.

Comstock, G. and Paik, H. (1991) *Television and the American Child*. New York: Academic Press.

Connolly, J.A. and Doyle, A.B. (1984) Relation of social fantasy play to social competence in pre-schoolers. *Developmental Psychology*, 20, pp. 797–806.

Cook, M. (1993) *Personnel Selection and Productivity*, 2nd edition. Chichester: Wiley.

Cook, M. and Mineka, S. (1989) Observational conditioning of fear to fear-relevant versus fear-irrelevant stimuli in rhesus monkeys. *Journal of Abnormal Psychology*, 98, pp. 448–459.

Coolican, H. (1994) *Research Methods and Statistics in Psychology*, 2nd edition. London: Hodder and Stoughton.

Cooper, C. (1972) The house as symbol. *Design and Environment*, 14, pp. 178–182.

Cooper, L. (1969) Athletics, activity and personality: A review of the literature. *Research Quarterly*, 40, pp. 17–22.

Cooper, W.H., Gallupe, R.G., Pollard, S. and Cadsby, J. (1998) Some liberating effects of anonymous electronic brainstorming. *Small Group Research*, 29, pp. 147–178.

Coopers and Lybrand (1996) *The SEN Initiative: Managing Budgets for Pupils with Special Educational Needs*. London: Coopers and Lybrand.

Copeland, J.T. (1994) Prophecies of power: motivational implications of social power for behavioural confirmation. *Journal of Personality and Social Psychology*, 67, pp. 264–277.

Copson, G. (1995) Coals to Newcastle? *Police Research Group Special Interest Series: Paper 7*. London: Home Office Police Department.

Copson, G. (1996) At last some facts about offender profiling in

Britain. *Forensic Update,* 46, Division of Criminological and Legal Psychology, Leicester. British.

Copson, G. and Holloway, K. (1997) Offender profiling. Paper presented to the annual conference of the Division of Criminological and Legal Psychology, British Psychological Society (October). Cited in Harrower, J. (1998*) Applying Psychology to Crime*. London: Hodder and Stoughton.

Corsaro, W.A. (1985) Friendship in the nursery school: social organisation in a peer environment. In Asher, S.R. and Gootman, J.M. (eds) *The Development of Children's Friendships*. Cambridge: Cambridge University Press.

Cose, E. (1994) Drawing up safer cities. *Newsweek*, July 11, p. 57.

Costa, P.T. and McCrae, R.R. (1992) *Revised NEO Personality Inventory (NEO-PI-R) and NEO Five Factor Inventory (NEO-FF): Professional manual*. Odessa, FL: Psychological Assessment Resources.

Costa, P.J. and Widiger, T.A. (1994) *Personality Disorders and the Five-Factor Model of Personality*. Washington DC: American Psychological Association.

Cottrell, N.B. (1968) Performance in the presence of other human beings: Mere presence, audience and affiliation effects. In Summell, E.C., Hoppe, R.A. and Milton, G.A. (eds) *Social Facilitation and Imitative Behaviour*. Boston: Allyn and Bacon.

Cox, M.J., Owen, M.T., Henderson, V.K. and Margand, N.A. (1992) Prediction of infant-father and infant-mother attachment. *Developmental Psychology, 28,* pp. 474–483.

Cox, R.H. (1994) *Sport Psychology: Concepts and Applications,* 3rd edition. Dubuque, IA: Wm Brown and Benchmark.

Crawford, J. (1981) *Crawford Small Parts Dexterity Test*. San Antonio, TX: The Psychological Corporation.

Croll, P. and Moses, D. (1990) Sex roles in the primary classroom. In Rogers, C. and Kutnick, P. (eds) *The Social Psychology of the Primary School*. London: Routledge.

Crowder (1955) cited in Child, D. (1999) *Psychology and the Teacher,* 6th edition (pp. 137–138). Cassell Education.

Crowe, R.R. (1974) An adoption study of antisocial personality. *Archives of General Psychiatry,* 31, pp. 785–791.

Crowe, R.R., Noyes, R., Pauls, D.L. and Slymen, D.J. (1983) A family study of panic disorder. *Archives of General Psychiatry,* 40, pp. 1065–1069.

Crutchfield, R.S. (1955) Conformity and character. *American Psychologist,* 10, pp. 191–198.

Csikszentmihalyi, M. (1975) *Flow: The Psychology of Optimal Experience*. New York: Harper Perennial.

Cumberbatch, G. (1992) Is television violence harmful? In Cochrane, R. and Carroll, D. (eds) *Psychology and Social Issues*. London: Falmer Press.

Cumberbatch, G. (1994) Legislating mythology: video violence and children. *Journal of Mental Health,* 3, pp. 485–494.

Cummings, E. and Henry, W.E. (1961) *Growing Old*. New York: Basic Books.

Cunningham, M.R. (1979) Weather, mood and helping behaviour: quasi experiments with the sunshine Samaritan. *Journal of Personality and Social Psychology,* 37, pp. 1947–1956.

Curry, N.E. and Arnaud, S. (1984) Play in preschool settings. In Yawkey, T. and Pellegrini, A. (eds) *Child's Play, Developmental and Applied*. London: Lawrence Erlbaum.

Curtiss, S. (1977) *Genie: A Psycholinguistic Study of a Modern-day 'Wild Child'*. London: Academic Press.

Dachler, M.P. (1994) *A social-relational perspective of selection*. Paper presented at the 23rd International Congress of Applied Psychology, Madrid, July.

Dalsheill, J.F. (1935) Experimental studies of the influence of social situations on the behaviour of individual human adults. In Murchison, C. (ed.) *A Handbook of Social Psychology*. Worcester, MA: Clark University Press.

Dane, F.C. and Wrightsman, L.S. (1982) Effects of defendants' and victims' characteristics on jurors' verdicts. In Kerr, N.L. and Bray, R.M. (eds) *The Psychology of the Courtroom*. London: Academic Press.

Davidowicz, L.C. (1975) *The War Against the Jews, 1933–1945*. New York: Holt, Rinehart and Winston.

Davies, G.M., Shepherd, J.W. and Ellis, H.D. (1979) Effects of interpolated mugshot exposure on accuracy of eyewitness identification. *Journal of Applied Psychology,* 64, pp. 232–237.

Davis, KL, Kahn, R.S., Ko, G. and Davidson, M. (1991) Dopamine in schizophrenia: A review and reconceptualisation. *American Journal of Psychiatry*, 148, pp. 1474–1486.

Davison, G.C. (1966) Differential relaxation and cognitive restructuring in therapy with a "paranoid schizophrenic" or "paranoid state". *Proceedings of the 74th Annual Conference of the Americal Psychological Association*. Washington, DC: American Psychological Association.

Davison, G.C. and Neale, J.M. (1994) *Abnormal Psychology,* 6th edition New York: John Wiley and Sons.

Dawes, R.M. (1980) Social dilemmas. *Annual Review of Psychology,* 31, pp. 169–193.

Deaux, K. and Wrightsman, L.S. (1988) *Social Psychology*, 5th edition. Belmont, CA: Brooks/Cole.

Deci, E.L., Betley, G., Kahle, J., Abrams, L. and Porac, J. (1981) When trying to win: Competition and instrinsic motivation. *Personality and Social Psychology Bulletin,* 7, pp. 79–83.

Deci, E.L. and Ryan, R.M. (1985) *Intrinsic Motivation and Self Determination in Human Behaviour*. New York: Plenum.

Decker, J.B. and Stubblebine, J.M. (1972) Crisis intervention and prevention and psychiatric disability: A follow-up study. *American Journal of Psychiatry,* 129, pp. 725–729.

Deffenbacher, J., Zwemer, W., Whisman, M., Hill, R. and Sloan, R. (1986) Irrational beliefs and anxiety. *Cognitive Therapy and Research,* 10, pp. 281–292.

Deffenbacher, K.A. (1983) The influence of arousal on reliability of testimony. In Lloyd-Bostock, S.M.A. and Clifford, B.R. (eds) *Evaluating Witness Evidence: Recent Psychological Research and New Perspectives*. Chichester: Wiley.

DeGroot, I. (1967) Trends in public attitudes towards air pollution. *Journal of the Air Pollution Control Association,* 17, pp. 679–681.

DeLeon, P.H., Fox, R.E. and Graham, S.R. (1991) Prescription privileges: Psychology's next frontier? *American Psychologist,* 46, pp. 384–393.

Dennis, W. (1960) Causes of retardation amongst institutional children: Iran. *Journal of Genetic Psychology,* 96, pp. 47–59.

Devine, P.G. and Malpass, R.S. (1985) Orienting strategies in differential face recognition. *Personality and Social Psychology Bulletin,* 11, pp. 33–40.

DeYoung, R., Duncan, A., Frank, J. *et al.* (1993) Promoting source reduction behaviour: the role of motivational information. *Environment and Behaviour,* 25, pp. 70–85.

Diamond, W.D. and Loewy, B.Z. (1991) Effects of probabilistic rewards on recycling attitudes and behaviour. *Journal of Applied Social Psychology,* 21, pp. 1590–1607.

Diener, E. (1980) Deindividuation: the absence of self-awareness and self-regulation in group members. In Paulus, P.B. (ed.) *Psychology of Group Influence*. Hillsdale, NJ: Erlbaum.

Diener, E., Fraser, S.C., Beaman, A.L. and Kelem, R.T. (1976) Effects of deindividuation variables on stealing by Halloween trick-or-treaters. *Journal of Personality and Social Psychology,* 33, pp. 178–183.

DiMatteo, M.R., Shugars, D.A. and Hays, R.D. (1993) Occupational stress, life stress and mental health among dentists. *Journal of Occupational and Organisational Psychology,* 66, pp. 153–162.

Dion, K.K. (1973) Young children's stereotyping of facial attractiveness. *Developmental Psychology,* 9, pp. 183–188.

Dipboye, R.L. (1994) Structured and unstructured selection

interviews: Beyond the job-fit model. *Research in Personnel and Human Resources Management,* 12, pp. 79–123.

Dodge, K.A., Coie, J.D., Pettit, G.S. and Price, J.M. (1990) Peer status and aggression in boys' groups: Developmental and contextual analyses. *Child Development,* 61, pp. 1289–1309.

Dodge, K.A., Schlundt, D.C., Shocken, I. and Delugach, J.D. (1983) Social competence and children's sociometric status: the role of peer group entry strategies. *Merrill-Palmer Quarterly,* 29, pp. 309–336.

Dodson (1908) cited in Morris, T. and Summers, J. (eds) (1995) *Sport Psychology Theory, Applications and Issues* (p. 49). Brisbane: John Wiley and Sons.

Dolan, B. (1991) Cross-cultural aspects of anorexia nervosa and bulimia: A review. *International Journal of Eating Disorders,* 10, pp. 67–79.

Donovan, J.E. and Jessor, R. (1985) Structure of problem behaviour in adolescence and young adulthood. *Journal of Consulting and Clinical Psychology,* 53, pp. 890–904.

Dubos, R. (1965) *Man Adapting.* New Haven, CT: Yale University Press.

Duck, J.M., Terry, D.J. and Hogg, M.A. (1995) The perceived influence of AIDS advertising: third-person effects in the context of positive media content. *Basic and Applied Social Psychology,* 17, pp. 305–325.

Duke, M.P. and Nowicki, S. (1972) A new measure and social–learning model for interpersonal distance. *Journal of Experimental Research in Personality,* 6, pp. 119–132.

Duncan, S.L. (1976) Differential social perception and attribution of intergroup violence: Testing the lower limits of stereotyping of blacks. *Journal of Personality and Social Psychology,* 34, pp. 590–598.

Dunn, J. (1984) *Sisters and Brothers.* Glasgow: Fontana/Open Books.

Dunn, J. and Kendrick, C. (1982a) Siblings and their mothers: developing relationships within the family. In Lamb, M.E. and Sutton-Smith, B. (eds) *Sibling Relationships: Their Nature and Significance Across the Lifespan.* Hillsdale, NJ: Erlbaum.

Dunn, J. and Kendrick, C. (1982b) *Siblings: Love, Envy, and Understanding.* Cambridge,MA: Harvard University Press.

Dunn, L. (1968) Special education for the mildly retarded: is much of it justifiable? *Exceptional Children,* 35, pp. 5–22.

Dunn, L., Wheton, C. and Burley, J. (1997) *The British Picture Vocabulary Scale,* 2nd edition. Slough: NFER-Nelson.

Durrett, M.E., Otaki, M. and Richards, P. (1984) Attachment and mothers' perception of support from the father. *Journal of the International Society for the Study of Behavioural Development,* 7, pp. 167–176.

Dweck, C. (1975) The role of expectations and attributes in the alleviation of learned helplessness. *Journal of Personality and Social Psychology,* 31, pp. 674–685.

Dwyer, D.J. and Ganster, D.C. (1991) The effects of job demands and control on employee attendance and satisfaction. *Journal of Organisational Behaviour,* 12, pp. 595–608.

Eagly, A.H. and Carli, L.L. (1981) Sex of researchers and sex-typed communication as determinants of sex differences in influencability: a meta-analysis of social influence studies. *Psychological Bulletin,* 100, pp. 282–306.

Eastwood, L. (1985) Personality, intelligence and personal space among violent and non-violent delinquents. *Personality and Individual Differences,* 6, pp. 717–723.

Eden, D. (1990) Pygmalion without interpersonal contrast effects: Whole groups gain from raising manager expectations. *Journal of Applied Psychology,* 75, pp. 394–398.

Edney, J.J. (1975) Territoriality and control: a field experiment. *Journal of Personality and Social Psychology,* 31, pp. 1108–1115.

Edney, J.J. (1977) Theories of human crowding: a review. *Environment and Planning: A,* 9, pp. 1211–1232.

Edney, J.J. (1979) The nuts game: a concise commons dilemma analog. *Environmental Psychology and Nonverbal Behaviour,* 3, pp. 252–254.

Edney, J.J. (1981) Paradoxes on the commons: Scarcity and the problem of equality. *Journal of Community Psychology,* 9, pp. 3–34.

Edney, J.J. and Bell, P.A. (1983) The commons dilemma: comparing altruism, the Golden Rule, perfect equality of outcomes, and territoriality. *Social Science Journal,* 20, pp. 23–33.

Edney, J.J. and Harper, C.S. (1978) The commons dilemma: a review of contributions from psychology. *Environmental Management,* 2, pp. 491–507.

Effective Reading Tests (1985) Macmillan/NFER-Nelson.

Elliott, C., Smith, P. and McCulloch, K. (1996) *British Ability Scales II.* Windsor: NFER-Nelson.

Ellis, A. (1962) *Reason and Emotion in Psychotherapy.* New York: Stuart.

Ellis, A. (1977) The basic clinical theory of rational-emotive therapy. In Ellis, A. and Grieger, R. (eds) *Handbook of Rational-Emotive Therapy.* New York: Springer.

Ellis, H.D. (1975) Recognising faces. *British Journal of Psychology,* 66, pp. 409–426.

Ellis, H.D. (1984) Practical aspects of face memory. In Wells, G.L. and Loftus, E.F. (eds) *Eyewitness Testimony: Psychological Perspectives.* Cambridge: Cambridge University Press.

Engel, G.L. (1977) The need for a new medical model: A challenge for biomedicine, *Science,* 196, pp. 129–135.

Engel,, G.L. (1980) The clinical application of the biopsychosocial model, *American Journal of Psychiatry,* 137, pp. 535–44.

Epstein, J.L. (1989) The selection of friends: Changes across the grades and in different school environments. In Berndt, T.J. and Ladd, G.W. (eds) *Peer Relations in Child Development.* New York: Wiley.

Erez, M. and Arad, R. (1986) Participative goal setting: social, motivational and cognitive factors. *Journal of Applied Psychology,* 71, pp. 591–597.

Erez, M. and Zidon, I. (1984) Effect of goal acceptance on the relationship of goal difficulty to performance. *Journal of Applied Psychology,* 69, pp. 69–78.

Erikson, E.H. (1963) *Childhood and Society* 2nd edition. New York: Norton.

Eron, L.D. (1994) Theories of aggression: From drives to cognitions. In Huesman, L.R. (ed.) *Aggressive Behaviour: Current Perspectives.* New York: Plenum.

Evans, B.K. and Fischer, D.G. (1993) The nature of burnout: A study of the three-factor model of burnout in human service and non-human service samples. *Journal of Occupational and Organisational Psychology,* 66, pp. 29–38.

Evans, G.W. (1978) Human spatial behaviour: the arousal model. In Baum, A. and Epstein, Y. (eds) *Human Response to Crowding.* Hillsdale, NJ: Erlbaum.

Evans, G.W. and Jacobs, S.V. (1981) Air pollution and human behaviour. *Journal of Social Issues,* 37, pp. 95–125.

Evans, G.W. and Jacobs, S.V. (1982) Air pollution and human behaviour. In Evans, G.W. (ed.) *Environmental Stress.* New York: Cambridge University Press.

Evans, G.W., Jacobs, S.V., Dooley, D. and Catalano, R. (1987) The interaction of stressful life events and chronic strains on community mental health. *American Journal of Community Psychology,* 15, pp. 23–34.

Evans, G.W., Palsane, M.N, Lepore, S.J. and Martin, J. (1989) Residential density and psychological health: the mediating effects of social support. *Journal of Personality and Social Psychology,* 15, pp. 23–34.

Evans, J. (1986) Physical education and the challenge of youth sport. *The ACHPER National Journal,* December, pp. 13–16.

Ewart, C.K. (1991) Social action theory for a public health psychology. *American Psychologist*, 46, pp. 931–946.

Eysenck, H.J. (1947) In Gross, R.D. (ed.) (1996) *Psychology: The Science of Mind and Behaviour*. London: Hodder and Stoughton.

Eysenck, H.J. (1953) Cited in Gross, R.D. (1999) *Psychology, The Science of Mind and Behaviour*, 3rd edition, p. 753. London: Hodder and Stoughton.

Eysenck, H.J. (1965) *Fact and Fiction Psychology*. Harmondsworth: Penguin.

Eysenck, H.J. (1967) *The Biological Basis of Personality*. Springfield, IL: Thomas.

Eysenck, H.J. (1993a) Creativity and personality: an attempt to bridge the divergent tradition, *Psychological Inquiry*, 4, pp. 238–246.

Eysenck, H.J. (1993b) Creativity and personality: suggestions for a theory, *Psychological Inquiry*, 4, pp. 147–178.

Eysenck, M.W. (1995) *Anxiety: The Cognitive Perspective*. Hove, UK: Lawrence Erlbaum.

Eysenck, H.J. and Eysenck, M.W. (1985) *Personality and Individual Differences: A Natural Science Approach*. New York: Plenum.

Fairburn, C.G. (1984) Cognitive behavioural treatment for bulimia. In Garner, D. and Garfinkle, P. (eds) *Handbook of Psychotherapy for Anorexia and Bulimia*. New York: Guilford Press.

Fairburn, C.G. and Beglin, S.J. (1990) Studies of the epidemiology of bulimia nervosa. *American Journal of Psychiatry*, 147, pp. 401–408.

Farrington, D.P. (1991b) Anti-social personality from childhood to adulthood. *Psychologist*, 4, pp. 389–394.

Farrington, D.P. and West, D.J. (1990) The Cambridge study in delinquent development: a long term follow up of 411 London males. In Kaiser, G. and Kerner, H.J. (eds) *Criminal: Personality, Behaviour, Life History*. Heidelberg: Springer-Verlag.

Fava, M. et al (1989) Neurochemical abnormalities of anorexia nervosa and bulimia nervosa. *American Journal of Psychiatry*, 146, pp. 963–971.

Fazey, J. and Hardy, L. (1988) The inverted-U hypothesis: a catastrophe for sport psychology? *British Association of Sports Sciences Monograph No. 1*. Leeds: The National Coaching Foundation.

Fein et al (1997), cited in K. Brewer (2000) *Psychology and Crime* (p58) Oxford: Heinemann.

Feldman, D.C. (1984) The development and enforcement of group norms. *Academy of Management Review*, 9, pp. 47–53.

Feldman, M.P. (1977) *Criminal behaviour: A Psychological Analysis*. Chichester: Wiley.

Felner, R.B., DuBois, D. and Adan, A. (1991) Community-based intervention and prevention: Conceptual underpinnings and progress towards a science of community intervention and evaluation. In Walker, C.E. (ed.) *Clinical Psychology: Historical and Research Foundations*. New York: Plenum.

Feltz, D.L. (1992) Understanding motivation in sport: A self-efficacy perspective. In Roberts, G.C. (ed.) *Motivation in Sport and Exercise*. Champaign, IL: Human Kinetics.

Feltz, D.L., Landers, D.M. and Raeder, U. (1979) Enhancing self-efficacy in high avoidance motor tasks: A comparison of modeling techniques. *Journal of Sport Psychology*, 5, pp. 263–277.

Festinger, L., Pepitone, A. and Newcomb, T.M. (1952) Some consequences of deindividuation in a group. *Journal of Personality and Social Psychology*, 47, pp. 382–389.

Festinger, L., Shacter, S. and Back, K. (1950) *Social Pressures in Informal Groups: A Study of Human Factors in Housing*. Stanford, California: Stanford University Press.

Fiedler, F.E. (1967) *A Theory of Leadership*. New York: McGraw-Hill.

Fiedler, F.E. and Chemers, M.M. (1984) *Improving leadership Effectiveness: The Leader Match Concept*, revised edition. New York: John Wiley and Sons.

Field, T. (1979) Differential behaviour and cardiac responses of 3–month-old infants to a mirror and a peer. *Infant Behavior and Development*, 2, pp. 179–184.

Fine, S.A. and Getkate, M. (1995) *Benchmark Tasks for Job Analysis: A Guide for Functional Job Analysis (FJA) Scales*. Hillsdale, NJ: Lawrence Erlbaum Associates.

Fischer, C.S. (1976) *The Urban Experience*. New York: Harcourt, Brace Jovanovich.

Fischer, C.S. (1982) *To Dwell Among Friends: Personal Networks in Town and City*. Chicago, IL: University of Chicago Press.

Fishbein, M. and Ajzen, I. (1975) *Belief, Attitude, Intention and Behavior*. Reading, MA: Addison-Wesley.

Fisher, J.D., Bell, P.A. and Baum, A. (1984) *Environmental Psychology*. New York: Holt, Rinehart and Winston.

Fisher, J.D. and Byrne, D. (1975) Too close for comfort: sex differences in response to invasions of personal space. *Journal of Personality and Social Psychology*, 32, pp. 15–21.

Fisher, S. (1993) Identifying video game addiction in children and adolescents. *Addictive Behaviours*, 19, pp. 545–555.

Fiske, S.T. and Neuberg, S.L. (1990) Continuum of impression from category-based to individuating processes: Influences of information and motivation on attention and interpretation. In Berkowitz, L. (ed.) *Advances in Experimental Social Psychology, Vol. 23*. New York: Academic Press.

Fiske, S.T. and Taylor, S.E. (1991) *Social Cognition*, 2nd edition. New York: McGraw-Hill.

Fitzsimmons, P.A., Landers, D. M., Thomas, J.R. and van der Mars, H. (1991) Does self-efficacy predict performance in experienced weightlifters? *Research Quarterly for Exercise and Sport*, 62, pp. 424–431.

Flanagan, C. (1996) *Applying Psychology to Early Child Development*. London: Hodder and Stoughton.

Flay, B.R. (1987) Psychosocial approaches to smoking prevention: A review of findings. *Health Psychology*, 4, pp. 449–488.

Fleishman, J.A. (1988) The effects of decision framing and others' behaviour on cooperation in a social dilemma. *Journal of Conflict Resolution*, 32, pp. 162–180.

Forston, R.F. and Larson, C.U. (1968) The dynamics of space: an experimental study in proxemic behaviour among Latin Americans and North Americans. *Journal of Communication*, 18, pp. 109–116.

Forsyth, D.R. (1990) *Group dynamics*, 2nd edition. Monterey, CA: Brooks/Cole.

Fox, N.A., Kimmerly. N.L. and Schafer, W.D. (1991) Attachment to mother/Attachment to father: A meta-analysis. *Child Development*, 62, pp. 210–225.

Fradkin, B. and Firestone, P. (1986) Premenstrual tension, expectancy and mother–child relations. *Journal of Behavioural Medicine*, 9, pp. 245–259.

Fraiberg, S.H. (1977) *Every Child's Birthright: In Defense of Mothering*. New York: Basic Books.

Frank, E., Winkleby, M.A., Atlman, D.G., Rockhill, B. and Fortmann, S.P. (1991) Predictors of physicians' smoking cessation advice. *Journal of the American Medical Association*, 266, pp. 3139–3144.

Frankl, V.E. (1960) Paradoxical intention: A logotherapeutic technique. *American Journal of Psychotherapy*, 14, pp. 520–535.

Freedman, J.L. (1975) *Crowding and Behaviour*. New York: Viking Press.

Freedman, J.L. (1984) Effect of television violence on aggressiveness. *Psychological Bulletin*, 96, pp. 227–246.

Freeman, J. (1991) *Gifted Children Growing Up*. London: Cassell.

Freides, D. (1974) Human information processing and sensory modality: Cross-modal functions, information, complexity and deficit. *Psychological Bulletin*, 81, pp. 284–310.

French, J.R., Caplan, R.D. and Harrison, R.V. (1982) *The Mechanisms of Job Stress and Strain*. Chichester: Wiley.

Frese, M. and Zapf, D. (1988) Methodological issues in the study of work stress: Objective versus subjective measurement of work stress and the question of longitudinal studies. In Cooper, C.L. and Payne, R. (eds) *Courses, Coping and Consequences of Stress at Work*. New York: Wiley.

Friedman, M. and Rosenman, R.H. (1974) *Type A Behaviour and Your Heart*. New York: Knopf.

Frisch, H. (1977) Sex stereotype in adult-infant play. *Child Development*, 48, pp. 1671–1675.

Fromm-Reichmann, F. (1948) Notes on the development of treatment of schizophrenia by psychoanalytic psychotherapy. *Psychiatry*, 11, pp. 263–273.

Fuller. R.K. and Roth, H.P. (1979) Disulfiram for the treatment of alcoholism: An evaluation in 128 men. *Annals of Internal Medicine*, 90, pp. 901–904.

Furman, W. (1987) Acquaintanceship in middle childhood. *Developmental Psychology*, 23, pp. 565–570.

Furnham, A. (1997) *The Psychology of Behaviour at Work*. Hove: Psychology Press.

Gabrielli, W.F., Jr and Plomin, R. (1985) Drinking behavior in the Colorado adoptee and twin sample. *Journal of Studies on Alcohol*, 46, pp. 24–31.

Gagné, R. (1965) *The Conditions of Learning*. New York: Holt, Reinhart and Winston.

Gagné, R., Brigg, L. and Wagner, W. (1988) *Principles of Instructional Design*. New York: Holt, Rinehart and Winston.

Gahagan, J. (1975) *Interpersonal and Group Hehaviour*. London: Methuen.

Galle, O.R. and Gove, W.R. (1979) Crowding and behaviour in Chicago, 1949–1970. In Aiello, J.R. and Baum, A. (eds) *Residential Crowding and Design*. New York: Plenum.

Gallupe, R.B., Bastianutti, L. and Cooper, W.H. (1991) Unblocking brainstorms. *Journal of Applied Psychology*, 76, pp. 137–142.

Galton, F. (1879) Psychometric experiments. *Brain*, 2, pp. 149–162.

Galton, M., Hargreaves, L., Comber, C., Wall, D. and Pell, A. (1999) *Inside the Primary Classroom: 20 Years On*. London: Routledge.

Galton, M. and Simon, B. (eds) (1980) *Progress and Performance in the Primary Classroom*. London: Routledge and Kegan Paul.

Galton, M., Simon, B. and Croll, P. (1980) *Inside the Primary School*. London: Routledge and Kegan Paul.

Ganster, D.C., Fusilier, M.R. and Mayes, B.T. (1986) Role of social support in the experience of stress at work. *Journal of Applied Psychology*, 71, pp. 102–110.

Gardner, H. (1983) *Frames of Mind: The Theory of Multiple Intelligence*. New York: Basic Books.

Gardner, H. (1990) *Frames of Mind: The Theory of Multiple Intelligence*, 2nd edition. London: Heinemann.

Garfinkel, H. (1964) Studies of the routine grounds of everyday activities. *Social Problems*, 11, pp. 225–250.

Garner, D.M. and Bemis, K.M. (1984) A cognitive-behavioural approach to anorexia nervosa. In Garner, D.M. and Garfinkel, P. (eds) *A Handbook of Psychotherapy for Anorexia Nervosa and Bulimia*. New York: Guilford Press.

Garry, M., Loftus, E.F. and Brown, S.W. (1994) Memory: a river flows through it. *Consciousness and Cognition*, 3, pp. 438–451.

Geberth, V. (1996) *Practical Homicide Investigation*, 3rd edition. New York: CRC Press.

Geiselman and Machlowitz (1987), cited in Brewer, K. *Psychology and Crime* (p. 48). Oxford: Heinemann.

Geller, E.S., Winett, R.A. and Everett, P.B. (1982) *Preserving the Environment: New Strategies for Behaviour Change*. New York: Pergammon.

George, J.M. (1995) Asymmetrical effects of rewards and punishments: The case of social loafing. *Journal of Occupational and Organisational Psychology*, 68, pp. 327–338.

George, T.R., Feltz, D.L. and Chase, M.A. (1992) Effects of model similarity on self-efficacy and muscular endurance: A second look. *Journal of Sport and Exercise Psychology*, 14, pp. 237–248.

Gerbner, G., Gross, L., Morgan, M. and Signorelli, N. (1986) Living with television: The dynamics of the cultivation process. In Bryant, J. and Zillman, D. (eds) *Perspectives on Media Effects*. Hillsdale, NJ: Erlbaum.

Ghorpade, J.V. (1988) *Job Analysis: A Handbook for the Human Resource Director*. Englewood Cliffs, NJ: Prentice-Hall.

Gibson, H.B. (1982) The Home Office attitude to forensic hypnosis: A victory for scientific evidence or medical conservatism? *British Journal of Experimental and Clinical Hypnosis*, 6, pp. 25–27.

Gifford, R. (1982) Projected interpersonal distance and orientation choices: personality, sex and social situation. *Social Psychology Quarterly*, 45, pp. 145–152.

Gifford, R. (1997) *Environmental Psychology*, 2nd edition. Needham Heights, MA: Allyn and Bacon.

Gifford, R. and Price, J. (1979) Personal space in nursery school children. *Canadian Journal of Behavioural Science*, 11, pp. 318–326.

Gifford, R. and Sacilotto, P. (1993) Social isolation and personal space: A field study. *Canadian Journal of Behavioural Science*, 25, pp. 165–174.

Gill, D.E. and Deeter, T.E. (1988) Development of the SQQ. *Research Quarterly for Exercise and Sport*, 59, pp. 191–202.

Gipps, C. and Stobart, G. (1990) *Assessment: A Teacher's Guide to the Issues*. London: Hodder and Stoughton.

Gitlin, MJ (1990) *The Psychotherapist's Guide to Psychopharmacology*. New York: Free Press.

Glaser, R. and Kiecolt-Glaser, J. (eds) (1994) *Handbook of Human Stress and Immunity*. San Diego, CA: Academic Press.

Glass, D.E. and Singer, J.E. (1972) *Urban Stress*. New York: Academic Press.

Gleitman, H. (1994) *Psychology*, 4th edition. London: W. W. Norton and Company.

Goethals, G.R. and Nelson, R.E. (1973) Similarity in the influence process: The benefit–value distinction. *Journal of Personality and Social Psychology*, 25, pp. 117–122.

Goldenhar, L.M. (1991) Understanding, predicting, and influencing recycling behaviour: the future generation. *Dissertation Abstracts International*, 53, p. 1379.

Goldfarb, W. (1943) The effects of early institutional care on adolescent personality. *Journal of Experimental Education*, 12, pp. 106–129.

Goldman, M.S. (1983) Cognitive impairment in chronic alcoholics: Some cause for optimism. *American Psychologist*, 38, pp. 1045–1054.

Goldstein, A.G., Chance, J.E. and Gilbert, B. (1984) Facial stereotypes of good guys and bad guys: a replication and extension. *Bulletin of the Psychonomic Society*, 22, pp. 549–552.

Goldstein, A.P., Glick, B., Irwin, N.J., Pask-McCartney, C. and Rubama, I. (1989) *Reducing Delinquency: Intervention in the Community*. New York: Pergammon.

Goldstein, M.J. (1988) Gender differences in the course of schizophrenia. *American Journal of Psychiatry*, 145, pp. 684–689.

Good, T. and Grouws, D. (1977) Teaching effects: a process-product study in fourth grade mathematics classrooms. *Journal of Teacher Education*, 28, pp. 49–54.

Gordon, J.R. (1983) *A Diagnostic Approach to Organisational Behaviour*. Boston: Allyn and Bacon.

Gorenstein, G.W. and Ellsworth, P.C. (1980) Effects of choosing an incorrect photograph on a later identification by an eyewitness. *Journal of Applied Psychology*, 65, pp. 616–622.

Gottesman, I.I. (1991) *Schizophrenia Genesis*. New York: Freeman.

Gottfried, A.W. and Gottfried, A.E. (1984) Home environment and cognitive development in young children of middle-socioeconomic-status families. In Gottfried, A.W. (ed.) *Home*

Environment and Early Cognitive Development. Orlando: Academic Press.

Gottlieb, M., Zinkus, P. and Thompson, A. (1980) Chronic middle ear disease and auditory perceptual deficits. *Clincial Paediatrics*, 18, pp. 725–732.

Gottman, J.M. (1983) How children become friends. *Monographs of the Society for Research in Child Development, 48* (3, Serial No. 201).

Gough, H.G. (1987) *California Psychological Inventory*. Palo Alto, CA: Consulting Psychologists Press.

Gould, D. and Weiss, M. (1981) Effect of model similarity and model self-talk on self-efficacy in muscular endurance. *Journal of Sport Psychology*, 3, pp. 17–29.

Gouldner, A.W. (1960) The norm of reciprocity: A preliminary statement. *American Sociological Review*, 25, pp. 161–178.

Gray, J. (1987) The mind–brain identity as a scientific hypothesis: A second look. In Blakemore, C.and Greenfield, S. (eds) *Mindwaves*. Oxford: Blackwell.

Gray, J.A. (1991) On the morality of speciesism. *The Psychologist*, 4, pp196–198.

Green, S. (1994) *Principles of Biopsychology*. Hove: Lawrence Erlbaum.

Green, S. (1996) Ecstasy. *Psychology Review*, 3, p. 34.

Greene, J. (1975) *Thinking and Language*. London: Methuen.

Greenhaus, J.H. and Beutell, N.J. (1985) Sources of conflict between work and family roles. *Academy of Management Review*, 10, pp. 76–88.

Griffit, W. (1970) Environmental effects on interpersonal affective behaviour: ambient effective temperature and attraction. *Journal of Personality and Social Psychology*, 15, pp. 240–244.

Griffiths, M. (1997) Video games and aggression. *Psychologist*, 10, pp. 397–401.

Griffiths, M.D. and Dancaster, I. (1995) The effect of Type A personality on physiological arousal while playing computer games. *Addictive Behaviours*, 20, pp. 543–548.

Grint, K. (1991) *The Sociology of Work: An Introduction*. Cambridge: Polity press.

Gross, R.D. (1992) *Psychology, The Science of Mind and Behaviour*. London: Hodder and Stoughton.

Gross, R. (1995) *Themes, Issues and Debates in Psychology.* London: Hodder and Stoughton.

Gross, R.D. (1996) *Psychology: The Science of Mind and Behaviour*, 3rd edition. London: Hodder and Stoughton.

Gross, R. (1999) *Key Studies in Psychology*, 3rd edition. London: Hodder and Stoughton.

Grossman, K., Grossman, K.E., Spangler, S., Suess, G. and Unzner, L. (1985) Maternal sensitivity and newborn orientation responses as related to quality of attachment in Northern Germany. *Monographs of the Society for Research in Child Development*, 50, (102 Serial No. 209).

Grossman, K.E. and Grossman, K. (1990) The wider concept of attachment in cross-cultural research. *Human Development*, 33, pp. 31–47.

Grove, W.M., Lebow, B.S., Clementz, B.A., Cerri, A., Medus, C. and Iacono, W.G. (1991) Familial prevalence and coaggregation of schizotypy indicators: A multitrait family study. *Journal of Abnormal Psychology*, 100, pp. 115–121.

Guardo, C.J. and Meisels, M. (1971) Factor structure of children's personal space schemata. *Child Development*, 42, pp. 1307–1312.

Gudjonsson, G.H. and Haward, L.R.C. (1998) *Forensic Psychology. A Guide to Practice*. London and New York: Routledge.

Guilford, J.P. (1959) *Personality.* New York: McGraw-Hill.

Halford, W.K. and Hayes, R. (1991) Psychological rehabilitation of chronic schizophrenic patients: recent findings on social skills training and family psychoeducation. *Clinical Psychology Review*, 11, pp. 23–44.

Hall, E.T. (1966) *The Hidden Dimension*. New York: Doubleday.

Halpern, D. (1995) *Mental Health and the Built Environment*. London: Taylor and Francis.

Hamburg, D.A. and Adams, J.E. (1967) A perspective on coping behaviour: Seeking and utilising information in major transitions. *Archives of General Psychiatry*, 19, pp. 277–284.

Handler, L. (1988) Monkey see, monkey do; The prescription-writing controversy. *The Clinical Psychologist*, 41, pp. 44–49.

Hanewicz, M.B. (1978) Police personality: A Jungian perspective. *Journal of Crime and Delinquency*, 24, pp. 152–172.

Hansen, W.B., Graham, J.W., Sobel, J.L., Shelton, D.R., Flay, B.R. and Johnson, C.A. (1987) The consistency of peer and parent influences on tobacco, alcohol, and marijuana use among young adolescents. *Journal of Behavioural Medicine*, 10, pp. 559–579.

Hardin, G. (1986a) Denial and the gift of history. In Hardin, G. (ed) *Population, Evaluation and Birth Control*. San Francisco: W.H. Freeman.

Hardin, G. (1986b) The tragedy of the commons. *Science*, 162, pp. 1243–1248.

Hargreaves, D.H. (1980) Classrooms, schools and juvenile deliquency. *Educational Analysis*, 2, pp. 75–87.

Harkins and Green (1975) cited in R.D. Gross (1996) *Psychology The Science of Mind and Behaviour* (p. 755). London: Hodder and Stoughton.

Harlow, H.F. and Harlow, M.K. (1969) Effects of various mother–infant relationships on rhesus monkey behaviours. In Foss B.M. (ed.) *Determinants of Infant Behaviour, Volume 4*. London: Methuen.

Harries, K.D. and Stadler, S.J. (1983) Determinism revisited: assault and heat stress in Dallas, 1980. *Environment and Behaviour*, 15, pp. 235–256.

Harris, C.S. (1973) The effects of different types of acoustic stimulation on performance. In Ward, W.D. (ed.) *Proceedings of the International Congress on Noise as a Public Health Problem*. Washington, DC: US Environmental Protection Agency.

Harris, D.M. and Guten, S. (1979) Health-protective behaviour: An exploratory study. *Journal of Health and Social Behaviour, 29*, pp. 17–29.

Harris, R.A., Brodie, M.S. and Dunwiddie, T.V. (1992) Possible substrates of ethanol reinforcement: GABA and dopamine. *Annals of the New York Academy of Sciences*, 654, pp. 61–69.

Harrop, A. and Williams, T. (1992) Rewards and punishments in the primary school: pupils' perceptions and teachers' usage. *Educational Psychology in Practice*, 7, pp. 211–215.

Harrower, J. (1998) *Applying Psychology to Crime*. Hodder and Stoughton.

Harter, S. (1978) Effectance motivation reconsidered. *Human Development*, 21, pp. 34–64.

Hartup, W.W. (1983) Peer relations. In Mussen, P.H. (ed.) *Handbook of Child Psychology*, 4th edition. New York: Wiley.

Hartup, W.W. (1992) Friendships and their developmental significance. In McGurk, H. (ed.) *Childhood Social Development: Contemporary Perspectives*. London: Erlbaum.

Harvey, R.J. and Lozada-Larsen, S.R. (1988) Influence of amount of job descriptive information on job analysis rating accuracy. *Journal of Applied Psychology*, 73, pp. 457–461.

Hathaway, S.R. and McKinley, J.C. (1970) *MMPI: Minnesota Multiphasic Personality Inventory*. Minneapolis: University of Minnesota Press.

Havinghurst, R.J. (1964) Flexibility and the social roles of the retired. *American Journal of Sociology*, 59, pp. 309–311.

Hay, D.E., Nash, A. and Pedersen, J. (1983) Interaction between six-month-old peers. *Child Development*, 54, pp. 557–562.

Hayduk, L.A. (1983) Personal space: where we now stand. *Psychological Bulletin*, 94, pp. 293–335.

Hayes, N.J. (1997) Qualitative research and research in psychology. In Hayes, N.J. (ed.) *Doing Qualitative Analysis in Psychology*. Hove: Psychology Press.

Hayes, N. (2000) *Foundations of Psychology*, 3rd edition. London: Thomson Learning.

Healy, W. and Bronner, A.F. (1936) *New Light on Delinquency and its Treatment*. New Haven, Conn: Yale University Press.

Hebb, D.O. (1949) *The Organisation of Behaviour*. New York: Wiley.

Heim, A. (1970) *Intelligence and Personality – Their Assessment and Relationship*. Harmondsworth: Penguin.

Heim, A. (1975) *Psychological Testing*. London: Oxford University Press.

Heim, A.W. (1970) *The Appraisal of Intelligence*. Slough: NFER.

Heimberg, R.G. (1989) Social phobia: No longer neglected. *Clinical Psychology Review*, 9, pp. 1–3.

Helzer, J.E., Canino, G.J., Yeh, E.-K., Bland, R.C., Lee, C.K., Hwu, H.-G. and Newman, S. (1990) Alcoholism – North America and Asia. *Archives of General Psychiatry*, 47, pp. 313–319.

Hemery, D. (1986) *Sporting Excellence*. Champaign, IL: Human Kinetics Publishers.

Henderson, D. and Gillespie, R.D. (1950) *A Text-book of Psychiatry for Students and Practitioners*, 7th edition. Oxford: Oxford University Press.

Hernandez, J.T. and Smith, F.J. (1990) Inconsistencies and misperceptions putting college students at risk of HIV infection. *Journal of Adolescent Health Care*, 11, pp. 295–297.

Herzberg, F. (1966) *Work and the Nature of Man*. Cleveland, OH: World.

Herzberg, F., Mausner, B. and Snyderman, B. (1959) *The Motivation to Work*. London: Granada.

Hetherington, E.M., Cox, M. and Cox, R. (1979) Play and social interaction in children following divorce. *Journal of Social Issues*, 35, pp. 26–49.

Hetherington, M., Law, T. and O'Connor, T. (1993) Divorce: Challenges, changes and new chances. In Walsh, F. (ed.) *Normal Family Process*, 2nd edition. New York: Guilford.

Hewstone, M., Stroebe, W. and Stephenson, G. (1996) *Introduction to Social Psychology*, 2nd edition. Oxford: Blackwell.

Heymann, T. (1989) *On an average day*. New York: Fawcett Columbine.

Hine, D.W. and Gifford, R. (1993) *Individual Restraint and Group Efficiency in The Commons: The Effects of Uncertainty in Pool Size and Regeneration Rate*. Manuscript submitted for publication.

Hines, J.M., Hungerford, H.R. and Tomera, A.N. (1986) Analysis and synthesis of research on responsible environmental behaviour: A meta-analysis. *Journal of Environmental Education*, 18, pp. 1–8.

Hoek, H.W. (1991) The incidence and prevalence of anorexia nervosa and bulimia nervosa in primary care. *Psychological Medicine*, 21, pp. 455–460.

Hoekstra, M. and Wilke, H. (1972) Wage recommendations in management groups: a cross-cultural study. *Nederlands, Tijdschrift voor de Psychlogie*, 27, pp. 266–272.

Hoffman, C., Mischel, W. and Mazze, K. (1981) The role of purpose in the organisation of information about behaviour: Trait-based versus goal-based categories in person cognition. *Journal of Personality and Social Psychology*, 40, pp. 211–225.

Hoffman, L.W. (1974) Effects of maternal employment on the child: A review of the research. *Developmental Psychology*, 10, pp. 204–208.

Hoffman, M.L. (1981) Is altruism part of human nature? *Journal of Personality and Social Psychology*, 40, pp. 121–137.

Hoffman, M.L. (1984) Empathy, social cognition and moral action. In Kurtines, W. and Gerwitz, J. (eds) *Moral Behaviour and Development: Advances in Theory, Research and Applications*. New York: John Wiley.

Hogarty, G.E. (1984) Depot neuroleptics: The relevance of psychosocial factors. *Journal of Clinical Psychiatry*, 45, pp. 36–42.

Hogg, M.A. and Vaughan, G.M. (1998) *Social Psychology*, 2nd edition. Sydney: Prentice Hall.

Holland, A.J., Sicotte, N. and Treasure, J. (1988) Anorexia nervosa – evidence for a genetic basis. *Journal of Psychosomatic Research*, 32, pp. 561–572.

Hollin, C.R. (1989) *Psychology and Crime. An Introduction to Criminological Psychology*. Routledge.

Hollin, C.R. (1992) *Criminal Behaviour*. London: Falmer Press.

Hollis, J.F., Carmody, T.P., Connor, S.L., Fey, S.G. and Matarazzo, J.D. (1986) The nutrition attitude survey: Associations with dietary habits, psychological and physical well-being, and coronary risk factors. *Health Psychology*, 5, pp. 359–374.

Holmes, D.S. (1994) *Abnormal Psychology*, 2nd edition. New York: Harper Collins.

Holzman, P.S., Kringlen, E., Matthysse, S., Flanagan, S.D., Lipton, R.B., Cramer, G., Levin, S., Lange, K. and Levy, D.L. (1988) A single dominant gene can account for eye tracking dysfunctions and schizophrenia in offspring of discordant twins. *Archives of General Psychiatry*, 45, pp. 641–647.

Honig, A.S. and Park, K.J. (1993) Effects of day care on preschool sex-rate development. *American Journal of Orthopsychiatry*, 36, pp. 481–486.

Hood, R. and Sparks, R. (1970) *Key Issues in Criminology*. London: Weidenfeld and Nicholson.

Hopper, J.R. and Neilson, J.M. (1991) Recycling as altruistic behaviour: normative and behavioural strategies to expand participation in a community recycling programme. *Environment and Behaviour*, 23, pp. 195–220.

Hopper, M.S. and Garner, D.M. (1986) Applications of the Eating Disorders Inventory to a sample of black, white and mixed race schoolgirls in Zimbabwe. *The International Journal of Eating Disorders*, 5, pp. 161–168.

Horn, T. and Glenn, S. (1988) The relationship between athletes' psychological characteristics and their preference for particular coaching behaviours. Paper presented at the meeting of the North American Society for the Psychology of Sport and Physical Activity, Knoxville, Tennesee, USA.

Horowitz, M.J. (1968) Spatial behaviour and psychopathology. *Journal of Nervous and Mental Diseases*, 146, pp. 24–35.

Horowitz, M.J., Duff, D.F. and Stratton, L.O. (1964) Body-buffer zone. *Archives of General Psychiatry*, 11, pp. 651–656.

Hough, M. and Mayhew, P. (1983) *The British Crime Survey: First Report*. London: HMSO.

Hough, M. and Mayhew, P. (1985) *Taking Account of Crime: Key Findings from the Second British Crime Survey*. London: HMSO.

House, R.J. (1971) A path-goal theory of leadership effectiveness. *Administrative Science Quarterly*, 16, pp. 321–338.

House, R.J. (1996) Path-goal theory of leadership: Lessons, legacy and a reformulated theory. *Leadership Quarterly*, 7, pp. 323–352.

Hovland, C.I. and Weiss, W. (1952) The influence of source credibility in communication effectiveness. *Public Opinion Quarterly*, 15, pp. 635–650.

Hovland, C.I., Janis, I.L. and Kelly, H.H. (1953) *Communication and Persuasion*. New Haven, CT: Yale University Press.

Hovland, C.I., Lumsdaine, A.A. and Sheffield, F.D. (1949) *Experiments in Mass Communication*. Princeton, NJ: Princeton University Press.

Howard, J.L. and Ferris, G.R. (1996) The employment interview context: Social and situational influences on interviewer decisions. *Journal of Applied Social Psychology*, 26, pp. 112–136.

Howe, M. (1988) Intelligence as an explanation. *British Journal of Psychology*, 79, pp. 349–360.

Howenstine, E. (1993) Market segmentation for recycling. *Environment and Behaviour*, 25, pp. 86–102.

Howes, C. and Olenick, M. (1986) Family and childcare influences on toddlers' compliance. *Child Development*, 57, pp. 202–216.

Howes, C. (1983) Patterns of friendship. *Child Development*, 54, pp. 1041–1053.

Hudson, L. (1966) *Contrary Imaginations: A Psychological Study of the English Schoolboy*. London: Methuen.

Huesmann, L.R. (1988) An information processing model for the development of aggression. *Aggressive Behaviour*, 14, pp. 13–24.

Huesmann, L.R. and Eron, L.D. (1986) *Television and the Aggressive Child: A Cross-national comparison*. Hillsdale, NJ: Erlbaum.

Huesmann. L.R., Eron, L.D., Lefkowitz, M.M. and Walder, L.O. (1984) Stability of aggression over time and generations. *Developmental Psychology*, 20, pp. 1120–1134.

Huesmann, L.R. and Miller, L.S. (1994) Long-term effects of repeated exposure to media violence in childhood. In Huesmann L.R. (ed.) *Aggressive Behaviour: Current Perspectives*. New York: Plenum.

Huffcutt, A.I., Roth, P.L. and McDaniel, M.A. (1996) A meta-analytic investigation of cognitive ability in employment interview evaluations: Moderating characteristics and implications for incremental validity. *Journal of Applied Psychology*, 81, pp. 459–473.

Hughes, J.R. (1986) Genetics of smoking: A brief review. *Behaviour Therapy*, 17, pp. 335–345.

Hull, C.L. (1943) *Principles of Behaviour*. New York: Appleton-Century-Crofts.

Humphrey, P.P.A., Hartig, P. and Hoyer, D. (1993) A proposed new nomenclature for 5–HT receptors. *Trends in Pharmacological Sciences*, 14, pp. 233–236.

Hunter, J.E. and Hunter, R.F. (1984) Validity and utility of alternative predictors of job performance. *Journal of Vocational Behaviour*, 29, pp. 340–362.

Hymel, S. (1986) Interpretations of peer behaviour: Affective bias in childhood and adolescence. *Child Development*, 57, pp. 431–445.

Iacono, W.G. and Beiser, M. (1992) Where are the women in first-episode studies of schizophrenia? *Schizophrenia Bulletin*, 18, pp. 471–480.

Isabella, R.S. (1993) Origins of attachment: Maternal interactive behaviour across the first year. *Child Development*, 64, pp. 605–621.

Jaccard, J. and Turrisi, R. (1987) Cognitive processes and individual differences in judgements relevant to drink driving. *Journal of Personality and Social Psychology*, 53, pp. 135–145.

Jackson, D.W., Jarrett, H., Bailey, D., Kausek, J., Swanson, J. and Powell, J.W. (1978) Injury prediction in the young athlete: A preliminary report. *American Journal of Sports Medicine*, 6, pp. 6–14.

Jackson, S.E. (1983) Participation in decision making as a strategy for reducing job-related strain. *Journal of Applied Psychology*, 68, pp. 3–19.

Jahoda, G. (1982) *Psychology and Anthropology: A Psychological Perspective*. London: Academic Press.

Jamison, D., Suppes, P. and Wells, S. (1974) The effectiveness of alternative instructional media: a survey. *Review of Educational Research*, 44, pp. 1–68.

Janis, I.L. (1954) Personality correlates of susceptibility to persuasion. *Journal of Personality*, 22, pp. 504–518.

Janis, I.L. (1967) Effects of fear arousal on attitude change: Recent developments in theory and experimental research. In Berkowitz, L. (ed.) *Advances in Experimental Social Psychology*, Vol. 3. New York: Academic Press.

Janis, I.L. (1972) *Victims of Groupthink*. Boston: Houghton Mifflin.

Janis, I.L. (1982) *Groupthink: A Study of Foreign Policy Decisions and Fiascos*, 2nd edition. Boston: Houghton Mifflin.

Janis, I.L. (1984) The patient as decision maker. In Gentry, W.D. (ed.) *Handbook of Behavioural Medicine*. New York: Guilford.

Jeffrey, C.R. (1965) Criminal behaviour and learning theory. *Journal of Criminal Law, Criminology and Police Science*, 56, pp. 294–300.

Jensen, A. (1973) *Educability and Group Differences*. London: Methuen.

Jerdee, T.H. and Rosen, B. (1974) The effects of opportunity to communicate and visibility of individual decisions on behaviour in the common interest. *Journal of Applied Psychology*, 59, pp. 712–716.

Jermier, J.M., Gaines, J. and McIntosh, N.J. (1989) Reaction to physically dangerous work: a conceptual and empirical analysis. *Journal of Organisational Behaviour*, 10, pp. 15–33.

Johnson, D. and Johnson, R. (1987) *Learning Together and Alone*. Englewood Cliffs, NJ: Prentice-Hall.

Johnson, R.D. and Downing, L.L. (1979) Deindividuation and valence of cues: effects on prosocial and antisocial behaviour. *Journal of Personality and Social Psychology*, 37, pp. 1532–1538.

Johnston, L.D., O'Malley, P.M. and Bachman, J.G. (1991) *Drug Use Among American High School Seniors, College Students and Young Adults, 1975–1990. Volume 2. College Students and Young Adults*. (DHHS Publication No. ADM91–1835). Rockville, MD: National Institute on Drug Abuse.

Jones R.A. (1987) Cigarettes, respiratory rate, and the relaxation paradox. *International Journal of the Addictions*, 22, pp. 803–809.

Jones, C. and Aronson, E. (1973) Attribution of fault to a rape victim as a function of respectability of the victim. *Journal of Personality and Social Psychology*, 26, pp. 415–419.

Jones, E.E. (1985) Major developments in social psychology during the past four decades. In Lindzey, G. and Aronson, E. (eds) *The Handbook of Social Psychology*, 3rd edition. New York: Random.

Jones, J.W. and Bogat, A.G. (1978) Air pollution and human aggression. *Psychological Reports*, 43, pp. 721–722.

Joyce, C.R.B. and Hudson, L. (1968) Student style and teaching style: an experimental study. *British Journal of Medical Education*, 2, pp. 28–32.

Jung, C.G. (1946) *Psychological Types or the Psychology of Individuation*. New York: Harcourt Brace (originally published 1932).

Jussim, L., Eccles, J. and Madon, S. (1996) Social perception, social stereotypes and teacher expectations: Accuracy and the quest for the powerful self-fulfilling prophecy. *Advances in Experimental Social Psychology*, 28, pp. 281–388.

Kabanoff, B. (1981) A critique of Leader Match and its implications for leadership research. *Personnel Psychology*, 34, pp. 749–764.

Kagan, J. (1971) *Learning Styles E281, Units 1 and 2*, Open University materials, cited in Childs, D. (1999) *Psychology and the Teacher*, 6th edition (p.327). Cassell Education.

Kagan, J., Kearsley, R.B. and Zelazo, P.R. (1978) *Infancy: Its Place in Human Development*. Cambridge, MA: Harvard University Press.

Kagan, J., Reznick, J.S. and Snidman, N. (1988) Biological bases of childhood shyness. *Science*, 240, pp. 167–171.

Kagan, J., Reznick, J.S., Snidman, N., Gibbons, J. and Johnson, M. (1988) Childhood derivatives of inhibition and lack of inhibition to the unfamiliar. *Child Development*, 59, pp. 1580–1589.

Kagehiro, D.K. (1990) Psycholegal research on the Fourth Amendment. *Psychological Science*, 1, pp. 187–193.

Kahle, L.R. and Beatty, S.E. (1987) cognitive consequences of legislating postpurchase behaviour: growing up with the bottle bill. *Journal of Applied Social Psychology*, 17, pp. 828–843.

Kalven, H. and Zeisel, H. (1966) *The American Jury*. Boston, MA: Little, Brown.

Kane, J., Honigfeld, G., Singer, J., Meltzer, H. and the Clozaril Collaborative Study Group (1988) Clozapine for the treatment-resistant schizophrenic: A double-bind comparison with chlorpromazine. *Archives of General Psychiatry*, 45, pp. 789–796.

Kao, J.J. (1979) *Three Millennia of Chinese Psychiatry*. Brooklyn: Institute for Advanced Research in Asian Science and Medicine.

Kaplan, M. (1983) A woman's view of DSM-III. *American Psychologist*, 38, pp. 786–792.

Kaplan, M.F. and Schersching, C. (1981) Juror deliberation: an information integration analysis. In Sales, B.D. (ed.) *The Trial Process: Perspectives in Law and Psychology*, Volume 2. London: Plenum.

Kaplan, R.L. (1990) Behaviour as the central outcome in health care, *American Psychologist*, 45, pp. 1211–20.

Karasek, R.A. (1979) Job demands, job decision latitude and mental strain: Implications for job redesign. *Administrative Science Quarterly*, 24, pp. 285–308.

Karau, S.J. and Hart, J.W. (1998) Group cohesiveness and social loafing: Effects of a social interaction manipulation on individual motivation within groups. *Group Dynamics: Theory, Research and Practice*, 2, pp. 185–191.

Karno, M., Hough, R.L., Burnam, M.A., Escobar, J.I., Timbers, D.M., Santana, F. and Boyd, J.H. (1987) Lifetime prevalence of specific psychiatric disorders among Mexican Americans and non-Hispanic whites in Los Angeles. *Archives of General Psychiatry*, 44, pp. 695–701.

Kass, F., Spitzer, R.L. and Williams, J.B. (1983) An empirical study of the issue of sex bias in the diagnostic criteria of DSM-III Axis II Personality Disorders. *American Psychologist*, 38, pp. 799–801.

Kassin and Kiechel (1996) cited in Feldman, R.S. (1998) *Social Psychology*, 4th edition. Englewood Cliffs, NJ: Prentice Hall.

Kassin, S.M. and Wrightsman, L.S. (1983) The construction and validation of a juror bias scale. *Journal of Research in Personality*, 17, pp. 423–442.

Katsev, R., Blake, G. and Messer, B. (1993) Determinants of participation in multi-family recycling programmes. *Journal of Applied Social Psychology*, 23, pp. 374–385.

Katz, P. (1937) *Animals and Men*. New York: Longmans, Green.

Katzell, R.A. and Austin, J.T. (1992) From then to now: the development of industrial-organisational psychology in the United States. *Journal of Applied Psychology*, 77, pp. 803–835.

Katzev, R. and Mishima, H.R. (1992) The use of posted feedback to promote recycling. *Psychological Reports*, 71, pp. 259–264.

Kavanagh, D. and Hausfeld, S. (1986) Physical performance and self-efficacy under happy and sad moods. *Journal of Sports Psychology*, 8, pp. 112–123.

Kelley, H.H. and Grzelak, J. (1972) Conflict between individuals and common interest in an n-person relationship. *Journal of Personality and Social Psychology*, 21, pp. 190–197.

Kellett, J. (1989) Health and housing. *Journal of Psychometric Research*, 33, pp. 255–268.

Kelvin, P. and Jarrett, J. (1985) *The Social Psychological Effects of Unemployment*. Cambridge: Cambridge University Press.

Kendall, P.C. and Hammen, C. (1995) *Abnormal Psychology*. Boston: Houghton Mifflin Company.

Kendler, K.S., Neale, M.C., Kessler, R.C., Heath, A.C. and Eaves, L.J. (1992a) Generalised anxiety disorder in women: A population-based twin study. *Archives of General Psychiatry*, 49, pp. 267–272.

Kendler, K.S., Neale, M.C., Kessler, R.C., Heath, A.C. and Eaves, L.J. (1992b) The genetic epidemiology of phobias in women: The interrelationships of agoraphobia, social phobia, situational phobia, and simple phobia. *Archives of General Psychiatry*, 49, pp. 273–281.

Kennedy, J.K. (1982) Middle LPC leaders and the contingency model of leadership effectiveness. *Organisational Behaviour and Human Performance*, 30, pp. 1–14.

Kennedy, M. (1978) Findings from follow through planned variation study. *Educational Researcher*, 7, pp. 3–11.

Kenrick, D.T. (1994) Evolutionary social psychology: from sexual selection to social cognition. *Advances in Experimental Social Psychology*, 26, pp. 75–121.

Kerr, N.L. (1982) The jury trial. In Konecni, V.J. and Ebbeson, E.B. (eds) *The Criminal Justice System: A Social-Psychological Analysis*. San Fransisco: Freeman.

Kerr, N.L. (1983) Motivation loss in small group: A social dilemma analysis. *Journal of Personality and Social Psychology*, 45, pp. 819–828.

Kerr, N.L. and Bruun, S.E. (1983) Dependability of member effort and group motivation loss: Free rider effects. *Journal of Personality and Social Psychology*, 44, pp. 78–94.

Kerr, N.L., Harmon, D.L. and Graves, J.K. (1982) Independence of multiple verdicts by jurors and juries. *Journal of Applied Psychology*, 12, pp. 12–29.

Kessler, R.C., McGonagle, K.A., Zhao, S., Nelson, C.B., Hughes, M., Eshleman, S., Wittchen, H. and Kendler, K.S. (1994) Lifetime and 12-month prevalence of DSM-III-R psychiatric disorders in the United States. *Archives of General Psychiatry*, 51, pp. 8–19.

Kiesler, C.A. (1977) The training of psychiatrists and psychologists [Editorial]. *American Psychologist*, 32, pp. 107–108.

Kiesler, C.A. and Kiesler, S.B. (1969) *Conformity*. Reading, MA: Addison-Wesley.

Kimble, G. (1961) *Hilgard and Maquis' Conditioning and Learning*, second edition. New York: Appleton.

Kinzel, A.S. (1970) Body buffer zone in violent prisoners. *American Journal of Psychiatry*, 127, pp. 59–64.

Kirchner, G. (1992) *Physical Education for Elementary School Children*, 8th edition. Dubuque, IA: Wm C. Brown.

Kirmeyer, S.L. and Dougherty, T.W. (1988) Work load, tension and coping: Moderating effects of supervisor support. *Personnel Psychology*, 41, pp. 125–139.

Kirscht, J.P. (1983) Preventive health behaviour: A review of research and issues. *Health Psychology*, 2, pp. 277–301.

Kirton, M.J. (1976) Adaptors and innovators: a description and measure. *Journal of Applied Psychology*, 61, pp. 622–629.

Klahr, D. (1982) Nonmonotone assessment of monotone development: an information processing analysis. In Straus, S. (ed.) *U-Shaped Behavioural Growth*. New York: Academic Press.

Klahr, D. and Wallace, J.G. (1976) *Cognitive Development: An Information Processing View*. New Jersey: Lawrence Erlbaum.

Klaus, M.H. and Kennell, J.H. (1976) *Maternal-Infant Bonding: The Impact of Early Separation or Loss on Family Development*. St. Louis, MO: Mosby.

Kline, P. (1981) Personality. In Fontana, D. (ed.) *Psychology for Teachers*. British Psychological Society/Macmillan Press.

Kline, P. (1983) *Personality – Measurement and Theory*. London: Hutchinson.

Klitzman, S. and Stellman, J.M. (1989) The impact of the physical environment on the psychological well-being of office workers. *Social Science and Medicine*, 29, pp. 733–742.

Knouse, S.B. (1994) Impressions of the resume: The effects of applicant education, experience, and impression management. *Journal of Business and Psychology*, 9, pp. 33–45.

Knowles, E.S. (1983) Social physics and the effects of others: tests of the effects of audience size and distance on social judgements and behaviour. *Journal of Personality and Social Psychology*, 45, pp. 1263–1279.

Knowles, E.S. and Brickner, M.A. (1981) Social cohesion effects on spatial cohesion. *Personality and Social Psychology Bulletin*, 7, pp. 309–313.

Kocsis, R., Lincoln, R. and Wilson, P. (1998) Validity, utility and ethics of profiling for serial violent and sexual offenders. *Psychiatry, Psychology and Law*, 6, pp. 1–11.

Kohn, I., Franck, K. and Fox, A.S. (1975) *Defensible Space Modification in Row-house Communities*. National Science Foundation Report.

Koller, K. and Gosden, S. (1984) On living alone, social isolation, and psychological disorder. *Australian and New Zealand Journal of Sociology*, 20, pp. 81–92.

Kolt, G.S. and Kirkby, R.J. (1991) Injury, anxiety, and mood in competitive gymnasts. Paper presented at the First Asian South Pacific Association of Sport Psychology Congress, Melbourne, Australia.

Koluchova, J. (1972) Severe deprivation in twins: A case study. *Journal of Child Psychology and Psychiatry*, 13, pp. 107–114.

Koluchova, J. (1976) A report on the further development of twins after severe and prolonged deprivation. In Clarke, A.M. and Clarke, A.D.B. (eds) *Early Experience: Myth and Evidence*. London: Open Books.

Komorita, S.S. and Barth, J.M. (1985) Components of reward in social dilemmas. *Journal of Personality and Social Psychology*, 48, pp. 364–373.

Kontos, S., Hsu, H. and Dunn, L. (1994) Children's cognitive and social competence in child care centers and family day-care homes. Special Issue: Diversity and development of Asian-Americans. *Journal of Applied Developmental Psychology*, 15, pp. 387–411.

Kopnecni, V.J., Libuser, L., Morton, H. and Ebbesen, E.B. (1975) Effects of a violation of personal space on escape and helping responses. *Journal of Experimental Social Psychology*, 11, pp. 288–299.

Korunka, C.,Weiss, A. and Karetta, B. (1993) Effects of new technologies with special regard for the implementation process per se. *Journal of Organisational Behaviour*, 14, pp. 331–348.

Kotelchuck, M. (1976) The infant's relationship to the father: Experimental evidence. In Lamb, M.E. (ed.) *The Role of the Father in Child Development*. New York: Wiley.

Kraepelin, E. (1883) Lehrbuch der psychiatrie. *Clinical Psychiatry*. Translated from the 7th German edition by A.R. Diefendorf. Delmar, NY: Scholars' Facsimiles and Reprints.

Krakowski, A.J. (1982) Stress and the practice of medicine II – stressors, stresses and strains. *Psychotherapeutics and Psychosomatics*, 38, pp. 11–23.

Kroll, W. and Crenshaw, W. (1970) Multivariate personality profile analysis of four athletic groups. In Kenyon, G.S. (ed.) *Contemporary Psychology of Sport: Second International Congress of Sport Psychology*. Chicago: The Athletic Institute.

Krupat, E. and Kubzansky, P.E. (1987) Designing to deter crime. *Psychology Today*, 21, pp. 58–61.

Kuethe, J.L. (1962) Social schemas and the reconstruction of social object displays from memory. *Journal of Abnormal and Social Psychology*, 65, pp. 71–74.

Kuhn, T. (1962) *The Nature of Scientific Revolutions*. Chicago: University of Chicago Press.

Kulik, J. and Kulik, C. (1992) Meta-analytic findings on grouping programs. *Gifted Child Quarterly*, 36, pp. 73–77.

Kumchy, C. and Sayer, L.A. (1980) Locus of control and delinquent adolescent populations. *Psychological Reports*, 46, pp. 1307–1310.

Labov, W. (1970) The logic of non-standard English. In Cashdan, A. and Grugeon, E. (eds) *Language in Education*. London: Routledge and Kegan-Paul.

Labov W. (1972) The logic of non-standard English. In Giglioli, P.P. (ed.) *Language and Social Context*. Harmondsworth: Penguin.

Laing, R.D. (1961) *The Self and Others*. London: Tavistock Publications.

Laing, R.D. (1967) *The Politics of Experience*. New York: Ballantine.

Lamb, M.E. (1976) Interactions between eight-month old children and their fathers and mothers. In Lamb, M.E. (ed.) *The Role of the Father in Child Development*. New York: Wiley.

Lamb, M.E., Pleck, J.H., Charnov, E.L. and Levine, J.A. (1987) A biosocial perspective on paternal behaviour and involvement. In Lancaster, J.B., Altman, J., Rossi, A. and Sherrod, L.R. (eds) *Parenting Across the Lifespan: Biosocial Perspectives*. Hawthorne, NY: Aldine de Gruyter.

Lambert, M.J., Shapiro, D.A. and Bergin, A.E. (1986) The effectiveness of psychotherapy. In Garfield, S.L. and Bergin, A.E. (eds) *Handbook of Psychotherapy and Behavior Change*, 3rd edition. New York: Wiley.

Lamm, H. (1988) Review of our research on group polarisation: Eleven experiments on the effects of group discussion on risk acceptance, probability estimation, and negotiation positions. *Psychological Reports*, 62, pp. 807–813.

Landy, F.J. (1997) Early influences on the development of industrial and organisational psychology. *Journal of Applied Psychology*, 82, pp. 467–477.

Langlois, J.H., Roggman, L.A. and Rieser-Danner, L.A. (1990) Infants' differential social responses to attractive and unattractive faces. *Developmental Psychology*, 27, pp. 803–818.

Last, C., Hersen, M., Kazdin, A., Orvaschel, H. and Perrin, S. (1991) Anxiety disorders in children and their families. *Archives of General Psychiatry*, 48, pp. 928–934.

Latane, B. (1981) The psychology of social impact. *American Psychologist*, 36, pp. 343–356.

Latané, B., Harkins, S.G. and Williams, K.D. (1980) *Many Hands Make Light Work: Social Loafing as a Social Disease*. Unpublished manuscript, Columbus: Ohio State University.

Latané, B., Williams, K. and Harkins, S. (1979) Many hands make light the work: the causes and consequences of social loafing. *Journal of Personality and Social Psychology*, 37, pp. 822–832.

Latham, G. and Saari, L. (1984) Do people do what they say? Further studies on situational interview. *Journal of Applied Psychology*, 69, pp. 569–573.

Laughery, K.R. and Fowler, R.H. (1977) *Factors Affecting Facial Recognition*. Mug File Project (Report Number UHMUG-3). Houston, TX: University of Houston.

Lave, L.B. and Seskin, E.P. (1970) Air pollution and human health. *Science*, 169, pp. 723–733.

Lazarus, R.S. (1991) Psychological stress in the workplace. *Journal of Social Behaviour and Personality*, 6, pp. 1–13.

Lazarus, R.S. and Folkman, S. (1984) *Stress, Appraisal and Coping*. New York: Springer.

Lazarus, R. and Monat, A. (1979) *Personality*. Prentice-Hall.

Le Bon, G. (1895) *Psychologie des Foules*. Paris: Alcan.

Le Bon, G. (1903) *The Crowd*. Translated from *Psychologie des Foules*. London: Allen and Unwin.

Lee, S. and Chiu, H.F. (1989) Anorexia nervosa in Hong Kong – why not more in Chinese? *British Journal of Psychiatry*, 154, pp. 683–688.

Leippe, M.R., Wells, G.L. and Ostrom, T.M. (1978) Crime seriousness as a determinant of accuracy in eyewitness identification. *Journal of Applied Psychology*, 63, pp. 345–351.

Leister, A., Borden, D. and Fiedler, E.E. (1977) Validation of contingency model leadership training: Leader Match. *Academy of Management Journal*, 20, pp. 464–470.

Leiter, M.P. and Harvie, P. (1998) Conditions for staff acceptance of organisational change; Burnout as a mediating construct. *Anxiety, Stress and Coping*, 11, pp. 1–25.

Leiter, M.P. and Maslach, C. (1988) The impact of interpersonal environment on burnout and organisational commitment. *Journal of Organisational Behaviour*, 9, pp. 297–308.

Leiter, M.P. and Schaufeli, W.B. (1996) Consistency of the burnout construct across occupations. *Anxiety, Stress and Coping*, 9, pp. 229–243.

Lenney, E. (1977) Women's self-confidence in achievement situations. *Psychological Bulletin*, 84, pp. 1–13.

Leon, G.R. and Phelan, P.W. (1985) Anorexia nervosa. In Lahey, B. and Kazdin, A.E. (eds) *Advances in Clinical Child Psychology, Volume 8*. New York: Plenum Press.

Lepper, M. and Greene, D. (1978) *The Hidden Costs of Reward*. Hillsdale, NJ: Lawrence Erlbaum.

Lerner, M.J. and Miller, D.T. (1978) Just-world research and the attribution process: Looking back and ahead. *Psychohlogical Bulletin*, 85, pp. 1030–1051.

Lerner, M.J. and Simmons, C.H. (1966) Observers' reaction to the innocent victim: compassion or rejection. *Journal of Personality and Social Psychology*, 4, pp. 203–210.

Leventhal, H., Prohaska, T.R. and Hirschman, R.S. (1985) Preventive health behavior across the life span. In Rosen, J.C. and Solomon, L.J. (eds) *Prevention in Health Psychology*. Hanover, NH: University Press of New England.

Leventhal, H., Singer, R. and Jones, S. (1965) Effects of fear and specificity of recommendations upon attitudes and behaviour. *Journal of Personality and Social Psychology*, 2, pp. 20–29.

Levy, A. and Kahan, B. (1991) *The Pindown Experience and the Protection of Children. Report of the Staffordshire Child Care Inquiry*. London: HMSO.

Lewin, K. (1943) Forces behind food habits and methods of change. *Bulletin of National Research Council*, 108, pp. 35–65.

Lewin, K., Lippitt, R. and White, R.K. (1939) Patterns of aggressive behaviour in experimentally created social climates. *Journal of Social Psychology*, 10, pp. 271–279.

Lewine, R.R.J. (1991) Ontogenetic implications of sex differences in schizophrenia. In Walker, E.F. (ed.) *Schizophrenia: A Life-course Developmental Perspective*. San Diego: Academic Press.

Leyens, J.P., Camino, L., Parke, R.D. and Berkowitz, L. (1975) Effects of movie violence on aggression in a field setting as a function of group dynamics and cohesiveness. *Journal of Personality and Social Psychology*, 32, pp. 346–360.

Leyens, J-P, Herman, G. and Dunand, M. (1982) The influence of an audience upon the reactions to filmed violence. *European Journal of Social Psychology*, 12, pp. 131–142.

Liberman, R.P. and Green, M.F. (1992) Whither cognitive-behavioural therapy for schizophrenia? *Schizophrenia Bulletin*, 18, pp. 27–36.

Liebert, R.N. and Baron, R.A. (1972) Some immediate effects of televised violence on children's behaviour. *Developmental Psychology*, 6, pp. 469–478.

Lightdale, J.R. and Prentice, D.A. (1994) Rethinking sex differences in aggression: aggressive behaviour in the absence of social roles. *Personality and Social Psychology Bulletin*, 20, pp. 34–44.

Linz and Penrod (1992) cited in Brewer, K. (2000) *Psychology and Crime* (p. 59). Oxford: Heinemann.

Lippman, W. (1922) *Public Opinion*. New York: Harcourt, Brace and Co.

Livermore, B. (1991) What reflexology can do for you. *Self*, p. 50.

Locke, E.A. (1968) Toward a theory of task motivation and incentives. *Organisational Behaviour and Human Performance*, 3, pp. 157–189.

Locke, E.A. and Henne, D. (1986) Work motivation theories. In Cooper, C.L. and Robertson, I.T. (eds) *International Review of Industrial and Organisational Psychology 1986*. Chichester: Wiley.

Locke, E.A. and Latham, G.P. (1990) *A Theory of Goal-Setting and Task Performance*. Englewood Cliffs: Prentice Hall.

Locke, E.A., Shaw, K.N., Saari, L.M. and Latham, G.P. (1981) Goal setting and task performance: 1969–1980. *Psychological Bulletin*, 90, pp. 125–152.

Loehlin, J.C., Lindzey, G. and Spuhler, J.N. (1975) *Race Differences in Intelligence*. San Fransisco: Freeman.

Loftus, E.F. (1974) The incredible eyewitness. *Psychology Today*, December, pp. 117–119.

Loftus, E.F. (1975) Leading questions and the eyewitness report. *Cognitive Psychology*, 7, pp. 560–572.

Loftus, E.F. (1979) *Eyewitness Testimony*. Cambridge, MA: Harvard University Press.

Loftus, E.F. (1980) Impact of expert psychological testimony on the unreliability of eyewitness identification. *Journal of Applied Psychology*, 65, pp. 9–15.

Loftus, E.F. (1997) Creating False Memories. *Scientific American*, 279, pp. 50–55.

Loftus, E.F. and Burns, T.E. (1982) Mental shock can produce retrograde amnesia. *Memory and Cognition*, 10, pp. 318–323.

Loftus, E.F. and Greene, E. (1980) Warning: even memory for faces may be contagious. *Law and Human Behaviour*, 4, pp. 323–334.

Loftus, E.F., Loftus, G.R. and Messo, J. (1987) Some facts about 'weapon focus'. *Law and Human Behaviour*, 11, pp. 55–62.

Loftus, E.F., Manber, M. and Keating, J.P. (1983) Recollection of naturalistic events: context enhancement vs negative cueing. *Human Learning*, 3, pp. 83–92.

Loftus, E.F. and Palmer, J.C. (1974) Reconstruction of automobile destruction: an example of the interaction between language and memory. *Journal of Verbal Learning and Verbal Behaviour*, 13, pp. 585–589.

Loftus, E.F., Miller, D.G. and Burns, H.J. (1978) Semantic integration of verbal information into a visual memory. *Journal of Experimental Psychology: Human Learning and Memory*, 4, pp. 19–31.

Lombroso, C. (1911) *Crime: Its Causes and Remedies*. Boston: Little, Brown.

London, E.D., Cascella, N.G., Wong, D.F., Phillips, R.L., Dannals, R.F., Links, J.M., Herning, R., Grayson, R., Jaffe, J.H. and Wagner, H.N. (1990) Cocaine-induced reduction of glucose utilization in human brain. *Archives of General Psychiatry*, 47, pp. 567–574.

Long, M. (2000) *The Psychology of Education*. London: Routledge Falmer.

Lonsana, F.M. (1992) Distinguishing potential recyclers from non-recyclers: A basis for developing recycling strategies. *Journal of Environmental Education*, 23, pp. 16–23.

Loomis, S.D., Bohnert, P.J. and Huncke, S. (1967) Predictions of EEG abnormalities in adolescent delinquents. *Archives of General Psychiatry*, 17, pp. 494–497.

Lopez, S.R. (1989) Patient variable biases in clinical judgement: Conceptual overview and methodological considerations. *Psychological Bulletin*, 106, pp. 184–203.

Lord, K.R. (1994) Motivating recycling behaviour: a quasi-experimental investigation of message and source strategies. *Psychology and Marketing*, 11, pp. 393–416.

Lorenz, K. (1935) Der Kumpan in der Umwelt des Vogels. *Journal of Ornithology*, 83, pp. 137–213. (Published in English (1937) The companion in the bird's world. *Auk*, 54, pp. 245–274.)

Lorr, M. (1986) Classifying psychotics: Dimensional and categorical approaches. In Milton, T. and Klerman, G.L. (eds) *Contemporary Directions in Psychopathology: Toward the DSM-IV*. New York: Guilford Press.

Losel (1995) cited in Brewer, K. (2000) *Psychology and Crime* (p. 77). Oxford: Heinemann.

Lovell, K. (1961) A follow up study of Inhelder and Piaget's The Growth of Logical Thinking. *British Journal of Psychology*, 52, pp. 143–154.

Lyman, S.M. and Scott, M.B. (1967) Territoriality: a neglected sociological dimension. *Social Problems*, 15, pp. 235–249.

Lynch, J.J. (1977) *The Broken Heart: The Medical Consequences of Loneliness*. New York: Basic Books.

Lyons-Ruth, K., Repacholi, B., McLeod, S., Silva, E. (1991) Disorganised attachment behaviour in infancy: Short-term stability, maternal and infant correlates, and risk-related subtypes. *Development of Psychopathology*, 3, pp. 377–396.

Macan, T.H. and Dipboye, R.L. (1994) The effects of the application on processing of information from the employment interview. *Journal of Applied Social Psychology*, 24, pp. 1291–1314.

Maccoby, E.E. (1980) *Social Development: Psychological Growth and the Parent–Child Relationship*. New York: Harcourt-Brace Jovanovich.

Maccoby, E. and Jacklin, C. (1974) *The Psychology of Sex Differences*. London: Oxford University Press.

MacFarlane, A. (1975) Olfaction in the development of social preferences in the human neonate. *Parent–Infant Interaction*. CIBA Foundation Symposium 33. New York: Elsevier.

Machlowitz, M.M. (1976) Working the 100 hour week – and loving it. *New York Times*, October 3.

Madsen, C.H., Becker, W.C. and Thomas, D.R. (1968) Rules, praise and ignoring: elements of classroom control. *Journal of Applied Behaviour Analysis*, 1, pp. 139—150.

Maher, B.A. (1966) *Principles of Psychopathology: An Experimental Approach*. New York: McGraw Hill.

Mahoney, B. and Dixon, J. (1997) A fair and just system. *Psychology Review, November*, pp. 30–32.

Male, D. (1996) Who goes to MLD schools? *British Journal of Special Education*, 23, pp. 35–41.

Malgady, R.G., Rogler, L.H. and Constantino, G. (1987) Ethnocultural and linguistic bias in mental health evaluation of Hispanics. *American Psychologist*, 42, pp. 228–234.

Malpass, R.S. and Devine, P.G. (1983) Measuring the fairness of eyewitness identification lineups. In Lloyd-Bostock, S.M.A. and Clifford, B.R. (eds) *Evaluating Witness Evidence: Recent Psychological Research and New Perspectives*. Chichester: Wiley.

Malpass, R. S. and Kravitz, J. (1969) Recognition for faces of own and other race. *Journal of Personality and Social Psychology*, 13, pp. 330–334.

Mandal, M.K. and Maitra, S. (1985) Perception of facial affect and physical proximity. *Perceptual and Motor Skills*, 60, p 782.

Mandler, J. (1983) Representation. In Mussen, P.H. (ed.) *Handbook of Child Psychology*. New York: Wiley.

Manning, R.E. (1985) Crowding norms in backcountry settings: a review and synthesis. *Journal of Leisure Research*, 17, pp. 75–89.

Marks, M.L. and Mirvis, P.H. (1998) *Joining Forces: Making One Plus One Equal Three in Mergers, Acquisitions and Alliances*. San Fransisco: Jossey-Bass.

Marshall, J. and Heslin, R. (1975) Boys and girls together: sexual composition and the effect of density and group size on cohesiveness. *Journal of Personality and Social Psychology*, 31, pp. 952–961.

Marshall, P. (1995) *The Experiences of Gifted Children Growing: Triangulation with the GULB*. PhD Dissertation, University of Manchester, cited in Long, M. (2000) *The Psychology of Education*. London: Routledge Falmer.

Martens, R. (1975) The paradigmatic crisis in American sport personology. *Sportwissenschaft*, 1, pp. 9–24.

Martens, R.A. (1976) *Competitiveness in Sport*. Paper presented at the International Congress of Physical Activity Sciences, Quebec City.

Martens, R. (1987) Science, knowledge and sport psychology. *The Sport Psychologist*, 1, pp. 29–55.

Martinson, R. (1974) What works? – Questions and answers about prison reform. *The Public Interest*, 35, pp. 22–54.

Maser, A.L., Sorenson, P.H. and Kryter, K.D. (1978) Effects of intrusive sound on classroom behaviour: data from a successful lawsuit. Paper presented at the Annual Meeting of the Western Psychological Association, San Fransisco.

Maslach, C. and Jackson, S.E. (1986) *Maslach Burnout Inventory*. Palo Alto, CA: Consulting Psychologists Press.

Maslow, A. (1954) *Motivation and Personality*. New York: Harper and Row.

Maslow, A.H. (1965) *Eupsychian Management*. Homewood, IL: Richard D.Irwin.

Maslow, A. H. (1970) *Motivation and Personality*, 2nd edition. New York: Harper and Row.

Mason, J.W. (1975) A historical view of the stress field. *Journal of Human Stress*, 1, pp. 22–36.

Masson, J. (1992) The tyranny of psychotherapy. In Dryden, W. and Feltham, C. (eds) *Psychotherapy and its Discontents*. Buckingham: Open University Press.

Masten, A.S. (1986) Humor and competence in school-aged children. *Child Development*, 57, pp. 461–473.

Mathews, K.E. and Canon, L.K. (1975) Environmental noise level as a determinant of helping behaviour. *Journal of Personality and Social Psychology*, 32, pp. 571–577.

Mattson, M.E., Pollack, E.S. and Cullen, J.W. (1987) What are the odds that smoking will kill you? *American Journal of Public Health*, 77, pp. 425–431.

Mawhinney, T.C. (1992) Total quality management and organisational behaviour management: An integration for continual improvement. *Journal of Applied Behaviour Analysis*, 25, pp. 525–543.

Mayer, R. (1979) Can advance organisers influence meaningful learning? *Review of Educational Resarch*, 49, pp. 371–383.

Mayer, R. (1987) *Educational Psychology: A Cognitive Approach*. Boston: Little, Brown.

Mayo, E. (1933) *The Human Problems of Industrial Civilisation*. New York: Macmillan.

Mazur, A. (1977) Interpersonal spacing on public benches in 'contact' and 'noncontact' cultures. *Journal of Social Psychology*, 101, pp. 53–58.

McAllister, H.A. and Bregman, N.J. (1986) Juror under-utilisation of eyewitness non-identifications: theoretical and practical implications. *Journal of Applied Psychology*, 71, pp. 168–170.

McAuley, E. (1985a) Modeling and self-efficacy: A test of Bandura's model. *Journal of Sport Psychology*, 7, pp. 283–295.

McAuley, E. (1985b) Success and causality in sport: The influence of perception. *Journal of Sport Psychology*, 7, pp. 283–295.

McAuley, E. (1992) Understanding exercise behaviour: A self-efficacy perspective. In Roberts, G.C. (ed.) *Motivation in Sport and Exercise*. Champaign, IL: Human Kinetics.

McClelland, D.C. and Franz, C.E. (1993) Motivational and other sources of work accomplishments at midlife: A longitudinal study. *Journal of Personality*, 60, pp. 679–707.

McClelland, D.C. (1961) *The Achieving Society*. New York: Free Press.

McClelland, D.C. (1975) *Power: The Inner Experience*. New York: Irvington Press.

McCord, J. (1979) Some childrearing antecedents of criminal behaviour in adult men. *Journal of Personality and Social Psychology*, 37, pp. 1477–1486.

McCormick, E.J. (1979) *Job Analysis: Methods and Applications*. New York: AMACOM.

McDougall et al. (1987), cited in Brewer, K. (2000) *Psychology and Crime* (p. 76). Oxford: Heinemann.

McGinnis, M., Richmond, J.B., Brandt, E.N., Windom, R.E. and Mason, J.O. (1992) Health progress in the United States: Results of the 1990 objectives for the nation. *Journal of the American Medical Association*, 268, pp. 2545–2552.

McGue, M. (1992) When assessing twin concordance, use the probandwise not the pairwise rate. *Schizophrenia Bulletin*, 18, pp. 171–176.

McGuire, J. and Priestley, P. (1983) Life skills training in prisons and the community. In: Spence, S. and Shepherd, G. (eds) *Developments in Social Skills Training*. London: Academic Press.

McGuire, R.H. (1984) Recycling: great expectations and garbage outcomes. Special issue: household refuse analysis theory, method, and applications in social science. *American Behavioural Scientist*, 28, pp. 93–114.

McGurk, H. (1975) *Growing and Changing*. London: Methuen.

McNamara, E. (1979) Pupil self-management in the secondary school: the goal of behavioural intervention. *AEP Journal*, 3, p1.

Mednick, S.A., Moffit, T.E., Pollock, V., Talovic, S., Gabrielli, W.F. and VanDusen, K.T. (1983) The inheritance of human deviance. In Magnusson, D. and Allen, V.L. (eds) *Human Development: An Interactional Perspective*. London: Academic Press.

Meehl P.E. (1977) Why do I not attend case conferences. In Meehl, P.E. (ed.) *Psychodiagnosis: Selected Papers*. New York: Norton.

Mehler et al. (1978), cited in Lea, S.E.G. (1984) *Instinct, Environment and Behaviour*. London: Methuen.

Mehrabian, A. and Diamond, S.G. (1971) Effects of furniture arrangement, props and personality on social interaction. *Journal of Personality and Social Psychology*, 20, pp. 18–30.

Melamed, S., Ben-Avi, I., Luz, J. and Green, M.S. (1995) Objective and subjective work monotony: Effects on job satisfaction, psychological distress, and absenteesim in blue collar workers. *Journal of Applied Psychology*, 80, pp. 29–42.

Mellenger, G.D. and Balter, M.B. (1981), cited in Kendall, P.C. and Hammen, C. (1995) *Abnormal Psychology* (p. 188). Boston: Houghton Mifflin Company.

Mendelsohn, R. and Orcutt, G. (1979) An empirical analysis of air pollution dose-response curves. *Journal of Environmental Economics and Management*, 6, pp. 85–106.

Michelson, W. (1977) *Environmental Choice, Human Behaviour and Residential Satisfaction*. New York: Oxford University Press.

Miklowitz, D.J., Velligan, D.I., Goldstein, M.J., Nuechterlein, K.H., Gitlin, M.J., Ranlett, G. and Doane, J. A. (1991) Communication deviance in families of schizophrenic and manic patients. *Journal of Abnormal Psychology*, 100, pp. 163–173.

Milgram, S. (1970) The experience of living in cities. *Science*, 167, pp. 1461–1468.

Milgram, S. (1977) The experience of living in cities. In Milgram, S. (ed.) *The Individual in a Social World*. Reading, MA: Addison-Wesley.

Miller, N. and Maruyama, G. (1976) Ordinal position and peer popularity. *Journal of Personality and Social Psychology*, 33, pp. 123–131.

Miller, N., Maruyama, G., Beaber, R.J. and Valone, K. (1976) Speed of speech and persuasion. *Journal of Personality and Social Psychology*, 34, pp. 615–625.

Miner, J.B. (1983) The unpaved road from theory: over the mountains to application. In Kilmann, R.H., Thomas, K.W., Slevin, D.P., Naith, R. and Ferrel, S.L. (eds) *Producing Useful Knowledge for Organisations*. New York: Praeger.

Miner. J.B. (1984) The unpaved road over the mountains: from theory to applications. *The Industrial/Organisational Psychologist*, 21, pp. 9–20.

Mintz, A. (1951) Nonadaptive group behaviour. *Journal of Abnormal Social Psychology*, 46, pp. 150–159.

Mintz, L.I., Lieberman, R.P., Miklowitz, D.J. and Mintz, J. (1987). Expressed emotion: A call for partnership among relatives, patients, and professionals. *Schizophrenia Bulletin*, 13, pp. 227–235.

Minuchin, S., Roseman, B.L. and Baker, L. (1978) *Psychosomatic Families: Anorexia Nervosa in Context*. Cambridge, MA: Harvard University Press.

Mischel, W. (1968) *Personality and Assessment*. New York: John Wiley and Sons.

Mitchell, K.J., Livosky, M. and Mather, M. (1998) The weapon focus effect revisited: the role of novelty. *Legal and Criminological Psychology*, 3, pp. 287–303.

Mitchell, R. (1971) Some social implications of high-density housing. *American Sociology Review*, 36, pp. 18–29.

Miyake, K., Chen, S. and Campos, J.J. (1985) Infant temperament, mother's mode of interaction, and attachment in Japan. An interim report. *Monographs of the Society for Research in Child Development*, 50 (1–2, Serial No. 209).

Moede, W. (1927) Die Richtlinien der Leistungs-Psychologie. *Industrielle Psychotechnik*, 4, pp. 193–207.

Mohler, S.R. (1983) The human element in air traffic control: Aeromedical aspects, problems and prescriptions. *Aviation, Space and Environmental Medicine*, 54, pp. 511–516.

Monroe, R.R. (1978) *Brain Dysfunction in Aggressive Criminals*. Lexington, MA: D.C. Heath.

Moore, N.C. (1975) Social aspects of flat dwelling. *Public Health*, 89, pp. 109–115.

Moos, R.H. (1988) Life stressors and coping resources influence health and wellbeing. *Psychological Assessment*, 4, pp. 133–158.

Morgan, W.P. (1980a) Sport personology: The credulous-skeptical argument in perspective. In Straub, W.F. (ed.) *Sport Psychology: An Analysis of Athlete Behaviour*. Ithaca, NY: Mouvement.

Morgan, W.P. (1980b) The trait psychology controversy. *Research Quarterly for Exercise and Sport*, 51, pp. 50–76.

Morgeson, F.P. and Campion, M.A. (1997) Social and cognitive sources of potential inaccuracy in job analysis. *Journal of Applied Psychology*, 82, pp. 627–655.

Moscovici, S., Lage, E. and Naffrechoux, M. (1969) Influence of a consistent minority on the reponses of a majority in a colour perception task. *Sociometry*, 32, pp. 365–380.

Moser, G. (1988) Urban stress and helping behaviour: effects of environmental overload and noise on behaviour. *Journal of Environmental Psychology*, 8, pp. 278–298.

Motowidlo, S.J., Carter, G.W., Dunnette, M.D., Tippins, N., Werner, S., Burnett, J.R. and Vaughan, M.J. (1992) Studies of the structured behavioural interview. *Journal of Applied Psychology*, 77, pp. 571–587.

Motowidlo, S.J., Dunnette, M.D. and Carter, G.W. (1990) An alternative selection procedure: The low-fidelity simulation. *Journal of Applied Psychology*, 75, pp. 640–647.

Muchinsky, P.M. (1993*) Psychology Applied to Work*. Pacific Grove, CA: Brooks/Cole.

Munsteberg (1913) *Psychology and Industrial Efficiency*. Boston, MA: Houghton Mifflin.

Murphy, K. (1976) In Oyer, H. (ed.) *Communication for the Hearing Handicapped*. Baltimore: University Park Press.

Murray, H.A. (1938) *Explorations in Personality*. New York: Free Press.

Murray, M., Swan, A.V., Johnson, M.R.D. and Bewley, B.R. (1983) Some factors associated with increased risk of smoking by children. *Journal of Child Psychology and Psychiatry*, 24, pp. 223–232.

Murrell, H. (1976) *Motivation at Work*. London: Methuen.

Myers, D.G. and Lamm, H. (1976) The group polarisation phenomenon. *Psychological Bulletin*, 83, pp. 602–627.

Myers, J.K., Weissman, M.M., Tischler, G.L., Holzer, C.E., Leaf, P.J., Orvaschel, H.A., Anthony, J.C., Boyd, J.H., Burke, J.E., Kramer, M. and Stolzman, R. (1984) Six-month prevalence of psychiatric disorders in three communities: 1980–1982. *Archives of General Psychiatry*, 41, pp. 959–967.

Myers, K., Hale, C.S., Mykytowycs, R. and Hughes, R.L. (1971) Density space, sociability and health. In Esser, A.H. (ed.) *Behaviour and Environment*. New York: Plenum.

Nemeth, C. and Owens, J. (1996) Value of minority dissent. In West, M.A. (ed.) *Handbook of Work Group Psychology*. Chichester: Wiley.

Newman, O. (1973) *Defensible Space*. London: Architectural Press.

Newson, E. (1994) Video violence and the protection of children. *Journal of Mental Health*, 3, pp. 221–226.

Nicholson, R.A. and Berman, J.S. (1983) Is follow-up necessary in evaluating psychotherapy? *Psychological Bulletin*, 93, pp. 261–278.

Norcross, J.C., Karg-Bray, R.S. and Prochaska, J.O. (1995) *Clinical Psychologists in the 1990s*. Unpublished manuscript.

Norcross, J.C. and Prochaska, J.O. (1982) A national survey of clinical psychologists: Characteristics and activities. *The Clinical Psychologist*, 35, pp. 1, 5–8.

Novaco, R.W. (1975) *Anger Control: The Development and Evaluation of an Experimental Treatment*. Lexington: D.C. Heath.

O'Conner, M.C. (1989) Aspects of differential performance by minorities on standardised tests: Linguistic and socio-cultural factors. In Gifford, B.R. (ed.) *Test Policy and Test Performance: Education, Language and Culture*. Boston: Kluwer Academic Publishers.

O'Driscoll, M.P. and Beehr, T.A. (1994) Supervisor behaviours, role stressors and uncertainty as predictors of personal outcomes for subordinates. *Journal of Organisational Behaviour*, 15, pp. 141–155.

O'Leary, D., Kaufman, K., Kass, R. and Drabman, R. (1970) The effects of loud and soft reprimands on the behaviour of disruptive students. *Exceptional Children*, 37, pp. 145–155.

O'Leary, D. and O'Leary, S. (1977) *Classroom Management: The Successful Use of Behaviour Modification*. New York: Pergammon.

Oakley, A. (1992) *Social Support and Motherhood*. Oxford: Basil Blackwell.

Oden, M.H. (1968) The fulfilment of promise: 40-year follow-up of the Terman gifted group. *Genetic Psychological Monographs*, 77, pp. 3–93.

Ogden, J. (2000) *Health Psychology: A Textbook*, 2nd edition. Open University Press.

Ogilvie, B. and Tutko, T. (1966) *Problem Athletes and How to Handle Them*. Palham Books.

Organ, D.W. (1988) *Organizational Citizenship Behaviour: The Good Soldier Syndrome*. Lexington, MA: Lexington.

Orlick, T.D. and Mosher, R. (1978) Extrinsic rewards and participant motivation in a sport related task. *International Journal of Sports Psychology*, 9, pp. 27–39.

Orne, M.D. (1979) The use and misuse of hypnosis in course. *International Journal of Clinical and Experimental Hypnosis*, 27, pp. 311–341.

Osborn, A.F. (1957) *Applied Imagination*. New York: Scribner.

Osborn, S.G. and West, D.J. (1979) Conviction records of fathers and sons compared. *British Journal of Criminology*, 19, pp. 120–133.

Oskamp, S., Harrington, M.J., Edwards, T.C. *et al.* (1991) Factors influencing household recycling behaviour. *Environment and Behaviour*, 23, pp. 494–519.

Otis, A.S. (1929) *Self-Administering Test of Mental Ability*. Tarrytown-on-Hudson, NY: World.

Overall, J.E. and Gorham, D.R. (1962) The brief psychiatric rating scale. *Psychological Reports*, 10, pp. 799–812.

Owen, D.R. (1972) The 47, XYY male: a review. *Psychological Bulletin*, 78, pp. 209–233.

Page, R.A. (1978) Environmental influences on prosocial behaviour: the effect of temperature. Paper presented to the Midwestern Psychological Association, Chicago.

Palmer, E.J. and Hollin, C.R. (1998) A comparison of patterns of moral development in young offenders and non-offenders. *Legal and Criminological Psychology*, 3, pp. 225–235.

Parke, R.D., Berkowitz, L., Leyens, J.P., West, S.G. and Sebastian, R.J. (1977) Some effects of violent and non-violent movies on the behaviour of juvenile delinquents. In Berkowitz, L. (ed.) *Advances in experimental social psychology, vol. 10*. New York: Academic Press.

Parten, M. (1932) Social play among preschooler children. *Journal of Abnormal and Social Psychology*, 27, pp. 243–269.

Passer, M.N. (1981) Children in sport: Participation motives and psychological stress. *Quest*, 33, pp. 231–244.

Patri, P. (1971) Personal communication. In Ittelson, W.H., Proshansky, H.M., Rivlin, L.G. and Winkel, G.H. (1974) *An Introduction to Environmental Psychology*. New York: Holt, Rinehart and Winston.

Patterson, M.L., Mullens, S. and Romano, J. (1971) Compensatory reactions to spatial intrusion. *Sociometry*, 34, pp. 114–121.

Paul, G.L. and Lentz, R.J. (1977) *Psychosocial Treatment of Chronic Mental Patients (Milieu vs. Social Learning Programs)*. Cambridge, MA: Harvard University Press.

Paulus, P.B. and Dzindolet, M.T. (1993) Social influence processes in group brainstorming. *Journal of Personality and Social Psychology*, 64, pp. 575–586.

Pavkov, T.W., Lewis, D.A. and Lyons, J.S. (1989) Psychiatric diagnoses and racial bias: An empiricial investigation. *Professional Psychology: Research and Practice*, 20, pp. 364–368.

Peers, I. and Johnston, M. (1994) Influence of learning context on the relationship between A-level attainment and final degree performance: A meta-analytic review. *British Journal of Education*, 64 pp. 1–18.

Pennebaker, J.W. (1990) *Opening Up: The Healing Power of Confiding in Others*. New York: William Morrow.

Pennington, D.C., Gillon, K. and Hill, P. (1999) *Social Psychology*. London: Arnold.

Pennington, N. and Hastie, R. (1990) Practical implications of psychological research on juror and jury decision-making. *Personality and Social Psychology Bulletin*, 16, pp. 90–105.

Penrod, S.D. and Cutler, B.L. (1987) Assessing the competence of juries. In Weiner, I.B. and Hess, A.K. (eds) *Handbook of Forensic Psychology*. New York: Wiley.

Perrin, S. and Spencer, C. (1981) Independence of conformity in the Asian experiment as a reflection of cultural and situational factors. *British Journal of Social Psychology*, 20, pp. 205–209.

Perris, C. (1989) *Cognitive Psychotherapy and the Schizophrenic Disorders*. New York: Guilford Press.

Peters, L.H., Hartke, D.D. and Pohlmann, J.T. (1985) Fiedler's contingency theory of leadership: an application of the meta-analysis procedures of Schmidt and Hunter. *Psychological Bulletin*, 97, pp. 224–285.

Petty, R.E. and Cacioppo, J.T. (1981) *Attitudes and Persuasion: Classic and Contemporary Approaches*. Dubuque, IA: Brown.

Pfeifer, J.E. and Ogloff, J.R. (1991) Ambiguity and guilt determinations: a modern racism perspective. *Journal of Applied Social Psychology*, 21, pp. 1713–1725.

Phares, E.J. and Trull, T.J. (1996) *Clinical Psychology*, 5th edition. Pacific Grove, CA: Brooks/Cole.

Piaget, J. (1970) *Science of Education and the Psychology of the Child*. Longman.

Piaget, J. (1973) *The Psychology of Intelligence*. Totowa, NJ: Littlefield and Adams.

Pinizzotto, A.J. and Finkel, N.J. (1990) Criminal personality profiling: an outcome and process study. *Law and Human Behaviour*, 14, pp. 215–233.

Plomin, R. (1994) *Genetics and Experience: The Interplay Between Nature and Nurture* Thousand Oaks, CA: Sage.

Plowden Report (1967) *Children and their Primary Schools: Report of The Central Advisory Council For Education In England*. London: HMSO.

Polivy, J. and Herman, C.P. (1987) Diagnosis and treatment of normal eating. *Journal of Consulting and Clinical Psychology*, 55, pp. 635–644.

Pope, A.W., Bierman, K.L. and Mumma, G.H. (1991) Aggression, hyperactivity, and inattention-immaturity: Behaviour dimensions associated with peer rejection in elementary school boys. *Developmental Psychology*, 27, pp. 663–671.

Popper, K. (1959) *The Logic of Scientific Discovery*. London: Hutchinson.

Prentice-Dunn, S. and Rogers, R.W. (1982) Effects of public and private self-awareness on deindividuation and aggression. *Journal of Personality and Social Psychology*, 43, pp. 503–513.

Pressey (1926) cited in Childs, D. (1999) *Psychology and the Teacher*, 6th edition (p. 136). Cassell Education.

Primoff, E. (1975) *How to Prepare and Conduct Job Element Examinations*. Personnel Research and Development Center, Washington, DC: U.S. Government Printing Office.

Quay, L.C. (1971) Language, dialect, reinforcement, and the intelligence test performance of Negro children. *Child Development*, 45, pp. 5–15.

Rada, P., Pothos, E., Mark, G.P. and Hoebel, B.G. (1991) Microdialysis evidence that acetylcholine in the nucleus accumbens is involved in morphine withdrawal and in its treatment with clonidine. *Brain Research*, 561, pp. 354–356.

Raphael, B. (1984) *The Anatomy of Bereavement*. London: Hutchinson.

Rappaport, J. (1977) *Community Psychology: Values, Research and Action*. New York: Holt, Rinehart and Winston.

Ratliff-Crain, J. and Baum, A. (1990) Individual differences in health: Gender, coping and stress. In Friedman, H.S. (ed.) *Personality and Disease*. New York: Wiley.

Raven, J. (1993) *Manual for Raven's Progressive Matrices and Vocabulary Scales*. Windsor: NFER-Nelson.

Reicher, S.D. (1982) The determination of collective behaviour. In Tajfel, H. (ed.) *Social Identity and Intergroup Relations*. Cambridge: Cambridge University Press.

Resnick, J.H. (1991) Finally, a definition of clinical psychology: A message from the President, Division 12. *The Clinical Psychologist*, 44, pp. 3–11.

Reynolds, D. and Farrell, S. (1996) *Worlds Apart: A Review of*

International Surveys of Educational Achievement Involving England. London: The Stationery Office.

Richards, J.E. (1987) Infant visual sustained attention and respiratory sinus arrhythmia. *Child Development*, 58, pp. 488–496.

Rickels, K., Schweizer, E., Case, W. and Greenblatt, D. (1991) Long-term therapeutic use of benzodiazepines: 1. Effects of abrupt discontinuation. *Archives of General Psychiatry*, 47, pp. 899–907.

Riemer, S. (1948) Maladjustment to the family home. *American Sociological Review*, 10, pp. 642–648.

Riggio, R.E. (2000) *Introduction to Industrial/Organisational Psychology*, 3rd edition. New Jersey: Prentice Hall.

Riggio, R.E. and Cole, E.J. (1995) Stress and coping processes in on-duty firefighters. Paper presented at meeting of the American Psychological Association, Toronto, Canada. Cited in Riggio, R.E. (2000) *Introduction to Industrial/Organisational Psychology*, 3rd edition. New Jersey: Prentice Hall.

Rimm, E.B., Giovannucci, E.L., Willett, W.C., Colditz, G.A., Ascherio, A., Rosner, B. and Stampfer, M.J. (1991) Prospective study of alcohol consumption and risk of coronary disease. *Lancet*, 338, pp. 464–468.

Ringelmann (1913), cited in Hogg, M.A. and Vaughan, G.M. (1998) *Social Psychology*, 2nd edition. Prentice Hall.

Riordan, S. (1999) Indecent exposure: the impact upon the victim's fear of sexual crime. *Journal of Forensic Psychiatry*, 10, pp. 309–316.

Rivano-Fischer, M. (1984) Interactional space: invasion as a function of the type of social interaction. *Psychological Research Bulletin*, 24, p. 15.

Robbins, T.L. (1995) Social loafing on cognitive tasks: An examination of the 'sucker effect'. *Journal of Business and Psychology*, 9, pp. 337–342.

Roberts, G.C. (1992) Motivation in sport and exercise: Conceptual constraints and convergence. In Roberts, G.C. (ed.) *Motivation in Sport and Exercise*. Champaign, IL: Human Kinetics.

Robertson, I.T. and Kinder, A. (1993) Personality and job competencies: the criterion-related validity of some personality variables. *Journal of Occupational and Organisational Psychology*, 66, pp. 225–244.

Robertson, J. and Robertson, J. (1968) Young children in brief separation: a fresh look. *Psychoanalytic Study of the Child*, 26, pp. 264–315.

Robins, L.N. and Guze, S.B. (1970) Establishment of diagnostic validity in psychiatric illness: Its application to schizophrenia. *American Journal of Psychiatry*, 126, pp. 107–111.

Robins, L.N., Helzer, J., Weissman, M.M., Orvaschel, H., Gruenberg, E., Burke, J.D. and Reiger, D.A. (1984) Life time prevalence of specific psychiatric disorders in three sites. *Archives of General Psychiatry*, 41, pp. 942–949.

Rodin, J. (1976) Crowding, perceived choice and response to controllable and uncontrollable outcomes. *Journal of Experimental Social Psychology*, 12, pp. 564–578.

Rodin, J., Solomon, S. and Metcalf, J. (1978) Role of control in mediating perceptions of density. *Journal of Personality and Social Psychology*, 36, pp. 989–999.

Roethlisberger, F.J. and Dickson, W.J. (1939) *Management and the Worker*. Cambridge, MA: Harvard University Press.

Rogers, C. (1982) *A Social Psychology of Schooling: The Expectancy Process*. London: Routledge and Kegan Paul.

Rohner, R.P. (1974) Proxemics and stress: an empirical study of the relationship between living space and roommate turnover. *Human Relations*, 27, pp. 697–702.

Rollinson, D., Broadfield, A. and Edwards, D.J. (1998) *Organisational Behaviour and Analysis*. Harlow: Addison-Wesley.

Roopnarine, J.L. and Johnson, J.E. (1984) Socialisation in a mixed-age experimental program. *Developmental Psychology*, 20, pp. 828–832.

Rose, E.F. and Rose, M. (1971) Carbon monoxide: a challenge to the physician. *Clinical Medicine*, 78, pp. 12–19.

Rosenfeld, P., Giacalone, R.A. and Kennedy, J.G. (1987) Of status and suits: personal space invasions in an administrative setting. *Social Behaviour and Personality*, 15, pp. 97–99.

Rosenhan, D.L. and Seligman, M.E.P. (1984) *Abnormal Psychology*. New York: Norton.

Rosenman, R.H. (1990) Type A behaviour pattern: A personal overview. *Journal of Social Behaviour and Personality*, 5, pp. 1–24.

Rosenstock, I.M. and Kirscht J.P. (1979) Why people seek health care. In Stone, G.C., Cohen, F. and Adler, N.E. (eds) *Health Psychology – A Handbook*. San Francisco: Jossey-Bass.

Rosenthal, R. (1985) From unconscious experimenter bias to teacher expectancy effects. In Dusek, J. (ed.) *Teacher Expectancies*. London: Lawrence Erlbaum.

Rosenthal, R. and Jacobson, L.F. (1968) *Pygmalion in the Classroom*. New York: Holt, Rinehart and Winston.

Ross, R.R. and Fabiano, E.A. (1985) *Time to Think: A Cognitive Model of Delinquency Prevention and Offender Rehabilitation*. Johnson City, TN: Institute of Social Sciences and Arts.

Rotenberg, M. and Nachshon, I. (1979) Impulsiveness and aggression among Israeli delinquents. *British Journal of Social and Clinical Psychology*, 18, pp. 59–63.

Roth, W.T., Margraf, J., Ehler, A., Taylor, B., Maddock, R.J., Davies, S. and Agras, S. (1992) Stress test reactivity in panic disorder. *Archives of General Psychiatry*, 49, pp. 301–310.

Rotter, J.B. (1966) Generalised expectancies for the internal versus external control of reinforcement. *Psychological Monographs*, 90, pp. 1–28.

Rotton, J. (1983) Affective and cognitive consequences of malodorous pollution. *Basic and Applied Social Psychology*, 4, pp. 171–191.

Rotton, J. (1993) Atmospheric and temporal correlates of sex crimes: endogenous factors do not explain seasonal differences in rape. *Environmental Behaviour*, 25, pp. 625–642.

Rotton, J., Barry, T., Frey, J. and Soler, E. (1978) Air pollution and interpersonal attraction. *Journal of Applied Social Psychology*, 8, pp. 57–71.

Rotton, J. and Frey, J. (1984) Psychological costs of air pollution: atmospheric conditions, seasonal trends and psychiatric emergencies. *Population and Environment*, 7, pp. 3–16.

Rotton, J., Frey, J., Barry, T., Milligan, M. and Fitzpatrick, M. (1979) The air pollution experience and interpersonal aggression. *Journal of Applied Social Psychology*, 9, pp. 397–412.

Rowell, J., Simon, J. and Wiseman, R. (1969) Verbal reception, guided discovery, and the learning of schemata. *British Journal of Educational Psychology*, 39, pp. 235–244.

Ruback, R.B. and Pandey, J. (1992) Very hot and really crowded: quasi-experimental investigations of Indian 'Tempos'. *Environment and Behaviour*, 24, pp. 527–554.

Rubin, J.Z. (1980) *Children's Friendships*. Cambridge, MA: Harvard University Press.

Rubin, J.Z., Provenzano, F.J. and Luria, Z. (1974) The eye of the beholder: parents' views on sex of newborns. *American Journal of Orthopsychiatry*, 44, pp. 512–519.

Rubin, K.H., Fein, G.G. and Vandenberg, B. (1983) Play. In Mussen, P.H. (ed.) *Handbook of Child Psychology: Vol. 4 Socialisation, Personality and Social Behaviour*. New York: Wiley.

Rubin, K.H., Lynch, D., Coplan, R., Rose-Krasnor, L. and Booth, C.L. (1994) 'Birds of a feather...': Behavioural concordance and preferential personal attraction in children. *Child Development*, 64, pp. 1778–1785.

Rutte, C.G., Wilke, H.A. and Messick, D.M. (1987) Scarcity or abundance caused by people or the environment as determinants of behaviour in the resource dilemma. *Journal of Experimental Social Psychology*, 23, pp. 208–216.

Rutter, M. (1970), cited in Gross, R.D. (1996) *Psychology The Science of Mind and Behaviour* (p. 563). London: Hodder and Stoughton.

Rutter, M. (1979) Maternal deprivation 1972–1978: new findings, new concepts, new approaches. *Child Development*, 50, pp. 283–305.

Rutter, M. (1981) *Maternal Deprivation Reassessed*, 2nd edition. Harmondsworth: Penguin.

Rutter, M., Maughan, B., Mortimore, P. and Ouston, J. (1979) *Fifteen Thousand Hours: Secondary Schools and their Effects*. Wells, Somerset: Open Books.

Rutter, M. and Rutter, M. (1992) *Developing Minds: Challenge and Continuity Across the Life Span*. Harmondsworth: Penguin.

Sabin, J.E. (1975) Translating despair. *American Journal of Psychiatry*, 132, pp. 197–199.

Sabini, J. (1994) *Social Psychology*, 2nd edition. New York: W.W. Norton and Company.

Sagar, H.A., Schofield, J.W. and Snyder, H.N. (1983) Race and gender barriers: Preadolescent peer behaviour in academic classrooms. *Child Development*, 54, pp. 1032–1040.

Sagi, A., Lamb, M.E., Lewkowicz, K.S., Shoham, R., Dvir, R. and Estes, D. (1985) Security of infant-mother, -father, and metapelet attachments among kibbutz reared Israeli children. *Monographs of the Society for Research in Child Development*, 50 (1–2 Serial No. 209).

Saks, A.M. (1994) A psychological process investigation of the effects of recruitment source and organisation information on job survival. *Journal of Organisational Behaviour*, 15, pp. 225–244.

Salzman, C. (1991) Why don't clinical trial results always correspond to clinical experience? *Neuropsychopharmacology*, 4, pp. 265–267.

Sandberg, A.A., Koepf, G.F., Ishiara, T. and Hauschka, T.S. (1961) An XXY human male. *Lancet*, 262, pp. 488–489.

Sanders, G.S. and Simmons, W.L. (1983) Use of hypnosis to enhance eyewitness accuracy: does it work? *Journal of Applied Psychology*, 68, pp. 70–77.

Sanders, J.L., Hakky, U.M. and Brizzolara, M.M. (1985) Personal space amongst Arabs and Americans. *International Journal of Psychology*, 20, pp. 13–17.

Sanna, L.J. and Parks, C.D. (1997) Group research trends in social and organisational psychology: Whatever happened to intragroup research? *Psychological Science*, 8, pp. 261–267.

Sarafino, E.P. (1986) *The Fears of Childhood; A Guide to Recognizing and Reducing Fearful States in Children*. New York: Human Sciences Press.

Sarafino, E.P. (1994) *Health Psychology: Biophysical Interactions*, 2nd edition. New York: John Wiley and Sons.

Sarason, S.B. (1973) Jewishness, blackness, and the nature nurture controversy. *American Psychologist*, 28, pp. 926–971.

Saunders, J.T., Reppuci, N.D. and Sarata, B.P. (1973) An examination of impulsivity as a trait characterising delinquent youth. *American Journal of Orthopsychiatry*, 43, pp. 789–795.

Scanlan, T. (1984) Competitive stress and the child athlete. In Silva, J.M. and Weinberg, R.S. (eds) *Psychological Foundations of Sport*. Champaign, IL: Human Kinetics.

Scarr, S. (1992) Developmental theories for the 1990s: Development and individual differences *Child Development*, 63, pp. 1–19.

Schacter, S. and Singer, J.E. (1962) Cognitive, social and physiological determinants of emotional state. *Psychology Review*, 69, pp. 379–399.

Schacter, S., Silverstein, B., Kozlowski, L. T., Perlick, D., Herman, C.P. and Liebling, B. (1977) Studies of the interaction of psychological and pharmacological determinants of smoking. *Journal of Experimental Psychology: General*, 106, pp. 3–40.

Schafer, S. (1976) *Introduction to Criminology*. New York: McGraw-Hill.

Schaffer, H.R. and Emerson, P.E. (1964) The development of social attachments in infancy. *Monographs of the Society for Research in Child Development*, 29 (3, Serial No. 94).

Schaubroeck, J., Ganster, D.C. and Kemmerer, B.E. (1994) Job complexity, Type A behaviour, and cardiovascular disorder: A prospective study. *Academy of Management Journal*, 37, pp. 426–439.

Schaubroeck, J., Ganster, D.C., Sime, W.E. and Ditman, D. (1993) A field experiment testing supervisory role clarification. *Personnel Psychology*, 46, pp. 1–25.

Schmidt, D.E. and Keating. J.P. (1979) Human crowding and personality control: an integration of research. *Psychological Bulletin*, 86, pp. 680–700.

Schmitt, N., Gilliland, S.W., Landis, R.S. and Devine, D. (1993) Computer-based testing applied to selection of secretarial applicants. *Personnel Psychology*, 46, pp. 149–165.

Schneider, D.J., Hastorf, A.H. and Ellsworth, P.C. (1979) *Person Perception*. Reading, MA: Addison-Wesley.

Schofield, J.W. and Francis, W.D. (1982) An observational study of peer interaction in racially mixed 'accelerated' classrooms. *Journal of Educational Psychology*, 74, pp. 722–732.

Schrodt, P.A. (1981) Conflict as a determinant of territory. *Behavioural Science*, 26, pp. 37–50.

Schulte, J.H. (1963) Effects of mild carbon monoxide intoxication. *Archives of Environmental Health*, 7, pp. 524–530.

Schwarzer, R., Jerusalem, M. and Hahn, A. (1994) Unemployment, social support and health complaints: A longitudinal study of stress in East German refugees. *Journal of Community and Applied Social Psychology*, 4, pp. 31–45.

Schweinhart, L.J. and Weikart, D.P. (1997) *Lasting Differences*. Ypsilanti, MI: High/Scope Press.

Schwerin, H.S. and Newell, H.H. (1981) *Persuasion in Marketing*. New York: Wiley.

Scott, D.W. (1986) Anorexia nervosa: A review of possible genetic factors. *International Journal of Eating Disorders*, 5, pp. 1–20.

Seggie (1983), cited in Brewer, K. (2000) *Psychology and Crime* (p. 68). Oxford: Heinemann.

Self, C.A. and Rogers, R.W. (1990) Coping with threat to health: effects of persuasive appeals on depressed, normal and antisocial personalities. *Journal of Behavioural Medicine*, 13, pp. 343–357.

Seligman, M.E.P. (1971) Phobias and preparedness. *Behaviour Research and Therapy*, 2, pp. 307–320.

Seligman, M.E.P. (1975) *Helplessness on Depression, Development and Death*. San Francisco: Freeman.

Selman, R.L., Schorin, M.Z., Stone, C.R. and Phelps, E. (1983) A naturalistic study of children's social understanding. *Developmental Psychology*, 19, pp. 81–102.

Selye, H. (1956) *The Stress of Life*. New York: McGraw-Hill.

Selye, H. (1976) *The Stress of Life*, revised edition. New York: McGraw-Hill.

Sethi, A.S., Caro, D.H.J. and Schuler, R.S. (1987*)* Strategic Management of Technostress in an Information Society*. Leviston, NY: C.J. Hogrefe.

Severy, L.J., Forsyth, D.R. and Wagner, P.J. (1979) A multi-method assessment of personal space development in female and male, black and white children. *Journal of Nonverbal Behaviour*, 4, pp. 68–86.

Sexton, M.M. (1979) Behavioural epidemiology. In Pomerleau, O.F. and Brady, J.P. (eds) *Behaviour Medicine: Theory and Practice*. Baltimore, MD: Williams and Wilkins.

Shackleton, V.J. and Fletcher, C.A. (1984) *Individual Differences – Theory, Research and Applications*. Monterey, CA: Brooks Cole.

Shackleton, V.J. and Newell, S. (1997) International selection and assessment. In Anderson, N. and Herriot, P. (eds) *International Handbook of Selection and Assessment*. Chichester: Wiley.

Shaffer, D.R. (1993) *Developmental Psychology*, 3rd edition. Pacific Grove, CA: Brooks/Cole.

Shanahan, M.J. and Mortimer, J.T. (1996) Understanding the positive consequences of psychosocial stressors. *Advances in Group Processes*, 13, pp. 189–209.

Shapira. A. and Madsen, M.C. (1969) Cooperative and competitive behaviour of kibbutz and urban children in Israel. *Child Development*, 4, pp. 609–617.

Shapiro, P.N. and Penrod, S. (1986) Meta-analysis of facial identification studies. *Psychological Bulletin*, 100, pp. 139–156.

Shaw, M.E. (1976) *Group Dynamics: The Psychology of Small Group Behaviour*. New York: McGraw-Hill.

Sheehan, P.W. (1983) Age trends and the correlates of children's television viewing. *Australian Journal of Psychology*, 35, pp. 417–431.

Sheldon, W.H. (1942) *The Varieties of Temperament: A Psychology of Constitutional Differences*. New York: Harper and Row.

Sheldon, W.H. (1949) *Varieties of Delinquent Youth: An Introduction to Constitutional Psychiatry*. New York: Harper and Row.

Shenton, M.E., Kikinis, R., Jolesz, F.A., Pollak, S.D., Le May, M., Wible, C.G., Hokama, H., Martin, J., Metcalf, D., Coleman, M. and McCarley, R.W. (1992) Abnormalities of the left temporal lobe and thought disorder in schizophrenia: A quantitative magnetic resonance imaging study. *New England Journal of Medicine*, 327, pp. 604–612.

Sherman, L.W. and Berk, R.A. (1984) The specific deterrent effects of arrest for domestic assault. *American Sociological Review*, 49, pp. 261–272.

Sherrington, R., Brynjolfsson, J., Petursson, H. and Potter, M. (1988) Localisation of a susceptibility locus for schizophrenia on chromosome 5. *Nature*, 336, pp. 164–167.

Shimmin, S. and Wallis, D. (1994) *Fifty Years of Occupational Psychology in Britain*. Leicester: Division and Section of Occupational Psychology, British Psychological Society.

Shoham-Solomon, V. and Rosenthal R. (1987) Paradoxical intervention: A meta-analysis. *Journal of Consulting and Clinical Psychology*, 55, pp. 22–28.

Shore, B.M. and Kanevsky, L.S. (1993) Thinking processes: being and becoming gifted. In Heller, K.H., Monks, F.J. and Passow, A.H. *International Handbook of Research and Development of Giftedness and Talent*. Oxford: Pergammon.

Shouksmith, G. and Burrough, S. (1988) Job stress factors for New Zealand and Canadian air-trafffic controllers. *Applied Psychology: An International Review*, 37, pp. 263–270.

Shrum, L.J., Lowrey, T.M. and McCarty, J.A. (1994) Recycling as a marketing problem: a framework for strategy development. *Psychology and Marketing*, 11, pp. 393–416.

Shuter, R. (1976) Proxemics and tactility in Latin America. *Journal of Communication*, 26, pp. 46–52.

Simonoff, E., Bolton, P., and Rutter, M. (1996) Mental retardation: genetic findings, clinical implications and research agenda. *Journal of Child Psychology and Psychiatry*, 37, pp. 259–280.

Singer, J., Brush, C. and Lublin, S. (1965) Some aspects of deindividuation: identification and conformity. *Journal of Experimental Social Psychology*, 1, pp. 356–378.

Singer, J.L. and Singer, D.G. (1981) *Television, Imagination and Aggression: a Study of Preschoolers*. Hillsdale: Erlbaum.

Skeels, H.R. (1966) Adult status of children with contrasting early life experiences: a follow-up study. *Monographs of the Society for Research in Child Development*, 31.

Skeels, H. and Dye, H.B. (1939) A study of the effects of differential stimulation on mentally retarded children. *Proceedings and Addresses of the American Association on Mental Deficiency*, 44, pp. 114–136.

Skinner, B. (1954) The science of learning and the art of teaching. *Harvard Educational Review*, 24, pp. 86–94.

Skolnick and Shaw (1997), cited in Brewer, K. (2000) *Psychology and Crime* (p. 67). Oxford: Heinemann.

Skorjanc, A.D. (1991) Differences in interpersonal distance among non-offenders as a function of perceived violence of offenders. *Perceptual and Motor Skills*, 73, pp. 659–662.

Slade, A. (1987) A longitudinal study of maternal involvement and symbolic play during the toddler period. *Child Development*, 58,

pp. 367–375.

Sluckin, W. (1965) *Imprinting and Early Learning*. London: Methuen.

Smith, A. (1991) *The Wealth of Nations*. Harmondsworth: Penguin.

Smith, C. and Lloyd, B. (1978) Maternal behaviour and perceived sex of infant: Revised. *Child Development*, 49, pp. 1263–1265.

Smith, K.G., Locke, E.A. and Barry, D. (1990) Goal setting, planning and organisational performance: An experimental simulation. *Organisational Behaviour and Human Decision Processes*, 46, pp. 118–134.

Smith, P.K. and Vollstedt, R. (1985) On defining play: An empirical study of the relationship between play and various play criteria. *Child Development*, 56, pp. 1042–1050.

Smith, R.E., Smoll, F.L. and Curtis, B. (1979) Coach effectiveness training: A cognitive-behavioural approach to enhancing relationship skills in youth sports coaches. *Journal of Sport Psychology*, 1, pp. 59–75.

Smith, S.S., O'Hara, B.F., Persico, A.M., Gorelick, D.A., Newlin, D.B., Vlahav, D., Solomon, L., Pickens, R. and Uhl, G.R. (1992) Genetic vulnerability to drug abuse: The D2 dopamine receptor Taq1B1 restriction fragment length polymorphism appears more frequently in polysubstance abusers. *Archives of General Psychiatry*, 49, pp. 723–727.

Smith, T.W. and Pope, M.K. (1990) Cynical hostility as a health risk: Current status and future directions. *Journal of Social Behaviour and Personality*, 5, pp. 77–88.

Snow, R. (1969) Unfinished pygmalion. *Contemporary Psychology*, 14, pp. 197–199.

Snyder, M., Tanke, E.D. and Berscheid, E. (1977) Social perception and interpersonal behaviour: On the self-fulfilling nature of social stereotypes. *Journal of Personality and Social Psychology*, 35, pp. 656–666.

Snyder, R.L. (1966) Fertility and reproductive performance of grouped male mice. In Benirschke, K. (ed.) *Symposium on Comparative Aspects of Reproductive Behaviour*. Berlin: Springer Press.

Snyder, S.H. (1984) Drug and neurotransmitter receptors in the brain. *Science*, 224, pp. 22–31.

Sommer, R. (1959) Studies in personal space. *Sociometry*, 22, pp. 247–260.

Sommer, R. (1968) Intimacy ratings in five countries. *International Journal of Psychology*, 3, pp. 109–114.

Sommer, R. (1969) *Personal Space*. Englewood Cliffs, NJ: Prentice-Hall.

Sommer, R. (1972) *Design Awareness*. San Fransisco: Rinehart Press.

Sommers, P., Van Dort, B. and Moos, R. (1976) Noise and air pollution. In Moos, R. (ed.) *The Human Context: Environmental Determinants of Behaviour*. New York: Wiley.

Soyland, A.J. (1994) *Psychology as a Metaphor*. London: Sage.

Spangler, W. (1992) Validity of questionnaire and TAT measures of achievement: Two meta-analyses. *Psychological Bulletin*, 112, pp. 140–154.

Sparks, R.F. (1981) Surveys of victimisation – an optimistic assessment. In Tonry, M. and Morris,N. (eds) *Crime and Justice: An Annual Review of Research, Vol. 3*. Chicago, IL: University of Chicago Press.

Spector, P.E. (1987) Interactive effects of perceived control and job stressors on alternative and health outcomes for clerical workers. *Work and Stress*, 1, pp. 155–162.

Spence, K.W. (1956) *Behaviour Theory and Conditioning*. New Haven, CT: Yale University Press.

Spencer, H. (1873) *Principles of Psychology*. New York: Appleton.

Spender, D. (1982) *Invisible Women: The Schooling Scandal*. London: Writers and Readers Publishing Cooperative.

Spitz, R.A. (1945) Hospitalism. An inquiry into the genesis of psychiatric conditions in early childhood. *Psychoanalytic Study of the Child*, 1, pp. 53–74.

Srivastava, P. and Mandal, M.K. (1990) Proximal spacing to facial affect expressions in schizophrenia. *Comprehensive Psychiatry*, 11, pp. 651–656.

Stacey, M., Dearden, R., Pill, R. and Robinson, D. (1970) *Hospitals,*

Children and Their Families: The Report of a Pilot Study. London: Routledge and Kegan Paul.

Steers, R.M. and Porter, L.W. (eds) (1991) *Motivation and Work Behaviour*, 5th edition. New York: McGraw-Hill.

Steiner, I.D. (1972) *Group Processes and Productivity*. New York: Academic Press.

Steinhausen, H.C. (1994) Anorexia and bulimia nervosa. In Rutter, M., Taylor, E. and Hersov, L. (eds) *Child and Adolescent Psychiatry*. Oxford: Blackwell Scientific Publications.

Steinmetz, K.A., Kushi, L., Bostick, R., Folsom, A. and Potter, J. (1994) Vegetables, fruit, and colon cancer in the Iowa Women's Health Study. *American Journal of Epidemiology*, 139, pp125–129.

Stern, cited in Childs, D. (1999) *Psychology and the Teacher*, 6th edition (p. 248). Cassell Education.

Sternberg, R. (1988) Explaining away intelligence: a reply to Howe. *British Journal of Psychology*, 79, pp. 527–533.

Stevens, C.K. (1998) Antecedents of interview interactions, interviewers' ratings, and applicants reactions. *Personnel Psychology*, 51, pp. 55–85.

Stewart, J.E. (1980) Defendant's attractiveness as a factor in the outcome of criminal trials: an observational study. *Journal of Applied Social Psychology*, 10, pp. 348–361.

Stewart, R., Baretta, E., Platte, L., Stewart, M.T., Kalbfleisch, J., Van Yserloo, B. and Rimm, A. (1974) Carboxyhemoglobin levels in American blood donors. *Journal of the American Medical Association*, 229, pp. 1187–1195.

Stewart, R.B. (1983) Sibling attachment relationships: child-infant interactions in the strange-situation. *Developmental Psychology*, 19, pp. 192–199.

Stodgill, R. (1974) *Handbook of Leadership*. New York: Free Press.

Stokols, D., Ohlig, W. and Resnick, S. M. (1979) Perceptions of residential crowding, classroom experiences, and student health. In Aiello, J. R. and Baum, A. (eds) *Residential Crowding and Design*. New York: Plenum.

Stokols, D., Shumaker, S.A. and Martinez, J. (1983) Residential mobility and personal well-being. *Journal of Environmental Psychology*, 3, pp. 5–19.

Stoner, J.A.F. (1961) A comparison of individual and group decisions involving risk. Unpublished masters thesis. Cambridge, MA: MIT.

Stones, E. (1984) *Psychology of Education: A Pedagogical Approach*. London: Methuen.

Storfer, M. (1990) *Intelligence and Giftedness*. San Francisco: Jossey-Bass.

Strahilevitz, M., Strahilevitz, A. and Miller, J. (1979) Air pollutants and the admission rate of psychiatric patients. *American Journal of Psychiatry*, 132, pp. 205–207.

Strasser, G., Kerr, N.L. and Bray, R.M. (1982) The social psychology of jury deliberations: structure, process and product. In Kerr, N.L. and Bray, R.M. (eds) *The Psychology of the Courtroom*. New York: Academic Press.

Stroebe, W. (2000) *Social Psychology and Health*, 2nd edition. Buckingham: Open University Press.

Strube, M.J. and Garcia, J.E. (1981) A meta-analytic investigation of Fiedler's contingency model of leadership effectiveness. *Psychological Bulletin*, 90, pp. 307–321.

Subotnik, R., Kassa, L., Summers, E. and Wasser, A. (1993) *Genius Revisited: High IQ Children Grown Up*. Norwood, NJ: Ablex.

Suematsu, H., Kuboki, T. and Itoh, T. (1985) Statistical studies on the prognosis of anorexia nervosa. *Psychosomatics*, 43, pp. 104–112.

Suls, J. and Fletcher, B. (1985) The relative efficacy of avoidant and nonavoidant coping strategies: A meta-analysis. *Health Psychology*, 4, pp. 249–288.

Suls, J. and Mullen, B. (1981) Life change and psychological distress: The role of perceived control and desirability. *Journal of Applied Social Psychology*, 11, pp. 379–389.

Sundstrom, E. (1978) Crowding as a sequential process: review of research on the effects of population density on humans. In Baum, A. and Epstein, Y.M. (eds) *Human Response to Crowding*. Hillsdale, NJ: Erlbaum.

Sundstrom, E., Town, J.P., Rice, R.W., Osborn, D.P. and Brill, M. (1994) Office noise, satisfaction and performance. *Environment and Behaviour*, 26, pp. 195–222.

Sutherland, E.H. (1939) *Principles of Criminology*. Philadelphia, PA: Lippincott.

Sutherland, E.H. and Cressey, D.R. (1960) *Principles of Criminology*, 6th edition. Philadelphia, PA: Lippincott.

Sutton-Smith, B. (1981) *A History of Children's Play: The New Zealand Playground 1840–1950*. University of Pennsylvania Press.

Svartberg, M. and Stiles, T. (1991) Comparative effects of short-term psychodynamic psychotherapy. *Journal of Consulting and Clinical Psychology*, 59, pp. 704–714.

Szasz, T.S. (1960) The myth of mental illness. *American Psychologist*, 15, pp. 113–118.

Tajfel, H. (ed.) (1978) *Differentiation Between Social Groups: Studies in the Social Psychology of Intergroup Relations*. London: Academic Press.

Taylor, S.E. (1983) Adjustment to threatening events: A theory of cognitive adaptation. *American Psychologist*, 41, pp. 1161–1173.

Taylor, S.E. (1999) *Health Psychology*, 4th edition. McGraw-Hill.

Tennes, K. and Kreye, M. (1985) Children's adrenocortical responses to classroom activities and tests in elementary school. *Psychosomatic Medicine*, 47, pp. 451–460.

Tennis, G.H. and Dabbs, J.M. (1975) Sex, setting and personal space: first grade through college. *Sociometry*, 38, pp. 385–394.

Terman, L. (1925) *Genetic Studies of Genius*, volumes 1 to 5. Stanford, CA: Stanford University Press.

Teti, D.M., Sakin, J.W., Kucera, E.M. and Corns, K.M. (1996) And baby makes four: predictors of attachment security among preschool-age firstborns during the transition to siblinghood. *Child Development*, 67, pp. 579–596.

Thomas, J.R. (1978) Attribution theory and motivation through reward: Practical implications for children's sports. In Magill, R.A., Ash, M.J. and Smoll, F.L. (eds) *Children in Sport: A Contemporary Anthology*. Champaign, IL: Human Kinetics.

Thornton, D.M. (1987) Treatment effects on recidivism: a reappraisal of the 'nothing works' doctrine. In McGurk, B.J., Thornton, D.M. and Williams, M. (eds) *Applying Psychology to Imprisonment: Theory and Practice*. London: HMSO.

Tindall, D.B. and O'Connor, B. (1987) Attitudes, social identity, social values, and behaviour in a commons dilemma. Paper presented at the Canadian Psychological Association Conference, Vancouver, B.C.

Tizard, B. and Hodges, J. (1978) The effects of early institutional rearing on the development of eight-year old children. *Journal of Child Psychology and Psychiatry*, 19, pp. 99–118.

Toles, T. (1985) Video games and American military ideology. In Mosco, A. and Wasco, R. (eds) *Critical Communications Review, Vol III: Popular Culture and Media Events*. Norwood: Ablex Press.

Tolman, E. (1932) *Purposive Behaviour in Animals and Men*. New York: Appleton Century Crofts.

Tomkins, S. (1966) Psychological model for smoking behaviour. *American Journal of Public Health*, 56, pp. 17–20.

Tomkins, S. (1968) A modified model of smoking behaviour. In Borgatta, E.F. and Evans, R.R. (eds) *Smoking, Health and Behaviour*. Chicago: Aldine.

Torrey, E.F. (1992) Are we overestimating the genetic contribution to schizophrenia? *Schizophrenia Bulletin*, 18, pp. 159–170.

Triplett, N. (1898) The dynamogenic factors in pacemaking and competition. *American Journal of Psychology*, 9, pp. 507–533.

Trull, T.J. (1992) DSM-III-R personality disorders and the Five-Factor Model of personality: An empirical comparison. *Journal of Abnormal Psychology*, 103, pp. 350–360.

Tryon, G.S. (1985) An exploratory study of the relationship between residence hall, design and student alcohol consumption. *Journal of College Student Personnel*, 26, pp. 372–373.

Tuckman, B.W. (1965) Developmental sequences in small groups. *Psychological Bulletin*, 63, pp. 384–399.

Turco, R. (1993) Psychological profiling. *International Journal of Offender Therapy and Comparative Criminology*, 34, pp. 147–154.

Turk, D.C., Rudy, T.E. and Salovey, P. (1984) Health protections: attitudes and behaviours of LPNS teachers and college students. *Health Psychology*, 3, pp. 189–210.

Turk, D.C., Rudy, T.E. and Salovey, P. (1986) Implicit models of illness. *Journal of Behavioural Medicine*, 9, pp. 453–474.

Turner, J.S. and Helms, D.B. (1989) *Contemporary Adulthood*, 4th edition. Fort Worth, FL: Holt, Rinehart and Winston.

Turner, R.H. (1974) Collective behaviour. In Faris, R.E.L. (ed.) *Handbook of Modern Sociology*. Chicago, IL: Rand-McNally.

Turvey, B. (1999) *Criminal Profiling: An Introduction to Behavioural Evidence Analysis*. London: Academic Press.

Unger, R. and Crawford, M. (1992) *Women and gender: A feminist Psychology*. London: McGraw-Hill.

Valliant, P.M. (1981) Personality and injury in competitive runners. *Perceptual and Motor Skills*, 53, pp. 251–253.

Vance, R.J. and Colella, A. (1990) Effects of two types of feedback on goal acceptance and personal goals. *Journal of Applied Psychology*, 75, pp. 68–76.

Vandell, D.L. and Mueller, E.C. (1980) Peer play and friendships during the first two years. In Foot, H.C., Chapman, A.J. and Smith, J.R. (eds) *Friendships and Social Relations in Children*. New York: Wiley.

Vandenberg, B. (1981) Environmental and cognitive factors in social play. *Journal of Experimental Child Psychology*, 31, pp. 169–175.

VanYperen, N.W. (1998) Informational support, equity and burnout: The moderating effect of self-efficacy. *Journal of Occupational and Organisational Psychology*, 71, pp. 29–33.

Vaughn, B.E., Lefevre, G.B., Seifer, R. and Barglow, P. (1989) Attachment behaviour, attachment security and temperament during infancy. *Child Development*, 60, pp. 728–737.

Vealey, R.S. (1992) Personality and sport: A comprehensive view. In Horn, T.S. (ed.) *Advances in Sport Psychology*. Champaign, IL: Human Kinetics.

Vecchio, R.P. (1977) An empirical examination of the validity of Fiedler's model of leadership effectiveness. *Organisational Behaviour and Human Performance*, 19, pp. 180–206.

Vener, A.M. and Krupka, L.R. (1990) AIDS knowledge and attitudes revisited (1987–1989). *American Biology Teacher*, 52, pp. 461–466.

Vernon, P.E. (1960) *Intelligence and Attainment Tests*. London: University of London Press.

Vernon, P.E. (1969) *Intelligence, Heredity and Environment*. San Fransisco: Freeman.

Veroff, J. (1969) Social comparison and the development of achievement motivation. In Smith, C.P. (ed.) *Achievement-related Motives in Children*. New York: Russell Sage Foundation.

Wachs, T.D. (1988) Relevance of physical environment influences for toddler temperament. *Infant Behaviour and Development*, 11, pp. 431–445.

Wachtel, P. (1977) *Psychoanalysis and Behaviour Therapy: Towards an Integration* New York: Basic Books.

Wageman, R. and Baker, G. (1997) Incentives and cooperation: The joint effects of task and reward interdependence on group performance. *Journal of Organisational Behaviour*, 18, pp. 138–158.

Wall, G. (1973) Public response to air pollution in South Yorkshire, England. *Environment and Behaviour*, 5, pp. 219–248.

Wallach, M.A. and Kogan, N. (1965) *Modes of Thinking in Young Children*. New York: Holt, Rinehart and Winston.

Wallach, M.A., Kogan, N. and Bem, D.J. (1962) Group influence on individual risk taking. *Journal of Abnormal and Social Psychology*, 65, pp. 75–86.

Walsh, W.D. and Snyder, C.W. (1982) Young participants' perception of Australian football. *The Australian Journal of Sport Sciences*, Spring, pp. 22–25.

Walster, E. and Festinger, L. (1962) The effectiveness of 'overheard' persuasive communications. *Journal of Abnormal and Social Psychology*, 65, pp. 395–402.

Walton, D. (1989) *Informal Logic: A Handbook for Critical Argumentation*. New York: Cambridge University Press.

Wang, T.H. and Katsev, R.D. (1990) Group commitment and resource conservation: two field experiments on promoting recycling. *Journal of Applied Social Psychology*, 20, pp. 265–275.

Warnick, D.H. and Sanders, G.S. (1980) The effects of group discussion on eyewitness accuracy. *Journal of Applied Social Psychology*, 10, pp. 249–259.

Warr, P.B. (1984) Work and unemployment. In Drenth, P.J.D. (ed.) *Handbook of Work and Organisational Psychology*. Chichester: Wiley.

Watson, O.M. (1970) *Proxemic Behaviour: A Cross-cultural Study*. The Hague: Mouton.

Watson, O.M. and Graves, T.D. (1966) Quantitative research in proxemic behaviour. *American Anthropologist*, 68, pp. 971–985.

Watson, R. I. (1959) Historical review of objective personality testing: The search for objectivity. In Bass, B.M. and Berg, I.A. (eds) *Objective Approaches to Personality Assessment*. Princeton, NJ: Van Nostrand.

Watzke, G.E., Dana, J.M., Doktor, R.H. and Rubenstein, F.D. (1972) An experimental study of individual vs. group interest. *Acta Sociologica*, 15, pp. 366–370.

Weinberg, R. and Gould, D. (1995) *Foundations of Sport and Exercise Psychology*. Champaign, IL: Human Kinetics.

Weiner, B. (1972) *Theories of Motivation: From Mechanism to Cognition*. Chicago: Rand McNally.

Weiner, B. (1986) *An Attribution Theory of Motivation and Emotion*. Springer-Verlag.

Weiss, G. (1983) Long-term outcome: findings, concepts and practical implications. In Rutter, M. (ed.) *Developmental Neuropsychiatry*. New York: Guilford Press.

Weiss, M.R. and Chaumeton, N. (1992) Motivational orientation in sport. In Horn, T.S. (ed.) *Advances in Sport Psychology*. Champaign, IL: Human Kinetics.

Wells, G.L. and Turtle, J.W. (1988) What is the best way to encode faces? In Gruneberg, M., Morris, P.E. and Sykes, R.N. (eds) *Practical Aspects of Memory: Current Research and Issues, vol. 1*. Chichester: Wiley.

Wells, G.L., Lieppe, M.R. and Ostrom, T.M. (1979a) Guidelines for empirically assessing the fairness of a lineup. *Law and Human Behaviour*, 3, pp. 285–293.

Wells, G.L., Lindsay, R.C.L. and Ferguson, T.J. (1979b) Accuracy, confidence and juror perceptions in eyewitness identification. *Journal of Applied Psychology*, 64, pp. 440–448.

Wentzel, K.R. and Asher, S.R. (1995) The academic level of neglected, rejected, popular and controversial children. *Child Development*, 66, pp. 754–763.

Weschler, cited in Child, D. (1999) *Psychology and the Teacher*, 6th edition (p. 248). Cassell Education.

Wesson, K., Wiggins, N., Thompson, G. and Harrison, S. (2000) *Sport and PE, A Complete Guide to Advanced Level Study*, 2nd edition. London: Hodder and Stoughton.

Westin, A.F. (1970) *Privacy and Freedom*. New York: Athenaeum.

Wheaton, G.R. and Whetzel, D.L. (1997) Contexts for developing applied measurement instruments. In Whetzel, D.L. and Wheaton, G.R. (eds) *Applied Measurement Methods in Industrial Psychology*. Palo Alto, CA: Davies-Black.

Wheldall, K. and Glynn, T. (1989) *Effective Classroom Learning: A Behavioural Interactionist Approach to Teaching*. Oxford: Blackwell.

Wicker, A.W. (1979) *An Introduction to Ecological Psychology*. Cambridge: Cambridge University Press.

Widiger, T.A. and Spitzer, R. (1991) Sex bias in the diagnosis of personality disorders: Conceptual and methodological issues. *Clinical Psychology Review*, 11, pp. 1–22.

Widmeyer, W.N., Brawley, L.R. and Carron, A.V. (1990) The effects of group size in sport. *Journal of Sport and Exercise Psychology*, 12, pp. 177–199.

Wilfley, D., Agras, W.S., Telch, C., Rossiter, E., Schneider, J., Cole, A., Sifford, L. and Raeburn, S. (1993) Group cognitive-behavioural therapy and group interpersonal psychotherapy for the nonpurging bulimic individual: A controlled comparison. *Journal of Consulting and Clinical Psychology*, 61, pp. 296–305.

Wilkes, R.L. and Summers, J.J. (1984) Cognitions, mediating variables and strength performance. *Journal of Sports Psychology*, 6, pp. 351–359.

Williams, D.R., Roggenbuck, J.W. and Bange, S.P. (1991) The effect of norm-encounter compatibility on crowding perceptions, experience and behaviour in river recreation settings. *Journal of Leisure Research*, 23, pp. 154–172.

Williams, E. (1991) College students and recycling: Their attitudes and behaviours. *Journal of College Student Development*, 32, pp. 86–88.

Williams, L.R.T. and Parkin, W.A. (1980) Personality profiles of three hockey groups. *International Journal of Sports Psychology*, 11, pp. 113–120.

Williams, S. and Taormina, R.J. (1992) Unanimous versus majority influences on group polarisation in business decision making. *The Journal of Social Psychology*, 133, pp. 199–205.

Williamson, D.F., Kahn, H.S., Remington, P.L. and Anda, R.F. (1990).The 10–year incidence of overweight and major weight gain in U.S. adults. *Archives of Internal Medicine*, 150, p. 665.

Wills, T.A. (1986) Stress and coping in early adolescence: Relationships to substance use in urban school samples. *Health Psychology*, 5, pp. 503–529.

Wilner, D.M., Walkley, R.P., Pinkerton, T.C. and Tayback, M. (1962) *The Housing Environment and Family Life*. Baltimore, MD: Johns Hopkins University Press.

Wilson, E.O. (1976) Personality. In Eysenck, H.J. and Wilson, G.D. (eds) *A Textbook of Human Psychology*. Lancaster: MTP.

Wilson, J.Q. and Kelling, G. (1982) Broken windows. *The Atlantic Monthly*, March, pp. 29–38.

Winger, G., Hofmann, F.G. and Woods, J.H. (1992) *A Handbook on Drug and Alcohol Abuse: The Biomedical Aspects*, 3rd edition. New York: Oxford University Press.

Winkler, R.C. and Winett, R.A. (1982) Behavioural interventions in resource management: a systems approach based on behavioural economics. *American Psychologist*, 37, pp. 421–435.

Wit, A. and Wilke, H.A. (1990) The presentation of rewards and punishments in a simulated social dilemma. *Social Behaviour*, 5, pp. 231–245.

Witkin (1965) in *Learning Styles*, E281, Units 1 and 2, Open University materials, cited in Child, D. (1999) *Psychology and the Teacher*, 6th edition (p. 327). Cassell Education.

Witmer, J.F. and Geller, E.S. (1976) Facilitating paper recycling: effects of prompts, raffles, and contests. *Journal of Applied Behavioural Analysis*, 9, pp. 315–322.

Wofford, J.C., Goodwin, V.L. and Premack, S. (1992) Meta-analysis of the antecedents of personal goal level and of the antecedents and consequences of goal commitment. *Journal of Management*, 18, pp. 595–615.

Wofford, J.C. and Liska, L.Z. (1993) Path-goal theories of leadership: A meta-analysis. *Journal of Management*, 19, pp. 857–874.

Wolfgang, A. and Wolfgang, J. (1968) Personal space: an unobtrusive measure of attitudes toward the physically handicapped. *Proceedings of the 76th Annual Convention of the American Psychological Association,* pp. 653–654.

Wolfgang, A.P. (1988) Job stress in the health professions: A study of physicians, nurses, and pharmacists. *Behavioural Medicine*, 14, pp. 43–47.

Wood, D. (1998) *How Children Think and Learn*, 2nd edition. Oxford: Blackwell.

Wood, W., Wong, F.Y. and Chachere, J.G. (1991) Effects of media violence on viewers' aggression in unconstrained social interaction. *Psychological Bulletin*, 109, pp. 371–383.

Wright, G.E. and Multon, K.D. (1995) Employer's perception of nonverbal communication in job interviews for persons with physical disabilities. *Journal of Vocational Behaviour*, 47, pp. 214–227.

Wyer, R.S. and Gordon, S.E. (1982) The recall of information about persons and groups. *Journal of Experimental Social Psychology*, 18, pp. 128–164.

Wyer, R.S. and Martin, L.L. (1986) Person memory: The role of traits, group stereotypes and specific behaviours in the cognitive representation of persons. *Journal of Personality and Social Psychology*, 50, pp. 661–675.

Wyer, R.S. Jr., and Carlston, D.E. (1994) The cognitive representation of persons and events. In Wyer, R.S. Jr and Srull, T.K. (eds) *Handbook of Social Cognition*, 2nd edition. Hillsdale, NJ: Erlbaum.

Yan Lan, L. and Gill, D.L. (1984) The relationships among self-efficacy, stress responses, and a cognitive feedback manipulation. *Journal of Sports Psychology*, 6, pp. 227–238.

Yancey, W.L. (1971) Architecture interaction and social control: the case of a large-scale public housing project. *Environment and Behaviour*, 3, pp. 3–21.

Yarmey, A.D. (1986) Verbal, visual, and voice identification of a rape suspect under different levels of illumination. *Journal of Applied Psychology*, 71, pp. 363–370.

Yearta, S.K., Maitlis, S. and Briner, R.B. (1995) An explanatory study of goal setting in theory and practice: a motivational technique that works? *Journal of Occupational and Organisational Psychology*, 68, pp. 237–252.

Yerkes (1908), cited in Morris, T. and Summers, J. (eds) (1995) *Sport Psychology Theory, Applications and Issues* (p. 49). Brisbane: John Wiley and Sons.

Yetton, P.W. and Bottger, P.C. (1982) Individual versus group problem solving: An empirical test of a best-member strategy. *Organisational Behaviour and Human Performance*, 29, pp. 307–321.

Yochelson, S. and Samenow, S.E. (1976) *The Criminal Personality, Vol. 1: A Profile for Change*. New York: Jason Aronsen.

Youngblade, L.M. and Belsky, J. (1992) Parent–child antecedents of 5-year-olds' close friendships: a longitudinal analysis. *Developmental Psychology*, 28, pp. 700–713.

Yuille, J.C. and Cutshall, J.L. (1986) A Case study of eyewitness memory to a crime. *Journal of Applied Psychology*, 71, pp. 291–301.

Yukl, G.A. (1989) *Leadership in Organisations*, 2nd edition. Englewood Cliffs, NJ: Prentice Hall.

Yukl, G.A. and Van Fleet, D.D. (1992) Theory and research on leadership in organisations. In Dunnette, M.D. and Hough, L.M. (eds) *Handbook of Industrial and Organisational Psychology, Vol. 3*, 2nd edition. Palo Alto, CA: Consulting Psychologists Press.

Zajonc, R.B. (1965) Social facilitation. *Science*, 149, pp. 269–274.

Zanni, G.R. and Offerman, J.T. (1978) Eyewitness testimony: an exploration of question wording upon recall as a function of neuroticism. *Perceptual and Motor Skills*, 46, pp. 163–166.

Zimbardo, P.G. (1970) The human choice: individuation, reason, and order versus deindividuation, impulse and chaos. In Arnold, W.J. and Levine, D. (eds) *Nebraska Symposium on Motivation 1969, vol. 17*. Lincoln, NB: University of Nebraska Press.

Index

Glossary and reference sections have not been indexed. However, when authors are mentioned in the text they have been indexed when appropriate. Page references in *italics* indicate figures or tables.